MASTER THE™
ASVAB

23RD EDITION

Dr. Scott A. Ostrow
Lt. Col., USAF (Ret.)

PETERSON'S®

PETERSON'S®

About Peterson's

Peterson's® has been your trusted educational publisher for over 50 years. It's a milestone we're quite proud of, as we continue to offer the most accurate, dependable, high-quality educational content in the field, providing you with everything you need to succeed. No matter where you are on your academic or professional path, you can rely on Peterson's for its books, online information, expert test-prep tools, the most up-to-date education exploration data, and the highest quality career success resources—everything you need to achieve your education goals. For our complete line of products, visit **www.petersons.com**.

For more information about Peterson's range of educational products, contact Peterson's, 8740 Lucent Blvd., Suite 400 Highlands Ranch, CO 80129, or find us online at **www.petersons.com**.

ISBN-13: 978-0-7689-4241-5

Printed in the United States of America

10 9 8 7 6 5 4 3 2 1   20 19 18

Twenty-Third Edition

Petersonspublishingcom/publishing updates

Check out our website at *www.petersonspublishing.com/publishingupdates* to see if there is any new information regarding the test and any revisions or corrections to the content of this book. We've made sure the information in this book is accurate and up-to-date; however, the test format or content may have changed since the time of publication.

Access an additional ASVAB® Practice Test online

For access to Peterson's online practice tests, visit *www.petersonspublishing.com/asvab.*

Contents

Acknowledgments...xi

Before You Begin xiii
    How This Book Is Organized...xiii
    You're Well on Your Way to Success xiii

PART I: ASVAB BASICS

1   **All About the ASVAB** 3
    The Student ASVAB...3
    The Enlistment ASVAB 4
    The Armed Forces Classification Test (AFCT) 4
    Subject Tests 4
    Armed Forces Qualification Test (AFQT) 7
    Computerized Adaptive Testing (CAT) 8
    Prescreen Internet Computerized Adaptive Test (PICAT) 10
    Preparing for the ASVAB 12
    Taking the ASVAB 13
    Your ASVAB Results 14
    Percentile Scores 15
    Composite Scores 15
    Frequently-Asked Questions About the ASVAB 18
    Self-Evaluation Chart..22
    Are You Ready To Move Forward? 24

PART II: DIAGNOSING STRENGTHS AND WEAKNESSES

2   **Practice Test 1: Diagnostic**...27
    Answer Sheet Practice Test 1: Diagnostic...28
    Part 1: General Science 31
    Part 2: Arithmetic Reasoning 35
    Part 3: Word Knowledge 40
    Part 4: Paragraph Comprehension 44
    Part 5: Mathematics Knowledge 49
    Part 6: Electronics Information..53
    Part 7: Auto & Shop Information 57
    Part 8: Mechanical Comprehension 62
    Part 9: Assembling Objects 69
    Answer Key and Explanations 74

PART III: ASVAB SUBJECT REVIEW

3   General Science **97**
    Life Science 98
    Physical Science...122
    Earth Science...139
    Practice Questions 144
    Answer Key and Explanations 145
    Summing It Up 146

4   Arithmetic Reasoning **147**
    Review of Basic Arithmetic 147
    Practice Questions 155
    Answer Key and Explanations 159
    Summing It Up 162

5   Word Knowledge Review..**163**
    Word Formation—A Key to Word Recognition...........................164
    Practice Questions 172
    Answer Key and Explanations 173
    Summing It Up 174

6   Paragraph Comprehension **175**
    Practice Questions 181
    Answer Key and Explanations 182
    Summing It Up 183

7   Mathematics Knowledge **185**
    Adding Fractions 186
    Adding Mixed Numbers 187
    Adding Percents 187
    Subtracting Fractions...188
    Subtracting Mixed Numbers 188
    Subtracting Percents 188
    Multiplying Fractions 189
    Multiplying Mixed Numbers 190
    Multiplying Percents 191
    Other Multiplication Properties...191
    Dividing Fractions 192
    Dividing Percents 193
    Dividing Mixed Numbers 193
    Other Division Properties 194
    Factors of a Product 195
    Roots 196
    Algebra 197
    Geometry...199
    Practice Questions 205
    Answer Key and Explanations 210
    Summing It Up...214

8 Electronics Information **217**
Electricity 217
Basic Electronic Theory 222
Practice Questions 226
Answer Key and Explanations 227
Summing It Up 228

9 Auto & Shop Information **229**
Basic Auto Information 229
Basic Shop Information 241
Practice Questions 295
Answer Key and Explanations 296
Summing It Up 297

10 Mechanical Comprehension **299**
Levers 299
Block and Tackle 303
The Wheel and Axle 307
The Inclined Plane and the Wedge 310
The Screw 312
Gears 315
Work 321
Power 324
Force and Pressure 324
Machine Elements and Basic Mechanisms 328
Basic Mechanisms 331
Clutches 335
Practice Questions 338
Answer Key and Explanations 340
Summing It Up 341

11 Assembling Objects **343**
Practice Questions 346
Answer Key and Explanations 348
Summing It Up 350

PART IV: THREE ASVAB PRACTICE TESTS

Practice Test 2 .... **353**
Answer Sheet Practice Test 2 354
Part 1: General Science 357
Part 2: Arithmetic Reasoning 361
Part 3: Word Knowledge 366
Part 4: Paragraph Comprehension 370
Part 5: Mathematics Knowledge 374
Part 6: Electronics Information..................................... 378
Part 7: Auto & Shop Information 382
Part 8: Mechanical Comprehension 386
Part 9: Assembling Objects 393
Answer Key and Explanations 398

Practice Test 3 .... **419**
Answer Sheet Practice Test 3 420
Part 1: General Science 423
Part 2: Arithmetic Reasoning 427
Part 3: Word Knowledge 432
Part 4: Paragraph Comprehension 436
Part 5: Mathematics Knowledge 441
Part 6: Electronics Information 445
Part 7: Auto & Shop Information 449
Part 8: Mechanical Comprehension 453
Part 9: Assembling Objects 460
Answer Key and Explanations 465

Practice Test 4 .... **485**
Answer Sheet Practice Test 4 486
Part 1: General Science 489
Part 2: Arithmetic Reasoning 493
Part 3: Word Knowledge 498
Part 4: Paragraph Comprehension 502
Part 5: Mathematics Knowledge 507
Part 6: Electronics Information 511
Part 7: Auto & Shop Information 515
Part 8: Mechanical Comprehension 519
Part 9: Assembling Objects 526
Answer Key and Explanations 531

APPENDIXES

A   Military Enlisted Occupations and Civilian Counterparts **555**
Occupational Index 556
Accounting, Budget, and Finance Occupations 559
Arts, Communications, Media, and Design Occupations 560
Aviation Occupations 569
Business Administration and Operations Occupations................................575
Combat Operations Occupations 579
Communications Equipment Technologists and Technicians Occupations 584
Construction, Building, and Extraction Occupations 590
Counseling, Social Work, and Human Services Occupations 596
Education and Training Occupations 599
Engineering and Scientific Research Occupations 601
Environmental Health and Safety Occupations... 605
Healthcare Practitioners Occupations 610
Human Resources Management and Services Occupations 616
Information Technology, Computer Science, and Mathematics Occupations.....619
Intelligence Occupations 621
International Relations, Linguistics, and Other Social Sciences Occupations ... 625
Law Enforcement, Security, and Protective Services Occupations.................... 628
Legal Professions and Support Services Occupations 630
Mechanic and Repair Technologists and Technicians Occupations 632

B   Enlisted Opportunities In The U.S. Military **653**

General Enlistment Qualifications 653

Enlisting In The Military 655

Military Training 656

Pay and Benefits 658

C   Coding Speed **665**

Sample Questions 665

Answer Key 676

Acknowledgments

Thanks go out to the following organizations for contributing to this book:

U.S. Military Entrance Processing Command, North Chicago, Illinois 60064-3094, for making available the following resource material:

> *ASVAB 25/26 Student and Parent Guide*
>
> *ASVAB 25/26 Educator and Counselor Guide*
>
> *ASVAB 25/26 Counselor Manual*
>
> *ASVAB Career Exploration Program*
>
> *ASVAB Technical Manual for the ASVAB 25/26 Career Exploration Program*
> *Exploring Careers: The ASVAB Workbook*

U.S. Department of Defense, Washington, DC, for:

> *Military Careers*

Bureau of Naval Personnel, Dover Publications, Inc., New York, for:

> *Tools and Their Uses*
>
> *Basic Machines*

General Motors Corporation, Detroit, Michigan, for:

> *What Makes Autos Run*

Before You Begin

Congratulations on making the decision to take the Armed Services Vocational Aptitude Battery (ASVAB)! By doing this, you are on the right path to determining your next step in life: college, the military, or a civilian career. A high score on the ASVAB is important for determining your potential for careers in both the military and civilian life.

Peterson's *Master the ASVAB* will help you gain the confidence you need to score higher by providing you with a comprehensive review of the ASVAB content, as well as four practice tests. You can spend your time wisely and focus on your weak areas by studying the subject reviews and build confidence in your test-taking abilities by taking the practice tests. Knowing the format of the ASVAB and feeling at ease on test day is an important factor for your success.

HOW THIS BOOK IS ORGANIZED

Divided into sections, this book provides four main parts that can help you with your preparation. Use Part One to learn more about each exam subject and how the exam is scored. Use Part Two to diagnose your strengths and weaknesses by taking your first practice test. Part Three includes the subject reviews that will help you strengthen your weak areas. Part Four includes three practice tests.

Start at Part One of the book and carefully read through the introductory sections so you fully understand the ASVAB and how the test is scored. Then take the Diagnostic Test in Part Two to assess what kind of review you might need. Devote extra time to those sections that deal with the subjects in which you need to improve your skills.

Next spend time in Part Three reviewing the subjects that will be tested on the ASVAB. Here you will find exercises with answers and explanations to help you strengthen your skills.

Then, take the practice tests in Part Four. Each test is especially designed to help you prepare with little anxiety. As you complete each test, take some time to review your answers. Always take the time to check the review section for clarification.

As a bonus, the Appendixes at the back of the book provide you with military enlisted occupations and civilian counterparts, as well as profiles of 120 military careers.

YOU'RE WELL ON YOUR WAY TO SUCCESS

Remember that knowledge is power. By using Peterson's *Master the ASVAB*, you will be studying the most comprehensive ASVAB preparation guide available. We look forward to helping you raise your ASVAB scores and get that career you deserve! Good luck!

TOP 10 STRATEGIES TO RAISE YOUR SCORES

Follow the 10 steps listed below to maximize your efforts and make the most of your test preparation.

1. **Read "ASVAB Basics."** This will give you a better understanding of the ASVAB, the different reasons to take the test, when and where you can take it, strategies for preparing for the test, and much more.

2. **Take the first ASVAB practice test.** After completing this practice test, you can evaluate your strengths and weaknesses and record your scores on the Self-Evaluation chart on page 22. Don't worry if you do not do well; the first time you take the test will be the hardest because you are not familiar with it.

3. **Review the areas you need more practice on in "ASVAB Subject Reviews."** This chapter provides a dedicated section to each ASVAB subject test. You can spend your time wisely and focus on the areas you need to work on and any area of which you are unsure.

4. **Take the second ASVAB practice test.** You should feel more comfortable with this the second time and know what to expect for the test format. Be sure to record your scores in the Self-Evaluation chart on page 22.

5. **Refer to the review section.** If you need more review in specific areas, go back to the review section to get the help you need.

6. **Take the third ASVAB practice test.** You are gaining familiarity with the test and are striving to surpass your scores from the previous test. Record your scores in the Self-Evaluation chart and take note of the progress you have made.

7. **Go back to the review section if needed.** The more you study the sections you are unsure of, the more you will learn.

8. **Take the fourth and final ASVAB practice test.** You should feel confident in your progress and knowledge about the test. Record your scores in the Self-Evaluation chart.

9. **Review your progress on the four practice tests you have completed.** You can now go on to "Your ASVAB Results" to help you determine how the military interprets ASVAB scores.

10. **Turn to the Appendixes to look for career areas that interest you.** Note that the military careers listed include their civilian counterparts. Also included are the Military Careers Score required for each career.

Don't hesitate to reread the review section or retake one or more of the practice tests. Remember, the more confident you are about the test subjects and the test format, the higher you will score on the ASVAB.

PART I
ASVAB BASICS

CHAPTER 1   All About the ASVAB

All About the ASVAB

OVERVIEW

- **The Student ASVAB**
- **The Enlistment ASVAB**
- **The Armed Forces Classification Test (AFCT)**
- **Subject Tests**
- **Armed Forces Qualification Test (AFQT)**
- **Computerized Adaptive Testing (CAT)**
- **Prescreen Internet Computerized Adaptive Test (PICAT)**
- **Preparing for the ASVAB**
- **Taking the ASVAB**
- **Your ASVAB Results**
- **Percentile Scores**
- **Composite Scores**
- **Frequently-Asked Questions About the ASVAB**
- **Self-Evaluation Chart**
- **Are You Ready To Move Forward?**

If you plan to join the military or want to find out what type of career you are suited for, your first step is to take the Armed Services Vocational Aptitude Battery, or ASVAB. The ASVAB is a multiple-aptitude battery consisting of either nine or ten subject tests. More than 1 million people each year take it to join the military or as part of a student testing program offered in high schools. Its primary purpose is to determine your basic skills and your aptitude for other skills. There are three main versions and purposes for taking the ASVAB.

THE STUDENT ASVAB

The *student* ASVAB, also known as the *institutional* ASVAB, is sponsored by high schools and is offered to all interested students (some schools make the ASVAB mandatory for all students). It was created for high school students in their sophomore, junior, or senior year or in a postsecondary school to help identify their abilities. It is a great tool, and it has helped many students decide on their future educational or career path. The student ASVAB also helps the military attract well-qualified volunteers for enlistment and to place them in military occupational programs.

More than 1 million people take the student ASVAB each year as part of the military's Career Exploration Program. With this program, students take surveys about their interests, identify personal characteristics, and use their ASVAB scores to match their background to possible careers.

If you choose to take the student ASVAB, you will take the exam with other students at your school. More than likely, there will be one or more military recruiters present as proctors of the exam. This is their sole purpose for being there, and they are prohibited by regulations from actively recruiting during the ASVAB. However, the ASVAB answer sheet contains questions about your plans after high school. Those plans may be attending a two- or four-year college, attending a vocational (or trade) school, or enlisting in the military. If you do well on the ASVAB, military recruiters may contact you regardless of your intended plans. If you list "plans military," you are a prime candidate for enlistment and will be pursued by recruiters from all of the military services. If you do choose to enlist in the military, your student ASVAB scores can be used for qualification for enlistment. Note that your scores remain valid for two years.

THE ENLISTMENT ASVAB

Another form of the ASVAB is referred to as the *enlistment* ASVAB, also known as the *production* ASVAB. This version is given to those pursuing enlistment who either did not take the student version or want to retake the exam in the hope that they will improve their scores. Your enlistment ASVAB scores determine your learning ability and vocational aptitude. More than 500,000 potential recruits take the enlistment ASVAB each year.

The enlistment ASVAB is given in one of two places, either at the Military Entrance Processing Station (MEPS) or at a Mobile Examining Team (MET) site. In either place, you take the exam with others who have also decided to join the military. All tests given at the MEPS, and some MET sites, are computer-adaptive tests. For more information on the computer-based ASVAB, see *Computerized Adaptive Testing*.

Note that your recruiter may arrange for you to take a pre-ASVAB test called the Entrance Screening Test (EST) or a computer version called the CAST (Computerized Adaptive Screening Test). These pretests are given at the recruiter's office. It gives the recruiter an idea of your potential for scoring high enough on the ASVAB to qualify, and it contains only subjects pertaining to math and English skills.

THE ARMED FORCES CLASSIFICATION TEST (AFCT)

The AFCT, also known as the *in-service* ASVAB, is required when military personnel want to change career fields and do not currently have qualifying ASVAB scores for that career field. The only difference between the AFCT and the ASVAB is the name. Presently, the AFCT is given only in the traditional paper-and-pencil version.

SUBJECT TESTS

The ASVAB consists of subject tests designed to measure acquired knowledge as well as general abilities acquired from interests or hobbies. Listed in the following chart are specifics about the tests and the times allotted for each section.

ASVAB CONTENT	
Testing Time	Approximately 149 minutes: student ASVAB (or paper-and-pencil enlistment ASVAB)
	Approximately 154 minutes: CAT-ASVAB and AFCT
Administrative Time	46 minutes
Total Testing Time	Approximately 195 minutes: student ASVAB (or paper-and-pencil enlistment ASVAB)
	Approximately 190 minutes: CAT-ASVAB and AFCT
Total Number of Items	225: student ASVAB (or AFCT paper-and-pencil enlistment ASVAB)
	145: CAT-ASVAB

TEST	TIME	ITEMS	DESCRIPTION
General Science	11 minutes	25	Measures knowledge of the physical and biological sciences
Arithmetic Reasoning	36 minutes	30	Measures ability to solve arithmetic word problems
Word Knowledge	11 minutes	35	Measures ability to select the correct meaning of words presented in context and to identify the best synonym for a given word
Paragraph Comprehension	13 minutes	15	Measures ability to obtain information from written passages
Mathematics Knowledge	24 minutes	25	Measures knowledge of general mathematics principles, including algebra and geometry
Electronics Information	9 minutes	20	Measures knowledge of electricity, radio principles, and electronics
Auto & Shop Information	11 minutes	25	Measures knowledge of automobiles, tools, and shop terminology and practices
Mechanical Comprehension	19 minutes	25	Measures knowledge of mechanical and physical principles and ability to visualize how illustrated objects work
Assembling Objects	15 minutes	25	Measures spatial aptitude—the ability to perceive spatial relations

You can become more familiar with the ASVAB by getting an overview of the subject tests and the areas that they cover. The following list contains the general contents and purpose of the tests, shows you what to expect on the tests, and provides you with a better understanding of the content areas covered on the official test battery. Part Three of this book, ASVAB Review Basics, contains a section for each of the subject areas.

Part 1—General Science (GS)

The General Science test consists of 25 items and covers the material generally taught in junior and senior high school science courses. Most of the questions deal with life science and physical science, with a few questions on earth science. Specifics about what each area covers are:

- Life Science: basic biology, human nutrition, and health
- Physical Science: elementary chemistry and physics
- Earth Science: geology, meteorology, and astronomy

Part 2—Arithmetic Reasoning (AR)

The Arithmetic Reasoning test consists of 30 items and covers basic mathematical problems you may come across in everyday life. These questions are designed to measure general reasoning and the ability to solve mathematical problems.

Part 3—Word Knowledge (WK)

The Word Knowledge test consists of 35 items and is designed to test your ability to understand the meaning of words through synonyms (words having the same or nearly the same meaning as other words). Vocabulary is one of many factors that characterizes reading comprehension, but it also provides a good measure of verbal comprehension.

The words used in these synonym questions are used in everyday language. The questions can appear in either of two forms:

1. The key word appears in the stem and is followed by "most nearly means."
2. The key word is used in a sentence.

Part 4—Paragraph Comprehension (PC)

The Paragraph Comprehension test consists of 15 items and is designed to measure ability to obtain information from written material. The reading passages vary in length from one paragraph to several paragraphs and may be used for one or more questions. Each question in this section is to be answered solely on the basis of the information contained in the reading passage.

Part 5—Mathematics Knowledge (MK)

The Mathematics Knowledge test consists of 25 items and is designed to measure general mathematical knowledge. It is a test of your ability to solve problems using high school mathematics, including algebra and some basic geometry. Scrap paper is provided for any figuring you may wish to do.

Part 6—Electronics Information (EI)

The Electronics Information test consists of 20 items dealing with electricity, radio principles, and electronics. This information can be learned through working on radios, working on electrical equipment, reading books, or taking courses.

Part 7—Auto & Shop Information (AS)

The Auto & Shop Information test consists of 25 items and covers the material generally taught in automobile mechanics in vocational-technical schools and in shop instruction. It is designed to measure knowledge of automobiles, tools, and shop terminology and practices.

The automotive information may also be acquired as a hobby or by working with automobiles. The questions generally pertain to diagnosing malfunctions of a car, the use of particular parts on a car, or the meaning of terminology. The shop information may also be acquired as a hobby or through shop experience using a variety of tools and materials.

Part 8—Mechanical Comprehension (MC)

The Mechanical Comprehension test consists of 25 items designed to measure your understanding of mechanical and physical principles. Many of the questions use drawings to illustrate specific principles.

Understanding of these principles comes from observing the physical world, working with or operating mechanical devices, or reading and studying.

Part 9—Assembling Objects (AO)

The Assembling Objects test consists of 25 items designed to measure your spatial aptitude—the ability to perceive spatial relations. The items involve a series of five drawings and require identification of an assembled puzzle or correctly connected objects.

ARMED FORCES QUALIFICATION TEST (AFQT)

Four ASVAB subject tests count toward your AFQT score, which is the score that determines eligibility for enlistment. The composite of the ASVAB subject tests is formed from the following:

Word Knowledge	35 items
Paragraph Comprehension	15 items
Arithmetic Reasoning	30 items
Mathematics Knowledge	25 items

The actual scores you get on your subject tests are considered *raw scores*. The military uses raw scores to compute scoring for specific purposes, such as the AFQT. The following equation shows you how to calculate your AFQT raw score:

(2 × the number correct on Word Knowledge) + (2 × the number correct on Paragraph Comprehension) + the number correct on Arithmetic Reasoning + the number correct on Mathematics Knowledge = AFQT raw score, which is then converted into a percentile score.

Note that if you have a General Education Development (GED) test or do not have a high school diploma and take the ASVAB for enlistment, the military may require a higher AFQT score. Check with your recruiter for more details about this because each branch of the service has different score requirements.

While the AFQT score is very important and you must score a minimum score to qualify for enlistment, do not just focus on the AFQT. It is possible to qualify for more jobs by scoring a lower AFQT and higher "line scores" in sub-tests.

It is entirely possible for you to score higher on the sub-tests even though you may not currently have knowledge in those areas by studying this book.

If you are in a time crunch and need to take the ASVAB next week, by all means, concentrate on the areas that make up the AFQT. If not, take the time to make yourself eligible for a broad range of military occupations.

COMPUTERIZED ADAPTIVE TESTING (CAT)

The CAT-ASVAB is the computerized version of the ASVAB. All MEPS now use this version of the ASVAB. On rare occasions, a paper-and-pencil version will be administered—usually only if the computer system is down.

Computerized ASVAB vs. the Paper-and-Pencil Test

The computerized ASVAB subtests measure the same abilities as the former paper-and-pencil ASVAB subject tests. The only differences are:

- Auto & Shop Information subject test has been split into two separate tests.
- All subject tests in the computerized version of the ASVAB are adaptive.

In the paper-and-pencil ASVAB, all test-takers, regardless of their ability, took the same questions. The computerized ASVAB is adaptive, which means that it tailors questions to the ability level of each test-taker. For example, the first test question is given in the middle ability range, not too difficult and not too easy. If it is answered correctly, the next question is more difficult. If the first item is answered incorrectly, the next item is less difficult. The test continues this way until your proficiency level is determined. You will answer questions that are appropriate for your ability level, so you will not waste time answering questions that are too easy or too difficult. Although you can skip a question, you cannot go back to answer that question or to check your answers as you might have done on a paper-and-pencil ASVAB.

Computerized ASVAB subtest raw scores are not equal to the total number of correct answers. ASVAB subtest scores are computed using formulas that consider the difficulty of the test item and the correctness of the answer. By equating computerized ASVAB raw scores with paper-and-pencil ASVAB raw scores, both scores become equivalent.

Taking The CAT-ASVAB

The computer keyboard used for the ASVAB has a simple design. Even if you do not have computer experience, you can learn how to take computerized tests after only a brief lesson.

When you arrive for the test session, the test administrator will give you a few instructions and verify your Social Security number. You will then be directed to an assigned test examination station and seated at a table with a computer monitor and keyboard.

A modified keyboard, similar to the one that follows, is used for the ASVAB. The keyboard has been modified so that only the keys needed to answer the test questions are labeled. On the main keyboard, all but six keys and the space bar are covered. The modifications include:

- Relocating keys A, B, C, and D
- Labeling the space bar to become ENTER
- Relabeling the F1 key to become HELP
- Covering all the keys on the numerical keyboard except 0–9

The computer screen begins the programmed orientation session by describing the keyboard and explaining how to use the keys labeled ENTER, A, B, C, D, and HELP. You are then given instructions on the following:

- How to answer test items by pressing the response key for the option selected
- Answering every question, even if it means guessing
- How to change answers by pressing another response key before requesting the next question
- Pressing ENTER to verify that the test item was answered and to bring the next item on the screen

The instructions are clear and simple, and practice is provided until you are comfortable with taking the actual test on the computer.

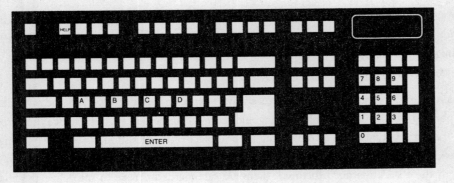

You should only press the red HELP key if a problem arises that requires the assistance of the test administrator or a monitor. When the HELP key is pressed, subject test timing stops until you return to the test questions. Note that the time spent reading instructions does not count against the subject test time limit either. A practice period is provided until you are ready for the actual tests.

The ten subject tests that compose the ASVAB and the order in which they are administered follows.

Title	Time Limit (Minutes)	Number of Questions
General Science (GS)	8	16
Arithmetic Reasoning (AR)	39	16
Word Knowledge (WK)	8	16
Paragraph Comprehension (PC)	22	11
Auto Information (AI)	7	11
Mathematics Knowledge (MK)	20	16
Mechanical Comprehension (MC)	20	16
Electronics Information (EI)	8	16
Shop Information (SI)	6	11
Assembling Objects (AO)	16	16
TOTAL	154	145

The ten subject tests are administered sequentially. For each of these subject tests, you are first given an easy sample item and instructed to press the correct response key. The screen indicates whether the answer is correct or incorrect. The actual test items follow, and you can begin to answer each test item displayed by pressing the appropriate response key (A, B, C, or D). You will need to confirm your answers by pressing the ENTER key after each response. The next test item then appears on your computer screen.

PRESCREEN INTERNET COMPUTERIZED ADAPTIVE TEST (PICAT)

Undoubtedly, the most significant change to come to the ASVAB process since the last edition of this study guide, the introduction of the Prescreen Internet Computerized Adaptive Test (PICAT), has brought ASVAB testing into the twenty-first century and has made taking the ASVAB as convenient as online shopping.

Originally set up to give military applicants a way to experience a "live" ASVAB and give recruiters, and applicants, an idea of how applicants would score on the actual ASVAB (hence the "Prescreen" part of the name), the PICAT is now being used in place of the traditional ASVAB. No longer is it necessary for military applicants to travel to a MEPS or MET site to take a proctored examination. Although the PICAT is not proctored, there are safeguards in place to minimize the chance of cheating, which will be discussed later.

Registering for the PICAT

Only those individuals who have never taken the ASVAB (except the high school version) are authorized to take the PICAT. Just like taking the ASVAB, you must see a recruiter in order to take the PICAT. Instead of your recruiter scheduling you to take the examination at MEPS or an MET site, he or she will give you an authorization code. You may take the PICAT anywhere you have access to the Internet but remember, once you are given the code you must take the PICAT within 30 days, and once you start the examination you have just 48 hours to complete it.

Preparing for the PICAT

There is, in essence, no difference between the PICAT and the ASVAB and, therefore, you should approach studying for the PICAT in the same way you would approach studying for the ASVAB. Review the "Top 10 Strategies to Raise Your Scores" found in the beginning of this book and apply them. Just as with the traditional ASVAB, PICAT success comes from proper preparation, and you've taken a major step by using this guide!

Taking the PICAT

Your recruiter will provide you with an access code and the URL necessary to access the online PICAT. Once you have accessed the website, you will be prompted to enter your last name and the Access Code provided to you by your recruiter. To maximize your success, follow the guidelines outlined below.

Guidelines for Success

- Find a quiet place where you will not be interrupted. This means that you may need to go somewhere other than home, such as a library, or school study area.
- Get plenty of rest prior to the PICAT
- Ensure you have reliable, uninterrupted Internet access
- Rid yourself of distractions, such as your cell phone
- Make sure you have plenty of pencils and plenty of scrap paper
- If you are using a laptop, or other portable device, make sure that it is fully charged or that it is plugged in
- Ensure that you have enough time to complete the PICAT. Most people can complete the PICAT in two hours. If you are interrupted, you can return to the test by logging in again, but you only have 48 hours from your first login to complete the PICAT.
- Do not use any outside assistance, including calculators, mobile aps, search engines, websites, etc.

After the PICAT

Once you have completed the PICAT, your recruiter will be able to immediately see your results. Let your recruiter know that you have completed the test and set up an appointment to go over your results. While there are minimum scores required for enlistment, that vary by service, a higher score on the PICAT increases the number of job opportunities available to you. For this reason, you should consider retesting if you are not satisfied with your PICAT results. While recruiters are professionals, their job is to get applicants through the enlistment process and not to ensure that you get the best possible military job.

WARNING

You will be given a verification test (outlined in the section below) when you get to the MEPS for processing; if your verification test results differ from your PICAT results by more than 20 points your PICAT score will be invalidated and you will be required to take the ASVAB. In other words, don't cheat!

Assuming that you are satisfied with your PICAT results, the next step will be to complete all the necessary documents to prepare you for further enlistment processing. Once that is done, your recruiter will schedule you to go to the Military Entrance Processing Station (MEPS) for final processing, including a physical exam and enlistment. As previously mentioned, you will also be required to take a 20-30 minute Verification Test at the MEPS.

The verification test is a much shorter version of the PICAT and is used to "weed-out" applicants who may have cheated when taking the PICAT. Applicants who score within 20 points of their PICAT score will move on with enlistments processing. However, those who score more than 20 points less on the verification test will be required to take the full-length ASVAB. Additionally, 20 percent of applicants will be randomly chosen to take the ASVAB upon arrival at the MEPS. These measures are in place to ensure the integrity of the PICAT because it is not a proctored exam and the opportunity for cheating is great.

If your score on the verification test is within 20 points of your PICAT score you will continue with your enlistment processing without delay. If you score higher on the verification test than you did on the PICAT, your PICAT score will be the score of record. In other words, the verification test does not result in a new score.

PREPARING FOR THE ASVAB

To score high on the ASVAB, you should begin preparing for the tests. You can do this by studying subject matter, reviewing sample questions in practice exercises, and taking practice test batteries. By using the following strategies, you can prepare yourself to achieve the scores you want on test day.

1. **Become familiar with the format of multiple-choice test items.** These items are used exclusively in the ASVAB.
2. **Become familiar with the keyboard layout used in the exam.** Read the section in this chapter about how the keyboard is set up for your use during the ASVAB.
3. **Find out what the test will cover.** This book and your recruiter are excellent sources for test-taking tips and strategies as well as information about what type of questions to expect.
4. **Review subject matter covered in the test.** Review the content in the ASVAB Review Basics section of this book. This reviews the basics for each subject test.
5. **Take each Practice Test in this book under actual test conditions.** Answer all questions in these practice tests within the allotted time of the actual test. Refer to the chart of the ASVAB contents in this section that contains the allotted test times for each section.
6. **Check your answers with the answer keys and explanations at the end of each practice test.** For questions answered incorrectly, determine why your original answers are incorrect. Be sure that you also understand the rationale for arriving at the correct answer. This is important to expand your knowledge in the subject areas and have a better understanding of the types of questions that may appear on the test.
7. **Set aside time every day for concentrated study.** Adhere closely to the schedule you set for yourself, and do not waste time with too many breaks.
8. **Study with a friend or a group.** This can be helpful and may ease the stress of studying. You can also quiz each other on different subjects as needed.

9. **Eliminate distractions.** Studying is easier when there are few or no distractions. Disturbances caused by family and neighbor activities (telephone calls, television, radio, conversations, etc.) will work to your disadvantage. Try to find a quiet room in which to study and, if necessary, use the library.

10. **Keep physically fit.** You cannot study as effectively when you are tired, ill, or tense. Because you are at your mental best when you are in good physical health, make sure you get a good night's sleep, daily exercise, and recreation and maintain a balanced diet.

Should You Guess on Test Day?

If you do not know the answer to a multiple-choice test item, should you guess? **Yes!** There is no penalty for incorrect answers on the ASVAB, so it is to your advantage to answer every question. If you can eliminate any answer choices you know are definitely wrong and can then make your selection from one of the remaining answer choices, you have made an "educated" guess rather than having guessed blindly. You also have increased your probabilities of guessing correctly.

Tips on Guessing

Be sure to remember these three important points when preparing for the ASVAB and making a decision about guessing:

1. Answer all items. There is no penalty for wrong answers.

2. An "educated" guess is better than guessing "blindly."

3. Guessing "blindly" is better than not guessing at all.

TAKING THE ASVAB

Here are some tips to help you succeed on your test day:

1. **If possible, avoid taking the test when you are tired, ill, injured, or emotionally upset.** Go to bed early the night before the test and get a good night's sleep.

2. **Eat a light meal.** Eating a heavy meal just before the test can make you sleepy and dull your senses.

3. **Bring a watch to help you budget your time.** Be sure that you know the amount of time you have for each subject test.

4. **Refrain from drinking excessive amounts of liquids.** Don't create the need to waste valuable testing time by going to the restroom during the test. Use the restroom before or after the test, not during the test.

5. **Arrive on time at the test location.** Choose a comfortable seat, if you have a choice, with good lighting and away from possible distractions, such as friends, the proctor's desk, the door, open windows, etc.

6. **Inform the proctor of your special needs.** If you are left-handed, have any special physical requirements, or have other needs, ask if some arrangements can be made so you can compete equally with the other candidates.

7. **Call uncomfortable conditions to the attention of the person in charge.** This includes the examination room being too cold, too warm, or not well ventilated.

8. **Be confident and calm.** If you follow this study plan of evaluating your strengths and weaknesses, reading the subject reviews of the areas you are unsure of, and completing the four practice tests in this book, you will have the confidence you need to score high on the ASVAB.

9. **Give the test your complete attention.** Block out all other thoughts, pleasant or otherwise, and concentrate solely on the test.

10. **Listen carefully to all instructions.** Carefully read the directions for taking the test and using the computer. If you don't understand the instructions or directions, raise your hand and ask the proctor for clarification. Failure to follow instructions or misreading directions can only result in a loss of points.

11. **When the signal is given to begin the test, start with the first question.** Don't jump to conclusions. Carefully read the question and all the choices before selecting the answer.

12. **Answer the question as given.** Do not answer what you *believe* the question should be.

13. **Work steadily and quickly but not carelessly.** Be sure to keep an eye on the time so you can complete each section. Note that you will not be permitted to go back and check your answers on the subject tests that you have already completed.

14. **Do not spend too much time on any one question.** If you can't figure out the answer in a few seconds, make an educated guess and go on to the next question. Continue this way through the subject tests. Remember, each question carries the same weight in terms of scoring.

YOUR ASVAB RESULTS

Your student ASVAB results are mailed to your school within thirty days after you take the ASVAB. ASVAB results consist of a combined Student Results Sheet and Counselor Summary for each student tested, as well as School Summary Reports.

The Student Results Sheet contains the following information:

- Student identification information (name, grade, Social Security number, test date, and school)
- Percentile scores for academic composites and all ten tests by same grade/same sex and same grade/opposite sex
- Graphic representation of student same grade/same sex percentile scores showing score bands
- The student's ASVAB Codes and Military Careers Score
- An explanation of percentile scores
- An explanation of score bands
- An explanation of the ASVAB Codes and the Military Careers Score
- An explanation of how to use ASVAB scores for career exploration
- A description of the ASVAB tests
- A brief description of *Exploring Careers: The ASVAB Workbook*

- An explanation of what information is released, to whom, and for what purposes

Also included is a *Counselor Summary* containing all the information that is provided to the student, plus percentile scores for academic composites and tests by same grade/gender. A sample of the student ASVAB Summary Results form is provided at the end of Part One. General information of interest to counselors is given on the back of the summary form. This summary can be detached and filed in the student's cumulative record.

If you took the enlistment ASVAB, your recruiter informs you of your scores. The recruiter also explains the breakdown of your scores, including the percentiles, composites, and military scores.

For more information about what your student ASVAB scores mean, check the ASVAB website at *www.ASVABProgram.com*.

PERCENTILE SCORES

ASVAB scores are reported as percentile scores, which indicate your standing in relation to a national sample of students. Since test results are not exact measures of ability, ASVAB percentile scores are reported within a score band. The score band indicates the range within which your true score probably lies. The ASVAB score report indicates score bands with dashes surrounded by brackets.

When bands for two tests overlap substantially, such as the Paragraph Comprehension and Arithmetic Reasoning tests, it is unlikely that the student has scored better on one than on the other. Where there is little or no overlap, it can be said with more confidence that the student's ability ranking is higher in one area than the other.

Both same grade/same sex and same grade/opposite sex percentile scores are reported. The scores that are most important are those for the student's same grade level and sex. These scores allow you to see your performance compared to that of your peers. The same grade/opposite sex percentiles are reported since men and women tend to perform differently on some ASVAB tests. On those tests that make up the academic composites, the differences are slight. On the more technical tests, the differences are more significant. Men tend to perform better on the Electronics Information test, for example, and women on the Coding Speed subtest. The goal of reporting these differences is for students to determine if they need to gain additional experience through course work or independent study to compete effectively and achieve their career goals.

COMPOSITE SCORES

The composite scores you receive are combinations of results of two or more parts of the ASVAB. The following indicates what each composite score measures and shows the various tests that contribute to each composite score.

ASVAB Codes

Your score report includes two ASVAB Codes, a primary ASVAB Code and a secondary ASVAB Code. These codes can be used with *Exploring Careers: The ASVAB Workbook* to identify occupations in which workers have aptitude levels similar to your own. ASVAB Codes are based on a five-level reduction of the Academic Ability Composite according to the following chart.

The first number in the ASVAB Code spot is your primary code. It can be used to find the occupations most suited to your aptitude levels. The second number is your secondary code, and it can be used to locate the occupations next most suited to your aptitude levels. Using two ASVAB Codes greatly expands the list of possible occupations to be explored. The codes summarize your level of general ability, and, together with interest inventory results and personal preferences, they can be used to evaluate different occupations as possible career choices.

Primary Code	Academic Ability Percentiles		Secondary Code
1	90–99		2
2	70–89	80–89	1
		70–79	3
3	50–69	60–69	2
		50–59	4
4	30–49	40–49	3
		30–39	5
5	01–29		4

Military Career Score

The Military Career Score is a combination of scores from the Academic Ability, Mechanical Comprehension, and Electronics Information tests. It estimates your likelihood of qualifying for various enlisted occupations described in *Military Careers*, a Department of Defense publication that details occupations available in the military. The Military Career Score is reported in a range between 140 and 240, with a mean of 200. Appendix A, Military Enlisted Occupations and Civilian Counterparts, is a condensed version of enlisted occupations described in *Military Careers* and can be used to estimate your chances of qualifying for such occupations.

Although the military uses sets of composites and scoring slightly different from the student ASVAB composites, most enlistment composites have test content the same as or similar to that of the student ASVAB composites. The two composites both predict successful performance in military technical training courses.

Academic Ability

Academic Ability is a general indicator of future academic success. It is a measure of how well you did on the Verbal Ability and Math Ability sections combined.

$$\text{ACADEMIC ABILITY} = \left[\text{WORD KNOWLEDGE} + \text{PARAGRAPH COMPREHENSION}\right] + \left[\text{ARITHMETIC REASONING} + \text{MATHEMATICS KNOWLEDGE}\right]$$

Scores of tests in brackets are combined and weighted as one unit.

Verbal Ability

Verbal Ability measures your performance on the Word Knowledge and Paragraph Comprehension tests combined. It is a general indicator of one's ability to learn from written material.

$$\text{VERBAL ABILITY} = \text{WORD KNOWLEDGE} + \text{PARAGRAPH COMPREHENSION}$$

Math Ability

Math Ability measures how well you did on the Arithmetic Reasoning and Mathematics Knowledge tests combined. It is a general indicator of success in future math courses.

$$\text{MATH ABILITY} = \text{ARITHMETIC REASONING} + \text{MATHEMATICS KNOWLEDGE}$$

Using Individual Test Scores

Individual test scores that are not used in computing ASVAB Codes—General Science, Auto & Shop Information, Mechanical Comprehension, Electronics Information, and Assembling Objects—can be used to provide additional direction for career explorations. Scores on individual ASVAB tests that are significantly higher or lower than the rest may point out particular strengths or weaknesses that might be considered in selecting the careers to be explored.

Using Military Scores

Enlistment processing occurs at Military Entrance Processing Stations (MEPs) and Mobile Examining Team (MET) sites located throughout the country. ASVAB results are used to determine if you qualify for entry into a service and if you have the specific aptitude level required for job specialty training programs. If you took the ASVAB in high school or postsecondary school, you can use your scores to determine whether you qualify for entry into the military services, provided the scores are not more than two years old.

Using Armed Forces Qualification Scores

The Armed Forces Qualification Test (AFQT) raw score is derived from the raw scores obtained on the ASVAB, as follows:

$$\begin{array}{c} \text{AFQT} \\ \text{RAW} \\ \text{SCORE} \end{array} = \begin{bmatrix} \begin{array}{cc} \begin{array}{l}\text{WORD} \\ \text{KNOWLEDGE} \\ \text{RAW SCORE}\end{array} + \begin{array}{l}\text{PARAGRAPH} \\ \text{COMPREHENSION} \\ \text{RAW SCORE}\end{array} \end{array} \end{bmatrix} + \begin{bmatrix} \begin{array}{cc} \begin{array}{l}\text{ARITHMETIC} \\ \text{REASONING} \\ \text{RAW SCORE}\end{array} + \begin{array}{l}\text{MATHEMATICS} \\ \text{KNOWLEDGE} \\ \text{RAW SCORE}\end{array} \end{array} \end{bmatrix}$$

This AFQT Raw Score is then converted into a Percentile Score, which is used to determine eligibility for entrance into the military.

Applicants without prior military service who receive an AFQT percentile score of 10 or higher are eligible for continued processing at a MEPS. However, the services usually reject those who fail to score in the top three categories. Typically, the services prefer applicants who score in the following categories:

Category	Percentile Score
Category I	93 and higher
Category II	65 to 92
Category III	31 to 64

A limited number of Category IV (Percentile score: 10 to 30) may be accepted under certain circumstances. Final determination of acceptability remains with the services. Also, applicants with prior military service who wish to return to the military are processed for enlistment at the discretion of the service, regardless of the AFQT score.

FREQUENTLY-ASKED QUESTIONS ABOUT THE ASVAB

What is the Armed Services Vocational Aptitude Battery?

The ASVAB, sponsored by the Department of Defense, is a multi-aptitude test battery that includes nine or ten individual tests covering General Science, Arithmetic Reasoning, Word Knowledge, Paragraph Comprehension, Mathematics Knowledge, Electronics Information, Auto & Shop Information, and Mechanical Comprehension. If you take the production (enlistment) ASVAB, there is an additional test called Assembling Objects. Your ASVAB results provide scores for each individual test as well as three academic composite scores—Verbal, Math, and Academic Ability—and two career exploration composite scores.

What is an aptitude?

An aptitude measures your readiness to excel when given the opportunity. This means that you have the ability to learn one type of work or indicates your potential for general training. The ASVAB measures aptitudes that relate to how successful you may be in different jobs.

Why should I take the ASVAB?

As a high school student nearing graduation, a student in a postsecondary school, or a recent high school graduate, you are faced with important career choices. Should you go on to college or a technical or vocational school? Would it be better to enter the job market? Should you consider a military career? As stated, your ASVAB scores are measures of aptitude. Three of the composite scores measure your aptitude for higher academic learning. The other two general composite scores are provided for career exploration purposes.

The ASVAB is a requirement for entrance into the military. It is also used to determine your eligibility for enlisted occupations.

Another reason to take the ASVAB is to change career fields when you are already in the military. This is needed if you do not have qualifying ASVAB scores on file for that particular career.

When and where is the ASVAB given?

ASVAB is given once or twice a year at more than 14,000 high schools and postsecondary schools in the United States. It is also given year-round at either a Military Entrance Processing Station (MEPS) or at a Mobile Examining Team (MET) site for anyone interested in enlistment.

Is there a charge or fee to take the ASVAB?

There are no fees for taking any version of the ASVAB.

How long does it take to complete the ASVAB?

It takes approximately 3 hours to complete the ASVAB. This includes the time it takes for you to take the test (which is about 2.5 hours long) as well as time for administrative needs (giving instructions, passing out the tests, etc.).

If I want to take the student ASVAB but my school doesn't offer it (or I missed it), what should I do?

If you want to take the ASVAB to join the military, contact your local recruiter to arrange it. If you want to take the student version of the ASVAB for career exploration, you may be able to take it at another school that offers the exam. Ask your guidance counselor to locate a school and make arrangements for you.

How do I find out what my scores mean and how to use them?

If you take the student ASVAB, your scores are given to you, your guidance counselor, and possibly to recruiting services in a report called the ASVAB Student Results Sheet. You will also receive a copy of *Exploring Careers: The ASVAB Workbook* from your guidance counselor. This contains information that will help you understand your ASVAB results and show you how to use them for career exploration. Test results are sent to schools within 30 days of your test date.

If you take the enlistment ASVAB, your recruiter will contact you with your results. Note that CAT-ASVAB results are automatically computed when you finish the test and your score report is printed out. This report contains raw and standard scores for each subject test as well as composite scores. If you qualify for enlistment, you are told the same day when to return for further processing.

Can a high school give the ASVAB test without having scores released to local military recruiters?

Yes. Schools have eight options regarding the release of test information. One option is "Option 8. No release to recruiters." If your school chooses Option 8, recruiters will not receive students' scores. Another option for schools is "Option 1. No special instructions." Under this option, recruiters can obtain scores and use them however they wish. If a school does not select an option, it will automatically be categorized as Option 1. Between Option 1 and Option 8 are other options specifying when recruiters may receive full information or whether they will be given access to phone numbers. Check with your guidance counselor if you wish to confirm what option your school selects or if you wish to have your scores withheld from recruiters.

What is a passing score on the ASVAB?

No one "passes" or "fails" the ASVAB. The ASVAB helps you to identify your abilities in different areas and can help you choose a career path. You can also compare your student ASVAB scores to other students at your grade level. If you plan to join the military, you need to meet minimum score requirements that vary from branch to branch. Your enlistment scores also identify your potential for military career areas.

If I take the ASVAB, am I obligated to join the military?

No. Taking the ASVAB does not obligate you to the military in any way.

Is there any relationship between taking the ASVAB and Selective Service registration?

There is no relationship between taking the ASVAB and Selective Service registration. The Selective Service System keeps a list of men from 18 to 25 years old who register to make themselves available in the case of a national emergency for draft purposes. ASVAB information is not available to the Selective Service System.

If I am planning to go to college, should I take the ASVAB?

Yes. ASVAB results provide you with information that can help you determine your capacity for advanced academic education. You can also use your ASVAB results, along with other personal information, to identify areas for career exploration.

If I take the ASVAB in school, can my scores be used if I decide to enlist in the military?

Yes. You can use your ASVAB results for up to two years for military enlistment if you are a junior, a senior, or a postsecondary school student. The military services encourage everyone to finish high school before joining the armed forces.

How long can I use my ASVAB test results for entrance into the military?

If you are a junior, senior, or a postsecondary student, you can use your ASVAB scores for up to two years for military enlistment. If you are a sophomore, you can't use the scores for enlistment and need to take the ASVAB in your junior or senior year or when you apply for military service.

If you take the enlistment ASVAB, your scores are good for two years from your test date.

Should I take the ASVAB if I plan to become a commissioned officer?

Yes. Taking the ASVAB is a valuable experience for any student who wants to become a military officer. The aptitude information you receive could help you in career planning.

Should I take the ASVAB if I am considering entering the Reserve or National Guard?

Yes. The Reserve and National Guard also use the ASVAB for enlistment purposes.

What should I do if a service recruiter contacts me after I take the student ASVAB?

A service recruiter may contact you before you graduate. If you want to learn about the many opportunities available through military service, arrange for a follow-up meeting. You are under no obligation to the military as a result of taking the ASVAB. If you do decide to meet with a recruiter, we suggest that you read the most recent edition of another book, *Guide to Joining the Military* (3rd edition), which is full of essential information about the enlistment process.

Is the ASVAB administered other than in the school testing program?

Yes. ASVAB is also used in the regular military enlistment program. This version is known as the enlistment ASVAB and is administered at MEPS and MET sites located throughout the United States. Each year, hundreds of thousands of young men and women who are interested in enlisting in the uniformed services (Army, Navy, Air Force, Marines, and Coast Guard), but did not take the ASVAB while in high school or postsecondary school are examined and processed at these military stations.

Is the ASVAB used in the regular military enlistment program the same as the student ASVAB?

Yes and no. The enlistment ASVAB given at MEPS is a Computerized Adaptive Testing program known as CAT-ASVAB. These tests are not paper-and-pencil tests but are computer administered. An additional section called Assembling Objects is part of the CAT-ASVAB but not the student ASVAB.

The paper-and-pencil enlistment ASVAB given at MET sites contains the same subject tests as the CAT-ASVAB.

What is Military Careers?

This is a career information book created by the U.S. Department of Defense. It describes up to 200 enlisted and officer occupations in all of the military services. A condensed version of *Military Careers* is included at the end of this book. High schools that sponsor the ASVAB are sent copies of *Military Careers* for interested students.

Is any special preparation necessary before taking the ASVAB?

Yes. Preparation is required for taking any examination, and it is a *must* to achieve the best results. Your test scores reflect not only your ability but also the time and effort you put into preparing for the test. The military services use ASVAB scores to help determine a person's qualification for enlistment and to help indicate the vocational areas for which that person is best suited. Getting the highest score you can increases your career and vocational opportunities.

SELF-EVALUATION CHART

This chart is a great way to see the progress you make after studying the subject review chapters and taking the sample practice tests. Start by recording the test results of the first ASVAB practice test. Be sure to read each subject review section, giving more time to those tests on which you scored low. As you take and record your results on the second, third, and fourth ASVAB practice test, you will see the progress made through your test preparation.

Number Answered Correctly					
Number of Questions		**Practice Test 1: Diagnostic**	**Practice Test 2**	**Practice Test 3**	**Practice Test 4**
1. General Science	25				
2. Arithmetic Reasoning	30				
3. Word Knowledge	35				
4. Paragraph Comprehension	15				
5. Mathematics Knowledge	25				
6. Electronics Information	20				
7. Auto & Shop Information	25				
8. Mechanical Comprehension	25				
9. Assembling Objects	16				

ASVAB SUMMARY RESULTS

Student
12th Gr Female (Form 23G)
SSN: XXX-XX-9999
Old Dominion H.S.
Hometown DC

Print No.:XXXXX

ASVAB Results

12th Grade Standard Score Bands

	Percentile Scores			12th Grade Standard Score
	12th Grade Females	12th Grade Males	12th Grade Students	
Career Exploration Scores				
Verbal Skills	97	95	96	65
Math Skills	22	17	19	42
Science and Technical Skills	81	48	64	53
ASVAB Tests				
General Science	91	81	86	61
Arithmetic Reasoning	43	30	37	47
Word Knowledge	98	95	96	66
Paragraph Comprehension	92	91	91	62
Mathematics Knowledge	14	12	13	37
Electronics Information	13	10	11	38
Auto and Shop Information	53	21	37	45
Mechanical Comprehension	95	76	85	59

Military Entrance Score (AFQT) 57

EXPLANATION OF YOUR ASVAB PERCENTILE SCORES

Your ASVAB results are reported as percentile scores in the three highlighted columns to the left of the graph. Percentile scores show how you compare to other students - males and females, and for all students - in your grade. For example, a percentile score of 65 for an 11th grade female would mean she scored the same or better than 65 out of every 100 females in the 11th grade.

For purposes of career planning, knowing your relative standing in these comparison groups is important. Being male or female does not limit your career or educational choices. There are noticeable differences in how men and women score in some areas. Viewing your scores in light of your relative standing both for men and women may encourage you to explore areas that you might otherwise overlook.

You can use the **Career Exploration Scores** to evaluate your knowledge and skills in three general areas (Verbal, Math, and Science and Technical Skills). You can use the **ASVAB Test Scores** together with information on specific skill areas. *Together, these scores provide a snapshot of your current knowledge and skills.* This information will help you develop and review your career goals and plans.

EXPLANATION OF YOUR ASVAB STANDARD SCORES

Your ASVAB results are reported as standard scores in the above graph. Your score on each test is identified by the "X" in the corresponding bar graph. You should view these scores as *estimates* of your true skill level in that area. If you took the test again, you probably would receive a somewhat different score. Many things, such as how you were feeling during testing, contribute to this difference. This difference is shown with gray score bands in the graph of your results. Your standard scores are based on the ASVAB tests and composites based on your grade level.

The score bands provide a way to identify some of your strengths. Overlapping score bands mean your true skill level is similar in both areas, so the real difference between specific scores might not be meaningful. If the score bands do not overlap, you probably are stronger in the area that has the higher score band.

The ASVAB is an aptitude test. It is neither an absolute measure of your skills and abilities nor a perfect predictor of your success or failure. A high score does not guarantee success, and a low score does not guarantee failure, in a future educational program or occupation. For example, if you have never worked with shop equipment or cars, you may not be familiar with the terms and concepts

assessed by the Auto and Shop Information test. Taking a course or obtaining a part-time job in this area would increase your knowledge and improve your score if you were to take it again.

USING ASVAB RESULTS IN CAREER EXPLORATION

Your career and educational plans may change over time as you gain more experience and learn more about your interests. *Exploring Careers: The ASVAB Career Exploration Guide* can help you learn more about yourself and the world of work, to identify and explore potential goals, and develop an effective strategy to realize your goals. The *Guide* will help you identify occupations in line with your interests and skills. As you explore potentially satisfying careers, you will develop your career exploration and planning skills.

Meanwhile, your ASVAB results can help you in making well-informed choices about your future high school courses.

We encourage you to discuss your ASVAB results with a teacher, counselor, parent, family member or other interested adult. These individuals can help you to view your ASVAB results in light of other important information, such as your interests, school grades, motivation, and personal goals.

USE OF INFORMATION

Personal identity information (name, social security number, street address, and telephone number) and test scores will not be released to any agency outside of the Department of Defense (DoD), the Armed Forces, the Coast Guard, and your school. Your school or local school system can determine any further release of information. The DoD will use your scores for recruiting and research purposes for up to two years. After that the information will be used by the DoD for research purposes only.

MILITARY ENTRANCE SCORES

The **Military Entrance Score** (also called AFQT, which stands for the Armed Forces Qualification Test) is the score used to determine your qualifications for entry into any branch of the United States Armed Forces or the Coast Guard. The Military Entrance Score predicts in a general way how well you might do in training and on the job in military occupations. Your score reflects your standing compared to American men and women 18 to 23 years of age.

www.asvabprogram.com

SEE YOUR COUNSELOR FOR FURTHER INFORMATION

ARE YOU READY TO MOVE FORWARD?

If you've reviewed the information in this chapter carefully, then congratulations—you have a solid understanding of what the ASVAB is all about and what you can expect when you take the test.

You're now ready to move forward in *Master the ASVAB*. The chapters in this book provide an in-depth look at all subject tests on the ASVAB, with thorough practice and careful review for every concept and topic tested. You'll also get advice and strategies for getting the best possible score—so make sure you pay close attention.

We wish you the very best of luck on your road to ASVAB success—but you have more than luck on your side. With *Master the ASVAB*, you're equipped with the practical preparation tools you need to achieve your goals.

PART II
DIAGNOSING STRENGTHS AND WEAKNESSES

CHAPTER 2   Practice Test 1: Diagnostic

Practice Test 1: Diagnostic

You are now ready to take the ASVAB practice test to assess your strengths and weaknesses. The scores you get on this practice test will help pinpoint the areas you need to focus on for review and extra practice.

The practice test answer sheets and answer keys are included to help you determine your scores. Answer explanations are also provided to give you the reasoning behind each answer. Note that the format of this practice test is the same format and content as an actual ASVAB test. Follow these guidelines to make the most of this practice test:

- Take this test under "real" test conditions (time yourself, take it in a quiet room without distractions, and use the sample answer sheets).

- Time each test carefully and do not go over the time allotted for each section.

- Use the answer keys to get your test scores and to evaluate your performance on each test.

- Record the number of questions you answered correctly and incorrectly for each section in the answer chart provided at the end of the test. Also, record the number of questions you want to review further or were unsure about.

- Carefully review and understand the answer explanations to all questions you answered incorrectly.

- Don't forget to review each of the questions that you answered correctly but may not be sure of. This is a necessary step to gain the knowledge and expertise you need to get the highest scores possible on the real ASVAB tests.

- Transfer your scores for each section of Practice Test 1: Diagnostic to the Self-Evaluation Chart on page 22. This will enable you to track your progress as you continue to prepare for the actual test.

- Use the practice test answer sheets provided to record your answers. If you prefer, you can cut them out to make them easier to use and to simulate actual test conditions.

ANSWER SHEET PRACTICE TEST 1: DIAGNOSTIC

Part 1: General Science

1.Ⓐ Ⓑ Ⓒ Ⓓ   2.Ⓐ Ⓑ Ⓒ Ⓓ   3.Ⓐ Ⓑ Ⓒ Ⓓ   4.Ⓐ Ⓑ Ⓒ Ⓓ   5.Ⓐ Ⓑ Ⓒ Ⓓ
6.Ⓐ Ⓑ Ⓒ Ⓓ   7.Ⓐ Ⓑ Ⓒ Ⓓ   8.Ⓐ Ⓑ Ⓒ Ⓓ   9.Ⓐ Ⓑ Ⓒ Ⓓ   10.Ⓐ Ⓑ Ⓒ Ⓓ
11.Ⓐ Ⓑ Ⓒ Ⓓ   12.Ⓐ Ⓑ Ⓒ Ⓓ   13.Ⓐ Ⓑ Ⓒ Ⓓ   14.Ⓐ Ⓑ Ⓒ Ⓓ   15.Ⓐ Ⓑ Ⓒ Ⓓ
16.Ⓐ Ⓑ Ⓒ Ⓓ   17.Ⓐ Ⓑ Ⓒ Ⓓ   18.Ⓐ Ⓑ Ⓒ Ⓓ   19.Ⓐ Ⓑ Ⓒ Ⓓ   20.Ⓐ Ⓑ Ⓒ Ⓓ
21.Ⓐ Ⓑ Ⓒ Ⓓ   22.Ⓐ Ⓑ Ⓒ Ⓓ   23.Ⓐ Ⓑ Ⓒ Ⓓ   24.Ⓐ Ⓑ Ⓒ Ⓓ   25.Ⓐ Ⓑ Ⓒ Ⓓ

Part 2: Arithmetic Reasoning

1.Ⓐ Ⓑ Ⓒ Ⓓ   2.Ⓐ Ⓑ Ⓒ Ⓓ   3.Ⓐ Ⓑ Ⓒ Ⓓ   4.Ⓐ Ⓑ Ⓒ Ⓓ   5.Ⓐ Ⓑ Ⓒ Ⓓ
6.Ⓐ Ⓑ Ⓒ Ⓓ   7.Ⓐ Ⓑ Ⓒ Ⓓ   8.Ⓐ Ⓑ Ⓒ Ⓓ   9.Ⓐ Ⓑ Ⓒ Ⓓ   10.Ⓐ Ⓑ Ⓒ Ⓓ
11.Ⓐ Ⓑ Ⓒ Ⓓ   12.Ⓐ Ⓑ Ⓒ Ⓓ   13.Ⓐ Ⓑ Ⓒ Ⓓ   14.Ⓐ Ⓑ Ⓒ Ⓓ   15.Ⓐ Ⓑ Ⓒ Ⓓ
16.Ⓐ Ⓑ Ⓒ Ⓓ   17.Ⓐ Ⓑ Ⓒ Ⓓ   18.Ⓐ Ⓑ Ⓒ Ⓓ   19.Ⓐ Ⓑ Ⓒ Ⓓ   20.Ⓐ Ⓑ Ⓒ Ⓓ
21.Ⓐ Ⓑ Ⓒ Ⓓ   22.Ⓐ Ⓑ Ⓒ Ⓓ   23.Ⓐ Ⓑ Ⓒ Ⓓ   24.Ⓐ Ⓑ Ⓒ Ⓓ   25.Ⓐ Ⓑ Ⓒ Ⓓ
26.Ⓐ Ⓑ Ⓒ Ⓓ   27.Ⓐ Ⓑ Ⓒ Ⓓ   28.Ⓐ Ⓑ Ⓒ Ⓓ   29.Ⓐ Ⓑ Ⓒ Ⓓ   30.Ⓐ Ⓑ Ⓒ Ⓓ

Part 3: Word Knowledge

1.Ⓐ Ⓑ Ⓒ Ⓓ   2.Ⓐ Ⓑ Ⓒ Ⓓ   3.Ⓐ Ⓑ Ⓒ Ⓓ   4.Ⓐ Ⓑ Ⓒ Ⓓ   5.Ⓐ Ⓑ Ⓒ Ⓓ
6.Ⓐ Ⓑ Ⓒ Ⓓ   7.Ⓐ Ⓑ Ⓒ Ⓓ   8.Ⓐ Ⓑ Ⓒ Ⓓ   9.Ⓐ Ⓑ Ⓒ Ⓓ   10.Ⓐ Ⓑ Ⓒ Ⓓ
11.Ⓐ Ⓑ Ⓒ Ⓓ   12.Ⓐ Ⓑ Ⓒ Ⓓ   13.Ⓐ Ⓑ Ⓒ Ⓓ   14.Ⓐ Ⓑ Ⓒ Ⓓ   15.Ⓐ Ⓑ Ⓒ Ⓓ
16.Ⓐ Ⓑ Ⓒ Ⓓ   17.Ⓐ Ⓑ Ⓒ Ⓓ   18.Ⓐ Ⓑ Ⓒ Ⓓ   19.Ⓐ Ⓑ Ⓒ Ⓓ   20.Ⓐ Ⓑ Ⓒ Ⓓ
21.Ⓐ Ⓑ Ⓒ Ⓓ   22.Ⓐ Ⓑ Ⓒ Ⓓ   23.Ⓐ Ⓑ Ⓒ Ⓓ   24.Ⓐ Ⓑ Ⓒ Ⓓ   25.Ⓐ Ⓑ Ⓒ Ⓓ
26.Ⓐ Ⓑ Ⓒ Ⓓ   27.Ⓐ Ⓑ Ⓒ Ⓓ   28.Ⓐ Ⓑ Ⓒ Ⓓ   29.Ⓐ Ⓑ Ⓒ Ⓓ   30.Ⓐ Ⓑ Ⓒ Ⓓ
31.Ⓐ Ⓑ Ⓒ Ⓓ   32.Ⓐ Ⓑ Ⓒ Ⓓ   33.Ⓐ Ⓑ Ⓒ Ⓓ   34.Ⓐ Ⓑ Ⓒ Ⓓ   35.Ⓐ Ⓑ Ⓒ Ⓓ

Part 4: Paragraph Comprehension

1.Ⓐ Ⓑ Ⓒ Ⓓ   2.Ⓐ Ⓑ Ⓒ Ⓓ   3.Ⓐ Ⓑ Ⓒ Ⓓ   4.Ⓐ Ⓑ Ⓒ Ⓓ   5.Ⓐ Ⓑ Ⓒ Ⓓ
6.Ⓐ Ⓑ Ⓒ Ⓓ   7.Ⓐ Ⓑ Ⓒ Ⓓ   8.Ⓐ Ⓑ Ⓒ Ⓓ   9.Ⓐ Ⓑ Ⓒ Ⓓ   10.Ⓐ Ⓑ Ⓒ Ⓓ
11.Ⓐ Ⓑ Ⓒ Ⓓ   12.Ⓐ Ⓑ Ⓒ Ⓓ   13.Ⓐ Ⓑ Ⓒ Ⓓ   14.Ⓐ Ⓑ Ⓒ Ⓓ   15.Ⓐ Ⓑ Ⓒ Ⓓ

Part 5: Mathematics Knowledge

1. Ⓐ Ⓑ Ⓒ Ⓓ   2. Ⓐ Ⓑ Ⓒ Ⓓ   3. Ⓐ Ⓑ Ⓒ Ⓓ   4. Ⓐ Ⓑ Ⓒ Ⓓ   5. Ⓐ Ⓑ Ⓒ Ⓓ
6. Ⓐ Ⓑ Ⓒ Ⓓ   7. Ⓐ Ⓑ Ⓒ Ⓓ   8. Ⓐ Ⓑ Ⓒ Ⓓ   9. Ⓐ Ⓑ Ⓒ Ⓓ   10. Ⓐ Ⓑ Ⓒ Ⓓ
11. Ⓐ Ⓑ Ⓒ Ⓓ   12. Ⓐ Ⓑ Ⓒ Ⓓ   13. Ⓐ Ⓑ Ⓒ Ⓓ   14. Ⓐ Ⓑ Ⓒ Ⓓ   15. Ⓐ Ⓑ Ⓒ Ⓓ
16. Ⓐ Ⓑ Ⓒ Ⓓ   17. Ⓐ Ⓑ Ⓒ Ⓓ   18. Ⓐ Ⓑ Ⓒ Ⓓ   19. Ⓐ Ⓑ Ⓒ Ⓓ   20. Ⓐ Ⓑ Ⓒ Ⓓ
21. Ⓐ Ⓑ Ⓒ Ⓓ   22. Ⓐ Ⓑ Ⓒ Ⓓ   23. Ⓐ Ⓑ Ⓒ Ⓓ   24. Ⓐ Ⓑ Ⓒ Ⓓ   25. Ⓐ Ⓑ Ⓒ Ⓓ

Part 6: Electronics Information

1. Ⓐ Ⓑ Ⓒ Ⓓ   2. Ⓐ Ⓑ Ⓒ Ⓓ   3. Ⓐ Ⓑ Ⓒ Ⓓ   4. Ⓐ Ⓑ Ⓒ Ⓓ   5. Ⓐ Ⓑ Ⓒ Ⓓ
6. Ⓐ Ⓑ Ⓒ Ⓓ   7. Ⓐ Ⓑ Ⓒ Ⓓ   8. Ⓐ Ⓑ Ⓒ Ⓓ   9. Ⓐ Ⓑ Ⓒ Ⓓ   10. Ⓐ Ⓑ Ⓒ Ⓓ
11. Ⓐ Ⓑ Ⓒ Ⓓ   12. Ⓐ Ⓑ Ⓒ Ⓓ   13. Ⓐ Ⓑ Ⓒ Ⓓ   14. Ⓐ Ⓑ Ⓒ Ⓓ   15. Ⓐ Ⓑ Ⓒ Ⓓ
16. Ⓐ Ⓑ Ⓒ Ⓓ   17. Ⓐ Ⓑ Ⓒ Ⓓ   18. Ⓐ Ⓑ Ⓒ Ⓓ   19. Ⓐ Ⓑ Ⓒ Ⓓ   20. Ⓐ Ⓑ Ⓒ Ⓓ

Part 7: Auto & Shop Information

1. Ⓐ Ⓑ Ⓒ Ⓓ   2. Ⓐ Ⓑ Ⓒ Ⓓ   3. Ⓐ Ⓑ Ⓒ Ⓓ   4. Ⓐ Ⓑ Ⓒ Ⓓ   5. Ⓐ Ⓑ Ⓒ Ⓓ
6. Ⓐ Ⓑ Ⓒ Ⓓ   7. Ⓐ Ⓑ Ⓒ Ⓓ   8. Ⓐ Ⓑ Ⓒ Ⓓ   9. Ⓐ Ⓑ Ⓒ Ⓓ   10. Ⓐ Ⓑ Ⓒ Ⓓ
11. Ⓐ Ⓑ Ⓒ Ⓓ   12. Ⓐ Ⓑ Ⓒ Ⓓ   13. Ⓐ Ⓑ Ⓒ Ⓓ   14. Ⓐ Ⓑ Ⓒ Ⓓ   15. Ⓐ Ⓑ Ⓒ Ⓓ
16. Ⓐ Ⓑ Ⓒ Ⓓ   17. Ⓐ Ⓑ Ⓒ Ⓓ   18. Ⓐ Ⓑ Ⓒ Ⓓ   19. Ⓐ Ⓑ Ⓒ Ⓓ   20. Ⓐ Ⓑ Ⓒ Ⓓ
21. Ⓐ Ⓑ Ⓒ Ⓓ   22. Ⓐ Ⓑ Ⓒ Ⓓ   23. Ⓐ Ⓑ Ⓒ Ⓓ   24. Ⓐ Ⓑ Ⓒ Ⓓ   25. Ⓐ Ⓑ Ⓒ Ⓓ

Part 8: Mechanical Comprehension

1. Ⓐ Ⓑ Ⓒ Ⓓ   2. Ⓐ Ⓑ Ⓒ Ⓓ   3. Ⓐ Ⓑ Ⓒ Ⓓ   4. Ⓐ Ⓑ Ⓒ Ⓓ   5. Ⓐ Ⓑ Ⓒ Ⓓ
6. Ⓐ Ⓑ Ⓒ Ⓓ   7. Ⓐ Ⓑ Ⓒ Ⓓ   8. Ⓐ Ⓑ Ⓒ Ⓓ   9. Ⓐ Ⓑ Ⓒ Ⓓ   10. Ⓐ Ⓑ Ⓒ Ⓓ
11. Ⓐ Ⓑ Ⓒ Ⓓ   12. Ⓐ Ⓑ Ⓒ Ⓓ   13. Ⓐ Ⓑ Ⓒ Ⓓ   14. Ⓐ Ⓑ Ⓒ Ⓓ   15. Ⓐ Ⓑ Ⓒ Ⓓ
16. Ⓐ Ⓑ Ⓒ Ⓓ   17. Ⓐ Ⓑ Ⓒ Ⓓ   18. Ⓐ Ⓑ Ⓒ Ⓓ   19. Ⓐ Ⓑ Ⓒ Ⓓ   20. Ⓐ Ⓑ Ⓒ Ⓓ
21. Ⓐ Ⓑ Ⓒ Ⓓ   22. Ⓐ Ⓑ Ⓒ Ⓓ   23. Ⓐ Ⓑ Ⓒ Ⓓ   24. Ⓐ Ⓑ Ⓒ Ⓓ   25. Ⓐ Ⓑ Ⓒ Ⓓ

Part 9: Assembling Objects

1. Ⓐ Ⓑ Ⓒ Ⓓ   2. Ⓐ Ⓑ Ⓒ Ⓓ   3. Ⓐ Ⓑ Ⓒ Ⓓ   4. Ⓐ Ⓑ Ⓒ Ⓓ   5. Ⓐ Ⓑ Ⓒ Ⓓ
6. Ⓐ Ⓑ Ⓒ Ⓓ   7. Ⓐ Ⓑ Ⓒ Ⓓ   8. Ⓐ Ⓑ Ⓒ Ⓓ   9. Ⓐ Ⓑ Ⓒ Ⓓ   10. Ⓐ Ⓑ Ⓒ Ⓓ
11. Ⓐ Ⓑ Ⓒ Ⓓ   12. Ⓐ Ⓑ Ⓒ Ⓓ   13. Ⓐ Ⓑ Ⓒ Ⓓ   14. Ⓐ Ⓑ Ⓒ Ⓓ   15. Ⓐ Ⓑ Ⓒ Ⓓ
16. Ⓐ Ⓑ Ⓒ Ⓓ

answer sheet

PART 1: GENERAL SCIENCE

Time: 11 Minutes—25 Questions

> **Directions:** This is a test of 25 questions to find out how much you know about general science as usually covered in high school courses. Pick the best answer for each question, then blacken the space on your answer sheet that has the same number and letter as your choice.

Here are three sample questions.

1. Water is an example of a   Ⓐ Ⓑ ● Ⓓ
   A. solid.
   B. gas.
   C. liquid.
   D. crystal.

Notice that choice C has been marked for question 1. Now do practice questions 2 and 3 by yourself. Find the correct answer to the question, then mark the space that has the same letter as the answer you picked.

Do this now.

2. Lack of iodine is often related to which of the following diseases?   Ⓐ Ⓑ Ⓒ Ⓓ
   A. Beriberi
   B. Scurvy
   C. Rickets
   D. Goiter

3. An eclipse of the sun throws the shadow of the   Ⓐ Ⓑ Ⓒ Ⓓ
   A. earth on the moon.
   B. moon on the earth.
   C. moon on the sun.
   D. earth on the sun.

You should have marked choice D for question 2 and choice B for question 3. If you made any mistakes, erase your mark carefully and blacken the correct answer space. Do this now.

Your score on this test will be based on the number of questions you answer correctly. You should try to answer every question. Do not spend too much time on any one question.

When you begin, be sure to start with question number 1 in Part 1 in your test booklet and number 1 in Part 1 on your answer sheet.

1. Under natural conditions, large quantities of organic matter decay after each year's plant growth has been completed. As a result of such conditions
   A. many animals are deprived of adequate food supplies.
   B. soil erosion is accelerated.
   C. soils maintain their fertility.
   D. earthworms are added to the soil.

2. Which is NOT a fruit?
   A. Tomato
   B. Cucumber
   C. Green pepper
   D. Potato

3. The most likely reason why dinosaurs became extinct was that they
   A. were killed by erupting volcanoes.
   B. were eaten as adults by the advancing mammalian groups.
   C. failed to adapt to a changing environment.
   D. killed each other in combat.

4. Which of the following is a chemical change?
   A. Magnetizing a rod of iron
   B. Burning one pound of coal
   C. Mixing flake graphite with oil
   D. Vaporizing 1g of mercury in a vacuum

5. In the process of manufacturing food, plants
   A. create energy.
   B. destroy energy.
   C. store energy of the sun.
   D. do not need the energy of the sun.

6. One-celled animals belong to the group of living things known as
   A. protozoa.
   B. annelida.
   C. porifera.
   D. arthropoda.

7. Spiders can be distinguished from insects by the fact that spiders have
   A. hard outer coverings.
   B. large abdomens.
   C. four pairs of legs.
   D. biting mouth parts.

8. What temperature is shown on a Kelvin thermometer when a centigrade thermometer reads 0°?
   A. 32°
   B. 0°
   C. 273°
   D. −32°

9. Of the following, the lightest element known on Earth is
   A. hydrogen.
   B. oxygen.
   C. helium.
   D. air.

10. Of the following gases in the air, the most plentiful is
    A. argon.
    B. oxygen.
    C. nitrogen.
    D. carbon dioxide.

11. Which of the following is the result of a bacterial infection?
    A. Measles
    B. Mumps
    C. Smallpox
    D. Syphilis

12. Which alcohol would be present in alcoholic beverages?
    A. Grain alcohol
    B. Glyceryl alcohol
    C. Wood alcohol
    D. Isopropyl alcohol

13. A new drug for treatment of tuberculosis was being tested in a hospital. Patients in Group A actually received doses of the new drug; those in Group B were given only sugar pills. Group B represents a(n)
    A. scientific experiment.
    B. scientific method.
    C. experimental error.
    D. experimental control.

14. Of the following, the simple machine that provides a mechanical advantage of 1 is the
    A. screw.
    B. second-class lever.
    C. single fixed pulley.
    D. single movable pulley.

15. Radium is stored in lead containers because
    A. the lead absorbs the harmful radiation.
    B. radium is a heavy substance.
    C. lead prevents the disintegration of the radium.
    D. lead is cheap.

16. The type of joint that attaches the arm to the shoulder blade is known as a(n)
    A. hinge.
    B. pivot.
    C. immovable.
    D. ball and socket.

17. Limes were eaten by British sailors to
    A. justify their nickname, "limeys."
    B. pucker their mouths to resist the wind.
    C. satisfy their craving for something acidic.
    D. prevent scurvy.

18. The time that it takes for the earth to rotate 45° is
    A. 1 hour.
    B. 4 hours.
    C. 3 hours.
    D. 10 hours.

19. Which gas is exhaled by mammals?
    A. Oxygen
    B. Carbon dioxide
    C. Hydrogen
    D. Carbon monoxide

20. All of the following are amphibia EXCEPT the
    A. salamander.
    B. frog.
    C. lizard.
    D. toad.

21. Of the following planets, the one that has the shortest revolutionary period around the sun is
    A. Earth.
    B. Jupiter.
    C. Mercury.
    D. Venus.

22. The rate of doing work is known as
    A. effort.
    B. energy.
    C. mechanical advantage.
    D. power.

practice test 1

23. A circuit breaker is used in many homes instead of a
   A. switch.
   B. fire extinguisher.
   C. fuse.
   D. meter box.

24. What is the name of the negative particle that circles the nucleus of the atom?
   A. Neutron
   B. Meson
   C. Proton
   D. Electron

25. Which of the following rocks can be dissolved with a weak acid?
   A. Sandstone
   B. Gneiss
   C. Granite
   D. Limestone

STOP!
IF YOU FINISH BEFORE THE TIME IS UP, YOU MAY CHECK OVER YOUR WORK ON THIS PART ONLY.

PART 2: ARITHMETIC REASONING

Time: 36 Minutes—30 Questions

Directions: This test has 30 questions about arithmetic. Each question is followed by four possible answers. Decide which answer is correct, then blacken the space on your answer sheet that has the same number and letter as your choice. Use scratch paper to do any figuring.

Here are two sample questions.

1. A person buys a sandwich for $4.00, soda for $1.25, and pie for $1.75.

   What is the total cost?　　　　　　　　　　　　　　　Ⓐ Ⓑ Ⓒ Ⓓ
   A. $6.85
   B. $6.95
   C. $7.00
   D. $7.15

   The total cost is $7.00; therefore, choice C is the correct answer.

2. If 8 workers are needed to run 4 machines, how many workers are
   needed to run 20 machines?　　　　　　　　　　　　Ⓐ Ⓑ Ⓒ Ⓓ
   A. 16
   B. 32
   C. 36
   D. 40

   The number needed is 40; therefore, choice D is the correct answer.

Your score on this test will be based on the number of questions you answer correctly. You should try to answer every question. Do not spend too much time on any one question.

Notice that Part 2 begins with question number 1. When you begin, be sure to start with question number 1 in Part 2 in your test booklet and number 1 in Part 2 on your answer sheet.

1. A man owns 50 shares of stock worth $30 each. The corporation declared a dividend of 6% payable in stock. How many shares did he then own?
   A. 47 shares
   B. 53 shares
   C. 56 shares
   D. 62 shares

2. If a load of snow contains 3 tons, it will weigh how many pounds?
   A. 3,000
   B. 1,500
   C. 12,000
   D. 6,000

3. A pint of milk is what part of half a gallon?
   A. $\frac{1}{8}$
   B. $\frac{1}{4}$
   C. $\frac{1}{2}$
   D. $\frac{1}{16}$

4. At the rate of 4 peaches for a half dollar, 20 peaches will cost
   A. $1.60
   B. $2.00
   C. $2.40
   D. $2.50

5. A student deposited in his savings account the money he had saved during the week. Find the amount of his deposit if he had 10 one-dollar bills, 9 half dollars, 8 quarters, 16 dimes, and 25 nickels.
   A. $16.20
   B. $17.42
   C. $18.60
   D. $19.35

6. How many minutes are there in 1 day?
   A. 60
   B. 1,440
   C. 24
   D. $1,440 \times 60$

7. One year the postage rate for sending 1 ounce of mail first class was increased from 25 cents to 29 cents. The percent of increase in the 29-cent postage rate was most nearly
   A. 14 percent
   B. 16 percent
   C. 18 percent
   D. 20 percent

8. On a scale drawing, a line $\frac{1}{4}$ inch long represents a length of 1 foot. On the same drawing, what length represents 4 feet?
   A. 1 inch
   B. 2 inches
   C. 3 inches
   D. 4 inches

9. What is the greatest number of half-pint bottles that can be filled from a 10-gallon can of milk?
   A. 160
   B. 170
   C. 16
   D. 17

10. If a boat is towed at the rate of 4 miles per hour, how much time will be needed to tow the boat 17 miles?
    A. 5 hours, 15 minutes
    B. 4 hours, 30 minutes
    C. 4 hours, 15 minutes
    D. 5 hours, 30 minutes

11. If 3 apples cost 48¢, how many dozen apples can be bought for $3.84?

   A. 1

   B. $1\frac{1}{2}$

   C. 2

   D. $5\frac{1}{3}$

12. How much time is there between 8:30 a.m. today and 3:15 a.m. tomorrow?

   A. $17\frac{3}{4}$ hours

   B. $18\frac{1}{3}$ hours

   C. $18\frac{1}{2}$ hours

   D. $18\frac{3}{4}$ hours

13. If a fire truck is 55 feet away from a hydrant, it is how many feet nearer to the hydrant than a truck that is 105 feet away?

   A. 40 feet

   B. 50 feet

   C. 55 feet

   D. 60 feet

14. A woman's weekly salary is increased from $350 to $380. The percent of increase is most nearly

   A. 6 percent.

   B. $8\frac{1}{2}$ percent.

   C. 10 percent.

   D. $12\frac{1}{2}$ percent.

15. A truck going at a rate of 20 miles an hour will reach a town 40 miles away in how many hours?

   A. 3 hours

   B. 4 hours

   C. 1 hour

   D. 2 hours

16. If a barrel has a capacity of 100 gallons, how many gallons will it contain when it is two-fifths full?

   A. 20

   B. 40

   C. 60

   D. 80

17. If a salary of $20,000 is subject to a 20 percent deduction, the net salary is

   A. $14,000

   B. $15,500

   C. $16,000

   D. $18,000

18. If $2,000 is the cost of repairing 100 square yards of pavement, the cost of repairing 1 square yard is

   A. $20

   B. $100

   C. $150

   D. $200

19. A car can travel 24 miles on a gallon of gasoline. How many gallons will be used on a 192-mile trip?

   A. 8

   B. 9

   C. 10

   D. 11

20. If an annual salary of $21,600 is increased by a bonus of $720 and by a service increment of $1,200, the total annual pay is

   A. $22,320

   B. $22,800

   C. $23,320

   D. $23,520

practice test 1

21. A man takes out a $5,000 life insurance policy at a yearly rate of $29.62 per $1,000. What is the yearly premium?
   A. $90.10
   B. $100.10
   C. $126.10
   D. $148.10

22. On her maiden voyage, the *S.S. United States* made the trip from New York to England in 3 days, 10 hours, and 40 minutes, beating the record set by the *R.M.S. Queen Mary* in 1938 by 10 hours and 2 minutes. How long did it take the *Queen Mary* to make the trip?
   A. 3 days, 20 hours, 42 minutes
   B. 3 days, 15 hours, 38 minutes
   C. 3 days, 12 hours, 2 minutes
   D. 3 days, 8 hours, 12 minutes

23. A carpenter spent his 40-hour workweek as follows:

   $\frac{1}{4}$ of his time ordering materials;

   $\frac{1}{2}$ of his time doing the woodwork; and

   $\frac{1}{8}$ of his time talking to customers.

   The rest of his time was devoted to cleanup. What is the approximate percentage of time the carpenter spent doing cleanup?
   A. 8%
   B. 10%
   C. 12.5%
   D. 15%

24. My friend bought some skateboards for $195. He sold them for $770 making $25 profit on each skateboard. How many skateboards were there?
   A. 20
   B. 23
   C. 32
   D. 36

25. An inch on a map represents 200 miles. On the same map, a distance of 375 miles is represented by
   A. $1\frac{1}{2}$ inches.
   B. $1\frac{7}{8}$ inches.
   C. $2\frac{1}{4}$ inches.
   D. $2\frac{3}{4}$ inches.

26. The number of half-pound packages of tea that can be made up from a box that holds of tea is
   A. 5
   B. $10\frac{1}{2}$
   C. 20
   D. $20\frac{1}{2}$

27. A pile of magazines is 4 feet high. If each magazine is $\frac{3}{4}$ of an inch thick, the number of magazines in the pile is
   A. 36
   B. 48
   C. 64
   D. 96

28. If one kilometer is approximately $\frac{5}{8}$ of a mile. Then approximately how many miles are in 42 kilometers?
   A. 22
   B. 26
   C. 32
   D. 44

29. Five girls each ate 3 cookies from a box containing 2 dozen. What part of a dozen was left?

A. $\frac{1}{8}$

B. $\frac{1}{4}$

C. $\frac{3}{4}$

D. $\frac{7}{8}$

30. A folding chair regularly sells for $29.50. How much money is saved if the chair is bought at a 20% discount?

A. $4.80

B. $5.90

C. $6.20

D. $7.40

STOP!
IF YOU FINISH BEFORE THE TIME IS UP,
YOU MAY CHECK OVER YOUR WORK ON THIS PART ONLY.

practice test 1

PART 3: WORD KNOWLEDGE

Time: 11 Minutes—35 Questions

> **Directions:** This test has 35 questions about the meanings of words. Each question has an underlined word. You are to decide which one of the four words in the choices most nearly means the same as the underlined word, then mark the space on your answer sheet that has the same number and letter as your choice.

Here are the two sample questions.

1. <u>Mended</u> most nearly means   Ⓐ Ⓑ Ⓒ Ⓓ
    - A. repaired.
    - B. torn.
    - C. clean.
    - D. tied.

    Repaired, choice A, is the correct answer. *Mended* means *fixed* or *repaired*. *Torn*, choice B, might be the state of an object before it is mended. The repair might be made by *tying*, choice D, but not necessarily. *Clean*, choice C, is wrong.

2. It was a <u>small</u> table.   Ⓐ Ⓑ Ⓒ Ⓓ
    - A. Sturdy
    - B. Round
    - C. Cheap
    - D. Little

    Little means the same as *small*, so choice D is the best answer.

Your score on this test will be based on the number of questions you answer correctly. You should try to answer every question. Do not spend too much time on any one question.

When you begin, be sure to start with question number 1 in Part 3 in your test booklet and number 1 in Part 3 on your answer sheet.

1. Double most nearly means
   A. almost.
   B. half.
   C. twice.
   D. more than.

2. Purchase most nearly means
   A. charge.
   B. supply.
   C. order.
   D. buy.

3. Hollow most nearly means
   A. empty.
   B. brittle.
   C. rough.
   D. smooth.

4. Candor most nearly means
   A. untruthful.
   B. directness.
   C. flightless.
   D. round about.

5. Customary most nearly means
   A. curious.
   B. necessary.
   C. difficult.
   D. common.

6. The clerk was criticized for his slipshod work.
   A. Slow
   B. Careful
   C. Careless
   D. Original

7. The captive was treated kindly.
   A. Savage
   B. Jailer
   C. Spy
   D. Prisoner

8. Benevolent most nearly means
   A. frugal.
   B. generous.
   C. thoughtful.
   D. peaceful.

9. Fictitious most nearly means
   A. imaginary.
   B. well known.
   C. odd.
   D. easy to remember.

10. The policeman consoled the weeping child.
    A. Found
    B. Scolded
    C. Carried home
    D. Comforted

11. The preface of the book was interesting.
    A. Title page
    B. Introduction
    C. Table of contents
    D. Appendix

12. To penetrate most nearly means to
    A. enter into.
    B. bounce off.
    C. dent.
    D. weaken.

13. Villainous most nearly means
    A. untidy.
    B. dignified.
    C. homely.
    D. wicked.

14. To defraud most nearly means
    A. to reward.
    B. to donate.
    C. to cheat.
    D. to save.

practice test 1

15. <u>Punctual</u> most nearly means
    A. polite.
    B. thoughtful.
    C. proper.
    D. prompt.

16. <u>Counterfeit</u> most nearly means
    A. questionable.
    B. mysterious.
    C. false.
    D. incomprehensible.

17. <u>Permissible</u> most nearly means
    A. considerable.
    B. allowable.
    C. negative.
    D. safe.

18. <u>Unite</u> most nearly means
    A. improve.
    B. serve.
    C. uphold.
    D. combine.

19. The foreman <u>defended</u> the striking workers.
    A. Delayed
    B. Shot at
    C. Protected
    D. Informed on

20. The <u>aim</u> of the enlistee was to join the navy.
    A. Bull's-eye
    B. Goal
    C. Duty
    D. Promise

21. To <u>nestle</u> most nearly means
    A. to snuggle.
    B. to cast out.
    C. to toss.
    D. to squirm.

22. <u>Merchants</u> most nearly means
    A. producers.
    B. advertisers.
    C. bankers.
    D. storekeepers.

23. <u>Compel</u> most nearly means
    A. tempt.
    B. persuade.
    C. force.
    D. disable.

24. The eagle has a <u>keen</u> eye.
    A. Bright
    B. Shiny
    C. Sharp
    D. Tiny

25. <u>Startled</u> most nearly means
    A. surprised.
    B. chased.
    C. punished.
    D. arrested.

26. <u>Forthcoming</u> events are published daily.
    A. Weekly
    B. Interesting
    C. Social
    D. Approaching

27. The <u>juncture</u> was crowded.
    A. Mansion
    B. Place where things join
    C. Division
    D. Group

28. <u>Self-sufficient</u> most nearly means
    A. independent.
    B. conceited.
    C. stubborn.
    D. clever.

29. In his hand, the hiker carried a sturdy <u>staff</u>.
    A. Pack
    B. Stick
    C. Loaf
    D. Musical instrument

30. <u>Insignificant</u> most nearly means
    A. unimportant.
    B. unpleasant.
    C. secret.
    D. thrilling.

31. <u>Acquired</u> most nearly means
    A. sold.
    B. plowed.
    C. desired.
    D. obtained.

32. <u>Exhaustion</u> most nearly means
    A. fear.
    B. overconfidence.
    C. extreme tiredness.
    D. unsteadiness.

33. The door was left <u>ajar</u>.
    A. Blocked
    B. Locked
    C. Unlocked
    D. Open

34. <u>Inferior</u> most nearly means
    A. noticeable.
    B. second-rate.
    C. lasting.
    D. excellent.

35. The hikers found several <u>crevices</u> in the rocks.
    A. Plants
    B. Uneven spots
    C. Cracks
    D. Puddles

STOP!
IF YOU FINISH BEFORE THE TIME IS UP,
YOU MAY CHECK OVER YOUR WORK ON THIS PART ONLY.

PART 4: PARAGRAPH COMPREHENSION

Time: 13 Minutes—15 Questions

> **Directions:** This test contains 15 items measuring your ability to obtain information from written passages. You will find one or more paragraphs of reading material followed by incomplete statements or questions. You are to read the paragraph(s) and select the lettered choice that best completes the statement or answers the question.

Here are two sample questions.

1. From a building designer's standpoint, three things that make a home livable are the needs of the client, the building site, and the amount of money the client has to spend. According to the passage, to make a home livable   Ⓐ Ⓑ Ⓒ Ⓓ
   A. the prospective piece of land makes little difference.
   B. it can be built on any piece of land.
   C. the design must fit the owner's income and site.
   D. the design must fit the designer's income.

   The correct answer is that the designer must fit the owner's income and site, so choice C is the correct response.

2. In certain areas, water is so scarce that every attempt is made to conserve it. For instance, on one oasis in the Sahara Desert, the amount of water necessary for each date palm tree has been carefully determined.   Ⓐ Ⓑ Ⓒ Ⓓ

   How much water is each tree given?
   A. No water at all
   B. Exactly the amount required
   C. Water only if it is healthy
   D. Water on alternate days

   The correct answer is exactly the amount required, so choice B is the correct response. Your score on this test will be based on the number of questions you answer correctly. You should try to answer every question. Do not spend too much time on any one question.

When you begin, be sure to start with question number 1 in Part 4 in your test booklet and number 1 in Part 4 on your answer sheet.

1. Few drivers realize that steel is used to keep the road surface flat despite the weight of buses and trucks. Steel bars, deeply embedded in the concrete, are sinews to take the stresses so that the stresses cannot crack the slab or make it wavy.

   The passage best supports the statement that a concrete road

   A. is expensive to build.

   B. usually cracks under heavy weights.

   C. looks like any other road.

   D. is reinforced with other material.

2. Blood pressure, the force that the blood exerts against the walls of the vessels through which it flows, is commonly meant to be the pressure in the arteries. The pressure in the arteries varies with the contraction (work period) and the relaxation (rest period) of the heart. When the heart contracts, the blood in the arteries is at its greatest, or systolic, pressure. When the heart relaxes, the blood in the arteries is at its lowest, or diastolic, pressure. The difference between these pressures is called the *pulse pressure*.

   According to the passage, which one of the following statements is most accurate?

   A. The blood in the arteries is at its greatest pressure during contraction.

   B. Systolic pressure measures the blood in the arteries when the heart is relaxed.

   C. The difference between systolic and diastolic pressure determines the blood pressure.

   D. Pulse pressure is the same as blood pressure.

3. More patents have been issued for inventions relating to transportation than for those in any other line of human activity. These inventions have resulted in a great financial savings to the people and have made possible a civilization that could not have existed without them.

   One of the following statements that is best supported by the passage is that transportation

   A. would be impossible without inventions.

   B. is an important factor in our civilization.

   C. is still to be much improved.

   D. is more important than any other activity.

4. The Supreme Court was established by Article 3 of the Constitution. Since 1869, it has been made up of nine members—the chief justice and eight associate justices—who are appointed for life. Supreme Court justices are named by the president and must be confirmed by the Senate.

   The Supreme Court

   A. was established in 1869.

   B. consists of nine justices.

   C. consists of justices appointed by the Senate.

   D. changes with each presidential election.

5. With the exception of Earth, all of the planets in our solar system are named for gods and goddesses in Greek or Roman legends. This is because the other planets were believed to be in heaven like the gods and our planet lay beneath, like the earth.

   All the planets EXCEPT Earth
   A. were part of Greek and Roman legends.
   B. were believed to be in heaven.
   C. are part of the same solar system.
   D. were worshipped as gods.

6. Both the high school and the college should take the responsibility for preparing the student to get a job. Because the ability to write a good application letter is one of the first steps toward this goal, every teacher should be willing to do what he or she can to help the student learn to write such letters.

   The paragraph best supports the statement that
   A. inability to write a good letter often reduces one's job prospects.
   B. the major responsibility of the school is to obtain jobs for its students.
   C. success is largely a matter of the kind of work the student applies for first.
   D. every teacher should teach a course in the writing of application letters.

7. Many people think that only older men who have a great deal of experience should hold public office. These people lose sight of an important fact. Many of the founding fathers of our country were comparatively young men. Today more than ever, our country needs young, idealistic politicians.

   The best interpretation of what this author believes is that
   A. only experienced men should hold public office.
   B. only idealistic men should hold public office.
   C. younger men can and should take part in politics.
   D. young people don't like politics.

8. The X-ray has gone into business. Developed primarily to aid in diagnosing human ills, the machine now works in packing plants, foundries, and service stations and in a dozen ways contributes to precision and accuracy in industry.

   The X-ray
   A. was first developed to aid business.
   B. is being used to improve the functioning of industry.
   C. is more accurate in packing plants than in foundries.
   D. increases the output of such industries.

9. In large organizations, some standardized, simple, inexpensive method of giving employees information about company policies and rules, as well as specific instructions regarding their duties, is practically essential. This is the purpose of all office manuals of whatever type.

The paragraph best supports the statement that office manuals

A. are all about the same.

B. should be simple enough for the average employee to understand.

C. are necessary to large organizations.

D. act as constant reminders to the employee of his or her duties.

10. In the relations of man to nature, the procuring of food and shelter is fundamental. With the migration of man to various climates, ever-new adjustments to the food supply and to the climate became necessary.

According to the passage, the means by which man supplies his material needs are

A. accidental.

B. inadequate.

C. limited.

D. varied.

11. Many experiments on the effects of alcohol consumption show that alcohol decreases alertness and efficiency. It decreases self-consciousness and at the same time increases confidence and feelings of ease and relaxation. It impairs attention and judgment. It destroys fear of consequences. Usual cautions are thrown to the winds. Drivers who use alcohol tend to disregard their usual safety practices. Their reaction time slows down; normally quick reactions are not possible for them. They cannot judge the speed of their car or any other car. They become highway menaces.

The above passage states that the drinking of alcohol makes drivers

A. more alert.

B. less confident.

C. more efficient.

D. less attentive.

12. It is reasonable to assume that drivers may overcome the bad effects of drinking by

A. relying on their good driving habits to a greater extent than normally.

B. waiting for the alcohol to wear off before driving.

C. watching the road more carefully.

D. being more cautious.

practice test 1

Questions 13–15 are based on the following passage.

Arsonists are persons who set fires deliberately. They don't look like criminals, but they cost the nation millions of dollars in property loss and sometimes loss of life. Arsonists set fires for many different reasons. Sometimes a shopkeeper sees no way out of losing his business and sets fire to it to collect the insurance. Another type of arsonist wants revenge and sets fire to the home or shop of someone he feels has treated him unfairly. Some arsonists just like the excitement of seeing the fire burn and watching the firefighters at work; arsonists of this type have even been known to help fight the fire.

13. According to the previous passage, an arsonist is a person who
    A. intentionally sets a fire.
    B. enjoys watching fires.
    C. wants revenge.
    D. needs money.

14. Arsonists have been known to help fight fires because they
    A. felt guilty.
    B. enjoyed the excitement.
    C. wanted to earn money.
    D. didn't want anyone hurt.

15. According to the previous passage, we may conclude that arsonists
    A. would make good firefighters.
    B. are not criminals.
    C. are mentally ill.
    D. are not all alike.

STOP!
IF YOU FINISH BEFORE THE TIME IS UP,
YOU MAY CHECK OVER YOUR WORK ON THIS PART ONLY.

PART 5: MATHEMATICS KNOWLEDGE

Time: 24 Minutes—25 Questions

> **Directions:** This is a test of your ability to solve 25 general mathematical problems. You are to select the correct response from the choices given. Then mark the space on your answer sheet that has the same number and letter as your choice. Use scratch paper to do any figuring.

Now look at the two sample problems below.

1. If $x + 6 = 7$, then x is equal to   Ⓐ Ⓑ Ⓒ Ⓓ
    A. 0
    B. 1
    C. −1
    D. $\frac{7}{6}$

    The correct answer is 1, so choice B is the correct response.

2. What is the area of the square above?   Ⓐ Ⓑ Ⓒ Ⓓ
    A. 1 square foot
    B. 5 square feet
    C. 10 square feet
    D. 25 square feet

    The correct answer is 25 square feet, so choice D is the correct response.

Your score on this test will be based on the number of questions you answer correctly. You should try to answer every question. Do not spend too much time on any one question.

When you are told to begin, be sure to start with question number 1 in Part 5 in your test booklet and number 1 in Part 5 on your answer sheet.

1. A box contains 20 marbles. There are equal amounts of blue, green, red, and yellow ones. If one of the marbles is picked out at random, what is the probability that it will be yellow?

   A. $\frac{1}{2}$

   B. $\frac{1}{3}$

   C. $\frac{1}{4}$

   D. $\frac{1}{5}$

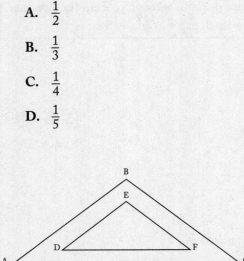

2. In the figure above, the sides of $\triangle ABC$ are respectively parallel to the sides of $\triangle DEF$. If the complement of A is 65°, then the measure of angle D is

   A. 25°

   B. 35°

   C. 55°

   D. 65°

3. The cube of 4 is

   A. 12

   B. 32

   C. 64

   D. 128

4. In the formula $l = p + prt$, what does l equal when $p = 500$, $r = 20\%$, $t = 2$?

   A. 10,000

   B. 700

   C. 8,000

   D. 12,000

5. $(x + 3)(x + 3) =$

   A. $x^2 + 9x + 6$

   B. $x^2 + 9x + 9$

   C. $x^2 + 6x + 6$

   D. $x^2 + 6x + 9$

6. $2.4 \times 104 =$

   A. 9,600

   B. 2,400

   C. 24,000

   D. 240,000

7. $x^2 \times x^3 =$

   A. x^6

   B. x^5

   C. $2x^6$

   D. $2x^5$

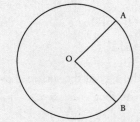

8. In the figure above, m∧ AOB = 60°. If O is the center of the circle, then minor arc AB is what part of the circumference of the circle?

   A. $\frac{1}{2}$

   B. $\frac{1}{3}$

   C. $\frac{1}{6}$

   D. $\frac{1}{8}$

9. In a bag there are red, green, black, and white marbles. If there are 6 red, 8 green, 4 black, and 12 white and one marble is to be selected at random, what is the probability it will be white?

   A. $\frac{1}{5}$

   B. $\frac{2}{5}$

   C. $\frac{4}{15}$

   D. $\frac{2}{15}$

10. A man has T dollars to invest; after he invests \$1,000, how much money does he have remaining?
   A. $T + 1,000$
   B. $T - 1,000$
   C. $1,000 - T$
   D. $1,000T$

11. A rectangular field is 900 yards by 240 yards. What is the greatest number of rectangular lots 120 yards by 60 yards that it can be divided into?
   A. 20
   B. 60
   C. 30
   D. 40

12. The sum of the measures of the interior angles of a pentagon is
   A. 540°
   B. 720°
   C. 900°
   D. 1,080°

13. If $\frac{3}{4}$ of a class is absent and $\frac{2}{3}$ of those present leave the room, what fraction of the original class remains in the room?

   A. $\frac{1}{24}$

   B. $\frac{1}{4}$

   C. $\frac{1}{12}$

   D. $\frac{1}{8}$

14. If $a^2 + b^2 = c^2$, then $b =$
   A. $\sqrt{a - c}$
   B. $\sqrt{c - a}$
   C. $\sqrt{a^2 - c^2}$
   D. $\sqrt{c^2 - a^2}$

15. If $a + b + 7 = 24$ and $a + b = c$, then $24 - c =$
   A. 0
   B. 7
   C. 14
   D. 24

16. If $0.04y = 1$, then $y =$
   A. 0.025
   B. 25
   C. 0.25
   D. 250

17. $\sqrt{45}$
   A. $5\sqrt{3}$
   B. $9\sqrt{5}$
   C. $9\sqrt{3}$
   D. $3\sqrt{5}$

18. Triangle *ABC* is a(n)

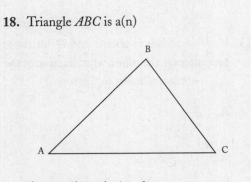

- **A.** equilateral triangle.
- **B.** right triangle.
- **C.** scalene triangle.
- **D.** obtuse triangle.

19. From a temperature of 15°, a drop of 21° would result in a temperature of
- **A.** −36°
- **B.** 36°
- **C.** −6°
- **D.** −30°

20. A certain highway intersection has had *A* accidents over a ten-year period, resulting in *B* deaths. What is the yearly average death rate for the intersection?
- **A.** $A + B - 10$
- **B.** $\dfrac{B}{10}$
- **C.** $10 - \dfrac{A}{B}$
- **D.** $\dfrac{A}{10}$

21. A cube has a volume of 27 cubic inches. What is the surface area?
- **A.** 18 square inches
- **B.** 36 square inches
- **C.** 45 square inches
- **D.** 54 square inches

22. $(10^3)^2 =$
- **A.** 10^6
- **B.** 10^9
- **C.** 20^6
- **D.** 20^9

23. The sum of the measures of the interior angles of an octagon is
- **A.** 720°
- **B.** 900°
- **C.** 1,080°
- **D.** 1,260°

24. $8! = 8 \times 7 \times 6 \times 5 \times 4 \times 3 \times 2 \times 1$. Therefore, $4! =$
- **A.** 44
- **B.** 32
- **C.** 42
- **D.** 24

25. If *T* tons of snow fall in 1 second, how many tons fall in *M* minutes?
- **A.** $60MT$
- **B.** $MT + 60$
- **C.** MT
- **D.** $\dfrac{60M}{T}$

STOP!
IF YOU FINISH BEFORE THE TIME IS UP,
YOU MAY CHECK OVER YOUR WORK ON THIS PART ONLY.

PART 6: ELECTRONICS INFORMATION

Time: 9 Minutes—20 Questions

> **Directions:** This is a test of your knowledge of electrical, radio, and electronics information. There are 20 questions. You are to select the correct response from the choices given. Then mark the space on your answer sheet that has the same number and letter as your choice.

Now look at the two sample questions below.

1. What does the abbreviation AC stand for?   Ⓐ Ⓑ Ⓒ Ⓓ
   A. Additional charge
   B. Alternating coil
   C. Alternating current
   D. Ampere current

   The correct answer is alternating current, so choice C is the correct response.

2. Which of the following has the LEAST resistance?   Ⓐ Ⓑ Ⓒ Ⓓ
   A. Wood
   B. Silver
   C. Rubber
   D. Iron

   The correct answer is silver, so choice B is the correct response.

Your score on this test will be based on the number of questions you answer correctly. You should try to answer every question. Do not spend too much time on any one question.

When you are told to begin, be sure to start with question number 1 in Part 6 in your test booklet and number 1 in Part 6 on your answer sheet.

practice test 1

1. The core of an electromagnet is usually
   A. aluminum.
   B. brass.
   C. lead.
   D. iron.

2. An electrician should consider all electrical equipment "live" unless he or she definitely knows otherwise. The main reason for this practice is to avoid
   A. doing unnecessary work.
   B. energizing the wrong circuit.
   C. personal injury.
   D. de-energizing a live circuit.

3. If *voltage* is represented by V, current by I, and *resistance* by R, then the one of the following that correctly states Ohm's Law is
   A. $R = V \times I$
   B. $R = \dfrac{I}{V}$
   C. $V = IR$
   D. $V = \dfrac{I}{R}$

4. The device used to change AC to DC is a
   A. frequency changer.
   B. transformer.
   C. regulator.
   D. rectifier.

5. A "centi" measures a(n)
   A. eighth.
   B. millionth.
   C. hundredth.
   D. ten-thousandth.

6. The device that is often used to change the voltage in alternating current circuits is the
   A. contactor.
   B. converter.
   C. rectifier.
   D. transformer.

7. What does LED stand for?
   A. Light Emitting Display
   B. Low Energy Display
   C. Light Emitting Diode
   D. Light Emitting Detector

8. To determine directly whether finished wire installations possess resistance between conductors and ground, use
   A. clamps.
   B. set screws.
   C. shields.
   D. a megger.

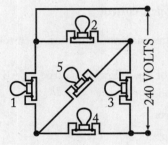

9. The five lamps shown above are each rated at 120 volts, 60 watts. If all are good lamps, lamp 5 will be
   A. much brighter than normal.
   B. about its normal brightness.
   C. much dimmer than normal.
   D. completely dark.

10. Microfarads are units of measurement usually associated with
   A. sockets.
   B. switches.
   C. capacitors.
   D. connectors.

11. What are the three leads of a common transistor?

A. Collector, Base, Emitter

B. Base, Collector, Case

C. Emitter, Collector, Bias

D. Collector, Bias, Omiter

12. Is it proper procedure to ground the frame of a portable motor?

A. No.

B. No, if it is AC.

C. Yes, unless the tool is specifically designed for use without a ground.

D. Yes, if the operation takes place only at less than 150 volts.

13. In comparing Nos. 00, 8, 12, and 6 A.W.G. wires, the smallest of the group is

A. No. 00

B. No. 8

C. No. 12

D. No. 6

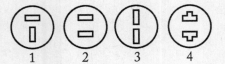

14. The convenience outlet above that is known as a *polarized* outlet is number

A. 1

B. 2

C. 3

D. 4

15. In a house bell circuit, the push button for ringing the bell is generally connected in the secondary of the transformer feeding the bell. One reason for doing this is to

A. save power.

B. keep line voltage out of the push button circuit.

C. prevent the bell from burning out.

D. prevent arcing of the vibrator contact points in the bell.

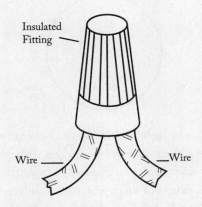

Insulated Fitting

Wire   Wire

16. Wires are often spliced by the use of a fitting like the one shown above. The use of this fitting does away with the need for

A. skinning.

B. cleaning.

C. twisting.

D. soldering.

17. To control a lamp from two different positions, it is necessary to use

A. two single-pole switches.

B. one single-pole switch and one four-way switch.

C. two three-way switches.

D. one single-pole switch and two four-way switches.

18. In electronic circuits, the symbol shown above usually represents a

    A. resistor.

    B. battery.

    C. capacitor.

    D. transformer.

19. The sketch above shows a head-on view of a three-pronged plug used with portable electrical power tools. Considering the danger of shock when using such tools, it is evident that the function of the U-shaped prong is to

    A. ensure that the other two prongs enter the outlet with the proper polarity.

    B. provide a half-voltage connection when doing light work.

    C. prevent accidental pulling of the plug from the outlet.

    D. connect the metallic shell of the tool motor to ground.

20. Connecting a lead for the anode to the cathode of a battery will produce

    A. a high resistance circuit.

    B. a short circuit.

    C. a low current path.

    D. an open circuit.

STOP!
IF YOU FINISH BEFORE THE TIME IS UP,
YOU MAY CHECK OVER YOUR WORK ON THIS PART ONLY.

PART 7: AUTO & SHOP INFORMATION

Time: 11 Minutes—25 Questions

Directions: This test has 25 questions about automobiles, shop practices, and the use of tools. Pick the best answer for each question, then blacken the space on your answer sheet that has the same number and letter as your choice.

Here are four sample questions.

1. The most commonly used fuel for running automobile engines is
   A. kerosene.
   B. benzene.
   C. crude oil.
   D. gasoline.

   Ⓐ Ⓑ Ⓒ Ⓓ

   Gasoline is the most commonly used fuel, so choice D is the correct answer.

2. A car uses too much oil when which parts are worn?
   A. Pistons
   B. Piston rings
   C. Main bearings
   D. Connecting rods

   Ⓐ Ⓑ Ⓒ Ⓓ

   Worn piston rings cause the use of too much oil, so choice B is the correct answer.

3. The saw shown above is used mainly to cut
   A. plywood.
   B. odd-shaped holes in wood.
   C. along the grain of the wood.
   D. across the grain of the wood.

   Ⓐ Ⓑ Ⓒ Ⓓ

   The compass saw is used to cut odd-shaped holes in wood, so choice B is the correct answer.

4. Thin sheet metal should be cut with
   A. ordinary scissors.
   B. a hacksaw.
   C. tin shears.
   D. a jigsaw.

   Ⓐ Ⓑ Ⓒ Ⓓ

   Tin shears are used to cut thin sheet metal, so choice C is the correct answer.

Your score on this test will be based on the number of questions you answer correctly. You should try to answer every question. Do not spend too much time on any one question.

When you are told to begin, be sure to start with question number 1 in Part 7 in your test booklet and number 1 in Part 7 on your answer sheet.

1. Most automobile engines run according to the
   A. rotary cycle.
   B. intake-exhaust cycle.
   C. four-stroke cycle.
   D. two-stroke cycle.

2. When referring to engine configuration, an automobile with a V6 engine means
   A. the engine is connected to a 6-speed transmission.
   B. the engine has 6 valves.
   C. the engine operates on 6 volts.
   D. the engine has 6 cylinders arranged in a V configuration.

3. A torque wrench measures torque in
   A. centimeters.
   B. foot-pounds.
   C. pounds-per-square-inch.
   D. millimeters.

4. A governor is used on an automobile primarily to limit its
   A. rate of acceleration.
   B. maximum speed.
   C. fuel consumption.
   D. stopping distance.

5. Automobile headlights are ordinarily connected in
   A. parallel.
   B. series.
   C. diagonal.
   D. perpendicular.

6. The most commonly used engine in an automobile is called a(an)
   A. external-combustion engine.
   B. diesel engine.
   C. two-cycle engine.
   D. internal combustion engine.

7. A mechanic sets the proper electrode gap on a spark plug most accurately if he or she uses a
   A. dial gauge.
   B. round wire feeler gauge.
   C. square wire feeler gauge.
   D. conventional flat feeler gauge.

8. When reference is made to the "compression ratio" of an automotive gasoline engine, this is best described as the
   A. volume above the piston at top dead center.
   B. displacement volume as the piston moves down to bottom dead center.
   C. total volume of a cylinder divided by its clearance volume.
   D. displacement volume of a cylinder divided by its clearance volume.

9. Reverse flushing of a clogged gasoline engine block and radiator cooling system is done properly by
   A. not removing the thermostat from the engine block.
   B. connecting the flushing gun at the bottom of the engine block.
   C. using air and water.
   D. using low-pressure steam.

10. Ethylene glycol is put into the radiator of an automobile in cold weather because it
   A. lowers the boiling point of the mixture.
   B. lowers the freezing point of the mixture.
   C. raises the boiling point of the mixture.
   D. raises the freezing point of the mixture.

11. If the "alternator," or charging system light comes on while the car is in normal operation, it is best to
    A. stop the car immediately and have it towed in for repairs.
    B. stop immediately and have a new battery installed.
    C. drive as usual and wait to see if the light goes out.
    D. drive to the nearest auto repair shop to have the problem checked out.

12. The tool that is best suited for use with a wood chisel is

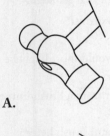
A.

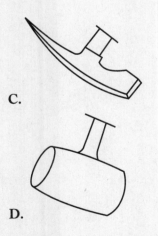
B.

C.

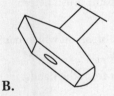
D.

13. An expansion bolt is used to
    A. enlarge a hole.
    B. fasten into hollow tile.
    C. allow for expansion and contraction.
    D. fasten into solid masonry.

14. The length of a 10-penny nail, in inches, is
    A. $2\frac{1}{2}$
    B. 3
    C. $3\frac{1}{2}$
    D. 4

15. Glazier's points are used to
    A. hold glass in a wooden window sash.
    B. scratch glass so that it can be broken to size.
    C. force putty into narrow spaces between glass and sash.
    D. remove broken glass from a pane.

16. The most likely reason for a total loss of oil pressure while driving is
    A. an oil level that is too high.
    B. the use oil whose viscosity is too thick.
    C. an oil level that is too low.
    D. dirty oil.

17. The reason that a lubricant prevents rubbing surfaces from becoming hot is that the oil
    A. is cold and cools off the rubbing metal surfaces.
    B. is sticky, preventing the surfaces from moving over each other too rapidly.
    C. forms a smooth layer between the two surfaces, preventing their coming into contact.
    D. makes the surfaces smooth so that they move easily over each other.

practice test 1

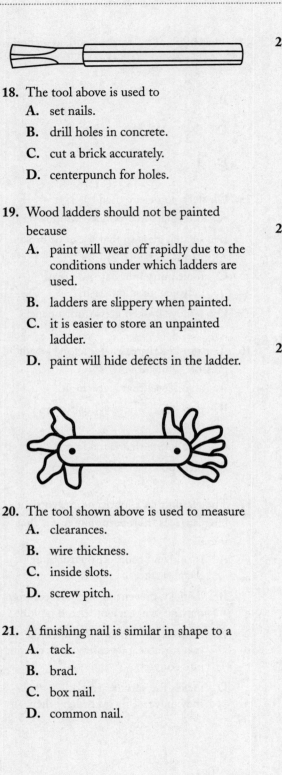

18. The tool above is used to
  A. set nails.
  B. drill holes in concrete.
  C. cut a brick accurately.
  D. centerpunch for holes.

19. Wood ladders should not be painted because
  A. paint will wear off rapidly due to the conditions under which ladders are used.
  B. ladders are slippery when painted.
  C. it is easier to store an unpainted ladder.
  D. paint will hide defects in the ladder.

20. The tool shown above is used to measure
  A. clearances.
  B. wire thickness.
  C. inside slots.
  D. screw pitch.

21. A finishing nail is similar in shape to a
  A. tack.
  B. brad.
  C. box nail.
  D. common nail.

22. The term *whipping* when applied to rope means
  A. binding the ends with cord to prevent unraveling.
  B. coiling the rope in as tight a ball as possible.
  C. lubricating the strands with tallow.
  D. wetting the rope with water to cure it.

23. The set in the teeth of a hand saw primarily
  A. prevents the saw from binding.
  B. makes the saw cut true.
  C. gives the saw a sharper edge.
  D. removes the sawdust.

24. Lacquer thinner would most likely be used to
  A. clean oil paint from a brush immediately after use.
  B. rinse a new paint brush before using it.
  C. clean a paint brush on which paint has hardened.
  D. remove paint from the hands.

25. The tool used to measure the depth of a hole is

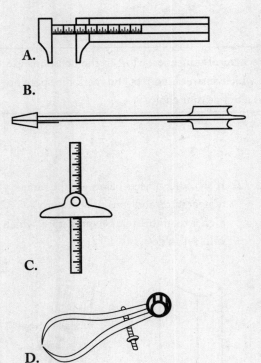

A.

B.

C.

D.

STOP!
IF YOU FINISH BEFORE THE TIME IS UP,
YOU MAY CHECK OVER YOUR WORK ON THIS PART ONLY.

PART 8: MECHANICAL COMPREHENSION

Time: 19 Minutes—25 Questions

> **Directions:** This test has 25 questions about mechanical principles. Most of the questions use drawings to illustrate specific principles. Decide which answer is correct and mark the space on your answer sheet that has the same number and letter as your choice.

Here are two sample questions.

1. Which bridge is the strongest?

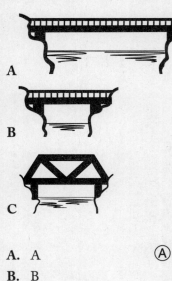

    A. A   Ⓐ Ⓑ Ⓒ Ⓓ
    B. B
    C. C
    D. All are equally strong.

Choice C is correct.

2. If all of the objects below are the same temperature, and your temperature is higher than the item's temperature, which will feel coldest?

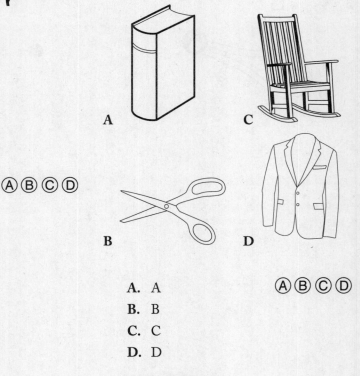

    A. A   Ⓐ Ⓑ Ⓒ Ⓓ
    B. B
    C. C
    D. D

Choice B is correct.

Your score on this test will be based on the number of questions you answer correctly. You should try to answer every question. Do not spend too much time on any one question.

When you are told to begin, be sure to start with question number 1 in Part 8 in your test booklet and number 1 in Part 8 on your answer sheet.

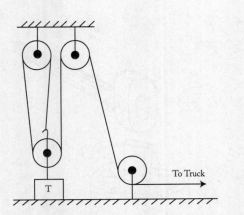

1. The tank, T, is to be raised as shown, in the above figure, by attaching the pull rope to a truck. If the tank is to be raised 10 feet, the truck will have to move
   A. 10 feet.
   B. 30 feet.
   C. 40 feet.
   D. 20 feet.

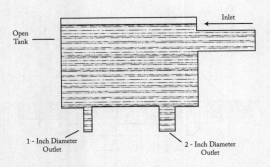

2. Eight gallons of water per minute are flowing at a given time from the 1-inch outlet in the tank shown above. What is the amount of water flowing at that time from the 2-inch outlet?
   A. 64 gallons per minute
   B. 32 gallons per minute
   C. 16 gallons per minute
   D. 2 gallons per minute

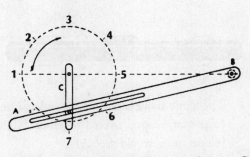

3. In the above illustration, crank arm C revolves at a constant speed of 400 rpm and drives the lever AB. When lever AB is moving the fastest, arm C will be in position
   A. 5.
   B. 6.
   C. 7.
   D. 1.

4. Assume that the color of the flame from a gas stove is bright yellow. To correct this, you should
   A. close the air flap.
   B. increase the size of the gas opening.
   C. increase the gas pressure.
   D. open the air flap.

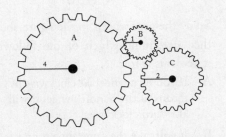

5. In the above illustration, if gear A makes one clockwise revolution per minute, which of the following is correct?
   A. Gear B makes four clockwise revolutions every minute.
   B. Gear C makes one counterclockwise revolution every 8 minutes.
   C. Gear B makes one counterclockwise revolution every 4 minutes.
   D. Gear C makes two clockwise revolutions every minute.

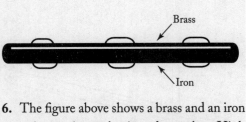

6. The figure above shows a brass and an iron strip continuously riveted together. High temperatures would probably
   A. have no effect at all.
   B. bend the strips.
   C. separate the strips.
   D. shorten the strips.

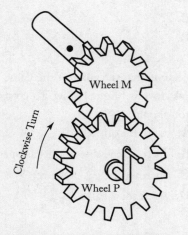

7. Study the gear wheels in the figure above, then determine which of the following statements is true.
   A. If you turn wheel M clockwise by means of the handle, wheel P will also turn clockwise.
   B. It will take the same time for a tooth of wheel P to make a full turn as it will for a tooth of wheel M.
   C. It will take less time for a tooth of wheel P to make a full turn than it will take a tooth of wheel M.
   D. It will take more time for a tooth of wheel P to make a full turn than it will for a tooth of wheel M.

8. The simple machine pictured above is a form of
   A. pulley.
   B. spur gear.
   C. inclined plane.
   D. worm gear.

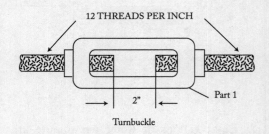

9. For the turnbuckle shown above, the number of complete turns of Part 1 required to make the ends of the threaded rods meet is
   A. 6
   B. 18
   C. 12
   D. 24

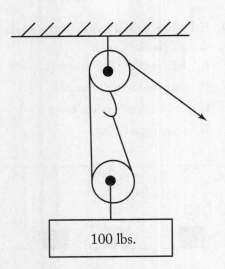

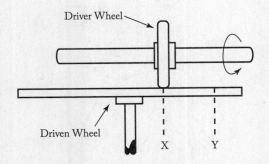

10. When the 100-pound weight is being slowly hoisted up by the pulley, as shown in the figure above, the downward pull on the ceiling to which the pulley is attached is

A. 50 pounds.

B. 100 pounds.

C. 150 pounds.

D. 200 pounds.

11. When the driver wheel in the figure above is moved from location X to location Y, the driven wheel will

A. reverse its direction of rotation.

B. turn slower.

C. not change its speed of rotation.

D. turn faster.

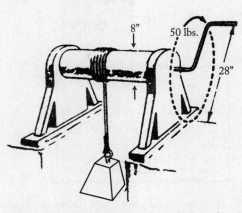

12. In the diagram above, the axle 8 inches in diameter has attached a handle 28 inches in diameter. If a force of 50 pounds is applied to the handle, the axle will lift a weight of

A. 224 pounds.

B. 175 pounds.

C. 200 pounds.

D. 88 pounds.

13. The main purpose of expansion joints in steam lines is to

A. provide for changes in length of heated pipe.

B. allow for connection of additional radiators.

C. provide locations for valves.

D. reduce breakage of pipe due to minor movement of the building frame.

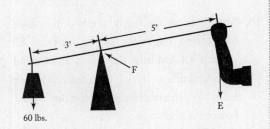

14. What effort must be exerted to lift a 60-pound weight in the figure of a first-class lever shown above (disregard the weight of the lever in your computation)?

A. 30 pounds

B. 36 pounds

C. 45 pounds

D. 60 pounds

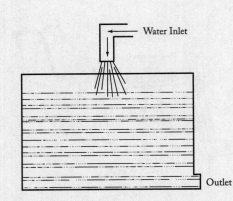

15. If water is flowing into the tank shown above at the rate of 120 gallons per hour and flowing out of the tank at a constant rate of 1 gallon per minute, the water level in the tank will
    A. rise 1 gallon per minute.
    B. rise 2 gallons per minute.
    C. fall 2 gallons per minute.
    D. fall 1 gallon per minute.

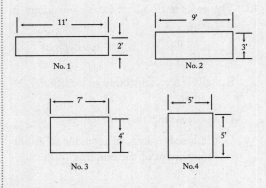

16. Shown above are the bottoms of four bins for storing materials. If the bins are all capable of holding the same amount of any particular material, then the bin whose sides have the least height is the one whose bottom is shown as
    A. No. 1.
    B. No. 2.
    C. No. 3.
    D. No. 4.

17. If the flush tank of a toilet fixture overflows, the fault is likely to be
    A. failure of the ball to seat properly.
    B. excessive water pressure.
    C. defective trap in the toilet bowl.
    D. waterlogged float.

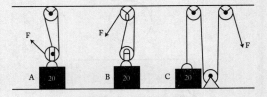

18. Which pulley arrangement shown above requires the LEAST force at F to lift the weight?
    A. A
    B. B
    C. C
    D. All three require the same force.

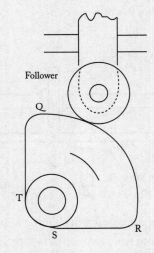

19. In the figure above, the follower is at its highest position between points
    A. Q and R.
    B. R and S.
    C. S and T.
    D. T and Q.

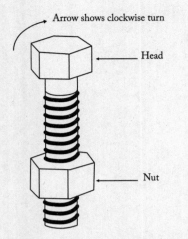

Arrow shows clockwise turn

Head

Nut

20. Which of the following statements is true about the figure above?

   A. If the nut is held stationary and the head turned clockwise, the bolt will move up.

   B. If the head of the bolt is held stationary and the nut is turned clockwise, the nut will move down.

   C. If the head of the bolt is held stationary and the nut is turned clockwise, the nut will move up.

   D. If the nut is held stationary and the bolt is turned counterclockwise, the nut will move up.

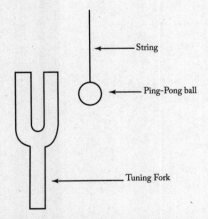

String

Ping-Pong ball

Tuning Fork

21. When the tuning fork shown above is struck, the ping-pong ball will

   A. remain stationary.

   B. bounce up and down.

   C. hit the tuning fork.

   D. swing away from the tuning fork.

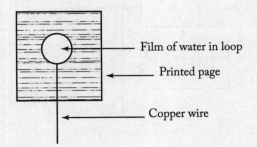

Film of water in loop

Printed page

Copper wire

22. The print in the figure above looked at through the film of water will

   A. be too blurred to read.

   B. look the same as the surrounding print.

   C. be enlarged.

   D. appear smaller.

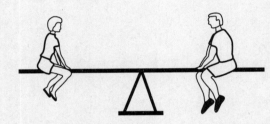

23. In the illustration above, if the man backs to the end of the seesaw, the woman will

   A. remain stationary.

   B. rise in the air.

   C. hit the ground hard.

   D. slide to her end of the seesaw.

24. Condensation on cold water pipes is frequently prevented by

   A. insulating the pipe.

   B. keeping the temperature of cold water at least 10° above the freezing point.

   C. keeping the cold water lines near the hot water lines.

   D. oiling or greasing the outside of the pipe.

practice test 1

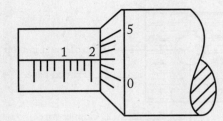

25. The micrometer above reads
- **A.** 0.2270
- **B.** 0.2120
- **C.** 0.2252
- **D.** 0.2020

STOP!
IF YOU FINISH BEFORE THE TIME IS UP,
YOU MAY CHECK OVER YOUR WORK ON THIS PART ONLY.

PART 9: ASSEMBLING OBJECTS*

Time: 9 Minutes—16 Questions

> **Directions:** This test contains 16 items measuring your ability to determine how an object will look when its parts are mentally assembled. Each item consists of five drawings. The problem is presented in the first drawing. Each problem is followed by four answers, only one of which is correct. Decide which answer is correct, then blacken the space on your answer sheet that has the same number and letter as your choice.

Now look at the two sample problems below.

1.

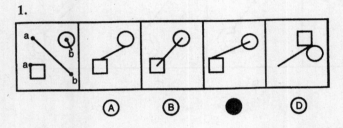

In the previous figure, the parts to be assembled are simple geometric figures (lines, squares, rectangles, etc.) that are labeled at one or more points with small letters. By matching corresponding letters on the different parts, you can see where the parts touch when the object is put together, or connected, properly.

Choice C is the correct answer.

2.

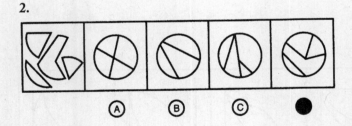

In this figure, the parts are not labeled. Instead, they fit together like pieces of a puzzle. Choice D is the correct answer.

Your score on this test will be based on the number of questions you answer correctly. You should try to answer every question. Do not spend too much time on any one question.

When you are told to begin, be sure to start with question number 1 in Part 9 in your test booklet and number 1 in Part 9 on your answer sheet.

---

*NOTE: This section is not included on paper-and-pencil versions of the ASVAB. It is included on the ASVAB computer-adaptive test (CAT) but may be eliminated in the future. Check with your recruiter for details.

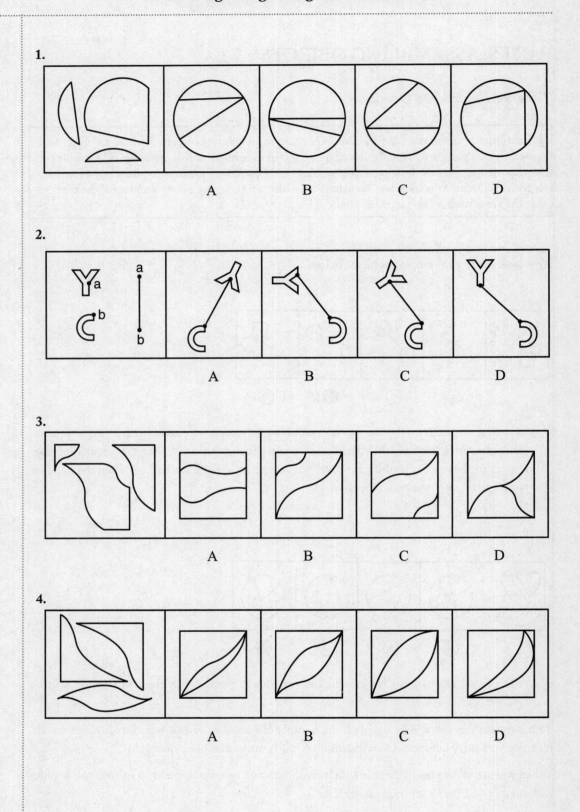

5.

6.

7.

8.

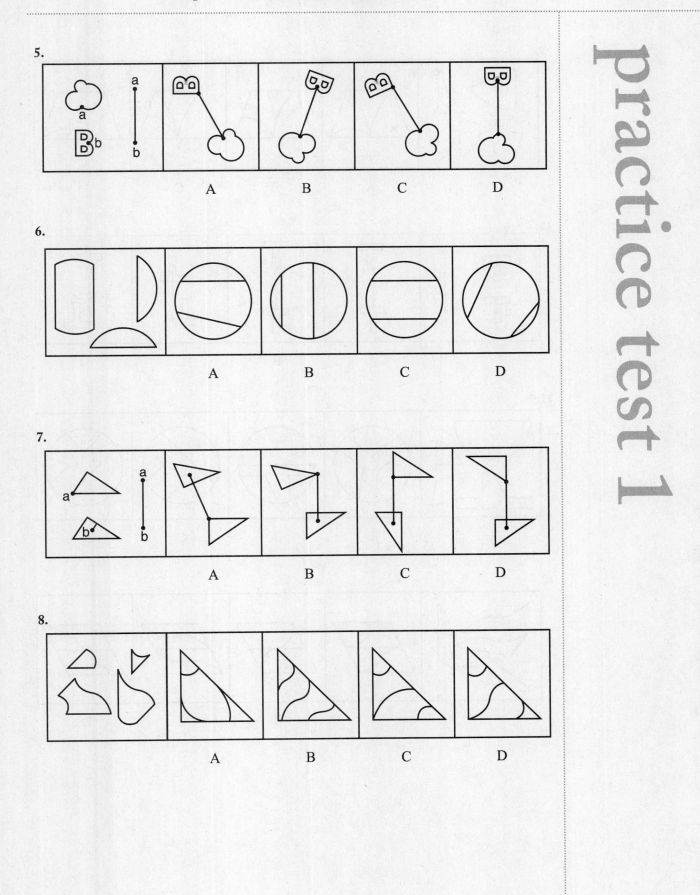

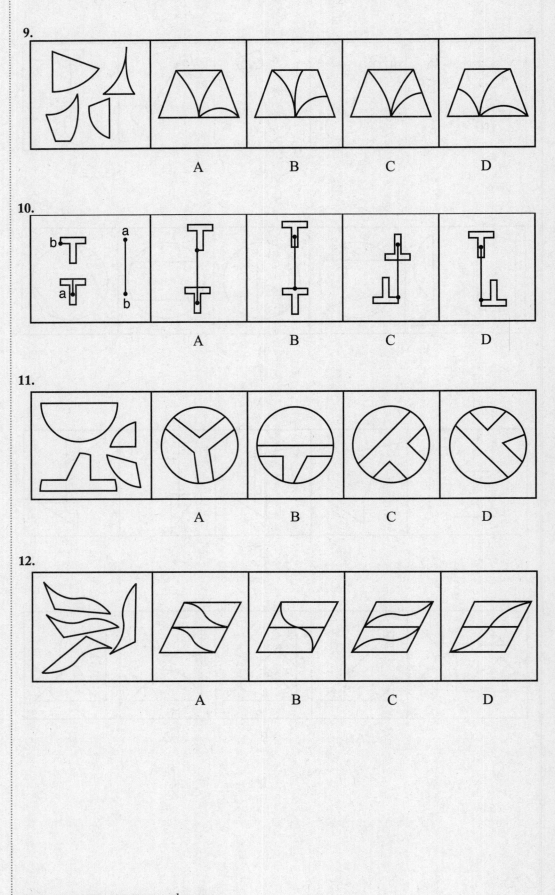

13.

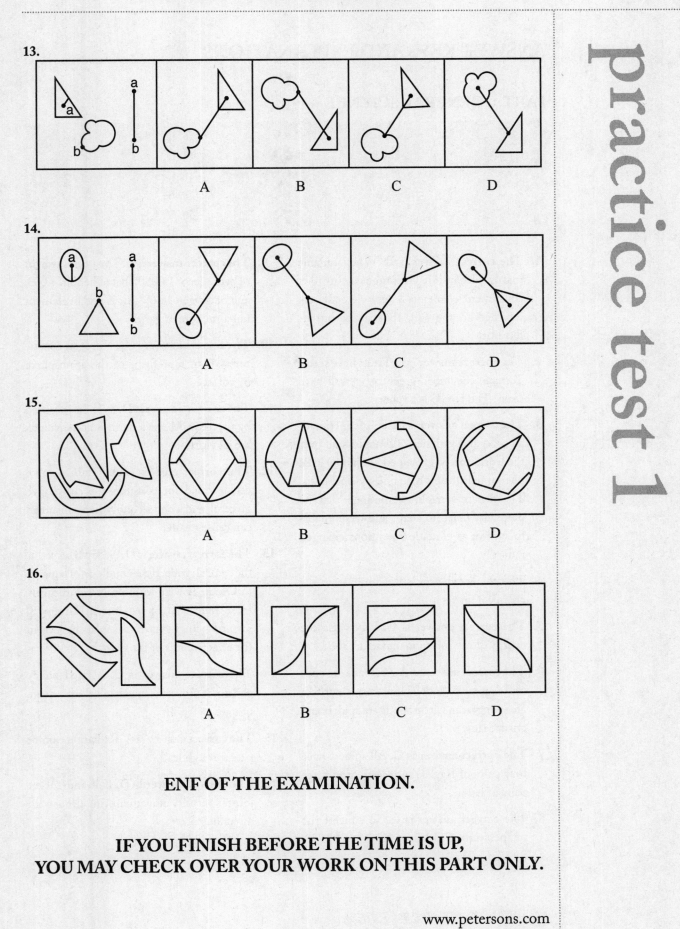

14.

15.

16.

ENF OF THE EXAMINATION.

**IF YOU FINISH BEFORE THE TIME IS UP,
YOU MAY CHECK OVER YOUR WORK ON THIS PART ONLY.**

ANSWER KEYS AND EXPLANATIONS

PART 1: GENERAL SCIENCE

1. C	**6.** A	**11.** D	**16.** D	**21.** C
2. D	**7.** C	**12.** A	**17.** D	**22.** D
3. C	**8.** C	**13.** D	**18.** C	**23.** C
4. B	**9.** A	**14.** C	**19.** B	**24.** D
5. C	**10.** C	**15.** A	**20.** C	**25.** D

1. **The correct answer is B.** When organic matter decays, it decomposes into its constituent elements. These elements are returned to the soil, thus increasing its fertility.

2. **The correct answer is D.** Fruits have seeds. Tomato, cucumber, green pepper all have seeds. The potato is a tuber.

3. **The correct answer is C.** The extinction of all sizes and varieties of dinosaurs all over the world can be explained neither by local phenomena nor on a one-by-one basis. The most reasonable assumption is that the dinosaurs failed to adapt and were unable to survive as climatic conditions changed radically.

4. **The correct answer is B.** Combustion is a chemical process.

5. **The correct answer is C.** Plants use the energy of the sun to manufacture food.

6. **The correct answer is A.** Protozoa are one-celled animals. Annelida are worms, porifera are sponges, and arthropoda are spiders and crustaceans.

7. **The correct answer is C.** All spiders have four pairs of legs. True insects have three pairs of legs.

8. **The correct answer is C.** To convert the temperature of Celsius to Kelvin add 273. 0 + 273 = 273.

9. **The correct answer is A.** The atomic weight of hydrogen is 1.0080, that of helium 4.003, and of oxygen 16.00. Air is not an element but a mixture of gases.

10. **The correct answer is C.** Nitrogen constitutes about four-fifths of the atmosphere by volume.

11. **The correct answer is D.** Syphilis is caused by a bacteria. Measles, mumps, and smallpox are all viruses.

12. **The correct answer is A.** Grain alcohol can be used for consumption. Isopropyl, glycerol, and wood alcohol when consumed can cause death.

13. **The correct answer is D.** Group B served as the control group. If the condition of patients in Group A were to improve significantly more than that of patients in Group B, scientists might have reason to believe in the effectiveness of the drug.

14. **The correct answer is C.** A fixed pulley and rope provide a mechanical advantage of one.

15. **The correct answer is A.** Radiation cannot pass through lead.

16. **The correct answer is D.** Ball-and-socket joints permit movement in almost all directions.

17. **The correct answer is D.** Scurvy is a disease caused by a Vitamin C deficiency. Limes are rich in Vitamin C.

18. **The correct answer is C.** The earth rotates 360° in 24 hours; therefore, it rotates 45° in 3 hours.

19. **The correct answer is B.** In the process of respiration, mammals inhale oxygen and exhale carbon dioxide.

20. **The correct answer is C.** A lizard is a reptile.

21. **The correct answer is C.** Mercury is closest to the sun; therefore, it has the shortest revolutionary period around the sun.

22. **The correct answer is D.** Power is the rate or speed of doing work.

23. **The correct answer is C.** Circuit breakers serve exactly the same function as fuses. Should wires become overheated for any reason, the circuit breaker will "trip," thus breaking the circuit and interrupting the flow of electricity. Fuse burnout creates the same protective interruption of current.

24. **The correct answer is D.** An electron is a negative particle. A proton is positively charged; a neutron is neutral and without charge; a meson has both positive and negative charges.

25. **The correct answer is D.** Limestone, a sedimentary rock composed of calcium carbonate, can be dissolved with a weak acid.

Items Answered Incorrectly: _____ ; _____ ; _____ ; _____ ; _____ ; _____ ; _____ ; _____ ; _____

Items Unsure Of: _____ ; _____ ; _____ ; _____ ; _____ ; _____ ; _____ ; _____ ; _____

Total Number Answered Correctly: _____

answers practice test 1

PART 2: ARITHMETIC REASONING

1. B	**7.** B	**13.** B	**19.** A	**25.** B
2. D	**8.** A	**14.** B	**20.** D	**26.** D
3. B	**9.** A	**15.** D	**21.** D	**27.** C
4. D	**10.** C	**16.** B	**22.** A	**28.** B
5. D	**11.** C	**17.** C	**23.** C	**29.** C
6. B	**12.** D	**18.** A	**24.** B	**30.** B

1. **The correct answer is B.** 50 shares x $30 = $1500. 6% payable stock => it means 6% of the total value of 50 shares => 1500 x 6% = 90. With $90, the man can buy 3 more shares, so the total he owns then are 53 shares.

2. **The correct answer is D.** 1 ton = 2,000 lbs.; $3 \times 2,000$ lbs. = 6,000 lbs.

3. **The correct answer is B.** There are 8 pts. in 1 gal.; therefore, there are 4 pts. in $\frac{1}{2}$ gal., so,

   1 pt. $= \frac{1}{4}$ of $\frac{1}{2}$ gal.

4. **The correct answer is D.** 20 peaches are 5×4 peaches; 4 peaches cost $.50; $5 \times \$.50 = \$2.50$

5. **The correct answer is D.**

$$
\begin{array}{r}
10 \times \$1.00 = \$10.00 \\
9 \times .50 = 4.50 \\
8 \times .25 = 2.00 \\
16 \times .10 = 1.60 \\
25 \times .05 = \underline{1.25} \\
\$19.35
\end{array}
$$

6. **The correct answer is B.** 60 minutes in 1 hour; 24 hours in one day; $60 \times 24 = 1,440$ minutes.

7. **The correct answer is B.** To find the percent of increase, subtract the original figure from the new figure. Then divide the amount of change by the original figure. 29¢ − 25¢ = 4¢; $4 \div 25 = .16 = 16\%$

8. **The correct answer is A.**

   $4 \times \frac{1}{4}$ inch = 1 inch

9. **The correct answer is A.** 8 pts. in 1 gal.; 80 pts. in 10 gal.; 160 half-pints in 10 gal.

10. **The correct answer is C.** Since distance = rate × time, substituting you get 17 = 4 × time. Dividing both sides by 4, you get $4\frac{1}{4} = t$. So, 4 hours and $\frac{1}{4}$ of an hour equals 4 hours, 15 minutes.

11. **The correct answer is C.** 3 apples cost 48¢, so one apple costs 48 ÷ 3 = 16¢. $3.84 ÷ 16 = 24 apples; 24 = 2 dozen.

12. **The correct answer is D.**

    From 8:30 a.m. until noon today:

$$
\begin{array}{r}
12:00 = 11:60 \\
-8:30 = \underline{8:30} \\
3 \text{ hrs. } 30 \text{ mins.}
\end{array}
$$

$$
\begin{array}{lr}
\text{From noon till midnight:} & 12 \text{ hrs.} \\
\text{From midnight until 3:15 a.m.:} & \underline{+\ 3 \text{ hrs. } 15 \text{ mins.}} \\
\text{Total Time:} & 18 \text{ hrs. } 45 \text{ mins.} \\
& = 18\frac{3}{4} \text{ hrs.}
\end{array}
$$

13. **The correct answer is B.** 105 feet − 55 feet = 50 feet.

14. **The correct answer is B.** To find percent of increase, subtract the original figure from the new figure. Then divide the amount of change by the original figure.

    $380 − $350 = $30; $30 ÷ $350 = .0857 (which is approximately $8\frac{1}{2}\%$).

15. **The correct answer is D.**
    40 miles ÷ 20 mph = 2 hrs.

16. **The correct answer is B.**

    $$\frac{2}{\cancel{5}_1} \times \frac{\cancel{100}^{20}}{1} = 40 \text{ gal.}$$

17. **The correct answer is C.** If 20% is deducted, the net salary is 80%. $20,000 × 80% = $20,000 × .80 = $16,000.

18. **The correct answer is A.** $2,000 ÷ 100 = $20

19. **The correct answer is A.** 192 ÷ 24 = 8 gal.

20. **The correct answer is D.**
    $21,600 + $720 + $1,200 = $23,520

21. **The correct answer is D.** $29.62 × 5 = $148.10

22. **The correct answer is A.**

    3 days 10 hrs. 40 min.
    +   10 hrs. 2 min.
    ―――――――――――――――――――
    3 days 20 hrs. 42 min.

23. **The correct answer is C.**

    $$40\left(\frac{1}{4}\right) + 40\left(\frac{1}{2}\right) + 40\left(\frac{1}{8}\right) \Rightarrow 10 + 20 + 5 \Rightarrow 35$$

40 − 35 = 5, so 5 hours was spent cleaning:

$$\frac{5}{40} = 12.5\%.$$

24. **The correct answer is B.** $770 − $195 = $575. $575 ÷ 25 = 23 skateboards.

25. **The correct answer is B.**

    $1 : 200 = x : 375$; $200x = 375$;

    $x = 375 ÷ 200 = 1.875 = 1\frac{7}{8}$ inches

26. **The correct answer is D.**

    $10\frac{1}{4}$ lbs. $÷ \frac{1}{2} = \frac{41}{4} \times \frac{2}{1} = 20\frac{1}{2}$ boxes

27. **The correct answer is C.** 4 feet = 48 inches;

    $48 ÷ \frac{3}{4} = \frac{48}{1} \times \frac{4}{3} = 64$ magazines

28. **The correct answer is B.** If 1 km = $\frac{5}{8}$ mile, then

    $$\frac{1 \text{ km}}{\frac{5}{8}} = \frac{42 \text{ km}}{x \text{ miles}}$$

    $$x = 42\frac{5}{8}$$

    The approximate answer is 26.

29. **The correct answer is C.** There were 2 × 12 = 24 cookies. The girls ate 5 × 3 = 15 cookies. Therefore, 24 − 15 = 9 cookies left; $9 = \frac{3}{4}$ dozen.

30. **The correct answer is B.** $29.50 × 20% = $29.50 × 0.20 = $5.90 saved.

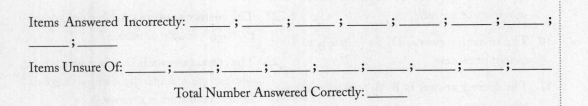

Items Answered Incorrectly: _____ ; _____ ; _____ ; _____ ; _____ ; _____ ; _____ ; _____ ; _____

Items Unsure Of: _____ ; _____ ; _____ ; _____ ; _____ ; _____ ; _____ ; _____ ; _____

Total Number Answered Correctly: _____

PART 3: WORD KNOWLEDGE

1. C	8. B	15. D	22. D	29. B
2. D	9. A	16. C	23. C	30. A
3. A	10. D	17. B	24. C	31. D
4. B	11. B	18. D	25. A	32. C
5. D	12. A	19. C	26. D	33. D
6. C	13. D	20. B	27. B	34. B
7. D	14. C	21. A	28. A	35. C

1. **The correct answer is C.** *Double* means *twofold* or *twice* as much.

2. **The correct answer is D.** To *purchase* is to *buy* for a price.

3. **The correct answer is A.** *Hollow* means *unfilled* or *empty*.

4. **The correct answer is B.** *Candor* means *directness*; telling someone how you feel.

5. **The correct answer is D.** That which is *customary* is *habitual* or established by *common* usage.

6. **The correct answer is C.** *Slipshod* means *exceedingly slovenly* or *careless*.

7. **The correct answer is D.** The *captive* is the one who was *captured* and made *prisoner*, regardless of the reason for his capture.

8. **The correct answer is B.** *Benevolent* means to be *generous, compassionate,* and *kind*.

9. **The correct answer is A.** *Fictitious* means *imaginary* or *not real*.

10. **The correct answer is D.** To *console* is to *comfort* or *reassure*.

11. **The correct answer is B.** A *preface* is an *introduction*.

12. **The correct answer is A.** To *penetrate* is to *enter into* or *to pierce*.

13. **The correct answer is D.** *Villainous* means *wicked* or *evil*.

14. **The correct answer is C.** To *defraud* means to *cheat, deceive, trick,* or *swindle*.

15. **The correct answer is D.** *Punctual* means *prompt* or *on time*.

16. **The correct answer is C.** *Counterfeit* most nearly means *false*, or *not real*, as in counterfeit money.

17. **The correct answer is B.** *Permissible* is synonymous with *allowable, acceptable,* and *tolerable*.

18. **The correct answer is D.** To *unite* is to *put together*, to *combine*, or to *join*.

19. **The correct answer is C.** To *defend* is to *protect* from harm, verbal or bodily.

20. **The correct answer is B.** An *aim* is an *intention* or *goal*. To aim is to direct toward the goal.

21. **The correct answer is A.** To *nestle* means to *snuggle, huddle,* or *nuzzle*.

22. **The correct answer is D.** A *merchant* is one who *sells goods*. A merchant who sells goods from a retail store is a *storekeeper*.

23. **The correct answer is C.** To *compel* is to *require*, to *coerce*, or to *force*. Compel is a much stronger word than persuade.

24. **The correct answer is C.** *Keen* means *acute, sensitive,* or *sharp.*

25. **The correct answer is A.** *Startled* means *frightened suddenly*, though not seriously, hence *surprised.*

26. **The correct answer is D.** *Forthcoming* means *coming up* or *approaching.*

27. **The correct answer is B.** A *juncture* is where things *come together*, or may signify an *occasion at a specific time.*

28. **The correct answer is A.** One who is *self-sufficient* is able to accomplish his or her own aims without external aid, and so is *independent.*

29. **The correct answer is B.** The *staff* carried by a hiker is a *stick.* In music, a staff is the horizontal lines and spaces on which music is written.

30. **The correct answer is A.** *Insignificant* means *meaningless* or *unimportant.* The prefix *in* means *not*, so the word literally means *not significant.*

31. **The correct answer is D.** To *acquire* is to *get* or to *obtain* by any means.

32. **The correct answer is C.** *Exhaustion* is the *using up of energy or resources, extreme tiredness* or *fatigue.*

33. **The correct answer is D.** *Ajar* means *open.*

34. **The correct answer is B.** *Inferior* means of *lower* or *lesser quality, rank,* or *value,* in short, *second-rate.*

35. **The correct answer is C.** A *crevice* is a narrow *opening* or *crack.*

Items Answered Incorrectly: _____ ; _____ ; _____ ; _____ ; _____ ; _____ ; _____ ; _____ ; _____

Items Unsure Of: _____ ; _____ ; _____ ; _____ ; _____ ; _____ ; _____ ; _____ ; _____

Total Number Answered Correctly: _____

answers practice test 1

PART 4: PARAGRAPH COMPREHENSION

1. D	4. B	7. C	10. D	13. A
2. A	5. B	8. B	11. D	14. B
3. B	6. A	9. C	12. B	15. D

1. **The correct answer is D.** The first three options are not supported by the passage. The second sentence in the passage states that steel bars, deeply embedded in the concrete, are sinews (a source of strength) to take the stresses.

2. **The correct answer is A.** The third sentence in the passage states that when the heart contracts, the blood in the arteries is at its greatest pressure.

3. **The correct answer is B.** The second sentence states that inventions relating to transportation have made possible a civilization that could not have existed without them. This supports the correct answer—transportation is an important factor in our civilization.

4. **The correct answer is B.** One chief justice plus eight associate justices equals nine justices.

5. **The correct answer is B.** The second sentence states that the other planets were believed to be in heaven.

6. **The correct answer is A.** Step one in the job application process is often the application letter. If the letter is not effective, the applicant will not move on to the next step, and job prospects will be greatly lessened.

7. **The correct answer is C.** The last sentence states that the country needs young, idealistic politicians.

8. **The correct answer is B.** The passage states that the X-ray machine "contributes to precision and accuracy in industry."

9. **The correct answer is C.** The passage states that office manuals are a necessity in large organizations.

10. **The correct answer is D.** The first three options are not supported by the passage. The correct answer is supported by the second sentence, which states, "With the migration of man to various climates, ever-new adjustments to the food supply and to the climate became necessary."

11. **The correct answer is D.** The first three options are not supported by the passage. The third sentence in the passage states that the drinking of alcohol impairs attention—making the driver less attentive.

12. **The correct answer is B.** Drinking alcohol causes harmful effects on the driver. The implication is that these effects do not last forever but wear off in time.

13. **The correct answer is A.** The first sentence in the passage states that arsonists set fires deliberately or intentionally.

14. The correct answer is B. The last sentence in the passage states that some arsonists just like the excitement of seeing the fire burn and watching the firefighters at work and even helping fight the fire.

15. The correct answer is D. The first three options are not supported by the passage. Different types of arsonists mentioned in the passage leads to the conclusion that arsonists are not all alike.

Items Answered Incorrectly: _____ ; _____ ; _____ ; _____ ; _____ ; _____ ; _____ ; _____ ; _____

Items Unsure Of: _____ ; _____ ; _____ ; _____ ; _____ ; _____ ; _____ ; _____ ; _____

Total Number Answered Correctly: _____

answers practice test 1

PART 5: MATHEMATICS KNOWLEDGE

1. C	**6.** C	**11.** C	**16.** B	**21.** D
2. A	**7.** B	**12.** A	**17.** D	**22.** A
3. C	**8.** C	**13.** C	**18.** C	**23.** C
4. B	**9.** B	**14.** D	**19.** C	**24.** D
5. D	**10.** B	**15.** B	**20.** B	**25.** A

1. **The correct answer is C.** If there are equal amounts of each color, there would be 5 blue, 5 green, 5 red, and 5 yellow for a total of 20 marbles. The chance of drawing out a yellow would be $\frac{5}{20}$ or $\frac{1}{4}$.

2. **The correct answer is A.** Angles that are complementary add up to 90°. If the complement of angle A is 65°, then angle A is 25°. Since angle A and angle D are corresponding angles in similar triangles, then angle D is also 25°.

3. **The correct answer is C.** $4 \times 4 \times 4 = 64$

4. **The correct answer is B.**

   $I = 500 , (500 \times 0.20 \times 2)$

   $I = 500 , 200$

   $I = 700$

5. **The correct answer is D.** $(x + 3)(x + 3) =$

   $$\begin{array}{r} x + 3 \\ \times \ \ x + 3 \\ \hline x^2 + 3x \\ + 3x + 9 \\ \hline x^2 + 6x + 9 \end{array}$$

6. **The correct answer is C.** $2.4 \times 10^4 = 2.4 \times 10,000 = 24,000$

7. **The correct answer is B.** The product of two powers with the same base can be calculated by keeping the base and adding the exponents.

8. **The correct answer is C.** A circle is 360°; 60° is $\frac{1}{6}$ of 360°.

9. **The correct answer is B.** There are $6 + 8 + 4 + 12 = 30$ marbles. $12 \div 30 = 0.40 = \frac{2}{5}$

10. **The correct answer is B.** If the man uses $1,000 of his T dollars, he has $T - \$1,000$ remaining.

11. **The correct answer is C.** The field is 900 yds. × 240 yds. = 216,000 sq. yds.

    Each lot is 120 yds. × 60 yds. = 7,200 sq. yds. 216,000 ÷ 7,200 = 30 lots

12. **The correct answer is A.** The formula for the sum of the measures of the interior angles of any polygon is $180(n - 2)$, where n = number of sides of the figure. Since a pentagon has 5 sides, $180(5 - 2) = 540°$.

13. **The correct answer is C.** If $\frac{3}{4}$ are absent, $\frac{1}{4}$ are present. If $\frac{2}{3}$ of the $\frac{1}{4}$ present leave, $\frac{1}{3}$ of the $\frac{1}{4}$ remain. $\frac{1}{3} \times \frac{1}{4} = \frac{1}{12}$ remain in the room.

14. **The correct answer is D.** In $a^2 + b^2 = c^2$, solving for b would mean subtracting a^2 from both sides leaving $b^2 = c^2 - a^2$. To solve for b, taking the square root of each side would yield $b = \sqrt{c^2 - a^2}$.

15. **The correct answer is B.** In equation $a + b + 7 = 24$, subtract 7 from both sides. That leaves $a + b = 17$. So, if $a + b = c$, then by transitive property $c = 17$. Then, $24 - (17) = 7$.

16. **The correct answer is B.**

$$.04y = 1$$
$$y = 1 \div .04 = 25$$

17. **The correct answer is D.** The goal of simplifying expressions with square roots is to factor the radicand (45) into a form that has no square factors. We can take out the square root of 9 in this case.

$$\sqrt{45} = \sqrt{9 \cdot 5} = 3\sqrt{5}$$

18. **The correct answer is C.** A triangle with no side of the same length is called scalene.

19. **The correct answer is C.** $15° - 21° = -6°$

20. **The correct answer is B.** The number of accidents is irrelevant to the question, so A has no place in the equation. B (total deaths) $\div$ 10 years $= \frac{B}{10}$ average deaths per year.

21. **The correct answer is D.** The cube has 3 edges 3 inches long. Area of one side = 3 × 3 = 9 square inches. There are six sides to a cube. 9 × 6 = 54 square inches.

22. **The correct answer is A.** $(10^3)^2 = (10^3)(10^3) = 10^6$

23. **The correct answer is C.** The sum of the interior angles of any polygon can be found using the formula (n-2) * 180 (insert degree symbol) where n is equal to the number of sides in the polygon. Since an octagon has 8 sides, substitute this value for n and calculate: (8-2) * 180 = 6 * 180 = 1,080 degrees.

24. **The correct answer is D.** 4! (read "four factorial") = 4 × 3 × 2 × 1 = 24

25. **The correct answer is A.** To find how many tons fall in a given number of minutes, multiply the number of tons that fall in 1 minute by the number of minutes. There are 60 seconds in 1 minute, and T tons fall in 1 second. In M minutes, the amount of snow that falls is $60MT$.

Items Answered Incorrectly: _____ ; _____ ; _____ ; _____ ; _____ ; _____ ; _____ ;
_____ ; _____

Items Unsure Of: _____ ; _____ ; _____ ; _____ ; _____ ; _____ ; _____ ; _____ ; _____

Total Number Answered Correctly: _____

PART 6: ELECTRONICS INFORMATION

1. D	5. A	9. D	13. C	17. C
2. C	6. D	10. C	14. A	18. B
3. C	7. C	11. A	15. B	19. D
4. D	8. D	12. C	16. D	20. B

1. **The correct answer is D.** Soft iron has the property of being easily magnetized or demagnetized. When the current is turned on in an electromagnet, it becomes magnetized. When the current is turned off, the iron loses its magnetism.

2. **The correct answer is C.** This is a general safety question. Never assume that there is no current in a piece of electrical equipment; the results could be shocking.

3. **The correct answer is C.** Using algebraic rules, Ohm's Law can be written in three equivalent ways:

$$R = \frac{V}{I}; \quad I = \frac{V}{R}; V = IR$$

4. **The correct answer is D.** A rectifier is a device that changes AC to DC and often includes one or more diodes.

5. **The correct answer is A.** The prefix *centi* refers to 100.

6. **The correct answer is D.** Converters change DC to AC. Rectifiers change AC to DC. Contactors are remote controlled switches frequently used as part of elevator controls. Transformers change voltages in AC circuits in accordance with the ratio of the number of turns in the secondary winding to the number of turns in the primary winding.

7. **The correct answer is C.** LED stands for Light Emitting Diode.

8. **The correct answer is D.** A megger (meg-ohmmeter) is a portable device that produces a voltage. It is used to check for high-voltage breakdown of insulation. In this case, it uses a resistance measurement to determine continuity.

9. **The correct answer is D.** This is the Wheatstone bridge circuit with balanced loads in each of its arms. Because there is no voltage across lamp No. 5, it will not be lit.

10. **The correct answer is C.** The farad is a unit of capacitance. Most capacitors used in electronics are small and their capacitance is only a tiny fraction of a farad. One microfarad is one millionth of a farad.

11. **The correct answer is A.** In a common transistor the common leads are collector, base, emitter.

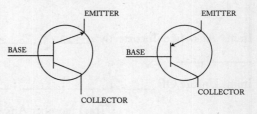

12. **The correct answer is C.** This is proper safety procedure and should be followed.

13. **The correct answer is C.** The number on the wires is in reverse order to the amount of current that they can carry. No. 12 is the smallest of the wires.

14. **The correct answer is A.** The plug can go into the outlet in only one way in a polarized outlet. In the other outlets, the plug can be reversed.

15. **The correct answer is B.** Connecting the bell to a 6- or 12-volt source on the secondary of a transformer is done as a safety precaution. The other way would be dangerous.

16. **The correct answer is D.** This is a mechanical or solderless connector. It does away with the need to solder wires and is found in house wiring.

17. **The correct answer is C.** Two three-way switches will control a lamp from two different positions.

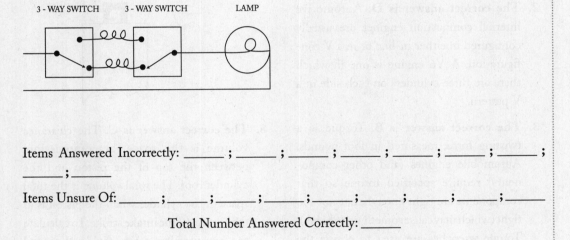

3 - WAY SWITCH   3 - WAY SWITCH   LAMP

18. **The correct answer is B.** A battery is an assembly of chemical cells. The common 9-volt battery found in transistor radios consists of six 1.5-volt cells connected in series to produce a total of six times 1.5 volts—or 9 volts.

19. **The correct answer is D.** The third prong in the plug is the grounding wire.

20. **The correct answer is B.** Connecting a lead from the anode to the cathode of a battery produces a short circuit.

Items Answered Incorrectly: _____ ; _____ ; _____ ; _____ ; _____ ; _____ ; _____ ; _____ ; _____ ;

Items Unsure Of: _____ ; _____ ; _____ ; _____ ; _____ ; _____ ; _____ ; _____ ; _____

Total Number Answered Correctly: _____

answers practice test 1

PART 7: AUTO & SHOP INFORMATION

1. C	**6.** D	**11.** D	**16.** C	**21.** B
2. D	**7.** B	**12.** D	**17.** C	**22.** A
3. B	**8.** C	**13.** D	**18.** B	**23.** A
4. B	**9.** C	**14.** B	**19.** D	**24.** C
5. A	**10.** B	**15.** A	**20.** D	**25.** C

1. **The correct answer is C.** The most popular engine has a four-stroke cycle. The four cycles are intake, compression, power, and exhaust.

2. **The correct answer is D.** Automotive internal combustion engines are usually configured in either in-line or in a V configuration. A V6 engine is one in which there are three cylinders on each side in a V pattern.

3. **The correct answer is B.** Torque is a twisting force, measured in foot-pounds. Automobile engines (and other components) require specified torque so that components are tight enough, but not too tight (which may cause something to break). Torque wrenches are used to ensure the appropriate torque is applied.

4. **The correct answer is B.** The governor is a device that is used to limit the maximum speed of an auto. It is used as a safety device.

5. **The correct answer is A.** Headlights are connected in parallel. In a parallel circuit, if one headlight goes out, the other will still light.

6. **The correct answer is D.** Automobiles use internal combustion engines. Fuel is ignited inside a cylinder to produce power.

7. **The correct answer is B.** The spark jumps across the arc at only one point on the electrode. A round wire feeler gauge gives the best spark plug gap at one point.

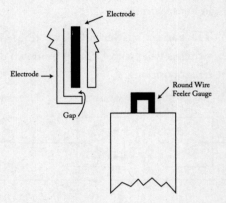

8. **The correct answer is C.** The clearance volume is the space, at compression, between the top of the piston and the cylinder roof. The total volume is the total space in the cylinder when the piston is at the bottom of the intake stroke. To calculate the compression ratio, divide the total volume by the clearance volume. Many modern engines run at a compression ratio of 8:1.

9. **The correct answer is C.** Choice C is the best answer. When the engine block and the radiator are clogged, a mechanic wants to remove any foreign material that prevents the antifreeze-water mixture from cooling the engine. Flushing with water and using compressed air remove the blockages. The other methods might not do the job adequately.

10. **The correct answer is B.** Water freezes at 32°F, or 0°C. Adding alcohol will cause the water to freeze at a lower temperature and will help prevent the engine block from cracking. *Note:* When water freezes, it expands, and the pressure created can crack an engine block.

11. **The correct answer is D.** Usually when a warning light of any kind comes on while driving, the best thing to do is to pull over and stop the car immediately. However, in the case of a charging system warning light, if you shut off the car, you may not be able to restart it. If the car is running, you have enough electrical power, and you should drive it to the nearest repair shop.

12. **The correct answer is D.** A wooden mallet is used in woodworking. The other hammers are made of steel. They are too hard and might crack a wood chisel. Choice A is a ball peen hammer, choice B is a straight peen hammer, and choice C is a brick hammer.

13. **The correct answer is D.** An expansion bolt is put into a hole that has been drilled into solid masonry. The bolt is then tightened, forcing apart the sides of the expansion bolt. This anchors into the concrete.

14. **The correct answer is B.** A 10-penny nail is 3 inches long. For each 2-penny increase, the length increases by $\frac{1}{2}$ inch. So, a 4-penny nail is $1\frac{1}{2}$ inches long and a 12-penny nail is $3\frac{1}{2}$ inches long.

15. **The correct answer is A.** Glazier's points are triangular-shaped pieces of metal that are inserted into a window frame to prevent the glass from being pushed out.

16. **The correct answer is C.** The key to this question is the complete loss of oil pressure. This would occur due to a lack of oil in the crankcase.

17. **The correct answer is C.** When two pieces of metal rub together, the friction causes a great deal of heat. Oil reduces the friction between the two pieces of metal.

18. **The correct answer is B.** The tool shown is a "star drill." It is hit with a hammer to make a hole in concrete.

19. **The correct answer is D.** One would not be able to see a defect in a painted ladder, such as a knot or a split in the wood. A ladder should *never* be painted.

20. **The correct answer is D.** When a blade in the gauge matches the threads in the screw, the measure is the screw pitch.

21. **The correct answer is B.** A finishing nail is similar in shape to a brad in that they both do not have flat heads and are designed to be countersunk into the wood.

22. **The correct answer is A.** A rope is made from many separate strands of hemp or synthetic fiber, such as nylon. When a rope is cut, the strands can unravel if the ends are not whipped or wrapped with cord.

23. **The correct answer is A.** The set is the angle at which the teeth are bent. It makes the teeth stand out from the rest of the saw and prevents the saw from getting stuck or binding to the stock.

24. **The correct answer is C.** Lacquer thinner is a strong solvent and will dissolve hardened paint.

25. **The correct answer is C.** The flattened part of the tool in choice C rests at the top of the hole and the ruler is then pushed down into the hole until it reaches the bottom. The depth of the hole is then read from the ruler.

Items Answered Incorrectly: _____ ; _____ ; _____ ; _____ ; _____ ; _____ ; _____ ; _____ ; _____

Items Unsure Of: _____ ; _____ ; _____ ; _____ ; _____ ; _____ ; _____ ; _____ ; _____

Total Number Answered Correctly: _____

answers practice test 1

PART 8: MECHANICAL COMPREHENSION

1. B	6. B	11. B	16. C	21. D
2. B	7. D	12. B	17. D	22. C
3. A	8. C	13. A	18. A	23. B
4. D	9. C	14. B	19. A	24. A
5. D	10. C	15. A	20. B	25. A

1. **The correct answer is B.** The truck will have to move 30 feet. Three ropes are supporting tank T. The mechanical advantage (the number of supporting wires holding the load) is three. The distance must be three times the height raised.

2. **The correct answer is B.** The volume is dependent on the area of the outlet. Since $A = I \, r^2$ and $r = \dfrac{d}{2}$, then $A = \pi\left(\dfrac{d^2}{4}\right)$ where A is the area and d is the diameter. The volume is proportional to the diameter squared (d^2). When the volumes of the 1-inch and 2-inch outlets are compared, we see that the latter will produce 4 times as great a volume. If the 1-inch outlet has an 8-gallon flow, then the 2-inch outlet will have a 32-gallon flow.

3. **The correct answer is A.** The slowest points for lever AB are 3 and 7 where the direction reverses and the velocity momentarily becomes zero. The midpoint, 5, represents the maximum speed, as it is halfway between these minimum points.

4. **The correct answer is D.** A yellow flame means too much fuel or too little oxygen is present during combustion. The best answer is to allow more air to enter and mix with the gas.

5. **The correct answer is D.** Gear A turns in the opposite direction from gear B. A clockwise turn of A results in a counterclockwise revolution of gear B. Since the distance traversed by A (perimeter = I × diameter = I × 4) is twice that of C (perimeter = I × 2), the speed of C is doubled.

6. **The correct answer is B.** The figure shown is a bimetallic strip that works like the wire in a thermostat. High temperatures will cause the metals to heat unevenly. The rivets will keep the strips together, so the only thing that they can do is bend.

7. **The correct answer is D.** Wheel P has 16 teeth; wheel M has 12 teeth. When wheel M makes a full turn, wheel P will still have 4 more teeth to turn. So, wheel P is slower and will take more time to turn.

8. **The correct answer is C.** An inclined plane is a sloping, triangular shape, used here as a wedge to force open an axe cut made in the log.

9. **The correct answer is C.** The trick with this question is that both of the rods will be pulled in at the same time when the turnbuckle is turned. If it is turned 12 times (12 threads per inch), both rods will be pulled in 1 inch.

10. **The correct answer is C.** The downward pull equals the 100-lb. weight being hoisted plus the 50-lb. effort required with the single movable block in the pulley, which has a mechanical advantage of 2. 100 lbs. + 50 lbs. = 150 lbs.

11. **The correct answer is B.** Imagine the driven wheel as a vinyl record. For one rotation of the record, point y travels much farther than point x. It takes more turns of the driver wheel to turn point y one complete revolution.

12. **The correct answer is B.** The diameter of the handle is $3\frac{1}{2}$ times $\left(\frac{28}{3}\right)$ the diameter of the axle. When 50 lbs. of force is applied to the handle, it is multiplied by $3\frac{1}{2}$ times, or, $\frac{28}{8} \times 50 = 175$ lbs.

13. **The correct answer is A.** When steam flows through pipes, it expands. The pipes would burst if extra space were not provided for expansion and contraction.

14. **The correct answer is B.** Let x = effort that must be exerted.

    $60 \times 3 = x \times 5$; $180 = 5x$; $x = \frac{80}{5} = 36$

15. **The correct answer is A.** The water is filling up in the tank at a rate of 120 gallons per hour, or 2 gallons per minute $\left(\frac{120}{60} = 2\right)$. The tank is also emptying at a rate of 1 gallon per minute. The net flow is increasing by 1 gallon per minute, because 2 gal./min. input − 1 gal./min. output = 1 gal./min. increase. Note: The easiest way to find the answer is to change all measurements to gallons per minute.

16. **The correct answer is C.** Figure No. 3 has the largest surface area and thus would need the shortest sides. Area = length × width. For No. 3, area = 7 ft. × 4 ft. = 28 sq. ft.

17. **The correct answer is D.** The water shut-off valve on a flush tank is closed by the force of a lightweight ball rising inside the tank. If this float becomes waterlogged, it will not rise and shut off the water.

18. **The correct answer is A.** The mechanical advantage is calculated by the number of strands supporting the weight. A has 3 strands, B has 2, and C has only 1.

19. **The correct answer is A.** Study the diagram and note that the follower is at its highest position between points Q and R.

20. **The correct answer is B.** Clockwise is right to left, so if the nut moves, it follows the threads of the bolt downward.

21. **The correct answer is D.** When the tuning fork vibrates, it causes a disturbance in the air that causes the ping-pong ball to swing away from the tuning fork.

22. **The correct answer is C.** The film of water inside the loop would form a lens that would enlarge the printing on the page. If you look through a water-filled globe, objects will also appear larger.

23. **The correct answer is B.** If the man moves to the back of the seesaw, his momentum (weight × distance from center) will increase. The woman, who is lighter, will rise in the air.

24. **The correct answer is A.** Insulating the pipes keeps warm moisture-laden air from coming into contact with the cold pipes. This stops condensation.

25. **The correct answer is A.** The measurements that can be made on the micrometer are: a) 2 major divisions and 1 minor division on the ruler-type scale, or 0.2 + 0.025 = 0.225; b) 2 minor divisions above 0 on the rotating scale, or 0.002. Summing, we find the final measurement is 0.225 + 0.002 = .227.

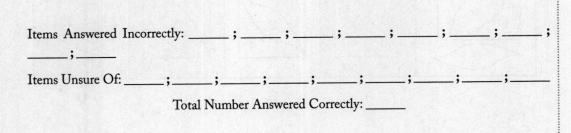

Items Answered Incorrectly: _____ ; _____ ; _____ ; _____ ; _____ ; _____ ; _____ ; _____ ; _____

Items Unsure Of: _____ ; _____ ; _____ ; _____ ; _____ ; _____ ; _____ ; _____ ; _____

Total Number Answered Correctly: _____

PART 9: ASSEMBLING OBJECTS

1. D	5. B	8. D	11. B	14. C
2. C	6. C	9. B	12. C	15. B
3. C	7. D	10. C	13. B	16. C
4. B				

1. **The correct answer is D.**

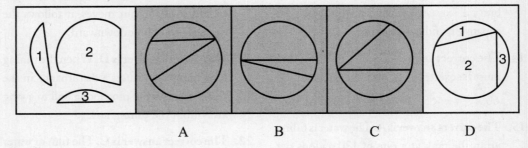

2. **The correct answer is C.**

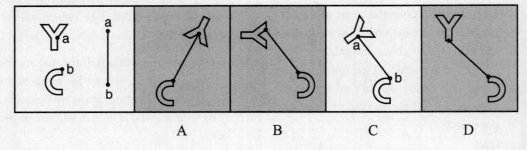

3. **The correct answer is C.**

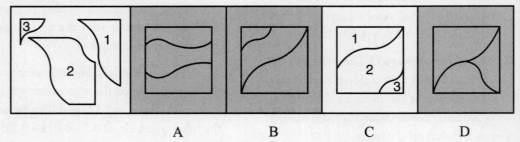

4. **The correct answer is B.**

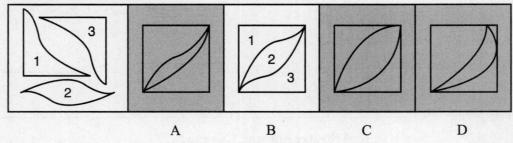

5. The correct answer is B.

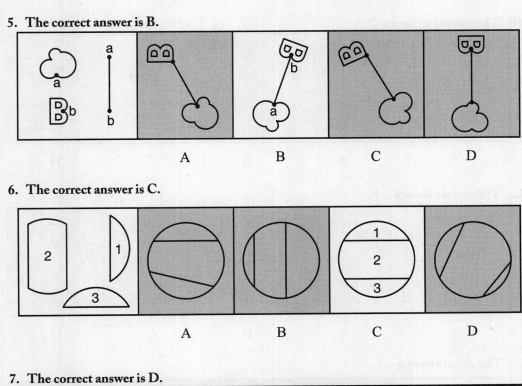

6. The correct answer is C.

7. The correct answer is D.

8. The correct answer is D.

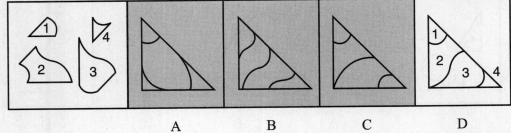

9. The correct answer is B.

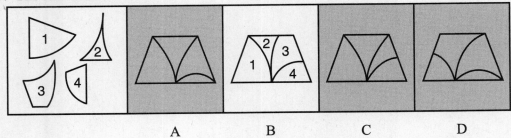

practice test 1

10. **The correct answer is C.**

11. **The correct answer is B.**

12. **The correct answer is C.**

13. **The correct answer is B.**

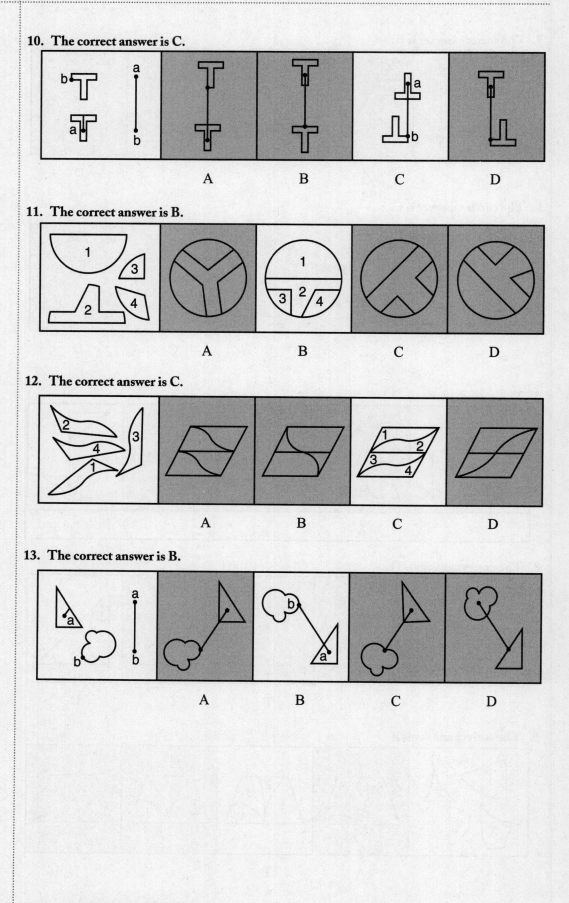

14. **The correct answer is C.**

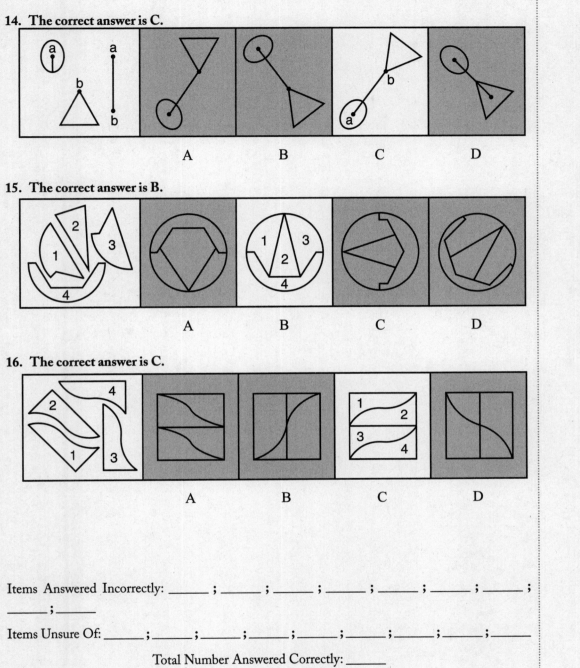

15. **The correct answer is B.**

16. **The correct answer is C.**

Items Answered Incorrectly: _____ ; _____ ; _____ ; _____ ; _____ ; _____ ; _____ ;
_____ ; _____

Items Unsure Of: _____ ; _____ ; _____ ; _____ ; _____ ; _____ ; _____ ; _____ ; _____

Total Number Answered Correctly: _____

PART III
ASVAB SUBJECT REVIEW

CHAPTER 3:   General Science

CHAPTER 4:   Arithmetic Reasoning

CHAPTER 5:   Word Knowledge Review

CHAPTER 6:   Paragraph Comprehension

CHAPTER 7:   Mathematics Knowledge

CHAPTER 8:   Electronics Information

CHAPTER 9:   Auto & Shop Information

CHAPTER 10: Mechanical Comprehension

CHAPTER 11: Assembling Objects

General Science

OVERVIEW

- **Life Science**
- **Physical Science**
- **Earth Science**
- **Practice Questions**
- **Answer Key and Explanations**
- **Summing It Up**

At this point in your ASVAB preparation, you should review your scores to pinpoint your weaknesses. Your next step is knowing what you can do to improve, to achieve your maximum scores, and to enhance your vocational opportunities.

Your test scores reflect a combination of your past learning experiences and the time and effort you put into preparing for the actual ASVAB test. If you have been a "reader," you probably have a good vocabulary and will do well on Word Knowledge and Paragraph Comprehension. If you have spent considerable time in "shop," chances are that you will score high on Auto & Shop Information, Mechanical Comprehension, and Electronics Information. If science has always fascinated you, then you are likely to have more knowledge in this area and will score high in General Science. And if you have always liked math, you probably will do well in Arithmetic Reasoning and Mathematics Knowledge.

It is also a big help to have a feel for the test by:

- Taking practice tests
- Timing yourself to the actual times for each test section
- Using the sample answer sheets
- Reviewing material in which you need extra help

The following basic reviews offer concise yet comprehensive coverage of the subject areas of the ASVAB. It is strongly recommended that you read the basic review for each test and spend extra time studying the reviews for the tests on which you scored low. After completing each of the remaining three ASVAB tests, you may find it helpful to return to this review chapter to better understand the answers or the reasoning for getting to the correct answer.

Your efforts preparing for the ASVAB will pay off in higher scores, broader knowledge of the subject matter covered, and better test-taking skills.

Chapter 3

Because general science covers a great deal of information, we provide only the most important findings and basic concepts of general science that are covered on the ASVAB. This will refresh your memory of what you learned in junior and senior high school science courses.

This review covers the following areas:

- **Life Science:** biology, human nutrition, and health
- **Physical Science:** elementary physics and chemistry
- **Earth Science:** geology, meteorology, and astronomy

LIFE SCIENCE

Classification of Animal and Plant Life

With more than a million different kinds of plants and animals living on Earth, there is a need for a system of classification. The system currently in use was developed by Linnaeus and is based on relationships and similarities in structure. The scientific name consists of two terms identifying the genus and species. Note that the first letter of each genus listed below is capitalized and the species is written in lowercase. For example:

Homo sapiens: scientific name for human beings

Escherichia coli: scientific name of the microorganism that inhabits the intestines of human beings

The classification system has seven levels. The top level contains the largest number of different kinds of organisms and is called the *kingdom*. The bottom level with the smallest number of different kinds of organisms is called the *species*. The seven levels are:

1. **KINGDOM**—contains several related *phyla*
2. **PHYLUM**—contains several related *classes*
3. **CLASS**—contains several related *orders*
4. **ORDER**—contains several related *families*
5. **FAMILY**—contains several related *genera*
6. **GENUS**—contains several related *species*
7. **SPECIES**—contains all organisms with the same characteristics

Scientists have struggled to find the best method of grouping organisms for hundreds of years. The most accepted theory is the five-kingdom system:

1. Animals
2. Monerans
3. Protists
4. Fungi
5. Plants

The animal and plant kingdoms are the two principal kingdoms and contain virtually all life. These two kingdoms are described in detail after Figure 1 on page 100. Brief descriptions of the other three kingdoms follow.

Monerans and Viruses

Monerans are simple one-celled microscopic organisms. They lack internal structures within their cells and have a simple circular molecule of DNA instead of a nucleus. This kingdom includes bacteria and blue-green algae. Many bacteria are known as parasites, which cause diseases (tetanus, gonorrhea, and strep throat), or as decomposers, which absorb food from decaying materials or living things. Blue-green algae make their own food by photosynthesizing.

Viruses are a type of life that scientists have difficulty defining. They do not fit easily into any classification scheme because they do not have a true cell structure. Some scientists describe them as nonliving things, even though they contain protein and nucleic acid. Many human diseases are caused by viruses (polio, influenza, AIDS, herpes, measles, etc.). Viruses cause diseases by using another cell's material to reproduce.

Protists

Protists are microscopic one-celled organisms that have a true nucleus, as well as many other structures found in more complex cells. Protists differ from each other in the way they obtain food. Some depend on other organisms for food, and some can photosynthesize. This kingdom includes protozoa, one-celled algae, and slime molds.

Fungi

Fungi are many-celled organisms with complex cell structure. Their cells lack chloroplasts that are necessary in photosynthesizing. They are decomposers. This kingdom includes bread molds, mushrooms, and yeasts.

Figure 1. The five-kingdom system.

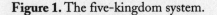

Animals	☐ Many-celled organisms	☐ Eat food and can move on their own

Sponges (porifera)
☐ Body has space in center
☐ Water flows through body

Finger sponge

Coelenterates
☐ One opening in body
☐ Have stinging cells

Jellyfish

Flatworms (platyhelminthes)
☐ Flat body
☐ One opening in digestive system

Tapeworm

Roundworms (nematoda)
☐ Smooth, round body
☐ Two openings in digestive system

Trichina worm

Segmented worms (annelida)
☐ Body divided into bands
☐ Has circulatory and nervous systems

Earthworm

Mollusks
☐ Soft bodies
☐ Most have a hard shell

Clam

Echinoderms
☐ Outer skeleton, usually with spines
☐ Water-pumping system

Starfish

Arthropods
☐ Hard outer skeleton
☐ At least 3 pairs of jointed legs
☐ Body divided into segments

Beetle

Millipede

Crab

Spider

Centipede

Vertebrates (chordata)
☐ Have inner skeleton

Lizard (reptile)

Salmon (fish)

Frog (amphibian)

Robin (bird)

Horse (mammal)

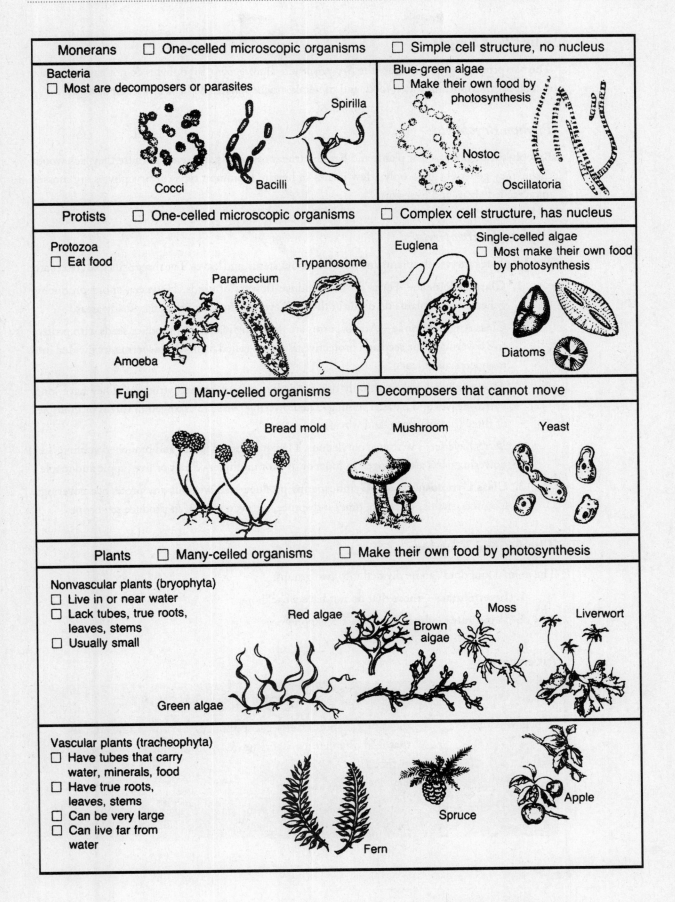

The Plant Kingdom

The two principal plant phyla are the *Bryophyta* and *Tracheophyta*. Bryophytes do not have a vascular system for transporting water, food, and minerals; tracheophytes do have a vascular system.

Phylum Bryophyta

Bryophytes are nonvascular plants and have no true roots, stems, or leaves. Because they lack woody tissue, they generally grow only a few inches in height. Common types of bryophytes are mosses, many-celled algae, and liverworts.

Phylum Tracheophyta

Tracheophytes are vascular plants and have true roots, stems, and leaves. The three principal classes are:

1. **Class Filicineae**—Ferns do not produce flowers or seeds. However, spore-producing generations of plants do occur in their life cycles. They require moist, shady areas.

2. **Class Angiospermae**—Angiosperms are flowering plants that produce seeds with protective coverings. The seed and protective tissue are called fruit. Angiosperms are divided into monocots and dicots.

   Monocots have seeds with only one cotyledon, a food-bearing structure. They have long, narrow leaves and parallel veining. The flowering parts are arranged in threes or multiples of three (banana, corn, and wheat).

   Dicots have seeds with two cotyledons. They have broad leaves and branched veining. The flowering parts are arranged in fours or fives or multiples of four or five (apple and maple).

3. **Class Gymnospermae**—Gymnosperms produce seed without any protective coverings. Conifers, such as cedar, fir, pine, and spruce, are evergreens that produce seed cones.

The Animal Kingdom

The animal kingdom can be divided into two groups:

1. **Invertebrates**—those that do not have a backbone
2. **Vertebrates**—those that have a backbone

Invertebrates

Phylum	Characteristics
Phylum Porifera	the simplest animals; also called sponges; mostly marine animals that feed on microscopic organisms; porous and lack bony skeletons or tissues. *Example: sponge*
Phylum Coelenterata	more complex organisms having simple tissues; marine animals *Examples: coral; jellyfish; sea anemone*

Phylum	Characteristics
Phylum Platyhelminthes	flatworms are the simplest animals with bilateral symmetry and organs; often live as parasites in humans; flat body *Examples: tapeworm; liver fluke*
Phylum Nematoda	roundworms have a digestive tract with two openings; most are parasitic *Examples: ascaris; hookworm; trichina*
Phylum Annelida	long, segmented, cylindrical bodies; the only parasitic annelid is the leech *Examples: earthworm; leech*

Phylum Mollusca	soft bodies enclosed in a mantle; move by means of a muscular foot; three principal classes:
	    Univalves—single-coil shell
	    Example: snail
	    Bivalves—two shells connected by a hinge
	    Examples: clam; mussel; oyster; scallop
	    Head-foot—no shell
	    Examples: squid; octopus

Phylum Echinodermata	aquatic animals with spiny skins; some have five or more arms that spread out in radial symmetry *Examples: starfish; sea urchin; sea cucumber*
Phylum Arthropoda	contains the largest number of animals; segmented bodies covered by an external skeleton; jointed appendages; generally have three distinct body regions (head, thorax, and abdomen) *Examples: lobster; shrimp; crab; centipede; millipede; spider; scorpion; insect*

The major classes of anthropoda and their characteristics are:

- **Crustaceans:** have five or more pairs of jointed legs and gills for respiration. The lobster, shrimp, and crab are common crustaceans.
- **Myriapods:** include the centipede and millipede. They have long bodies made up of numerous segments with legs on each segment. The centipede has one pair of legs per segment; the millipede has two pairs on each segment.
- **Arachnids:** have two body regions and four pairs of legs. The spider and scorpion are in this class.
- **Insects:** comprise the largest group of arthropods. Insects have three pairs of legs and generally one or two pairs of wings. The ant, bee, butterfly, fly, grasshopper, locust, louse, mosquito, and moth are common insects.

Vertebrates

There are five classes of vertebrates in the phylum Chordata:

Phylum Chordata	
Class	**Characteristics**
1. Fish	cold-blooded; use internal gills for respiration; use fins for locomotion
	Examples: bass; trout; perch; mackerel; shark
2. Amphibians	can live both in the water and on land; cold-blooded; develop lungs in the adult stage
	Examples: frog; toad; salamander
3. Reptiles	cold-blooded; breathe air through lungs; have legs for movement (except snakes); most lay eggs with tough shells
	Examples: alligator; crocodile; lizard; snake; turtle
4. Birds	warm-blooded with feathers and wings; lay eggs with brittle shells; there are many different kinds of birds with some raised for human consumption
	Examples: chicken; goose; turkey
5. Mammals	warm-blooded with hair or fur on bodies; breathe by means of lungs; newborns are fed milk from the mother's mammary glands; mammals are divided into many orders based on differences in body structure
	Examples: duckbill platypus; kangaroo; beaver; mouse; rat; squirrel; dolphin; porpoise; whale; cat; dog; fox; lion; wolf; cow; deer; horse; pig; sheep; ape; human; monkey

The major classes of mammals and their characteristics are:

- **Monotremes:** the most primitive mammals, lay eggs (*duckbill platypus*)
- **Marsupials:** carry their young in the pouch on the mother's body (*kangaroo*)
- **Rodents:** gnawing mammals (*beaver, mouse, rat, and squirrel*)
- **Cetaceans:** marine mammals with forelimbs that have been modified to flippers (*dolphin, porpoise, and whale*)
- **Carnivores:** have sharp claws and powerful jaws (*cat, dog, fox, lion, and wolf*)
- **Ungulates:** hoofed mammals with teeth adapted for grinding (*cow, deer, horse, pig, and sheep*)
- **Primates:** possess a highly developed brain, stand erect, and have the ability to grasp and hold objects with their two hands (*ape, human, and monkey*)

Humans

Humans are part of the primate order. They are unique in their species in that they have characteristics that set them apart from other primates. These characteristics include:

- Power of speech
- Bipedalism, or the ability to walk on two legs instead of four
- Adaptability to almost any environment
- Ability to remember
- Ability to make associations between ideas

Major Systems of the Human Body

The human body is a complex machine that operates in a most effective and precise manner. It consists of several major systems that work together with extreme efficiency.

The Skeletal System

The human skeleton is the supporting framework of the body. It consists of more than 200 bones connected by joints (see Figure 2). The four main types of joints are:

1. **Fixed joints**—as in the skull, hold the bones firmly together.
2. **Hinge joints**—as in the knee and finger, are partly movable and provide some flexibility.
3. **Pivot joints**—as in the elbow, are similar to hinge joints but can also be rotated.
4. **Ball and socket joints**—as in the hip or shoulder, provide greatest flexibility.

The surfaces of joints are lined and cushioned by a flexible material called *cartilage*. Cartilage is also found in the outer ear and the tip of the nose. Bands of tissue called ligaments support the bones of movable joints.

The Muscular System

This system enables the body to move. The body has more than 600 skeletal muscles that are made up of bundles of striated (or voluntary) muscle fibers. Each end of the muscle is attached to the bone by connective tissue called tendon. Movement results from the contraction of these muscles that always operate in pairs. For example, the contraction of the biceps while the triceps are relaxed causes the elbow to bend; the contraction of the triceps while the biceps are relaxed causes the elbow to straighten (see Figure 3). The skeletal muscles are known as voluntary muscles because they are controlled by the individual through conscious thought.

Figure 2. The human skeleton. Each bone pictured functions in supporting a part of the body.

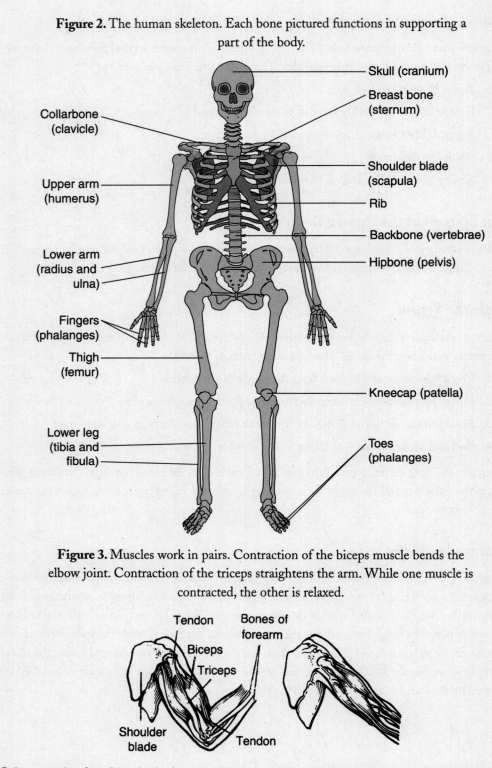

Skull (cranium)
Breast bone (sternum)
Collarbone (clavicle)
Shoulder blade (scapula)
Upper arm (humerus)
Rib
Backbone (vertebrae)
Lower arm (radius and ulna)
Hipbone (pelvis)
Fingers (phalanges)
Thigh (femur)
Kneecap (patella)
Lower leg (tibia and fibula)
Toes (phalanges)

Figure 3. Muscles work in pairs. Contraction of the biceps muscle bends the elbow joint. Contraction of the triceps straightens the arm. While one muscle is contracted, the other is relaxed.

Tendon
Bones of forearm
Biceps
Triceps
Shoulder blade
Tendon

Other muscles found in the body are smooth muscle in internal organs and cardiac muscle that enables the heart to pump blood. Smooth and cardiac muscles are known as *involuntary muscles* because they are not controlled by the individual. They play an important role in maintaining such body functions as circulation, respiration, and digestion.

The Digestive System

The digestive tract is essentially a long, winding tunnel that extends from the mouth to the anus. It includes the mouth, esophagus, stomach, small intestine, large intestine, rectum, and anus (see Figure 4).

Figure 4. The human digestive system.

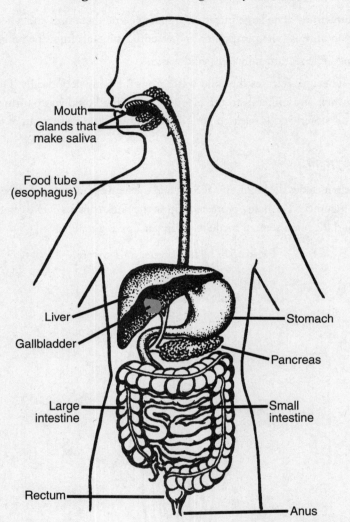

The digestive system controls food intake, digestion, and the absorption of the digested material by the body cells for energy and bodybuilding. The six important steps in digestion are as follows:

1. **Mouth**—The teeth and tongue aid in mechanical digestion. Amylase contained in the saliva acts on the starch.

2. **Stomach**—Food is mixed with acidic gastric juice and pepsin, which acts on the protein.

3. **Small intestine**—The bulk of digestion occurs in the small intestine. The food pulp mixes with alkali and digestive juices that are manufactured by the pancreas and the liver and released into the duodenum, the beginning of the small intestine. The juice manufactured by the pancreas contains lipase, which changes fat to glycerol and fatty acids; amylase, which changes complex carbohydrates to simple sugars; and trypsins, which change polypeptides

to amino acids. Bile produced by the liver and stored in the gallbladder aids in the digestion and absorption of fats and oils.

Absorption of all digested substances, except the fatty acids and glycerol, occurs in the small intestine through capillaries that carry the blood to the liver and then to all body cells. Fatty acids and glycerol are absorbed and transported by the lymphatic system to the neck before entering the bloodstream.

4. **Large intestine**—The large intestine produces certain vitamins and is responsible for the absorption of those vitamins, water, and essential minerals from the remaining material.

5. **Rectum**—The rectum stores the solid waste.

6. **Anus**—The anus releases the solid waste from the body periodically. The kidneys return needed water and minerals to the blood but send the liquid waste (urine) to the bladder, where it is stored and is released periodically through the urethra out of the body.

The Nervous System

The nervous system includes the brain, spinal cord, and the network of nerves. It receives and responds to all stimuli (see Figure 5). The brain, protected within the skull, consists of two cerebral hemispheres, the cerebellum, and the brain stem or medulla oblongata (see Figure 6).

Figure 5. The human nervous system.

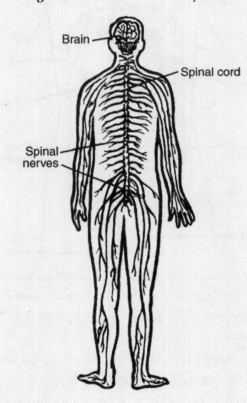

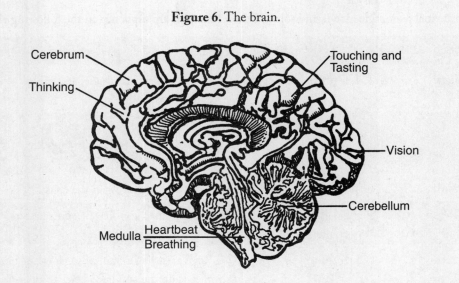

Figure 6. The brain.

The main components of the nervous system and their functions are:

- **Cerebrum or forebrain:** major part of the brain and is responsible for many human abilities, such as hearing, seeing, speaking, learning, etc.

- **Cerebellum:** concerned with muscular coordination and is responsible for the coordination of impulses sent out from the cerebrum. It also controls posture and balance.

- **Brain stem:** connects the brain with the spinal cord. It controls several involuntary activities, such as heartbeat rate and breathing rate.

- **Spinal cord:** major connecting center between the brain and the network of nerves. It is also the control center for many simple reflexes.

The Endocrine System

The endocrine system is a group of specialized organs and body tissues that produce, store, and secrete chemical substances. These chemical substances are known as *hormones* and are chemical regulators that control growth, metabolism, and reproduction. They are produced by endocrine glands and the brain controls their release into the bloodstream. When they are released, specific hormones affect specific tissues and processes in the body (see Figure 7).

The principal endocrine glands and some of their functions are explained in the following chart.

Endocrine Gland	Hormone	Process Regulated
Pituitary	1. Growth hormone	1. Growth of muscle, bone, and other connective tissue
	2. Vasopressin	2. Increases blood pressure; increases reabsorption of water into blood from kidneys
Thyroid	Thyroxin	Energy release process in the cells
Parathyroid	PTH (parathyroid hormone)	Nerve impulses and muscle contraction, strength of bones
Pancreas	1. Insulin	1. Regulates the amount of sugar in the blood; speeds up the storage of excess sugar
	2. Glucagon	2. Speeds up the removal of stored sugar
Adrenal glands	Adrenaline	Readies the body for strenuous physical activity; increases the amount of sugar in the blood
Testes	Androgens	Controls development of sex characteristics of adult males
Ovaries	Estrogens	Controls development of sex characteristics of adult females

Figure 7. The principal endocrine glands in the human body.

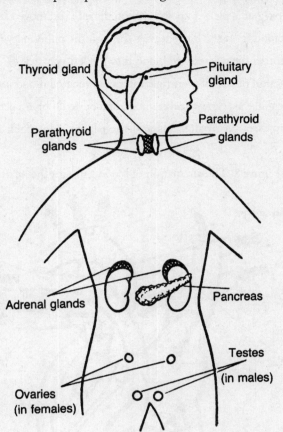

Endocrine organs have no ducts connecting them to specific body parts. The main functions of endocrine glands include:

- Body's growth and development
- Control of the function of various tissues
- Support of pregnancy and other reproductive functions
- Regulation of metabolism

The Circulatory System

The circulatory system's main organ is the heart. It pumps oxygenated blood at high pressure to every part of the body through arteries and capillaries, back to the heart at reduced pressure through small veins and large veins, back to the lungs for oxygenation, and then back to the heart to repeat the cycle.

The heart is a pear-shaped organ that lies in the center of the chest. The lungs are shaped like elongated ovoids and lie on either side of the heart. The heart has four chambers—the right atrium, the left atrium, the right ventricle, and the left ventricle (see Figure 8).

The nine principal steps in the circulation of blood are as follows:

1. Blood from the body enters the right atrium of the heart.
2. Contraction forces the blood into the right ventricle.

3. Contraction forces the blood into the pulmonary artery, which goes to the lungs.

4. In the lungs, oxygen is picked up and carbon dioxide is removed from the blood.

5. Oxygenated blood from the lungs travels through the pulmonary veins to the left atrium.

6. Contraction forces the oxygenated blood into the left ventricle.

7. Strong contraction of the left ventricle forces oxygenated blood into the aorta.

8. Arteries and capillaries carry the oxygenated blood to all blood cells.

9. Blood returns through small veins and then large veins back to the right atrium of the heart.

Figure 8. The circulation of blood through the heart.

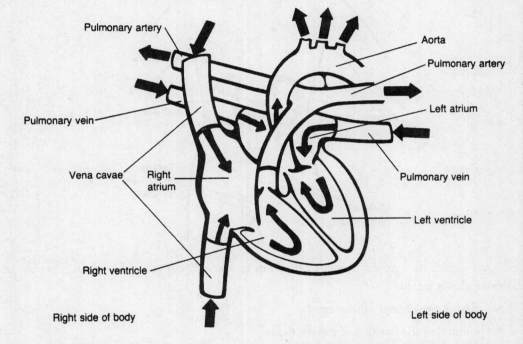

The heartbeat reflects the contraction of the heart. The normal adult heartbeat is 72 beats per minute. The pulse rate and the heartbeat rate are the same. Each heartbeat consists of two stages. The powerful muscular contraction of the ventricles is the *systolic* stage, when blood is pumped into the aorta. The other stage is the *diastolic*, or rest stage. Blood pressure is the ratio of systolic over diastolic pressure measured in millimeters of mercury. Normal adult blood pressure is approximately 120/80.

The four principal components of blood are:

1. **Red blood cells (erythrocytes)**—carry oxygen and carbon dioxide

2. **White blood cells (leukocytes)**—produce antibodies and fight off infections

3. **Platelets**—cell fragments involved in blood clotting

4. **Proteins**—involved in blood clotting and antibody production

The Respiratory System

The respiratory system's main function is to breathe air into and out of the lungs, oxygenating the blood while eliminating carbon dioxide. Oxygen diffuses into the blood, while carbon dioxide moves out of the blood via the lungs and out of the body via the mouth or nose. Using oxygen to oxidize the intracellular nutrients releases energy into the body. Exhalation of air rids the body of carbon dioxide, a waste product of oxidation.

The respiratory system consists of the following (see Figure 9):

- **Nose and nasal cavity**—filter, moisten, and warm inhaled air
- **Throat**—aids in protection against infection
- **Windpipe**—provides a passageway for the air
- **Bronchi**—two tubes that connect the windpipe with the lungs
- **Lungs**—capillary vessels of the lungs exchange gases between the air and the blood
- **Blood**—the oxygen combines with the hemoglobin in the red blood cells and is carried throughout the body to the cells. Carbon dioxide is carried back to the lungs where this waste product is exchanged for oxygen.

The Lymphatic System

The lymphatic system filters impurities out of the fluid that surrounds body tissues and comprises a network of organs, ducts, and tissues. The organs are divided into two categories:

1. **The primary lymphatic organs**—These consist of the thymus and bone marrow, which produce lymphocytes. Although the thymus is critical for T-cell development in children, it begins to shrink as they progress toward adulthood.

2. **The secondary lymphatic organs**—These include the spleen, appendix, tonsils, adenoids, lymph nodes, and Peyer's patches in the small intestine. Tonsils reach full size at approximately age 7, then gradually shrink until adulthood. Tonsils and adenoids were routinely removed surgically in the past in most children. Today, tonsils are not removed unless a child experiences repeated infections of the tonsils, known as tonsillitis.

Lymph nodes are mainly clustered in the pelvic area, the neck, and the armpits. They are the lymphatic system's way to fight infection and are connected to each other by lymphatic vessels. White blood cells in the nodes and other secondary organs surround and destroy debris to prevent it from reentering the bloodstream.

Figure 9. Organs of the respiratory system.

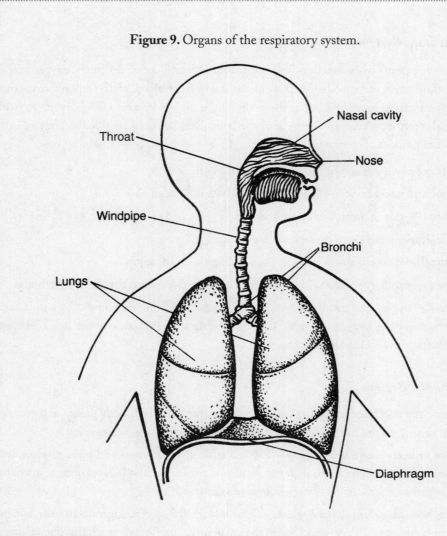

The Excretory System

The excretory system involves several organs, including some involved in digestion and respiration, and is responsible for the removal of waste substances from the body. The main organs of the excretory system are:

- **Skin:** excretes waste through perspiration
- **Large intestine:** absorbs water from solid food waste, stores and eliminates waste
- **Kidneys:** filter blood and excrete waste in the form of urea
- **Liver:** excretes bilirubin
- **Lungs:** excrete carbon dioxide

The Reproductive System

Humans reproduce by the union of a male sperm and a female ovum. The male organ ejaculates more than 250 million sperm into the vagina, for which some make their way to the uterus and the fallopian tubes that provide passage from the ovaries to the uterus. Ovulation, the release of an egg into a fallopian tube, occurs approximately every 28 days; meanwhile the uterus is prepared for the implantation of a fertilized ovum by the action of estrogen. If sperm unites with an ovum, a zygote is formed that eventually develops into a fetus. If no sperm unites with the ovum, other hormones cause the uterine wall to slough off during menstruation. From puberty to menopause, the process of ovulation, preparation, and menstruation is repeated monthly except for periods of pregnancy. The duration of pregnancy is approximately 280 days. After childbirth, prolactin, a hormone secreted by the pituitary, activates the production of milk.

Health and Nutrition

Humans obtain energy from food for maintenance, growth, and repair. A healthy diet contains sufficient quantities of *macronutrients*, such as proteins, carbohydrates, and fats, because they are energy producers.

- *Proteins* are necessary for the growth and repair of body tissues. Animal proteins are contained in meat, fish, eggs, and cheese. Vegetable proteins are found in peas, beans, and other legumes as well as in grains.

- *Carbohydrates* comprise the starches and sugars. Starches are found in bread, cereals, pasta, vegetables such as potatoes, and rice. Sugars are obtained from fruits, cane sugar, and beets. Cakes and pies contain excessive amounts of sugar and should be eaten sparingly.

- *Fats* may be of plant or animal origin. Although some fat is needed for body growth and repair, excess fat is retained in the body as fatty tissue that can cause health problems.

- *Micronutrients*, consisting of vitamins and minerals, are needed in smaller quantities because they do not contain calories but are essential for health.

- *Vitamins* are required by the body to function well. Some of the more important vitamins are listed in the following chart.

Vitamin	Source	Deficiency Result
A	Yellow and green leafy vegetables, eggs, butter, meat	Night blindness, rough and dry skin
B_1	Whole grain cereals, liver, beef, peas, beans, pork, nuts	Beriberi with loss of appetite, nervous disorders
B_2	Milk, leafy green vegetables, liver, enriched and fortified grain cereals	Skin infections, general weakness
B_{12}	Meat, eggs, dairy products	Pernicious anemia
C	Citrus fruits, strawberries, tomatoes, green peppers, broccoli	Scurvy
D	Milk, eggs, fish oil	Rickets
E	Green leafy vegetables, wheat germ, margarine, nuts	Sterility, hemolytic anemia
K	Green leafy vegetables, eggs, dairy products	Slow blood clotting

Minerals are needed in small quantities for proper metabolic functioning. Mineral salts are chemical compounds containing sodium, calcium, phosphorus, potassium, magnesium, iron, chlorine, fluorine, and iodine.

Fibers are needed for a healthy diet since they provide bulk, which enables the large intestine to carry away body wastes. Water is also essential. The body loses approximately four pints of water a day, which must be replaced. Since most foods contain water, replenishment generally occurs.

A balanced diet requires moderate eating of a variety of foods. Some foods are needed each day from each of the following four major groups:

1. **Milk and Dairy Products**—These foods provide the body with energy, protein, vitamins, and minerals.

2. **Breads, Cereals, Rice, Potatoes, and Pastas**—These foods provide energy for the body.

3. **Fruits and Vegetables**—Both raw and cooked fruits and vegetables provide the body with energy, minerals, vitamins, and roughage.

4. **Meats, Poultry, and Fish**—These foods or substitutes, such as eggs, nuts, peas, and beans, supply the body with energy, minerals, vitamins, and proteins.

Human Genetics

Human genetics is the study of heredity, the mechanism by which characteristics are passed from parents to offspring. Three basic laws of heredity were developed by Gregor Mendel in the late eighteenth century. These are:

1. **The Law of Segregation**—Individual heredity traits separate in the reproductive cells.

2. **The Law of Independent Assortment**—Each trait is inherited independently of other traits.

3. **The Law of Dominance**—When certain contrasting traits are crossed, one trait will be dominant and the other will be recessive.

Every child develops from a fertilized egg (zygote) that contains 23 pairs of chromosomes, or a total of 46. Each pair consists of one chromosome from the mother and one from the father (see Figure 10). Each chromosome contains large numbers of hereditary units called genes that determine physical and mental characteristics of the offspring. A gene is a unit of a DNA molecule that carries a code for the production of a specific protein.

Meiosis is a specialized process of cell division in which gametes, also known as sex cells, are produced by sexually mature adults. These gametes are in the haploid stage, which means they have only one of each pair, or half the number, of chromosomes. The 23 pairs of chromosomes split into two sets of 23 each. The chromosomes in the nucleus of each gamete are reduced from 46 to 23. At fertilization, the 23 chromosomes from one parent combine with the 23 chromosomes from the other parent to form a new cell with a total of 46 chromosomes. Sexual reproduction by meiosis and fertilization results in great variation among offspring.

Sex Determination

The sex of babies is determined by genes located on the pair of sex chromosomes. In the human female, the two sex chromosomes are alike and are designated as XX. In the male, the sex chromosomes are not alike and are designated as XY.

At fertilization, the zygote or fertilized egg receives an X chromosome from the mother but may receive either an X or Y chromosome from the father (see Figure 10). If the paired chromosomes are XX, the offspring will be female. If the paired chromosomes are XY, the offspring will be male.

Figure 10. Pairing of chromosomes.

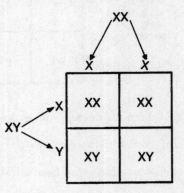

Dominant and Recessive Characteristics

Each person has two genes for each particular characteristic. These genes may be alike or not alike. If the genes are alike, that person is homozygous for that characteristic. If the genes are not alike, the person is heterozygous for that characteristic.

There are many common inherited characteristics and traits of people such as: hair color, eye color, nose size and shape, earlobe shape, color vision, and blood type.

A person's earlobe shape is determined by the gene received from each parent. To illustrate this, the free earlobe is designated with a capital E in Figure 11 because it is dominant, and the attached earlobe with a small letter e because it is recessive. Consider the following:

- If the genes are alike and the person is homozygous for free earlobes designated by EE, the individual will show free earlobes.

- If the genes are alike and the person is homozygous for attached earlobes designated by ee, the individual will show attached earlobes.

- If the person received an E gene from one parent and an e gene from the other, the person would be heterozygous for ear shape designated by Ee, but would show free earlobes, the dominant form.

- If both parents have a genetic makeup of EE, the offspring will have a genetic makeup of EE and will show free earlobes.

- If both parents have a genetic makeup of ee, the offspring will have a genetic makeup of ee and will show attached earlobes.

If both parents have free earlobes but are heterozygous with a genetic makeup of Ee, the different genetic combinations are those shown in Figure 11.

Figure 11. Two heterozygous parents.

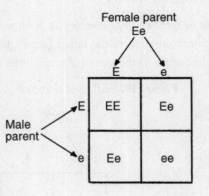

1-EE—homozygous with free earlobes

2-Ee—heterozygous with free earlobes (dominant trait)

1-ee—homozygous with fixed earlobes

If both parents have free earlobes but one is homozygous (EE) and the other is heterozygous (Ee), the different genetic combinations are those shown in Figure 12.

Figure 12. One homozygous, one heterozygous parent.

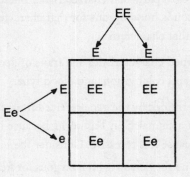

2-EE—homozygous with free earlobes

2-Ee—heterozygous with free earlobes (dominant trait)

Because of the genetic combination shown in Figure 12, the recessive characteristic does not appear in the offspring but may appear in the next generation, depending on the genetic makeup of both parents and chance.

Ecology

Ecology is the study of the relationship between organisms and their living and physical surroundings. Every plant and animal is a member of a complex system called an ecosystem. In all ecosystems, the following exist as interacting forces:

Producers (green plants): They make their own food via the photosynthesis process.

Consumers (animals): There are three types of consumers:

- **Primary consumers:** also known as herbivores, eat plants. Examples include grasshoppers, rabbits, and cows.
- **Secondary consumers:** also called carnivores, are flesh-eaters. These include wolves, snakes, and lions.
- **Tertiary consumers:** include carnivores in their diet. Tertiary consumers may be omnivores, organisms that consume producers and consumers. Humans are omnivores as a species.

Scavengers: feed on dead organic matter. A vulture is an example of a scavenger.

Decomposers (bacteria and fungi): break down dead organic matter and release minerals back into the soil.

Important factors that restrict green plants to certain parts of the earth include:

- Temperature
- Soil
- Sunlight
- Water
- Plant eaters

These and additional considerations restrict animals to those parts of the earth where they can survive. Some additional considerations are as follows:

- Food supply
- Mates
- Diseases
- Parasites
- Natural enemies

Energy captured by green plants is transferred from organism to organism in a pathway known as a food chain. Each organism in the chain provides food for the next organism. For example:

Barley → Grasshopper → Spider → Frog → Fish → Bear

In this food chain, the bear is the predator, the fish is its prey; the fish is the predator, the frog is its prey, and so on. An organism may be part of several food chains. Unconsumed dead organisms at every level are broken down by decomposers, returning organic matter and minerals to the soil.

This entire process is the traditional method of recycling by natural forces. Ecosystems are frequently unbalanced or destroyed as a result of human activities. Conservation of natural resources and control of pollution of air, water, and soil will help preserve existing ecosystems.

Biomes

Areas on the earth that have similar climate, plants, and animals are called *biomes*. Biomes are permanent ecosystems in a large geographical area. The seven major biomes are:

1. **Tundra**—Located in the high northern latitudes of the world, is the coldest of all the biomes. Because the ground is always frozen a few feet below the surface, there are no deep root systems; the tundra is known for its treeless plains.

2. **Taiga**—Located just south of the tundra. Contains mostly cold-tolerant evergreen trees. Its seasons are divided into short, moist, and moderately warm summers and cold, dry winters.

3. **Deciduous Forests**—Located south of the taiga in eastern North America, northeastern Asia, western and central Europe. Characterized by a moderate climate with distinct winters. Its trees have broad leaves that are shed annually.

4. **Grasslands**—Some locations include North America (the Great Plains) and the pampas of South America. The grasslands are dominated by grasses rather than large shrubs or trees due to insufficient rainfall.

5. **Tropical Rain Forests**—Located near the equator and known for high temperatures and constant rainfall. Trees grow very tall and form a thick layer of leaves (the canopy) that greatly reduces light at ground level.

6. **Deserts**—Deserts cover one-fifth of the earth's surface and are characterized by extreme dryness. Deserts may be hot or cold.

7. **Marine**—This is the largest part of the biosphere, since water covers almost 75 percent of the earth's surface.

Cell Structures and Processes

Cell Structures

Cells are the basic structural unit of living things and develop from other cells. *Protoplasm*, or living material, is contained within tiny cells. These cells differ in size and shape, depending on their function in the body (see Figure 13).

The major parts of cells and their functions follow.

1. The **nucleus** is the control center for all cellular activity. Small dark bodies found in the nucleus are called *nucleoli*. The protoplasm within the nucleus is called *nucleoplasm*. Within the nucleoplasm are long, thin fibers called chromatin on which genes are found.

2. The **cytoplasm**, the cells' manufacturing area, contains small *vacuoles*, which are storage areas, and several other structures or organelles.

3. **Ribosomes** combine amino acids to build proteins. The cytoplasm contains many ribosomes.

4. The **cell membrane** plays an important role in controlling the flow of materials entering and leaving the cell. It is semipermeable and allows only certain materials to enter and leave.

The movement of particles from an area of high concentration to an area of lower concentration until equilibrium is reached is termed *diffusion*.

5. The **endoplasmic reticulum** is a membrane network that extends from the nucleus to the cell membrane. It transports lipids and proteins through the cell.

6. The **Golgi body**, or Golgi apparatus, prepares and stores chemical products produced in the cell and then secretes them outside the cell.

7. **Lysosomes** are saclike structures that contain and release enzymes necessary for digesting certain substances within the cell.

8. **Mitochondria** are complex organelles in the cell that produce energy via cellular respiration to fuel the cell's activities.

Figure 13. Parts of cells.

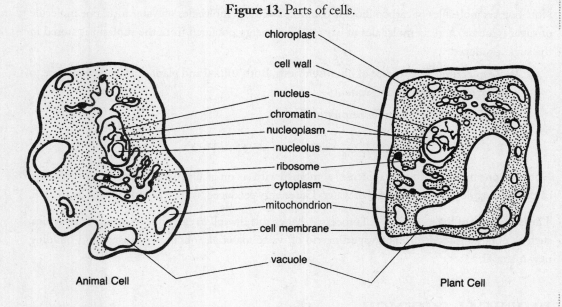

chloroplast
cell wall
nucleus
chromatin
nucleoplasm
nucleolus
ribosome
cytoplasm
mitochondrion
cell membrane
vacuole

Animal Cell   Plant Cell

Differences Between Plant and Animal Cells

Although all cells are similar in structure, plant and animal cells do differ. The major differences are as follows:

- Plant cells have a firm outer boundary called the *cell wall*. This wall supports and protects the plant cell.

- Vacuoles in the plant cell are much larger than those in the animal cell.

- Many plant cells contain within the cytoplasm small green structures called chloroplasts. These chloroplasts contain *chlorophyll* that enables the plant cell to make food.

Cell Processes

There are various processes carried out by the living cell. Some major examples are as follows:

- Water is the largest component of the cell protoplasm. Movement or diffusion of water through a semipermeable membrane is known as *osmosis*.

- The sum of all chemical reactions within a living cell, both the building up and the tearing down of complex molecules, is known as *metabolism*.
- Cells can also acquire material by engulfing particles. This process is termed *phagocytosis*. Certain white blood cells protect the body from infection by this method.

Two vital cellular reactions are:

1. **Photosynthesis:** The process by which green plants convert carbon dioxide and water into sugar and oxygen. Both sunlight and chlorophyll are needed for this reaction.

   The chemical reaction for photosynthesis is

$$6CO_2 + 6H_2O \xrightarrow[\text{chlorophyll}]{\text{sunlight}} C_6H_{12}O_6 + 6O_2$$

Note that six molecules of carbon dioxide combined with six molecules of water form one molecule of sugar (glucose) and six molecules of oxygen. The energy obtained from the sunlight is stored in the sugar produced.

2. **Respiration:** The reverse of photosynthesis. Both animal and plant cells oxidize glucose to form carbon dioxide and water.

   The chemical reaction for respiration is

$$C_6H_{12}O_6 + 6O_2 \longrightarrow 6CO_2 + 6H_2O$$

Note that one molecule of sugar (glucose) combined with six molecules of oxygen form six molecules of carbon dioxide and six molecules of water. The energy produced by this reaction is used by the cell.

These are some of the more vital cell processes that enable the cell to carry out essential life activities, such as obtaining food for energy, getting rid of waste materials, obtaining oxygen, and building new material.

PHYSICAL SCIENCE

Chemistry

Chemistry is the science that deals with the structure, composition, and properties of substances. It is also the study of elements and the compounds they form.

Classification of Matter into Elements and Compounds

Matter is anything that has mass and occupies space, although mass and weight are not the same. Mass is the amount of matter an object contains. Weight is the pull of gravity on that mass. For example, a 200-pound astronaut may be almost weightless in outer space without any reduction in mass.

Elements

Matter is composed of basic substances known as *elements*. The *atom* is the smallest part of an element that still acts like that element. The atom consists of a nucleus that contains *neutrons* and *protons* in the center. They are surrounded by flying particles called electrons. Atoms are electrically neutral as the positive protons neutralize the negative electrons. The number of electrons outside the nucleus is the same as the number of protons in the nucleus. The neutrons in the nucleus have no charge.

The negatively-charged electrons outside the nucleus are arranged in energy levels. When atoms bond to form substances, they complete their outer energy level. The first energy level needs two electrons to be complete, the second energy level needs eight, etc.

Atomic Numbers

The number of protons in an atom determines its atomic number. The atomic number of hydrogen is one because it has one proton in its nucleus. Helium has an atomic number of two because it has two protons in its nucleus. Carbon has an atomic number of 6; oxygen has an atomic number of 8 (see Figure 14).

Figure 14. Atomic structures.

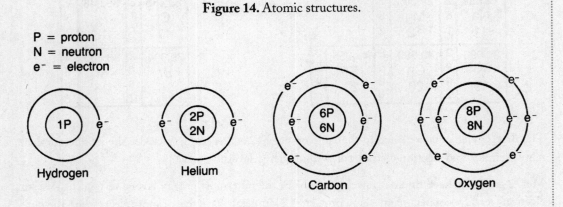

Periodic Table

The Periodic Table classifies all elements. The elements, listed by increasing atomic number, are arranged in vertical columns called groups or families. Each group contains elements with similar chemical properties (see Figure 15).

Note that hydrogen, lithium, sodium, and potassium, all with one electron in the outermost energy level, are in the same group. Helium, neon, and argon are in the group termed the noble gases. They are rare gases that are completely inert—having completed outermost energy levels.

Figure 15. A left-hand and right-hand portion of the Periodic Table of the Elements.

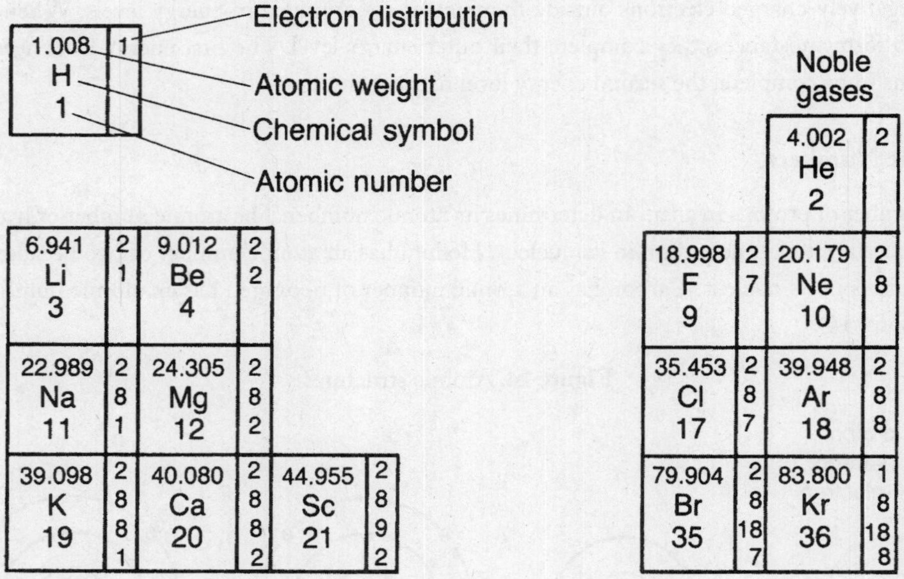

The first 22 elements are listed in the table on page 125. The listing includes the atomic number, name, symbol, and electron distribution within energy levels.

Metals generally have three or fewer electrons in the outermost energy level and tend to give up electrons readily (copper, magnesium, iron, etc.). Nonmetals have five or more electrons in the outermost energy level and tend to hold them tightly (nitrogen, oxygen, chlorine, etc.).

Compounds

Substances composed of atoms of two or more different elements are called *compounds*. Hydrogen atoms combine with oxygen to form a molecule of water (H_2O). A sodium atom combines with a chlorine atom to form an ionic particle of salt (NaCl). Properties of compounds differ greatly from the properties of the atoms that form the compound. Common salt, a relatively harmless substance, consists of sodium and chlorine, both highly toxic elements. The types of compounds follow.

- **Organic compounds:** contain carbon.
- **Hydrocarbons:** contain hydrogen and carbon only. Methane, ethylene, acetylene, and propane are hydrocarbons.
- **Carbohydrates:** contain only carbon, hydrogen, and oxygen. Common carbohydrates are sugars and starch. Glucose ($C_6H_{12}O_6$) is a simple sugar. Sucrose ($C_{12}H_{22}O_{11}$) or cane sugar is a disaccharide or more complex sugar.
- **Fats:** contain carbon, hydrogen, and oxygen. Fats may be classified as saturated or unsaturated compounds.
- **Proteins:** contain carbon, hydrogen, oxygen, and nitrogen. Some proteins contain, in addition, sulfur and phosphorus. Proteins consist of smaller molecules called *amino acids*.

Atomic Number	Element	Symbol	Electron Distribution
1	Hydrogen	H	1
2	Helium	He	2
3	Lithium	Li	2 - 1
4	Beryllium	Be	2 - 2
5	Boron	B	2 - 3
6	Carbon	C	2 - 4
7	Nitrogen	N	2 - 5
8	Oxygen	O	2 - 6
9	Fluorine	F	2 - 7
10	Neon	Ne	2 - 8
11	Sodium	Na	2 - 8 - 1
12	Magnesium	Mg	2 - 8 - 2
13	Aluminum	Al	2 - 8 - 3
14	Silicon	Si	2 - 8 - 4
15	Phosphorus	P	2 - 8 - 5
16	Sulfur	S	2 - 8 - 6
17	Chlorine	Cl	2 - 8 - 7
18	Argon	Ar	2 - 8 - 8
19	Potassium	K	2 - 8 - 8 - 1
20	Calcium	Ca	2 - 8 - 8 - 2
21	Scandium	Sc	2 - 8 - 9 - 2
22	Titanium	Ti	2 - 8 - 10 - 2

Mixtures

A *mixture* consists of different types of matter near each other but not chemically bound to each other. For example, granite rock has three different crystalline materials dispersed throughout the rock—quartz, feldspar, and mica. They each retain their own unique properties in the mixture.

- A *solution* is a mixture in which one type of molecule is dispersed throughout other molecules (sugar and water). The resulting solution has similar properties throughout.
- A *suspension* is a mixture in which the dispersed particles are larger than molecules and are dispersed throughout the system. Suspended particles eventually settle out (smoke).

- A *colloid* is a mixture containing dispersed particles larger than molecules but small enough not to settle out (gelatin).

Characteristics of Solids, Liquids, and Gases

The three different physical states in which matter normally exists are:

1. *Solids*—A solid has a definite shape and a definite volume. It generally consists of small crystals tightly joined together. The molecular particles in a solid are still in motion but to a much lesser extent. Ice is the solid state of water. Aluminum and copper are solids.

2. *Liquids*—A liquid has a definite volume but takes the shape of its container. Molecular particles in a liquid move about but not rapidly. Mercury is a liquid.

3. *Gases*—A gas has no shape and no definite volume. It is mostly empty space and can readily be expanded or compressed by either pressure or temperature. Particles in a gas move about rapidly. Steam is the gaseous state of water. Hydrogen and oxygen are gases.

When molecular particles of a substance have little kinetic energy, the substance will be in a solid state. If the solid is heated, the kinetic energy of the molecules increases and the physical state changes from a solid to a liquid (ice to water). The temperature at which a solid substance changes to a liquid is known as its *melting* point.

Further heating will increase the kinetic energy of the molecules still more and the physical state will change from a liquid to a gas (water to steam). The temperature at which a liquid substance changes to a gas is called its *boiling* point.

Lowering the temperature will change a gas to a liquid and a liquid to a solid. The temperature at which a liquid changes to a solid is called the *freezing* point. Movement of particles in matter ceases at absolute zero or −273°C.

Simple Solutions

A solution is a mixture of one substance dissolved in another substance. The substance being dissolved is the *solute*; the substance in which a solute is dissolved is the *solvent*. In a salt solution, the salt (NaCl) is the solute, and water (H_2O) is the solvent.

Solutes may be solids, liquids, or gases. Solvents are generally liquids. Water is the most common solvent. Solutions may be classified according to the relative amounts of solute to solvent.

- A *dilute* solution contains a relatively small amount of solute dissolved in a large amount of solvent.
- A *concentrated* solution contains a relatively large amount of solute dissolved in a small amount of solvent.
- An *unsaturated* solution is a solution that can still dissolve more solute at the prevailing temperature and pressure.
- A *saturated* solution is one containing the maximum amount of solute that can be dissolved at a given temperature and pressure.
- A *supersaturated* solution is one that contains more solute than it can normally hold at a given temperature.

Acids and Bases

Acids are substances that give up hydrogen ions (H^+) when dissolved in water. Acids react with metals and generally have a sour taste. Some common acids are hydrochloric acid, nitric acid, and sulfuric acid used in industry; acetic acid found in vinegar; lactic acid found in milk; and citric acid found in oranges and lemons.

Bases are substances that give up hydroxyl ions (OH) when dissolved in water. Bases generally contain a metal (the one exception is ammonia). Some common bases are sodium hydroxide (lye) used in making soap and ammonium hydroxide (ammonia) used as a cleaning agent.

When acids and bases react, *neutralization* occurs with the formation of water and a salt.

Hydrochloric acid plus sodium hydroxide yield common salt plus water:

$$HCl + NaOH \longrightarrow NaCl + H_2O$$

The *pH* of a solution is a number within the range of 1 to 14 that indicates the degree of acidity or alkalinity. A pH of 7 indicates a neutral solution; less than 7 shows increased acidity; more than 7 shows increased alkalinity.

Simple Chemical Reactions

Matter may change either by a physical change or by a chemical change. The form, size, or shape of matter is altered in a physical change, but the molecules remain unchanged. Changing water into ice or steam and dissolving sugar in water are examples of physical change. In a chemical change, molecules of new matter are formed that are different from the original matter. The burning of coal or the rusting of iron are examples of chemical change.

A chemical reaction is a reaction in which a chemical change occurs. The molecules that enter the reaction are called *reactants*. The molecules resulting from the reaction are called *products*.

When charcoal burns, the following occurs:

Carbon plus oxygen produce carbon dioxide

carbon + oxygen $\longrightarrow$ carbon dioxide

Using chemical symbols, the formula is:

$$C + O_2 \longrightarrow CO_2$$

This formula is the chemical equation for the oxidation of carbon. One atom of carbon combined with one molecule of oxygen to form one molecule of carbon dioxide.

Using the reaction of hydrogen and oxygen to form water:

$$H_2 + O_2 \longrightarrow H_2O$$

Note that this equation is not balanced; there are two oxygen atoms on the left side and only one oxygen atom on the right.

$$H_2 + O_2 \longrightarrow 2H_2O$$

But now the hydrogen atoms are not balanced. There are 4 hydrogen atoms on the right but only 2 on the left. This is corrected by placing "2" in front of the H_2 on the left side.

$$2H_2 + O_2 \longrightarrow 2H_2O$$

Is the following equation balanced?

$$H_2 + Cl_2 \longrightarrow HCl$$

No, it is not. There are 2 atoms of hydrogen and 2 atoms of chlorine on the left side but only 1 atom of hydrogen and 1 atom of chlorine on the right side.

This equation can be balanced by placing a "2" in front of the HCl.

$$H_2 + Cl_2 \longrightarrow 2HCl$$

There are four types of chemical reactions:

1. *Synthesis:* two or more elements or compounds unite to form one compound:

    carbon + oxygen $\longrightarrow$ carbon dioxide

    $$C + O_2 \longrightarrow CO_2$$

    calcium oxide + carbon dioxide $\longrightarrow$ calcium carbonate

    $$CaO + CO_2 \longrightarrow CaCO_3$$

2. *Decomposition:* a substance breaks down into two or more substances:

    Peroxide decomposes into water and oxygen

    $$2H_2O_2 \longrightarrow 2H_2O + O_2$$

3. *Single displacement:* one element displaces another in a compound.

    $$2KBr + Cl_2 \longrightarrow 2KCl + Br_2$$

    Chlorine displaced the bromine in the compound potassium bromide.

4. *Double displacement:* the positive part of each reactant unites with the negative part of the other reactant.

    $$3NaOH + FeCl_3 \longrightarrow 3\ NaCl + Fe(OH)_3$$

    Sodium hydroxide reacts with ferric chloride to form sodium chloride and ferric hydroxide.

Measurement

Measurement is an essential part of chemistry. Although the English system of measurement is used in everyday life in the United States, most of the people in the rest of the world, as well as scientists, use the modernized form of the metric system, a decimal system based on tens, multiples of tens, and fractions of tens.

Length

The meter is the standard unit of length in the metric system. The meter (m) may be divided into 100 equal parts called centimeters (cm).

> 100 cm = 1 m

The meter (m) may also be divided into 1,000 equal parts called millimeters (mm).

> 1 m = 100 cm = 1,000 mm
>
> 1 cm = 10 mm

Distances of considerable length are measured in kilometers (km).

> 1 km = 1,000 m

Changing from one unit to another is done by simply dividing or multiplying by multiples of 10.

Area

Area is calculated by multiplying length by width. The area of a rectangle 3 meters long and 4 meters wide is 12 square meters.

> $3 \text{ m} \times 4 \text{ m} = 12 \text{ m}^2$

Volume

Volume is the amount of space an object occupies. If the object is a cube or rectangular solid, the volume is obtained by multiplying length χ width χ height. The cubic meter is a standard metric unit of volume. However, it is a large unit containing 1 million cubic centimeters. The liter (L), equal to 1,000 cubic centimeters, is the metric unit commonly used. The milliliter (mL) is used for measuring still smaller volumes.

> 1 liter (L) = 1,000 milliliters (mL)
>
> $1 \text{ mL} = 1 \text{ cm}^3$

Mass

The more important units of mass in the metric system are the gram (g), kilogram (kg), and milligram (mg).

> 1 kg = 1,000 g = 1,000,000 mg
>
> 1 g = 1,000 mg

A comparison of the different metric units is shown in the following table.

COMPARISON OF METRIC UNITS			
Factor		**Metric Prefix**	**Symbols**
× 1,000	kilo-	(kilometer, kiloliter, kilogram)	km, kL, kg
× 100	hecto-	(hectometer, hectoliter, hectogram)	hm, hL, hg
× 10	deka-	(dekameter, dekaliter, dekagram)	dam, daL, dag
× 1		(meter, liter, gram)	m, L, g
× 0.1	deci-	(decimeter, deciliter, decigram)	dm, dL, dg
× 0.01	centi-	(centimeter, centiliter, centigram)	cm, cL, cg
× 0.001	milli-	(millimeter, milliliter, milligram)	mm, mL, mg

Temperature

Temperature is generally measured in scientific work by using the Celsius or centigrade scale. This temperature scale is based on the freezing and boiling points of water. The freezing point is at 0°C; the boiling point is at 100°C.

The Fahrenheit scale, used in everyday activities, is also based on the freezing and boiling points of water. The freezing point is at 32°F; the boiling point is at 212°F.

Use the following formulas to change from one scale to the other:

$$°C = \frac{5}{9}(°F - 32°)$$

$$°F = \frac{9}{5}°C + 32°$$

The Kelvin or absolute scale of temperature is also used in scientific work. This scale starts with absolute zero at −273°C. To change Celsius or centigrade temperature to Kelvin or absolute temperature, add 273°.

K = °C + 273°

Physics

Physics is the science of matter, energy, and their interactions. These are grouped into many different fields, such as mechanics, thermodynamics, magnetism, and electricity.

Force and Work

A *force* is the push or pull that forces an object to change its speed or direction. Weight is the force of gravity on an object. *Work* done on an object is defined as the force exerted on the object times the distance moved in the direction of the force.

If W = work; F = force; and d = distance,

$W = Fd$

The unit of work in the British system is expressed in foot-pounds (ft-lb). In the metric system, the unit of work is the newton-meter (n-m) or joule (j).

Power is the rate of doing work.

$$\text{Power} = \frac{\text{Work}}{\text{Time}}$$

If P = Power; W = work; and t = time,

$$P = \frac{W}{t} = \frac{Fd}{t}$$

In the British system, power is expressed in foot-pounds per second or foot-pounds per minute. In the metric system, power is expressed in newton-meters per second or joules per second (also known as watts). Machine power is generally expressed in *horsepower*. One horsepower is equal to 550 ft-lb/sec.

Newton's Laws

Sir Isaac Newton was an English physicist, philosopher, and mathematician. He formulated the three laws of motion that explain how objects move in response to forces and a law to explain the force of gravity as follows:

1. *Newton's first law of motion* predicts the behavior of objects for which all existing forces are balanced. If the net force acting on an object is zero, the object will remain at rest or remain moving at a constant velocity. If the force exerted on an object is zero, the object does not necessarily have zero velocity. Without any forces acting on it, including friction, an object in motion will continue to travel at constant velocity. In simpler terms, an object at rest tends to stay at rest, and an object in motion tends to stay in motion with the same speed and in the same direction unless acted on by an unbalanced force.

2. *Newton's second law of motion* pertains to the behavior of objects for which all existing forces are not balanced. The net force acting on an object equals the product of the mass and the acceleration of the object. A net force on an object will accelerate it or change its velocity, and the direction of the force is the same as that of the acceleration. The mass (m) of the object is measured in kilograms. Acceleration (a) is measured in meters per second per second. Force (f) is measured in *newtons*. A newton is the force necessary to impart a mass of 1kg an acceleration of 1/m/sec/sec. This theory is illustrated by the following equation: $F = ma$. Note that this law is also known as the *law of inertia* because the greater the mass of an object, the greater the force needed to overcome its *inertia* (its reluctance to change velocity).

3. *Newton's third law of motion.* An object experiences a force because it is interacting with some other object. When an object exerts force on another object, the second object exerts

on the first a force of the same magnitude but in the opposite direction. Simply stated, for every action, there is an equal and opposite reaction.

4. *Newton's law of gravity* states that all objects in the universe attract each other with a force that varies directly as the product of their masses and inversely as the square of their separation from each other. The force is known as gravity, the fundamental force responsible for interactions that occur because of mass between particles of matter. Note that the earth's, the moon's, and planets' attraction for objects is known as gravity.

Speed

Speed is a scalar quantity (a quantity that is fully described by a magnitude alone), which refers to how fast an object is moving or the distance an object travels per unit of time. A fast-moving object has a high speed, whereas a slow-moving object has a low speed. An object with no movement at all has no speed.

$$\text{Speed} = \frac{\text{distance}}{\text{time}}$$

Velocity

Velocity is a vector quantity (a quantity that is fully described by both a magnitude and a direction) that refers to the rate in which an object changes position. *Acceleration* is the rate of change of velocity. Velocity is also called momentum. Note that if an object is heavy, it will be difficult to stop it or change its direction.

Machines

Machines are devices for transferring energy. Simple machines are generally used to change the size or direction of a force.

Machines may be divided into the following classes:

- Lever (see-saw, crowbar, hammer, scissors, pliers, and shovel)
- Inclined plane (screw and wedge)
- Wheel and axle (doorknob and steering wheel)
- Pulley (elevator and power shovel)

The jackscrew—a screw-operated jack used for lifting something or adjusting its position—combines the lever and the inclined plane.

$$\text{Efficiency} = \frac{\text{Output Work}}{\text{Input Work}} \times 100$$

The force applied to a machine to do the work needed is known as *effort*. The greater the force that is applied, the greater the work that is done. The force that one must overcome is known as *resistance*.

Energy

Energy may be defined as the capacity to do work and can be either kinetic or potential. *Kinetic* energy is the energy possessed by a moving object. *Potential* energy is the work that can be done by an object because of its relative position. Energy is found in many different forms, such as the following:

- Chemical
- Heat
- Electrical
- Light
- Sound
- Mechanical
- Nuclear

Energy is neither created nor destroyed but can readily be changed from one form to another. This is known as conservation of energy. For example, chemical energy is changed to electrical energy with the storage battery. Friction may be used to change mechanical energy to heat. The radio may be used to change sound to electrical energy and electrical energy to sound. Note that some energy will be lost in the form of heat when energy is converted.

Heat Transfer

There are three methods by which heat is transferred from one object to another. These are conduction, convection, and radiation.

1. *Conduction* is the simplest method of heat transfer. It is accomplished by direct contact, such as placing your finger on a hot object. The heat is transferred directly from the hot object to the skin on your finger. Metals are generally good conductors of heat. Other materials, such as wood or plastic, are poor conductors and are termed *insulators*. Note that many metallic pots and pans have wooden handles that act as heat insulators.

2. *Convection* is the transfer of heat in liquids or gases when heated unevenly. The heated liquid or gas rises and the resulting movement is termed convection.

3. *Radiation* of heat, such as the heat from the sun, is transmitted by electromagnetic waves, which change into heat when they reach their destination.

Basic Electricity

There are two kinds of electric charge. One is positive (+); the other is negative (−). How objects become electrically charged may be explained by *electrons*, negatively charged particles of matter.

When two objects are rubbed together, electrons are taken away from one object and added to the other object. Combing your hair results in electrons moving from your hair to the comb, which then takes on a negative charge.

Protons are positively charged particles. Matter is generally neutral, because it contains an equal number of electrons and protons. The flow of electrons from one place to another results in electric current. Metallic materials allow electrons to flow freely. These materials are called conductors (copper, iron, silver, aluminum, etc.). Materials that do not allow the free flow of electrons are called insulators (air, rubber, wood, plastic, etc.).

Circuits

An electric circuit is the path along which electrons move from a place where there are many electrons to a place where there are fewer electrons. It consists of many parts, including the power source, conductors, switches, and the appliance or appliances to be operated. The circuits may be in *series* or in *parallel* (see Figure 16 and Figure 17).

In a *series* circuit, all parts are connected in a continuous line, one after another. If any part fails or is switched off, all other parts are turned off. For example, when using series-circuited lights to decorate a Christmas tree, one burned-out light will cause all the other lights on the tree to become unlit by breaking the flow of electrons in the circuit.

In a *parallel* circuit, the different parts are on separate branches and can be switched off without affecting the parts on the other branches.

There are two kinds of electric current:

1. *Direct current* (DC): electrons flow in one direction only. With the dry cell, the electrons move from the negative connector to the positive connector.

2. *Alternating current* (AC): alternating current generated in power stations changes direction many times per second. The electricity is produced by electromagnetic induction resulting from motion in a magnetic field.

Figure 16. This diagram shows a series circuit. If one bulb goes out, all the other bulbs will also go out.

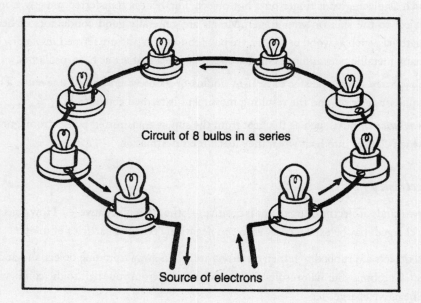

Circuit of 8 bulbs in a series

Source of electrons

Figure 17. These appliances are arranged in a parallel circuit. You can turn one of them off without affecting the others.

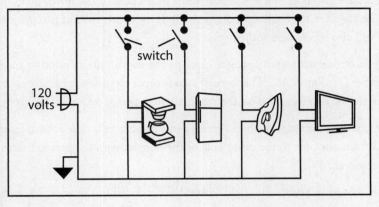

Except for battery-operated electrical systems, such as in the automobile, electrical energy is supplied as alternating current since it can be transmitted through wires at high voltage over great distances, unlike direct current. *Transformers* are used to change the voltage in power lines. *Step-up* transformers raise the voltage; *step-down* transformers reduce the voltage. Voltage supplied to our homes is generally at 110 to 120 volts.

The following terms are used in measuring electricity:

- **Volt:** measures the amount of work done when electrons are moved between two points in an electric circuit.

- **Ampere:** measures the amount of electrons moving past a certain point in a current in one second.

- **Ohm:** the unit of measurement of resistance, which consists of all conditions in an electric circuit that limit the flow of electrons. An electric circuit with a current of 3 amperes and a resistance of 4 ohms would have a voltage of 12. Ohm's law states:

  Volts = Amperes χ Ohms

- **Watt:** measures how much electricity is consumed. The amount of electricity used and the length of time used is measured in watt-hours for small amounts of energy or kilowatt-hours for larger amounts. A kilowatt-hour is the amount of energy used in one hour by one kilowatt of power.

- **Ammeter:** used to measure the amount of current in amperes.

- **Voltmeter:** used to measure potential difference in volts.

Fuses and *circuit breakers* are devices that limit current flow. In the fuse, a small section of wire will melt and break the current if a certain amount of electric current passes through it. Current capacity of the fuse is determined by the size (thickness) of the wire. *Circuit breakers* interrupt the flow of current mechanically when the current limit is reached.

Magnetism

Simple magnets have two poles—a north pole and a south pole. If the north poles of two magnets are brought close together, they will repel one another. If the south poles of two magnets are brought together, they will also repel one another.

If the north pole of one magnet is brought close to the south pole of another magnet, they will attract one another (see Figure 18). The force of attraction or repulsion is called magnetic force. The magnetic poles are the two locations on the magnet where magnetic forces are strongest.

The region surrounding the magnet where there is a magnetic force is called the magnetic field. Lines of force extend from one pole to the other pole of the magnet with the greatest force concentrated at the poles (see Figure 19).

When a wire is moved in a magnetic field, current is produced in the wire. This effect, known as *electromagnetic induction*, led to the development of generators. The electric generator produces current that flows in one direction and then in the opposite direction, producing an alternating current.

Figure 18. Like poles repel. Unlike poles attract.

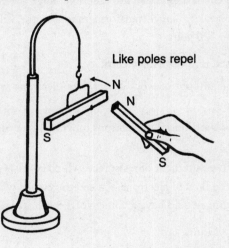

Figure 19. Lines of force in a magnetic field.

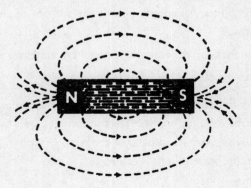

The strength of the magnetic force between two objects increases as the amount of electric charge on these objects increases. The strength of the magnetic charge between the objects decreases as the distance between them increases. Reducing the distance between the two objects by a half results in a magnetic force four times as great. For example, reducing the distance from 100 mm to 50 mm increases the magnetic force fourfold. Similarly, increasing the distance from 100 mm to 200 mm reduces the force to one fourth the original amount.

The magnetic compass contains a magnetic needle that rotates in a horizontal direction. The compass case is always made of a nonmagnetic substance, usually brass.

Light

Although light possesses many properties of waves (reflection, refraction, etc.), it differs somewhat from other waves. Compared with sound waves, light waves are much faster and can travel through empty space. Light or other waves that can travel through space at very high speed are called electromagnetic waves.

The different types of electromagnetic waves in increasing order of frequency and decreasing wavelength are as follows:

- Ordinary radio waves
- FM and television waves
- Radar and microwaves
- Infrared waves
- Light waves
- Ultraviolet waves
- X-rays
- Gamma waves

Two important characteristics of light are:

1. Light waves generally move in a straight path at approximately 186,000 miles per second.
2. Light may change its direction when moving from one material to another material (for example, from air to water).

Refraction occurs when light waves are bent (change direction) passing from one material into another. Refracted light can cause mirages or illusions.

Sunlight is a mixture of all the colors of the rainbow—a spectrum. When sunlight is passed through a prism, the colors are separated into a spectrum of red, orange, yellow, green, blue, indigo, and violet.

Reflection occurs when light rays strike a flat mirror and bounce off. The rays striking the mirror are called *incident* rays; those that bounce off are termed *reflected* rays.

Lenses refract light rays in different ways (see Figure 20).

Figure 20. Convex and concave lenses.

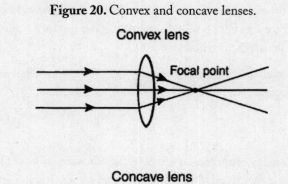

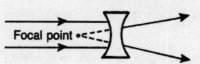

A *convex* lens is shaped so that the edges are thinner than the center. The light rays passing through the prism meet at a certain point. The *focal point* is the point at which the parallel light rays are brought together after being refracted by the lens.

A *concave* lens is shaped so that the edges are thicker than the center. The parallel light rays passing through the prism are spread apart after being refracted by the lens.

Sound

References to sound in physics are really references to *sound waves*. These are waves in gases, liquids, and solids that cannot be transmitted through a vacuum or empty space. There are three important properties of sound waves:

1. *Wavelength* is the distance between high points or between low points and is generally measured in millimeters or centimeters.

2. *Speed* is determined by measuring how fast the waves move. That is, how fast the high point (crest) or low point (trough) moves. Speed is generally measured in meters per second (see Figure 21).

3. *Frequency* is determined by measuring the number of waves (crests or troughs) that move past a certain point in one second. The unit of measurement is the hertz (Hz). One hertz is one wave moving past per second.

Figure 21. This diagram shows how speed, frequency, and wavelength are related.

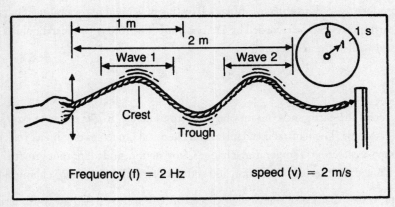

The relationship of these properties of sound may be shown by the formula:

$$\text{Wavelength} = \frac{\text{Speed}}{\text{Frequency}}$$

Sound waves have a vibrating or back-and-forth motion. They do not move as fast in air as in water. Similarly, sound waves do not move as fast in water as they do in wood or metals. A train approaching from the distance can be heard at a greater distance by the noise through the steel rails than by the noise made through the air.

The pitch of sound is closely related to the frequency of the sound waves. A high sound frequency is called a high pitch. The volume, or loudness of a sound, is determined by the amplitude of sound waves. The intensity of sound is expressed on a decibel scale. The amplitude and frequency of sound waves determine the sound intensity.

EARTH SCIENCE

This section includes several sciences that fall into the category of earth sciences. These include the basics of geology, meteorology, and astronomy.

Geology

The earth consists of three layers—the crust, the mantle, and the core:

1. The *crust* is a thin layer and compromises the earth's surface. It varies in thickness from a few miles beneath the oceans to nearly 50 miles beneath the Himalaya-Tibetan Plateau.

2. The *mantle* is the thick layer beneath the crust and represents more than 80 percent of the earth's volume. The mantle consists of solid rock. However, the top portion of the mantle has areas capable of sudden movement or continuous, slow movement.

3. The *core* is the earth's center and comprises almost 20 percent of the earth's volume.

The temperature of the earth's outer core is estimated to be between 3,500° C and 4,700° C. This heat is prevented from escaping by the solid rock in the upper mantle and the crust. Cracks in the earth's crust produce *faults*. Earthquakes are caused by the movement of rocks along faults. The waves produced by earthquakes can be recorded by a *seismograph*. The intensity of earthquakes is measured on a 1 to 10 scale called the *Richter scale*.

Rocks

Rocks are pieces of the earth and contain one or more minerals. Rocks differ in size, shape, color, and degree of hardness. The natural mechanical and chemical processes that break rock into smaller pieces are termed *weathering*. Temperature changes, frost action, and plant root growth are common forms of mechanical weathering. Oxidation and action of air pollutants cause chemical weathering.

The natural processes that cause the smaller pieces of rock to be carried away are termed *erosion*. Erosion is generally accomplished by running water, wind, and glaciers.

Based on their method of formation, the three classes of rock are igneous, sedimentary, and metamorphic.

- *Igneous* rock is formed by the cooling and hardening of molten material. Granite and pumice are two common igneous rocks.
- *Sedimentary* rock is formed by the joining together of small pieces of rock or sediment deposited when fast-moving streams slow down. The sediment may consist of different sized particles or pieces ranging from mud to gravel. In time, these particles may become compressed or cemented together to form sedimentary rock. Shale, sandstone, limestone, and soft coal are common types of sedimentary rock.
- *Metamorphic* rock is formed by changes resulting from great heat, pressure, and time. Both sedimentary and igneous rock may become metamorphosed. Slate, marble, and hard coal are common kinds of metamorphic rock.

Rocks beneath the earth's crust that are heated to the melting point are called *magma*. When the molten magma reaches the earth's surface, it is called *lava*. A *volcano* is the rock formation that results when lava reaches the earth's surface.

Meteorology

The earth's atmosphere consists of layers of air surrounding Earth's surface (see Figure 22). These gaseous layers are:

- The *troposphere* is the first or innermost layer of the atmosphere and extends 5 to 10 miles above the earth's surface. We live in this layer where virtually all weather changes and cloudiness occur. Most of the air surrounding the earth is found in this layer.
- The second layer is the *stratosphere* and extends up to about 25 to 30 miles above the earth.
- The third layer is the *mesosphere*, which extends to about 50 miles above the earth.
- The fourth or outermost layer is the *thermosphere*, which extends to approximately 350 miles above the earth. Air in this layer is extremely thin.

- The *ionosphere* is the layer between the mesosphere and the thermosphere. This is an important communication zone as it reflects various types of radio waves.

Figure 22. The important layers of the earth's atmosphere. (Note that the heights are not drawn to scale.)

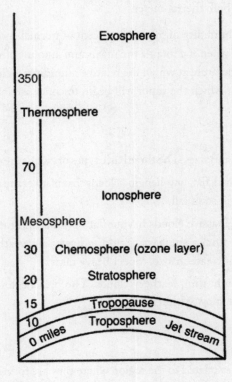

Almost half of the sun's radiation passes through the atmosphere and reaches the earth's surface where it is absorbed by the land and the water of the oceans, which warm the air above them. Land absorbs energy and warms up faster than water. Accordingly, during the daytime, air over land gets warmer than air over water; at night, air over land gets cooler than air over water. These temperature differences cause differences in air density.

The sun's rays strike the earth's surface at different angles. The equator receives direct rays, whereas the regions closer to the poles receive slanted rays. This also affects the air temperatures and causes differences in air density.

Air Pressure

The force with which air presses on the surface of the Earth is known as *air pressure*. Cold air is denser and presses down with greater pressure (high pressure). Warm air is less dense and presses down with less pressure (low pressure). A mercury *barometer* uses a thin tube of mercury to measure atmospheric pressure. At sea level, air pressure will normally support about 30 inches of mercury. This pressure may also be expressed as about 15 pounds per square inch.

Air generally flows from high pressure to low pressure. This air movement is called *wind*. Wind direction is identified by using a *weather vane*. Wind velocity is measured by an *anemometer*.

Humidity

The sun's energy evaporates the oceans' water, producing vapor. *Humidity* is the amount of water vapor in the air. *Relative humidity* is the amount of moisture in the air compared to the maximum amount it can hold at that temperature. Relative humidity is measured by means of a hygrometer consisting of a wet-and-dry bulb thermometer.

Most people find a relative humidity of 50 to 60 percent at normal room temperature to be quite comfortable. Air is *saturated* when it contains the maximum amount of water vapor it can hold at a given temperature. The temperature at which the relative humidity reaches 100 percent is called the *dew point*, the temperature at which the vapor will begin to condense into a liquid.

Clouds

Clouds have different shapes and sizes. The three basic types of clouds are stratus, cumulus, and cirrus.

1. *Stratus* clouds are broad, flat, low-hanging clouds that blanket the sky. Darkened stratus clouds indicate that rain will soon fall.
2. *Cumulus* clouds are massive clouds having flat bottoms and rounded tops. They resemble white smoke rising from a smokestack and indicate fair weather. When cumulus clouds darken and greatly increase in size, expect heavy rains.
3. *Cirrus* clouds are high, thin, feathery clouds. The presence of such clouds indicates the possibility of rain or snow within a few days.

Air Masses

Air masses have characteristics related to the region where they are formed. Air masses formed over land are dry; those formed over oceans are humid. Air masses formed in the northern regions of the northern hemisphere are cold; those formed at or near the equator are warm.

When two different air masses meet, they do not readily mix but form a boundary of separation called a *front*. When a cold air mass encounters a warm air mass, a cold front is created. The warmer air mass is pushed aside, cumulus clouds form, and there are heavy showers. When a warm air mass encounters a cold air mass, a warm front is created. The warm air passes over the cold air forming cirrus clouds. In time, the clouds thicken and move closer to the earth, causing precipitation and, sometimes, lingering fog.

Astronomy

Astronomy is the study of the stars, planets, and other heavenly bodies.

The earth's orbit around the sun is termed an ellipse, a slightly flattened circle. As the earth's axis (an imaginary line running through the earth from pole to pole) is not perpendicular to the orbit, but tilted at an angle of $23\frac{1}{2}°$, the North Pole is tilted toward the sun during part of the orbit and tilted away from the sun during another part of the orbit. This explains why daylight and darkness are not of equal length except on the first day of spring (vernal equinox) and the first day of autumn (autumnal equinox).

The earth spins on its axis and makes a complete rotation every 24 hours. It revolves around the sun every $365\frac{1}{4}$ days, necessitating a leap year every four years. The earth revolves and rotates in the same direction, from west to east.

The moon is a satellite of the earth. It makes a complete orbit around the earth every $27\frac{1}{3}$ days, turning once on its axis during this period. The moon is the earth's nearest neighbor. A lunar eclipse occurs when the moon moves into the earth's shadow. A solar eclipse occurs when the earth moves into the moon's shadow.

Solar System

The solar system consists of the sun and a multitude of smaller bodies held in orbit by the sun's huge mass. It is called the *solar system* because the sun's huge mass and its resulting force of gravity control the movement of these smaller bodies.

The planets of the solar system are among its largest bodies. Currently, there are eleven recognized planets in the solar system: Mercury, Venus, Earth, Mars, Ceres, Jupiter, Saturn, Uranus, Neptune, Pluto, and Eris. Note that along with Ceres and Eris, Pluto is now considered a dwarf planet. Six of the planets (Earth, Mars, Jupiter, Saturn, Uranus, and Neptune) have satellites.

The four smaller planets closest to the sun are frequently called the *inner* planets. These are:

- Mercury
- Venus
- Earth
- Mars

The four planets farthest from the sun are frequently termed the *outer* planets and are far larger than the inner planets. The outer planets are:

- Jupiter
- Saturn
- Uranus
- Neptune

Some of the small bodies in the solar system collide with the earth. Most of these bodies burn up because of the friction of the earth's atmosphere. These bodies are called *meteors* or "shooting stars." Those that reach the earth's surface are termed *meteorites*.

The *North Star*, or Polaris, is a most important star because it is virtually in direct line with the North Pole of the earth and therefore appears to remain stationary in the sky. This star has long been used by navigators as a directional guide.

PRACTICE QUESTIONS

1. The chief nutrient in lean meat is
   A. fat.
   B. starch.
   C. protein.
   D. carbohydrates.

2. Which of the following is an invertebrate?
   A. Starfish
   B. Pigeon
   C. Gorilla
   D. Alligator

3. Substances that hasten chemical reaction time without themselves undergoing change are called
   A. buffers.
   B. colloids.
   C. reducers.
   D. catalysts.

4. The case of a compass would NOT be made of
   A. brass.
   B. copper.
   C. plastic.
   D. steel.

5. An eclipse of the sun throws the shadow of the
   A. moon on the sun.
   B. moon on the earth.
   C. earth on the sun.
   D. earth on the moon.

ANSWER KEY AND EXPLANATIONS

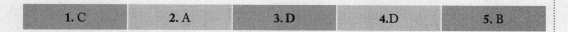

1. C	2. A	3. D	4. D	5. B

1. **The correct answer is C.** Protein is a nutrient found in lean meat. Starch is a form of carbohydrates. Fat may be found in meat, but it is not the chief nutrient in lean meat.

2. **The correct answer is A.** An invertebrate is an animal that lacks a backbone. Since all birds, mammals, and reptiles have backbones, starfish is the only possible choice.

3. **The correct answer is D.** Catalysts hasten chemical reaction time without undergoing change.

4. **The correct answer is D.** Since a compass uses the earth's magnetism to operate, a steel case would interfere with the compass operation.

5. **The correct answer is B.** A solar eclipse is an obstruction of the sun's rays by the moon. Therefore, the shadow of the moon would be cast on the earth.

SUMMING IT UP

The classification system for plant and animal life has seven levels. The top level includes the largest number of different kinds of organisms and is called the *kingdom*. The bottom level with the smallest number of different kinds of organisms is called the *species*. The seven levels are **kingdom**, **phylum**, **class**, **order**, **family**, **genus**, and **species**.

- The scientific name for an organism consists of two terms identifying the genus and the species. For example, the scientific name for humankind is Homo sapiens.

- The animal kingdom is divided into two groups: **invertebrates** (animals that do not have a backbone) and **vertebrates** (animals that have a backbone).

- The human body consists of the following major systems that work together: skeletal, muscular, digestive, nervous, endocrine, circulatory, respiratory, lymphatic, excretory, and reproductive.

- Every plant and animal is a member of an **ecosystem**. In all ecosystems, the following exist as interacting forces: **producers**, **consumers**, **scavengers**, and **decomposers**.

- Cells are the basic structural unit of living things and develop from other cells. **Protoplasm**, or living material, is contained within tiny cells. These cells differ in size and shape, depending on their function in the body.

- Matter is composed of basic substances known as **elements**. The **atom** is the smallest part of an element that still acts like that element. The atom consists of a **nucleus** that contains neutrons and protons in the center, which are surrounded by flying particles called **electrons**.

- A force is the push or pull that forces an object to change speed or direction. Weight is the force of gravity on an object. **Work** done on an object is defined as the force exerted on the object times the distance moved in the direction of the force.

- Earth consists of three layers—the **crust**, the **mantle**, and the **core**.

- Earth's atmosphere consists of layers of air surrounding Earth's surface. These layers are the **troposphere**, **stratosphere**, **mesosphere**, **ionosphere**, and **thermosphere**.

Arithmetic Reasoning

OVERVIEW

- **Review of Basic Arithmetic**
- **Practice Questions**
- **Answer Key and Explanations**
- **Summing It Up**

The Arithmetic Reasoning section in the ASVAB includes basic math processes like addition, subtraction, multiplication, and division, and applying these computational operations to solve simple math problems you come across in everyday life. The ability to perform basic math operations and to use computational skills to solve simple math problems is needed for activities at work, school, or home; in shopping and banking; or engaging in social, community, or recreational activities.

A concise review of basic arithmetic follows. It is provided to refresh your memory about basic math operations and give you practice for the math word problems that are on the ASVAB.

REVIEW OF BASIC ARITHMETIC

Whole Numbers

1.	One
10.	Ten
100.	One hundred
1,000.	One thousand
10,000.	Ten thousand
100,000.	One hundred thousand
1,000,000.	One million
10,000,000.	Ten million
100,000,000.	One hundred million
1,000,000,000.	One billion

Always start counting from the decimal point. Note that the value of a digit increases when the digit is moved to the left. Each time it is moved farther to the left of the decimal point, the value of a digit is multiplied by ten. To make it easier to read great numbers (numbers containing four or more digits), commas are placed every three spaces as you go left from the decimal point.

If the decimal point is not shown with the whole number, it is understood to be just to the right of the last digit on the right.

24 means 24. 12,528 means 12,528.

Decimals

0.1	One tenth
0.01	One hundredth
0.001	One thousandth
0.0001	One ten-thousandth
0.00001	One hundred-thousandth
0.000001	One millionth

Always start counting from the decimal point. Note that the value of a digit decreases when the digit in a decimal is moved to the right. The value of the digit is divided by ten each time it is moved one place farther to the right of the decimal point.

Decimals are also known as decimal fractions, since the denominator is a tenth, hundredth, thousandth, etc.

$$0.1 \text{ is } \frac{1}{10} \quad 0.01 \text{ is } \frac{1}{100} \quad 0.001 \text{ is } \frac{1}{1000}$$

Fractions

A fraction is a number that indicates one or more equal parts. A fraction has a *numerator*, a *division line*, and a *denominator*.

$$\frac{1}{4} \quad \text{or} \quad 1/4$$

The bottom number (*denominator*) shows the number of equal parts into which the whole has been divided.

The top number (*numerator*) shows how many of these equal parts are in the fraction.

A *proper fraction* has a numerator that is less than the denominator. It is also called a *common fraction* or *fraction*.

$$1/3 \text{ or } \frac{1}{3} \quad 3/4 \text{ or } \frac{3}{4} \quad 7/9 \text{ or } \frac{7}{9}$$

An *improper fraction* has a numerator that is equal to or greater than the denominator.

$$3/3 \text{ or } \frac{3}{3} \quad 9/8 \text{ or } \frac{9}{8} \quad 16/15 \text{ or } \frac{16}{15}$$

A *mixed number* consists of the sum of whole number and a fraction.

$$1\ 1/4 \text{ or } 1\frac{1}{4} \quad 12\ 1/2 \text{ or } 12\frac{1}{2}$$

Percent

Percent means hundredth. It may be expressed with the % symbol, as a fraction with a denominator of 100, or as a decimal.

Here is a quick chart to rename percents as fractions and decimals.

Percent	Fraction	Decimal
1%	$\frac{1}{100}$	0.01
50%	$\frac{50}{100}$ or $\frac{1}{2}$	0.50 or 0.5
$12\frac{1}{2}\%$	$\frac{12.5}{100}$ or $\frac{125}{1000}$	0.125

Addition

Addition is indicated by the plus (+) sign, the word *plus*, or the word *and*.

Addends are the numbers that are added. The *total* or *sum* is the number obtained by adding all the addends.

Adding Whole Numbers, Decimals, and Dollars and Cents

The numbers to be added are arranged in vertical columns. As additions consist of combining similar units, units must be placed directly under units, tens under tens, hundreds under hundreds, etc. If decimals are to be added, place tenths under tenths, hundredths under hundredths, etc.

		9					$4.32
4	167	82			6.40	$3.85	16.68
21	285	134	23,857	28.7	12.25	6.21	103.14
+153	+310	+2675	+71,204	+34.7	+107.125	+4.16	+421.08
178	762	2900	95,061	63.4	125.775	$14.22	$545.22

Note that in vertical additions of dollars and cents, the dollar sign ($) is placed to the left of the top addend and to the left of the total.

Subtraction

Subtraction is indicated by the subtraction sign (−), the word *minus*, the words *take away*, or the words *find the difference between*. There are three parts to a subtraction problem:

1. *Minuend:* Placed on the top of the vertical subtraction. It is the number from which another number is taken away.

2. *Subtrahend:* Placed below the minuend in vertical subtraction. It is the number that is taken away.

3. *Difference* or *remainder:* Result of the subtraction or what is left. This result is put at the bottom in vertical subtraction.

```
  581    minuend
− 350    subtrahend
  231    difference or remainder
```

Subtracting Whole Numbers, Decimals, and Dollars and Cents

As with addition, the numbers in the subtraction are arranged in vertical columns. Units must be placed directly under units, tens under tens, hundreds under hundreds, etc. If there are decimals, place the decimal point directly under the decimal point, tenths under tenths, hundredths under hundredths, etc.

```
  576      385      87.647     $743.65
− 342     − 57     − 8.350    − 418.45
  234      328      79.297     $325.20
```

Note that in vertical subtraction of dollars and cents, the $ is placed to the left of the minuend and to the left of the answer.

Multiplication

Multiplication is indicated by the multiplication sign (×), the word *multiply*, or the word *times*. There are three main parts to multiplication problems:

1. *Multiplicand:* Number being multiplied.
2. *Multiplier:* Number by which you multiply.
3. *Product:* Answer obtained by multiplying the multiplicand by the multiplier.

```
   12    multiplicand         483    multiplicand
  ×9    multiplier          × 24    multiplier
  108    product             1932    partial product (4 × 483)
                              966    partial product (2 × 483)
                            11592    product
```

Note that when the multiplier consists of more than one digit, the answer obtained by multiplying the multiplicand by each digit of the multiplier is called a *partial product*.

Multiplying Whole Numbers

In the multiplication process, first multiply units, then tens, then hundreds, etc. The answers to each of these separate multiplications are partial products. The final answer or product is obtained by adding all the partial products.

$$
\begin{array}{r}
365 \\
\times 124 \\
\hline
1460 \ \text{(ones)} \\
730 \ \text{(tens)} \\
365 \ \text{(hundreds)} \\
\hline
45,260
\end{array}
$$

Note that the right digit of each partial product is placed in a vertical line with the digit used as a multiplier. The addition of the partial products is made easier by placing the right digit of each succeeding partial product one place farther to the left.

Multiplying Decimals and Dollars and Cents

The multiplication process is the same as that for the whole numbers. However, it requires the additional step of fixing the decimal point in the answer. This is accomplished by counting the total number of digits to the right of the decimal points in both the multiplicand and the multiplier and then fixing the decimal point in the answer by counting off the same total number of places from right to left in the product.

$\begin{array}{r} 25.6 \\ \times\ .43 \\ \hline 768 \\ 1024 \\ \hline 11.008 \end{array}$	One digit to the right of the decimal point in the multiplicand plus two digits to the right of the decimal point in the multiplier equals three. Count off three places from right to left in the product to fix the decimal point.

$\begin{array}{r} \$\ 325.75 \\ \times\ 18 \\ \hline 260600 \\ 32575 \\ \hline \$5,863.50 \end{array}$	Two digits to the right of the decimal point in the multiplicand plus zero digits to the right of the decimal point in the multiplier equals two. Count off two from right to left in the product to fix the decimal point.

Division

Division is indicated by the division sign ($\div$), the fraction sign (— or /), the words *divided by*, the short-division symbol ⟩   , or the long-division symbol ⟩‾‾‾ . Division problems have four parts:

1. *Dividend:* Number being divided.
2. *Divisor:* Number by which you divide.
3. *Quotient:* Answer to division.
4. *Remainder:* Number that is left if division is not exact.

Dividing Whole Numbers

If the divisor is a single-digit number, use either short division or long division. If the divisor has more than one digit, use long division.

Short division:

Divisor   3)867   Dividend
            289   Quotient

1. 8 divided by 3 is 2 with a remainder of 2, change 6 to 26.
2. Record the 2 in the quotient under 8.
3. 26 divided by 3 is 8 with a remainder of 2, change 7 to 27.
4. Record the 8 in the quotient under 6.
5. 27 divided by 3 is 9 exactly.

To check if the division is correct, multiply the quotient by the divisor. If no error was made, the product should be the same as the dividend.

Check: 289
         $\times 3$
         867

Long division:

$$
\begin{array}{r}
35 \\
26)\overline{910} \\
-78 \\
\hline
130 \\
-130 \\
\hline
0
\end{array}
$$

1. Estimate 91 divided by 26 as 3.
2. Record the 3 in the quotient over 1 and multiply 26 by 3.
3. Record the product 78 under 91.

(If the product is greater than 91, it means that 3 is too great and that a lesser number should be used.)

4. Subtract the 78 from the 91 and record the 13.

    (If the difference is greater than 26, it means that 3 is too small and that a greater number should be estimated.)

5. Bring down the next digit (0 in this case) and join it to the difference.

6. Estimate 130 divided by 26 as 5.

7. Record the 5 in the quotient over the 0 and multiply 26 by 5.

8. Record the product under 130.

9. Subtract 130 from 130.

10. The difference is 0, so there is no remainder.

Check: 35
           $\underline{\times 26}$
            210
            $\underline{70}$
            910

Dividing Decimals

To divide a decimal by a whole number, proceed as if the dividend were a whole number. Then fix the decimal point in the quotient directly in line with the decimal point in the dividend.

$$
8\overline{)385.04} \qquad
\begin{array}{r}
48.13 \\
8\overline{)385.04} \\
\underline{-32} \\
65 \\
\underline{-64} \\
10 \\
\underline{-8} \\
24 \\
\underline{-24} \\
0
\end{array}
$$

48.13

Check: 48.13
           $\underline{\times\ 8}$
            385.04

To divide by a decimal, first rename the divisor as a whole number by moving the decimal point to the right of the last digit on the right. Then move the decimal point in the dividend to the right the same number of places. If necessary, add zeros. Finally, complete the division as you ordinarily would with a whole number as a divisor.

$.6\overline{)2.4}$	is changed to	$6\overline{)24}$
$.6\overline{)24.}$	is changed to	$6\overline{)240}$
$2.4\overline{)3.12}$	is changed to	$24\overline{)31.2}$
$2.46\overline{)3.198}$	is changed to	$246\overline{)319.8}$
$.005\overline{)30.}$	is changed to	$5\overline{)30000}$

Note that in all the above changes, the quotient is unchanged as both the divisor and the dividend are multiplied by the same amount.

Decimal division is also used when the division involves dollars and cents or just cents alone.

$$\frac{\$9.60}{3} = \$3.20 \qquad \frac{\$.75}{15} = \$.05$$

Note that when dollars or cents are divided by a number, the answer is in dollars or cents.

$$\frac{\$150}{\$5} = 30 \qquad \frac{\$5.50}{\$.25} = 22$$

Note that when dollars are divided by dollars or when dollars and cents are divided by dollars and cents, the answer is a number.

PRACTICE QUESTIONS

The following sample questions illustrate some of the question types in the Arithmetic Reasoning subtest that deal with the application of the four basic arithmetic operations just covered. Answers and explanations are located on pages 159–161.

Addition

1. 75 + 49 =
   The sum is
   A. 114
   B. 124
   C. 125
   D. 225

2. The sum of $51.75, $172.50, $39, $8.54, and $0.09 is
   A. $116.64
   B. $171.78
   C. $261.89
   D. $271.88

Subtraction

3. Subtract: 57,697
            − 9,748

   The difference is
   A. 40,945
   B. 47,949
   C. 48,949
   D. 67,445

4. Subtract $987.59 from $1,581.06. The difference is
   A. $593.47
   B. $603.47
   C. $693.47
   D. $694.47

5. Add $72.07 and $31.54, and then subtract $25.75. The correct answer is
   A. $77.86
   B. $82.14
   C. $88.96
   D. $129.36

Multiplication

6. Multiply 36
           × 8

   The product is
   A. 246
   B. 262
   C. 288
   D. 368

7. Multiply 312.77 by .04 and round the result to the nearest hundredth.
   A. 12.51
   B. 12.511
   C. 12.518
   D. 12.52

Division

8. Divide 5)455

   The quotient is
   A. 81
   B. 84
   C. 91
   D. 94

9. 7.95 ÷ 0.15 =
- **A.** 0.53
- **B.** 5.3
- **C.** 53
- **D.** 530

Additional Sample Arithmetic Problems Encountered in Everyday Life

10. Which of the following amounts of money has the greatest value?
- **A.** 3 quarters
- **B.** 8 dimes
- **C.** 15 nickels
- **D.** 79 pennies

11. Two weeks, five days plus three weeks, four days equals
- **A.** 5 weeks, 1 day.
- **B.** 5 weeks, 2 days.
- **C.** 6 weeks, 1 day.
- **D.** 6 weeks, 2 days.

12. Subtract:
$$2 \text{ feet, } 4 \text{ inches}$$
$$- 1 \text{ foot, } 6 \text{ inches}$$
- **A.** 8 inches
- **B.** 10 inches
- **C.** 1 foot
- **D.** 1 foot, 2 inches

13. Of the 36 students registered in a class, $\frac{2}{3}$ of them are females. How many males are registered in the class?
- **A.** 12
- **B.** 18
- **C.** 24
- **D.** 30

14. If a 200-mile trip takes 4 hours to complete, the average speed is
- **A.** 30 miles per hour.
- **B.** 40 miles per hour.
- **C.** 50 miles per hour.
- **D.** 60 miles per hour.

15. How many pounds are in 24 ounces?
- **A.** $\frac{1}{2}$
- **B.** 1
- **C.** $1\frac{1}{2}$
- **D.** 2

16. The sales tax of 8% on a purchase of $12 is
- **A.** $0.86
- **B.** $0.96
- **C.** $1.06
- **D.** $1.60

17. A dozen oranges cost $2.70. The cost per orange is most nearly
- **A.** 22¢
- **B.** 24¢
- **C.** 26¢
- **D.** 28¢

18. A $75 fund is available for a holiday party. If 75% of the available money is spent for food and beverages, how much is left for other expenses?
- **A.** $18.75
- **B.** $28.75
- **C.** $46.25
- **D.** $56.25

19. A certain employee is paid at the rate of $8.00 per hour with time-and-a-half for overtime. The regular work week is 40 hours. During the past week, the employee put in 44 working hours. What were the employee's gross wages for that week?

  A. $322.00

  B. $352.00

  C. $368.00

  D. $528.00

20. It takes 4 men 14 days to do a certain job. How long should it take 7 men working at the same rate to do the same job?

  A. 5 days

  B. 6 days

  C. 7 days

  D. 8 days

21. If one quart of floor wax covers 400 square feet, how many gallons of wax are needed to wax the floor of a 6,400-square-foot office?

  A. 4 gallons

  B. 8 gallons

  C. 12 gallons

  D. 16 gallons

22. A pole 15 feet high casts a shadow 5 feet long. A 6-foot man standing nearby would cast a shadow

  A. $1\frac{1}{2}$ feet long.

  B. 2 feet long.

  C. $2\frac{1}{2}$ feet long.

  D. 3 feet long.

23. If 1 foot of chain costs 17¢, then 4 yards of this chain would cost

  A. $0.68

  B. $1.53

  C. $2.04

  D. $2.75

24. Tires regularly priced at $44 each are on sale for $37. How much would a truck owner save by buying four tires at the sale price?

  A. $7

  B. $28

  C. $49

  D. $81

25. How many 32-passenger buses are needed to transport 180 persons?

  A. 4

  B. 5

  C. 6

  D. 7

26. If a service station greased 270 vehicles in a 31-day period, the daily average of vehicles greased is most nearly what number?

  A. 6

  B. 7

  C. 8

  D. 9

27. To check on a shipment of 500 articles, a sampling of 50 articles was carefully inspected. Of the sample, 4 articles were defective. On this basis, what is the probable percentage of defective articles in the original shipment?

  A. 0.04%

  B. 4%

  C. 8%

  D. 10%

28. If the total area of a four-room apartment is 3,600 square feet, the average area of each room is

    A. $\frac{1}{4}$ of the total area.

    B. $\frac{1}{3}$ of the total area.

    C. $\frac{1}{2}$ of the total area.

    D. $\frac{3}{4}$ of the total area.

29. A floor that is 9 feet wide and 12 feet long measures how many square feet?
    A. 12
    B. 21
    C. 108
    D. 118

30. The area of a room measuring 12 feet by 15 feet is
    A. 9 square yards.
    B. 12 square yards.
    C. 15 square yards.
    D. 20 square yards.

31. The circumference of a circle that has a radius of 70 feet is most nearly
    A. 220 feet.
    B. 440 feet.
    C. 660 feet.
    D. 690 feet.

32. Find the perimeter of the following square.

    1 in.

    A. 1 inch
    B. 2 inches
    C. 3 inches
    D. 4 inches

33. A swimming pool has an average depth of 4 feet and is 25 feet long and 15 feet wide. What is the volume of the pool?
    A. 375 cubic feet
    B. 1,000 cubic feet
    C. 1,500 cubic feet
    D. 4,500 cubic feet

34. Find the volume of the following cube.

    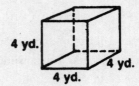

    4 yd.   4 yd.   4 yd.

    A. 12 cubic yards
    B. 16 cubic yards
    C. 46 cubic yards
    D. 64 cubic yards

35. Find the perimeter of the following figure.

    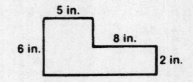

    5 in.   8 in.   6 in.   2 in.

    A. 21 inches
    B. 25 inches
    C. 33 inches
    D. 38 inches

ANSWER KEY AND EXPLANATIONS

1. B	8. C	15. C	22. B	29. C
2. D	9. C	16. B	23. C	30. D
3. B	10. B	17. A	24. B	31. B
4. A	11. D	18. A	25. C	32. D
5. A	12. B	19. C	26. D	33. C
6. C	13. A	20. D	27. C	34. D
7. A	14. C	21. A	28. A	35. D

1. **The correct answer is B.** The sum of the two numbers is 124.

    75
    +49
    124

2. **The correct answer is D.** Arrange the five amounts in the appropriate vertical columns and add. The sum is $271.88.

    $51.75
    172.50
    39.00
    8.54
    + 0.09
    $271.88

3. **The correct answer is B.** Arrange numbers in proper vertical columns and then subtract. The difference is 47,949.

    57,697
    −9,748
    47,949

4. **The correct answer is A.** Arrange numbers in proper vertical columns and then subtract. The difference is $593.47.

    $1581.06
    −987.59
    $593.47

5. **The correct answer is A.** This question consists of an addition and a subtraction. The sum of the first two amounts is $103.61. $25.75 from $103.61 gives us an answer of $77.86.

    $72.07
    +31.54
    $103.61
    −25.75
    $77.86

6. **The correct answer is C.** The product of the two numbers is 288.

    36
    × 8
    288

7. **The correct answer is A.** Multiply the two numbers and fix the decimal point in the answer to conform with the total number of digits to the right of the decimal points in both the multiplicand and the multiplier. Round off the product to the nearest hundredth.

    312.77
    × .04
    12.51

8. **The correct answer is C.** This is simple short division, and the quotient is 91.

    5)455
      91

9. **The correct answer is C.** Rename the divisor as a whole number and move the decimal point in the dividend the same number of places to the right. Complete the division. The quotient is 53.

$$0.15\overline{)7.95} =$$

$$
\begin{array}{r}
53 \\
15\overline{)795} \\
-75 \\
\hline
45 \\
-45 \\
\hline
0
\end{array}
$$

10. **The correct answer is B.** By computing the value of the coins in each option, we find that choice B has the greatest value.

$$3 \times 25\cent = 75\cent$$
$$8 \times 10\cent = 80\cent$$
$$15 \times 5\cent = 75\cent$$
$$79 \times 1\cent = 79\cent$$

11. **The correct answer is D.** The sum of the two time periods is 5 weeks and 9 days, which is equivalent to 6 weeks and 2 days.

$$
\begin{array}{r}
2 \text{ weeks, } 5 \text{ days} \\
+3 \text{ weeks, } 4 \text{ days} \\
\hline
5 \text{ weeks, } 9 \text{ days}
\end{array}
$$

12. **The correct answer is B.** Two feet, four inches is equal to one foot, 16 inches. This amount less one foot, six inches equals 10 inches.

$$
\begin{array}{r}
1'16'' \\
-1'6'' \\
\hline
10''
\end{array}
$$

13. **The correct answer is A.** Two thirds of 36 is 24, the number of females. This number subtracted from 36 gives the number of males.

14. **The correct answer is C.** Dividing the distance (200) by the number of hours (4) gives the average speed.

15. **The correct answer is C.** There are 16 ounces in a pound; therefore, 24 ounces would be equivalent to one pound, 8 ounces or $1\frac{1}{2}$ pounds.

16. **The correct answer is B.** 8% of $12 is 96 cents.

$$
\begin{array}{r}
\$12 \\
\times\ .08 \\
\hline
\$.96
\end{array}
$$

17. **The correct answer is A.** The price of a dozen oranges divided by 12 gives the cost per orange. $0.225 to the nearest cent is 22¢.

$$
\begin{array}{r}
.225 \\
12\overline{)2.700} \\
-24 \\
\hline
30 \\
-24 \\
\hline
60 \\
-60 \\
\hline
0
\end{array}
$$

18. **The correct answer is A.** The amount of money spent is .75 times $75, which equals $56.25. The fund available minus the amount spent equals the amount left. $75 minus $56.25 = $18.75.

19. **The correct answer is C.** $1\frac{1}{2} \times \$8.00 = \$12.00$

$$
\begin{array}{lr}
\$8.00 \text{ times } 40 \text{ equals} & \$320.00 \\
\$12.00 \text{ times } 4 \text{ equals} & +\ \underline{\$48.00} \\
& \$368.00
\end{array}
$$

20. **The correct answer is D.** 4 men times 14 days equals 56 man-days.

7 men times ? equals 56 man-days

56 divided by 7 = 8.

21. **The correct answer is A.** There are four quarts to a gallon. Therefore, 16 quarts divided by 4 equals 4 gallons.

22. **The correct answer is B.** The shadow will be 2 feet in length.

    $15 : 5 :: 6 : x$

    $15x = 30$

    $x = 2$

23. **The correct answer is C.** The chain would cost $2.04.

    4 yards = 12 feet

    $1 : .17 :: 12 : x$

    $x = 2.04$

24. **The correct answer is B.** $44 minus $37 equals $7, the savings on each tire.

    $7 times 4 equals $28, the savings on four tires.

25. **The correct answer is C.** The number of persons to be transported divided by the number of persons the bus can carry will give the number of buses needed. 180 divided by 32 equals 5.6.

26. **The correct answer is D.** The number of vehicles greased divided by the number of days gives the daily average 270/31 ≈ 8.71 The correct answer is 9.

27. **The correct answer is C.** If 4 out of 50 sampled articles were defective, the fraction 4/50 multiplied by 100 equals the percentage of defective articles in the sampling. Because 8% of the articles in the sample were defective, the probable percentage of defective articles in the original shipment would also be 8%.

28. **The correct answer is A.** The total area divided by the number of rooms gives the average area of each room. As there are four rooms, the total area divided by four gives the average area of each room.

29. **The correct answer is C.** 9 feet × 12 feet = 108 square feet.

30. **The correct answer is D.** 12 feet = 4 yards; 15 feet = 5 yards; 4 × 5 = 20 square yards.

31. **The correct answer is B.** Perimeter or circumference = $2\pi r$; r = 70 feet;

    $P = 2 \times \dfrac{22}{7} \times 70$; P = 440 feet.

32. **The correct answer is D.** Each side is 1 inch. Perimeter = 1 + 1 + 1 + 1 = 4 inches.

33. **The correct answer is C.** The volume is obtained by multiplying length times width times depth—25 feet times 15 feet times 4 feet. The answer is 1,500 cubic feet.

34. **The correct answer is D.** The volume of the cube is the cube of one side. $V = (4 \text{ yds.})^3$. V = 64 cubic yards.

35. **The correct answer is D.** The perimeter = 5 + (6 − 2) + 8 + 2 + 13 + 6 = 5 + 4 + 8 + 2 + 13 + 6 = 38 inches.

SUMMING IT UP

- A fraction is a number that indicates one or more equal parts. A fraction has a *numerator*, a *division line*, and a *denominator*.

    1/4   or   ¼

- Decimals are also known as decimal fractions, since the denominator is a tenth, hundredth, thousandth, etc.

    0.1= 1/10   0.01 = 1/100   0.001 = 1/1000

- Percent means *hundredth*. It may be expressed with the % symbol, as a fraction with a denominator of 100, or as a decimal.

- Addition is indicated by the plus (+) sign, the word *plus*, or the word *and*. *Addends* are the numbers that are added. The *total* or *sum* is the number obtained by adding all the addends.

- Subtraction is indicated by the subtraction sign (–), the word **minus**, the words **take away**, or the words **find the difference between**. There are three parts to a subtraction problem: the minuend, subtrahend, and difference or remainder.

- Multiplication is indicated by the multiplication sign (×), the word *multiply*, or the word *times*. There are three parts to multiplication problems: the multiplicand, multiplier, and product.

- Division is indicated by the division sign (÷), the fraction sign (— or /), the words *divided by*, the short-division symbol, or the long-division symbol. Division problems have four parts: the dividend, divisor, quotient, and remainder.

Word Knowledge Review

Chapter 5

OVERVIEW

- **Word Formation—A Key to Word Recognition**
- **Practice Questions**
- **Answer Key and Explanations**
- **Summing It Up**

The ability to understand other people and to be understood by other people is an important communication skill, both in speaking and in writing. This ability can be measured in a written test by including a section on synonyms—words having the same, or nearly the same, meaning as other words in the language.

Synonym questions are used to test for ability to understand the meaning of words. They are also good indicators of reasoning ability and ability to learn.

The Word Knowledge subtest determines breadth of word knowledge through synonyms. The words used in the synonym questions are those used in everyday language by high school graduates or those who have high school equivalency diplomas. The test questions are four-choice items and appear in either of the two following formats:

Format 1. Complete the definition of a key word.

Sample:

1. <u>Notorious</u> most nearly means
   - **A.** annoying.
   - **B.** condemned.
   - **C.** unpleasant.
   - **D.** well known.

   Notorious means *well known*, which is the same as choice D. Choices A and C are unrelated in meaning since a notorious person may or may not be annoying or unpleasant. Although choice B may be just slightly related in meaning, as *notorious* also implies being widely and unfavorably known, it does not necessarily imply being condemned. Choice D is the only correct answer of the options given.

Sample:

2. To <u>assent</u> means most nearly to
   - **A.** acquire.
   - **B.** climb.
   - **C.** consent.
   - **D.** participate.

To *assent* means to *express acceptance* or *concurrence*. Choice C is almost the same in meaning. Choices A, B, and D are unrelated in meaning. Choice B is similar in meaning to the word "ascend" but not to "assent."

Choice C is the correct answer.

Format 2. Choose the word that means the same as the key word in a sentence.

Sample:

Choose the lettered word that means most nearly the same as the underlined word as it is used in the sentence.

3. The rear of the truck should be washed.
   A. Back
   B. Front
   C. Hood
   D. Roof

Replace *rear* with each of the choices. The correct choice is the word that does not change the meaning of the sentence. In the previous question, the choice that is closest in meaning to the underlined word is *back*. Therefore, choice A is the correct answer.

An excellent method of increasing your vocabulary is by developing and maintaining your own word list. Write down every word you see or hear whose meaning you are not certain of. Look up its meaning in a dictionary and record it next to the word. Then follow up by using the word in a sentence.

A guide to word formation follows. This key to word recognition consists of commonly used prefixes and suffixes, as well as Latin and Greek word stems that have been absorbed into the English language. Use this guide as a reference to increase your knowledge of word meanings, an essential component of verbal ability.

Information about the Word Knowledge test and sample questions with accompanying answer explanations follow the Word Formation section and word parts list. Be sure to study these sections and then try the practice questions.

WORD FORMATION—A KEY TO WORD RECOGNITION

Many English words, especially the longer and more difficult ones, are built from basic parts or roots. One of the most efficient ways of increasing your vocabulary is to learn some of these parts. Once you know some basic building blocks, you will find it easier to remember words you've learned and to puzzle out unfamiliar ones.

The following chart lists more than 150 common word parts. Each part is defined, and an example is given of a word in which it appears. Study the chart a small section at a time. When you've learned one of the building blocks, remember to look for it in your reading. See if you can think of other words in which the word part appears. Use the dictionary to check your guesses.

Word Part	Meaning	Example
ab, abs	from, away	*abrade*—to wear off
		absent—away, not present
act, ag	do, act, drive	*action*—a doing
		agent—one who acts for another
alter, altr	other, change	*alternate*—to switch back and forth
am, ami	love, friend	*amorous*—loving
anim	mind, life, spirit	*animated*—spirited
annu, enni	year	*annual*—yearly
ante	before	*antedate*—to occur earlier
anthrop	man	*anthropology*—study of mankind
anti	against	*antiwar*—against war
arbit	judge	*arbiter*—a judge
arch	first, chief	*archetype*—first model
aud, audit, aur	hear	*auditorium*—place where performances are heard
auto	self	*automobile*—self-moving vehicle
bell	war	*belligerent*—warlike
bene, ben	good, well	*benefactor*—one who does good deeds
bi	two	*bilateral*—two-sided
bibli	book	*bibliophile*—book lover
bio	life	*biology*—study of life
brev	short	*abbreviate*—to shorten
cad, cas	fall	*casualty*—one who has fallen
cede, ceed, cess	go, yield	*exceed*—go beyond
		recession—a going backward
cent	hundred	*century*—hundred years
chrom	color	*monochrome*—having one color
chron	time	*chronology*—time order
cide, cis	cut, kill	*suicide*—a self-killing
		incision—a cutting into

Word Part	Meaning	Example
circum	around	*circumnavigate*—to sail around
clam, claim	shout	*proclaim*—to declare loudly
clin	slope, lean	*decline*—to slope downward
cogn	know	*recognize*—to know
com, co, col, con	with, together	*concentrate*—to bring closer together
		cooperate—to work with
contra, contro, counter	against	*contradict*—to speak against
		counterclockwise—against the clock's direction
corp	body	*incorporate*—to bring into a body
cosm	order, world	*cosmos*—universe
cre, cresc	grow	*increase*—to grow
cred	trust, believe	*incredible*—unbelievable
culp	blame	*culprit*—one who is to blame
cur, curr, curs	run, course	*current*—presently running
de	away from, down,	*detract*—to draw away from opposite
dec	ten	*decade*—ten years
dem	people	*democracy*—rule by the people
dic, dict	say, speak	*dictation*—a speaking
		predict—to say in advance
dis, di	not, away from	*dislike*—to not like
		digress—to turn away from the subject
doc, doct	teach, prove	*indoctrinate*—to teach
domin	rule	*domineer*—to rule over
du	two	*duo*—a couple
duc, duct	lead	*induct*—to lead in
dur	hard, lasting	*durable*—able to last
equ	equal	*equivalent*—of equal value
ev	time, age	*longevity*—age, length of life

Word Part	Meaning	Example
ex, e, ef	from, out	*expatriate*—one who lives outside his native country
		emit—to send out
extra	outside, beyond	*extraterrestrial*—from beyond the earth
fac, fact, fect, fic	do, make	*factory*—place where things are made
		fictitious—made up or imaginary
fer	bear, carry	*transfer*—to carry across
fid	belief, faith	*fidelity*—faithfulness
fin	end, limit	*finite*—limited
flect, flex	bend	*reflect*—to bend back
flu, fluct, flux	flow	*fluid*—flowing substance
		influx—a flowing in
fore	in front of, previous	*forecast*—to tell ahead of time
		foreleg—front leg
form	shape	*formation*—shaping
fort	strong	*fortify*—to strengthen
frag, fract	break	*fragile*—easily broken
fug	flee	*fugitive*—one who flees
gen	birth, kind, race	*engender*—to give birth to
geo	earth	*geology*—study of the earth
grad, gress	step, go	*progress*—to go forward
graph	writing	*autograph*—to write one's own name
her, hes	stick, cling	*adhere*—to cling
		cohesive—sticking together
homo	same, like	*homophonic*—sounding the same
hyper	too much, over	*hyperactive*—overly active
in, il, ig, im, ir	not	*incorrect*—not correct
		ignorant—not knowing
		illogical—not logical
		irresponsible—not responsible

Word Part	Meaning	Example
in, il, im, ir	on, into, in	*impose*—to place on
		invade—to go into
inter	between, among	*interplanetary*—between planets
intra, intro	within, inside	*intrastate*—within a state
ject	throw	*reject*—to throw back
junct	join	*juncture*—place where things join
leg	law	*legal*—lawful
leg, lig, lect	choose, gather, read	*legible*—readable
		eligible—able to be chosen
		select—to choose
lev	light, rise	*alleviate*—to make lighter
liber	free	*liberation*—a freeing
loc	place	*location*—place
log	speech, study	*dialogue*—speech for two characters
		psychology—study of the mind
luc, lum	light	*translucent*—allowing some light to pass through
		luminous—shining
magn	large, great	*magnify*—to make larger
mal, male	bad, wrong, poor	*maladjusted*—poorly adjusted
		malevolent—ill-wishing
mar	sea	*marine*—sea-dwelling
ment	mind	*demented*—out of one's mind
meter, metr, mens	measure	*chronometer*—time-measuring device
		commensurate—of equal measure
micr	small	*microwave*—small wave
min	little	*minimum*—least
mis	badly, wrongly	*misunderstand*—to understand wrongly
mit, miss	send	*remit*—to send back
		mission—a sending

Word Part	Meaning	Example
mono	single, one	*monorail*—train that runs on a single track
morph	shape	*anthropomorphic*—human-shaped
mov, mob, mot	move	*removal*—a moving away
		mobile—able to move
multi	many	*multiply*—to become many
mut	change	*mutation*—change
nasc, nat	born	*innate*—inborn
		native—belonging by or from birth
neg	deny	*negative*—no, not
neo	new	*neophyte*—beginner
nom	name	*nominate*—to name for office
non	not	*nonentity*—a nobody
nov	new	*novice*—newcomer, beginner
		innovation—something new
omni	all	*omnipresent*—present in all places
oper	work	*operate*—to work
		cooperation—a working together
path, pat, pass	feel, suffer	*patient*—suffering
		compassion—a feeling with
ped, pod	foot	*pedestrian*—one who goes on foot
pel, puls	drive, push	*impel*—to push
phil	love	*philosophy*—love of wisdom
phob	fear	*phobia*—irrational fear
phon	sound	*symphony*—a sounding together
phot	light	*photosynthesis*—synthesis of chemical compounds in plants with the aid of light
poly	many	*polygon*—many-sided figure
port	carry	*import*—to carry into a country
pot	power	*potency*—power
post	after	*postmortem*—after death

Word Part	Meaning	Example
pre	before, earlier than	*prejudice*—judgment in advance
press	press	*impression*—a pressing into
prim	first	*primal*—first, original
pro	in favor of, in front of, forward	*proceed*—to go forward
		prowar—in favor of war
psych	mind	*psychiatry*—cure of the mind
quer, quir, quis, ques	ask, seek	*query*—to ask
		inquisitive—asking many questions
		quest—a search
re	back, again	*rethink*—to think again
		reimburse—to pay back
rid, ris	laugh	*deride*—to make fun of
		ridiculous—laughable
rupt	break	*erupt*—to break out
sci, scio	know	*science*—knowledge
		conscious—having knowledge
scrib, script	write	*describe*—to write about
		inscription—a writing on
semi	half	*semiconscious*—half conscious
sent, sens	feel, think	*sensation*—feeling
		sentimental—marked by feeling
sequ, secut	follow	*sequential*—following in order
sol	alone	*desolate*—lonely
solv, solu, solut	loosen	*dissolve*—to loosen the bonds of
		solvent—loosening agent
son	sound	*sonorous*—sounding
spect	look	*inspect*—to look into
		spectacle—something to be looked at
spir	breathe	*respiration*—breathing

Word Part	Meaning	Example
stab, stat	stand	*establish*—to make stand, found
string, strict	bind	*restrict*—to bind, limit
stru, struct	build	*construct*—to build
super	over, greater	*superfluous*—overflowing beyond what is needed
tang, ting, tact, tig	touch	*tactile*—of the sense of touch
		contiguous—touching
tele	far	*telescope*—machine for seeing far
ten, tain, tent	hold	*tenacity*—holding power
		contain—to hold together
term	end	*terminal*—last, ending
terr	earth	*terrain*—surface of the earth
test	witness	*attest*—to witness
therm	heat	*thermos*—container that retains heat
tort, tors	twist	*contort*—to twist out of shape
tract	pull, draw	*attract*—to pull toward
trans	across	*transport*—to carry across a distance
un	not	*uninformed*—not informed
uni	one	*unify*—to make one
vac	empty	*evacuate*—to make empty
ven, vent	come	*convene*—to come together
ver	true	*verity*—truth
verb	word	*verbose*—wordy
vid, vis	see	*video*—means of seeing
		vision—sight
viv, vit	life	*vivid*—lively
voc, vok	call	*provocative*—calling for a response
		revoke—to call back
vol	wish, will	*involuntary*—not willed

PRACTICE QUESTIONS

1. Small most nearly means
   A. cheap.
   B. round.
   C. sturdy.
   D. little.

2. Impair most nearly means
   A. direct.
   B. weaken.
   C. improve.
   D. stimulate.

3. Cease most nearly means
   A. stop.
   B. start.
   C. change.
   D. continue.

4. The wind is variable today.
   A. Mild
   B. Steady
   C. Shifting
   D. Chilling

5. The student discovered an error.
   A. Found
   B. Entered
   C. Searched
   D. Enlarged

6. Do not obstruct the entrance to the building.
   A. Block
   B. Enter
   C. Leave
   D. Cross

ANSWER KEY AND EXPLANATIONS

1. D	3. A	4.C	5. A	6. A
2. B				

1. **The correct answer is D.** *Little* most closely means the same as *small*. The other choices are not related in any way to the word small.

2. **The correct answer is B.** Of all the choices, *weaken* most closely means the same as *impair*. *Impair* means to *decrease in strength, amount,* or *quality.*

3. **The correct answer is A.** *Stop* most nearly means *cease*. *Start* and *continue* are opposites of *cease*, while *change* is not related to the word *cease.*

4. **The correct answer is C.** The word *shifting* could replace *variable* in this sentence. *Variable* means "changing" or "subject to change."

5. **The correct answer is A.** The word *discovered* can be replaced by *found* in this sentence. *Discovered* means *to have uncovered* or *found.*

6. **The correct answer is A.** *Obstruct* can be replaced by the word *block. Obstruct* means to *impede* or *interfere.*

SUMMING IT UP

- The Word Knowledge subtest determines breadth of word knowledge through **synonyms** (words having the same, or nearly the same, meaning as other words in the language). The words used in the synonym questions are those used in everyday language. The test questions appear in either of the two following formats: 1) completing the definition of a key word, and 2) choosing the word that means the same as the key word in a sentence.

- Synonym questions are used to test for ability to understand the **meaning** of words. They are also good indicators of **reasoning ability** and ability to learn.

- An excellent method of increasing your vocabulary is by developing and maintaining your own **word list**. Write down every word you see or hear whose meaning you are not certain of. Look up its meaning in a dictionary and record it. Then follow up by using the word in a sentence.

- Many English words, especially the longer and more difficult ones, are built from basic parts or **roots**. One of the most efficient ways of increasing your vocabulary is to learn some of these roots.

- The key to word recognition consists of identifying commonly used **prefixes** and **suffixes**, as well as Latin and Greek word **stems** that have been absorbed into the English language.

Paragraph Comprehension

Chapter 6

OVERVIEW

- **Practice Questions**
- **Answer Key and Explanations**
- **Summing It Up**

Reading comprehension, the ability to read and understand written or printed material, is an important verbal skill. The reading material may be in the form of several paragraphs, a single paragraph, or a single sentence. This section includes reading selections that are samples of the type of material that you would be required to read, whether at school, in training, or on the job.

Before you try the following samples, note the eight general suggestions for answering reading comprehension questions. Keep these in mind as you take the practice tests in this book as well as on your ASVAB test day.

1. Scan the passage to get the general intent of the reading selection.

2. Reread the passage carefully to understand the main idea and any related ideas.

3. Read each question carefully. Be careful to base your answer on what is stated, implied, or inferred in the reading passage. Do not be influenced by your opinions, personal feelings, or any other information not expressed or implied in the passage.

4. Options that are partly true and partly false are incorrect.

5. Look for such words as *least, greatest, first, not,* etc., appearing in the comprehension question.

6. Be suspicious of options containing words such as *all, always, every, forever, never, none, wholly,* etc.

7. Be sure to consider all options given for the question before selecting your answer.

8. Speed is an important consideration in answering reading comprehension questions. Try to proceed as rapidly as you can without sacrificing careful thinking or reasoning.

When answering Paragraph Comprehension questions, refer back to the paragraph *as often as necessary*. Questions may focus on a particular sentence or phrase within the paragraph. You should refer back to make sure you answer the question correctly instead of trying to answer from memory. Keep in mind that wrong answer choices could be *subtly* wrong. With careful review of the paragraph and the details in the answer choices, it becomes clear which answers are correct and which ones aren't.

Here are samples of the four main types of paragraph comprehension questions you may find on the ASVAB Paragraph Comprehension section of your test. Each type of question is explained, a sample is given, and an explanation of the correct answer is given in detail. After these samples are practice questions to try on your own.

The four main types of questions are:

Type 1. Finding specific information or directly stated details contained in the reading passage.

This is a common type of item found in paragraph comprehension tests. It requires the ability to pick out specific facts provided in a passage or, sometimes, the ability to pick out the fact that is not mentioned in a particular passage.

Sample:

There are many signs by which people predict the weather. Some of these have a true basis but many do not. There is, for example, no evidence that it is more likely to storm during one phase of the moon than during another. If it happens to rain on Easter, there is no reason to think that it will rain for the next seven Sundays. The groundhog may or may not see his shadow on Groundhog Day, but it probably won't affect the weather anyway.

1. Which of the following is NOT mentioned as a sign of weather phenomenon?
    A. Rain on Easter
    B. The phases of the moon
    C. Pain in a person's joints
    D. The groundhog's shadow

The correct answer is choice C. The other choices were mentioned in the passage.

Below are some typical "detail" questions:

- The first toll road in the United States was completed in _____.
- Helping to prevent accidents is the responsibility of _____.
- The principal reason for issuing traffic summonses is to _____.
- The side margins of a typewritten letter are most pleasing when _____.
- The reason for maintaining ongoing safety education is that _____.
- It would be desirable when planning a departmental reorganization to _____.

Type 2. Recognizing the main idea or concept expressed in the passage.

Although questions of this type may be phrased differently, they generally require the ability to summarize the principal purpose or idea expressed in the reading passage. These questions require the ability to analyze and interpret as well as to read and understand the material presented.

Sample:

Specific types of lighting are required at first-class airports by the Department of Commerce. To identify an airport, there must be a beacon of light of not less than 100,000 candlepower, with a beam that properly distributes light up in the air so that it can be seen all around the horizon from an altitude of from 500 to 2,000 feet. All flashing beacons must have a definite Morse code characteristic to aid in identification. Colored lights are required to indicate where the safe area for landing ends, red lights being used where landing is particularly dangerous.

2. The best title for this selection is
   A. "Landing Areas."
   B. "Colored Lights at Airports."
   C. "Identification of Airports."
   D. "Airport Lighting Requirements."

The correct answer is choice D because every sentence in the paragraph describes a lighting requirement for airports. The other choices are each mentioned in only one of the four sentences.

Below are other typical "main idea" questions:

- This paragraph is mainly about _____.
- The passage best supports the statement that _____.
- The passage means most nearly that _____.
- One may conclude from the above statement that_____.

Type 3. Determining the meaning of certain words as used in context.

The particular meaning of a word as actually used in the passage requires an understanding of the central or main theme of the reading passage, as well as the thought being conveyed by the sentence containing the word in question.

Sample:

The maritime and fishing industries find perhaps 250 applications for rope and cordage. There are hundreds of different sizes, constructions, tensile strengths, and weights in rope and twine. Rope is sold by the pound but ordered by length and is measured by circumference rather than by diameter.

3. In this context, the word "application" means
   A. use.
   B. description.
   C. size.
   D. types.

The correct answer is choice A, "use." Try it in the sentence in place of the word "application"; "use" makes sense in that context and keeps the meaning of the sentence intact.

Type 4. Finding implications or drawing inferences from a stated idea.

This type of item requires the ability to understand the stated idea and then to reason by logical thinking to the implied or inferred idea. *Implied* means not exactly stated but merely suggested; *inferred* means derived by reasoning. Although these terms are somewhat similar in meaning, *inferred* implies being further removed from the stated idea. Much greater reasoning ability is required to arrive at the proper inference. Because the answer to an inference question will not be found in the passage, it is the most difficult type of comprehension question to answer.

Sample:

The facts, as we see them, on drug use and the dangerous behaviors caused by drugs are that some people do get into trouble while using drugs, and some of those drug users are dangerous to others. Sometimes a drug is a necessary element in order for a person to commit a crime, although it may not be the cause of his or her criminality. On the other hand, the use of a drug sometimes seems to be the only convenient excuse by means of which the observer can account for the undesirable behavior.

4. The author apparently feels that
   A. the use of drugs always results in crime.
   B. drugs and crime are only sometimes related.
   C. drug use does not always cause crime.
   D. drugs are usually an element in accidents and suicides.

The author states that drugs are sometimes a necessary element in a crime but at other times are just an excuse for criminal behavior. Therefore, choice B is the correct answer.

Other typical "implication" or "inference" questions include any of the following:

- Which of the following is implied by the above passage? _____.
- Of the following, the most valid implication of the above paragraph is _____.
- The author probably believes that _____.
- It can be inferred from the above passage that_____.
- The best of the following inferences that can be made is that_____.

Now try the **sample Paragraph Comprehension questions** that follow. Detailed explanations of the answers are given immediately after each question to help you understand the logic of the answers. Once you feel comfortable with these, continue on to try the next set of sample questions on your own.

1. Investigations show that activation analysis of wipings taken from a suspect's hands will reveal not only whether he or she has fired a gun recently but also the type of ammunition used, the number of bullets fired, and the hand in which the gun was held.

   Activation analysis of wipings taken from the hands of a person suspected of firing a gun CANNOT be used to reveal the
   A. exact time the gun was fired.
   B. hand in which the gun was fired.
   C. number of bullets fired.
   D. type of ammunition used.

The paragraph states that activation analysis can be used to reveal choices B, C, and D. Although activation analysis can reveal whether the suspect fired a gun recently, it *cannot* ascertain the exact time the gun was fired; therefore, choice A is correct.

The ability of activation analysis to detect and identify very tiny amounts of certain elements has come to the aid of law-enforcement officers in a variety of ways. Hair, even hundreds of years old, can be analyzed successfully for arsenic and other residues.

2. English scientists recently found an unusual amount of arsenic in a relic of hair from Napoleon's head. The suspicion now is that he was slowly poisoned to death.

The case of King Eric XIV of Sweden is similar. When the king's body was exhumed recently, activation analysis showed that his body contained traces of poisonous arsenic.

Both King Eric XIV of Sweden and Napoleon could have been
   A. killed by gunshot.
   B. killed in military combat.
   C. poisoned by arsenic.
   D. poisoned by lead.

For this question, the possibility of poisoning by arsenic is indicated for both Napoleon and King Eric XIV. There is nothing in the reading passage suggesting that their deaths were due to gunshot or occurred in military combat; nor is there any reference to poisoning by lead. Choice C is the only correct answer.

3. In spite of the fact that the latitude of Scandinavia corresponds to that of Alaska and Siberia, the climate is surprisingly mild. Even in winter, the temperatures in Scandinavia are often higher than those of Central Europe and sometimes even Southern Europe. The average temperature is higher in Scandinavia than for other places on the same latitude, thanks to the Gulf Stream that washes the Scandinavian Atlantic coastline.

According to the quotation above, it may be concluded that the latitude of Scandinavia is
   A. higher than that of Alaska.
   B. lower than that of Siberia.
   C. higher than that of Southern Europe.
   D. lower than that of Central Europe.

Nothing in the passage suggests that the latitude is either higher or lower than that of Alaska or Siberia; nor is there any indication that it is lower than that of Central Europe. The implication is that it is higher than that of Southern Europe. Choice C is the correct answer.

Answer the next two questions on the basis of the following passage.

4. It is important for every office to have proper lighting. Inadequate lighting is a common cause of fatigue and tends to create a dreary atmosphere in the office. Appropriate light intensity is essential for proper lighting. It is generally recommended that for "casual seeing" tasks, such as in reception rooms or inactive file rooms, the amount of lighting be 30-foot candles. For "ordinary seeing" tasks, such as reading or for work in active file rooms and mail rooms, the recommended lighting is 100-foot candles. For "very difficult seeing" tasks, such as transcribing, accounting, and business machine use, the recommended lighting is 150-foot candles.

For copying figures onto a payroll, the recommended lighting is
   A. less than 30-foot candles.
   B. 30-foot candles.
   C. 100-foot candles.
   D. 150-foot candles.

For this question, it is necessary to determine the proper lighting task for copying figures onto a payroll. This activity requires much more light than either "casual seeing" or "ordinary seeing." As it is a "very difficult seeing" task, choice D is the correct answer.

5. It can be inferred from the passage above that a well-coordinated lighting scheme is likely to result in
   A. greater employee productivity.
   B. lower lighting costs.
   C. more use of natural light.
   D. windowless offices.

In this question, there is no mention of lighting costs or the need for windowless offices in the reading passage. Nor is there any suggestion for greater use of natural light. Choices B, C, and D are therefore eliminated. If inadequate lighting is a common cause of fatigue, one can *infer* that proper lighting would eliminate this fatigue element and should result in greater employee productivity. Choice A is the correct answer.

PRACTICE QUESTIONS

1. In the relations of man to nature, the pro-curing of food and shelter is fundamental. With the migration of man to various cli-mates, ever-new adjustments to the food supply and to the climate became necessary.

   According to the passage, the means by which man supplies his material needs are
   A. accidental.
   B. inadequate.
   C. limited.
   D. varied.

2. From a building designer's standpoint, three things that make a home livable are the needs of the client, the building site, and the amount of money the client has to spend.

   According to the passage, to make a home livable,
   A. it can be built on any piece of land.
   B. the design must fit the designer's income.
   C. the design must fit the owner's income and site.
   D. the prospective piece of land makes little difference.

3. Twenty-five percent of all household burglaries can be attributed to unlocked windows or doors. Crime is the result of opportunity plus desire. To prevent crime, it is each individual's responsibility to
   A. provide the desire.
   B. provide the opportunity.
   C. prevent the desire.
   D. prevent the opportunity.

4. In certain areas, water is so scarce that every attempt is made to conserve it. For instance, on one oasis in the Sahara Desert, the amount of water necessary for each date palm has been carefully determined.

   How much water is each tree given?
   A. No water at all
   B. Water on alternate days
   C. Exactly the amount required
   D. Water only if it is healthy

ANSWERS AND EXPLANATIONS

1. D	2. C	3. D	4. C

1. **The correct answer is D.** The author talks about "adjustments" to the food supply and climate. Of the available choices, the only word related to adjustment is "varied."

2. **The correct answer is C.** The author mentions three necessary items: the needs of the clients, the building site, and amount of money available. Choice C is the only answer that makes any sense.

3. **The correct answer is D.** Choices A and B can be immediately eliminated, and since individuals cannot control the desires of burglars, choice D is the only logical answer.

4. **The correct answer is C.** The only conclusion that can be drawn from information given is contained in choice C. The author talks about "...the amount of water necessary..." This is the key to the correct answer.

SUMMING IT UP

- Note the eight general suggestions for answering reading comprehension questions:

  1. Scan the passage to get the general intent of the reading selection.

  2. Reread the passage carefully to understand the main idea and any related ideas.

  3. Read each question carefully. Be careful to base your answer on what is stated, implied, or inferred in the reading passage. Do not be influenced by your opinions, personal feelings, or any other information not expressed or implied in the passage.

  4. Options that are partly true and partly false are incorrect.

  5. Look for such words as *least, greatest, first, not,* etc., that appear in the comprehension question.

  6. Be suspicious of options including words such as *all, always, every, forever, never, none, wholly,* etc.

  7. Be sure to consider all options given for the question before selecting your answer.

  8. Speed is an important consideration in answering reading comprehension questions Try to proceed as rapidly as you can without sacrificing careful thinking or reasoning.

- The four main types of Paragraph Comprehension questions are:

  Type 1. Finding specific information or directly stated details included in the reading passage.

  Type 2. Recognizing the main idea or concept expressed in the passage.

  Type 3. Determining the meaning of certain words as used in context.

  Type 4. Finding implications or drawing inferences from a stated idea.

- When answering Paragraph Comprehension questions, refer back to the paragraph *as often as necessary*. Questions may focus on a specific sentence or phrase within the paragraph. You should refer back to make sure you answer the question correctly instead of trying to answer from memory.

Mathematics Knowledge

Chapter 7

OVERVIEW

- **Adding Fractions**
- **Adding Mixed Numbers**
- **Adding Percents**
- **Subtracting Fractions**
- **Subtracting Mixed Numbers**
- **Subtracting Percents**
- **Multiplying Fractions**
- **Multiplying Mixed Numbers**
- **Multiplying Percents**
- **Other Multiplication Properties**
- **Dividing Fractions**
- **Dividing Percents**
- **Dividing Mixed Numbers**
- **Other Division Properties**
- **Factors of a Product**
- **Roots**
- **Algebra**
- **Geometry**
- **Practice Questions**
- **Answer Key and Explanations**
- **Summing It Up**

The Mathematics Knowledge subtest of the ASVAB deals with the ability to use basic mathematical relationships learned in math courses, such as algebra, geometry, and trigonometry. This subtest tests your knowledge of math principles, concepts, and procedures. This review section can also be considered a continuation of Arithmetic Reasoning given previously. Reread that section as background material for Mathematics Knowledge.

ADDING FRACTIONS

With the Same Denominator

Fractions with the same denominator are added directly, as each part represents a part of the same value. Add the numerators and place the sum over the common denominator. If necessary, simplify to the simplest form.

$$\begin{array}{r} \frac{1}{5} \\ +\frac{3}{5} \\ \hline \frac{4}{5} \end{array} \qquad \begin{array}{r} \frac{1}{5} \\ \frac{3}{5} \\ +\frac{4}{5} \\ \hline \frac{8}{5} = 1\frac{3}{5} \end{array}$$

With Different Denominators

Fractions with different denominators may not be added directly because parts of different values are involved. They must be renamed as equivalent fractions having the same common denominator. After all the fractions have the same denominator, add the numerators and place the total over the common denominator. If necessary, simplify to the simplest form.

$$\frac{1}{2}+\frac{1}{4}; \ \frac{1}{2}+\frac{1}{3}+\frac{3}{4}$$

$$\begin{array}{r} \frac{1}{2} \\ +\frac{1}{4} \end{array} \qquad \begin{array}{r} \frac{2}{4} \\ +\frac{1}{4} \\ \hline \frac{3}{4} \end{array} \qquad \begin{array}{r} \frac{1}{2} \\ \frac{1}{3} \\ +\frac{3}{4} \end{array} \qquad \begin{array}{r} \frac{6}{12} \\ \frac{4}{12} \\ +\frac{9}{12} \\ \hline \frac{19}{12} = 1\frac{7}{12} \end{array}$$

ADDING MIXED NUMBERS

In adding mixed numbers, first add all the whole numbers, then add all fractions, and then add the sum of the whole numbers to the sum of the fractions.

$$4\frac{1}{4}+3\frac{1}{2}+2\frac{1}{2}$$

$$
\begin{array}{cc}
4\frac{1}{4} & 4\frac{1}{4} \\[2mm]
3\frac{1}{2} & 3\frac{2}{4} \\[2mm]
+2\frac{1}{2} & +2\frac{2}{4} \\[2mm]
\hline
& 9+\frac{5}{4}=9+1\frac{1}{4}=10\frac{1}{4}
\end{array}
$$

ADDING PERCENTS

As percents are actually fractions with 100 as the same common denominator, they may be added directly.

$$
\begin{array}{ccc}
6\% & & 20\% \\
4\% & 8\% & 25\% \\
+9\% & +17\% & +35\% \\
\hline
19\% & 25\% & 80\%
\end{array}
$$

If fractional parts of a percent are involved in the addition, the addends may be added as decimals or added directly after the fractional parts are renamed with the same common denominator.

$$15\frac{1}{2}\%+8\frac{1}{4}\%$$

$$
\begin{array}{ccc}
& 15\frac{1}{2}\% & 15\frac{2}{4}\% \\[2mm]
.155 & +8\frac{1}{4}\% & +8\frac{1}{4}\% \\[2mm]
+.0825 & \hline & \hline \\
\hline
.2375 & & 23\frac{3}{4}\%
\end{array}
$$

SUBTRACTING FRACTIONS

With the Same Denominator

Fractions with the same denominator may be subtracted directly.

$$\frac{3}{5} - \frac{2}{5} = \frac{1}{5} \qquad \frac{7}{8} - \frac{1}{8} = \frac{6}{8}, \text{ which simplifies to } \frac{3}{4}.$$

With Different Denominators

Fractions with different denominators are not subtracted directly because parts of different values are involved. They must be renamed as equivalent fractions having the same common denominator. After the fractions have the same denominator, subtract the numerators and place the remainder over the common denominator.

$$\frac{3}{4} - \frac{2}{3} = \frac{9}{12} - \frac{8}{12} = \frac{1}{12} \qquad \frac{4}{5} - \frac{1}{2} = \frac{8}{10} - \frac{5}{10} = \frac{3}{10}$$

SUBTRACTING MIXED NUMBERS

With the Same Denominator

If mixed numbers have the same denominator, rename them as improper fractions and subtract directly.

$$4\frac{1}{3} - 2\frac{2}{3} = \frac{13}{3} - \frac{8}{3} = \frac{5}{3} = 1\frac{2}{3}$$

With Different Denominators

If mixed numbers have different denominators, first rename as improper fractions, then rename as equivalent fractions with the same common denominator and subtract directly.

$$3\frac{1}{3} - 2\frac{3}{4} = \frac{10}{3} - \frac{11}{4} = \frac{40}{12} - \frac{33}{12} = \frac{7}{12}$$

SUBTRACTING PERCENTS

Percents are fractions with 100 as the same common denominator and may be subtracted directly.

70% minus 30% = 40%

If fractional parts of a percent are involved in the subtraction, rename them as decimals or rename the fractional parts with the same common denominator.

$$8\frac{1}{4}\% - 5\frac{2}{5}\%$$

$$
\begin{array}{ccc}
8\frac{1}{4}\% & 8\frac{5}{20}\% & 7\frac{25}{20}\% \\
-5\frac{2}{5}\% & -5\frac{8}{20}\% & -5\frac{8}{20}\% \\
\hline
& & 2\frac{17}{20}\%
\end{array}
$$

$$
\begin{array}{r}
0.0825 \\
-\,0.0540 \\
\hline
0.0285
\end{array}
$$

MULTIPLYING FRACTIONS

With fractions, the product of the numerators divided by the product of the denominators gives the final answer or product.

$$\frac{1}{2} \times \frac{2}{3} = \frac{2}{6}, \text{ which simplifies to } \frac{1}{3}.$$

Dividing a number in the numerator by the same number in the denominator simplifies the computation.

$$\frac{1}{\cancel{2}} \times \frac{\cancel{2}}{3} = \frac{1}{3}$$

Dividing a common factor is particularly useful when multiplying many fractions.

$$\frac{3}{5} \times \frac{1}{2} \times \frac{2}{3} \times \frac{5}{8} = \frac{3 \times 1 \times 2 \times 5}{5 \times 2 \times 3 \times 8} = \frac{30}{240} = \frac{1}{8}$$

With dividing common factors:

$$\frac{3}{5} \times \frac{1}{2} \times \frac{2}{3} \times \frac{5}{8} = \frac{\cancel{3} \times 1 \times \cancel{2} \times \cancel{5}}{\cancel{5} \times \cancel{2} \times \cancel{3} \times 8} = \frac{1}{8}$$

Note that dividing common factors is permitted when only multiplication is involved.

When multiplying fractions and whole numbers, use the same procedure as when multiplying fractions only. Whole numbers are basically fractions with the whole number as the numerator and one as the denominator.

$$4 = \frac{4}{1} \qquad 10 = \frac{10}{1} \qquad 150 = \frac{150}{1}$$

When multiplying a fraction and a whole number, the word *of* means *multiply by*.

$$\frac{1}{2} \text{ of 48 means } \frac{1}{2} \times \frac{48}{1}, \text{ which equals } \frac{48}{2} \text{ and equals 24.}$$

MULTIPLYING MIXED NUMBERS

There are several methods that may be used in multiplying mixed numbers.

When the numbers are small-valued, rename the mixed numbers as improper fractions and then multiply in the usual manner.

$$3\frac{1}{4} \times 16 = \frac{13}{4} \times \frac{16}{1} = \frac{208}{4} = 52$$

$$2\frac{2}{3} \times 1\frac{1}{4} = \frac{8}{3} \times \frac{5}{4} = \frac{40}{12} = \frac{10}{3} = 3\frac{1}{3}$$

$$1\frac{1}{2} \times 2\frac{2}{3} \times 3\frac{3}{4} = \frac{\cancel{3}^1}{\cancel{2}_1} \times \frac{\cancel{8}^1}{\cancel{3}_1} \times \frac{15}{\cancel{4}_1} = 15$$

When the numbers are great and the fractional parts have exact decimal equivalents, rename the fractional parts as decimals and then multiply.

$$342\frac{1}{4} \times 609\frac{3}{4} = 342.25 \times 609.75$$

$$\begin{array}{r} 342.25 \\ \times 609.75 \\ \hline 171125 \\ 239575 \\ 308025 \\ 2053500 \\ \hline 208,686.9375 \end{array}$$

When the numbers are not small-valued and the fractional parts have no exact decimal equivalents, use the partial product method as follows:

$$386\frac{3}{7} \times 245\frac{1}{3}$$

$$386\frac{3}{7}$$

$$\times 245\frac{1}{3}$$

$$\frac{3}{21} \qquad \left(\frac{1}{3}\times\frac{3}{7}\right)$$

$$128\frac{2}{3} \qquad \left(\frac{1}{3}\times 386\right)$$

$$105 \qquad \left(\frac{3}{7}\times 245\right)$$

$$94,570 \qquad \left(245\times 386\right)$$

$$94,803\frac{17}{21}$$

Find the partial products of the

    a. fractional parts of the multiplier and the multiplicand.

    b. fractional part of the multiplier and the whole number of the multiplicand.

    c. fractional part of the multiplicand and the whole number of the multiplier.

    d. whole number part of the multiplier and the whole number part of the multiplicand.

Add the partial products and, if necessary, simplify the fractional part of the answer.

MULTIPLYING PERCENTS

Since a percent is actually a fraction with a denominator of 100, it may be multiplied after renaming the percent as a decimal or as a fraction.

$$33\%\times 8\% = .33\times .08 = .0264 = 2\frac{64}{100}\% = 2\frac{32}{50}\% = 2\frac{16}{25}\%$$

$$75\%\times 50\% = \frac{3}{4}\times\frac{1}{2} = \frac{3}{8} = 37\frac{1}{2}\%$$

OTHER MULTIPLICATION PROPERTIES

    1. If the multiplier and the multiplicand are interchanged, the product will remain the same.

        5 × 4 = 20   4 × 5 = 20

2. If the numbers being multiplied are associated in different ways, the product will remain the same.

$$3 \times (5 \times 2) = 2 \times (3 \times 5) = 5 \times (2 \times 3)$$

3. Multiplying any number by 1 does not change the number.

$$8 \times 1 = 8 \qquad 1.5 \times 1 = 1.5 \qquad \frac{3}{4} \times 1 = \frac{3}{4}$$

4. Zero times any number equals zero.

$$8 \times 0 = 0 \qquad 1.5 \times 0 = 0 \qquad \frac{3}{4} \times 0 = 0$$

5. a. To multiply by 10, move the decimal point in the number one place to the right:

$$1.36 \times 10 = 13.6, 13.6 \times 10 = 136, 136 \times 10 = 1,360$$

b. To multiply by 100, move the decimal point in the number two places to the right.

$$3.61 \times 100 = 361, 36.1 \times 100 = 3,610, 361 \times 100 = 36,100$$

c. To multiply by 1,000, move the decimal point in the number three places to the right.

$$4.875 \times 1,000 = 4,875$$
$$48.75 \times 1,000 = 48,750$$
$$487.5 \times 1,000 = 487,500$$
$$4,875 \times 1,000 = 4,875,000$$

When multiplying by 10, 100, 1,000, etc., move the decimal point in the number as many places to the right as there are zeros in the multiplier. If necessary, add zero(s) to the product.

DIVIDING FRACTIONS

With fractions, multiply by the reciprocal of the divisor.

$$\frac{3}{4} \div \frac{1}{2} \text{ is rewritten as } \frac{3}{4} \times \frac{2}{1}, \text{ which equals } \frac{6}{4} = 1\frac{1}{2}$$

$$\frac{2}{3} \div \frac{3}{4} \text{ is rewritten as } \frac{2}{3} \times \frac{4}{3}, \text{ which equals } \frac{8}{9}$$

$$3 \div \frac{3}{4} \text{ is rewritten as } \frac{3}{1} \times \frac{4}{3}, \text{ which equals } \frac{12}{3} = 4$$

$$\frac{1}{4} \div 2 \text{ is rewritten as } \frac{1}{4} \times \frac{1}{2}, \text{ which equals } \frac{1}{8}$$

DIVIDING PERCENTS

A percent divided by a percent is similar to dividing two fractions with 100 as the common denominator.

$$25\% \div 50\% \text{ is rewritten as } \frac{25}{100} \times \frac{100}{50} \text{, which equals } \frac{25}{50} = \frac{1}{2}$$

$$40\% \div 40\% \text{ is rewritten as } \frac{40}{100} \times \frac{100}{40} \text{, which equals } 1$$

Note that when a percent is divided by a percent, the result is a whole number or a fraction.

$$\frac{1}{2} \div 25\% \text{ is rewritten as } \frac{1}{2} \times \frac{100}{25} \text{, which equals } \frac{100}{50} = 2$$

$$25\% \div \frac{1}{2} \text{ is rewritten as } \frac{25}{100} \times \frac{2}{1} \text{, which equals } \frac{50}{100} = \frac{1}{2}$$

Similarly, when a fraction is divided by a percent or a percent is divided by a fraction, the result is also a whole number or a fraction.

Percents may also be renamed to decimal form before division.

$$25\% \div 50\% \text{ is rewritten as } \frac{.25}{.50} \text{, which equals } \frac{25}{50} = \frac{1}{2}$$

$$\frac{1}{2} \div 25\% \text{ is rewritten as } \frac{1}{2} \div .25 = \frac{1}{2} \times \frac{1}{.25} = \frac{1}{.50} = \frac{100}{50} = 2$$

$$25\% \div \frac{1}{2} \text{ is rewritten as } .25 \div \frac{1}{2} = .25 \times 2 = .50 = \frac{1}{2}$$

DIVIDING MIXED NUMBERS

There are several methods that are used to divide mixed numbers.

When the numbers are small valued, rename the mixed numbers as improper fractions and then divide in the usual manner.

$$2\frac{1}{4} \div 1\frac{1}{2} \text{ is rewritten as } \frac{9}{4} \div \frac{3}{2} \text{, which becomes } \frac{9}{4} \times \frac{2}{3} \text{ and equals } \frac{3}{2} = 1\frac{1}{2}$$

$$1\frac{1}{2} \div 2\frac{1}{4} \text{ is rewritten as } \frac{3}{2} \div \frac{9}{4} \text{, which becomes } \frac{3}{2} \times \frac{4}{9} \text{ and equals } \frac{2}{3}$$

When the mixed numbers are great and the fractional parts have exact decimal equivalents, rename the fractional parts as decimals and then divide.

$$432\frac{3}{5} \text{ divided by } 156\frac{1}{2} \text{ is rewritten as } 432.6 \div 156.5$$

$$1565\overline{)4326}$$

When the mixed numbers are great and the fractional parts do not have exact decimal equivalents,

1. Multiply both the dividend and the divisor by the denominator of the fraction if only one fraction is involved:

$$475 \div 28\frac{2}{3} = \frac{475 \times 3}{28\frac{2}{3} \times 3} = \frac{475 \times 3}{\frac{86}{3} \times 3} = \frac{1425}{86}$$

$$27\frac{1}{6} \div 39 = \frac{27\frac{1}{6} \times 6}{39 \times 6} = \frac{\frac{163}{6} \times 6}{39 \times 6} = \frac{163}{234}$$

2. Multiply both the dividend and the divisor by the least common denominator if two fractions are involved:

$$42\frac{2}{3} \div 12\frac{1}{6} = \frac{42\frac{2}{3} \times 6}{12\frac{1}{6} \times 6} = \frac{\frac{128}{3} \times 6}{\frac{73}{6} \times 6} = \frac{256}{73}$$

OTHER DIVISION PROPERTIES

1. If the division is not exact, the number that is left is the remainder. This remainder becomes the numerator, and the divisor becomes the denominator of this common fraction that is added to the quotient:

4)1207

$301\frac{3}{4}$

2. The remainder may also be shown as a decimal. The decimal point is placed to the right of the unit digit of the dividend and zero digits are added. Divide to the desired number of decimal places:

4)1207.00

301.75

3. Dividing any number by 1 does not change the number:

$$25 \div 1 = 25 \qquad 4.7 \div 1 = 4.7 \qquad \frac{3}{5} \div 1 = \frac{3}{5}$$

4. Dividing by zero is not permissible, because the answer indicated would be undefined.

5. a. To divide by ten, move the decimal point in the number one place to the left:

$$\frac{136}{10} = 13.6 \qquad \frac{13.6}{10} = 1.36 \qquad \frac{1.36}{10} = .136$$

b. To divide by 100, move the decimal point in the number two places to the left:

$$\frac{350}{100} = 3.50 \qquad \frac{35}{100} = 0.35 \qquad \frac{3.5}{100} = .035$$

c. To divide by 1,000, move the decimal point in the number three places to the left:

$$\frac{4055}{1000} = 4.055 \qquad \frac{40.55}{1000} = .04055$$

$$\frac{405.5}{1000} = .4055 \qquad \frac{4.055}{1000} = .004055$$

When dividing by 10, 100, 1000, etc., move the decimal point in the number as many places to the left as there are zeros in the divisor. If necessary, use zeros at the left of the dividend.

FACTORS OF A PRODUCT

When two or more numbers are multiplied to produce a certain product, each number is known as a *factor* of the product.

$1 \times 8 = 8$ (1 and 8 are factors of the product)

$2 \times 4 = 8$ (2 and 4 are factors of the product)

Base

A *base* is a number used as a factor two or more times. $2 \times 2 \times 2$ may be written 2^3, which is read "2 cubed" or "2 to the third power." In the equation $2^3 = 8$, 2 is called the base.

Exponent

The *exponent* is the number that shows how many times the base is to be used as a factor. 10^2 is a short way of writing 10×10. 10 is called the base in 10^2; 2 is called the exponent.

$a^4 = a \times a \times a \times a$ (*a* is the base, 4 is the exponent)

$5^3 = 5 \times 5 \times 5$ (5 is the base, 3 is the exponent)

Power

Power is an expression such as 3^2. 3^2 is the second power of three (3×3) and is equal to 9. 2^4 is the fourth power of two ($2 \times 2 \times 2 \times 2$) and is equal to 16. Note that all the factors of the product are equal.

Reciprocal

If the product of two numbers is 1, either number is called the *reciprocal* of the other number. 4 is the reciprocal of $\frac{1}{4}$; $\frac{1}{4}$ is the reciprocal of 4; $4 \times \frac{1}{4} = 1$. Similarly, $\frac{3}{5}$ is the reciprocal of $\frac{5}{3}$; $\frac{5}{3}$ is the reciprocal of $\frac{3}{5}$; $\frac{3}{5} \times \frac{5}{3} = 1$.

Factorial

The *factorial* of a natural or counting number is the product of that number and all the natural numbers less than it. **4 factorial**, written as 4! = 4 × 3 × 2 × 1 = 24.

Prime Number

A *prime number* is a natural or counting number with exactly two factors, namely itself and 1. Examples of prime numbers are 2, 3, 5, 7, 11, 13, 17, etc.

ROOTS

Square Root

The *square root* of a number is a number that, when raised to the second power, produces the given number. For example, the square root of 16 is 4 because $4^2 = 16$. $\sqrt{}$ is the symbol for square root.

The square roots of the most common perfect squares are given in the following table below.

Number	Perfect Square	Number	Perfect Square
1	1	10	100
2	4	11	121
3	9	12	144
4	16	13	169
5	25	14	196
6	36	15	225
7	49	20	400
8	64	25	625
9	81	30	900

For example, to find $\sqrt{81}$, note that 81 is the perfect square of 9, or $9^2 = 81$. Therefore, $\sqrt{81} = 9$.

Cube Root

Cube root is the procedural inverse of raising to a cube. If $2^3 = 8$, then $\sqrt[3]{8} = 2$. The cube root of $27 = 3$; $3^3 = 27$.

ALGEBRA

Algebra is the branch of mathematics that focuses on addition, subtraction, multiplication, and division operations applied to variables, or unknowns, instead of specific numbers.

Here are these operations in algebraic form:

Operation	Algebraic Form
Addition: The sum of two numbers	$x + y$
Subtraction: The difference between two numbers	$x - y$
Multiplication: The product of two numbers	$x \times y$ or xy
Division: The quotient of two numbers	$\dfrac{x}{y}$

Algebraic Equations

An *equation* states that two quantities are equal. The solution to an equation is a number that can be substituted for the letter, or *variable*, to give a true statement.

For example, in the equation $x + 7 = 10$, if 5 is substituted for x, the equation becomes $5 + 7 = 10$, which is false. If 3 is substituted for x, the equation becomes $3 + 7 = 10$, which is true. Therefore, $x = 3$ is a solution for the equation $x + 7 = 10$.

An equation has been solved when it is transformed or rearranged so that a variable or unknown is on one side of the equal sign and a number is on the other side.

There are two basic principles that are used to transform equations:

1. The same quantity may be added to, or subtracted from, both sides of an equation.

    To solve the equation $x - 3 = 2$, add 3 to both sides:

$$
\begin{aligned}
x - 3 &= 2 \\
+3 \quad &\quad +3 \\
\hline
x \quad &= 5
\end{aligned}
$$

    Adding 3 isolates x on one side and leaves a number on the other side. The solution to the equation is
    $x = 5$.

To solve the equation $y + 4 = 10$, subtract 4 from both sides (adding -4 to both sides will have the same effect):

$$
\begin{aligned}
y + 4 &= 10 \\
\underline{-4} &\quad \underline{-4} \\
y &= 6
\end{aligned}
$$

The variable has been isolated on one side of the equation. The solution is $y = 6$.

2. Both sides of an equation may be multiplied by, or divided by, the same quantity.

To solve $2a = 12$, divide both sides by 2:

$$
\frac{2a}{2} = \frac{12}{2}
$$
$$
a = 6
$$

To solve $\dfrac{b}{5} = 10$, multiply both sides by 5:

$$
5 \cdot \frac{b}{5} = 10 \cdot 5
$$
$$
b = 50
$$

To solve equations containing more than one operation:

First, eliminate any number that is being added to or subtracted from the variable. Then eliminate any number that is multiplying or dividing the variable. (A number that is multiplying the variable is called a *coefficient*.)

Solve:

$$
\begin{aligned}
3x - 6 &= 9 \\
\underline{+6} &\quad \underline{+6} \qquad \text{Adding 6 eliminates } -6. \\
3x &= 15 \\[4pt]
\frac{3x}{3} &= \frac{15}{3} \qquad \text{Dividing by 3 eliminates the 3 that is} \\
&\qquad\qquad\;\; \text{multiplied by the } x. \\
x &= 5 \qquad \text{The solution to the original equation is} \\
&\qquad\qquad\;\; x = 5.
\end{aligned}
$$

GEOMETRY

Angles

An *angle* is the figure formed by two rays meeting at a point.

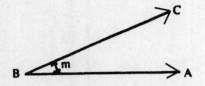

The point B is the *vertex* of the angle, and $\overrightarrow{BA}$ and $\overrightarrow{BC}$ are the *sides* of the angle. The symbol for an angle is ∠. The letter *m* stands for the measure of the angle in degrees.

Types of Angles

1. When two straight lines intersect (cut each other), four angles are formed. If these four angles are equal, each angle is a *right angle* and contains 90°. The symbol ∟ is used to indicate a right angle, as shown below.

    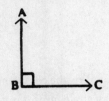

    ∠ABC is a right angle.

2. An angle that is smaller than a right angle is an *acute angle*.

3. If the two sides of an angle extend in opposite directions forming a straight line, the angle is a *straight angle* and measures 180°.

4. An angle that is bigger than a right angle (90°) and smaller than a straight angle (180°) is an *obtuse angle*.

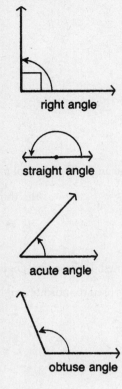

right angle

straight angle

acute angle

obtuse angle

5. *Complementary angles* are two angles whose measures sum to 90°. Each angle is the complement of the other. If an angle measures 30°, its complement measures 60°. If an angle measures x°, its complement measures $(90 - x)$°.

6. *Supplementary angles* are two angles whose measures sum to 180°. Each angle is the supplement of the other. If an angle measures 140°, its supplement measures 40°. If an angle measures x°, its supplement measures $(180 - x)$°.

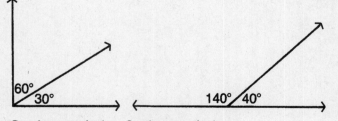

Complementary Angles   Supplementary Angles

Triangles

A *triangle* is a closed, three-sided figure. The following figures are triangles.

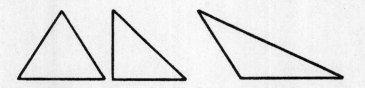

The sum of the measures of three angles of a triangle is 180°.

To find the measure of an angle of a triangle given the measure of the other two angles, add the measures and subtract their sum from 180°.

For example, if the measures of two angles of a triangle are 60° and 40°, the measure of the third angle is:

$$180° - (60° + 40°) =$$
$$180° - 100° = 80°$$

- A triangle with two congruent sides is called an *isosceles triangle*. In an isosceles triangle, the angles opposite the congruent sides are also congruent.

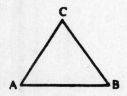

If AC = BC, then m∠A = m∠B

- A triangle with all three sides congruent is called an *equilateral triangle*. Each angle of an equilateral triangle measures 60°.

- A triangle with a right angle is called a *right triangle*. In a right triangle, the two acute angles are complementary.

In a right triangle, the side opposite *the right angle* is called the *hypotenuse* and is the longest side. The other two sides are called *legs*.

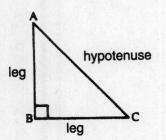

In right triangle ABC, $\overline{AC}$ is the hypotenuse. $\overline{AB}$ and $\overline{BC}$ are the legs.

The *Pythagorean theorem* states that in a right triangle, the square of the hypotenuse equals the sum of the squares of the legs.

In right triangle ABC: $(AC)^2 = (AB)^2 + (BC)^2$

Circles

A *circle* is a closed plane curve, all points of which are equidistant from a point within called the center.

A complete circle contains 360°.

A *radius* of a circle is a line segment connecting the center with any point on the circle.

A *diameter* of a circle is a line segment connecting any two points on the circle and passing through the center of the circle. The diameter of any circle is twice the radius of that circle.

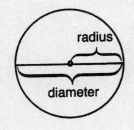

Perimeter

The *perimeter* of a two-dimensional figure is the distance around the figure. The perimeter of a rectangle equals twice the sum of the length and the width.

$$P = 2(l + w)$$
$$P = 2(8 + 4) = 2(12)$$
$$P = 24$$

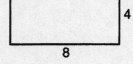

The perimeter of a triangle is the sum of the three sides.

$$P = 7 + 6 + 5 = 18$$

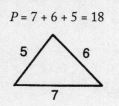

The perimeter of a circle is called the *circumference*. The circumference of a circle is equal to the product of the diameter multiplied by π. The formula is:

$$C = \pi d$$

Pi (π) is a mathematical value equal to approximately 3.14 or $\frac{22}{7}$.

$$C = \pi d$$
$$C = \pi(3) = 3\pi$$

Area

In a two-dimensional figure, the total space within the figure is called the *area*.

Area is expressed in square denominations, such as square inches, square centimeters, or square miles.

The area of a rectangle equals the product of the length (or base) multiplied by the width (or height).

$$A = lw$$
$$A = 9 \text{ ft.} \times 3 \text{ ft.}$$
$$A = 27 \text{ sq. ft.}$$

The area of a triangle is equal to one half the product of the base and the height. The height (or altitude) of a triangle is a line drawn from a vertical perpendicular to the opposite side, called the base.

$$A = \frac{1}{2}bh$$
$$A = \frac{1}{2}(9 \text{ in.})(5 \text{ in.}) = \frac{45}{2}$$
$$A = 22\frac{1}{2} \text{ sq. in.}$$

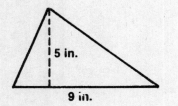

The area of a circle is equal to the radius squared multiplied by π.

$$A = \pi r^2$$
$$A = \pi \left(4 \ cm.\right)^2$$
$$A = 16\pi \ sq. \ cm.$$

For some ASVAB questions, you may leave the area in terms of pi.

PRACTICE QUESTIONS

Sample questions illustrating some of the types of questions found in the Mathematics Knowledge subtest follow. Explanatory answers are given at the end of this section and show how the correct answers are obtained.

1. The sum of $2\frac{5}{8}$, $3\frac{3}{16}$, $1\frac{1}{2}$, and $4\frac{1}{4}$ is

   A. $9\frac{13}{16}$

   B. $10\frac{7}{16}$

   C. $11\frac{9}{16}$

   D. $13\frac{3}{16}$

2. Which fraction is equal to 0.20?

   A. $\frac{1}{5}$

   B. $\frac{2}{7}$

   C. $\frac{3}{16}$

   D. $\frac{1}{50}$

3. Which of the following fractions is the LEAST?

   A. $\frac{3}{4}$

   B. $\frac{5}{6}$

   C. $\frac{7}{8}$

   D. $\frac{19}{24}$

4. The product of $11\frac{2}{13}$ times $13\frac{7}{9}$ is most nearly

   A. 152.58

   B. 152.68

   C. 153.58

   D. 153.68

5. The sum of $\sqrt{81}$ and $\sqrt{25}$ is

   A. 106

   B. 86

   C. 24

   D. 14

6. Find the value of $\left(3\sqrt{2}\right)^2$

   A. $9\sqrt{2}$

   B. 18

   C. 24

   D. 36

7. $\sqrt[3]{216}$ is equal to

   A. 6

   B. 12

   C. 36

   D. 72

8. The fourth root of 81 is

   A. 324

   B. 27

   C. 9

   D. 3

9. The numerical value of 5! is
   A. 110
   B. 115
   C. 120
   D. 125

10. The numerical value of $\frac{4!}{3!}$ is
    A. 0.75
    B. 1.25
    C. 1.33
    D. 4

11. Which one of the following is a prime number?
    A. 9
    B. 11
    C. 15
    D. 21

12. The reciprocal of 4 is
    A. 0.25
    B. 0.40
    C. 1.25
    D. 1.40

13. 1,000 is equivalent to
    A. 10^2
    B. 10^3
    C. 10^4
    D. 10^5

14. $10^3 \times 10^4 =$
    A. 10^7
    B. 10^{12}
    C. 100^7
    D. 100^{12}

15. When +5 is added to –7, the sum is
    A. +2
    B. –2
    C. +12
    D. –12

16. Find the product of (–5)(–4)(–3).
    A. +12
    B. –12
    C. +60
    D. –60

17. Solve the following: $\frac{5}{9}(41 + 40) - 40 =$
    A. 55
    B. 5
    C. 22.30
    D. 73.80

18. If you subtract –1 from +1, the result will be
    A. –2
    B. –1
    C. +1
    D. +2

19. If $a + 6 = 7$, then a is equal to
    A. 0
    B. $\frac{7}{6}$
    C. +1
    D. –1

20. If $4y = 12$, then $y =$
    A. $\frac{1}{4}$
    B. $\frac{1}{3}$
    C. 3
    D. 8

21. If 50% of $x = 66$, then $x =$
    A. 132
    B. 99
    C. 66
    D. 33

22. $8 \times 8 = 4x$. Find x.
- **A.** 1
- **B.** 2
- **C.** 3
- **D.** 4

23. If $2n - 3 = 32$, then n equals
- **A.** 5
- **B.** 6
- **C.** 7
- **D.** 8

24. What percent of a is b?

- **A.** $\dfrac{b}{a}$

- **B.** $\dfrac{a}{b}$

- **C.** $\dfrac{100b}{a}$

- **D.** $\dfrac{100a}{b}$

25. Using the formula $A = P(1 + rt)$, find A when $P = 500$, $r = .03$, and $t = 15$.
- **A.** 625
- **B.** 725
- **C.** 795
- **D.** 800

26. If $a = 5b$, then $\dfrac{3}{5}a =$

- **A.** $\dfrac{5}{3}b$

- **B.** $\dfrac{3}{5}b$

- **C.** $3b$

- **D.** $\dfrac{b}{3}$

27. If you multiply $x + 3$ by $2x + 5$, what will be the coefficient of x?
- **A.** 11
- **B.** 10
- **C.** 9
- **D.** 6

28. $\dfrac{x-2}{x^2 - 6x + 8}$ can be simplified to

- **A.** $\dfrac{1}{x-4}$

- **B.** $\dfrac{1}{x-2}$

- **C.** $\dfrac{1}{x+4}$

- **D.** $\dfrac{1}{x+2}$

29. If $2x = 3y$ and $5x + y = 34$, $y =$
- **A.** 4
- **B.** 5
- **C.** 6
- **D.** 7

30. Solve for x: $x + y = a$
$$x - y = b$$

- **A.** $a + b$

- **B.** $a - b$

- **C.** $\dfrac{1}{2}(a+b)$

- **D.** $\dfrac{1}{2}(a-b)$

31. Solve for x: $\dfrac{x+1}{8} = \dfrac{28}{32}$

- **A.** 5
- **B.** 6
- **C.** 7
- **D.** 8

32. If $\dfrac{a}{b} \times \dfrac{b}{c} \times \dfrac{c}{d} \times \dfrac{d}{e} \times x = 1$, then x must be equal to

A. $\dfrac{a}{e}$

B. $\dfrac{e}{a}$

C. $\dfrac{1}{a}$

D. $\dfrac{1}{e}$

33. If $\dfrac{a}{b} = \dfrac{3}{4}$, then $12a =$

A. $3b$

B. $6b$

C. $9b$

D. $12b$

34. The average of two numbers is A. If one of the numbers is x, the other number is

A. $\dfrac{A}{2} - x$

B. $\dfrac{A + x}{2}$

C. $A - x$

D. $2A - x$

35. Two angles that are both congruent and supplementary are

A. acute angles.

B. obtuse angles.

C. right angles.

D. straight angles.

36. In one hour, the minute hand of a clock rotates through an angle of

A. 45°

B. 90°

C. 180°

D. 360°

37. At 6:00 a.m., the angle between the hands of the clock is

A. 90°

B. 120°

C. 180°

D. 360°

38. In the triangle given below, if m∠B = 90°,

A. $\overline{AB}$ is longer than $\overline{AC}$.

B. m∠ABC is less than m∠ACB.

C. m∠ABC = m∠ACB.

D. m∠ABC is greater than m∠ACB.

39. A circle is inscribed in a square whose side is 6. What is the circumference of the circle in terms of π?

A. 3π

B. 6π

C. 9π

D. 12π

40. The hypotenuse of a right triangle whose legs are 5 inches and 12 inches is

A. 7 inches.

B. 13 inches.

C. 14 inches.

D. 17 inches.

41. Approximately how many meters will a point on the rim of a wheel travel if the wheel makes 50 rotations and its radius is 1 meter?

A. 314

B. 298

C. 283

D. 157

42. The area of a square is 36 square inches. If the side of this square is doubled, the area of the new square will be

A. 72 square inches.

B. 144 square inches.

C. 216 square inches.

D. 244 square inches.

43. The circumference of a circle that has a radius of 70 feet is most nearly

A. 440 feet.

B. 660 feet.

C. 690 feet.

D. 15,300 feet.

44. The distance between two points on a graph whose rectangular coordinates are (2, 4) and (5, 8) is most nearly

A. 5.0

B. 5.5

C. 6.0

D. 6.5

45. In triangle ABC, AB = BC and $\overline{AC}$ is extended to D. If angle BCD measures 110°, find the number of degrees in angle B.

A. 20°

B. 40°

C. 60°

D. 80°

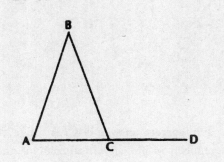

ANSWER KEY AND EXPLANATIONS

1. C	10. D	19. C	28. A	37. C
2. A	11. B	20. C	29. A	38. D
3. A	12. A	21. A	30. C	39. B
4. D	13. B	22. C	31. B	40. B
5. D	14. A	23. D	32. B	41. A
6. B	15. B	24. C	33. C	42. B
7. A	16. D	25. B	34. D	43. A
8. D	17. B	26. C	35. C	44. A
9. C	18. D	27. A	36. D	45. B

1. **The correct answer is C.** Arrange the numbers in proper vertical columns, then rename fractions as equivalent fractions having the same common denominator and, finally, add.

   The sum of $10\frac{25}{16}$ is actually $11\frac{9}{16}$.

2. **The correct answer is A.** $0.2 = \frac{2}{10} = \frac{1}{5}$

3. **The correct answer is A.** Rename all fractions as 24ths and then compare numerators.

   $A = \frac{18}{24}$, $B = \frac{20}{24}$, $C = \frac{21}{24}$, $D = \frac{19}{24}$

4. **The correct answer is D.** Rename the mixed numbers as improper fractions and then multiply:

   $\frac{145}{13} \times \frac{124}{9} = \frac{17980}{117} = 153.68$

5. **The correct answer is D.**
   $\sqrt{81} = 9$; $\sqrt{25} = 5$; $9 + 5 = 14$

6. **The correct answer is B.**
   $\left(3\sqrt{2}\right)^2 = 3\sqrt{2} \times 3\sqrt{2} = 9 \times 2 = 18$

7. **The correct answer is A.** $6 \times 6 \times 6 = 216$

8. **The correct answer is D.** $3 \times 3 \times 3 \times 3 = 81$

9. **The correct answer is C.** 5 factorial is $5 \times 4 \times 3 \times 2 \times 1 = 120$

10. **The correct answer is D.** The factorial of a natural number is the product of that number and all the natural numbers less than it. $4! = 4 \times 3 \times 2 \times 1 = 24$.

    $3! = 3 \times 2 \times 1 = 6$

    $\frac{4!}{3!} = \frac{24}{6} = 4$

11. **The correct answer is B.** Of the numbers given, only 11 has no other factor except 1 and itself.
    $3 \times 3 = 9$; $3 \times 5 = 15$; $7 \times 3 = 21$.

12. **The correct answer is A.** If the product of two numbers is 1, either number is called the reciprocal or multiplicative inverse of the other. For example, since $4 \times \frac{1}{4} = 1$, 4 is the reciprocal of $\frac{1}{4}$ and $\frac{1}{4}$ is the reciprocal of 4. $\frac{1}{4}$ is equivalent to 0.25.

13. **The correct answer is B.** $10 \times 10 \times 10 = 1,000$

14. **The correct answer is A.** $10^3 = 1,000$; $10^4 = 10,000$; $1,000 \times 10,000 = 10,000,000$ or 10^7. To multiply numbers of the same base, add the exponents. $10^3 \times 10^4 = 10^{(3+4)} = 10^7$.

15. **The correct answer is B.** To add numbers with different signs, subtract the magnitude of the numbers and use the sign of the number with the greater magnitude.

16. **The correct answer is D.** If there is an odd number of negative factors when multiplying, the product is negative. $(-5)(-4)(-3) = -60$.

17. **The correct answer is B.**

$$\left(\frac{5}{9} \times 81\right) - 40 = 45 - 40 = 5$$

18. **The correct answer is D.** Subtracting -1 from $+1$, change -1 to $+1$ and add to $+1 = +2$.

19. **The correct answer is C.** $a = 7 - 6 = +1$

20. **The correct answer is C.** $y = \frac{12}{4} = 3$

21. **The correct answer is A.**

$$\frac{1}{2} \text{ of } x = 66; \ x = 66 \times 2 = 132$$

22. **The correct answer is C.** $8 \times 8 = 64$; $4 \times 4 \times 4 = 64$; $x = 3$

23. **The correct answer is D.** $2^5 = 32$; $n - 3 = 5$; $n = 8$

24. **The correct answer is C.** $\dfrac{b}{a} \times 100 = \dfrac{100b}{a}$

25. **The correct answer is B.** $A = 500(1 + .03 \times 15) = 500(1 + .45) = 500(1.45) = 725$

26. **The correct answer is C.** $\dfrac{3}{5} \times 5b = 3b$

27. **The correct answer is A.**

$$
\begin{array}{r}
x + 3 \\
\underline{2x + 5} \\
2x^2 + 6x \\
\underline{+\,5x + 15} \\
2x^2 + 11x + 15
\end{array}
$$

28. **The correct answer is A.** The factors of $x^2 - 6x + 8$ are $(x-4)$ and $(x-2)$.

Therefore,

$$\frac{x-2}{x^2-6x+8} = \frac{x-2}{(x-4)(x-2)} = \frac{1}{x-4} \ .$$

29. **The correct answer is A.** Solve for x:

$2x = 3y$.

$$x = \frac{3y}{2}$$

Substitute in the second equation and solve

for y: $5\left(\dfrac{3y}{2}\right) + y = 34$

$$\frac{15y}{2} + y = 34$$

$$15y + 2y = 68$$

$$17y = 68$$

$$y = 4$$

30. **The correct answer is C.** Add the two equations to eliminate y:

$$x + y = a$$
$$\underline{x - y = b}$$
$$2x = a + b$$

Solve for x:

$$x = \frac{a+b}{2}$$

31. **The correct answer is B.** Solve for x:

$$\frac{x+1}{8} = \frac{28}{32}$$

$$(x+1)32 = 8 \times 28$$

$$32x + 32 = 224$$

$$32x = 192$$

$$x = \frac{192}{32} = 6$$

32. **The correct answer is B.** Divide common factors, and then solve.

$$\frac{a}{\cancel{b}} \times \frac{\cancel{b}}{\cancel{c}} \times \frac{\cancel{c}}{\cancel{d}} \times \frac{\cancel{d}}{e} \times x = 1$$

$$\frac{a}{e} \times x = 1$$

$$\frac{ax}{e} = 1$$

$$ax = e$$

$$x = \frac{e}{a}$$

33. **The correct answer is C.** Solve for a:

$$\frac{a}{b} = \frac{3}{4}$$

$$4a = 3b$$

$$a = \frac{3b}{4}$$

$$12a = \cancel{12}^{\,3}\left(\frac{3b}{\cancel{4}}\right)$$

$$12a = 9b$$

34. **The correct answer is D.** Let $x =$ one of the numbers and $y =$ the other number. $\dfrac{x+y}{2} = A; x+y = 2A; y = 2A - x$.

35. **The correct answer is C.** If the angles are congruent and supplementary, they must be of the same measure and add up to 180°. Each measures 90° or a right angle.

36. **The correct answer is D.** In 1 hour, the minute hand rotates a full circle of 360°.

37. **The correct answer is C.** At 6 a.m., one hand is at 6 and the other is at 12, forming a straight angle of 180°.

38. The correct answer is D. In this right triangle, angle ABC is a right angle. Each of the measures of the other angles in the triangle must be less than 90°. $\overline{AC}$, the hypotenuse, is longer than either leg of the triangle.

39. The correct answer is B. Side = 6; therefore, diameter = 6. Circumference = π × diameter = 6π.

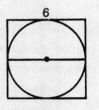

40. The correct answer is B. The Pythagorean theorem states that for any right triangle, the sum of the square of the legs is equal to the square of the length of the hypotenuse.
$5^2 + 12^2 = h^2$, $25 + 144 = h^2$, $h^2 = 169$. $\sqrt{169} = 13$. $h = 13$. The correct answer is 13 inches.

41. The correct answer is A. If the radius of the wheel is 1 meter, its diameter is 2 meters. The circumference is π × diameter = 2 × 3.14. The distance traveled is 50 × 2 × 3.14 = 100 × 3.14 = 314.

42. The correct answer is B. If the area of a square = 36 square inches, the side of the square = 6 inches. If doubled to 12 inches, the area of the new square will be 12 inches by 12 inches = 144 square inches.

43. The correct answer is A. If the radius is 70 feet, the diameter is 140 feet. Circumference = π × diameter = $140 \times \dfrac{22}{7} = 440$ feet.

44. The correct answer is A. As shown in the following graph, we have a right triangle with one leg of 3 and the other leg of 4. Using the Pythagorean theorem, the hypotenuse, or the distance between the two points, is obtained as follows: $h^2 = 3^2 + 4^2$; $h^2 = 9 + 16$; $h^2 = 25$; $h = \sqrt{25}$; $h = 5$.

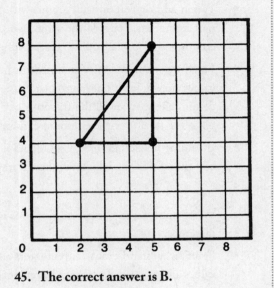

45. The correct answer is B.

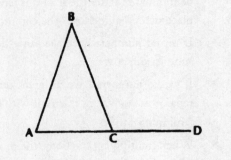

ACD is a straight line. Therefore, if m∠BCD = 110°, m∠BCA = 70°. AB = BC. Therefore, triangle ABC is an isosceles triangle and m∠BAC = m∠BCA = 70°. The sum of the measures of the angles of a triangle = 180°. Therefore, m∠ABC = 180° − (70° + 70°) = 180° − 140° = 40°.

SUMMING IT UP

- The Mathematics Knowledge subtest tests your knowledge of math principles, concepts, and procedures. This chapter can also be considered a continuation of Arithmetic Reasoning presented previously. Reread that section as background material for Mathematics Knowledge.

Addition

- When **adding fractions**, fractions with the same denominator are added directly, as each part represents a part of the same value. Add the numerators and place the sum over the common denominator. If necessary, simplify to the simplest form.

- Fractions with different denominators may not be added directly because parts of different values are involved. They must be renamed as equivalent fractions having the same common denominator. After all the fractions have the same denominator, add the numerators and place the total over the common denominator.

- In adding mixed numbers, first add all the whole numbers, then add all fractions, and then add the sum of the whole numbers to the sum of the fractions.

Subtraction

- When **subtracting fractions**, fractions with the same denominator may be subtracted directly.

- Fractions with different denominators are not subtracted directly because parts of different values are involved. They must be renamed as equivalent fractions having the same common denominator. After the fractions have the same denominator, subtract the numerators and place the remainder over the common denominator.

- If mixed numbers have the same denominator, rename them as improper fractions and subtract directly.

- If mixed numbers have different denominators, first rename as improper fractions, then rename as equivalent fractions with the same common denominator and subtract directly.
  Multiplication

- When multiplying fractions, the product of the numerators divided by the product of the denominators gives the final answer or product. Dividing a number in the numerator by the same number in the denominator simplifies the computation.

- There are several methods that may be used in multiplying mixed numbers:

  o When the numbers are small-valued, rename the mixed numbers as improper fractions and then multiply in the usual manner.

  o When the numbers are great and the fractional parts have exact decimal equivalents, rename the fractional parts as decimals and then multiply.

  o When the numbers are not small-valued and the fractional parts have no exact decimal equivalents, use the partial product method.

Division

- When **dividing fractions**, multiply by the reciprocal of the divisor.

- There are several methods that are used to divide mixed numbers:

- When the numbers are small-valued, rename the mixed numbers as improper fractions and then divide in the usual manner.

- When the mixed numbers are great and the fractional parts do not have exact decimal equivalents:

    1. Multiply both the dividend and the divisor by the denominator of the fraction if only one fraction is involved.

    2. Multiply both the dividend and the divisor by the least common denominator if two fractions are involved.

- The *square root* of a number is a number that, when raised to the second power, produces the given number.

- **Algebra** is the branch of mathematics that focuses on addition, subtraction, multiplication, and division operations applied to variables, or unknowns, instead of specific numbers.

Electronics Information

Chapter 8

OVERVIEW

- **Electricity**
- **Basic Electronic Theory**
- **Practice Questions**
- **Answer Key and Explanations**
- **Summing It Up**

ELECTRICITY

Electricity is a form of energy resulting from the existence of charged particles. It is an invisible force that we know about only through the effects it produces. The exact nature of electricity is not known, but the laws governing electrical phenomena are clearly understood and defined. The same is true for the laws of gravitation that are known, while the nature of gravity cannot be defined.

To understand basic electronic theory, it is important to be familiar with the basics of electricity.

The Movement of Electricity

In many ways electricity in motion is like flowing water, and electrical phenomena can be more easily understood if this analogy is borne in mind. In dealing with the flow of electricity, which is similar to the flow of water, we consider three factors:

1. **Electrical Current**—Flow of electricity, usually along a conductor
2. **Electrical Pressure**—Causes the current to flow
3. **Electrical Resistance**—Regulates the flow of the current

Electrical Current

To know about the flow of water in a pipe, one would determine how many gallons of water flow through the pipe in a second. In exactly the same way, an electrician determines the number of *coulombs* of electricity that flow through a wire in a second. Just as the gallon is a measure of the quantity of water, the coulomb is a measure of the quantity of electricity. There is an abbreviated method of describing the flow of electrical current. An electrician speaks of the *ampere*, which means one coulomb per second and is thus saved the trouble of saying "per second" every time he wants to describe the current flow. Very small currents drawn by electronic devices are frequently measured in terms of milliamperes (ma), or thousandth's of an ampere.

Electrical Pressure

Water pressure is measured in pounds per square inch. There is also a measure of electrical pressure. This electrical pressure has a definite effect on the number of amperes flowing along a wire. The electrical unit of pressure is the *volt*. A volt means the same thing in speaking of a current of electricity that a pound-per-square-inch pressure does in speaking of a current of water. Just as a higher pressure is required to force the same current of water through a small pipe than through a large pipe, so a higher electrical pressure is required to force the same current of electricity through a small wire than through a large wire. The voltage (pressure) between two points in an electric circuit is sometimes spoken of as the difference in potential, the drop in potential, or merely the "drop" between those two points.

The main distinction between amperes and volts is that the amperes represent the amount of the current flowing through a circuit; the volts represent the pressure causing it to flow.

Electrical Resistance

The electrical unit of resistance is the ohm. A wire has one ohm resistance when a pressure of one volt forces a current of one ampere through it. Ohms are often represented by the symbol Ω.

Ohm's Law

In any circuit through which a current is flowing, the three following factors are present:

1. The pressure or potential difference or electromotive force (emf), expressed in volts, causing the current to flow
2. The opposition or resistance of the circuit, expressed in ohms, which must be overcome
3. The current strength, expressed in amperes, which is maintained in the circuit as a result of the pressure overcoming the resistance

A definite and exact relation exists between the three factors: the pressure, current strength, and resistance in any circuit, whereby the value of any one factor may always be calculated when the values of the other two factors are known. This relation is known as Ohm's Law. It may be summarized as follows:

The current in any electric circuit is equal to the voltage applied to the circuit, divided by the resistance of the circuit.

Let V = voltage applied to the circuit, expressed in volts

R = resistance of the circuit, expressed in ohms

I = current strength in amperes, to be maintained through the circuit

Then, by the above statement of Ohm's Law,

$$\text{Current} = \frac{\text{Voltage}}{\text{Resistance}} \text{ or Amperes} = \frac{\text{Volts}}{\text{Ohms}} \text{ or } I = \frac{V}{R}$$

An easier way to solve for unknowns using Ohm's Law is to use the "Ohm's Law Triangle" (see Figure 1). Simply cover the unknown value and perform the calculation shown. For instance, to solve for voltage, cover the "V," which leaves $I \times R$ ($V = I \times R$). To solve for resistance, cover the "R," which leaves $\frac{V}{I}\left(R = \frac{V}{I}\right)$. To solve for current, cover the "I," which leaves $\frac{V}{R}\left(I = \frac{V}{R}\right)$.

Figure 1. Ohm's Law Triangle.

$$V = IR$$
$$R = \frac{V}{I}$$

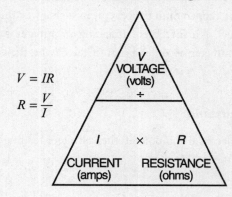

Electrical Power

The product of the voltage across a device and the current flowing through it is defined as the power consumed by the device. The power consumed by a device that draws one ampere when one volt is applied to it is one watt.

$$P = VI$$

where P = power in watts, V = volts, and I = amperes.

The Circuit

Electricity is not as simple as water; it cannot be piped from one point to another. To flow, electricity must be sent along a closed circuit. Except through a generator or a battery cell, electricity always flows from a higher to a lower level. The higher level or positive is marked +, and the lower level or negative is marked − to indicate the direction in which the current is flowing. A given point is + to all points below its level and − to all points above its level.

If any of the wires leading from the + to the − terminal is broken, the current cannot flow, for the circuit has been interrupted and is incomplete.

Measurements

There are different ways to determine measurements for current, pressure, and electrical resistance.

Measuring Electrical Current

To find out how much current is flowing through an electric circuit, insert a current meter into the circuit so that all the current that you wish to measure flows through the meter. A current meter, known as an *ammeter*, measures an electric current and is read in amperes. The ammeter must be of very low resistance so as not to hinder the current and must be handled carefully since it is very delicate.

Measuring Electrical Pressure

When it is necessary to measure the pressure causing an electric current to flow through a circuit, the terminals of a *voltmeter* are tapped onto that circuit in such a way that the voltmeter is made to register not current but pressure. The method of attaching a voltmeter is different from that used in attaching an ammeter. The ammeter becomes a part of the circuit; the voltmeter does not become a part of the circuit.

Measuring Electrical Resistance

To find the resistance of an electrical component, the voltmeter reading is divided by the ammeter reading, or an ohmmeter or "megger" is used.

Regulating and Controlling Electrical Current

By inserting or removing resistance into or from a circuit, you regulate and control the current required for various electrical purposes. An adjustable resistance, or any apparatus for changing the resistance without opening the circuit, is called a *rheostat*. The function of a rheostat is to absorb electrical energy. This energy, which appears as heat, is wasted instead of performing any useful work.

The Effects of a Current

A current of electricity is believed to be a transfer of electrons through a circuit, and, because these carriers are so minute, a direct measurement of them is impractical. Consequently, the effects it produces, all of which are commercially used, measure an electric current. The effects manifested by a current of electricity are:

Heating Effect

Every wire that conducts a current of electricity becomes heated to some extent as a result of the current because even the best conductors offer some opposition (resistance) to the flow of the current. It is in overcoming this resistance that the heat is developed. If the wire is large in a cross-sectional area and the current is small, the heat developed will be so small in amount as not to be recognized by the touch. Nevertheless, the wire releases some heat energy. On the other hand, with a small wire and a large current, it becomes quite hot.

Magnetic Effect

A wire carrying a current of electricity deflects a magnetic needle. When the wire is insulated and coiled around an iron core, the current magnetizes the core.

Chemical Effect

Electrical current is capable of decomposing certain chemical compounds when it is passed through them, breaking up the compounds into their constituent parts. In the production of electrical energy by a simple primary cell, electrolytic decomposition occurs inside the cell when the current is flowing. Electroplating, or the art of depositing a coating of metal on any object, is based on the principles of electrolytic decomposition.

Physiological Effect

A current of electricity passed through the body produces muscular contractions that result from the physiological effects of an electrical current. Electrotherapeutics deals with the study of this effect.

The Dynamo and Electromagnetic Induction

The electrical generator and the electric motor are intimately related. The term *dynamo* is applied to machines that convert either mechanical energy into electrical energy or electrical energy into mechanical energy by using the principles of electromagnetic induction. A dynamo is called a generator when mechanical energy supplied in the form of rotation is converted into electrical energy. When the energy conversion occurs in the reverse order, the dynamo is called a motor. Thus, a dynamo is a reversible machine capable of operation as a generator or motor as desired.

The generator consists fundamentally of numerous loops of insulated wires revolving in a strong magnetic field in such a way that these wires cut across the lines of magnetic force. This cutting of the lines of force sets up an electromotive force along the wires.

Wherever there is an electric current present, there is also present a magnetic field. It is not true that wherever a magnetic field exists, there also exists an electric current, in the ordinary sense; but you can say that wherever a conductor moves in a magnetic field in such a way as to cut lines of force, an electromotive force is set up. It is on this principle that the electric generator works.

Alternating Current (AC) and Direct Current (DC)

A direct or continuous current always flows in the same direction. In many cases it has a constant strength for definite periods of time. A pulsating current has a uniform direction, but the current strength varies. Most direct current generators furnish pulsating current; but since the pulsations are very small, the current is practically constant.

An alternating current of electricity is one that changes its direction of flow at regular intervals of time. These intervals are usually much shorter than one second. During an interval, the current strength is capable of varying in any way. In practice, the strength rises and then falls smoothly. Most electricity today comes in the form of alternating current since high voltage can more easily be obtained with alternating current than with direct current. High voltages are much more cheaply transmitted over power lines than are low voltages.

The alternating current (AC) supplied to our homes ordinarily changes its direction of flow 60 times per second. The term used to describe the frequency with which a current changes its direction of flow per second is the Hertz (Hz). House current, therefore, has a frequency of 60 Hz.

BASIC ELECTRONIC THEORY

Electronic devices and systems frequently operate at very high frequencies. These high frequencies are measured in terms of kilohertz (KHz), which represents a thousand Hz, or in megahertz (MHz), which represents a million Hz.

Some representative frequencies used by electronic systems are:

- AM radio broadcasts: 535 KHz to 1,605 KHz
- FM radio broadcasts: 88 MHz to 108 MHz
- TV Channel 2: 54 MHz
- Radar: 400 MHz to 100,000 MHz

Visible light is an ultrahigh frequency form of radiation that occurs at frequencies in the order of a billion MHz.

Impedance

The flow of AC is impeded not only by a circuit's resistance but also by its reactance. Reactance results from the presence of capacitance and inductance. *Capacitive* reactance and *inductive* reactance are both measured in ohms (Ω). The total of the resistances and reactances in an AC circuit is called its *impedance*.

Some kinds of electrical circuits, especially those used in electronics, require particular values of capacitive or inductive reactance to function properly. Electronic components such as capacitors, typically rated in microfarads (MFD), and inductors, typically rated in millihenries (MH), are introduced into circuits as required to provide capacitive and inductive reactances.

Rectification

Electronic circuits are frequently used to change alternating current to direct current. These circuits, called rectifiers, usually contain solid-state semiconductor diodes that conduct electricity in only one direction. The current output of the diodes contains ripples that are smoothed into a steady DC output by means of filters consisting of combinations of inductors and capacitors.

Transistors

The transistor is another solid-state device frequently found in electronic circuits. It consists of two types of semiconductor material: N-type and P-type. An NPN transistor consists of P-type material sandwiched between two sections of N-type material. Another version is called a PNP transistor and consists of N-type material sandwiched between two sections of P-type material. Each transistor has an emitter, a collector, and a base section. The common symbolic representations of transistors are shown in Figure 2.

Figure 2. Transistors.

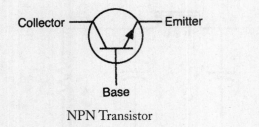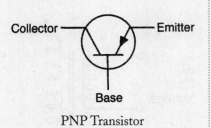

NPN Transistor   PNP Transistor

Electronic Circuits

Some of the other common symbols used to represent components of electronic circuits are shown in Figure 3.

Figure 3. Symbols for electronic circuit components.

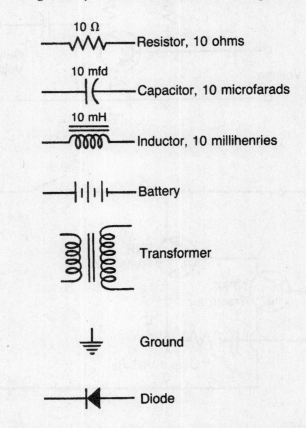

These elements are combined to create typical electronics circuits (see Figure 4 and Figure 5).

Figure 4. Half-wave filtered rectifier.

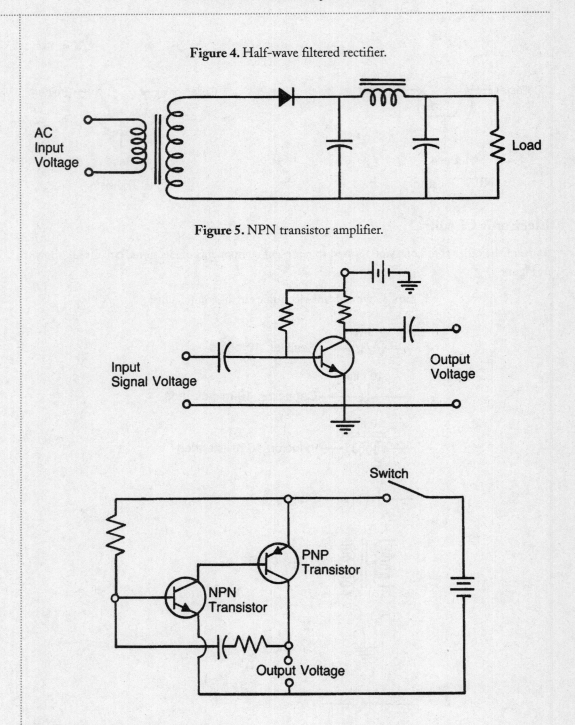

Figure 5. NPN transistor amplifier.

Communications Electronics

Combinations of basic electronic circuits make up complex communications systems. Block diagrams, such as the one that follows, can help you to understand these systems by defining basic components within an overall complex system. Radio transmitters send out high-frequency electromagnetic radiation whose frequency or maximum voltage swing (amplitude) is varied or modulated, in accordance with the frequency of the sound waves required for transmission. We therefore have amplitude modulated (AM) and frequency modulated (FM) radio stations and receivers. The basic block diagram of an AM radio receiver of the modern superheterodyne type is shown in Figure 6.

Figure 6. Superheterodyne AM receiver.

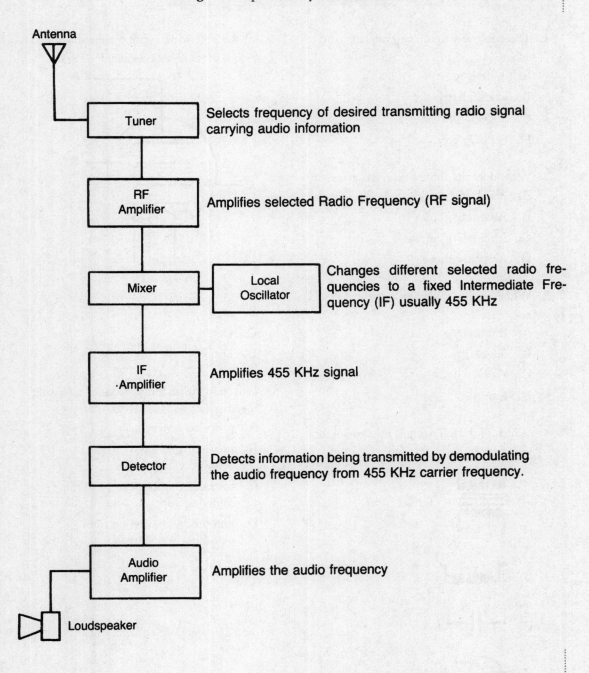

PRACTICE QUESTIONS

1. The safest way to run an extension cord to a lamp is
   A. under a rug.
   B. along a baseboard.
   C. under a sofa.
   D. behind a sofa.

2. What does the abbreviation AC stand for?
   A. Additional charge
   B. Alternating coil
   C. Alternating current
   D. Ampere current

3. Which of the following has the LEAST resistance?
   A. Rubber
   B. Silver
   C. Wood
   D. Iron

4. Which of the following is the symbol for a transformer?

   A.

   B.

   C. ─┤├─

   D. ─⊗─

5. In the schematic vacuum tube illustrated below, the cathode is element

   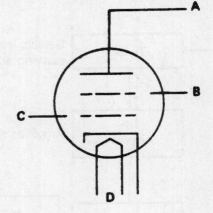

   A. A
   B. B
   C. C
   D. D

6. Flux is used in the process of soldering together two conductors to
   A. provide a luster finish.
   B. prevent oxidation when the connection is heated.
   C. maintain the temperature of the soldering iron.
   D. prevent the connection from becoming overheated.

ANSWER KEY AND EXPLANATIONS

1. B **2.** C	**3.** B	**4.** A	**5.** D	**6.** B

1. **The correct answer is B.** The safest place to run an extension cord to protect against fire hazard is along the baseboard. Running an extension cord near furniture or under a rug increases the potential of a fire in case of an electrical short.

2. **The correct answer is C.** AC, Alternating Current (as opposed to DC, Direct Current), is the type of current that is used to operate household appliances.

3. **The correct answer is B.** Since silver is the best conductor of electricity, it also has the least resistance.

4. **The correct answer is A.** Diagram A is the symbol for a transformer.

5. **The correct answer is D.** Element D represents the cathode in the illustration of the vacuum tube.

6. **The correct answer is B.** The process of soldering causes oxidation on the connections being heated. Flux is added to the process to prevent oxidation from occurring.

SUMMING IT UP

- **Electricity** is a form of energy resulting from the existence of charged particles. It is an invisible force that we know about only through the effects it produces. The exact nature of electricity is not known, but the laws governing electrical phenomena are clearly understood and defined.

- Consider three factors when dealing with the flow of electricity:

  1. **Electrical Current**—Flow of electricity, usually along a conductor
  2. **Electrical Pressure**—Causes the current to flow
  3. **Electrical Resistance**—Regulates the flow of the current

- **Ohm's Law**: In any circuit through which a current is flowing, the three following factors are present:

  1. The pressure or potential difference or electromotive force (emf), expressed in volts, causing the current to flow
  2. The opposition or resistance of the circuit, expressed in ohms, which must be overcome
  3. The current strength, expressed in amperes, which is maintained in the circuit as a result of the pressure overcoming the resistance

- To **flow**, electricity must be sent along a closed circuit. Electricity always flows from a higher to a lower level (except through a generator or a battery cell). The higher level, or positive, is marked +, and the lower level, or negative, is marked – to indicate the direction that the current is flowing.

- The effects manifested by a current of electricity are the **heating** effect, **magnetic** effect, **chemical** effect, and **physiological** effect.

- The term *dynamo* is applied to machines that convert either mechanical energy into electrical energy or electrical energy into mechanical energy by using the principles of electromagnetic induction.

- A **direct** or **continuous** current always flows in the same direction. An **alternating** current changes its direction of flow at regular intervals of time.

- Electronic devices and systems frequently operate at very high frequencies. These high frequenciesare measured in terms of **kilohertz** (KHz), which represent a thousand hertz (Hz), or in **megahertz** (MHz), which represent a million Hz.

Auto & Shop Information

Chapter 9

OVERVIEW

- **Basic Auto Information***
- **Basic Shop Information†**
- **Practice Questions**
- **Answer Key and Explanations**
- **Summing It Up**

BASIC AUTO INFORMATION*

At the very least, an automobile needs an engine and some means of connecting the engine to the wheels to make it go. The engine turns the shaft, which runs back toward the rear wheels. It has a gear on the end, which meshes with a gear on the axle, connecting the rear wheels. As the first shaft turns, it rotates the axle and the wheels propel the car.

If there were no hills around and we didn't want to go very fast and didn't want to turn any corners, this arrangement might work. But in an actual automobile, there are additional parts between the engine and the wheels. The rest of this chapter will detail these additional parts, explaining what they are as well as what they do.

Engine

The power of an automobile engine comes from the burning of a mixture of gasoline and air in a small, enclosed space. When this mixture burns, it expands greatly and pushes out in all directions. It happens so quickly that we sometimes call it an explosion. This push or pressure can be used to move a part of the engine, and the movement of this part is eventually transmitted back to the wheels to drive the car.

Looking at an engine under the hood of an automobile, it seems to be a complicated sort of thing with hundreds of pieces and attachments and what-nots. But we can forget about most of these for the present and consider only the basic parts.

Cylinders and Pistons

First, we must have a cylinder. This is something like a tall metal can, or a pipe closed at one end. In fact, some of the early automobiles used cast iron pipes for cylinders.

---

* The "Basic Auto Information" section is based on *What Makes Autos Run*.

229

Inside the cylinder we have a piston. This is a plug that is close-fitting but can slide up and down easily. It is the part of the engine that is moved by the expanding gases, being driven down on each power impulse or explosion.

Connecting Rod and Crankshaft

Now, we must find some way to change that up-and-down motion to rotary motion to propel the car. For this we have a connecting rod and crankshaft. The crankshaft is a shaft with an offset portion, the crank, which moves in a circular motion as the shaft rotates. The top end of the connecting rod is fastened to the piston, so it goes up and down in a straight line. The bottom end is fastened to the crank, so that it has to go around in a circle as the piston moves up and down.

On one end of the crankshaft is a heavy wheel called the flywheel. If we turn a grindstone or emery wheel rapidly by hand and then let go, the wheel will keep on rotating. This is the same action as the flywheel. It keeps the engine turning between power impulses.

These are the basic parts of an engine, but what we have shown here would make only a single-cylinder engine. Most automobile engines today have four or more cylinders. They can be arranged in one straight row, which we call an in-line engine, or in two rows set at an angle, descriptively called a V-type engine. In either case we have only one crankshaft, but it has a number of cranks instead of only one. With a number of cylinders the flywheel does not have such a big job to do because the power impulses occur more often and thus keep the crankshaft turning.

Valves

This basic engine we have put together so far has no way of getting the fuel-air mixture into it or burned gases out of it. We need some "doors," which in this case we call valves. Two holes are cut in the top of the cylinder, one for intake and one for exhaust. Metal discs are arranged to fit tightly over the holes to close them, but when pushed down they open the holes to allow passage of the gases through them. They work very much like the familiar stopper in a washbowl but turned upside down.

The valves are controlled by rocker arms and rods, which are moved by a camshaft. This is a shaft with cams or bumps on it—one bump for each valve—which push up on the rods to open the valves. The camshaft is driven by the crankshaft, at one-half speed. The cams are accurately shaped and located, and the shaft rotates at just the proper speed, because the valves must open and close at exactly the right moment.

Carburetor

To produce power, the engine needs a supply of gasoline and air mixed in the proper proportions. The carburetor does the mixing job. Gasoline is pumped from the tank to the carburetor by the fuel pump. This operates in much the same manner as the old-fashioned water pump, each stroke pushing a little fuel on to the carburetor where it goes first to the float chamber.

Air enters the carburetor through the air cleaner, being pulled in by the pumping action of the engine pistons working in the cylinders. This air flows through a venturi (a reduced passage in the carburetor) at high speed, then past the end of a tube leading from the float chamber. This sucks out the fuel into the air stream, breaking the liquid up into a fine mist and mixing it thoroughly with the air. An atomizer, or garden sprayer, works in a similar manner. Then the fuel and air mixture goes on into the engine, the amount being controlled by a throttle valve at the base of the carburetor, which is opened or closed by movement of the accelerator pedal.

A good mixture for burning in an engine is about 15 pounds of air to 1 pound of gasoline. Air being so much lighter than gasoline, this means that for every gallon of gasoline we burn, we use enough air to fill a room 10 feet square and more than 10 feet high. We call them gasoline engines, but it is easy to see that in some ways air plays the more important part.

Spark Plug

Now we have everything we need to make an engine run except something to start the mixture burning in the cylinder. Any kind of a spark will do it. In a cigarette lighter we make a spark by friction against a special metal. In an engine we do it electrically. A spark plug is inserted in the top of each cylinder, and a spark is created by electricity jumping across the gap between the two electrodes of the plug.

Battery

A battery furnishes the electricity, but several additional pieces of equipment are necessary for a complete ignition system. The coil and the breaker cooperate to develop a very high voltage, and the distributor is responsible for getting the high-voltage electricity to the right spark plug at the right time.

All of this must occur very rapidly. In an eight-cylinder engine driving a car 55 miles per hour, the ignition system would have to furnish approximately 7,350 sparks per minute, or 123 each second. And it must do this at exactly the right time and without a miss.

The reason the valve mechanism and ignition system must perform their duties at just the right time is that an engine operates with a certain definite cycle of events—over and over again, at a high rate of speed. Now that we have all the necessary parts of an engine, we can see how it actually works.

Four-Cycle Engines

Most automobile engines are four-cycle engines. This means they operate on a four-stroke cycle, taking four strokes of the piston—down, up, down, up—for one complete cycle of events.

On the first stroke, the intake valve is open and the piston moves down, pulling in the fuel-air mixture until the cylinder is full. This is the *intake stroke*.

Then the intake valve closes and the piston starts up on the *compression stroke*. It squeezes the mixture into a small space at the top of the cylinder, which increases the pressure in the cylinder to almost 200 pounds per square inch.

Between the second and third strokes, ignition or firing occurs. The spark, jumping the gap of the spark plug, ignites the mixture of fuel and air squeezed at the top of the cylinder. In burning, the mixture, of course, gets very hot and tries to expand in all directions. The pressure rises to about 600 or 700 pounds per square inch. The piston is the only thing that can move, so the expanding gases push it down to the bottom of the cylinder. This is the *power stroke*.

The fuel is burned and the energy in the gases has been used up in pushing the piston downward. Now it is necessary to clear these burned gases out of the cylinder to make room for a new charge. On the *exhaust stroke*, the exhaust valve opens and the piston pushes the gases out through the opening.

The cycle continues through the same series of actions. The crankshaft is going around continuously while the piston is going up and down, but we should note that it is only on the power stroke that the piston is driving it around. On the other three strokes, the crankshaft is driving the piston. There is one power stroke to every two revolutions of the crankshaft. This is for each cylinder, of course; with an eight-cylinder engine there are four power strokes for each revolution.

It is a fundamental fact of internal combustion engines that the more we compress the mixture, the harder we squeeze it, the more power we get from it. Compression ratio is a measure of how much we squeeze the mixture. If the cylinder holds 100 cubic inches when the piston is all the way down in its lowest position and 10 cubic inches when the piston is up as far as it can go, we say the compression ratio is 10:1. The mixture has been compressed into a space 1/10 as large as it originally occupied. Fifty years ago, 4:1 was a common figure for the compression ratio of automobile engines. This has increased over the years, and today compression ratios range upward of 8:1.

If we did not have a cooling system our engine would not last long. The usual way of cooling the engine is to put water jackets around the hottest parts. Water is constantly circulated through these by a small pump. The heat of the cylinder makes the water hot, and it then goes to the radiator where it is cooled by the outside air passing through. Then it starts back to the engine again to do more cooling. It is actually very much like a steam or hot-water heating system in a home. The engine is our boiler that heats up the water, which then goes to a radiator where it gives up its heat to the air.

Lubrication System

We also need a lubrication system for our engine. If all the rotating and reciprocating parts were running metal against metal, with no film of oil between them, they would soon heat up and stick. The friction would also make it harder for the parts to turn. So we have a reservoir of oil in the crankcase, where a pump forces it to the bearings and more critical points in the engine. Some of it flows through tubes and some through passages drilled in the crankshaft and connecting rods. The lubrication system might be compared to the water system in a house. The liquid is forced from one central place through pipes to many different locations where it is needed.

Electric Motor

We must have some way of starting the engine. It has to be turning over before it can run under its own power, and we give it this initial start by means of an electric motor. This is somewhat similar to the motor in our vacuum cleaner or washing machine. It runs on electricity from the battery, and the starter switch is similar to the electric wall switch that turns on the lights in our home.

Alternator

There is one more important piece of electrical equipment: the alternator. It looks something like the starter motor, but its job is just the opposite. Instead of taking electricity from the battery to start the engine, the alternator is driven by the engine and generates electric current, which feeds back into the battery to keep it charged for starting. The alternator also supplies power for the ignition system, lights, radio, and other electrical units.

Emissions Systems

There are three major pollutants that are emitted from automobiles into the atmosphere:

1. **Hydrocarbons**—Hydrocarbons, which we can think of as essentially unburned gasoline, come from the exhaust pipe and the engine's crankcase as a result of the combustion process. They also enter the atmosphere from the carburetor and the fuel tank through an evaporation process.

2. **Carbon monoxide**—Carbon monoxide (CO) results from partially burned fuel when rich fuel/air mixtures do not allow complete combustion all the way to carbon dioxide (CO_2).

3. **Oxides of nitrogen**—Oxides of nitrogen, on the other hand, are gases formed during combustion resulting from the high temperatures.

Today's cars have built-in systems designed to reduce the three major pollutants emitted from these sources. The systems may vary somewhat between different makes of cars, but they all work to perform the same job: reducing emissions of hydrocarbons, carbon monoxide, and oxides of nitrogen. Let's see what the systems are and what they do.

The first emission control applied to automobile engines was called the positive crankcase ventilation (PCV) system. This system, introduced in the early 1960s, is still in use today. During the "compression strokes" of the pistons, small amounts of gasoline vapors are forced past the piston rings from the combustion chamber and into the engine crankcase. These infinitesimal amounts of vapors expelled each engine cycle would add up to significant quantities of hydrocarbon (HC) emissions if they were allowed to enter the atmosphere. They don't, however, because the PCV system directs these vapors back to the intake system so that they are burned in the combustion chambers.

There is another system, air injection, that helps control hydrocarbon and carbon monoxide emissions in the exhaust. Air is injected by a pump into the engine's exhaust ports to cause further burning of the hot gasoline vapors before they pass out the exhaust pipe. (See Figure 1.)

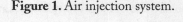

Figure 1. Air injection system.

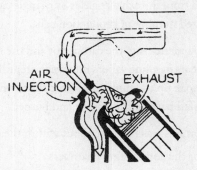

A *catalytic converter* was first introduced on most 1975 model cars made in the United States. This emission control system oxidizes HC and CO into harmless water vapor and carbon dioxide as the exhaust gases pass through a canister containing pellets that are coated with a catalyst material. A catalyst promotes chemical reactions, allowing them to take place at much lower than normal temperatures and more rapidly than a chemical reaction ordinarily would proceed. In the case of the catalytic converter emission control system, this means that catalysts allow more nearly complete oxidation of hydrocarbons and carbon monoxide at a much lower temperature than ordinary "burning." (See Figure 2.)

Figure 2. Catalytic converter.

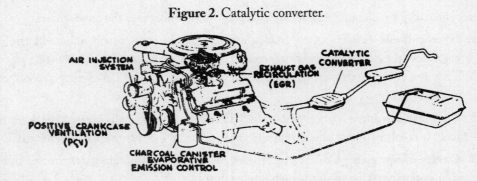

The catalytic converter has played a major role in reducing the emission of hydrocarbons and carbon monoxide from exhaust pipes into the atmosphere. It has also promoted improved fuel economy and has helped engineers "tune" the engine for a more pleasant car to drive.

Although the present catalytic converter, an oxidizing converter, does an excellent job in controlling HC and CO emissions, it isn't effective in controlling oxides of nitrogen (NOx), the third type of pollutant in exhaust gases. Oxides of nitrogen are different from HC and CO because they will not burn to harmless combustion products. Instead, control of NOx in the engine exhaust usually requires measures to prevent their formation.

Oxides of nitrogen are formed any time you have very high temperatures in the oxidation process when air is used to provide the oxygen. This is because air contains mostly nitrogen (more than 78%) along with the oxygen (nearly 21%).

The formation of NOx in an engine is minimized by diluting the fuel/air mixture entering the combustion chamber. This helps reduce the peak combustion temperature. One system being used to control NOx emission is called Exhaust Gas Recirculation (EGR). With this system, small quantities of exhaust gases are recirculated back into the intake system of the engine to dilute the fuel/air mixture. Engineers are also looking at a "Three-Way Closed Catalyst Loop System" in which all three pollutants can be removed from the exhaust gases by a single catalytic converter. Such a system has been used already in a limited number of production cars.

To reduce hydrocarbons that evaporate from the carburetor and the fuel tank when the engine is not running, there's a system that vents gasoline vapors into a canister filled with carbon granules. These granules act like a sponge and soak up the fumes and store them while the car is parked. When the engine starts up, the fumes are fed back to the engine and burned.

Further control of exhaust emissions was brought about within the engine by:

- Changing the shape of the combustion chambers
- Using a leaner air-fuel ratio (more air in the mixture that goes to the cylinders for combustion)
- Regulating the temperature of the air entering the carburetor
- Increasing the speed at which the engine idles
- Modifying spark timing for stop-and-go driving

These changes to the engine all combine to help achieve more complete combustion and decrease exhaust emissions.

Drive System

The first thing needed in the drive system (Figure 3) is a device that completely disconnects the engine from the rear wheels and the rest of the power transmission system. This allows the engine to run when the car is standing still.

Suppose we mount two ordinary pie tins, each on a shaft, as shown in the following figure. As long as they are not touching each other, we can spin one as fast as we want to without affecting the other at all. But if we move them together when one of them is spinning, the other will begin to turn and almost immediately both shafts will be turning together as one unit. This is the general principle of operation of the disc, or friction, clutch used in automobiles having manual shift transmissions. The discs are forced together by strong springs and are separated by pushing down on the clutch pedal in the driver's compartment.

Cars equipped with automatic transmissions do not have a friction clutch or clutch pedal. We will discuss those shortly, but first we will cover the manual shift type transmission and drive system.

Figure 3. Drive system.

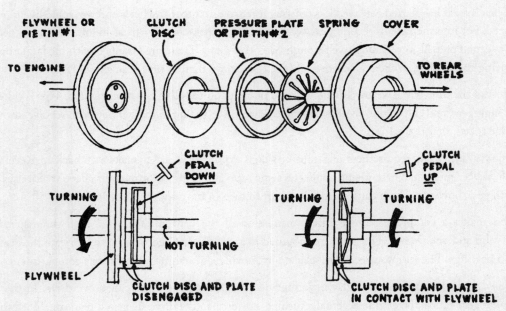

Manual Transmissions

A transmission enables us to change the speed of the engine in relation to the speed of the rear wheels by functioning as a system of gears (see Figure 4). Suppose we have a small gear with 12 teeth driving a larger gear with 24 teeth. When the first gear has made one complete revolution, we might say that it has gone a distance equivalent to 12 teeth. The second one has gone around the same distance—12 teeth—but this means only one half a revolution for the larger gear. So this second gear and the shaft it is fastened to always turn at one half the speed of the first gear and its shaft.

Figure 4. Gear system.

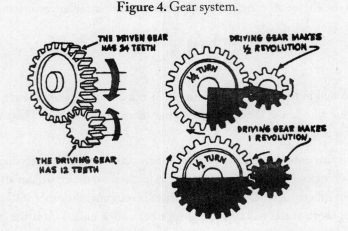

In a manual-shift automobile transmission, we have several combinations of gears arranged so that we can select the one we want to use at any moment. For low gear, or first, a small gear on the engine shaft drives a large gear on another shaft. This reduces the speed and increases the twisting force. Then a small gear on the second shaft drives a large gear on the drive shaft that goes to the rear axle. This reduces the speed and increases the twist still more, giving a ratio of about 3:1 for starting up or heavy pulling.

When the car has started, we need less twisting force to turn the rear wheels and we would like more speed. For intermediate or second gear, we use the same first pair of gears as in low. We disconnect the second pair, however, and drive through two other gears. These are arranged with the larger one driving the smaller, so there is less overall speed reduction than in first gear, about $1\frac{2}{3} : 1$.

Most of the time while we are driving we need no reduction at all in the transmission. This is third, or high gear, and the engine shaft is connected directly to the drive shaft. They both revolve at the same speed, that is a 1:1 ratio.

One very important requirement of a transmission is to provide means to make a car back up. Reverse gear is very much like first, giving about the same ratio and using the same four gears. It also uses a fifth gear, however, which causes the drive shaft to turn in the opposite direction.

This makes a complete manual-shift transmission of the conventional type, with three speeds forward and one reverse. The gears are mounted in a metal case filled with oil to lubricate the gears and bearings. The various speeds are selected by moving a gearshift in the driver's compartment.

Many manual transmissions today have four or five speeds, sometimes called overdrive. In these higher gear ratios, the engine is actually turning slower than the drive shaft and rear axle. With the high gear ratios and lower engine speeds, fuel economy can be significantly improved.

Automatic Transmissions

Most cars built today have some form of automatic transmission, which eliminates the clutch and the need to shift gears manually to obtain the right gear ratios. There are various types, but most of them are similar in the way they affect the driving of the car.

They usually have a hydraulic drive of some sort. The type that is in wide use today is the three-element torque converter. Imagine taking a doughnut, slicing it in two, and putting blades on the inside of each half. Both halves represent two elements of the torque converter:

1. Pump (or driving element)
2. Turbine (or driven element)

The pump is mechanically connected to the engine's crankshaft, so it always rotates when the engine runs. When the engine is started, the pump begins rotating and sends oil, spinning in a clockwise direction, against the blades of the turbine to start it turning. The spinning oil has energy that the turbine absorbs and converts into torque, or twisting force, which then is sent to the rear wheels. When the oil leaves the turbine it spins in a counterclockwise direction, and if it went back to the pump spinning in this direction it would slow it down. We would lose any torque that had been gained. To make sure this doesn't happen, we use the blades of the stator, which does not rotate (not just yet, anyway), to change the direction of the oil flow so it spins again in a clockwise direction. When the oil now enters the pump it adds to the torque the pump receives from the engine, the pump starts to turn faster, and we start to obtain torque multiplication. The cycle of oil going from the pump to the turbine, then through the stator, and back to the pump is repeated over and over until the car reaches a speed where torque multiplication is no longer needed. When this happens, the stator starts to turn freely (it's fixed to rotate only clockwise). The pump and turbine then rotate at nearly the same speed and act like a fluid coupling, or clutch. We now have a situation similar to high gear in a manual-shift transmission where the engine crankshaft is connected directly to the driveshaft and both revolve at nearly the same speed. The stator stops rotating when torque multiplication is needed.

The turbine is connected by a shaft to a gear transmission located behind the converter. The transmission usually used contains planetary gear sets and provides the desired number of forward speed gear ratios automatically. These gear ratios may also be selected manually for greater engine braking or exceptionally hard pulling. A reverse gear and neutral are also provided. The planetary type of gear transmission has its gears in mesh at all times. Gear ratios for different driving conditions are obtained using hydraulic controls that cause friction bands and clutches to grab and hold certain gears of the set stationary while the others rotate.

Hydraulic torque converters can have variations in the design of their basic components. Some elements may have their blades set at a fixed angle to the flow of oil. Others may have blades that are hydraulically operated to provide varying blade angles automatically. For example, a stator could have a low angle for maximum efficiency during the average operating range of the transmission and a high angle for increased acceleration and performance (when more torque is needed at the rear wheels). There also are variations in the way the components are arranged in hydraulic torque converters. Some have two stators, others have multiple sets of pump and turbine blades. Differences can exist, too, in the way the planetary gears are combined with the pump, turbine, and stator elements. (See Figure 5.)

Figure 5. Hydraulic torque converter.

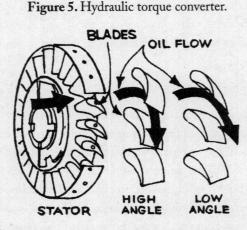

Under ordinary circumstances, however, these variations will not make a great deal of difference to the driver of the car. He still will find no clutch pedal and will have no shifting to do, except when he wants to back up. And for forward driving, all he has to do is step on the accelerator to go and the brake pedal to stop.

Rear Axle

From the transmission, the propeller shaft, or drive shaft, goes back to the rear axle. (See Figure 6.) This is simply a solid or tubular steel shaft. The universal joint allows the rear axle to move up or down in relation to the transmission without bending or breaking the shaft. It is something like the gimbals of a compass on a boat, which allows the compass to remain level at all times, no matter how the boat rolls or pitches.

In the rear axle we have two sets of gears. The first, ring gear and pinion, is simply to transmit the power around a corner. It enables the propeller shaft to drive the axle shafts, which are at right angles to it. The old-fashioned ice-cream freezer has a set of gears to do the same thing.

When we turn a corner, the outside wheel has to travel farther than the inside wheel, and so it has to go faster during that time. We have a set of gears called the differential to take care of this. The differential consists of two small bevel gears on the ends of the axle shafts meshed with two bevel gears (for simplicity we show only one) mounted in the differential frame. This frame is fastened solidly to the ring gear. When the car is going straight ahead, the frame and the gears all rotate as a unit, with no motion between one another. But when the car is turning, one wheel wants to go faster than the other, so the gears on the axle shafts rotate relative to the other small gear. If the ring gear were stationary, one axle would turn frontward and the other one backward. But inasmuch as the ring gear is turning the whole unit, it means that one axle is turning faster than the ring gear and the other is turning slower by the same amount. This can be carried to the point where one wheel is stationary and the other one is turning at twice ring gear speed, which is the situation we sometimes get when one wheel is on a slippery spot and the other isn't. Some cars, however, can be equipped with a limited slip differential, a type of differential that allows the major driving force to go to the wheel having greater traction.

Figure 6. Complete power path—Engine to rear wheels.

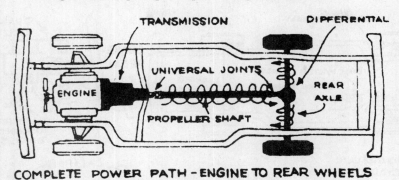

The Axle Shafts

The axle shafts, of course, drive the wheels and make the car move, which is the point we have been getting to all this time. We now have a complete rear wheel drive system, just as outlined at the beginning. Power starts at the engine and eventually gets to the rear wheels after passing through various mechanisms so that it will arrive there in the proper form.

There also are cars that have front-wheel drive. The same basic components are used as for the rear-wheel drive system, but all the components are arranged up front of the driver. The power flow from the engine is to the front wheel axle shafts. Instead of the rear wheels pushing the car forward, the front wheels pull the car along.

Brakes

There is one more part of the car we should mention before we are through. We have shown how we get the car to move, but another very important point is to be able to stop it.

Brakes are provided for this purpose. There is one in each of the four wheels, and they are simply a method of applying friction to the rotating wheels to stop them. It is like rubbing a stick against the rim of a child's wagon wheels.

Two types of brake systems (Figure 7) are common on today's cars:

1. Drum brake
2. Disc brake

Figure 7. Brake systems.

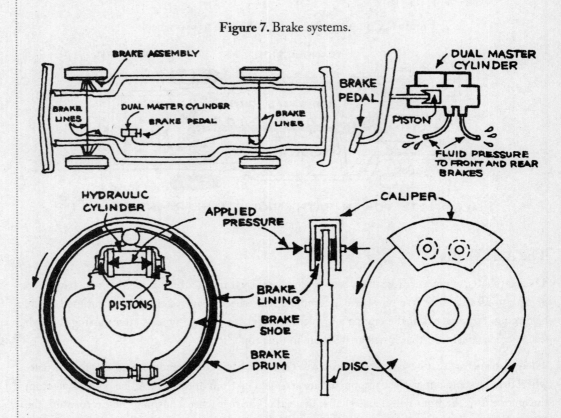

In the drum brake system, two stationary brake shoes covered with a special friction material, called brake lining, are forced outward by hydraulic pressure against the inside of a metal drum that rotates with the wheel. A system of steel tubes filled with a special hydraulic brake fluid runs from a master cylinder to each brake. When the driver steps on the brake pedal, pressure is built up in the master cylinder and this pressure is transmitted through the tubes, called brake lines, to pistons located inside a hydraulic cylinder in each wheel. The pistons move outward and push the shoes against the brake drum. As a safety feature, today's cars have a dual master cylinder that provides two independent hydraulic systems, one for the front wheels and one for the rear.

In the disc brake system, brake pads are attached to a caliper that has parts positioned on each side of a rotating disc located in the wheel. When the brake pedal is applied, hydraulic pressure transmitted from the dual master cylinder causes the caliper to clamp the opposing pads against the disc (it's like taking your thumb and forefinger and squeezing them together against a rotating plate).

The brake is a friction device that converts work into heat, and the amount of heat created by the brakes during a fast stop from high speed is amazing. Because of this, proper cooling of the brakes is an important consideration during their design.

BASIC SHOP INFORMATION†

Common Hand Tools

Tools are designed to make a job easier and enable you to work more efficiently and are a craftsman's best friend. Here are examples of tools by category.

Striking Tools

Hammers, mallets, and sledges (Figure 8) are used to apply a striking force.

Figure 8. Hammers, mallets, and sledges.

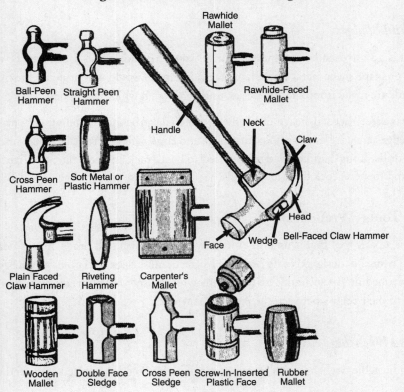

Hammers

Carpenter's Hammer

The primary use of the carpenter's hammer is to drive or draw (pull) nails. Note the names of the various parts of the hammer shown in **Figure 8**. The carpenter's hammer has either a curved or a straight claw. The face may be either bell-faced or plain-faced, and the handle may be made of wood or steel.

† Condensed from *Tools and Their Uses*, Bureau of Naval Personnel, Dover Publications, Inc., New York

Machinist's Hammer

Machinist's hammers are used mostly by people who work with metal or who work around machinery. These hammers are distinguished from carpenter's hammers by a variable-shaped peen, rather than a claw, at the opposite end of the face. The ball peen hammer is probably most familiar to you. It has a ball that is smaller in diameter than the face. It is therefore useful for striking areas that are too small for the face to enter.

Machinist's hammers may be further divided into hard-face and soft-face classifications. The hard-faced hammer is made of forged tool steel, whereas the soft-faced hammer has a head made from brass, lead, or a tightly rolled strip of rawhide. Plastic-tipped hammers, or solid plastic with a lead core for added weight, are also popular.

Mallets and Sledges

The mallet is a short-handled tool used to drive wooden-handled chisels, gouges, or wooden pins or to form or shape sheet metal where hard-faced hammers would mar or injure the finished work. Mallet heads are made from a soft material, usually wood, rawhide, or rubber.

The sledge is a steel-headed, heavy-duty driving tool that can be used for numerous purposes. Short-handled sledges are used to drive bolts, driftpins, and large nails and to strike cold chisels and small hand rock drills. Long-handled sledges are used to break rock and concrete; to drive spikes, bolts, or stakes; and to strike rock drills and chisels.

Turning Tools (Wrenches)

A wrench is a basic tool that is used to exert a twisting force on bolt heads, nuts, studs, and pipes. The special wrenches designed to do certain jobs are, in most cases, variations of the basic wrenches that are described in this section. The size of any wrench used on bolt heads or nuts is determined by the size of the opening between the jaws of the wrench.

Open-End Wrenches

Solid, nonadjustable wrenches with openings in one or both ends are called open-end wrenches.

Usually they come in sets of from six to ten wrenches with sizes ranging from $\frac{5}{16}$ to 1 inch. Wrenches with small openings are usually shorter than wrenches with large openings.

Open-end wrenches may have their jaws parallel to the handle or at angles anywhere up to 90 degrees. The average angle is 15 degrees (see Figure 9). This angular displacement variation permits selection of a wrench suited for places where there is room to make only a part of a complete turn of a nut or bolt.

Figure 9. Open-end wrenches.

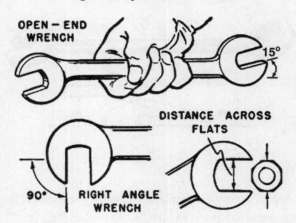

Box Wrenches

Box wrenches (see Figure 10) are safer than open-end wrenches because there is less likelihood they will slip off the work. They completely surround or box a nut or bolt head. The most frequently used box wrench has 12 points or notches arranged in a circle in the head and can be used with a minimum swing angle of 30 degrees. Six- and eight-point wrenches are used for heavy, 12 for medium, and 16 for light-duty only.

Figure 10. 12-point box-end wrench.

One disadvantage of the box-end wrench is the loss of time that occurs whenever a craftsman has to lift the wrench off and place it back on the nut in another position in case there is insufficient clearance to spin the wrench in a full circle.

Combination Wrench

After a tight nut is broken loose, it can be unscrewed much more quickly with an open-end wrench than with a box wrench. This is where a combination box-open end wrench (see Figure 11) comes in handy. You can use the box end for breaking nuts loose or for snugging them down and the open end for faster turning.

The box-end portion of the wrench can be designed with an offset in the handle. Notice in **Figure 11** how the 15-degree offset allows clearance over nearby parts.

Figure 11. Combination wrench.

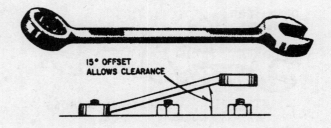

Socket Wrench

The socket wrench is one of the most versatile wrenches in the toolbox. Basically, it consists of a handle and a socket type wrench that can be attached to the handle.

The "Spintite" wrench shown in **Figure 12** is a special type of socket wrench. It has a hollow shaft to accommodate a bolt protruding through a nut, has a hexagonal head, and is used like a screwdriver. It is supplied in small sizes only and is useful for assembly and electrical work. When used for the latter purpose, it must have an insulated handle.

A complete socket wrench set consists of several types of handles along with bar extensions, adapters, and a variety of sockets.

Figure 12. Socket set components.

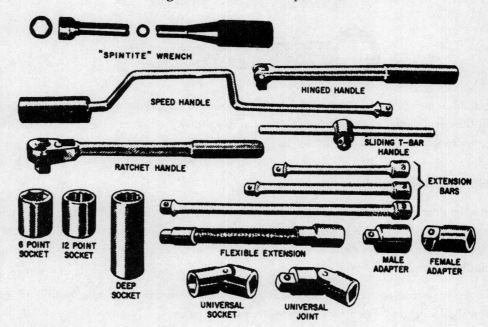

Torque Wrenches

There are times when, for engineering reasons, a specific force must be applied to a nut or bolt head. In such cases a torque wrench must be used. For example, equal force must be applied to all the head bolts of an engine. Otherwise, one bolt may bear the brunt of the force of internal combustion and ultimately cause engine failure.

The three most commonly used torque wrenches are the deflecting beam, dial indicating, and micrometer setting types (see Figure 13).

Figure 13. Torque wrenches.

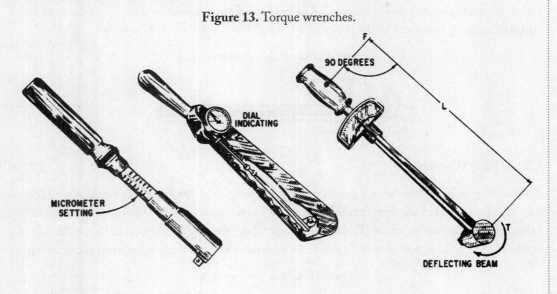

Adjustable Wrenches

A handy all-round wrench that is generally included in every toolbox is the adjustable open-end wrench. This wrench is not intended to take the place of the regular solid open-end wrench. In addition, it is not built for use on extremely hard-to-turn items. Its usefulness is achieved by being capable of fitting odd-sized nuts. This flexibility is achieved although one jaw of the adjustable open-end wrench is fixed because the other jaw is moved along a slide by a thumbscrew adjustment (see Figure 14). By turning the thumbscrew, the jaw opening may be adjusted to fit various sizes of nuts.

Adjustable wrenches are available in varying sizes ranging from 4 to 24 inches in length. The size of the wrench selected for a particular job depends on the size of nut or bolt head to which the wrench is to be applied. As the jaw opening increases, the length of the wrench increases.

Figure 14. Adjustable wrenches.

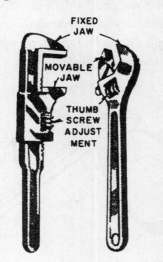

Pipe Wrench (Stillson)

When rotating or holding round work, an adjustable pipe wrench (Stillson) may be used (see Figure 15). The movable jaw on a pipe wrench is pivoted to permit a gripping action on the work. This tool must be used with discretion, because the jaws are serrated and always make marks on the work unless adequate precautions are observed. The jaws should be adjusted so the bite on the work will be taken at about the center of the jaws.

Figure 15. Adjustable pipe wrench.

Chain Pipe Wrench

A different type pipe wrench, used mostly on large sizes of pipe, is the chain pipe wrench (see Figure 16). This tool works in one direction only but can be backed partly around the work and a fresh hold taken without freeing the chain. To reverse the operation, the grip is taken on the opposite side of the head. The head is double ended and can be reversed when the teeth on one end are worn out.

Figure 16. Chain pipe wrench.

Strap Wrench

The strap wrench (see Figure 17) is similar to the chain pipe wrench but uses a heavy web strap in place of the chain. This wrench is used for turning pipe or cylinders where you do not want to mar the surface of the work. To use this wrench, the webbed strap is placed around the cylinder and passed through the slot in the metal body of the wrench. The strap is then pulled up tight and as the mechanic turns the wrench in the desired direction, the webbed strap tightens further around the cylinder. This gripping action causes the cylinder to turn.

Figure 17. Strap wrench.

Spanner Wrenches

Many special nuts are made with notches cut into their outer edge. For these nuts a hook spanner (see Figure 18) is required. This wrench has a curved arm with a lug or hook on the end. This lug fits into one of the notches of the nut and the handle turned to loosen or tighten the nut. This spanner may be made for just one particular size of notched nut, or it may have a hinged arm to adjust it to a range of sizes.

Another type of spanner is the pin spanner. Pin spanners have a pin in place of a hook. This pin fits into a hole in the outer part of the nut. Face pin spanners are designed so that the pins fit into holes in the face of the nut.

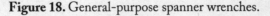

Figure 18. General-purpose spanner wrenches.

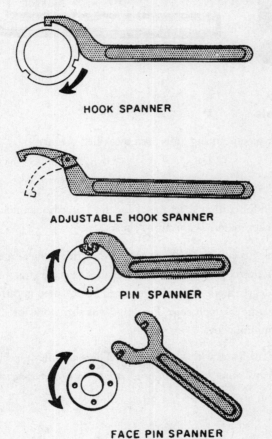

HOOK SPANNER

ADJUSTABLE HOOK SPANNER

PIN SPANNER

FACE PIN SPANNER

Setscrew Wrenches (Allen and Bristol)

In some places it is desirable to use recessed heads on setscrews and capscrews. One type (Allen) is used extensively on office machines and in machine shops. The other type (Bristol) is used infrequently.

Recessed head screws usually have a hex-shaped (six-sided) recess. To remove or tighten this type of screw requires a special wrench that will fit in the recess. This wrench is called an Allen wrench. Allen wrenches are made from hexagonal L-shaped bars of tool steel (see Figure 19). They range in size up to ¾-inch. When using an Allen wrench, make sure you use the correct size to prevent rounding or spreading the head of the screw. A snug fit within the recessed head of the screw is an indication that you have the correct size.

The Bristol wrench is made from round stock. It is also L-shaped, but one end is fluted to fit the flutes or little splines in the Bristol setscrew (see Figure 19).

Figure 19. Allen and Bristol wrenches.

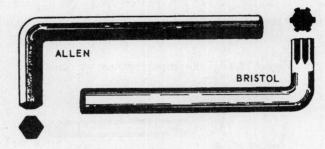

Metal-Cutting Tools

There are many types of metal-cutting tools used by skilled mechanics.

Snips and Shears

Snips and shears are used for cutting sheet metal and steel of various thicknesses and shapes. Normally, the heavier or thicker materials are cut by shears.

One of the handiest tools for cutting light (up to ¹⁄₁₆-inch thick) sheet metal is the hand snip (tin snips). The *straight hand snips* (see Figure 20) have blades that are straight and cutting edges that are sharpened to an 85-degree angle. Snips like this can be obtained in different sizes ranging from the small 6-inch to the large 14-inch snip. Tin snips will also work for slightly heavier gauges of soft metals, such as aluminum alloys.

It is hard to cut circles or small arcs with straight snips. There are snips especially designed for circular cutting. They are called *circle snips, hawks-bill snips, trojan snips, and aviation snips.*

Figure 20. Snips.

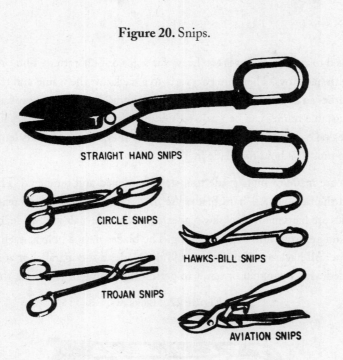

Bolt Cutters

Bolt cutters (see Figure 21) are giant shears with short blades and long handles. The handles are hinged at one end. The cutters are at the ends of extensions that are jointed in such a way that the inside joint is forced outward when the handles are closed, thus forcing the cutting edges together with great force.

Bolt cutters are made in lengths of 18 to 36 inches. The larger ones will cut mild steel bolts and rods up to one-half inch. The material to be cut should be kept as far back in the jaws as possible. Never attempt to cut spring wire or other tempered metal with bolt cutters. This will cause the jaws to be sprung or nicked.

Adjusting screws near the middle hinges provide a means for ensuring that both jaws move the same amount when the handles are pressed together. Keep the adjusting screws just tight enough to ensure that the cutting edges meet along their entire length when the jaws are closed. The hinges should be kept well oiled at all times.

Figure 21. Bolt cutters.

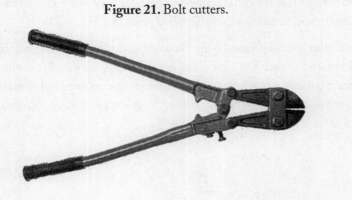

Hacksaws

Hacksaws are used to cut metal that is too heavy for snips or bolt cutters. Thus, metal bar stock can be cut readily with hacksaws. There are two parts to a hacksaw: the frame and the blade. Common hacksaws have either an adjustable or solid frame (see Figure 22). Most hacksaws are of the adjustable frame type. Adjustable frames can be made to hold blades from 8 to 16 inches long, whereas those with solid frames take only the length blade for which they are made. This length is the distance between the two pins that hold the blade in place.

Hacksaw blades are made of high-grade tool steel, hardened and tempered. There are two types, the all-hard and the flexible. All-hard blades are hardened throughout, whereas only the teeth of the flexible blades are hardened. Hacksaw blades are about one-half inch wide, have from 14 to 32 teeth per inch, and are from 8 to 16 inches long. The blades have a hole at each end that hooks to a pin in the frame. All hacksaw frames that hold the blades either parallel or at right angles to the frame are provided with a wingnut or screw to permit tightening or removing the blade.

Figure 22. Hacksaws.

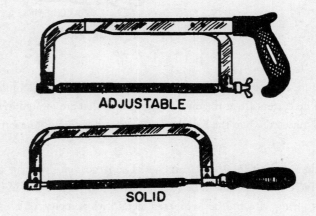

ADJUSTABLE

SOLID

Chisels

Chisels are tools that can be used for chipping or cutting metal. They will cut any metal that is softer than the materials of which they are made. Chisels are made from a good grade tool steel and have a hardened cutting edge and beveled head. Metal-cutting chisels are classified according to the shape of their points, and the width of the cutting edge denotes their size. The most common shapes of chisels are flat (cold chisel), cape, round nose, and diamond point (see Figure 23).

The type of chisel most commonly used is the flat cold chisel, which serves to cut rivets, split nuts, chip castings, and thin metal sheets. The cape chisel is used for special jobs like cutting keyways, narrow grooves, and square corners. Round-nose chisels make circular grooves and chip inside corners with a fillet. Finally, the diamond point is used for cutting V-grooves and sharp corners.

Figure 23. Types of points on metal-cutting chisel.

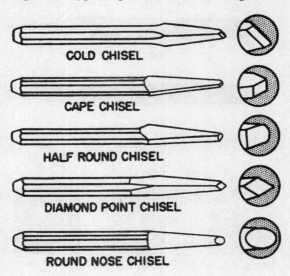

COLD CHISEL

CAPE CHISEL

HALF ROUND CHISEL

DIAMOND POINT CHISEL

ROUND NOSE CHISEL

Files

A toolkit is not complete unless it contains an assortment of files. There are a number of different types of files in common use, and each type may range in length from 3 to 18 inches.

Grades

Files are graded according to the degree of fineness and according to whether they have single- or double-cut teeth. The difference is apparent when you compare the files in **Figure 24A**.

Single-cut files have rows of teeth cut parallel to each other. These teeth are set at an angle of about 65 degrees with the centerline. You will use single-cut files for sharpening tools, finish filing, and drawfiling. They are also the best tools for smoothing the edges of sheet metal.

Files with crisscrossed rows of teeth are double-cut files. The double cut forms teeth that are diamond shaped and fast cutting. You will use double-cut files for quick removal of metal and for rough work.

Files are also graded according to the spacing and size of their teeth and their coarseness or fineness. Some of these grades are pictured in **Figure 24B**. In addition to the three grades shown, you may use some *dead smooth* files, which have very fine teeth, and some rough files with very coarse teeth. The fineness or coarseness of file teeth is also influenced by the length of the file. (The length of a file is the distance from the tip to the heel and does not include the tang [see Figure 24C].) When you have a chance, compare the actual size of the teeth of a 6-inch, single-cut smooth file and a 12-inch, single-cut smooth file. You will notice the 6-inch file has more teeth per inch than the 12-inch file.

Shapes

Files come in different shapes. Therefore, in selecting a file for a job, the shape of the finished work must be considered. Some of the cross-sectional shapes are shown in **Figure 24D**.

Triangular files are tapered (longitudinally) on all three sides. They are used to file acute internal angles and to clear out square corners. Special triangular files are used to file saw teeth.

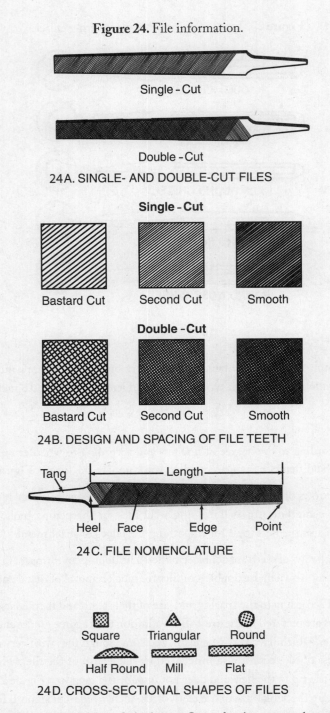

Figure 24. File information.

Single - Cut

Double - Cut

24A. SINGLE- AND DOUBLE-CUT FILES

Single - Cut

Bastard Cut   Second Cut   Smooth

Double - Cut

Bastard Cut   Second Cut   Smooth

24B. DESIGN AND SPACING OF FILE TEETH

Tang   Length

Heel   Face   Edge   Point

24C. FILE NOMENCLATURE

Square   Triangular   Round

Half Round   Mill   Flat

24D. CROSS-SECTIONAL SHAPES OF FILES

Mill files are tapered in both width and thickness. One edge has no teeth and is known as a *safe edge*. Mill files are used for smoothing lathe work, drawfiling, and other fine, precision work. Mill files are always single-cut.

Flat files are general-purpose files and may be either single- or double-cut. They are tapered in width and thickness. *Hard* files, not shown, are somewhat thicker than flat files. They taper slightly in thickness, but their edges are parallel. The flat or hard files most often used are the double-cut for rough work and the single-cut, smooth file for finish work.

Square files are tapered on all four sides and are used to enlarge rectangular-shaped holes and slots. *Round* files serve the same purpose for round openings. Small round files are often called "rattail" files.

The *half round* file is a general-purpose tool. The rounded side is used for curved surfaces and the flat face on flat surfaces. When you file an inside curve, use a round or half round file whose curve most nearly matches the curve of the work.

Twist Drills

The most common tool for making holes in metal is the twist drill. It consists of a cylindrical piece of steel with spiral grooves. One end of the cylinder is pointed, whereas the other end is shaped so that it may be attached to a drilling machine. The grooves, usually called flutes, may be cut into the steel cylinder, or the flutes may be formed by twisting a flat piece of steel into a cylindrical shape.

The principal parts of a twist drill are the body, the shank, and the point (see Figure 25). The dead center of a drill is the sharp edge at the extreme tip end of the drill. It is formed by the intersection of the cone-shaped surfaces of the point and should always be in the exact center of the axis of the drill. The point of the drill should not be confused with the dead center. The point is the entire cone-shaped surface at the end of the drill.

Figure 25. Twist drill nomenclature.

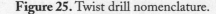
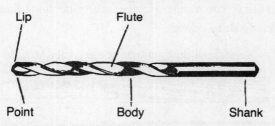

The lip or cutting edge of a drill is that part of the point that actually cuts away the metal when drilling a hole. It is ordinarily as sharp as the edge of a knife. There is a cutting edge for each flute of the drill.

The lip clearance of a drill is the surface of the point that is ground away or relieved just back of the cutting edge of the drill. The strip along the inner edge of the body is called the margin. It is the greatest diameter of the drill and extends the entire length of the flute. The diameter of the margin at the shank end of the drill is smaller than the diameter at the point. This allows the drill to revolve without binding when drilling deep holes.

Countersinks

Countersinking is the operation of beveling the mouth of a hole with a rotary tool called a countersink (see Figure 26). The construction of the countersink is similar to the twist drill. There are four cutting edges, which are taper-ground to the angle marked on the body.

A countersink is used primarily to set the head of a screw or rivet flush with the material in which it is being placed. Countersinks are made in a number of sizes. One size usually takes care of holes of several different sizes. That is, the same countersink can be used for holes from ¼- to ½-inch in diameter. Remove only enough material to set the screw or rivet head flush with the material. If you remove too much material, the hole will enlarge and weaken the work.

Select the countersink with the correct lip angle to correspond with the screw or rivet head being used. This type of countersink can be turned by any machine that will turn a twist drill.

Figure 26. Countersink.

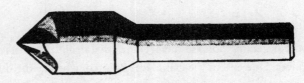

Reamers

Reamers are used to enlarge and true a hole. The reamer consists of three parts—the body, the shank, and the blades. The shank has a square tang to allow the reamer to be held with a wrench for turning. The main purpose of the body is to support the blades.

Reamers of the types shown in **Figure 27** are available in any standard size. They are also available in size variations of .001 inch for special work. A solid straight flute reamer lasts longer and is less expensive than the solid spiral flute reamer. However, the solid spiral flute reamer is preferred by craftsmen because it is less likely to chatter.

Figure 27. Top: solid spiral flute reamer; Bottom: solid straight flute reamer.

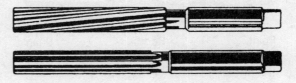

For general purposes, an expansion reamer (see Figure 28) is the most practical. This reamer can usually be obtained in standard sizes from ¼ inch to 1 inch, by 32nds. It is designed to allow the blades to expand $\frac{1}{32}$ of an inch. For example, the ¼-inch expansion reamer will ream a ¼- to $\frac{9}{32}$-hole. A $\frac{9}{32}$-inch reamer will enlarge the hole from $\frac{9}{32}$ to $\frac{5}{16}$ of an inch. This range of adjustment allows a few reamers to cover sizes up to 1 inch.

Figure 28. Expansion reamer.

Punches

A hand punch (see Figure 29) is a tool that is held in the hand and struck on one end with a hammer. The part held in the hand is usually octagonal shaped, or it may be knurled. This prevents the tool from slipping around in the hand. The other end is shaped to do a particular job.

The center punch is used for marking the center of a hole to be drilled. If you try to drill a hole without first punching the center, the drill will "wander" or "walk away" from the desired center. Automatic center punches are useful for layout work. They are operated by pressing down on the shank by hand. An inside spring is compressed and released automatically, striking a blow on the end of the punch. The impression is light, but adequate for marking, and serves to locate the point of a regular punch when a deeper impression is required.

Drift punches, sometimes called "starting punches," have a long taper from the tip to the body. This allows them to withstand the shock of heavy blows. They may be used for knocking out rivets after the heads have been chiseled off or for freeing pins that are "frozen" in their holes.

After a pin has been loosened or partially driven out, the drift punch may be too large to finish the job. The follow-up tool to use is the *pin punch*. It is designed to follow through the hole without jamming. Always use the largest drift or pin punch that will fit the hole. These punches usually come in sets of three to five assorted sizes. Both of these punches will have flat points, never edged or rounded.

Figure 29. Punches.

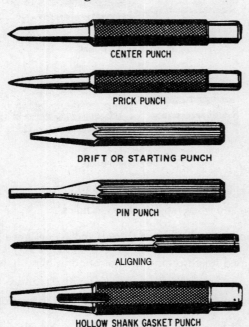

CENTER PUNCH

PRICK PUNCH

DRIFT OR STARTING PUNCH

PIN PUNCH

ALIGNING

HOLLOW SHANK GASKET PUNCH

For assembling units of a machine, an *alignment* (aligning) punch is invaluable. It is usually about 1 foot long and has a long gradual taper. Its purpose is to line up holes in mating parts.

Hollow metal-cutting punches are made from hardened tool steel. They are made in various sizes and are used to cut holes in light-gauge sheet metal.

Taps and Dies

Taps and dies are used to cut threads in metal, plastics, or hard rubber. The taps arc is used for cutting internal threads, and the dies are used to cut external threads. The most common taps are shown in **Figure 30.**

Figure 30. Types of common taps.

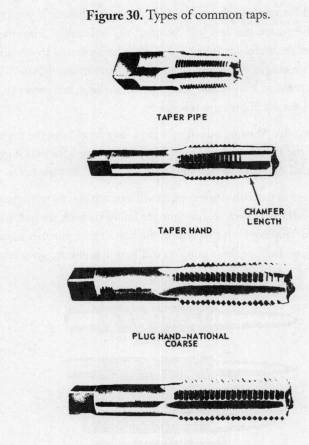

The taper (starting) hand tap has a chamfer length of 8 to 10 threads. These taps are used when starting a tapping operation and when tapping through holes.

Plug hand taps have a chamfer length of 3 to 5 threads and are designed for use after the taper tap.

Bottoming hand taps are used for threading the bottom of a blind hole. They have a very short chamfer length of only 1 to 1½ threads for this purpose. This tap is always used after the plug tap has already been used. Both the taper and plug taps should precede the use of the bottoming hand tap.

Pipe taps are used for pipefittings and other places where extremely tight fits are necessary. The tap diameter, from end to end of threaded portion, increases at the rate of ¾ inch per foot. All the threads on this tap do the cutting, as compared to the straight taps where only the nonchamfered portion does the cutting.

Dies are made in several different shapes and are of the solid or adjustable type. The square pipe die (see Figure 31) will cut American Standard Pipe Thread only. It comes in a variety of sizes for cutting threads on pipe with diameters of ⅛ to 2 inches.

Figure 31. Types of solid dies.

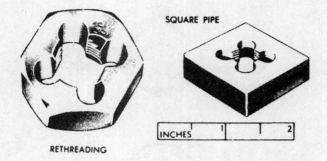

A rethreading die (see Figure 31) is used principally for dressing over bruised or rusty threads on screws or bolts. It is available in a variety of sizes for rethreading American Standard Coarse and Fine Threads. These dies are usually hexagonal in shape and can be turned with a socket, box, open-end, or any wrench that will fit. Rethreading dies are available in sets of 6, 10, 14, and 28 assorted dies in a case.

Round split adjustable dies (see Figure 32) are called "Button" dies and can be used in either hand diestocks or machine holders. The adjustment in the adjusting screw type is made by a fine-pitch screw that forces the sides of the die apart or allows them to spring together. The adjustment in the open adjusting types is made by means of three screws in the holder, one for expanding and two for compressing the dies. Round split adjustable dies are available in a variety of sizes to cut American Standard Coarse and Fine Threads, special form threads, and the standard sizes of threads that are used in Britain and other European countries. For hand threading, these dies are held in diestocks (see Figure 33). One type of die stock has three-pointed screws that will hold round dies of any construction, although it is made specifically for open adjusting-type dies.

Figure 32. Types of adjustable dies.

Figure 33. Diestocks.

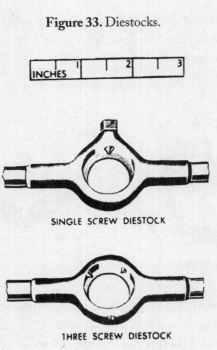

Screw and Tap Extractors

Screw extractors are used to remove broken screws without damaging the surrounding material or the threaded hole. Tap extractors are used to remove broken taps. Some screw extractors are straight, having flutes from end to end. These extractors are available in sizes to remove broken screws having ¼- to ½-inch outside diameters. *Spiral tapered extractors* are sized to remove screws and bolts from ³⁄₁₆ - to 2 ⅛ -inch outside diameters.

Tap extractors are similar to the screw extractors and are sized to remove taps ranging from ³⁄₁₆ to 2 ⅛ inches to outside diameter.

To remove a broken screw or tap with a spiral extractor first drill a hole of proper size in the screw or tap. The size hole required for each screw extractor is stamped on it. The extractor is then inserted in the hole and turned counterclockwise to remove the defective component.

Pipe and Tubing Cutters and Flaring Tools

Pipe cutters (see Figure 34) are used to cut pipe made of steel, brass, copper, wrought iron, and lead. Tube cutters are used to cut tubing made of iron, steel, brass, copper, and aluminum. The essential difference between pipe and tubing is that tubing has considerably thinner walls. Flaring tools (see Figure 35) are used to make single or double flares in the ends of tubing.

Figure 34. Pipe and tubing cutters.

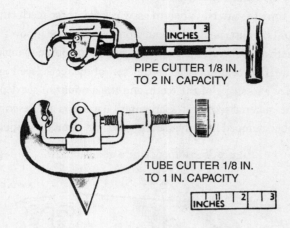

Figure 35. Single-flaring tool.

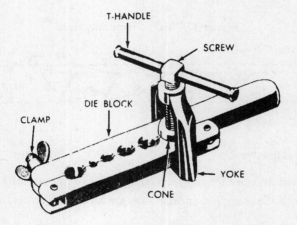

Woodcutting Hand Tools

A person working with wood uses a variety of hand tools and should be familiar with these tools, their proper names, the purpose for which they are used, and how to keep them in good condition.

Handsaws

The most common carpenter's handsaw consists of a steel blade with a handle at one end. The blade is narrower at the end opposite the handle. This end of the blade is called the "point" or "toe." The end of the blade nearest the handle is called the "heel" (see Figure 36). One edge of the blade has teeth, which act as two rows of cutters. When the saw is used, these teeth cut two parallel grooves close together. The chips (sawdust) are pushed out from between the grooves (kerf) by the beveled part of the teeth. The teeth are bent alternately to one side or the other, to make the kerf wider than the thickness of the blade. This bending is called the "set" of the teeth (see Figure 37). The number of teeth per inch, the size and shape of the teeth, and the amount of set depend on the use to be made of the saw and the material to be cut. Carpenter's handsaws are described by the number of points per inch. A number stamped near the handle gives the number of points of the saw.

Figure 36. Nomenclature of a handsaw.

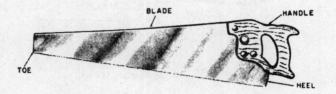

Figure 37. "Set" of handsaw teeth.

Crosscut Saws and Ripsaws

Woodworking handsaws designed for general cutting consist of ripsaws and crosscut saws. Ripsaws are used for cutting with the grain, and crosscut saws are for cutting across the grain.

The major difference between a ripsaw and a crosscut saw is the shape of the teeth. A tooth with a square-faced chisel-type cutting edge, like the ripsaw tooth (see Figure 38), does a good job of cutting with the grain (called ripping) but a poor job of cutting across the grain (called crosscutting). A tooth with a beveled, knife-type cutting edge, like the crosscut-saw tooth (see Figure 38), does a good job of cutting across the grain but a poor job of cutting with the grain.

Figure 38. Comparing ripsaw and crosscut-saw teeth.

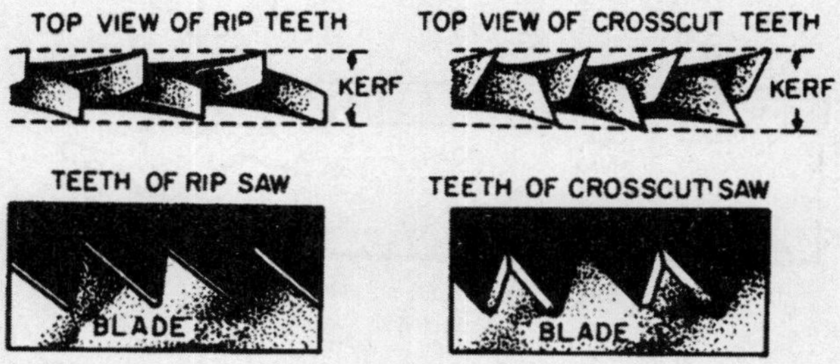

Special-Purpose Saws

The more common types of saws used for special purposes are shown in **Figure 39.** The *backsaw* is a crosscut saw designed for sawing a perfectly straight line across the face of a piece of stock. A heavy steel backing along the top of the blade keeps the blade perfectly straight.

The *dovetail saw* is a special type of backsaw with a thin, narrow blade and a chisel-type handle.

The *compass saw* is a long, narrow, tapering ripsaw designed for cutting out circular or other non-rectangular sections from within the margins of a board or panel. A hole is bored near the cutting line to start the saw. A *keyhole saw* is simply a finer, narrower compass saw. The *coping saw* is used to cut along curved lines.

Figure 39. Special saws.

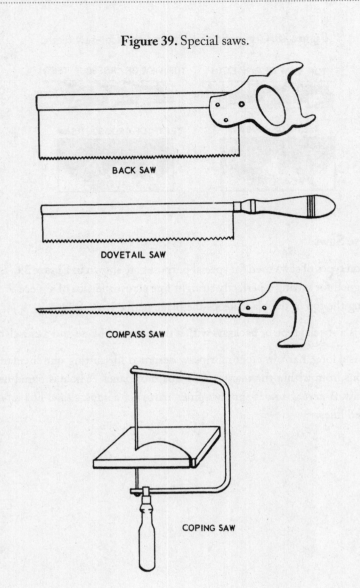

Planes

The plane is the most extensively used of the hand-shaving tools. Most of the lumber handled by anyone working with wood is dressed on all four sides, but when performing jobs such as fitting doors and sash and interior trim work, planes must be used.

Bench and block planes are designed for general surface smoothing and squaring. Other planes are designed for special types of surface work.

The principal parts of a bench plane and the manner in which they are assembled are shown in **Figure 40.** The part at the rear that you grasp to push the plane ahead is called the handle; the part at the front that you grasp to guide the plane along its course is called the knob. The main body of the plane, consisting of the bottom, the sides, and the sloping part that carries the plane iron, is called the frame. The bottom of the frame is called the sole, and the opening in the sole, through which the blade emerges, is called the mouth. The front end of the sole is called the toe; the rear end, the heel.

There are three types of bench planes (see Figure 41): *the smooth plane*, the *jack plane*, and the *jointer plane* (sometimes called the *fore plane* or the *gage plane*). All are used primarily for shaving and smoothing with the grain; the chief difference is the length of the sole. The sole of the smooth plane is about 9 inches long, the sole of the jack plane about 14 inches long, and the sole of the jointer plane from 20 to 24 inches long.

Figure 40. Parts of a bench plane.

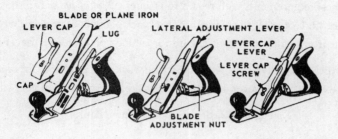

Figure 41. Types of bench planes and block plane.

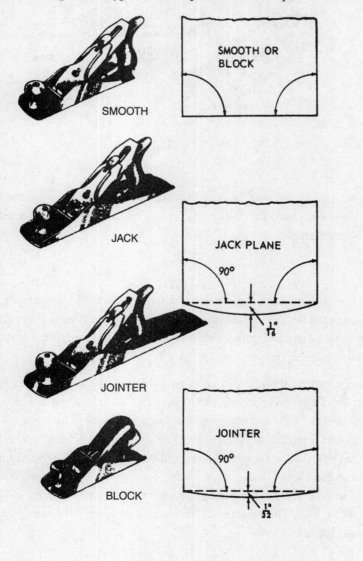

The longer the sole of the plane is, the more uniformly flat and true the planed surface will be. Consequently, which bench plane you should use depends on the requirements regarding surface trueness. The smooth plane is, in general, a smoother only; it will plane a smooth but not an especially true surface in a short time. It is also used for cross-grain smoothing and squaring of end stock.

The jack plane is the general "jack-of-all-work" of the bench plane group. It can take a deeper cut and plane a truer surface than the smooth plane. The jointer plane is used when the planed surface must meet the highest requirements with regard to trueness. A *block plane* and the names of its parts are shown in **Figure 42.** Note that the plane iron in a block plane does not have a plane iron cap and also that, unlike the iron in a bench plane, the iron in a block plane goes in bevel-up.

The block plane, which is usually held at an angle to the work, is used chiefly for cross-grain squaring of end stock. It is also useful, however, for smoothing all plane surfaces on very small work.

Figure 42. Block-plane nomenclature.

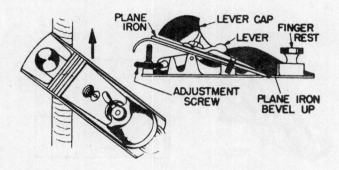

Boring Tools

When working with wood, you are frequently required to bore holes. It is important, therefore, that you know the proper tools used for this job. Auger bits and a variety of braces and drills are used extensively for boring purposes.

Auger Bits

Bits are used for boring holes for screws, dowels, and hardware; as an aid in mortising (cutting a cavity in wood for joining members); and in shaping curves and for many other purposes. Like saws and planes, bits vary in shape and structure with the type of job to be done. Some of the most common bits are described in this section.

Auger bits are screw-shaped tools consisting of six parts: the cutter, screw, spur, twist, shank, and tang (see Figure 43). The twist ends with two sharp points called the spurs, which score the circle, and two cutting edges, which cut shavings within the scored circle. The screw centers the bit and draws it into the wood. The threads of the screw are made in three different pitches: steep, medium, and fine. The steep pitch makes for quick boring and thick chips, and the fine or slight pitch makes for slow boring and fine chips. For end-wood boring, a steep- or medium-pitch screw bit should be used because end wood is likely to be forced in between the fine screw threads, and that will prevent the screw from taking hold. The twist carries the cuttings away from the cutters and deposits them in a mound around the hole.

Figure 43. Nomenclature of an auger bit.

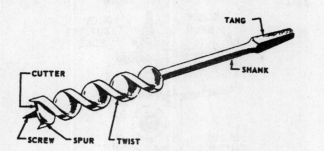

The sizes of auger bits are indicated in sixteenths of an inch and are stamped on the tang (see Figure 44). A number 10 stamped on the tang means $^{10}/_{16}$ or $^{5}/_{8}$ inches, number 5 means $^{5}/_{16}$ inches, and so on. The most common woodworker's auger bit set ranges in size from $^{1}/_{4}$ to 1 inch.

Figure 44. Size markings on auger bits.

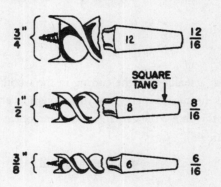

Ordinary auger bits up to 1 inch in diameter are from 7–9 inches long. Short auger bits that are about 3½ inches long are called *dowel* bits.

Expansive auger bits have adjustable cutters for boring holes of different diameters (see Figure 45). Expansive bits are generally made in two different sizes. The larger size has three cutters and bores holes up to 4 inches in diameter. A scale on the cutter blade indicates the diameter of the hole to be bored.

Figure 45. Expansive bit.

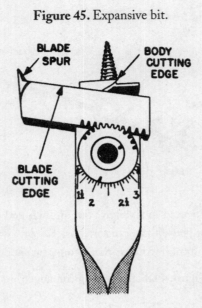

Braces and Drills

The auger bit is the tool that actually does the cutting in the wood; however, it is necessary that another tool be used to hold the auger bit and give you enough leverage to turn the bit. The tools most often used for holding the bit are the carpenter's or hand brace, the breast drill, and the push or spiral hand drill (see Figure 46).

Figure 46. Brace and drill.

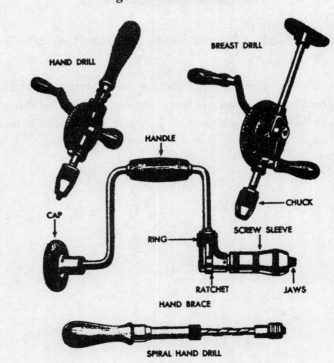

Wood Chisels

A *wood chisel* is a steel tool fitted with a wooden or plastic handle. It has a single beveled cutting edge on the end of the steel part, or blade. According to their construction, chisels may be divided into two general classes: *tang chisels*, in which part of the chisel enters the handle, and *socket chisels*, in which the handle enters into a part of the chisel (see Figure 47).

A *socket chisel* is designed for striking with a wooden mallet (never a steel hammer), whereas a tang chisel is designed for hand manipulation only.

Figure 47. Tang and socket wood chisels.

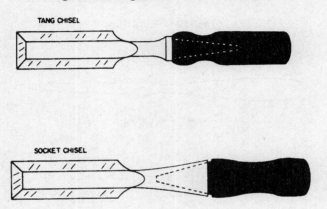

Wood chisels are also divided into types, depending on their weights and thicknesses, the shape or design of the blade, and the work they are intended to do.

The shapes of the more common types of wood chisels are shown in **Figure 48**. The *firmer chisel* has a strong, rectangular cross-section blade, designed for both heavy and light work. The blade of the *paring chisel* is relatively thin and is beveled along the sides for the fine paring work. The *butt chisel* has a short blade, designed for work in hard-to-get-at places.

The butt chisel is commonly used for chiseling the *gains* (rectangular depressions) for the *butt* hinges on doors; hence the name. The *mortising chisel* is similar to a socket firmer but has a narrow blade, designed for chiseling out the deep, narrow mortises for mortise-and-tenon joints. This work requires a good deal of levering out of chips; consequently, the mortising chisel is made extra thick in the shaft to prevent breaking.

A *framing chisel* is shaped like a firmer chisel but has a very heavy, strong blade designed for work in rough carpentry.

Figure 48. Shapes of common types of wood chisels.

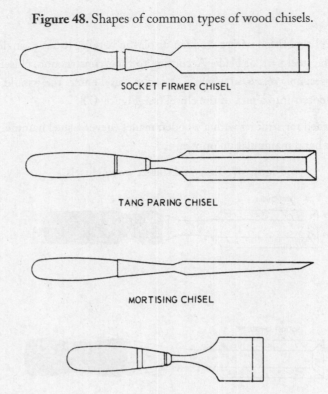

Screwdrivers

A screwdriver is one of the most basic of basic hand tools. It is designed for one function only: to drive and remove screws.

Standard

There are three main parts to a standard screwdriver (see Figure 49). The portion you grip is called the handle, the steel portion extending from the handle is the shank, and the end that fits into the screw is called the blade. The steel shank is designed to withstand considerable twisting force in proportion to its size, and the tip of the blade is hardened to keep it from wearing.

Standard screwdrivers are classified by size, according to the combined length of the shank and blade. The most common sizes range in length from 2½ to 12 inches. There are many screwdrivers smaller and some larger for special purposes. The diameter of the shank and the width and thickness of the blade are generally proportionate to the length, but again there are special screwdrivers with long thin shanks, short thick shanks, and extra wide or extra narrow blades.

Figure 49. Screwdriver parts.

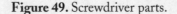

Screwdriver handles may be wood, plastic, or metal. When metal handles are used, there is usually a wooden hand grip placed on each side of the handle. In some types of wood- or plastic-handled screwdrivers, the shank extends through the handle, whereas in others the shank enters the handle only a short way and is pinned to the handle. For heavy work, special types of screwdrivers are made with a square shank. They are designed this way so that they may be gripped with a wrench, but this is the only kind on which a wrench should be used.

Recessed

Recessed screws are available in various shapes (see Figure 50). They have a cavity formed in the head and require a special-shaped screwdriver. The more common include the Phillips, Reed and Prince, and newer Torq-Set types. The most common type found is the Phillips-head screw. This requires a Phillips-type screwdriver.

Phillips Screwdriver

The head of a Phillips-type screw has a four-way slot into which the screwdriver fits. This prevents the screwdriver from slipping. Three standard-sized Phillips screwdrivers handle a wide range of screw sizes. Their ability to hold helps to prevent damaging the slots or the work surrounding the screw. It is a poor practice to try to use a standard screwdriver on a Phillips screw because both the tool and screw slot will be damaged.

Figure 50. Comparison of Phillips, Reed and Prince, and Torq-Set screwheads.

Reed and Prince Screwdriver

Reed and Prince screwdrivers (see Figure 51) are not interchangeable with Phillips screwdrivers. Therefore, always use a Reed and Prince screwdriver with Reed and Prince screws and a Phillips screwdriver with Phillips screws, or a ruined tool or ruined screwhead will result.

Figure 51. Reed and Prince and Phillips Screwdrivers.

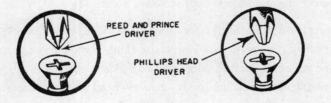

The Phillips screwdriver has approximately 30-degree flukes and a blunt end, whereas the Reed and Prince has 45-degree flukes and a sharper, pointed end. The Phillips screw has beveled walls between the slots; the Reed and Prince, straight, pointed walls. In addition, the Phillips screw slot is not as deep as the Reed and Prince slot.

"Torq-Set" Screws

"Torq-Set" machine screws (offset cross-slot drive) have recently begun to appear in new equipment. The main advantage of the newer type is that more torque can be applied to its head while tightening or loosening than any other screw of comparable size and material without damaging the head of the screw.

Offset Screwdrivers

An offset screwdriver (see Figure 52) may be used where there is not sufficient vertical space for a standard or recessed screwdriver. Offset screwdrivers are constructed with one blade forged in line and another blade forged at right angles to the shank handle. Both blades are bent 90 degrees to the shank handle. By alternating ends, most screws can be seated or loosened even when the swinging space is very restricted. Offset screwdrivers are made for both standard and recessed head screws.

Figure 52. Offset driver.

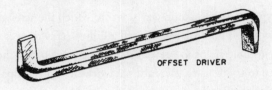

Ratchet Screwdriver

For fast easy work, the ratchet screwdriver (see Figure 53) is extremely convenient, because it can be used with one hand and does not require the bit to be lifted out of the slot after each turn. It may be fitted with either a standard type bit or a special bit for recessed heads. The ratchet screwdriver is most commonly used by the woodworker for driving screws in soft wood.

Figure 53. Ratchet and driver.

Pliers

Pliers are used for cutting purposes as well as holding and gripping small articles in situations where it may be inconvenient or impossible to use hands (see Figure 54).

Combination pliers are handy for holding or bending flat or round stock. The *long-nosed pliers* are less rugged and break easily if you use them on heavy jobs. Long-nosed pliers, commonly called needle-nose pliers, are especially useful for holding small objects in tight places and for making delicate adjustments. The round-nosed kind are handy when you need to crimp sheet metal or form a loop in a wire. *Diagonal cutting pliers*, commonly called "diagonals" or "dikes," are designed for cutting wire and cotter pins close to a flat surface and are especially useful in the electronic and electrical fields. *Duckbill pliers* are used extensively in aviation areas.

Figure 54. Pliers.

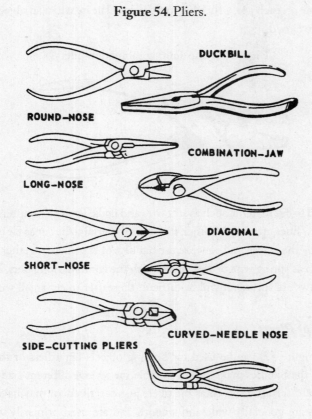

Slip-Joint Pliers

Slip-joint pliers (see Figure 55) are pliers with straight, serrated (grooved) jaws, and the screw or pivot with which the jaws are fastened together may be moved to either of two positions, in order to grasp small- or large-sized objects better.

To spread the jaws of slip-joint pliers, first spread the ends of the handles apart as far as possible. The slip-joint, or pivot, will now move to the open position. To close, again spread the handles as far as possible, then push the joint back into the closed position.

Figure 55. Slip-joint pliers.

Slip-joint combination pliers (see Figure 56) are similar to the slip-joint pliers just described but with the additional feature of a side cutter at the junction of the jaws. This cutter consists of a pair of square cut notches, one on each jaw, which act like a pair of shears when an object is placed between them and the jaws are closed.

Figure 56. Slip-joint combination pliers.

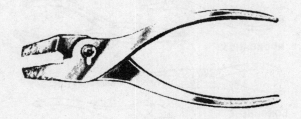

The cutter is designed to cut material such as soft wire and nails. To use the cutter, open the jaws until the cutter on either jaw lines up with the other. Place the material to be cut as far back as possible into the opening formed by the cutter, and squeeze the handles of the pliers together. Do not attempt to cut hard material such as spring wire or hard rivets with the combination pliers. To do so will spring the jaws; and if the jaws are sprung, it will be difficult thereafter to cut small wire with the cutters.

Wrench (Vise-Grip) Pliers

Vise-grip pliers (see Figure 57) can be used for holding objects regardless of their shape. A screw adjustment in one of the handles makes them suitable for several different sizes. The jaws of vise-grips may have standard serrations, such as the pliers just described, or may have a clamp-type jaw. The clamp-type jaws are generally wide and smooth and are used primarily when working with sheet metal.

Vise-grip pliers have an advantage over other types of pliers because you can clamp them on an object and they will stay. This will leave your hands free for other work.

Figure 57. Vise-grip pliers.

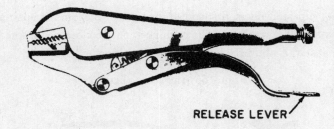

RELEASE LEVER

Vises and Clamps

Vises (see Figure 58) are used for holding work when it is being planed, sawed, drilled, shaped, sharpened, or riveted or when wood is being glued. Clamps are used for holding work that cannot be satisfactorily held in a vise because of its shape and size or when a vise is not available. Clamps are generally used for light work.

Figure 58. Common types of bench vises.

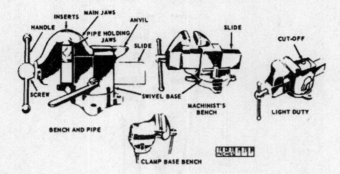

A *machinist's bench vise* is a large steel vise with rough jaws that prevent the work from slipping. Most of these vises have a swivel base with jaws that can be rotated, whereas others cannot be rotated. A similar light duty model is equipped with a cutoff. These vises are usually bolt mounted onto a bench.

The *bench and pipe vise* has integral pipe jaws for holding pipe from ¾ to 3 inches in diameter. The maximum working main jaw opening is usually 5 inches, with a jaw width of 4 to 5 inches. The base can be swiveled to any position and locked. These vises are equipped with an anvil and are also bolted onto a workbench.

The *clamp base vise* usually has a smaller holding capacity than the machinist's or the bench and pipe vise and is usually clamped to the edge of a bench with a thumbscrew. These vises can be obtained with a maximum holding capacity varying between 1½ and 3 inches. These vises normally do not have pipe holding jaws.

The *blacksmith's vise* (see Figure 59) is used for holding work that must be pounded with a heavy hammer. It is fastened to a sturdy workbench or wall, and the long leg is secured into a solid base on the floor.

Figure 59. Blacksmith's and pipe vises.

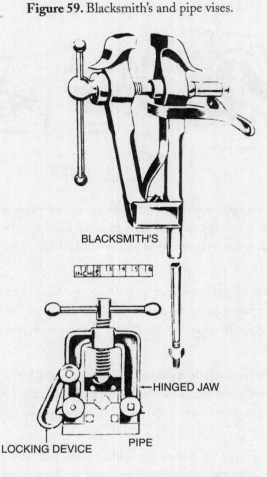

BLACKSMITH'S

HINGED JAW

LOCKING DEVICE   PIPE

The *pipe vise* (see Figure 59) is specially designed to hold round stock or pipe. The vise shown has a capacity of 1 to 3 inches. One jaw is hinged so that the work can be positioned and then the jaw brought down and locked. This vise is also used on a bench. Some pipe vises are designed to use a section of chain to hold down the work. Chain pipe vises range in size from ⅛ - to 2½-inch pipe capacity up to ½- to 8-inch pipe capacity.

A *C-clamp* (see Figure 60) is shaped like the letter C. It consists of a steel frame threaded to receive an operating screw with a swivel head. It is made for light, medium, and heavy service in a variety of sizes.

Figure 60. C-clamp and hand screw clamp.

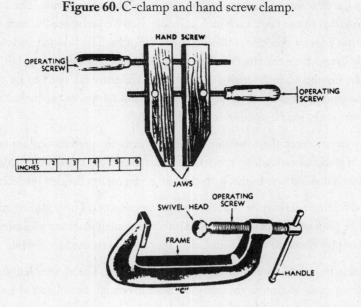

A *hand screw clamp* (see Figure 60) consists of two hard maple jaws connected with two operating screws. Each jaw has two metal inserts into which the screws are threaded.

Measuring Tools

Rules and Tapes

There are many different types of measuring tools in use. Where exact measurements are required, a micrometer caliper (mike) is used. Such a caliper, when properly used, gives measurements to within .001 of an inch accuracy. On the other hand, where accuracy is not extremely critical, the common rule or tape will suffice for most measurements.

Figure 61 shows some of the types of rules and tapes commonly used. Of all measuring tools, the simplest and most common is the steel rule. This rule is usually 6 or 12 inches in length, although other lengths are available. Steel rules may be flexible or nonflexible, but the thinner the rule, the easier it is to measure accurately because the division marks are closer to the work.

Figure 61. Some common types of rules.

Generally a rule has four sets of graduations, one on each edge of each side. The longest lines represent the inch marks. On one edge, each inch is divided into 8 equal spaces, so each space represents ⅛ inch. The other edge of this side is divided into sixteenths. The ¼ -inch and ½-inch marks are commonly made longer than the smaller division marks to facilitate counting, but the graduations are not, as a rule, numbered individually, as they are sufficiently far apart to be counted without difficulty. The opposite side is similarly divided into 32 and 64 spaces per inch, and it is common practice to number every fourth division for easier reading.

There are many variations of the common rule. Sometimes the graduations are on one side only, sometimes a set of graduations is added across one end for measuring in narrow spaces, and sometimes only the first inch is divided into 64ths, with the remaining inches divided into 32nds and 16ths.

A metal or wood folding rule may be used for measuring purposes. These folding rules are usually 2 to 6 feet long. The folding rules cannot be relied on for extremely accurate measurements because a certain amount of play develops at the joints after they have been used for a while.

Steel tapes are made from 6 to approximately 300 feet in length. The shorter lengths are frequently made with a curved cross-section so that they are flexible enough to roll up but remain rigid when extended. Long, flat tapes require support over their full length when measuring, or the natural sag will cause an error in reading.

Flexible-rigid tapes are usually contained in metal cases into which they wind themselves when a button is pressed or into which they can be easily pushed. A hook is provided at one end to hook over the object being measured so one person can handle it without assistance. On some models, the outside of the case can be used as one end of the tape when measuring inside dimensions.

Simple Calipers

Simple calipers are used in conjunction with a scale to measure diameters. The calipers most commonly used are shown in **Figure 62.**

Outside calipers for measuring outside diameters are bowlegged; those used for inside diameters have straight legs with the feet turned outward. Calipers are adjusted by pulling or pushing the legs to open or close them. Fine adjustment is made by tapping one leg slightly on a hard surface to close them or by turning them upside down and tapping on the joint end to open them.

Figure 62. Simple calipers—noncalibrated.

Spring-joint calipers have the legs joined by a strong spring hinge and linked together by a screw and adjusting nut. For measuring chamfered cavities (grooves) or for use over flanges, transfer calipers are available. They are equipped with a small auxiliary leaf attached to one of the legs by a screw. The measurement is made as with ordinary calipers; then the leaf is locked to the leg.

Slide Caliper

The main disadvantage of using ordinary calipers is that they do not give a direct reading of a caliper setting. As explained earlier, you must measure a caliper setting with a rule. To overcome this disadvantage, use slide calipers (see Figure 63). This instrument is occasionally called a *caliper rule*.

Figure 63. Caliper square (slide caliper).

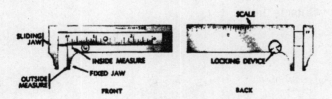

Slide calipers can be used for measuring outside, inside, and other dimensions. One side of the caliper is used as a measuring rule, while the scale on the opposite side is used in measuring outside and inside dimensions. Graduations on both scales are in inches and fractions thereof. A locking screw is incorporated to hold the slide caliper jaws in position during use. Stamped on the frame are two words, "IN" and "OUT." These are used in reading the scale while making inside and outside measurements, respectively.

To measure the outside diameter of round stock or the thickness of flat stock, move the jaws of the caliper into firm contact with the surface of the stock. Read the measurement at the reference line stamped OUT.

While measuring the inside diameter of a hole or the distance between two surfaces, insert only the rounded tips of the caliper jaws into the hole or between the two surfaces. Read the measurement on the reference line stamped IN.

Note that two reference lines are needed if the caliper is to measure both outside and inside dimensions and that they are separated by an amount equal to the outside dimension of the rounded tips when the caliper is closed.

Pocket models of slide calipers are commonly made in 3-inch and 5-inch sizes and are graduated to read in 32nds and 64ths. Pocket slide calipers are valuable when extreme precision is not required. They are frequently used for duplicating work when the expense of fixed gauges is not warranted.

Vernier Caliper

A *vernier caliper* (see Figure 64) consists of an L-shaped member with a scale engraved on the long shank. A sliding member is free to move on the bar and carries a jaw that matches the arm of the L. The vernier scale is engraved on a small plate that is attached to the sliding member.

Perhaps the most distinct advantage of the vernier caliper over other types of calipers is the ability to provide very accurate measurements over a large range. It can be used for both internal and external surfaces. Pocket models usually measure from 0 to 3 inches, but sizes are available all the way to 4 feet. In using the vernier caliper, you must be able to measure with a slide caliper and be able to read a vernier scale.

Figure 64. Vernier caliper.

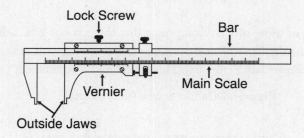

Micrometer

In much wider use than the vernier caliper is the *micrometer*, commonly called the "mike." It is important that a person who is working with machinery or in a machine shop thoroughly understands the mechanical principles, construction, use, and care of the micrometer. **Figure 65** shows an outside micrometer caliper with the various parts clearly indicated. Micrometers are used to measure distances to the nearest .001 of an inch. The measurement is usually expressed or written as a decimal, so you must know the method of writing and reading decimals.

Figure 65. Nomenclature of an outside micrometer caliper.

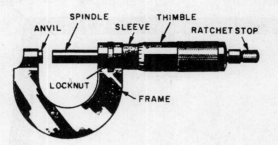

Types

There are three types of micrometers that are commonly used: the outside micrometer caliper (including the screw thread micrometer), the inside micrometer, and the depth micrometer. The outside micrometer is used for measuring outside dimensions, such as the diameter of a piece of round stock. The screw thread micrometer is used to determine the pitch diameter of screws. The inside micrometer is used for measuring inside dimensions; for example, the inside diameter of a tube or hole, the bore of a cylinder, or the width of a recess. The depth micrometer is used for measuring the depth of holes or recesses.

Squares

Squares are primarily used for testing and checking trueness of an angle or for laying out lines on materials. Most squares have a rule marked on their edge. As a result, they may also be used for measuring. There are several types of squares commonly used.

Carpenter's Square

The size of a carpenter's steel square (see Figure 66) is usually 12 × 8 inches, 24 × 16 inches, or 24 × 18 inches. The flat sides of the blade and the tongue are graduated in inches and fractions of an inch. (The square also contains information that helps to simplify or eliminate the need for computations in many woodworking tasks.) The most common uses for this square are laying out and squaring up large patterns and for testing the flatness and squareness of large surfaces. Squaring is accomplished by placing the square at right angles to adjacent surfaces and observing if light shows between the work and the square.

Figure 66. Carpenter's square.

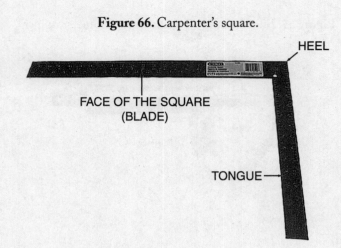

One type of carpenter's square (framing) has additional tables engraved on the square. With the framing square, the craftsman can perform calculations rapidly and lay out rafters, oblique joints, and stairs.

Try Square

The *try square* (see Figure 67) consists of two parts at right angles to one another: a thick wood or iron stock and a thin, steel blade. Most try squares are made with the blades graduated in inches and fractions of an inch. The blade length varies from 2 to 12 inches. This square is used for setting or checking lines or surfaces that have to be at right angles to each other.

Figure 67. Common try square.

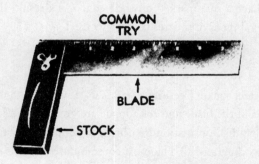

Sliding T-Bevel

The sliding T-bevel (see Figure 68) is an adjustable try square with a slotted beveled blade. Blades are normally 6 to 8 inches long. The sliding T-bevel is used for laying out angles other than right angles and for testing constructed angles such as bevels. These squares are made with either wood or metal handles.

Figure 68. Sliding T-bevel.

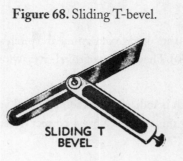

Miscellaneous Gages

There are a number of miscellaneous gages, or gauges. The depth gage, feeler gage, thread gage, dividers, and plumb bob are among some of the gages that are discussed.

Depth Gage

A depth gage is an instrument for measuring the depth of holes, slots, counterbores, and recesses and the distance from a surface to some recessed part.

Thickness (Feeler) Gage

Thickness (feeler) gages are used for checking and measuring small openings, such as contact point clearances, narrow slots, etc. These gages are made in many shapes and sizes, and, as shown in **Figure 69**, thickness gages can be made with multiple blades (usually 2 to 26). Each blade is a specific number of thousandths of an inch thick. This enables the application of one tool to the measurement of a variety of thicknesses. Some thickness gage blades are straight, whereas others are bent at 45- and 90-degree angles at the end. Thickness gages can also be grouped so that there are several short and several long blades together. Before using a feeler gage, remove any foreign matter from the blades. You cannot get a correct measurement unless the blades are clean.

Figure 69. Thickness gages.

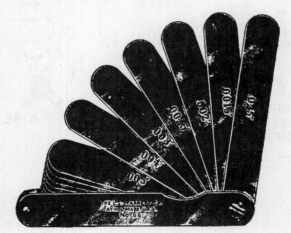

Thread Gage

Thread gages (screw-pitch gages) are used to determine the pitch and number of threads per inch of threaded fasteners (see Figure 70). They consist of thin leaves whose edges are toothed to correspond to standard thread sections.

The number of threads per inch is indicated by the numerical value on the blade that is found to fit the unknown threads. Using this value as a basis, correct sizes of nuts, bolts, tap cutters, and die cutters are selected for use.

Figure 70. Screw-pitch gage.

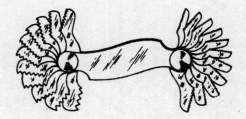

Wire Gage

The *wire gage* shown in **Figure 71** is used for measuring the diameters of wires or the thickness of sheet metal. This gage is circular in shape with cutouts in the outer perimeter. Each cutout gages a different size from No. 0 to No. 36. Examination of the gage will show that the larger the gage number, the smaller the diameter or thickness.

Figure 71. Using a wire gauge to measure wire and sheet metal.

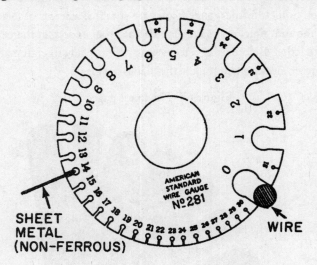

Marking Gages

A marking gage is used to mark off guidelines parallel to an edge, end, or surface of a piece of wood or metal. It has a sharp spur or pin that does the marking.

Marking gages (see Figure 72) are made of wood or steel. They consist of a graduated beam 8 inches long on which a head slides. The head can be fastened at any point on the beam by means of a thumbscrew. The thumbscrew presses a brass shoe tightly against the beam and locks it firmly in position. The steel pin or spur that does the marking projects from the beam about $\frac{1}{16}$ inch.

Figure 72. Marking gages.

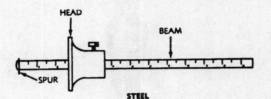
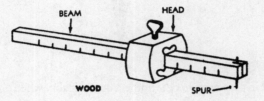

Dividers

Dividers (see Figure 73) are useful instruments for transferring measurements and are frequently used in scribing arcs and circles in layout work.

Figure 73. Setting a divider to a desired radius.

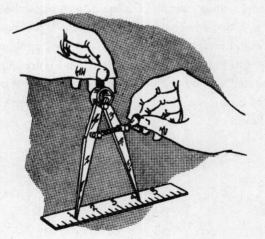

Plumb Bob

A *plumb bob* (see Figure 74) is a pointed, tapered brass or bronze weight that is suspended from a cord for determining the vertical or plumb line to or from a point on the ground. Common weights for plumb bobs are 6, 8, 10, 12, 14, 16, 18, and 24 oz. A plumb bob usually has a detachable tip so that if the tip should become damaged it can be renewed without replacing the entire instrument.

Figure 74. Plumb bob.

The plumb bob is used in carpentry to determine true verticality when erecting vertical uprights and corner posts of framework. Surveyors use it for transferring and lining up points.

Levels

Levels are tools designed to prove whether a plane or surface is true horizontal or true vertical. Some precision levels are calibrated so that they will indicate in degrees, minutes, and seconds the angle inclination of a surface in relation to a horizontal or vertical surface.

The level is a simple instrument consisting of a liquid, such as alcohol or chloroform, partially filling a glass vial or tube so that a bubble remains. The tube is mounted in a frame, which may be aluminum, wood, or iron. Levels are equipped with one, two, or more tubes. One tube is built in the frame at right angles to another. The tube indicated in **Figure 75** is slightly curved, causing the bubble to seek always the highest point in the tube. On the outside of the tube are two sets of graduation lines separated by a space. Leveling is accomplished when the air bubble is centered between the graduation lines.

Figure 75. Horizontal and vertical use of level.

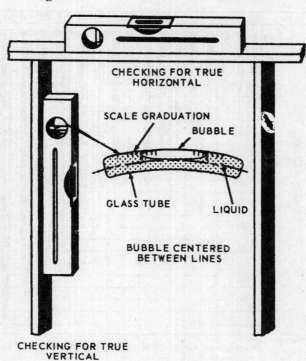

CHECKING FOR TRUE
HORIZONTAL

SCALE GRADUATION

BUBBLE

GLASS TUBE

LIQUID

BUBBLE CENTERED
BETWEEN LINES

CHECKING FOR TRUE
VERTICAL

Fastening Components

Woodworking Fasteners

Nails

Nails achieve their fastening or holding power when they displace wood fibers from their original position. The pressure exerted against the nail by these fibers, as they try to spring back to their original position, provides the holding power.

The usual type of shank is round, but there are various special-purpose nails with other types of shanks. Nails with square, triangular, longitudinally grooved, and spirally grooved shanks have a much greater holding power than smooth round wire nails of the same size.

The lengths of the most commonly used nails are designated by the *penny* system. The abbreviation for the word "penny" is the letter "d." Thus, the expression "a 2d nail" means a two-penny nail. The penny sizes and corresponding length and thicknesses (in gage sizes) of the common nails are shown in **Figure 76.** The thickness of a nail increases and the number of nails per pound decreases with the penny size.

Figure 76. Common nail sizes.

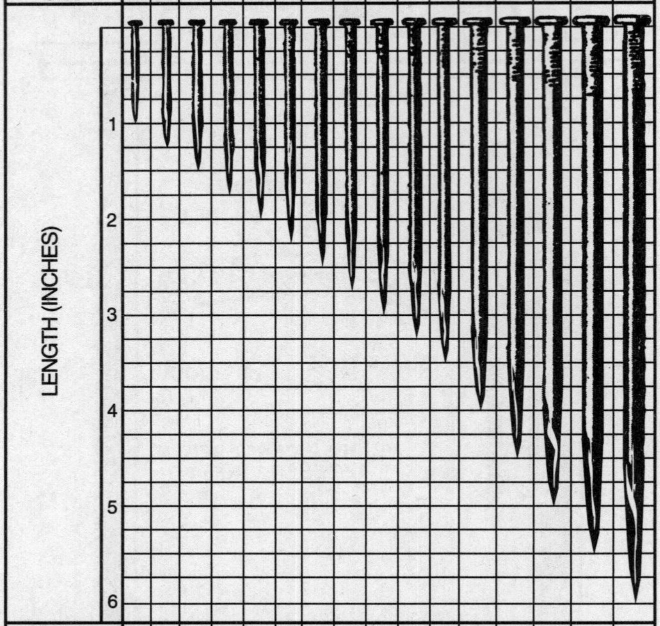

Size	2d	3d	4d	5d	6d	7d	8d	9d	10d	12d	16d	20d	30d	40d	50d	60d
Diameter (inches)	.072	.08	.098	.098	.113	.112	.131	.131	.148	.148	.162	.192	.207	.225	.244	.262
Steel wire gauge	15	14	12	12	11	11	10	10	9	9	8	6	5	4	3	2
Number per pound	900	615	322	254	200	154	106	85	74	57	46	29	23	17	14	11

LENGTH (INCHES)

Spikes have larger diameters than nails the same length and are designated by the penny system for lengths up to 6 inches (60d). Longer spikes are designated by diameter. Nails smaller than 2d are designated in fractions of an inch in length instead of in the penny system.

Following are the more common types of wire nails. The *brad* and the *finish* nail both have a deep countersink head that is designed to be "set" below the surface of the work. These nails are used for interior and exterior trimwork where the nails are "set" and puttied to conceal their location. The *casing* nail is used for the same purpose, but because of its flat countersink head, it may be driven flush and left that way.

The other nails shown in **Figure 77** are all flat-headed, without countersinks. One of these flat-headed nails (called the *common* nail) is one of the most widely used in general wood construction. Nails with large flat heads are used for nailing roof paper, plaster board, and similar thin or soft materials. *Duplex* or *double-headed* nails are used for nailing temporary structures, such as scaffolds, which are eventually to be dismantled. When using the double-headed nail, it is driven to the lowest head so that it can be easily drawn at a later time.

Figure 77. Nail varieties.

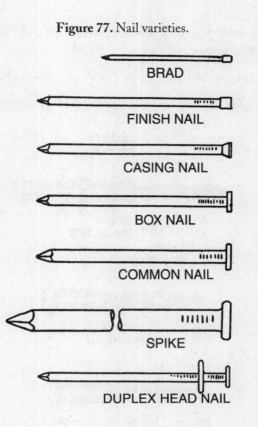

BRAD

FINISH NAIL

CASING NAIL

BOX NAIL

COMMON NAIL

SPIKE

DUPLEX HEAD NAIL

Wood Screws

Screws have several advantages over nails. They may be easily withdrawn at any time without injury to the material. They also hold the wood more securely, can be easily tightened, and, generally, are neater in appearance. Wood screws are designated by material, type of head (see Figure 78), and size.

Figure 78. Woodscrew heads.

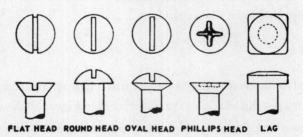

FLAT HEAD   ROUND HEAD   OVAL HEAD   PHILLIPS HEAD   LAG

Most wood screws are made of steel or brass, but other metals are used as well. Cost or special-purpose application will determine the selection of the material to be used.

The size of an ordinary wood screw is indicated by the length and body diameter (unthreaded part) of the screw. **Figure 79** shows the nomenclature and the three most common types of wood screws. Notice that the length is always measured from the point to the greatest diameter of the head.

Body diameters are designated by gauge numbers, running from 0 (for about a $\frac{1}{16}$ -inch diameter) to 24 (for about a $\frac{3}{8}$ -inch diameter).

Designation of length and gauge number appear as "1¼-9". This means a No. 9 screw is 1¼ inches long.

Figure 79. Nomenclature and types of wood screws.

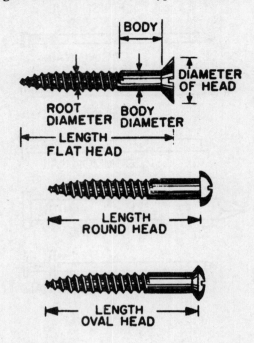

Metal Fastening Devices

Many mechanisms and devices are held together with metal fasteners. Only the more commonly used fasteners are discussed.

Metal parts can be fastened together with various fastening devices, such as rivets, bolts, screws, etc. Rivets provide a more permanent type of fastening, whereas bolts and screws are used to fasten together parts that may have to be taken apart later.

Bolts

A *bolt* is distinguished from a wood screw by the fact that it does not thread into the wood but goes through and is held by a nut threaded onto the end of the bolt. **Figure 80** shows four common types of bolts used in woodworking. *Stove* bolts are rather small, ranging in length from $\frac{3}{8}$ to 4 inches and in body diameter from $\frac{1}{8}$ to $\frac{3}{8}$ inches. *Carriage and machine bolts* run from ¾ to 20 inches long and from $\frac{3}{16}$ to ¾ inches in diameter. (The carriage bolt has a square section below the head, which is embedded in the wood to prevent the bolt from turning as the nut is drawn up.) The machine bolt has a hexagonal or square head, which is held with a wrench to prevent it from turning.

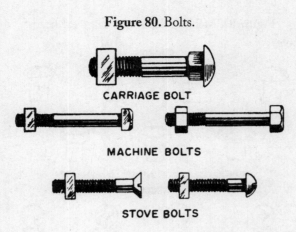

Figure 80. Bolts.

CARRIAGE BOLT

MACHINE BOLTS

STOVE BOLTS

Machine Screws

The term "machine screw" is the general term used to designate the small screws that are used in tapped holes for the assembly of metal parts. Machine screws may also be used with nuts, but usually they are screwed into holes that have been tapped with matching threads.

Machine screws are manufactured in a variety of lengths, diameters, (gauges) pitches (threads per inch), head shapes, materials, and finishes. A complete description of machine screws must include these factors. For example, "½ inch, 8-32, round head, brass, chromium-plated, machine screw." The first number is the length of the screw. Let's examine some of these other factors.

Diameter and Pitch

The diameters of American Standard machine screws are expressed in gage numbers or fractions of an inch. In the preceding paragraph, the "8-32" means that the screw gage is No. 8 and that it has 32 threads per inch. Note, particularly, that the "eight" and "thirty-two" are two separate numbers, indicating two individual measurements; they are never to be written as a fraction such as $\frac{8}{32}$ or pronounced "eight-thirty-seconds."

Materials and Finishes

Most machine screws are made of steel or brass. They may be plated to help prevent corrosion. Other special machine screws made of aluminum or Monel metal are also obtainable. The latter metal is highly resistant to the corrosive action of salt water.

Head Shapes

A variety of common and special machine screw head shapes are shown in **Figure 81.** Some of the heads require special tools for driving and removing. These special tools are usually included in a kit that comes with the machine or installation on which the screws are used.

Figure 81. Machine screw and capscrew heads.

Capscrews

Capscrews perform the same functions as machine screws but come in larger sizes for heavier work. Sizes range up to 1 inch in diameter and 6 inches in length.

Capscrews are usually used without nuts. They are screwed into tapped holes and are sometimes referred to as tap bolts. Capscrews may have square, hex, flat, button, or fillister heads. Fillister heads are best for use on moving parts when such heads are sunk into counterbored holes. Hex heads are usually used where the metal parts do not move.

The strongest capscrews are made of alloy steel and can withstand great stresses, strains, and shearing forces. Capscrews made of Monel metal are often specified on machinery that is exposed to salt water. Some capscrews have small holes through their heads. A wire, called a *safety wire*, is run through the holes of several capscrews to keep them from coming loose.

Setscrews

Setscrews are used to secure small pulleys, gears, and cams to shafts and to provide positive adjustment of machine parts. They are classified by diameter, thread, head shape, and point shape. The point shape is important because it determines the holding qualities of the setscrew.

Setscrews hold best if they have either a *cone point* or a *dog point*, shown in **Figure 82**. These points fit into matching recesses in the shaft against which they bear.

Headless setscrews—slotted, Allen, or Bristol types—are used with moving parts because they do not stick up above the surface. They are threaded all the way from point to head. *Common setscrews*, used on fixed parts, have square heads. They have threads all the way from the point to the shoulder of the head.

Figure 82. Setscrews and thumb screws.

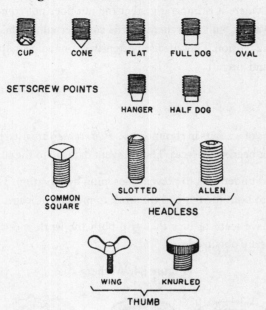

Thumb screws are used for setscrews, adjusting screws, and clamping screws. Because of their design they can be loosened or tightened without the use of tools.

Nuts

Square and hexagonal nuts are standard but they are supplemented by special nuts (see Figure 83). One of these is the *jam nut*, used above a standard hex nut to lock it in position. It is about half as thick as the standard hex nut and has a washer face.

Figure 83. Common kinds of nuts.

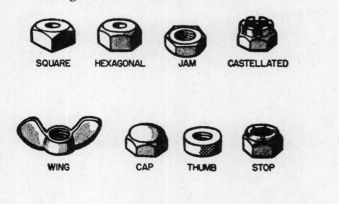

Castellated nuts are slotted so that a safety wire or *cotter key* may be pushed through the slots and into a matching hole in the bolt. This provides a positive method of preventing the nut from working loose. For example, you will see these nuts used with the bolts that hold the two halves of an engine connecting rod together.

Wing nuts are used where the desired degree of tightness can be obtained by the fingers. *Cap nuts* are used where appearance is an important consideration. They are usually made of chromium plated brass. *Thumb nuts* are knurled, so they can be turned by hand for easy assembly and disassembly.

Elastic stop nuts are used where it is imperative that the nut does not come loose. These nuts have a fiber or composition washer built into them that is compressed automatically against the screw threads to provide holding tension. They are used extensively on radio equipment, sound equipment, fire control equipment, and aircraft.

Washers

Figure 84 shows the types of washers in common use. *Flat washers* are used to back up bolt heads and nuts and to provide larger bearing surfaces. They prevent damage to the surfaces of the metal parts.

Split lock washers are used under nuts to prevent loosening by vibration. The ends of these spring-hardened washers dig into both the nut and the work to prevent slippage.

Shakeproof lock washers have teeth or lugs that grip both the work and the nut. Several patented designs, shapes, and sizes are obtainable.

Figure 84. Washers.

FLAT WASHER   SPLIT LOCK   SHAKEPROOF
WASHER   WASHER

Keys and Pins

Cotter keys (see Figure 85) are used to secure screws, nuts, bolts, and pins. They are also used as stops and holders on shafts and rods. *Square keys* and *woodruff keys* are used to prevent hand wheels, gears, cams, and pulleys from turning on a shaft. These keys are strong enough to carry heavy loads if they are fitted and seated properly.

Figure 85. Keys and pins.

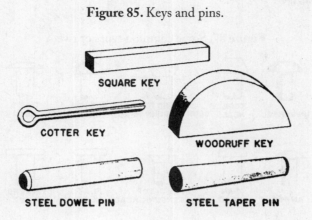

Taper pins are used to locate and position matching parts. They are also used to secure small pulleys and gears to shafts. They usually have a taper of ¼ inch per foot. Holes for taper pins must be reamed with tapered reamers. If this is not done, the taper pin will not fit properly.

Dowel pins are used to position and align the units or parts of an assembly. One end of a dowel pin is chamfered (grooved), and it is usually .001 to .002 inch greater in diameter than the size of the hole into which the pin will be driven.

Cotter Pins

Some cotter pins are made of low-carbon steel, where as others consist of stainless steel, and thus are more resistant to corrosion. Regardless of shape or material, all cotter pins are used for the same general purpose—safetying.

Dimension parameters of a cotter pin are shown in **Figure 86.** Whenever uneven prong cotter pins are used, the length measurement is to the end of the shortest prong.

Figure 86. Types of cotter pins.

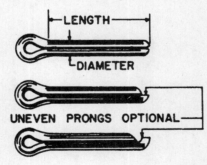

Rivets

Rivets are used extensively as a fastening device in aircraft. They are also used to join metal sheets when brazing, welding, or locking techniques will not provide a satisfactory joint.

Rivet Types

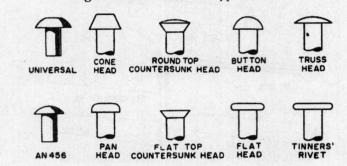

Figure 87. Some common types of rivets.

The major types of rivets used extensively include the standard type and pop rivets. Standard rivets must be driven using a bucking bar, whereas the pop rivets have a self-heading capability and may be installed where it is impossible to use a bucking bar.

- **Standard Rivets.** Wherever possible, rivets should be made of the same material as the material they join. They are classified by lengths, diameters, and their head shape and size. Some of the standard head shapes are shown in **Figure 87.**

Selection of the proper length of a rivet is important. Should too long a rivet be used, the formed head will be too large, or the rivet may bend or be forced between the sheets being riveted. Should too short a rivet be used, the formed head will be too small or the riveted material will be damaged. The length of the rivet should equal the sum of the thickness of the metal plus 1½ times the diameter of the rivet.

- **Pop Rivets.** Pop rivets have two advantages compared to standard rivets in that they can be set by one person and also be used for blind fastening. This means that they can be used when there is limited or no access to the reverse side of the work.

PRACTICE QUESTIONS

1. A fuel-injection system on an automobile engine eliminates the necessity for
   A. a manifold.
   B. a carburetor.
   C. spark plugs.
   D. a distributor.

2. A car uses too much oil when which parts are worn?
   A. Pistons
   B. Piston rings
   C. Main bearings
   D. Connecting rods

3. The function of the rotor is to
   A. distribute the electricity to the spark plugs.
   B. open and close the distributor points.
   C. rotate the distributor cam.
   D. rotate the distributor shaft.

4. What happens if cylinder head torquing is not done in proper sequence?
   A. It warps the piston rings.
   B. It cracks the intake manifold.
   C. It distorts the head.
   D. It reduces valve clearance.

5. The saw shown is used mainly to cut

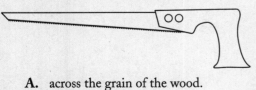

   A. across the grain of the wood.
   B. along the grain of the wood.
   C. plywood.
   D. odd-shaped holes in wood.

6. Sheet metal should be cut with
   A. household scissors.
   B. a hacksaw.
   C. tin shears.
   D. a jigsaw.

7. A lathe would normally be used in making which of the following items?
   A. A baseball bat
   B. A bookcase
   C. A hockey stick
   D. A picture frame

8. What tool is shown below?

   A. Countersink
   B. Keyhole saw
   C. Hole saw
   D. Grinding saw

ANSWER KEY AND EXPLANATIONS

| 1. B | 3. A | 5. D | 7. A | 8. C |
| 2. B | 4. C | 6. C | | |

1. **The correct answer is B.** Fuel-injected engines use injectors to spray the fuel mixture into the combustion chamber rather than using a carburetor to mix the fuel and air.

2. **The correct answer is B.** Piston rings carry small amounts of oil to coat the cylinders. Normally, the oil is not allowed to enter the combustion chamber. When piston rings are worn, they allow oil through to be burned during the combustion process.

3. **The correct answer is A.** The rotor turns inside the distributor connecting the charge from the coil to the spark plug at the exact time required to complete the combustion process.

4. **The correct answer is C.** Improper torque may cause distorting of the head because one side of the head may be too tight while the other side is not tight enough. This may also result in improper dissipation of heat also causing the head to warp.

5. **The correct answer is D.** The saw pictured is a "compass saw," which is used to cut circular or other nonrectangular shapes in wood.

6. **The correct answer is C.** Sheet metal work is best done using tin shears. Although a hacksaw or jigsaw may work, you will wind up with distorted metal. Household scissors just won't "cut it."

7. **The correct answer is A.** A lathe is a machine used to make objects that are made of one solid piece of material and usually has a rounded shape, such as table legs and baseball bats.

8. **The correct answer is C.** A hole saw uses a drill bit–like instrument to start the hole and then a rounded "saw" blade to cut the actual hole.

SUMMING IT UP

- The **power** of an automobile engine comes from the burning of a mixture of gasoline and air in a small, enclosed space. When this mixture burns, it expands greatly and pushes out in all directions.

- The **cylinder** resembles a tall metal can, or a pipe closed at one end. Some of the early automobiles used cast iron pipes for cylinders.

- Inside the cylinder there is a **piston**, which is a plug that is close-fitting but can slide up and down easily. It is the part of the engine that is moved by the expanding gases, being driven down on each power impulse or explosion.

- The **crankshaft** is a shaft with an off-set portion, the crank, which moves in a circular motion as the shaft rotates. The top end of the connecting rod is fastened to the piston, and the bottom end is fastened to the crank.

- **Valves** allow the fuel-air mixture into the engine and also release the burned gases. Two holes are cut in the top of the cylinder, one for intake and one for exhaust. Metal discs are arranged to fit tightly over the holes to close them, but when pushed down they open the holes to allow passage of the gases through them.

- To produce power, the **carburetor** supplies the engine with a mixture of gasoline and air blended in the proper proportions. Gasoline is pumped from the tank to the carburetor by the fuel pump.

- A **spark plug** is inserted in the top of each cylinder, and a spark is created by electricity jumping across the gap between the two electrodes of the plug.

- A **battery** furnishes the electricity, but additional pieces of equipment are necessary for acomplete ignition system. The coil and the breaker cooperate to develop a very high voltage, andthe distributor is responsible for getting the high-voltage electricity to the right spark plug at the right time.

- Most automobile engines are **four-cycle** engines. This means they operate on a four-stroke cycle, taking four strokes of the piston—down, up, down, up—for one complete cycle of events.

- There are three major pollutants that are emitted from automobiles into the atmosphere: **hydrocarbons, carbon monoxide**, and **oxides of nitrogen**.

- **Tools** are designed to make a job easier and enable you to work more efficiently. The types of tools used to work on automobiles can be categorized into the following groups: striking tools, turning tools, metal-cutting tools, files, woodcutting hand tools, screwdrivers, pliers, vises and clamps, measuring tools, gauges, levels, and fastening components.

Mechanical Comprehension

Chapter 10

OVERVIEW

- **Levers**
- **Block and Tackle**
- **The Wheel and Axle**
- **The Inclined Plane and the Wedge**
- **The Screw**
- **Gears**
- **Work**
- **Power**
- **Force and Pressure**
- **Machine Elements and Basic Mechanisms**
- **Basic Mechanisms**
- **Clutches**
- **Practice Questions**
- **Answer Key and Explanations**
- **Summing It Up**

LEVERS

The simplest machine, and perhaps the one that you are most familiar with, is the *lever*. A seesaw is a familiar example of a lever in which one weight balances the other. A lever consists of a rigid part that pivots about a point called the fulcrum.

The type, or class, of lever depends on the arrangement of these elements:

1. *Fulcrum* (F)
2. *Effort* (E)
3. *Resistance* (R)

Look at the lever in **Figure 1.** You see the pivot point F (fulcrum); the effort (E), which you apply at distance A from the fulcrum; and a resistance (R), which acts at distance a from the fulcrum. Distances A and a are the lever arms.

Figure 1. A simple lever.

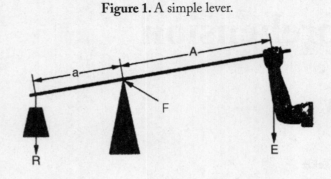

Classes of Levers

The three classes of levers are shown in **Figures 2 and 3**. The location of the fulcrum (the fixed or pivot point) with relation to the resistance (or weight) and the effort determines the lever class.

First-Class Levers

In the first-class lever (see Figure 2A), the fulcrum is located between the effort and the resistance. As mentioned earlier, the seesaw is a good example of the first-class lever. The amount of weight and the distance from the fulcrum can be varied to suit the need. Crowbars, shears, and pliers are common examples of this class of lever.

Figure 2. First- and second-class levers.

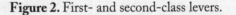
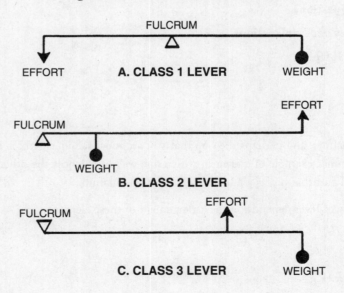

Second-Class Levers

The second-class lever (see Figure 2B) has the fulcrum at one end; the effort is applied at the other end. The resistance is somewhere between these two points.

Both first- and second-class levers are commonly used to help in overcoming big resistances with a relatively small effort.

Third-Class Levers

There are occasions when you will want to speed up the movement of the resistance even though you have to use a large amount of effort. Levers that help you accomplish this are third-class levers. As shown in **Figure 2C**, the fulcrum is at one end of the lever and the weight or resistance to be overcome is at the other end, with the effort applied at some point between. You can always spot third-class levers because you will find the effort applied between the fulcrum and the resistance. Look at **Figure 3**. It is easy to see that although point E is moving the short distance, e, the resistance, R, has been moved a greater distance, r. The speed of R must have been greater than that of E, because R covered a greater distance in the same length of time.

Figure 3. A third-class lever.

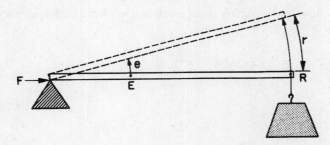

One convenient thing about machines is that you can determine in advance the forces required for their operation, as well as the forces they will exert. Consider for a moment the first-class lever. Suppose you have an iron bar, like the one shown in **Figure 4**. This bar is 9 feet long, and you want to use it to raise a 300-pound crate off the deck while you slide a dolly under the crate. But you can exert only 100 pounds to lift the crate. So you place the fulcrum—a wooden block—beneath one end of the bar, and force that end of the bar under the crate. Then you push down on the other end of the bar. After a few adjustments of the position of the fulcrum, you will find that your 100-pound force will just fit the crate when the fulcrum is 2 feet from center of the crate.

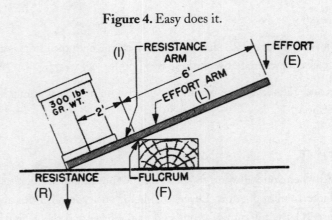

Figure 4. Easy does it.

This leaves a 6-foot length of bar from the fulcrum to the point where you push down. The 6-foot portion is three times as long as the distance from the fulcrum to the center of the crate. But you lifted a load three times as great as the force you applied—3 × 100 = 300 pounds. Here is an indication of a direct relationship between lengths of lever arms and forces acting on those arms.

You can state this relationship in general terms by saying the length of the effort arm is the same number of times greater than the length of the resistance arm as the resistance to be overcome is greater than the effort you must apply. Writing these words as a mathematical equation, it looks like this:

$$\frac{L}{\ell} = \frac{R}{E}$$

in which

      L = length of effort arm

      ℓ = length of resistance arm

      R = resistance weight or force

      E = effort force

Remember that all distances must be in the same units—such as feet—and all forces must be in the same units—such as pounds.

Mechanical Advantage

There is another thing about first- and second-class levers that you have probably noticed by now. Since they can be used to magnify the applied force, they provide positive mechanical advantages. The third-class lever provides what's called a fractional mechanical advantage, which is really a mechanical disadvantage. You use more force than the force of the load you lift.

$$\text{MECHANICAL ADVANTAGE} = \frac{\text{RESISTANCE}}{\text{EFFORT}}$$

or

$$\text{M.A.} = \frac{R}{E}$$

Mechanical advantage of levers may also be found by dividing the length of the effort arm A by the length of the resistance arm a. Stated as a formula, this reads:

$$\text{MECHANICAL ADVANTAGE} = \frac{\text{EFFORT ARM}}{\text{RESISTANCE ARM}}$$

$$\text{M.A.} = \frac{A}{a}$$

BLOCK AND TACKLE

Blocks, also known as pulleys, are simple machines that have many uses. Remember how your mouth hung open as you watched movers taking a piano out of a fourth-story window? The guy on the end of the tackle eased the piano safely to the sidewalk with a mysterious arrangement of blocks and ropes.

You rig a block and tackle to make some of your work easier. Learn the names of the parts of the block shown in **Figure 5**. Look at the single block and see some of the ways you can use it. If you lash a single block to a fixed object—an overhead, a yardarm, or a bulkhead—you give yourself the advantage of being able to pull from a convenient direction.

Figure 5. Look it over.

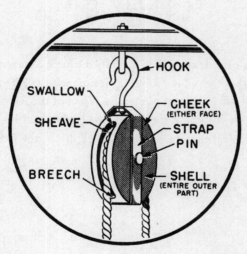

Mechanical Advantage

With a single fixed sheave, the force of your down-pull on the fall must be equal to the weight of the object being hoisted. You can't use this rig to lift a heavy load or resistance with a small effort; you can change only the direction of your pull.

A single fixed block is really a first-class lever with equal arms. The arms EF and FR are equal; hence, the mechanical advantage is one. When you pull down at A with a force of one pound, you raise a load of one pound at B. A single fixed block does not magnify force or speed (see Figure 6).

Figure 6. No advantage.

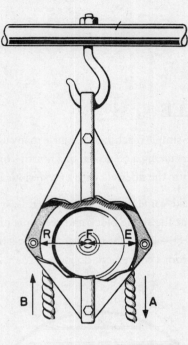

You can, however, use a single block-and-fall to magnify the force you exert. Notice, in **Figure 7**, that the block is not fixed, and that the fall is doubled as it supports the 200-pound cask. When rigged this way, a single block-and-fall is called a runner. Each half of the fall carries one half of the total load, or 100 pounds. Thus, by the use of the runner, the person is lifting a 200-pound cask with a 100-pound pull. The mechanical advantage is two. Check this by the formula:

$$\text{M.A.} = \frac{R}{E} = \frac{200}{100}, \text{ or } 2$$

Figure 7. A runner.

The single movable block in this setup is really a second-class lever (see Figure 8). Your effort, E, acts upward on the arm, EF, which is the diameter of the sheave, or pulley. The resistance, R, acts downward on the arm, FR, which is the radius of the sheave. Since the diameter is twice the radius, the mechanical advantage is two.

But, when the effort at E moves up two feet, the load at R is raised only about one foot. That's one thing to remember about blocks and falls—if you are actually getting a mechanical advantage from the system, the length of rope that passes through your hands is greater than the distance that the load is raised. However, if you can lift a big load with a small effort, you don't care how much rope you have to pull.

The person in **Figure 7** is in an awkward position to pull. If he had another single block handy, he could use it to change the direction of the pull, as in **Figure 9**. This second arrangement is known as a gun-tackle purchase. Because the second block is fixed, it merely changes the direction of pull—and the mechanical advantage of the whole system remains two.

You can arrange blocks in a number of ways, depending on the job to be done and the mechanical advantage you want to get. For example, a luff tackle consists of a double block and a single block, rigged as in **Figure 10**. Notice that the weight is suspended by the three parts of rope that extend from the movable single block. Each part of the rope carries its share of the load. If the crate weighs 600 pounds, then each of the three parts of the rope supports its share—200 pounds. If there's a pull of 200 pounds downward on rope B, you will have to pull down with a force of 200 pounds on A to counterbalance the pull on B. Neglecting the friction in the block, a pull of 200 pounds is all that is necessary to raise the crate. The mechanical advantage is:

$$\text{M.A.} = \frac{R}{E} = \frac{600}{200} = 3$$

Figure 8. It's 2 to 1.   **Figure 9.** A gun tackle.

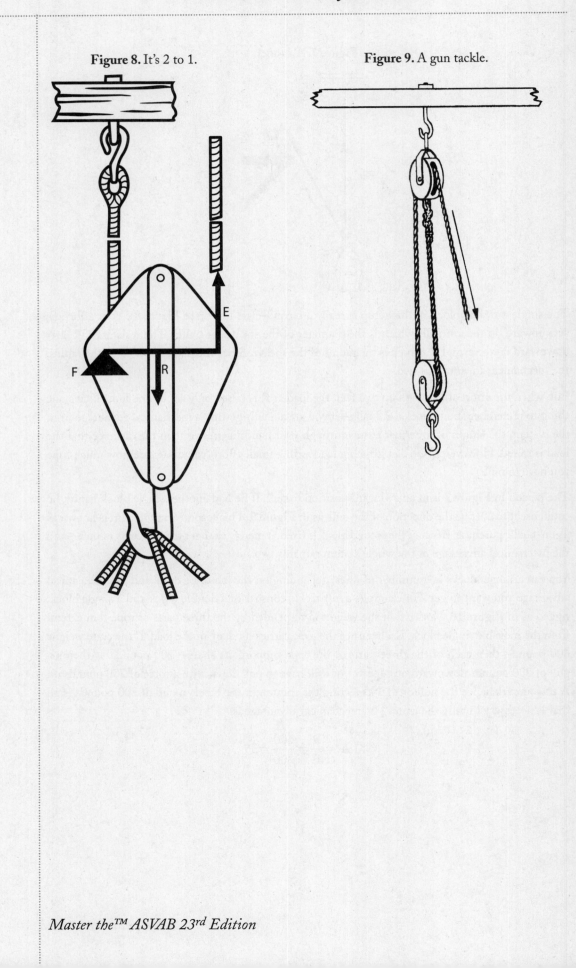

Figure 10. A luff tackle.

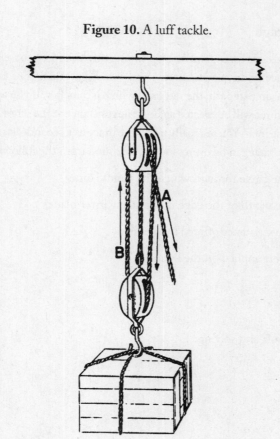

Here's a good tip. If you count the number of the parts of rope going to and from the movable block, you can figure the mechanical advantage at a glance. This simple rule will help you to quickly approximate the mechanical advantage of most tackles.

Many combinations of single-, double-, and triple-sheave blocks are possible.

THE WHEEL AND AXLE

Have you ever tried to open a door when the knob was missing? If you have, you know that trying to twist that small four-sided shaft with your fingers is tough work. That gives you some appreciation of the advantage you get by using a knob. The door knob is an example of a simple machine called a wheel and axle.

The steering wheel on an automobile, the handle of an ice-cream freezer, and a brace and bit are familiar examples of this type of simple machine. As you know from your experience with these devices, the wheel and axle is commonly used to multiply the force you exert. If a screwdriver won't do a job because you can't turn it, you stick a screwdriver bit in the chuck of a brace and the screw probably goes in with little difficulty.

There's one thing you'll want to get straight at the beginning. The wheel-and-axle machine consists of a wheel or crank rigidly attached to the axle, which turns with the wheel. Thus, the front wheel of an automobile is not a wheel-and-axle machine because the axle does not turn with the wheel.

Mechanical Advantage

How does the wheel-and-axle arrangement help to magnify the force you exert? Suppose you use a screwdriver bit in a brace to drive a stubborn screw (see Figure 11). Your effort is applied on the handle, which moves in a circular path, the radius of which is 5 inches. If you apply a 10-pound force on the handle, how big a force will be exerted against the resistance at the screw? Assume the radius of the screwdriver blade is ¼-inch. You are really using the brace as a second-class lever (see Figure 11). The size of the resistance that can be overcome can be found from the following formula, in which:

L = radius of the circle through which the handle turns

ℓ = one-half the width of the edge of the screwdriver blade

R = force of the resistance offered by the screw

E = force of effort applied on the handle

$$\frac{L}{\ell} = \frac{R}{E}$$

Substituting in the formula and solving:

$$\frac{5}{1/4} = \frac{R}{10}$$

$$R = \frac{5 \times 10}{1/4}$$

$$= 5 \times 10 \times 4$$

$$= 200 \text{ lb.}$$

This means that the screwdriver blade will tend to turn the screw with a force of 200 pounds. The relationship between the radii, or the diameters, or the circumferences, of the wheel and axle tells you how great a mechanical advantage you can get.

Figure 11. Wheel and axle advantage of a screwdriver bit in a brace.

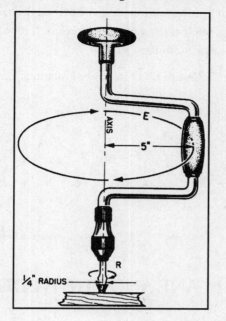

Moment of Force

In a number of situations, you can use the wheel and axle to speed up motion. The rear-wheel sprocket of a bike, along with the rear wheel itself, is an example. When you are pedaling, the sprocket is fixed to the wheel, so the combination is a true wheel-and-axle machine. Assume that the sprocket has a circumference of 8 inches, and the wheel circumference is 80 inches. If you turn the sprocket at a rate of one revolution per second, each sprocket tooth moves at a speed of 8 inches per second. Since the wheel makes one revolution for each revolution made by the sprocket, any point on the tire must move through a distance of 80 inches in one second. So, for every 8-inch movement of a point on the sprocket, you have moved a corresponding point on the wheel through 80 inches.

Since a complete revolution of the sprocket and wheel requires only one second, the speed of a point on the circumference of the wheel is 80 inches per second, or ten times the speed of a tooth on the sprocket. *NOTE: Both sprocket and wheel make the same number of revolutions per second, so the speed of turning for the two is the same.*

Here is an idea that you will find useful in understanding the wheel and axle, as well as other machines. You probably have noticed that the force you apply to a lever tends to turn or rotate it about the fulcrum. You also know that a heave on a fall tends to rotate the sheave of the block and that turning the steering wheel of a car tends to rotate the steering column. Whenever you use a lever, or a wheel and axle, your effort on the lever arm or the rim of the wheel tends to cause a rotation about the fulcrum or the axle in one direction or another. If the rotation occurs in the same direction as the hands of a clock, that direction is called clockwise. If the rotation occurs in the opposite direction from that of the hands of a clock, the direction of rotation is called counterclockwise. A glance at **Figure 12** will make clear the meaning of these terms.

You have already seen that the result of a force acting on the handle of the carpenter's brace depends not only on the amount of that force but also on the distance from the handle to the center of rotation. From here on you'll know this result as the moment of force, or torque (pronounced tork). Moment of force and torque have the same meaning.

Figure 12. Directions of rotation.

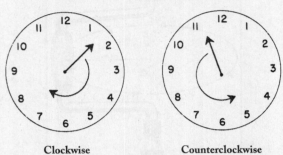

Clockwise   Counterclockwise

THE INCLINED PLANE AND THE WEDGE

The Barrel Roll

You have probably watched a driver load barrels on a truck. The truck is backed up to the curb. The driver places a long double plank or ramp from the sidewalk to the tailgate and then rolls the barrel up the ramp. A 32-gallon barrel may weigh close to 300 pounds when full, and it would be quite a job to lift one up into the truck. Actually, the driver is using a simple machine called the inclined plane. You have seen the inclined plane used in many situations. Cattle ramps, a mountain highway, and the gangplank are familiar examples.

The inclined plane permits you to overcome a large resistance by applying a relatively small force through a longer distance than the load is raised (see Figure 13). Here you see the driver easing the 300-pound barrel up to the bed of the truck, three feet above the sidewalk. He is using a plank nine feet long. If he didn't use the ramp at all, he'd have to apply a 300-pound force straight up through the three-foot distance. With the ramp, however, he can apply his effort over the entire nine feet of the plank as the barrel is slowly rolled up to a height of three feet. It looks, then, as if he could use a force only three-ninths of 300, or 100 pounds, to do the job. And that is actually the situation.

Figure 13. An inclined plane.

Here's the formula:

$$\frac{L}{\ell} = \frac{R}{E}$$

in which

L	=	Length of the ramp, measured along the slope
ℓ	=	Height of the ramp
R	=	Weight of object to be raised or lowered
E	=	Force required to raise or lower object

Now apply the formula to this problem.

In this case, L = 9 feet; ℓ = 3 feet; and R = 300 pounds. By substituting these values in the formula, you get:

$$\frac{9}{3} = \frac{300}{E}$$
$$9E = 900$$
$$E = 100 \text{ pounds}$$

Since the ramp is three times as long as its height, the mechanical advantage is three. You find the theoretical mechanical advantage by dividing the total distance through which your effort is exerted by the vertical distance through which the load is raised or lowered.

The Wedge

You have probably used wedges. The wedge is a special application of the inclined plane. Abe Lincoln used a wedge to help him split logs into rails for fences. The blades of knives, axes, hatchets, and chisels act as wedges when they are forced into a piece of wood. The wedge is two inclined planes, set base to base. By driving the wedge full length into the material to be cut or split, the material is forced apart a distance equal to the width of the broad end of the wedge (see Figure 14).

Long, slim wedges give high mechanical advantage. For example, the wedge of Figure 14 has a mechanical advantage of six. Their greatest value, however, lies in the fact that you can use them in situations where other simple machines won't work. Imagine the trouble you'd have trying to pull a log apart with a system of pulleys.

Figure 14. A wedge.

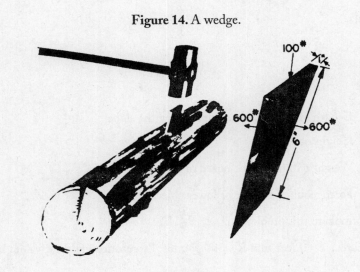

THE SCREW

A Modified Inclined Plane

The screw is a simple machine that has many uses. The vise on a workbench, the screw clamps used to hold a piece of furniture together, and many automobile jacks make use of the great mechanical advantage of the screw.

A screw is a modification of the inclined plane. Cut a sheet of paper in the shape of a right triangle—an inclined plane. Wind it around a pencil, as in **Figure 15**. Then you can see that the screw is actually an inclined plane wrapped around a cylinder. As the pencil is turned, the paper is wound up so that its hypotenuse forms a spiral thread similar to the thread on the screw shown at the right. The pitch of the screw, and of the paper, is the distance between identical points on the same threads, and measured along the length of the screw.

Figure 15. A screw is an inclined plane in spiral form.

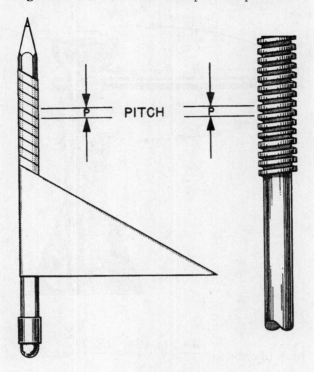

The Jack

To understand how the screw works, look at **Figure 16**. Here you see a jackscrew of the type that is used to raise a house or a piece of heavy machinery. The jack has a handle with a length R. If you pull the handle around one turn, its outer end has described a circle. The circumference of a circle is equal to pi × diameter, or 2 × pi × radius. (You remember that pi equals 3.14, or $\frac{22}{7}$.) That is the distance, or the lever arm, through which your effort is applied.

At the same time, the screw has made one revolution, and in doing so has been raised a height equal to its pitch p. You might say that one full thread has come up out of the base. At any rate, the load has been raised a distance p.

Remember that the theoretical mechanical advantage is equal to the distance through which the effort or pull is applied, divided by the distance the resistance or load is moved.

Assuming a 2-foot—24"—length for the lever arm, and a ¼-inch pitch for the thread, you can find the theoretical mechanical advantage by the formula:

$$\text{M.A. (theoretical) } \frac{2\pi r}{p}$$

in which

r = length of handle = 24 inches

p = pitch, or distance between corresponding points on successive threads = ¼ inch

Figure 16. A jack screw.

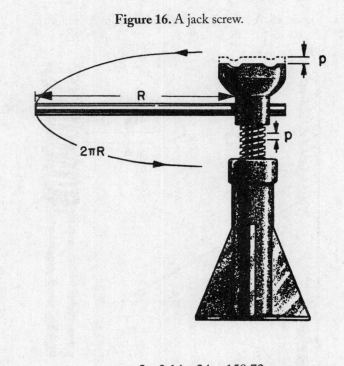

Substituting:

$$\text{M.A. (theoretical)} \quad \frac{2 \times 3.14 \times 24}{1/4} = \frac{150.72}{1/4} = 602.88$$

A 50-pound pull on the handle would result in a theoretical lift of 50 × 603 or 30,150 pounds. More than fifteen tons for fifty pounds.

But jacks have considerable friction loss. The threads are cut so that the force used to overcome friction is greater than the force used to do useful work. If the threads were not cut this way, if no friction were present, the weight of the load would cause the jack to spin right back down to the bottom as soon as the handle is released.

The Micrometer

In using the jack, you exerted your effort through a distance of $2\varpi r$, or 150 inches, in order to raise the screw ¼ inch. It takes a lot of circular motion to get a small amount of straight-line motion from the head of the jack. You will use this point to advantage in the micrometer, which is a useful device for making accurate small measurements, measurements of a few thousandths of an inch.

In **Figure 17**, you see a cutaway view of a micrometer. The thimble turns freely on the sleeve, which is rigidly attached to the micrometer frame. The spindle is attached to the thimble and is fitted with screw threads, which move the spindle and thimble to the right or left in the sleeve when the thimble is rotated. These screw threads are cut 40 threads to the inch. Hence, one turn of the thimble moves the spindle and thimble $\frac{1}{40}$ inch. This represents one of the smallest divisions on the micrometer.

Four of these small divisions make $\frac{4}{40}$ of an inch, or $\frac{1}{10}$ inch. Thus, the distance from 0 to 1 or 1 to 2 on the sleeve represents $\frac{1}{10}$ or 0.1 inch.

Figure 17. A micrometer.

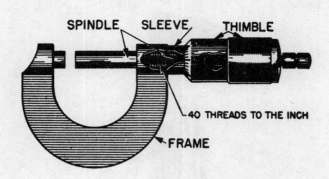

SPINDLE   SLEEVE   THIMBLE

40 THREADS TO THE INCH

FRAME

GEARS

Did you ever take a clock apart to see what made it tick? Of course you came out with some parts left over when you got it back together again. And they probably included a few gear wheels. Gears are used in many machines. Frequently the gears are hidden from view in a protective case filled with grease or oil, and you may not see them.

An eggbeater gives you a simple demonstration of the three things that gears do. They can change the direction of motion, increase or decrease the speed of the applied motion, and magnify or reduce the force that you apply. Gears also give you a positive drive. There can be, and usually is, creep or slip in a belt drive. But gear teeth are always in mesh, and there can be no creep or slip.

Follow the directional changes in **Figure 18**. The crank handle is turned in the direction indicated by the arrow—clockwise, when viewed from the right. The 32 teeth on the large vertical wheel A mesh with the 8 teeth on the right-hand horizontal wheel B, which rotates as indicated by the arrow. Notice that as B turns in a clockwise direction, its teeth mesh with those of wheel C and cause wheel C to revolve in the opposite direction. The rotation of the crank handle has been transmitted by gears to the beater blades, which also rotate.

Figure 18. A simple arrangement gear.

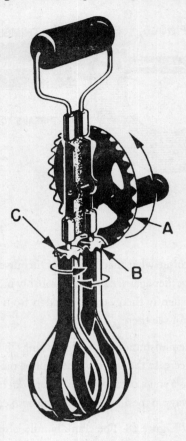

Now figure out how the gears change the speed of motion. There are 32 teeth on gear A and 8 teeth on gear B. But the gears mesh, so that one complete revolution of A results in four complete revolutions of gear B. And since gears B and C have the same number of teeth, one revolution of B results in one revolution of C. Thus, the blades revolve four times as fast as the crank handle.

Previously, you learned that third-class levers increase speed at the expense of force. The same thing happens with this eggbeater. The magnitude of the force is changed, and the force required to turn the handle is greater than the force applied to the frosting by the blades. Therefore, a mechanical advantage of less than one results.

Types of Gears

When two shafts are not lying in the same straight line but are parallel, motion can be transmitted from one to the other by means of spur gears. This setup is shown in **Figure 19**.

Figure 19. Spur gears coupling two parallel shafts.

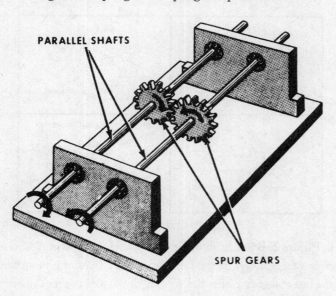

PARALLEL SHAFTS

SPUR GEARS

Spur gears are wheels with mating teeth cut in their surfaces so that one can turn the other without slippage. When the mating teeth are cut so that they are parallel to the axis of rotation, as shown in **Figure 19**, the gears are called straight spur gears.

When two gears of unequal size are meshed together, the smaller of the two is usually called a pinion. By unequal size, we mean an unequal number of teeth causing one gear to be of a larger diameter than the other. The teeth, themselves, must be of the same size to mesh properly.

The most commonly used type is the straight spur gear, but quite often you'll run across another type of spur gear called the helical spur gear.

In helical gears, the teeth are cut slantwise across the working face of the gear. One end of the tooth, therefore, lies ahead of the other. In other words, each tooth has a leading end and a trailing end. A look at these gears in **Figure 20** shows you how they're constructed.

In the straight spur gears, the whole width of the teeth comes in contact at the same time. But with helical (spiral) gears, contact between two teeth starts first at the leading ends and moves progressively across the gear faces until the trailing ends are in contact. This kind of meshing action keeps the gears in constant contact with one another. Therefore, less lost motion and smoother, quieter action is possible. One disadvantage of this helical spur gear is the tendency of each gear to thrust or push axially on its shaft. It is necessary to put a special thrust bearing at the end of the shaft to counteract this thrust. **Figure 20** also shows you three other gear arrangements in common use.

Figure 20. Gear types.

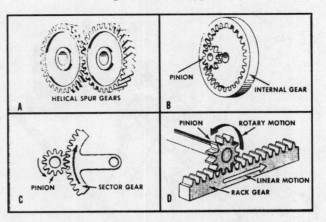

The internal gear in **Figure 20B** has teeth on the inside of a ring, pointing inward toward the axis of rotation. An internal gear is always meshed with an external gear, or pinion, whose center is offset from the center of the internal gear. Either the internal or the pinion gear can be the driver gear, and the gear ratio is calculated the same as for the other gears—by counting teeth.

Often, only a portion of a gear is needed where the motion of the pinion is limited. In this case, the sector gear (Figure 20C) is used to save space and material. The rack and pinion in **Figure 20D** are both spur gears. The rack may be considered as a piece cut from a gear with an extremely large radius. The rack-and-pinion arrangement is useful in changing rotary motion into linear motion.

The Bevel Gear

So far, most of the gears you've learned about transmit motion between parallel shafts. When shafts are not parallel, but at an angle, another type of gear is used—the bevel gear. This type of gear can connect shafts lying at any given angle because they can be beveled to suit the angle.

Figure 21A shows a special case of the bevel gear—the miter gear. A pair of miter gears is used to connect shafts having a 90-degree angle, which means the gear faces are beveled at a 45-degree angle.

You can see in **Figure 21B** how bevel gears are designed to join shafts at any angle. Gears cut at any angle other than 45 degrees are called just plain bevel gears.

The gears shown in **Figure 21** are called straight bevel gears, because the whole width of each tooth comes in contact with the mating tooth at the same time. However, you'll also run across spiral bevel gears with teeth cut so as to have advanced and trailing ends. **Figure 22** shows you what spiral bevel gears look like. They have the same advantages as other spiral (helical) gears—less lost motion and smoother, quieter operation.

Figure 21. Bevel gears.

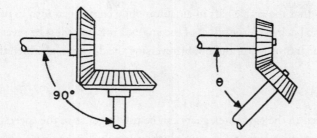

Figure 22. Spiral bevel gears.

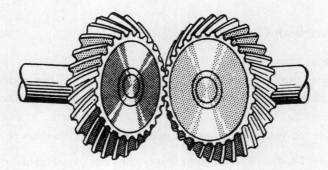

The Worm and Worm Wheel

Worm and worm-wheel combinations, like those in **Figure 23**, have many uses and advantages. But it's better to understand their operating theory before learning of their uses and advantages.

Figure 23A shows the action of a single-thread worm. For each revolution of the worm, the worm wheel turns one tooth. Thus, if the worm wheel has 25 teeth, the gear ratio is 25:1.

Figure 23. Worm gears.

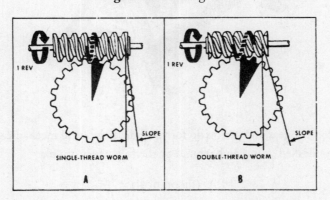

Figure 23B shows a double-thread worm. For each revolution of the worm in this case, the worm wheel turns two teeth. That makes the gear ratio 25:2 if the worm wheel has 25 teeth.

Likewise, a triple-threaded worm would turn the worm wheel three teeth per revolution of the worm.

Changing Direction with Gears

No doubt you know that the crankshaft in an automobile engine can turn in only one direction. If you want the car to go backward, the effect of the engine's rotation must be reversed. This is done by a reversing gear in the transmission and not by reversing the direction in which the crankshaft turns.

Changing Speed

As you've already seen in the eggbeater, gears can be used to change the speed of motion. Another example of this use of gears is found in your clock or watch. The mainspring slowly unwinds and causes the hour hand to make one revolution in 12 hours. Through a series—or train—of gears, the minute hand makes one revolution each hour, while the second hand goes around once per minute.

Magnifying Force with Gears

Gear trains are used to increase the mechanical advantage. In fact, wherever there is a speed reduction, the effect of the effort you apply is multiplied. Look at the cable winch in **Figure 24**. The crank arm is 30 inches long, and the drum on which the cable is wound has a 15-inch radius. The small pinion gear turned by the crank has 10 teeth, which mesh with the 60 teeth on the internal spur gear. You will find it easier to figure the mechanical advantage of this machine if you think of it as two machines.

Figure 24. The cable winch combines gears and the wheel and axle.

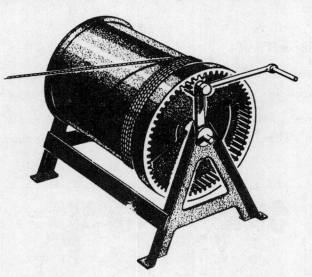

First, figure out what the gear and pinion do for you. The theoretical mechanical advantage of any arrangement of two meshed gears can be found by the following formula:

$$\text{M.A. (theoretical)} = \frac{T_o}{T_a}.$$

in which

T_o = number of teeth on driven gear

T_a = number of teeth on driver gear

In this case, T_o = 60 and T_a = 10. Then,

$$\text{M.A. (theoretical)} = \frac{T_o}{T_a} = \frac{60}{10} = 6$$

Now, for the other part of the machine, which is a simple wheel-and-axle arrangement consisting of the crank arm and the drum. The theoretical mechanical advantage of this can be found by dividing the distance the effort moves—$2\varpi R$—in making one complete revolution, by the distance the cable is drawn up in one revolution of the drum—$2\varpi r$.

$$\text{M.A. (theoretical)} = \frac{2\pi R}{2\pi r} = \frac{R}{r} = \frac{30}{15} = 2$$

You know that the total, or overall, theoretical mechanical advantage of a compound machine is equal to the product of the mechanical advantages of the several simple machines that comprise it. In this case, you considered the winch as being two machines—one having an M.A. of 6, and the other an M.A. of 2. Therefore, the overall theoretical mechanical advantage of the winch is 6 × 2, or 12. Because friction is always present, the actual mechanical advantage may be only 7 or 8. Even so, by applying a force of 100 pounds on the handle, you could lift a load of 700 or 800 pounds.

WORK

Measurement

You know that machines help you to do work. But just what is work? Work doesn't mean simply applying a force. Work, in the mechanical sense of the term, is done when a resistance is overcome by a force acting through a measurable distance.

Notice that two factors are involved—force and movement through a distance. The force is normally measured in pounds, and the distance in feet. Work, therefore, is commonly measured in units called foot-pounds. You do one foot-pound of work when you lift a one-pound weight through a height of one foot. But—you also do one foot-pound of work when you apply one pound of force on any object through a distance of one foot. Writing this as a formula, it becomes

WORK	=	FORCE	×	DISTANCE
(foot-pounds)		(pounds)		(feet)

Thus, if a person lifts a 90-pound bag through a vertical distance of 5 feet, he will do

WORK = 90 × 5 = 450 ft-lb.

There are two points concerning work that you should get straight right at the beginning.

First, in calculating the work done, you measure the actual resistance being overcome. This is not necessarily the weight of the object being moved. To make this clear, look at the job being done in

Figure 25A. A man is pulling a 900-pound load of supplies 200 feet along the dock. Does this mean that he is doing 900 × 200, or 180,000 foot-pounds of work? Of course not. He isn't working against the pull of gravity—or the total weight—of the load. He's pulling only against the rolling friction of the truck, and that may be as little as 90 pounds. That is the resistance that is being overcome. Always be sure that you know what resistance is being overcome by the effort, as well as the distance through which it is moved. The resistance in one case may be the weight of the object; in another it may be the frictional resistance of the object as it is dragged or rolled along the deck.

Figure 25A. Working against friction.

The second point to remember is that you have to move the resistance to do any work on it. If you hold a suitcase for 15 minutes while waiting for a bus, your arm will get tired. However, according to the definition of work, you aren't doing any—because you aren't moving the suitcase. You are merely exerting a force against the pull of gravity on the bag.

You already know about the mechanical advantage of a lever. Now consider it in terms of getting work done easily, and look at **Figure 25B**. The load weighs 300 pounds, and you want to lift it up onto a platform a foot above the floor. How much work must you do on it? Because 300 pounds must be raised one foot, 300 × 1, or 300 foot-pounds of work must be done. You can't make this weight any smaller by the use of any machine. However, if you use the eight-foot plank as shown, you can do that amount of work, by applying a smaller force through a longer distance. Notice that you have a mechanical advantage of 3 so that a 100-pound push down on the end of the plank will raise the 300-pound crate. How long of a distance will you have to exert that 100-pound push? Neglecting friction—and in this case you can safely do so—the work done on the machine is equal to the work done by the machine. Say it this way:

Work put in = Work put out

and because work = force × distance, you can substitute "force times distance" on each side of the work equation. Thus,

F_1 times S_1 = F_2 times S_2

in which

F_1 = Effort applied, in pounds

S_1 = Distance through which effort moves, in feet

F_2 = Resistance overcome, in pounds

S_2 = Distance resistance is moved, in feet

Now substitute the known values, and you obtain—

100 times S_1 = 300 times 1

S_1 = 3 feet

Figure 25B. Push 'em up.

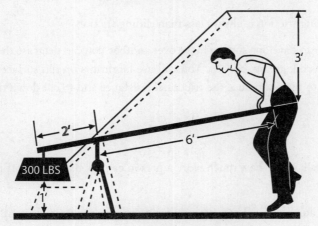

Friction

You are going to push a 400-pound crate up a 12-foot plank, the upper end of which is 3 feet higher than the lower end. You figure out that a 100-pound push will do the job, since the height the crate is to be raised is one-fourth of the distance through which you are exerting your push. The theoretical mechanical advantage is 4. Then you push 100 pounds worth and nothing happens! You've forgotten that there is friction between the surface of the crate and the surface of the plank. This friction acts as a resistance to the movement of the crate—and you must overcome this resistance to move the crate. In fact, you might have to push as much as 150 pounds to move it. Fifty pounds would be used to overcome the frictional resistance, and the remaining 100 pounds would be the useful push that would move the crate up the plank.

Friction is the resistance that one surface offers to its movement over another surface. The amount of friction depends on the nature of the two surfaces and the forces that hold them together.

In many instances, friction is useful to you. Friction helps you hold back the crate from sliding down the inclined ramp. The cinders you throw under the wheels of your car when it's slipping on an icy pavement increase the friction. You wear rubber-soled shoes in the gym to keep from slipping. And locomotives carry a supply of sand, which can be dropped on the tracks in front of the driving wheels to increase the friction between the wheels and the track. Nails hold structures together because of the friction between the nails and the lumber.

When you are trying to stop or slow down an object in motion, when you want traction, and when you want to prevent motion from taking place, you make friction work for you. But when you want a machine to run smoothly and at high efficiency, you eliminate as much friction as possible by oiling and greasing bearings and honing and smoothing rubbing surfaces.

Wherever you apply force to cause motion, friction makes the actual mechanical advantage fall short of the theoretical mechanical advantage. Because of friction, you have to make a greater effort to overcome the resistance that you want to move. If you place a marble and a lump of sugar on a table and give each an equal push, the marble will move farther. This is because rolling friction is always less than sliding friction. You take advantage of this fact whenever you use ball bearings or roller bearings.

Remember that rolling friction is always less than sliding friction.

When it is necessary to have one surface move over another, you can decrease the friction by the use of lubricants, such as oil, grease, or soap. You will use lubricants on flat surfaces, as well as on ball and roller bearings, to further reduce the frictional resistance and to cut down the wear.

POWER

It's all very well to talk about how much work a person can do, but the payoff is how long it takes that person to do it.

Power is the rate of doing work. Thus, power always includes the time element.

$$\text{By formula, } \text{Power} = \frac{\text{Work, in ft-lb.}}{\text{Time, in minutes}}$$

Horsepower

You measure force in pounds; distance in feet; work in foot-pounds. What is the common unit used for measuring power? The horsepower. If you want to tell someone how powerful an engine is, you could say that it is so many times more powerful than a man, or an ox, or a horse. But what man, and whose ox or horse? James Watt, the inventor of the steam engine, compared his early models with the horse. By experiment, he found that an average horse could lift a 330-pound load straight up through a distance of 100 feet in one minute. By agreement among scientists, that figure of 33,000 foot-pounds of work done in one minute has been accepted as the standard unit of power, and it is called a horsepower (hp).

Since there are 60 seconds in a minute, one horsepower is also equal to

$$\frac{33,000}{60} = 550 \text{ foot-pounds per second. By formula, } \text{Horsepower} = \frac{\text{Power (in ft-lb. per min.)}}{33,000}$$

FORCE AND PRESSURE

By now you should have a pretty good idea of what a force is. A force is a push or a pull exerted on, or by, an object. You apply a force on a machine, and the machine in turn transmits a force to the load. Men and machines, however, are not the only things that can exert forces. If you've been out in a sailboat you know that the wind can exert a force. Furthermore, you don't have to get knocked on your ear more than a couple of times by the waves to get the idea that water, too, can exert a force.

Measuring Forces

You've had a lot of experience in measuring forces. You can estimate or "guess" the weight of a package you're going to mail by "hefting" it. Or you can put it on a scale to find its exact weight. Weight is a common term that tells you how much force or pull gravity is exerting on the object.

You can readily measure force with a spring scale. An Englishman named Hooke discovered that if you hang a 1-pound weight on a spring, the spring stretches a certain distance. A 2-pound weight will extend the spring just twice as far, and 3 pounds will lengthen it three times as far as the 1-pound weight. Right there are the makings of the spring scale. All you need to do is attach a pointer to the spring, put a face on the scale, and mark on the face the positions of the pointer for various loads in pounds or ounces.

This type of scale can be used to measure the pull of gravity—the weight—of an object, or the force of a pull exerted against friction. Unfortunately, springs get tired, just as you do. When they get old, they don't always snap back to the original position. Hence, an old spring or an overloaded spring will give inaccurate readings.

Honest Weight—No Springs

Because springs do get tired, other types of force-measuring devices are made. Perhaps you've seen the sign, "Honest Weight—No Springs," on some scales. Scales of this type are shown in **Figure 26**. They are applications of first-class levers. The one shown in **Figure 26A** is the simplest type. Since the distance from the fulcrum to the center of each platform is equal, the scale is balanced when equal weights are placed on the platforms. With your knowledge of levers, you will be able to figure out how the steelyard shown in **Figure 26B** operates.

Figure 26. Balances.

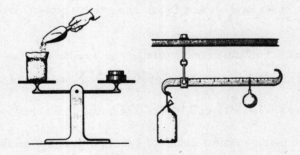

Pressure

Have you ever tried to walk on crusted snow only to break through once you put weight on it? But you could walk on the same snow if you put on snowshoes. Furthermore, you know that snowshoes do not reduce your weight—they merely distribute it over a larger area. In doing this, they reduce the pressure per square inch. Figure out how that works. If you weigh 160 pounds, that weight, or force, is more or less evenly distributed by the soles of your shoes. The area of the soles of an average man's shoes is roughly 60 square inches. Each one of those square inches has to carry 160 ÷ 60 = 2.7 pounds of your weight. Since 2.7 pounds per square inch is too much for the snow crust, you break through.

When you put on the snowshoes, you distribute your weight over an area of approximately 900 sq. in.—depending, of course, on the size of the snowshoes. Now the force on each one of those square inches is equal to only 160 ÷ 900 = 0.18 pound. The pressure on the snow has been decreased, and the snow can easily support you.

Pressure is force per unit area and is measured in pounds per square inch (psi). With showshoes on, you exert a pressure of 0.18 psi. To calculate pressure, divide the force by the area over which the force is applied. The formula is

$$\text{Pressure, in psi} = \frac{\text{Force, in lb.}}{\text{Area, in sq. in.}} \quad \text{Or, } P = \frac{F}{A}$$

To get this idea, follow this problem. A tank for holding fresh water is 10 feet long, 6 feet wide, and 4 feet deep. Therefore, it holds 10 × 6 × 4, or 240 cubic feet of water. Each cubic foot of water weighs about 62.5 pounds. The total force tending to push the bottom out of the tank is equal to the weight of the water—240 × 62.5, or 15,000 lbs. What is the pressure on the bottom? Since the weight is evenly distributed on the bottom, you apply the formula $P = \frac{F}{A}$ and substitute the proper values for F and A. In this case, F = 15,000 lbs., and the area of the bottom in square inches is 10 × 6 × 144, since 144 sq. in. = 1 sq. ft.

$$P = \frac{15,000}{10 \times 6 \times 144} = 1.74 \text{ psi}$$

Now work out the idea in reverse. You live at the bottom of the great sea of air that surrounds the earth. Because the air has weight—gravity pulls on the air, too—the air exerts a force on every object that it surrounds. Near sea level that force on an area of 1 square inch is roughly 15 pounds. Thus, the air pressure at sea level is about 15 psi. The pressure gets less and less as you go up to higher altitudes.

With your finger, mark out an area of one square foot on your chest. What is the total force that tends to push in your chest? Again, use the formula $P = \frac{F}{A}$. Now substitute 15 psi for P, and for A use 144 sq. in. Then, F = 144 × 15, or 2,160 lbs. The force on your chest is 2,160 lbs. per square foot—more than a ton pushing against an area of 1 sq. ft. If there was no air inside your chest to push outward with the same pressure, you'd be squashed flat.

Measuring Pressure

Fluids, which include both liquids and gases, exert pressure. A fluid at rest exerts equal pressure in all directions.

In many jobs, it is necessary to know the pressure exerted by gas or a liquid. For example, it is important at all times to know the steam pressure inside of a boiler. One device to measure pressure is the Bourdon gage, shown in **Figure 27**. Its working principle is the same as that of those snakelike paper tubes that you get at a New Year's party. They straighten out when you blow into them.

Figure 27. The Bourdon gage.

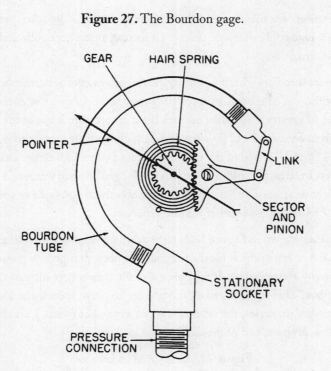

In the Bourdon gage, there is a thin-walled metal tube, somewhat flattened, and bent into the form of a C. Attached to its free end is a lever system that magnifies any motion of the free end of the tube. The fixed end of the gage ends in a fitting that is threaded into the boiler system so that the pressure in the boiler will be transmitted to the tube. Like the paper "snake," the metal tube tends to straighten out when the pressure inside it is increased. As the tube straightens, the pointer is made to move around the dial. The pressure, in psi, may be read directly on the dial.

Air pressure and pressures of steam and other gases and fluid pressures in hydraulic systems are generally measured in pounds per square inch. For convenience, however, the pressure exerted by water is commonly measured in pounds per square foot.

The Bourdon gage is a highly accurate but rather delicate instrument and can very easily be damaged. In addition, it develops trouble where pressure fluctuates rapidly. To overcome this, another type of gage, the Schrader, was developed. The Schrader gage is not as accurate as the Bourdon but is sturdily constructed and quite suitable for ordinary hydraulic pressure measurements. It is especially recommended for fluctuating loads. In the Schrader gage, a piston is directly actuated by the liquid pressure to be measured, and moves up a cylinder against the resistance of a spring, carrying a bar or indicator with it over a calibrated scale. In this manner, all levers, gears, cams, and bearings are eliminated, and a sturdy instrument can be constructed.

Where accurate measurements of comparatively slight pressures are desired, a diaphragm-type gage may be used. Diaphragm gages give sensitive and reliable indications of small pressure differences.

The Barometer

To the average person, the chief importance of weather is as an introduction to general conversation. But at sea and in the air, advance knowledge of what the weather will do is a matter of great concern to all hands. Operations are planned or cancelled on the basis of weather predictions. Accurate weather forecasts are made only after a great deal of information has been collected by many observers located over a wide area.

One of the instruments used in gathering weather data is the barometer. Remember, the air is pressing on you all the time. So-called normal atmospheric pressure is 14.7 psi. But as the weather changes, the air pressure may be greater or less than normal. If the air pressure is low in the area where you are, you know that air from one or more of the surrounding high-pressure areas is going to move in toward you. Moving air—or wind—is one of the most important factors in weather changes. In general, if you're in a low-pressure area, you may expect wind, rain, and storms, whereas a high-pressure area generally enjoys clear weather. The barometer can tell you the air pressure in your locality and give you a rough idea of what kind of weather may be expected.

The aneroid barometer, shown in **Figure 28**, is an instrument that measures air pressure. It contains a thin-walled metal box from which most of the air has been pumped. A pointer is mechanically connected to the box by a lever system. If the pressure of the atmosphere increases, it tends to squeeze in the sides of the box. This squeeze causes the pointer to move toward the high-pressure end of the scale. If the pressure decreases, the sides of the box expand outward. This causes the pointer to move toward the low-pressure end of the dial.

Figure 28. An aneroid barometer.

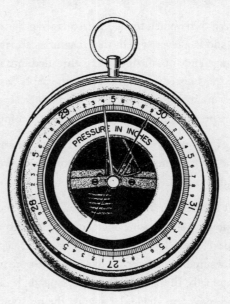

MACHINE ELEMENTS AND BASIC MECHANISMS

Machine Elements

Any machine, however simple, uses one or more basic machine elements or mechanisms in its makeup. In this section, we will take a look at some of the more familiar elements and mechanisms commonly used in machinery and equipment.

Bearings

Previously, we saw that whenever two objects rub against one another, friction is produced. If the surfaces are smooth, there will be little friction; if either or both are rough, there will be more friction. *Friction* is the resistance to any force that produces motion of one surface over another. When you are trying to start a loaded hand truck rolling, you have to give it a hard tug (to overcome the resistance of static friction) to get it started. Starting to slide the same load across the floor would require a harder push than starting it on rollers, because rolling friction is always less than sliding friction. To take advantage of this fact, rollers or bearings are used in machines to reduce friction. Lubricants on bearing surfaces reduce the friction even more.

A bearing is a support and guide that carries a moving part (or parts) of a machine and maintains the proper relationship between the moving part or parts and the stationary part. It usually permits only one form of motion, as rotation, and prevents any other. There are two basic types of bearings: sliding type (plain bearings), also called friction or guide bearings, and antifrictional type (roller and ball bearings).

Sliding-Type (Plain) Bearings

In bearings of this type, a film of lubricant separates the moving part from the stationary part. There are three types of sliding motion bearings in common use: reciprocal motion bearings, journal bearings, and thrust bearings.

Reciprocal motion bearings provide a bearing surface on which an object slides back and forth. They are found on steam reciprocating pumps, where connecting rods slide on bearing surfaces near their connections to the pistons. Similar bearings are used on the connecting rods of large internal-combustion engines and in many mechanisms operated by cams.

Journal bearings are used to guide and support revolving shafts. The shaft revolves in a housing fitted with a liner. The inside of the liner, on which the shaft bears, is made of babbitt metal or similar soft alloy (antifriction metal) to reduce friction. The soft metal is backed by a bronze or a copper layer that has a steel back for strength. Sometimes the bearing is made in two halves and is clamped or screwed around the shaft. It is also called a laminated sleeve bearing.

Thrust bearings are used on rotating shafts, such as those supporting bevel gears, worm gears, propellers, and fans. They are installed to resist axial thrust or force and to limit axial movement. They are used chiefly on heavy machinery.

Antifrictional or Roller and Ball Bearings

You may have had firsthand acquaintance with ball bearings when you were a child. They were what made your roller skates, skateboard, or bicycle wheels spin freely. If any of the little steel balls came out and were lost, your wheels screeched and groaned. The balls or rollers were of hard, highly polished steel. The typical bearing consisted of two hardened steel rings (called *races*), the hardened steel balls or rollers, and a *separator*. The motion occurred between the race surfaces and the rolling elements. Ball bearings of this type have since been replaced by more modern antifrictional bearings.

Springs

Springs are elastic bodies (generally metal) that can be twisted, pulled, or stretched by some force and that have the ability to return to their original shape when the force is released. Springs used in machinery are generally made of metal—usually steel, though some are of phosphor bronze, brass, or other alloys. A part that is subject to constant spring thrust or pressure is said to be *spring loaded*. (Some components that appear to be spring loaded are actually under hydraulic or pneumatic pressure or are moved by weights.)

Functions of Springs

Springs are used for many purposes, and one spring may serve more than one purpose. Following are some of the more common of these functional purposes. As you read them, try to think of at least one familiar application of each:

- To store energy for part of a functioning cycle.
- To force a component to bear against, to maintain contact with, to engage, to disengage, or to remain clear of some other component.
- To counterbalance a weight or thrust (gravitational, hydraulic, etc.). Such springs are usually called equilibrator springs.
- To maintain electrical continuity.
- To return a component to its original position after displacement.
- To reduce shock or impact by gradually checking the motion of a moving weight.
- To permit some freedom of movement between aligned components without disengaging them. These are sometimes called takeup springs.

Types of Springs

As you read different books, you will find that authors do not agree on classification of types of springs. The names are not as important as the types of work they can do and the loads they can bear. We may say there are three basic types: flat, spiral, and helical or coil.

Flat springs include various forms of elliptic or leaf springs (see Figure 29A[1 & 2]), made up of flat or slightly curved bars, plates, or leaves, and special flat springs (see Figure 29A[3]). A special flat spring is made from a flat strip or bar into whatever shape or design is calculated to be best suited for its position and purpose.

Spiral springs are sometimes called clock or power springs (see Figure 29B), and sometimes coil springs. A well-known example is a watch or clock spring, which is wound (tightened) and then gradually releases the power as it unwinds. Although there is good authority for calling this spring by other names, to avoid confusion we shall consistently call it *spiral*.

Helical springs, often called spiral, but not in this text (see Figure 29), are probably the most common type of spring. They may be used in compression (29D[1]), extension or tension (see Figure 29D[2]), or torsion (see Figure 29D[3]). A spring used in compression tends to shorten in action, while a tension spring lengthens in action. Torsion springs are made to transmit a twist instead of a direct pull and operate by coiling or uncoiling action.

In addition to straight helical springs, cone, double-cone, keg, and volute springs are also classed as helical. These are usually used in compression. A cone spring (see Figure 29D[4]), often called a valve spring because it is frequently used in valves, is shaped by winding the wire on a tapered mandrel instead of a straight one. A double-cone spring (not illustrated) is composed of two cones joined at the small ends, and a keg spring (not illustrated) is two cone springs joined at their large ends.

Figure 29. Types of springs.

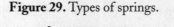

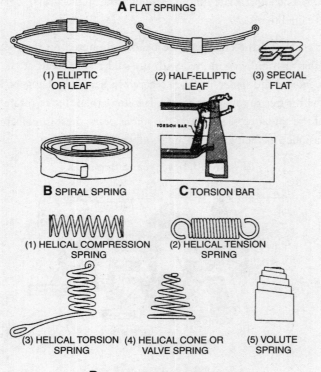

D HELICAL OR COIL SPRINGS

Volute springs (see Figure 29D[5]) are conical springs made from a flat bar, which is so wound that each coil partially overlaps the adjacent one. The width (and thickness) of the material gives it great strength or resistance.

A conical spring can be pressed flat so it requires little space, and it is not likely to buckle sidewise.

Torsion bars (see Figure 29C) are straight bars that are acted on by torsion (twisting force). The bar may be circular or rectangular in cross section or less commonly in other shapes. It may also be a tube.

BASIC MECHANISMS

The Gear Differential

A gear differential is a mechanism that is capable of adding and subtracting mechanically. To be more precise, it adds the total revolutions of two shafts—or subtracts the total revolutions of one shaft from the total revolutions of another shaft—and delivers the answer by positioning a third shaft. The gear differential will add or subtract any number of revolutions, or very small fractions of revolutions, continuously and accurately. It will produce a continuous series of answers as the inputs change.

Figure 30 is a cutaway drawing of a bevel gear differential showing all its parts and how they are related to each other. Grouped around the center of the mechanism are four bevel gears, meshed together. The two bevel gears on either side are called *end gears*. The two bevel gears above and below are called "spider gears." The long shaft running through the end gears and the three spur gears is called the *spider shaft*. The short shaft running through the spider gears, together with the spider gears themselves, is called the *spider*.

Each of the spider gears and the end gears are bearing mounted on their shafts and are free to rotate. The spider shaft is rigidly connected with the spider cross shaft at the center block where they intersect. The ends of the spider shaft are secured in flanges or hangers, but they are bearing mounted and the shaft is free to rotate on its axis. It follows then that to rotate the spider shaft, the spider, consisting of the spider cross shaft and the spider gears, must tumble, or spin, on the axis of the spider shaft, inasmuch as the two shafts are rigidly connected.

Figure 30. Bevel gear differential.

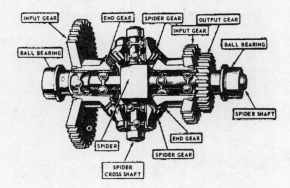

The three spur gears shown in **Figure 30** are used to connect the two end gears and the spider shaft to other mechanisms. They may be of any convenient size. Each of the two input spur gears is attached to an end gear. An input gear and an end gear together are called a *side* of a differential. The third spur gear is the output gear, as designated in **Figure 30**. This is the only gear that is pinned to the spider shaft. All of the other gears, both bevel and spur, in the differential are bearing mounted.

Linkages

A linkage may consist of either one or a combination of the following four basic parts:

1. Rod, shaft, or plunger
2. Lever
3. Rocker arm
4. Bell crank

These parts combined are used to transmit limited rotary or linear motion. To change direction of a motion, cams are used with the linkage.

Lever-type linkages are used in equipment that has to be opened and closed; for instance, valves in electric-hydraulic systems, gates, clutches, and clutch-solenoid interlocks. Rocker arms are merely a variation, or special use, of levers.

Bell cranks are used primarily to transmit motion from a link traveling in one direction to another link, which is to be moved in a different direction. The bell crank is mounted on a fixed pivot, and the two links are connected at two points in different directions from the pivot. By properly locating the connection points, the output links can be made to move in any desired direction.

All linkages require occasional adjustments or repair, particularly when they become worn. To make the proper adjustments, a person must be familiar with the basic parts that constitute a linkage. Adjustments are normally made by lengthening or shortening the rods and shafts by means of a clevis or turnbuckle.

Couplings

In a broad sense, the term *coupling* applies to any device that holds two parts together. Line shafts that are made up of several shafts of different lengths may be held together by any of several types of shaft couplings. When shafts are very closely aligned, the sleeve coupling may be used. It consists of a metal tube slit at each end. The slit ends enable the clamps to fasten the sleeve securely to the shaft ends. With the clamps tightened, the shafts are held firmly together and turn as one shaft. The sleeve coupling also serves as a convenient device for making adjustments between units. The weight at the opposite end of the clamp from the screw is merely to offset the weight of the screw and clamp arms. By distributing the weight more evenly, shaft vibration is reduced.

A universal joint is the answer when two shafts not in the same plane must be coupled. Universal joints may have various forms. They are used in nearly all types and classes of machinery. An elementary universal joint, sometimes called a Hooke joint (see Figure 31), consists of two U-shaped yokes fastened to the ends of the shafts to be connected. Within these yokes is a cross-shaped part that holds the yokes together and allows each yoke to bend, or pivot, one with respect to the other. With this arrangement, one shaft can drive the other even though the angle between the two is as great as 25 degrees from alignment. **Figure 32** shows a ring-and-trunnion type of universal joint. This is merely a slight modification of the old Hooke joint. This type is commonly used in automobile drive shaft systems. Two, and sometimes three, are used. Another type of universal joint is used where a smoother torque transmission is desired and less structural strength is required. This is the Bendix-Weiss universal joint (see Figure 33). In this type of joint, four large balls transmit the rotary force, with a smaller ball as a spacer. With the Hooke type of universal joint, a whipping motion occurs as the shafts rotate—the amount of whip depends on the degree of shaft misalignment. The Bendix-Weiss joint does not have this disadvantage; it transmits rotary motion with a constant angular velocity. This type of joint is both more expensive to manufacture and of less strength than the Hooke types, however.

Figure 31. Universal joint
(Hooke type).

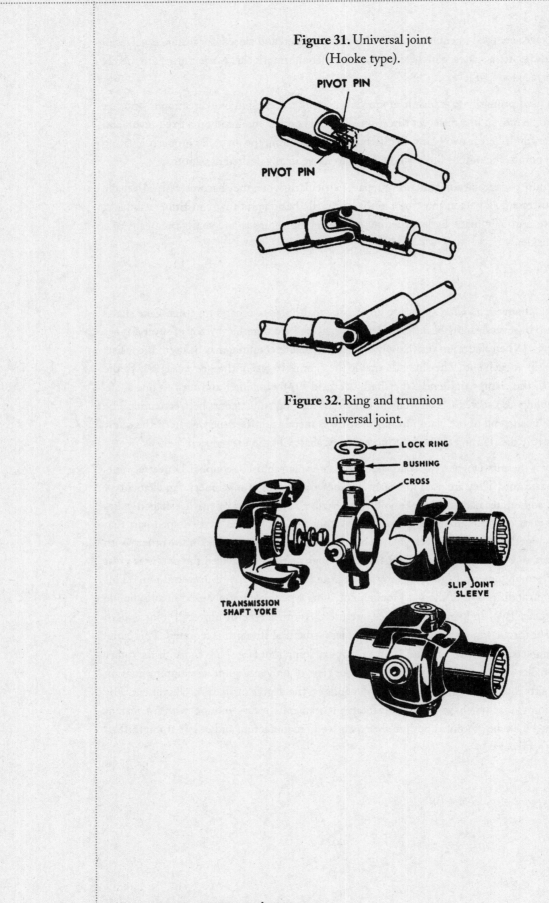

Figure 32. Ring and trunnion
universal joint.

Figure 33. Bendix-Weiss universal joint.

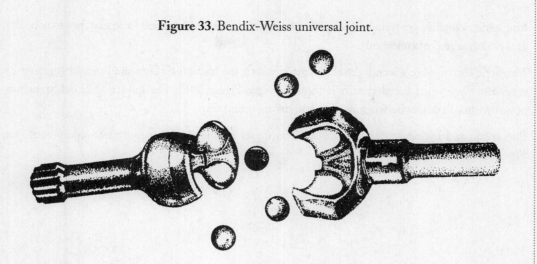

Cam and Cam Followers

A cam is a specially shaped surface, projection, or groove whose movement with respect to a part in contact with it (cam follower) drives the cam follower in another movement in response. A cam may be a projection on a revolving shaft (or on a wheel) for the purpose of changing the direction of motion from rotary to up-and-down, or vice versa. It may be a sliding piece or a groove to impart an eccentric motion. Some cams do not move at all but cause a change of motion in the contacting part. Cams are not ordinarily used to transmit power in the sense that gear trains are. They are generally used to modify mechanical movement, the power for which is furnished through other means. They may control other mechanical units or lock together or synchronize two or more engaging units.

CLUTCHES

Types

A clutch is a form of coupling that is designed to connect or disconnect a driving and a driven member for stopping or starting the driven part. There are two general classes of clutches—positive clutches and friction clutches.

Positive clutches have teeth that interlock. The simplest is the jaw or claw type (see Figure 34A), which is usable only at low speeds. The spiral claw or ratchet type (see Figure 34B) cannot be reversed. An example of a clutch is seen in bicycles—it engages the rear sprocket with the rear wheel when the pedals are pushed forward and lets the rear wheel revolve freely when the pedals are stopped.

Friction clutches. The object of a *friction clutch* is to connect a rotating member to one that is stationary, to bring it up to speed, and to transmit power with a minimum of slippage. **Figure 34C** shows a cone clutch commonly used in motor trucks. They may be single-cone or double-cone. **Figure 34D** shows a disc clutch, also used in autos. A disc clutch may also have a number of plates (multiple-disc clutch). In a series of discs, each driven disc is located between two driving discs. You may have had experience with a multiple-disc clutch on your car. The Hele-Shaw clutch is a combined conical-disc clutch (see Figure 34E). The groove permits circulation of oil and cooling.

Single-disc clutches are frequently dry clutches (no lubrication); multiple-disc clutches may be dry or wet (lubricated or run in oil).

Magnetic clutches are a recent development in which the friction surfaces are brought together by magnetic force when the electricity is turned on (see Figure 34F). The induction clutch transmits power without contact between driving and driven members.

Pneumatic and hydraulic clutches are used on diesel engines and transportation equipment (see Figure 34G).

Figure 34. Types of clutches.

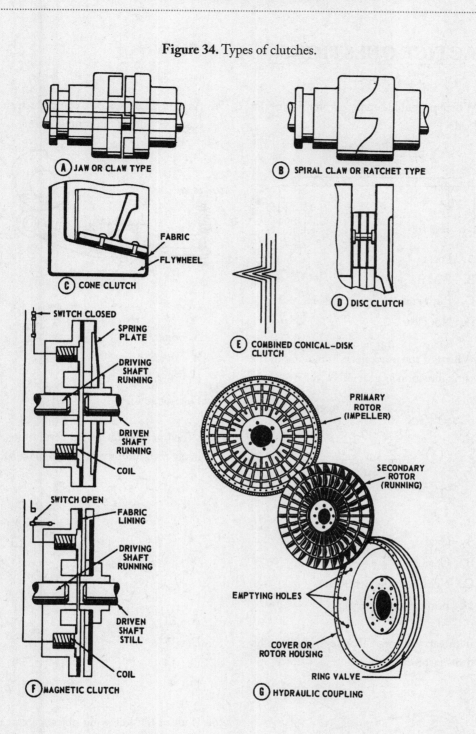

PRACTICE QUESTIONS

1. Which post holds up the greater part of the load?

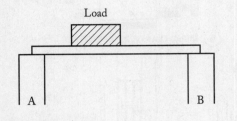

A. Post A
B. Post B
C. Both equal
D. Not clear

2. Which of the other gears is moving in the same direction as gear 2?

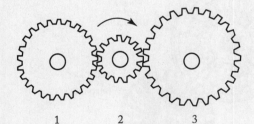

A. Gear 1
B. Gear 3
C. Neither of the other gears
D. Both of the other gears

3. In this arrangement of pulleys, which pulley turns fastest?

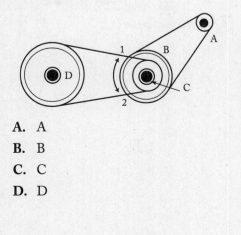

A. A
B. B
C. C
D. D

4. As cam A makes one complete turn, the setscrew will hit the contact point

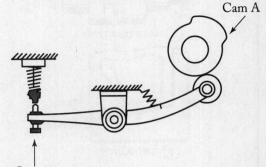

A. once.
B. twice.
C. three times.
D. not at all.

5. When gear A makes 14 revolutions, how many revolutions will gear B make?

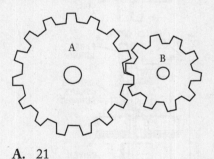

A. 21
B. 17
C. 14
D. 9

6. If all of the following objects are at room temperature, which will feel coldest?
A. Book
B. Metal spoon
C. Wooden chest
D. Blanket

7. In the illustration, liquid is being transferred from the barrel to the bucket by

A. the vacuum at the lower end of the hose.

B. the difference between the fluid volumes in the barrel and the bucket.

C. air pressure on top of the liquid.

D. capillary action.

ANSWER KEY AND EXPLANATIONS

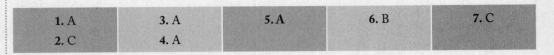

1. A	3. A	5. A	6. B	7. C
2. C	4. A			

1. **The correct answer is A.** The weight is distributed more on the side of post A. Therefore, it is holding up the greatest part of the load.

2. **The correct answer is C.** Because of the way the gears are meshed, both gear 1 and gear 3 will move in the opposite direction of gear 2.

3. **The correct answer is A.** Pulley A is the smallest gear. Therefore, it must turn faster (make more revolutions per minute).

4. **The correct answer is A.** The single lobe on cam A will cause the setscrew to hit the contact point once during the cam's revolution.

5. **The correct answer is A.** Since gear A has 15 teeth and gear B has 10 teeth, gear A is 1.5 the size of gear B. Therefore, $14 \times 1.5 = 21$.

6. **The correct answer is B.** Metal will feel coldest out of paper, wood, and the fabric of a blanket.

7. **The correct answer is C.** The siphon works, in part, because of air pressure on the top of the liquid.

SUMMING IT UP

- The simplest machine, and perhaps the one that you are most familiar with, is the *lever*. A seesaw is a familiar example of a lever in which one weight balances the other. A lever consists of a rigid part that pivots about a point called the fulcrum. The type, or class, of lever depends on the arrangement of these elements:

  1. *Fulcrum* (F)
  2. *Effort* (E)
  3. *Resistance* (R)

- **Blocks**, also known as pulleys, are simple machines that have many uses. You set up a block and tackle to make some of your work easier. If you lash a single block to a fixed object—an overhead, a yardarm, or a bulkhead—you give yourself the advantage of being able to pull from a convenient direction.

- The **wheel-and-axle machine** consists of a wheel or crank rigidly attached to the axle, which turns with the wheel. The steering wheel on an automobile and a door knob are familiar examples of the wheel-and-axle.

- The **inclined plane** permits you to overcome a large resistance by applying a relatively small force through a longer distance than the load is raised. You have seen the inclined plane used in many situations—cattle ramps, a mountain highway, and a gangplank are familiar examples.

- The **wedge** is a special application of the inclined plane. The blades of knives, axes, hatchets, and chisels act as wedges when they are forced into a piece of wood. The wedge is two inclined planes, set base to base. By driving the wedge full length into the material to be cut or split, the material is forced apart a distance equal to the width of the broad end of the wedge.

- The **screw** is a simple machine that has many uses. The vise on a workbench, the screw clamps used to hold a piece of furniture together, and many automobile jacks make use of the great mechanical advantage of the screw. A screw is a modification of the inclined plane.

- **Gears** are used in many machines. An eggbeater gives you a simple demonstration of the three things that gears do. They can change the direction of motion, increase or decrease the speed of the applied motion, and magnify or reduce the force that you apply.

- **Work**, in the mechanical sense of the term, is done when a resistance is overcome by a force acting through a measurable distance. Notice that two factors are involved—force and movement through a distance. The force is normally measured in pounds, and the distance in feet. Work, therefore, is commonly measured in units called foot-pounds.

- **Power** is the rate of doing work. Thus, power always includes the time element. Power is equal to the amount of work (measured in foot-pounds) divided by time (measured in minutes).

- **Pressure** is force per unit area and is measured in pounds per square inch (psi). To calculate pressure, divide the force by the area over which the force is applied.

- Any machine, however simple, uses one or more basic machine elements or mechanisms in its makeup, such as **bearings** and **springs**.

Assembling Objects

OVERVIEW

- **Practice Questions**
- **Answer Key and Explanations**
- **Summing It Up**

The Assembling Objects subtest of the ASVAB currently appears on both the computerized and the paper-and-pencil versions of the enlistment ASVAB. It is not currently included in the institutional (high school) ASVAB or the ASCT (Armed Services Classification Test) taken by military personnel who wish to change jobs within the military.

The score for the Assembling Objects subtest is currently used only by the Navy, and applies to a very few occupations within this branch of the armed services. As of this printing, no other branch of the military makes use of this score. You may wish to check with your high school guidance counselor or your recruiter for possible changes.

The Assembling Objects subtest consists of 16 problems that must be answered in 9 minutes. This subtest measures spatial aptitude. You must determine how an object will look when its parts are mentally assembled.

The test has two types of items, each consisting of five drawings. The first drawing (far left position) shows the parts to be put together; the other drawings show four possible ways this might be accomplished. You need to select the one correct solution.

Type 1. Connection items present simple geometric figures such as circles, stars, letter shapes, and lines. The shapes and lines are labeled with dots and small letters to indicate points of attachment.

Using the lines to connect the shapes, you must match corresponding letters to connect the parts at the right points, in the correct manner. While the shapes may be reoriented from problem to solution, the points of connection must faithfully reflect the points noted in the problem. If a connection point in or on a shape includes a line that goes through some part of the shape, the solution must also faithfully reflect this point-line relationship.

Chapter 11

For example,

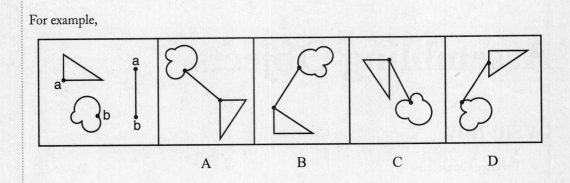

It may be helpful with this type of item to quickly add dots and letters to the possible solution to confirm that the connected shapes are joined at the right points and that any indicated point-line relationships are accurately represented. See below.

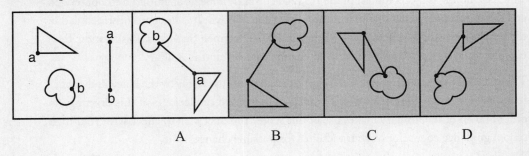

Type 2. Puzzle items present several unlabeled geometric shapes, some of which may be rather complex. Your job is to identify the solution that consists of precisely the same shapes, fitted together.

For example,

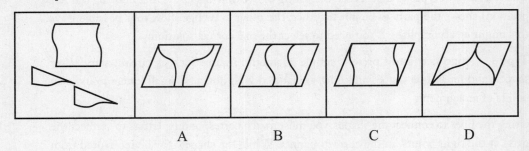

It may be helpful with this type of item to quickly number the shapes in the problem and the possible solution to ensure that all of the shapes are common to both. See below.

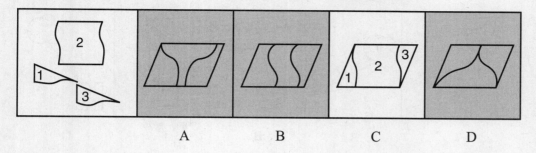

Keep in mind that you have just over half a minute to respond to each item, so you won't want to spend too much time on any one item. Remember also that your score on this test will be of interest to the Navy as it applies to certain naval occupations. You may wish to consult your recruiter if you think this test may be especially important for you. The practice questions here and in the three sample test batteries will familiarize you with these types of items and improve your chances to score well on this subtest.

The following questions are similar to those on the actual ASVAB. Answers and explanations follow the items.

PRACTICE QUESTIONS

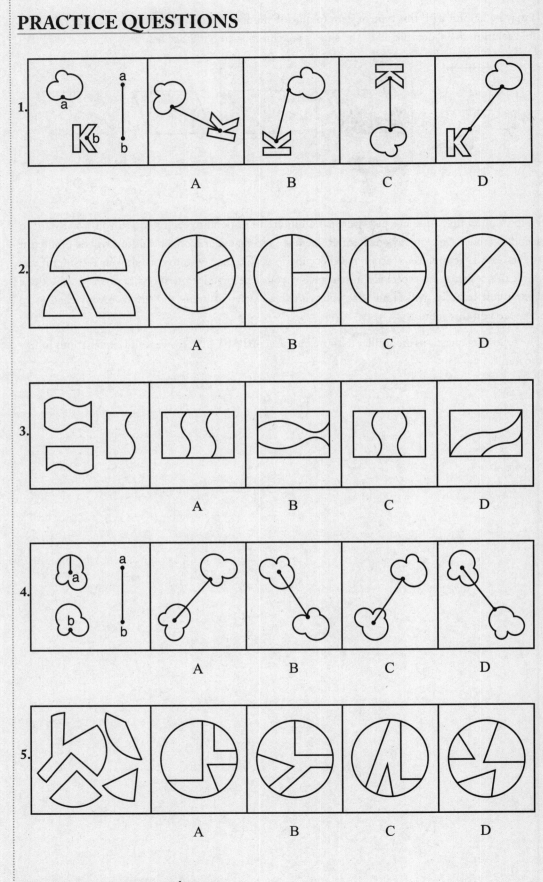

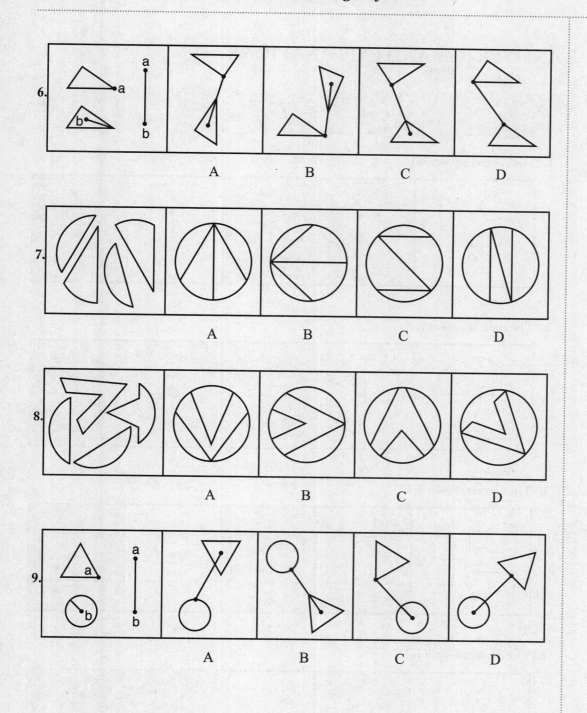

ANSWER KEY AND EXPLANATIONS

1. C	3. C	5. B	7. A	9. C
2. A	4. B	6. B	8. D	

1. The correct answer is C.

2. The correct answer is A.

3. The correct answer is C.

4. The correct answer is B.

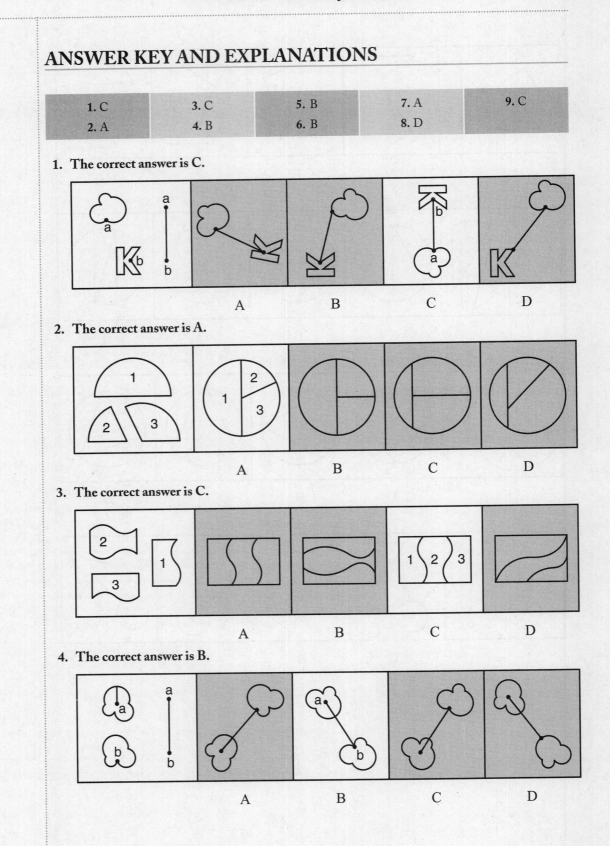

5. **The correct answer is B.**

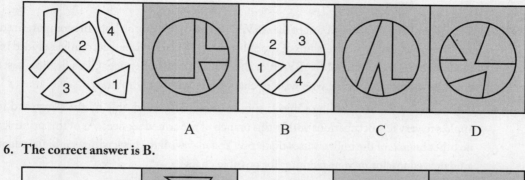

A   B   C   D

6. **The correct answer is B.**

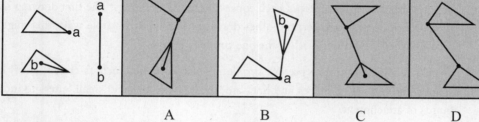

A   B   C   D

7. **The correct answer is A.**

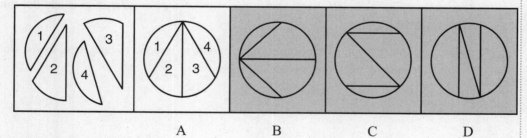

A   B   C   D

8. **The correct answer is D.**

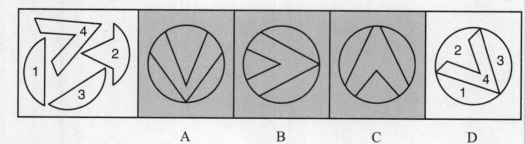

A   B   C   D

9. **The correct answer is C.**

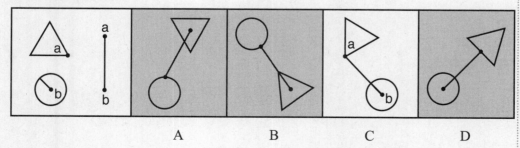

A   B   C   D

SUMMING IT UP

- The Assembling Objects subtest of the ASVAB currently appears on both the computerized and the paper-and-pencil versions of the enlistment ASVAB. It is not currently included in the institutional (high school) ASVAB or the ASCT (Armed Services Classification Test) taken by military personnel who wish to change jobs within the military.

- The score for the Assembling Objects subtest is currently used only by the Navy, and it applies to very few occupations within this branch of the armed services. As of this printing, no other branch of the military uses this score. You may wish to check with your high school guidance counselor or your recruiter for possible changes.

- The test has two types of items, each consisting of five drawings. The first drawing shows the parts to be put together; the other drawings show four possible ways this might be accomplished. You need to select the one correct solution.

  Type 1. Connection items present simple geometric figures such as circles, stars, letter shapes, and lines. The shapes and lines are labeled with dots and small letters to indicate points of attachment.

  Type 2. Puzzle items present several unlabeled geometric shapes, some of which may be rather complex. Your job is to identify the solution that consists of precisely the same shapes, fitted together.

- Keep in mind that you have just over half a minute to respond to each item, so you won't want to spend too much time on any one item.

PART IV
THREE ASVAB PRACTICE TESTS

PRACTICE TEST 2

PRACTICE TEST 3

PRACTICE TEST 4

Practice Test 2

You completed the Diagnostic Test, pinpointed your strengths and weaknesses, completed subject reviews, and are now prepared to take another practice test. Keep in mind that the more practice tests you take, the more confident you will be on your actual test day.

Here are the guidelines again to help you make the most of this practice test:

- Take this test under "real" test conditions (time yourself, take it in a quiet room without distractions, and use the sample answer sheets).

- Time each test carefully and do not go over the time allotted for each section.

- Use the answer keys to get your test scores and to evaluate your performance on each test.

- Record the number of questions you answered correctly and incorrectly for each section in the answer chart provided at the end of the test. Also, record the number of questions you want to review further or were unsure about.

- Carefully review and understand the answer explanations to all questions you answered incorrectly.

- Don't forget to review each of the questions that you answered correctly but of which you may not be sure. This is a necessary step to gain the knowledge and expertise you need to get the highest scores possible on the real ASVAB tests.

- Transfer your scores for each section of Practice Test 2 to the Self-Evaluation Chart on page 22. This will enable you to track your progress as you continue to prepare for the actual test.

- Use the sample answer sheets provided to record your answers. If you want, you can cut them out to make them easier to use and to simulate actual test conditions.

ANSWER SHEET PRACTICE TEST 2

Part 1: General Science

1. Ⓐ Ⓑ Ⓒ Ⓓ 2. Ⓐ Ⓑ Ⓒ Ⓓ 3. Ⓐ Ⓑ Ⓒ Ⓓ 4. Ⓐ Ⓑ Ⓒ Ⓓ 5. Ⓐ Ⓑ Ⓒ Ⓓ
6. Ⓐ Ⓑ Ⓒ Ⓓ 7. Ⓐ Ⓑ Ⓒ Ⓓ 8. Ⓐ Ⓑ Ⓒ Ⓓ 9. Ⓐ Ⓑ Ⓒ Ⓓ 10. Ⓐ Ⓑ Ⓒ Ⓓ
11. Ⓐ Ⓑ Ⓒ Ⓓ 12. Ⓐ Ⓑ Ⓒ Ⓓ 13. Ⓐ Ⓑ Ⓒ Ⓓ 14. Ⓐ Ⓑ Ⓒ Ⓓ 15. Ⓐ Ⓑ Ⓒ Ⓓ
16. Ⓐ Ⓑ Ⓒ Ⓓ 17. Ⓐ Ⓑ Ⓒ Ⓓ 18. Ⓐ Ⓑ Ⓒ Ⓓ 19. Ⓐ Ⓑ Ⓒ Ⓓ 20. Ⓐ Ⓑ Ⓒ Ⓓ
21. Ⓐ Ⓑ Ⓒ Ⓓ 22. Ⓐ Ⓑ Ⓒ Ⓓ 23. Ⓐ Ⓑ Ⓒ Ⓓ 24. Ⓐ Ⓑ Ⓒ Ⓓ 25. Ⓐ Ⓑ Ⓒ Ⓓ

Part 2: Arithmetic Reasoning

1. Ⓐ Ⓑ Ⓒ Ⓓ 2. Ⓐ Ⓑ Ⓒ Ⓓ 3. Ⓐ Ⓑ Ⓒ Ⓓ 4. Ⓐ Ⓑ Ⓒ Ⓓ 5. Ⓐ Ⓑ Ⓒ Ⓓ
6. Ⓐ Ⓑ Ⓒ Ⓓ 7. Ⓐ Ⓑ Ⓒ Ⓓ 8. Ⓐ Ⓑ Ⓒ Ⓓ 9. Ⓐ Ⓑ Ⓒ Ⓓ 10. Ⓐ Ⓑ Ⓒ Ⓓ
11. Ⓐ Ⓑ Ⓒ Ⓓ 12. Ⓐ Ⓑ Ⓒ Ⓓ 13. Ⓐ Ⓑ Ⓒ Ⓓ 14. Ⓐ Ⓑ Ⓒ Ⓓ 15. Ⓐ Ⓑ Ⓒ Ⓓ
16. Ⓐ Ⓑ Ⓒ Ⓓ 17. Ⓐ Ⓑ Ⓒ Ⓓ 18. Ⓐ Ⓑ Ⓒ Ⓓ 19. Ⓐ Ⓑ Ⓒ Ⓓ 20. Ⓐ Ⓑ Ⓒ Ⓓ
21. Ⓐ Ⓑ Ⓒ Ⓓ 22. Ⓐ Ⓑ Ⓒ Ⓓ 23. Ⓐ Ⓑ Ⓒ Ⓓ 24. Ⓐ Ⓑ Ⓒ Ⓓ 25. Ⓐ Ⓑ Ⓒ Ⓓ
26. Ⓐ Ⓑ Ⓒ Ⓓ 27. Ⓐ Ⓑ Ⓒ Ⓓ 28. Ⓐ Ⓑ Ⓒ Ⓓ 29. Ⓐ Ⓑ Ⓒ Ⓓ 30. Ⓐ Ⓑ Ⓒ Ⓓ

Part 3: Word Knowledge

1. Ⓐ Ⓑ Ⓒ Ⓓ 2. Ⓐ Ⓑ Ⓒ Ⓓ 3. Ⓐ Ⓑ Ⓒ Ⓓ 4. Ⓐ Ⓑ Ⓒ Ⓓ 5. Ⓐ Ⓑ Ⓒ Ⓓ
6. Ⓐ Ⓑ Ⓒ Ⓓ 7. Ⓐ Ⓑ Ⓒ Ⓓ 8. Ⓐ Ⓑ Ⓒ Ⓓ 9. Ⓐ Ⓑ Ⓒ Ⓓ 10. Ⓐ Ⓑ Ⓒ Ⓓ
11. Ⓐ Ⓑ Ⓒ Ⓓ 12. Ⓐ Ⓑ Ⓒ Ⓓ 13. Ⓐ Ⓑ Ⓒ Ⓓ 14. Ⓐ Ⓑ Ⓒ Ⓓ 15. Ⓐ Ⓑ Ⓒ Ⓓ
16. Ⓐ Ⓑ Ⓒ Ⓓ 17. Ⓐ Ⓑ Ⓒ Ⓓ 18. Ⓐ Ⓑ Ⓒ Ⓓ 19. Ⓐ Ⓑ Ⓒ Ⓓ 20. Ⓐ Ⓑ Ⓒ Ⓓ
21. Ⓐ Ⓑ Ⓒ Ⓓ 22. Ⓐ Ⓑ Ⓒ Ⓓ 23. Ⓐ Ⓑ Ⓒ Ⓓ 24. Ⓐ Ⓑ Ⓒ Ⓓ 25. Ⓐ Ⓑ Ⓒ Ⓓ
26. Ⓐ Ⓑ Ⓒ Ⓓ 27. Ⓐ Ⓑ Ⓒ Ⓓ 28. Ⓐ Ⓑ Ⓒ Ⓓ 29. Ⓐ Ⓑ Ⓒ Ⓓ 30. Ⓐ Ⓑ Ⓒ Ⓓ
31. Ⓐ Ⓑ Ⓒ Ⓓ 32. Ⓐ Ⓑ Ⓒ Ⓓ 33. Ⓐ Ⓑ Ⓒ Ⓓ 34. Ⓐ Ⓑ Ⓒ Ⓓ 35. Ⓐ Ⓑ Ⓒ Ⓓ

Part 4: Paragraph Comprehension

1. Ⓐ Ⓑ Ⓒ Ⓓ 2. Ⓐ Ⓑ Ⓒ Ⓓ 3. Ⓐ Ⓑ Ⓒ Ⓓ 4. Ⓐ Ⓑ Ⓒ Ⓓ 5. Ⓐ Ⓑ Ⓒ Ⓓ
6. Ⓐ Ⓑ Ⓒ Ⓓ 7. Ⓐ Ⓑ Ⓒ Ⓓ 8. Ⓐ Ⓑ Ⓒ Ⓓ 9. Ⓐ Ⓑ Ⓒ Ⓓ 10. Ⓐ Ⓑ Ⓒ Ⓓ
11. Ⓐ Ⓑ Ⓒ Ⓓ 12. Ⓐ Ⓑ Ⓒ Ⓓ 13. Ⓐ Ⓑ Ⓒ Ⓓ 14. Ⓐ Ⓑ Ⓒ Ⓓ 15. Ⓐ Ⓑ Ⓒ Ⓓ

answer sheet

Part 5: Mathematics Knowledge

1. Ⓐ Ⓑ Ⓒ Ⓓ   2. Ⓐ Ⓑ Ⓒ Ⓓ   3. Ⓐ Ⓑ Ⓒ Ⓓ   4. Ⓐ Ⓑ Ⓒ Ⓓ   5. Ⓐ Ⓑ Ⓒ Ⓓ
6. Ⓐ Ⓑ Ⓒ Ⓓ   7. Ⓐ Ⓑ Ⓒ Ⓓ   8. Ⓐ Ⓑ Ⓒ Ⓓ   9. Ⓐ Ⓑ Ⓒ Ⓓ   10. Ⓐ Ⓑ Ⓒ Ⓓ
11. Ⓐ Ⓑ Ⓒ Ⓓ   12. Ⓐ Ⓑ Ⓒ Ⓓ   13. Ⓐ Ⓑ Ⓒ Ⓓ   14. Ⓐ Ⓑ Ⓒ Ⓓ   15. Ⓐ Ⓑ Ⓒ Ⓓ
16. Ⓐ Ⓑ Ⓒ Ⓓ   17. Ⓐ Ⓑ Ⓒ Ⓓ   18. Ⓐ Ⓑ Ⓒ Ⓓ   19. Ⓐ Ⓑ Ⓒ Ⓓ   20. Ⓐ Ⓑ Ⓒ Ⓓ
21. Ⓐ Ⓑ Ⓒ Ⓓ   22. Ⓐ Ⓑ Ⓒ Ⓓ   23. Ⓐ Ⓑ Ⓒ Ⓓ   24. Ⓐ Ⓑ Ⓒ Ⓓ   25. Ⓐ Ⓑ Ⓒ Ⓓ

Part 6: Electronics Information

1. Ⓐ Ⓑ Ⓒ Ⓓ   2. Ⓐ Ⓑ Ⓒ Ⓓ   3. Ⓐ Ⓑ Ⓒ Ⓓ   4. Ⓐ Ⓑ Ⓒ Ⓓ   5. Ⓐ Ⓑ Ⓒ Ⓓ
6. Ⓐ Ⓑ Ⓒ Ⓓ   7. Ⓐ Ⓑ Ⓒ Ⓓ   8. Ⓐ Ⓑ Ⓒ Ⓓ   9. Ⓐ Ⓑ Ⓒ Ⓓ   10. Ⓐ Ⓑ Ⓒ Ⓓ
11. Ⓐ Ⓑ Ⓒ Ⓓ   12. Ⓐ Ⓑ Ⓒ Ⓓ   13. Ⓐ Ⓑ Ⓒ Ⓓ   14. Ⓐ Ⓑ Ⓒ Ⓓ   15. Ⓐ Ⓑ Ⓒ Ⓓ
16. Ⓐ Ⓑ Ⓒ Ⓓ   17. Ⓐ Ⓑ Ⓒ Ⓓ   18. Ⓐ Ⓑ Ⓒ Ⓓ   19. Ⓐ Ⓑ Ⓒ Ⓓ   20. Ⓐ Ⓑ Ⓒ Ⓓ

Part 7: Auto & Shop Information

1. Ⓐ Ⓑ Ⓒ Ⓓ   2. Ⓐ Ⓑ Ⓒ Ⓓ   3. Ⓐ Ⓑ Ⓒ Ⓓ   4. Ⓐ Ⓑ Ⓒ Ⓓ   5. Ⓐ Ⓑ Ⓒ Ⓓ
6. Ⓐ Ⓑ Ⓒ Ⓓ   7. Ⓐ Ⓑ Ⓒ Ⓓ   8. Ⓐ Ⓑ Ⓒ Ⓓ   9. Ⓐ Ⓑ Ⓒ Ⓓ   10. Ⓐ Ⓑ Ⓒ Ⓓ
11. Ⓐ Ⓑ Ⓒ Ⓓ   12. Ⓐ Ⓑ Ⓒ Ⓓ   13. Ⓐ Ⓑ Ⓒ Ⓓ   14. Ⓐ Ⓑ Ⓒ Ⓓ   15. Ⓐ Ⓑ Ⓒ Ⓓ
16. Ⓐ Ⓑ Ⓒ Ⓓ   17. Ⓐ Ⓑ Ⓒ Ⓓ   18. Ⓐ Ⓑ Ⓒ Ⓓ   19. Ⓐ Ⓑ Ⓒ Ⓓ   20. Ⓐ Ⓑ Ⓒ Ⓓ
21. Ⓐ Ⓑ Ⓒ Ⓓ   22. Ⓐ Ⓑ Ⓒ Ⓓ   23. Ⓐ Ⓑ Ⓒ Ⓓ   24. Ⓐ Ⓑ Ⓒ Ⓓ   25. Ⓐ Ⓑ Ⓒ Ⓓ

Part 8: Mechanical Comprehension

1. Ⓐ Ⓑ Ⓒ Ⓓ   2. Ⓐ Ⓑ Ⓒ Ⓓ   3. Ⓐ Ⓑ Ⓒ Ⓓ   4. Ⓐ Ⓑ Ⓒ Ⓓ   5. Ⓐ Ⓑ Ⓒ Ⓓ
6. Ⓐ Ⓑ Ⓒ Ⓓ   7. Ⓐ Ⓑ Ⓒ Ⓓ   8. Ⓐ Ⓑ Ⓒ Ⓓ   9. Ⓐ Ⓑ Ⓒ Ⓓ   10. Ⓐ Ⓑ Ⓒ Ⓓ
11. Ⓐ Ⓑ Ⓒ Ⓓ   12. Ⓐ Ⓑ Ⓒ Ⓓ   13. Ⓐ Ⓑ Ⓒ Ⓓ   14. Ⓐ Ⓑ Ⓒ Ⓓ   15. Ⓐ Ⓑ Ⓒ Ⓓ
16. Ⓐ Ⓑ Ⓒ Ⓓ   17. Ⓐ Ⓑ Ⓒ Ⓓ   18. Ⓐ Ⓑ Ⓒ Ⓓ   19. Ⓐ Ⓑ Ⓒ Ⓓ   20. Ⓐ Ⓑ Ⓒ Ⓓ
21. Ⓐ Ⓑ Ⓒ Ⓓ   22. Ⓐ Ⓑ Ⓒ Ⓓ   23. Ⓐ Ⓑ Ⓒ Ⓓ   24. Ⓐ Ⓑ Ⓒ Ⓓ   25. Ⓐ Ⓑ Ⓒ Ⓓ

Part 9: Assembling Objects

1. Ⓐ Ⓑ Ⓒ Ⓓ   2. Ⓐ Ⓑ Ⓒ Ⓓ   3. Ⓐ Ⓑ Ⓒ Ⓓ   4. Ⓐ Ⓑ Ⓒ Ⓓ   5. Ⓐ Ⓑ Ⓒ Ⓓ
6. Ⓐ Ⓑ Ⓒ Ⓓ   7. Ⓐ Ⓑ Ⓒ Ⓓ   8. Ⓐ Ⓑ Ⓒ Ⓓ   9. Ⓐ Ⓑ Ⓒ Ⓓ   10. Ⓐ Ⓑ Ⓒ Ⓓ
11. Ⓐ Ⓑ Ⓒ Ⓓ   12. Ⓐ Ⓑ Ⓒ Ⓓ   13. Ⓐ Ⓑ Ⓒ Ⓓ   14. Ⓐ Ⓑ Ⓒ Ⓓ   15. Ⓐ Ⓑ Ⓒ Ⓓ
16. Ⓐ Ⓑ Ⓒ Ⓓ

PART 1: GENERAL SCIENCE

Time: 11 Minutes—25 Questions

> **Directions:** This is a test of 25 questions to find out how much you know about general science as usually covered in high school courses. Pick the best answer for each question, then blacken the space on your answer sheet that has the same number and letter as your choice.

Here are three sample questions.

1. Water is an example of a   Ⓐ Ⓑ ● Ⓓ
   A. solid.
   B. gas.
   C. liquid.
   D. crystal.

   Notice that answer space C has been marked for question 1. Now do practice questions 2 and 3 by yourself. Find the correct answer to the question, then mark the space that has the same letter as the answer you picked. Do this now.

2. Lack of iodine is often related to which of the following diseases?   Ⓐ Ⓑ Ⓒ Ⓓ
   A. Beriberi
   B. Scurvy
   C. Rickets
   D. Goiter

3. An eclipse of the sun throws the shadow of the   Ⓐ Ⓑ Ⓒ Ⓓ
   A. earth on the moon.
   B. moon on the earth.
   C. moon on the sun.
   D. earth on the sun.

   You should have marked choice D for question 2 and choice B for question 3. If you made any mistakes, erase your mark carefully and blacken the correct answer space. Do this now.

Your score on this test will be based on the number of questions you answer correctly. You should try to answer every question. Do not spend too much time on any one question.

When you begin, be sure to start with question number 1 in Part 1 in your test booklet and number 1 in Part 1 on your answer sheet.

1. Citrus fruits include
   A. apples.
   B. bananas.
   C. oranges.
   D. peaches.

2. What temperature is shown on a Fahrenheit thermometer when a centigrade thermometer reads 0°?
   A. −40°
   B. −32°
   C. 0°
   D. 32°

3. The major chemical constituent of a cell, by weight, is
   A. protein.
   B. ash.
   C. water.
   D. carbohydrates.

4. Which of the following is NOT a viral disease?
   A. Measles
   B. Mumps
   C. Smallpox
   D. Syphilis

5. Alcoholic beverages contain
   A. wood alcohol.
   B. isopropyl alcohol.
   C. glyceryl alcohol.
   D. grain alcohol.

6. The air around us is composed mostly of
   A. carbon.
   B. nitrogen.
   C. hydrogen.
   D. oxygen.

7. The process that is responsible for the continuous removal of carbon dioxide from the atmosphere is
   A. respiration.
   B. oxidation.
   C. metabolism.
   D. photosynthesis.

8. Ringworm is caused by a(n)
   A. algae.
   B. fungus.
   C. bacterium.
   D. protozoan.

9. Light passes through the crystalline lens in the eye and focuses on the
   A. cornea.
   B. iris.
   C. pupil.
   D. retina.

10. Which of the following processes is responsible for the removal of oxygen from the atmosphere?
    A. respiration
    B. oxidation
    C. photosynthesis
    D. metabolism

11. The vitamin that helps coagulation of the blood is
    A. C
    B. E
    C. D
    D. K

12. Of the following, the part of a ship that gives it stability by lowering the center of gravity is the
    A. bulkhead.
    B. keel.
    C. anchor.
    D. prow.

13. To reduce soil acidity, a farmer should use
    A. lime.
    B. phosphate.
    C. manure.
    D. peat moss.

14. Which of the following will cause Athlete's foot?
    A. Algae
    B. Bacterium
    C. Fungus
    D. Protozoan

15. Bacteria of decay help
    A. deplete soil.
    B. enrich soil.
    C. form oxygen.
    D. form water.

16. Of the following, the food that contains the largest amount of Vitamin C is
    A. carrots.
    B. sweet potatoes.
    C. lima beans.
    D. tomatoes.

17. The cyclotron is used to
    A. measure radioactivity.
    B. measure the speed of the earth's rotation.
    C. split atoms.
    D. store radioactive energy.

18. The earth completes one trip around the sun approximately every
    A. 24 hours.
    B. 52 weeks.
    C. 7 days.
    D. 30 days.

19. A person is more buoyant when swimming in saltwater than in freshwater because
    A. he keeps his head out of saltwater.
    B. salt coats his body with a floating membrane.
    C. saltwater has greater tensile strength.
    D. saltwater weighs more than an equal volume of freshwater.

20. A volcanic eruption is caused by
    A. sunspots.
    B. pressure inside the earth.
    C. nuclear fallout.
    D. boiling lava.

21. The scientific name of an organism consists of its
    A. family and class.
    B. genus and species.
    C. order and family.
    D. species and kingdom.

22. Which organelle is responsible for the eye focusing?
    A. retina
    B. cornea
    C. iris
    D. pupil

23. Which of the following acids is found in the digestive system?
    A. sulfuric
    B. nitric
    C. hydrochloric
    D. phosphoric

24. When two forces act on an object in opposite directions, the resultant force is equal to the
    A. difference between the forces.
    B. ratio of the forces.
    C. product of the forces.
    D. sum of the forces.

25. Which vitamin can be intensified by the sun?
   A. C
   B. D
   C. E
   D. K

STOP!
IF YOU FINISH BEFORE THE TIME IS UP, YOU MAY CHECK OVER YOUR WORK ON THIS PART ONLY.

PART 2: ARITHMETIC REASONING

Time: 36 Minutes—30 Questions

Directions: This test has 30 questions about arithmetic. Each question is followed by four possible answers. Decide which answer is correct, then blacken the space on your answer sheet that has the same number and letter as your choice. Use scratch paper to do any figuring.

Here are two sample questions.

1. A person buys a sandwich for $4.00, soda for $1.25, and pie for $1.75. What is the total cost?   Ⓐ Ⓑ Ⓒ Ⓓ
   A. $6.85
   B. $6.95
   C. $7.00
   D. $7.15

   The total cost is $7.00; therefore, choice C is the correct answer.

2. If 8 workers are needed to run 4 machines, how many workers are needed to run 20 machines?   Ⓐ Ⓑ Ⓒ Ⓓ
   A. 16
   B. 32
   C. 36
   D. 40

   The number needed is 40; therefore, choice D is the correct answer.

Your score on this test will be based on the number of questions you answer correctly. You should try to answer every question. Do not spend too much time on any one question.

Notice that Part 2 begins with question number 1. When you begin, be sure to start with question number 1 in Part 2 in your test booklet and number 1 in Part 2 on your answer sheet.

1. A man owned 75 shares of stock worth $50 each. The corporation declared a dividend of 8%, payable in stock. How many shares did he then own?
   - A. 81 shares
   - B. 90 shares
   - C. 91 shares
   - D. 95 shares

2. If a scow is towed at the rate of 3 miles an hour, how many hours will be needed to tow the scow 28 miles?
   - A. 10 hours, 30 minutes
   - B. 9 hours, 20 minutes
   - C. 12 hours
   - D. 9 hours, 15 minutes

3. Fifteen dozen eggs were needed for baking four wedding cakes. The first cake needed one dozen eggs, and each successive cake needed twice as many eggs as the previous cake. How many eggs were used to make the fourth cake?
   - A. 24
   - B. 48
   - C. 96
   - D. 180

4. The local high school had 1,000 bottles of water on hand. The school issued $\frac{1}{4}$ of the supply to the 9th grade, $\frac{1}{5}$ of the supply to the 10th grade, and $\frac{2}{5}$ of the supply to the 11th grade. How many bottles remained for the 12th grade?
   - A. 240
   - B. 190
   - C. 170
   - D. 150

5. A dealer bought some bicycles for $4,000. He sold them for $6,200, making $50 on each bicycle. How many bicycles were there?
   - A. 40
   - B. 43
   - C. 38
   - D. 44

6. Many American cars feature speedometers that show kilometers per hour. If you are required to drive 500 miles, and you know that one kilometer is approximately $\frac{5}{8}$ of a mile, how many kilometers would you cover in that journey?
   - A. 625
   - B. 800
   - C. 850
   - D. 1,000

7. Six gross of special drawing pencils were purchased for use in a department. If the pencils were used at the rate of 24 a week, the maximum number of weeks that the 6 gross of pencils would last is
   - A. 6 weeks.
   - B. 24 weeks.
   - C. 12 weeks.
   - D. 36 weeks.

8. A stock clerk had 600 pads on hand. He then issued $\frac{3}{8}$ of his supply of pads to Division X, $\frac{1}{4}$ to Division Y, and $\frac{1}{6}$ to Division Z. The number of pads remaining in stock is
   - A. 48
   - B. 240
   - C. 125
   - D. 475

9. During a sale, CDs that normally cost $6.98 each were priced at 2 for $12.50. Pete bought 4 CDs at the sale price. How much money did he save by buying the 4 CDs on sale?
   A. $2.98
   B. $2.92
   C. $2.50
   D. $1.46

10. At the grocery store, boxes of coffee that normally cost $6.99 each were priced at 2 for $8.50. Jack bought 4 boxes at the sale price. How much money did he save by buying the 4 boxes of coffee on sale?
    A. $10.96
    B. $19.46
    C. $12.96
    D. $14.96

11. Two sailors traveled by bus from one point to another. The trip took 15 hours, and they left their point of origin at 8 a.m. What time did they arrive at their destination?
    A. 11 a.m.
    B. 10 p.m.
    C. 11 p.m.
    D. 12 a.m.

12. A team won 8 of the 24 games it played in one season. What percent of the games did it win?
    A. $33\frac{2}{3}\%$
    B. $33\frac{1}{3}\%$
    C. 50%
    D. 16%

13. The distance from my home to my school is 4 miles. If I can walk at an average rate of 3 miles per hour, how many minutes should it take to walk from home to school?
    A. 60 min
    B. 80 min
    C. 100 min
    D. 120 min

14. A shopper bought 4 pillow cases that cost $4.98 apiece, 2 fitted sheets that cost $8.29 apiece, and 2 flat sheets that cost $8.09 apiece. What was her total bill?
    A. $52.58
    B. $51.68
    C. $52.68
    D. $21.36

15. The wage rate in a certain trade is $8.60 an hour for a 40-hour week and $1\frac{1}{2}$ times the base pay for overtime. An employee who works 48 hours in a week earns
    A. $447.20
    B. $498.20
    C. $582.20
    D. $619.20

16. The temperature yesterday at noon was 68.5 degrees. Today at noon it was 59.9 degrees. What was the difference in temperature?
    A. 8.4 degrees
    B. 8.5 degrees
    C. 8.6 degrees
    D. 8.7 degrees

17. My family left at 4 a.m. this morning on a trip to the mountains. If the car averaged 60 miles per hour for 600 miles, what time would they arrive at their destination?
    A. 1 p.m.
    B. 2 p.m.
    C. 3 p.m.
    D. 4 p.m.

18. A woman bought a new color television with a $40 down payment and 16 monthly payments of $20 each. What was the total cost of the television?
    A. $450
    B. $360
    C. $320
    D. $280

19. A man paid $42.30 for gasoline in May, $38.60 in June, and $43 in July. What was his average monthly cost for gasoline?
    A. $40.45
    B. $41.30
    C. $61.95
    D. $123.90

20. A skier started a fire in the fireplace. Each log she put on burned for a half-hour. If she started with a supply of 10 logs, for how many hours could the fire burn?
    A. 5 hours
    B. $8\frac{1}{2}$ hours
    C. 10 hours
    D. 7 hours

21. To go from Poughkeepsie, New York, to West Palm Beach, Florida, you must travel 1,400 miles. If you can average a driving speed of 50 miles an hour, how many hours must you drive to make this trip?
    A. 25
    B. 28
    C. 30
    D. $27\frac{1}{2}$

22. Mrs. Jones wishes to buy 72 ounces of canned beans for the least possible cost. Which of the following should she buy?
    A. Six 12-ounce cans at 39¢ per can
    B. Seven 10-ounce cans at 34¢ per can
    C. Three 24-ounce cans at 79¢ per can
    D. Two 25-ounce cans at 62¢ per can

23. On a certain day, the temperature ranged from −2°F to 10°F. What is the difference between the high and low temperatures for that day?
    A. 6°
    B. 8°
    C. 10°
    D. 12°

24. My favorite football team won 13 out of 16 games this season. What percentage of the games did the team win?
    A. 44.83 %
    B. 78.25%
    C. 81.25%
    D. 18.75%

25. An officer traveled 1,200 miles in 20 hours. How many miles per hour did she average?
    A. 45
    B. 60
    C. 50
    D. 65

26. A boy sold $88.50 worth of stationery. If he received a $33\frac{1}{3}$ commission, what was the amount of his commission?
    A. $29.50
    B. $40
    C. $50
    D. $62.50

27. What is the shortest board a man must buy in order to cut 3 sections from it, each 4 feet 8 inches long?

   A. 12 feet

   B. 14 feet

   C. 16 feet

   D. 18 feet

28. A girl bought a sweater for $21, a blouse for $14.98, and a scarf for $4.97. What was the total cost of her purchases?

   A. $35.50

   B. $40.85

   C. $30.85

   D. $40.95

29. Don and Frank started from the same point and drove in opposite directions. Don's rate of travel was 50 miles per hour. Frank's rate of travel was 40 miles per hour. How many miles apart were they at the end of 2 hours?

   A. 90

   B. 160

   C. 140

   D. 180

30. A decorator went to a department store and ordered curtains for 5 windows. One pair of curtains cost $14.28; 2 pairs cost $33.26 apiece; and the remaining 2 pairs cost $65.38 apiece. What was the retail cost of the 5 pairs of curtains?

   A. $211.46

   B. $211.56

   C. $112.92

   D. $110.82

STOP!
IF YOU FINISH BEFORE THE TIME IS UP,
YOU MAY CHECK OVER YOUR WORK ON THIS PART ONLY.

practice test 2

PART 3: WORD KNOWLEDGE

Time: 11 Minutes—35 Questions

> **Directions:** This test has 35 questions about the meanings of words. Each question has an underlined word. You are to decide which one of the four words in the choices most nearly means the same as the underlined word, then mark the space on your answer sheet that has the same number and letter as your choice.

Now look at the two sample questions below.

1. <u>Mended</u> most nearly means   Ⓐ Ⓑ Ⓒ Ⓓ
   A. repaired.
   B. torn.
   C. clean.
   D. tied.

   Repaired, choice A, is the correct answer. *Mended* means *fixed* or *repaired*. *Torn*, choice B, might be the state of an object before it is mended. The repair might be made by *tying*, choice D, but not necessarily. *Clean*, choice C, is wrong.

2. It was a <u>small</u> table.   Ⓐ Ⓑ Ⓒ Ⓓ
   A. Sturdy
   B. Round
   C. Cheap
   D. Little

   Little means the same as *small*, so choice D is the best answer.

Your score on this test will be based on the number of questions you answer correctly. You should try to answer every question. Do not spend too much time on any one question.

When you begin, be sure to start with question number 1 in Part 3 in your test booklet and number 1 in Part 3 on your answer sheet.

1. <u>Revenue</u> most nearly means
   A. taxes.
   B. income.
   C. expenses.
   D. produce.

2. To <u>necessitate</u> most nearly means
   A. required.
   B. irrelevant.
   C. enter.
   D. depart.

3. The machine has <u>manual</u> controls.
   A. Self-acting
   B. Simple
   C. Hand-operated
   D. Handmade

4. <u>Deportment</u> most nearly means
   A. attendance.
   B. intelligence.
   C. neatness.
   D. behavior.

5. <u>Prior</u> most nearly means
   A. personal.
   B. more urgent.
   C. more attractive.
   D. earlier.

6. <u>Grimy</u> most nearly means
   A. ill-fitting.
   B. poorly made.
   C. dirty.
   D. ragged.

7. Her <u>malady</u> caused side effects.
   A. Accident
   B. Disease
   C. Parents
   D. Employment

8. The man <u>survived</u> his three sisters.
   A. Outlived
   B. Envied
   C. Excelled
   D. Destroyed

9. She is a <u>competent</u> worker.
   A. Busy
   B. Capable
   C. Friendly
   D. Good-natured

10. All service was <u>suspended</u> during the emergency.
    A. Turned back
    B. Checked carefully
    C. Regulated strictly
    D. Stopped temporarily

11. The <u>territory</u> is too large for one platoon to defend.
    A. Region
    B. Swamp
    C. Ranch
    D. Beach

12. <u>Huge</u> most nearly means
    A. ugly.
    B. tall.
    C. wide.
    D. immense.

13. <u>Myriad</u> most nearly means
    A. colorful.
    B absorption.
    C. many.
    D. chaos.

14. Mail will be <u>forwarded</u> to our new address.
    A. Sent
    B. Returned
    C. Canceled
    D. Received

15. The room was <u>vacant</u> when we arrived.
    A. Quiet
    B. Dark
    C. Available
    D. Empty

16. <u>Irritating</u> most nearly means
    A. nervous.
    B. unsuitable.
    C. annoying.
    D. noisy.

17. <u>Aspire</u> most nearly means to
    A. fail.
    B. strive for a goal.
    C. elevate.
    D. destroy.

18. <u>Power</u> most nearly means
    A. size.
    B. ambition.
    C. force.
    D. success.

19. The <u>accusation</u> was hurtful.
    A. Truth
    B. Statement of wrongdoing
    C. Joke
    D. Speech

20. <u>Flexible</u> most nearly means
    A. pliable.
    B. rigid.
    C. weak.
    D. athletic.

21. <u>Comprehend</u> most nearly means
    A. hear.
    B. listen.
    C. agree.
    D. understand.

22. <u>Instructor</u> most nearly means
    A. expert.
    B. assistant.
    C. teacher.
    D. foreman.

23. <u>Defunct</u> most nearly means
    A. useful.
    B. extinct.
    C. thriving.
    D. lost.

24. <u>Revolving</u> most nearly means
    A. rocking.
    B. working.
    C. vibrating.
    D. turning.

25. <u>Alert</u> most nearly means
    A. watchful.
    B. busy.
    C. helpful.
    D. honest.

26. The computer did not <u>function</u> yesterday.
    A. Finish
    B. Stop
    C. Operate
    D. Overheat

27. <u>Hazard</u> most nearly means
    A. damage.
    B. choice.
    C. opportunity.
    D. danger.

28. <u>Blemish</u> most nearly means
   A. color.
   B. insect.
   C. flaw.
   D. design.

29. The reply will be <u>conveyed</u> by messenger.
   A. Carried
   B. Guarded
   C. Refused
   D. Damaged

30. She committed an <u>egregious</u> error.
   A. Accidental
   B. Blinding
   C. Outrageous
   D. Unnoticeable

31. <u>Attorney</u> most nearly means
   A. banker.
   B. lawyer.
   C. foot doctor.
   D. accountant.

32. <u>Obsolete</u> most nearly means
   A. out of date.
   B. broken down.
   C. as good as new.
   D. improved.

33. The classroom has <u>stationary</u> desks.
   A. Heavy
   B. Carved
   C. Written-upon
   D. Not movable

34. We heard the <u>steady</u> ticking of the clock.
   A. Noisy
   B. Eerie
   C. Tiresome
   D. Regular

35. The letter <u>emphasized</u> two important ideas.
   A. Introduced
   B. Overlooked
   C. Contrasted
   D. Stressed

STOP!
IF YOU FINISH BEFORE THE TIME IS UP,
YOU MAY CHECK OVER YOUR WORK ON THIS PART ONLY.

practice test 2

PART 4: PARAGRAPH COMPREHENSION

Time: 13 Minutes—15 Questions

> **Directions:** This test contains 15 items measuring your ability to obtain information from written passages. You will find one or more paragraphs of reading material followed by incomplete statements or questions. You are to read the paragraph(s) and select the lettered choice that best completes the statement or answers the question.

Here are two sample questions.

1. From a building designer's standpoint, three things that make a home livable are the needs of the client, the building site, and the amount of money the client has to spend.

   Ⓐ Ⓑ Ⓒ Ⓓ

   According to the passage, to make a home livable
   A. the prospective piece of land makes little difference.
   B. it can be built on any piece of land.
   C. the design must fit the owner's income and site.
   D. the design must fit the designer's income.

   The correct answer is that the design must fit the owner's income and site, so choice C is the correct answer.

2. In certain areas, water is so scarce that every attempt is made to conserve it. For instance, on one oasis in the Sahara Desert, the amount of water necessary for each date palm tree has been carefully determined.

   Ⓐ Ⓑ Ⓒ Ⓓ

   How much water is each tree given?
   A. No water at all
   B. Exactly the amount required
   C. Water only if it is healthy
   D. Water on alternate days

   The correct answer is exactly the amount required, so choice B is the correct answer.

Your score on this test will be based on the number of questions you answer correctly. You should try to answer every question. Do not spend too much time on any one question.

When you begin, be sure to start with question number 1 in Part 4 in your test booklet and number 1 in Part 4 on your answer sheet.

1. The lead-acid storage battery is used for storing energy in its chemical form. The battery does not actually store electricity but converts an electrical charge into chemical energy that is stored until the battery terminals are connected to a closed external circuit. When the circuit is closed, the battery's chemical energy is transformed back into electrical energy and, as a result, current flows through the circuit.

   According to this passage, a lead-acid battery stores

   A. current.

   B. electricity.

   C. electric energy.

   D. chemical energy.

2. A good or service has value only because people want it. Value is an extrinsic quality wholly created in the minds of people and is not intrinsic in the property itself.

   According to this passage, it is correct to say that an object will be valuable if it is

   A. beautiful.

   B. not plentiful.

   C. sought after.

   D. useful.

3. You can tell a frog from a toad by its skin. In general, a frog's skin is moist, smooth, and shiny while a toad's skin is dry, dull, and rough or covered with warts. Frogs are also better at jumping than are toads.

   You can recognize a toad by its

   A. great jumping ability.

   B. smooth, shiny skin.

   C. lack of warts.

   D. dry, rough skin.

4. The speed of a boat is measured in knots. One knot is equal to a speed of one nautical mile an hour. A nautical mile is equal to 6,080 feet, while an ordinary mile is 5,280 feet.

   According to the passage, which of the following statements is true?

   A. A nautical mile is longer than an ordinary mile.

   B. A speed of 2 knots is the same as 2 miles per hour.

   C. A knot is the same as a mile.

   D. The distance a boat travels is measured in knots.

5. There are only two grooves on a record—one on each side. The groove is cut in a spiral on the surface of the record. For stereophonic sound, a different sound is recorded in each wall of the groove. The pick-up produces two signals, one of which goes to the left-hand speaker and one to the right-hand speaker.

   Stereophonic sound is produced by

   A. cutting extra grooves in a record.

   B. recording different sounds in each wall of the groove.

   C. sending the sound to two speakers.

   D. having left- and right-hand speakers.

practice test 2

6. It is a common assumption that city directories are prepared and published by the cities concerned. However, the directory business is as much a private business as is the publishing of dictionaries and encyclopedias. The companies financing the publication make their profits through the sales of the directories themselves and through the advertising in them.

   The paragraph best supports the statement that
   A. the publication of a city directory is a commercial enterprise.
   B. the size of a city directory limits the space devoted to advertising.
   C. many city directories are published by dictionary and encyclopedia concerns.
   D. city directories are sold at a cost to local residents and businesspeople.

7. Although rural crime reporting is spottier and less efficient than city and town reporting, sufficient data have been collected to support the statement that rural crime rates are lower than those in urban communities.

   The paragraph best supports the statement that
   A. better reporting of crime occurs in rural areas than in cities.
   B. there appears to be a lower proportion of crime in rural areas than in cities.
   C. cities have more crime than towns.
   D. no conclusions can be drawn regarding crime in rural areas because of inadequate reporting.

8. Iron is used in making our bridges and skyscrapers, subways and steamships, railroads and automobiles, and nearly all kinds of machinery—besides millions of small articles, from the farmer's scythe to the tailor's needle.

   The paragraph best supports the statement that iron
   A. is the most abundant of the metals.
   B. has many different uses.
   C. is the strongest of all metals.
   D. is the only material used in building skyscrapers and bridges.

9. Most solids, like most liquids, expand when heated and contract when cooled. To allow for this, roads, sidewalks, and railroad tracks are constructed with spacing between sections so that they can expand during the hot weather.

   If roads, sidewalks, and railroad tracks were not constructed with spacing between sections
   A. nothing would happen to them when the weather changed.
   B. they could not be constructed as easily as they are now.
   C. they would crack or break when the weather changed.
   D. they would not appear to be even.

10. Twenty-five percent of all household burglaries can be attributed to unlocked windows or doors. Crime is the result of opportunity plus desire.

    To prevent crime, it is each individual's responsibility to
    A. provide the desire.
    B. provide the opportunity.
    C. prevent the desire.
    D. prevent the opportunity.

Questions 11 and 12 are based on the following passage.

When demand for new buildings rises sharply, prices of such buildings usually increase rapidly while construction invariably lags behind. The relation of supply to demand is one of the factors that may greatly influence prices. When demand for new buildings suddenly declines, their prices fall because the available supply cannot be immediately curtailed.

11. According to the passage, a sharp increase in demand for new buildings usually results in
    A. fewer new buildings in proportion to buyers.
    B. a proportionate increase in construction.
    C. more builders of new buildings.
    D. more sellers.

12. When there is a sudden drop in the demand for new buildings, the immediately resulting effect on their prices is attributable mainly to the
    A. cessation in new construction.
    B. curtailment in the supply of such buildings.
    C. reduction in new construction.
    D. static condition in the supply of such buildings.

Questions 13–15 are based on the following passage.

A large proportion of the people behind bars are not convicted criminals, but people who have been arrested and are being held until their trial in court. Experts have often pointed out that this detention system does not operate fairly.

For instance, a person who can afford to pay bail usually will not get locked up. The person must show up in court when he is supposed to; otherwise, he will forfeit his bail. Sometimes, one who can show that he is a stable citizen with a job and a family will be released on "personal recognizance." The result is that the well-to-do, the employed, and the family men can often avoid the detention system. Those who do wind up in detention tend to be the poor, the unemployed, the single, and the young.

13. According to the passage, people who are put behind bars
    A. are almost always dangerous criminals.
    B. include many innocent people who have been arrested by mistake.
    C. are often people who have been arrested but have not yet come to trial.
    D. are all people who tend to be young and single.

14. The passage says that the detention system works unfairly against people who are
    A. rich.
    B. married.
    C. old.
    D. unemployed.

15. When someone is released on "personal recognizance," this means that
    A. the judge knows that he is innocent.
    B. he does not have to show up for a trial.
    C. he has a record of previous convictions.
    D. he does not have to pay bail.

STOP!
IF YOU FINISH BEFORE THE TIME IS UP,
YOU MAY CHECK OVER YOUR WORK ON THIS PART ONLY.

PART 5: MATHEMATICS KNOWLEDGE

Time: 24 Minutes—25 Questions

Directions: This is a test of your ability to solve 25 general mathematical problems. You are to select the correct response from the choices given. Then mark the space on your answer sheet that has the same number and letter as your choice. Use scratch paper to do any figuring.

Now look at the two sample problems below.

1. If $x + 6 = 7$, then x is equal to   Ⓐ Ⓑ Ⓒ Ⓓ
   A. 0
   B. 1
   C. −1
   D. $\frac{7}{6}$

   The correct answer is 1, so choice B is the correct answer.

2. What is the area of the square above?   Ⓐ Ⓑ Ⓒ Ⓓ
   A. 1 square foot
   B. 5 square feet
   C. 10 square feet
   D. 25 square feet

   The correct answer is 25 square feet, so choice D is the correct answer.

Your score on this test will be based on the number of questions you answer correctly. You should try to answer every question. Do not spend too much time on any one question.

When you are told to begin, be sure to start with question number 1 in Part 5 in your test booklet and number 1 in Part 5 on your answer sheet.

1. A box contains 3 black, 4 red, and 5 white marbles. If one marble is to be picked at random, what is the probability that it will be red?

    A. $\frac{1}{5}$

    B. $\frac{1}{2}$

    C. $\frac{1}{3}$

    D. $\frac{1}{4}$

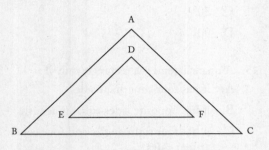

2. In the figure above, the sides of ABC are respectively parallel to the sides of DEF. If the complement of C is 40°, then the complement of F is

    A. 20°

    B. 50°

    C. 40°

    D. 60°

3. The sum of the measures of the angles of a hexagon is

    A. 540°

    B. 720°

    C. 900°

    D. 1,080°

4. If $A^2 + B^2 = A^2 + X^2$, then B equals

    A. $\pm X$

    B. $X^2 - 2A^2$

    C. $\pm A$

    D. $A^2 + X^2$

5. If $6 + x + y = 20$ and $x + y = k$, then $20 - k =$

    A. 6

    B. 0

    C. 14

    D. 20

6. $\sqrt{75} =$

    A. $3\sqrt{5}$

    B. $5\sqrt{3}$

    C. $5\sqrt{15}$

    D. $15\sqrt{5}$

7. $\sqrt{745}$ is a number between

    A. 30 and 40

    B. 40 and 50

    C. 70 and 80

    D. 20 and 30

8. If $m\angle 2 = 80°$ in figure above, $m\angle 4 =$

    A. 80°

    B. 100°

    C. 120°

    D. None of the above

9. $\frac{10^4}{10} =$

    A. 10^3

    B. 10^4

    C. 20^3

    D. 20^4

10. ∧ 1 and ∧ 2 form a linear pair and therefore are supplementary angles. If $m∧ 1 = 7x - 6$ and $m∧ 2 = 5x + 18$, $m∧ 2 =$
   A. 78°
   B. 82°
   C. 85°
   D. 88°

11. If $x = y$, find the value of $8 + 5(x - y)$.
   A. $8 + 5x - 5y$
   B. $8 + 5xy$
   C. $13x - 13y$
   D. 8

12. Look at the figures below.

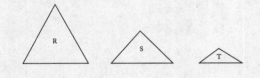

Triangle R is 3 times triangle S.

Triangle S is 3 times triangle T.

If triangle S = 1, what is the sum of the three triangles?

   A. $2\frac{1}{3}$

   B. $3\frac{1}{3}$

   C. $4\frac{1}{3}$

   D. 6

13. How many different combinations of jackets and pants are possible from a wardrobe that contains 3 jackets and 5 pairs of pants?
   A. 3
   B. 5
   C. 8
   D. 15

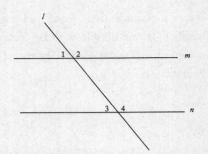

14. In the figure above m is parallel to n. If $m∧ 2 = 120°$, then what is $m∧ 3$?
   A. 120°
   B. 60°
   C. 30°
   D. 90°

15. A quadrilateral is a rectangle only if
   A. it has four congruent sides.
   B. it has opposite sides equal in length.
   C. it has four right angles and four congruent sides.
   D. it has four right angles and opposite side equal in length.

16. ∧ 1 and ∧ 2 form a linear pair and therefore are supplementary angles. If $m∧ 1 = 6x + 19$ and $m∧ 2 = 5x - 4$, then $m∧ 1 =$
   A. 71°
   B. 109°
   C. 45°
   D. 91°

17. Which is NOT a prime number?
   A. 23
   B. 37
   C. 87
   D. 53

18. A is older than B. With the passage of time, the
   A. ratio of the ages of A and B remains unchanged.
   B. ratio of the ages of A and B increases.
   C. ratio of the ages of A and B decreases.
   D. difference in their ages varies.

19. If you multiply $x + 3$ by $2x + 5$, what will the coefficient of x be?
    A. 3
    B. 6
    C. 9
    D. 11

20. $(x + 3)(x + 2) =$
    A. $x^2 + 5x + 5$
    B. $x^2 + 5x + 6$
    C. $x^2 + 6x + 5$
    D. $x^2 + 6x + 6$

21. The perimeter of a rectangle is 90. One side of the rectangle is twice the length of the other.

    What is the length of the longer side?
    A. 20
    B. 25
    C. 30
    D. 35

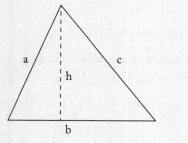

22. The area of the figure above can be determined by the formula
    A. $ac \div b$
    B. $\frac{1}{2}bh$
    C. $bc \div a$
    D. bh^2

23. If $2x = y$, then find the value of $(2x - y)4 + 6$
    A. 6
    B. $20x - 10y$
    C. $8x - 4y + 6$
    D. $8x - y + 6$

24. Look at the figures below.

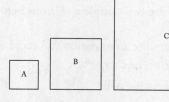

    Square B is 2 times Square A.

    Square C is 2 times Square B.

    If square B = 3, what is the sum of the three squares?

    A. $10\frac{1}{2}$

    B. $9\frac{1}{2}$

    C. $6\frac{1}{3}$

    D. $6\frac{1}{2}$

25. A quadrilateral is a square only if
    A. it has four right angles.
    B. it has at least one pair of parallel sides.
    C. it has four right angles and four congruent sides.
    D. both pairs of its opposite sides are parallel.

STOP!
IF YOU FINISH BEFORE THE TIME IS UP,
YOU MAY CHECK OVER YOUR WORK ON THIS PART ONLY.

practice test 2

PART 6: ELECTRONICS INFORMATION

Time: 9 Minutes—20 Questions

> **Directions:** This is a test of your knowledge of electrical, radio, and electronics information. There are 20 questions. You are to select the correct response from the choices given. Then mark the space on your answer sheet that has the same number and letter as your choice.

Now look at the two sample questions below.

1. What does the abbreviation AC stand for?   Ⓐ Ⓑ Ⓒ Ⓓ
   A. Additional charge
   B. Alternating coil
   C. Alternating current
   D. Ampere current

The correct answer is alternating current, so choice C is the correct response.

2. Which of the following has the LEAST resistance?   Ⓐ Ⓑ Ⓒ Ⓓ
   A. Wood
   B. Silver
   C. Rubber
   D. Iron

The correct answer is silver, so choice B is the correct response.

Your score on this test will be based on the number of questions you answer correctly. You should try to answer every question. Do not spend too much time on any one question.

When you are told to begin, be sure to start with question number 1 in Part 6 in your test booklet and number 1 in Part 6 on your answer sheet.

1. In lights controlled by three-way switches, the switches should be treated and put in as
   A. flush switches.
   B. single-pole switches.
   C. three double-pole switches.
   D. three-pole switches.

2. When working on live 600-volt equipment where rubber gloves might be damaged, an electrician should
   A. work without gloves.
   B. carry a spare pair of rubber gloves.
   C. reinforce the fingers of the rubber gloves with rubber tape.
   D. wear leather gloves over the rubber gloves.

3. A "mil" measures a(n)
   A. eighth of an inch.
   B. millionth of an inch.
   C. thousandth of an inch.
   D. ten-thousandth of an inch.

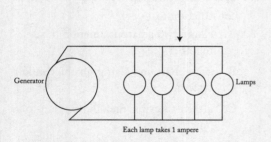

Each lamp takes 1 ampere

4. The current in the wire at the point indicated by the arrow above is
   A. 1 ampere.
   B. 2 amperes.
   C. 3 amperes.
   D. 4 amperes.

5. If a fuse of higher than the required current rating is used in an electrical circuit
   A. better protection will be afforded.
   B. the fuse will blow more often since it carries more current.
   C. serious damage may result to the circuit from overload.
   D. maintenance of the large fuse will be higher.

6. The electrical contacts in the tuner of a television set are usually plated with silver. Silver is used to
   A. avoid tarnish.
   B. improve conductivity.
   C. improve appearance.
   D. avoid arcing.

7. The following equipment is required for a "2-line return-call" electric bell circuit:
   A. 2 bells, 2 metallic lines, 2 ordinary push buttons, and 1 set of batteries
   B. 2 bells, 2 metallic lines, 2 return-call push buttons, and 2 sets of batteries
   C. 2 bells, 2 metallic lines, 2 return-call push buttons, and 1 set of batteries
   D. 2 bells, 2 metallic lines, 1 ordinary push button, 1 return-call push button, and 1 set of batteries

8. What is the approximate characteristic voltage that develops across a red LED?
   A. 1.7v
   B. 3.4v
   C. 5v
   D. 0.6v

9. Metal cabinets used for lighting circuits are grounded to
   A. eliminate electrolysis.
   B. ensure that the fuse in a defective circuit will blow.
   C. reduce shock hazard.
   D. simplify wiring.

10. If two resistors are placed in series, is the final resistance:

   A. Lower

   B. Higher

   C. The same

   D. Can't be determined

11. A value that is NOT common for resistance is:

   A. 4k4

   B. 2k7

   C. 1M8

   D. 330R

12. A polarized plug generally has

   A. two parallel prongs of the same size.

   B. prongs at an angle with one another.

   C. magnetized prongs.

   D. prongs marked plus and minus.

13. The reading of the kilowatt-hour meter shown above is

   A. 7972

   B. 1786

   C. 2786

   D. 6872

14. Commutators are found on

   A. mercury rectifiers.

   B. DC motors.

   C. circuit breakers.

   D. alternators.

15. Neutral wire can be quickly recognized by the

   A. greenish color.

   B. bluish color.

   C. natural or whitish color.

   D. black color.

16. The term that is NOT applicable in describing the *construction* of a microphone is

   A. dynamic.

   B. carbon.

   C. crystal.

   D. feedback.

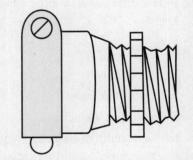

17. The fitting shown above is used in electrical construction to

   A. clamp two adjacent junction boxes together.

   B. act as a ground clamp for the conduit system.

   C. attach a flexible metallic conduit to a junction box.

   D. protect exposed wires where they pass through a wall.

18. A good magnetic material is

   A. copper.

   B. iron.

   C. tin.

   D. brass.

19. Rosin is a material generally used
   A. in batteries.
   B. for high-voltage insulation.
   C. as a dielectric.
   D. as a soldering flux.

20. If a small value of capacitance is connected in parallel with a large value, the combined capacitance will be
   A. lower.
   B. higher.
   C. the same.
   D. slightly higher.

STOP!
IF YOU FINISH BEFORE THE TIME IS UP,
YOU MAY CHECK OVER YOUR WORK ON THIS PART ONLY.

practice test 2

PART 7: AUTO & SHOP INFORMATION

Time: 11 Minutes—25 Questions

Directions: This test has 25 questions about automobiles, shop practices, and the use of tools. Select the best answer for each question, then blacken the space on your answer sheet that has the same number and letter as your choice.

Here are two sample questions.

1. A car uses too much oil when which parts are worn?   Ⓐ Ⓑ Ⓒ Ⓓ
   A. Pistons
   B. Piston rings
   C. Main bearings
   D. Connecting rods

   Worn piston rings cause the use of too much oil, so choice B is the correct answer.

2. The saw shown above is used mainly to cut   Ⓐ Ⓑ Ⓒ Ⓓ
   A. plywood.
   B. odd-shaped holes in wood.
   C. along the grain of the wood.
   D. across the grain of the wood.

   The compass saw is used to cut odd-shaped holes in wood, so choice B is the correct answer.

Your score on this test will be based on the number of questions you answer correctly. You should try to answer every question. Do not spend too much time on any one question.

When you are told to begin, be sure to start with question number 1 in Part 7 in your test booklet and number 1 in Part 7 on your answer sheet.

1. Which component of the charging system keeps the alternator from overcharging the battery?
   A. Current regulator
   B. Governor
   C. Voltage regulator
   D. Solenoid

2. In the four-stroke cycle gasoline engine, the sequence of the steps in each cylinder to complete a cycle is which one of the following?
   A. Intake stroke, power stroke, compression stroke, exhaust stroke
   B. Intake stroke, compression stroke, exhaust stroke, power stroke
   C. Intake stroke, exhaust stroke, compression stroke, power stroke
   D. Intake stroke, compression stroke, power stroke, exhaust stroke

3. Vapor-lock in a gasoline engine is most likely due to
   A. an over-rich gas-air mixture.
   B. fuel forming bubbles in the gas line.
   C. a tear in the fuel pump diaphragm.
   D. the carburetor being clogged with dirt.

4. What would be the most likely reason a car "turns over" slowly, and has weak headlights?
   A. Weak battery
   B. Faulty ignition cable
   C. Defective starter
   D. Worn sparkplug

5. After brakes have been severely overheated, what should be checked for?
   A. Water condensation in brake fluid
   B. Glazed brake shoes
   C. Wheels out of alignment
   D. Crystallized wheel bearings

6. A good lubricant for locks is
   A. graphite.
   B. grease.
   C. mineral oil.
   D. motor oil.

7. If an automobile won't "turn over," and the battery is fully charged, the next thing to check for would be
   A. a defective starter.
   B. bad switches.
   C. loose battery cables.
   D. a faulty alternator.

8. Manifolds are used to conduct
   A. gases out of an engine only.
   B. gases into an engine only.
   C. gases into or out of an engine.
   D. heat into the piston.

9. What forces fuel from the carburetor into the cylinder?
   A. The fuel pump
   B. Atmospheric pressure
   C. Temperature difference
   D. The distributor

10. If an automobile engine overheats while the radiator remains cold, the problem most likely is
    A. an overloaded engine.
    B. a stuck thermostat.
    C. improper ignition timing.
    D. low engine oil level.

11. To test for leaks around the intake manifold of an idling engine, the mechanic would most likely use
    A. soap bubbles.
    B. talc powder.
    C. oil.
    D. heavy grease.

practice test 2

12. If the intake manifold of a gasoline engine is warped to the extent that it leaks, the engine will most likely tend to
   A. check out with a vacuum gauge as running on a rich mixture.
   B. miss on one cylinder.
   C. perform better on acceleration.
   D. have a fast idle.

13. The type of screwdriver that will develop the greatest turning force is a
   A. screwdriver-bit and brace.
   B. straight handle with ratchet.
   C. standard straight handle.
   D. spiral push-type.

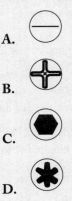

14. The tool shown above is used to
   A. ream holes in wood.
   B. countersink holes in soft metals.
   C. turn Phillips-head screws.
   D. drill holes in concrete.

15. A jointer plane is
   A. used for making close fits.
   B. used for heavy rough work.
   C. usually less than 12 inches long.
   D. used for squaring of end-stock.

16. A number 10 wood screw is
   A. thicker than a number 6.
   B. longer than a number 6.
   C. shorter than a number 6.
   D. thinner than a number 6.

17. Paint is "thinned" with
   A. linseed oil.
   B. varnish.
   C. turpentine.
   D. gasoline.

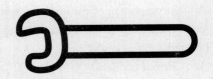

18. The tool shown above is a(n)
   A. offset wrench.
   B. box wrench.
   C. spanner wrench.
   D. open-end wrench.

19. What is used to fasten ceramic tiles to walls?
   A. Putty
   B. Caulking
   C. Plaster of paris
   D. Mastic

20. With which of these screw heads do you use an Allen wrench?
   A. ⊖
   B. ✚
   C. ⬡
   D. ✳

21. When sanding wood by hand, the best results are usually obtained in finishing the surface when the sanding block is worked
   A. across the grain.
   B. in a diagonal to the grain.
   C. in a circular motion.
   D. with the grain.

22. A 6-point saw is one that
   A. weighs 6 ounces per foot.
   B. is made of no. 6 gauge steel.
   C. has 6 teeth per inch.
   D. has 6 styles of teeth for universal work.

23. The tool that would be most useful in cutting a piece of wood at a 45-degree angle is a(n)
- **A.** binder.
- **B.** jointer.
- **C.** angle iron.
- **D.** miter box.

24. The carpenter's "hand screw" is

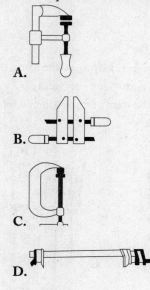

- **A.**
- **B.**
- **C.**
- **D.**

25. Of the following tools, the one that is LEAST like the others is a
- **A.** brace and bit.
- **B.** plane.
- **C.** draw-knife.
- **D.** spoke-shave.

STOP!
IF YOU FINISH BEFORE THE TIME IS UP,
YOU MAY CHECK OVER YOUR WORK ON THIS PART ONLY.

PART 8: MECHANICAL COMPREHENSION

Time: 19 Minutes—25 Questions

> **Directions:** This test has 25 questions about mechanical principles. Most of the questions use drawings to illustrate specific principles. Decide which answer is correct and mark the space on your answer sheet that has the same number and letter as your choice.

Here are two sample questions.

1. Which bridge is the strongest?

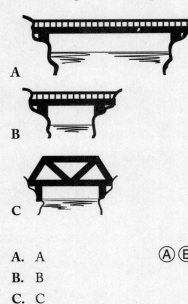

A

B

C

A. A
B. B
C. C
D. All are equally strong.

Ⓐ Ⓑ Ⓒ Ⓓ

Choice C is correct.

2. If all of the objects below are the same temperature, and your temperature is higher than the item's temperature, which will feel coldest?

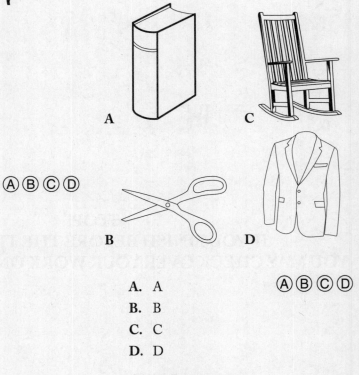

A

B

C

D

A. A
B. B
C. C
D. D

Ⓐ Ⓑ Ⓒ Ⓓ

Choice B is correct.

Your score on this test will be based on the number of questions you answer correctly. You should try to answer every question. Do not spend too much time on any one question.

When you are told to begin, be sure to start with question number 1 in Part 8 in your test booklet and number 1 in Part 8 on your answer sheet.

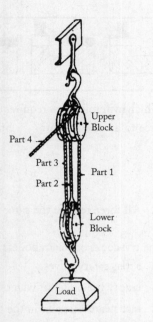

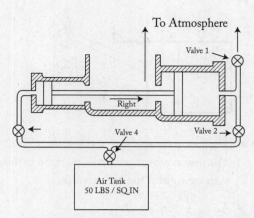

1. When a load is hoisted by means of the tackle shown above, the part that remains stationary is the

   A. load.
   B. lower block.
   C. lower hook.
   D. upper block.

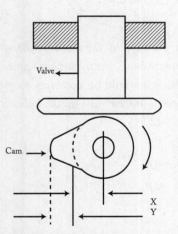

2. The figure above shows a cam and a valve. For each cam revolution, the vertical valve rise equals distance

   A. Y.
   B. X.
   C. X plus Y.
   D. twice X.

3. If all valves are closed at the start, in order to have air pressure from the tank move the pistons to the right, the valves to be opened are

   A. 2 and 4.
   B. 2, 3, and 4.
   C. 1 and 2.
   D. 1, 3, and 4.

4. Automatic operation of a sump pump is controlled by the

   A. pneumatic switch.
   B. float.
   C. foot valve.
   D. centrifugal driving unit.

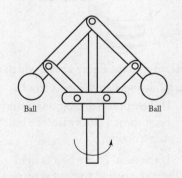

5. The figure above shows a governor on a rotating shaft. As the shaft speeds up, the governor balls will move

   A. down.
   B. upward and inward.
   C. upward.
   D. inward.

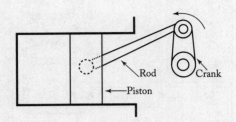

6. The figure above shows a crank and piston. The piston moves from mid-position to the extreme right if the crank makes

    A. a $\frac{1}{2}$ turn.

    B. a $\frac{3}{4}$ turn.

    C. 1 turn.

    D. $1\frac{1}{2}$ turn

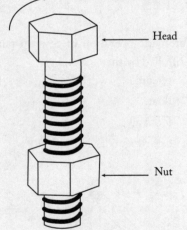

7. Referring to the figure above, which one of the following statements is true?

    A. If the nut is held stationary and the head turned clockwise, the bolt will move down.

    B. If the head of the bolt is held stationary and the nut is turned clockwise, the nut will move down.

    C. If the head of the bolt is held stationary and the nut is turned clockwise, the nut will move up.

    D. If the nut is held stationary and the head turned counterclockwise, the bolt will move up.

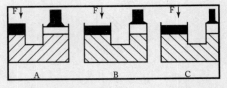

8. Which hydraulic press requires the LEAST force to lift the weight?

    A. A

    B. B

    C. C

    D. All three require the same force.

9. The try-cocks of steam boilers are used to

    A. act as safety valves.

    B. empty the boiler of water.

    C. test steam pressure in the boiler.

    D. find the height of water in the boiler.

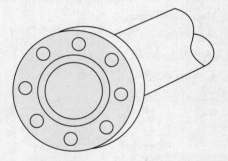

10. In the case of the standard flanged pipe shown above, the maximum angle through which it would be necessary to rotate the pipe in order to line up the holes is

    A. 22.5°

    B. 45°

    C. 30°

    D. 60°

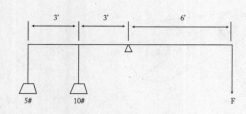

11. The force F needed to balance the lever shown above is, in pounds, most nearly

A. 7.5

B. 12.5

C. 10

D. 15

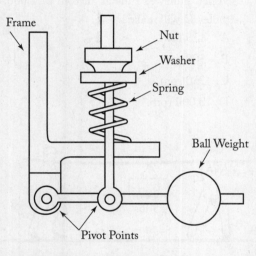

12. If the ball and spring mechanism is balanced in the position shown above, the ball will move upward if the

A. nut is loosened.

B. ball is moved away from the frame.

C. nut is loosened and the ball moved away from the frame.

D. nut is tightened.

RIVETED SPLICE

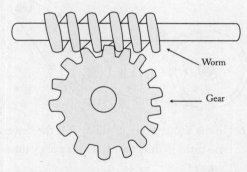

13. In the structural steel splice above, the different types of rivets are shown by different symbols. The number of different types of rivets is

A. 6

B. 4

C. 5

D. 3

14. The above illustration shows a worm and gear. If the worm rotates slowly on its shaft, the gear will

A. turn rapidly.

B. not turn.

C. turn very slowly.

D. oscillate.

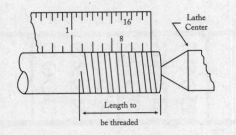

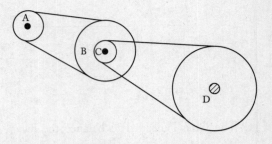

15. A very light cut (trace) is being measured as a check before cutting the thread on the lathe. The number of threads per inch shown above is

A. 12

B. 14

C. 13

D. 15

17. In the diagram above, pulley A drives a system of pulleys. Pulleys B and C are keyed to the same shaft. Use the following diameters in your computations: A = 1 inch; B = 2 inches; C = $\frac{1}{2}$ inch; and D = 4 inches. When pulley A runs at an rpm of 2,000, pulley D will make

A. 125 rpm.

B. 500 rpm.

C. 250 rpm.

D. 8,000 rpm.

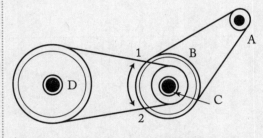

16. In the above figure, if pulley A is the driver and turns in direction 1, which pulley turns fastest?

A. A

B. B

C. C

D. D

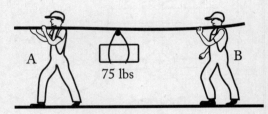

18. The weight is being carried entirely on the shoulders of the two people shown above. Which person bears more weight on the shoulder?

A. A

B. B

C. Both are carrying the same weight.

D. It cannot be determined.

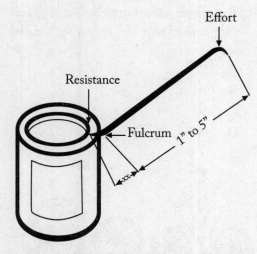

19. In the figure shown above, what force must be applied to the 6-inch file scraper to pry up the lid of the paint can? Assume that the average force holding the lid is 50 pounds (disregard weight of file scraper).

A. 10 pounds
B. 20 pounds
C. 30 pounds
D. 40 pounds

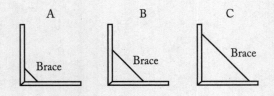

20. In the figure above, the flat sheet metal pattern that can be bent along the dotted lines to form the completely closed triangular box is

A. 1
B. 3
C. 2
D. 4

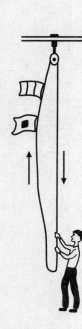

21. Neglecting friction, what is the mechanical advantage in using a single fixed pulley shown above?

A. 1
B. 2
C. 3
D. 4

22. In order to keep down the inside temperature of an oil tank that is exposed to the sun, the outside of the tank should be painted

A. white.
B. brown.
C. red.
D. black.

practice test 2

A.

B.

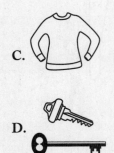

C.

D.

23. If all of the objects shown above are the same temperature, and your temperature is higher than the items' temperature, which will feel coldest?

A. A

B. B

C. C

D. D

24. The difference between the boiling point and the freezing point of water on the Celsius scale is

A. 112°

B. 0°

C. 180°

D. 100°

25. If both cyclists pedal at the same rate on the same surface, the cyclist in front will

A. travel at the same speed as the cyclist behind.

B. move faster than the cyclist behind.

C. move more slowly than the other cyclist.

D. have greater difficulty steering.

STOP!
IF YOU FINISH BEFORE THE TIME IS UP,
YOU MAY CHECK OVER YOUR WORK ON THIS PART ONLY.

PART 9: ASSEMBLING OBJECTS*

Time: 9 Minutes—16 Questions

Directions: This test contains 16 items measuring your ability to determine how an object will look when its parts are mentally assembled. Each item consists of five drawings. The problem is presented in the first drawing. Each problem is followed by four answers, only one of which is correct. Decide which answer is correct, then blacken the space on your answer sheet that has the same number and letter as your choice.

Now look at the two sample problems below.

1.

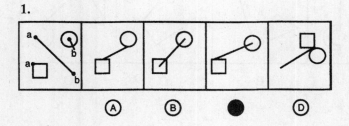

In the previous figure, the parts to be assembled are simple geometric figures (lines, squares, rectangles, etc.) that are labeled at one or more points with small letters. By matching corresponding letters on the different parts, you can see where the parts touch when the object is put together, or connected, properly.

Choice C is the correct answer.

2.

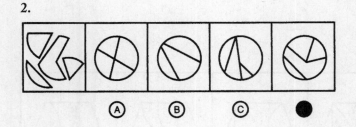

In this figure, the parts are not labeled. Instead, they fit together like pieces of a puzzle. Choice D is the correct answer.

Your score on this test will be based on the number of questions you answer correctly. You should try to answer every question. Do not spend too much time on any one question.

When you are told to begin, be sure to start with question number 1 in Part 9 in your test booklet and number 1 in Part 9 on your answer sheet.

---

*NOTE: This section is not included on paper-and-pencil versions of the ASVAB. It is included on the ASVAB computer-adaptive test (CAT) but may be eliminated in the future. Check with your recruiter for details.

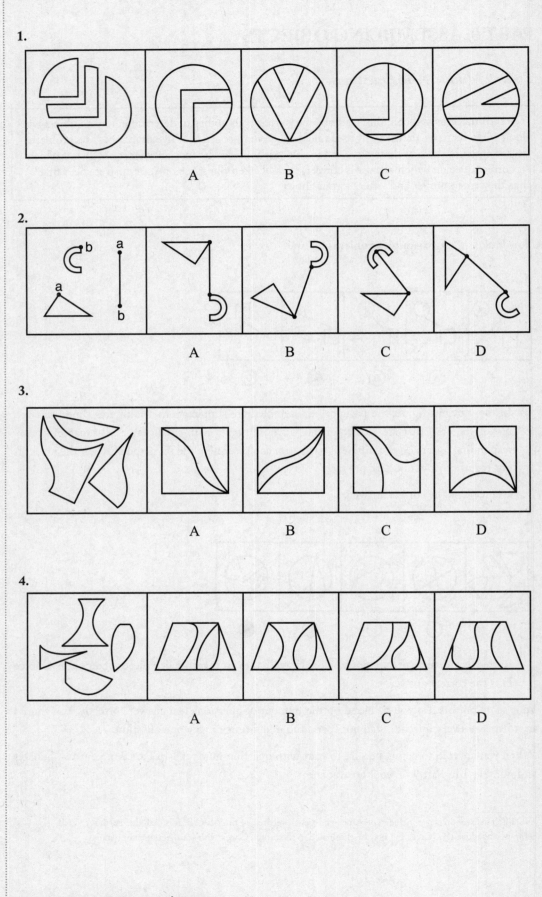

5.

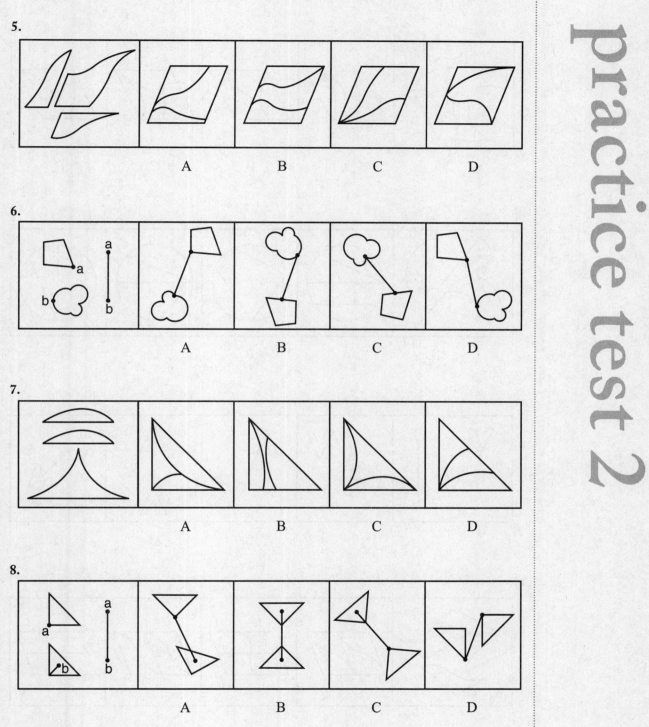

9.

10.

11.

12.

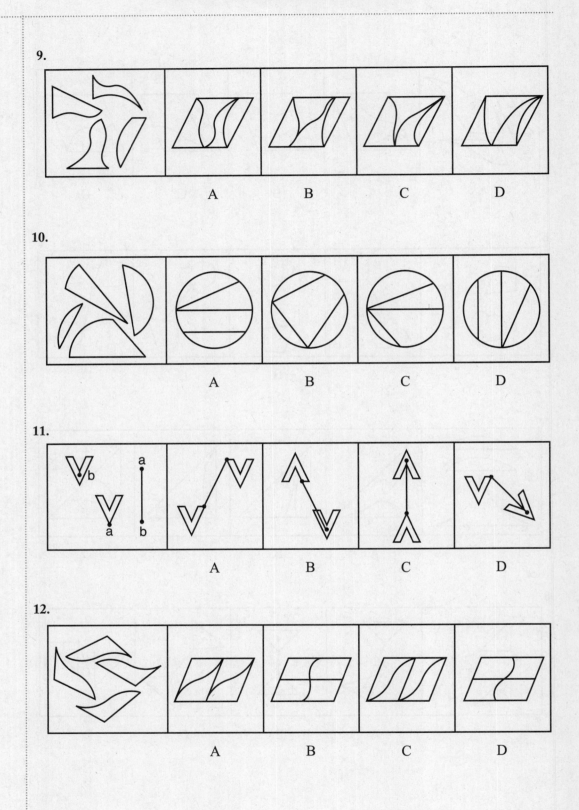

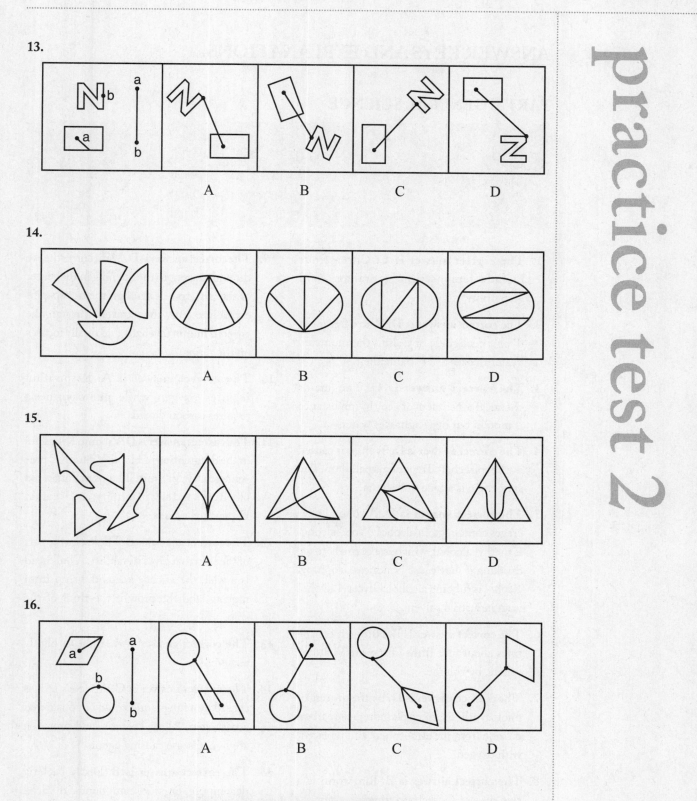

13.

          A   B   C   D

14.

          A   B   C   D

15.

          A   B   C   D

16.

          A   B   C   D

END OF THE EXAMINATION.

**IF YOU FINISH BEFORE THE TIME IS UP,
YOU MAY CHECK OVER YOUR WORK ON THIS PART ONLY.**

practice test 2

ANSWER KEYS AND EXPLANATIONS

PART 1: GENERAL SCIENCE

1. C	6. B	11. D	16. D	21. B
2. D	7. D	12. B	17. C	22. A
3. C	8. B	13. A	18. B	23. C
4. D	9. D	14. C	19. D	24. A
5. D	10. A	15. B	20. B	25. B

1. **The correct answer is C.** Citrus fruits include lemons, limes, oranges, and grapefruits.

2. **The correct answer is D.** Water freezes at 0° on a centigrade or Celsius thermometer. Water freezes at 32° Fahrenheit.

3. **The correct answer is C.** The major chemical constituent of a cell by importance is protein but by weight it is water.

4. **The correct answer is D.** Syphilis is caused by the spirochete Treponema pallidum. The spirochete is a type of bacteria.

5. **The correct answer is D.** Alcoholic beverages contain grain alcohol. Wood alcohol is methyl alcohol, which is extremely toxic; drinking it may cause blindness. Isopropyl alcohol is rubbing alcohol. Glyceryl alcohol is an industrial solvent.

6. **The correct answer is B.** Nitrogen constitutes about four fifths of the earth's atmosphere, by volume.

7. **The correct answer is D.** By the process of photosynthesis, green plants remove carbon dioxide from the atmosphere and replace it with oxygen.

8. **The correct answer is B.** Ringworm is a skin disease caused by a fungus.

9. **The correct answer is D.** Light enters the eye through the pupil (the opening in the center of the iris), travels through the transparent crystalline lens, then travels through the vitreous humor (eyeball), and finally focuses on the retina.

10. **The correct answer is A.** Respiration requires oxygen while photosynthesis requires carbon dioxide.

11. **The correct answer is D.** Vitamin K is useful in the coagulation of blood. Vitamin C prevents scurvy; Vitamin E helps maintain red blood cells and aids in fertility; and Vitamin D prevents rickets.

12. **The correct answer is B.** The keel is the part of the ship that gives it stability. A bulkhead is a wall, the anchor keeps the ship from moving, and the prow is the front of the ship.

13. **The correct answer is A.** Lime is highly alkaline.

14. **The correct answer is C.** Athlete's foot is caused by a fungus and could be considered a pathogen. Algae, bacteria, and protozoa are non-disease causing agents.

15. **The correct answer is B.** Decay bacteria decompose organic compounds of dead organisms to inorganic compounds, which enrich the soil.

16. **The correct answer is D.** All vegetables contain some Vitamin C, and yellow vegetables contain more Vitamin C than green ones. However, tomatoes contain nearly as much Vitamin C as citrus fruits.

17. **The correct answer is C.** The cyclotron is the machine that splits atoms.

18. **The correct answer is B.** It takes the earth one year to complete an orbit of the sun. A year contains 365 days, or 52 weeks.

19. **The correct answer is D.** The weight of the saltwater displaced by a human body is greater than the weight of freshwater displaced by that same body. Because the water displaced is heavier, the body is proportionally lighter and is more buoyant.

20. **The correct answer is B.** Boiling lava erupts from a volcano. The force that causes the eruption is pressure inside the earth.

21. **The correct answer is B.** The scientific name of an organism consists of the genus and the species.

22. **The correct answer is A.** The purpose of the retina is to receive light that the lens has focused, convert the light into neural signals, and send these signals on to the brain for visual recognition.

23. **The correct answer is C.** Gastric acid, gastric juice or stomach acid, is a digestive fluid formed in the stomach and is composed of hydrochloric acid (HCl), potassium chloride (KCl) and sodium chloride ($NaCl$).

24. **The correct answer is A.** When two forces act on an object in opposite directions, the resultant force produced is equal to the difference between the two forces.

25. **The correct answer is B.** Known as the sunshine vitamin, vitamin D is produced by the body in response to skin being exposed to sunlight.

Items Answered Incorrectly: _____ ; _____ ; _____ ; _____ ; _____ ; _____ ; _____ ; _____ ; _____

Items Unsure Of: _____ ; _____ ; _____ ; _____ ; _____ ; _____ ; _____ ; _____ ; _____

Total Number Answered Correctly: _____

answers *practice test 2*

PART 2: ARITHMETIC REASONING

1. A	**7.** D	**13.** B	**19.** B	**25.** B
2. B	**8.** C	**14.** C	**20.** A	**26.** A
3. C	**9.** B	**15.** A	**21.** B	**27.** B
4. D	**10.** A	**16.** C	**22.** A	**28.** D
5. D	**11.** C	**17.** B	**23.** D	**29.** D
6. B	**12.** B	**18.** B	**24.** C	**30.** B

1. **The correct answer is A.** 8% of 75 = 6 shares; 75 shares + 6 shares = 81 shares

2. **The correct answer is B.**

   28 miles ÷ 3 mph = 9.33 hrs. =

   $9\frac{1}{3}$ hrs. = 9 hrs. 20 mins.

3. **The correct answer is C.** 1st Cake = 1(12), 2nd Cake = 2(12), 3rd Cake = 4(12), 4th Cake = 8(12). The 4th cake will require 8(12) = 96 eggs.

4. **The correct answer is D.**

   $1,000\left(\frac{1}{4}\right) + 1,000\left(\frac{1}{5}\right) + 1,000\left(\frac{2}{5}\right)$

   250 + 200 + 400 = 850

   So, 1,000 − 850 = 150 bottles

5. **The correct answer is D.** $6,200 − $4,000 = $2,200 is the amount he made. $2,200 ÷ $50 (profit on each bicycle) = 44 bicycles sold.

6. **The correct answer is B.** Rename the miles as kilometers by dividing them by $\frac{5}{8}$.

   $500 \text{ miles } \div \frac{5}{8} = \frac{\overset{100}{\cancel{500}}}{1} \times \frac{8}{\underset{1}{\cancel{5}}} = 800 \text{ kilometers}$

7. **The correct answer is D.** There are 144 pencils in a gross; 144 × 6 = 864 pencils in all. 864 ÷ 24 = 36 weeks' worth of pencils.

8. **The correct answer is C.**

   $\frac{3}{8} = \frac{9}{24}$

   $\frac{1}{4} = \frac{6}{24}$

   $\frac{1}{6} = \frac{4}{24}$

   $\frac{19}{24}$ of the pads were issued; $\frac{5}{24}$ remained

   $\frac{5}{\underset{1}{\cancel{24}}} \times \frac{\overset{25}{\cancel{600}}}{1} = 125 \text{ pads remained}$

9. **The correct answer is B.** The regular cost of 4 CDs was $6.98 × 4 = $27.92. The sale price of 4 CDs was $12.50 × 2 = $25.

   $27.92 − $25 = $2.92

10. **The correct answer is A.** Coffee on sale is 2 for $8.50, so each cost $4.25. $4.25 ⨯ 4 = $17.00.

    The non-sale price is $6.99 ⨯ 4 = $27.96. So, $27.96 − $17.00 = $10.96.

11. **The correct answer is C.** 8 a.m. + 15 hours = 23 o'clock = 11 p.m.

12. **The correct answer is B.** Express the relationship of games won to games played as a fraction: $\frac{8}{24}$.

    Simplify: $\frac{8}{24} = \frac{1}{3}$

    Then rename as a percent:

    $\frac{1}{3} = .33\overline{3} = 33\frac{1}{3}\%$

13. **The correct answer is B.** Distance (d) = rate(r) χ time (t).

$4 = 3t$. Divide

$\dfrac{4}{3} = t = 1\dfrac{1}{3} t$

1 hour = 60 mins and $\dfrac{1}{3}$ hour = 20 minutes.

So, 60 mins + 20 mins = 80 minutes.

14. **The correct answer is C.**

$\$4.98 \times 4 = \$19.92$

$\$8.29 \times 2 = \$16.58$

$+ \$8.09 \times 2 = \$16.18$

$\$52.68$

15. **The correct answer is A.** 48 − 40 = 8 hours overtime

Salary for 8 hours overtime:

$1\dfrac{1}{2} \times \$8.60 \times 8 = \dfrac{3}{\underset{1}{2}} \times \$8.60 \times \overset{4}{\cancel{8}} = \$103.20$

Salary for 40 hours regular time: $\$8.60 \times 40 = \$344.00$

Total salary = $\$344.00 + \$103.20 = \$447.20$

16. **The correct answer is C.** $68.5° − 59.9° = 8.6°$

17. **The correct answer is B.** Distance (d) = rate (r) χ time (t).

$600 = 60 \chi\ t$ Divide

$10 = t$

Beginning at 4 a.m., moving forward 10 hours would be 2 p.m.

18. **The correct answer is B.** Multiply the number of monthly payments by amount to be paid each month: 16 × $20 = $320. Add the down payment to the total of monthly payments:

$320 + $40 = $360.

19. **The correct answer is B.** Add the three monthly totals, then divide by 3 to find the average monthly cost:

$ 42.30

    38.60 $123.90 ÷ 3 = $41.30

$+ 43.00$

$123.90

20. **The correct answer is A.**

$10 \times \dfrac{1}{2}$ hours = 5 hours

21. **The correct answer is B.** 1,400 miles ÷ 50 mph = 28 hours

22. **The correct answer is A.** Only choices A and C represent 72 ounces. 6 × $.39 = $2.34, which is less than 3 × $.79 = $2.37

23. **The correct answer is D.** From −2°F to 0°F = 2°

From 0°F to 10°F = 10°

10° + 2° = 12°

24. **The correct answer is C.** 13 ′ 16 = 0.8125 or 81.25%.

25. **The correct answer is B.**

Rate = Distance ÷ Time

1,200 miles ÷ 20 hours = 60 mph

26. **The correct answer is A.**

$33\dfrac{1}{3}\% = \dfrac{1}{3}$; $\$88.50 \times \dfrac{1}{3} = \$29.50$

27. **The correct answer is B.**

4 ft. 8 in. × 3 = 12 ft. 24 in. = 14 ft.

28. **The correct answer is D.** $21 + $14.98 + $4.97 = $40.95

answers practice test 2

29. **The correct answer is D.** Don drove 50 miles × 2 hours = 100 miles. Frank drove 40 miles × 2 hours = 80 miles. Since they drove in opposite directions, add the two distances to learn that they were 180 miles apart.

30. **The correct answer is B.**

$14.28 × 1 = $14.28
33.26 × 2 = 66.52
+ 65.38 × 2 = 130.76
$211.56

Items Answered Incorrectly: _____ ; _____ ; _____ ; _____ ; _____ ; _____ ; _____ ; _____ ; _____

Items Unsure Of: _____ ; _____ ; _____ ; _____ ; _____ ; _____ ; _____ ; _____

Total Number Answered Correctly: _____

PART 3: WORD KNOWLEDGE

1. B	8. A	15. D	22. C	29. A
2. A	9. B	16. C	23. B	30. C
3. C	10. D	17. B	24. D	31. B
4. D	11. A	18. C	25. A	32. A
5. D	12. D	19. B	26. C	33. D
6. C	13. C	20. A	27. D	34. D
7. B	14. A	21. D	28. C	35. D

1. **The correct answer is B.** *Revenue* means *income*. Taxes produce revenue but they are not in themselves revenue.

2. **The correct answer is A.** *Necessitate* most nearly means *required*; it may also mean *demand*, *dictate*, or *need*.

3. **The correct answer is C.** *Manual*, as opposed to automatic or mechanical, means *hand-operated*.

4. **The correct answer is D.** *Deportment* means *behavior* or *conduct*.

5. **The correct answer is D.** *Prior* means *previous* or *earlier*.

6. **The correct answer is C.** *Grimy* and *ragged* often go together, but *grimy* means *dirty*.

7. **The correct answer is B.** A *malady* is a *disease, disorder, condition,* or *illness*.

8. **The correct answer is A.** To *survive* is to *live beyond the life or existence of another*, in short, to *outlive*.

9. **The correct answer is B.** *Competent* means *qualified* or *capable*.

10. **The correct answer is D.** To *suspend* is to *stop temporarily*.

11. **The correct answer is A.** A *territory* is a *large expanse of land or water*, a *region*.

12. **The correct answer is D.** *Huge* means *very large, enormous,* or *immense*.

13. **The correct answer is C.** *Myriad* means *many* as in myriad reasons to study for the ASVAB.

14. **The correct answer is A.** To *forward* is to *transmit* or to *send on*.

15. **The correct answer is D.** *Vacant* means *unfilled* or *empty*.

16. **The correct answer is C.** To *irritate* is to *incite impatience or displeasure*, to *exasperate*, or to *annoy*.

17. **The correct answer is B.** To *aspire* means to *strive for something*. For example, he aspired to become a professional baseball player.

18. **The correct answer is C.** *Power* is *strength* or *force*. All the other choices are attributes that might help one to attain power.

19. **The correct answer is B.** An *accusation* is a *statement, or claim, of wrongdoing*.

20. **The correct answer is A.** *Flexible* means *capable of being adapted, elastic,* or *pliable*.

21. **The correct answer is D.** To *comprehend* is to *grasp the meaning of* or to *understand*.

22. **The correct answer is C.** To *instruct* is to *teach*. For example, an instructor is a teacher.

23. **The correct answer is B.** *Defunct* means to be *extinct*, but can also mean to be *obsolete*, or *outdated*.

24. **The correct answer is D.** To *revolve* is to *turn around* or to *rotate*.

25. **The correct answer is A.** To be *alert* is to be *wide awake* and *watchful.*

26. **The correct answer is C.** To *function* is to *operate* or to *work.*

27. **The correct answer is D.** A *hazard* is a *risk, peril,* or *danger.*

28. **The correct answer is C.** A *blemish* is a *mark of deformity,* a *defect,* or a *flaw.*

29. **The correct answer is A.** To *convey* is to *transmit,* to *transport,* or to *carry.*

30. **The correct answer is C.** *Egregious* means *outrageous, horrendous, awful, appalling,* or *shocking.*

31. **The correct answer is B.** An *attorney* is a *lawyer.*

32. **The correct answer is A.** *Obsolete* means *no longer in use* or *out-of-date.*

33. **The correct answer is D.** *Stationary* means *fixed in one place, not movable.*

34. **The correct answer is D.** *Steady* means *constant* and *regular.*

35. **The correct answer is D.** To *emphasize* is to *stress.*

Items Answered Incorrectly: _____ ; _____ ; _____ ; _____ ; _____ ; _____ ; _____ ; _____ ; _____

Items Unsure Of: _____ ; _____ ; _____ ; _____ ; _____ ; _____ ; _____ ; _____ ; _____

Total Number Answered Correctly: _____

PART 4: PARAGRAPH COMPREHENSION

1. D	4. A	7. B	10. D	13. C
2. C	5. B	8. B	11. A	14. D
3. D	6. A	9. C	12. D	15. D

1. **The correct answer is D.** The second sentence in the passage states that the battery converts an electrical charge into chemical energy that is stored until the battery terminals are connected to a closed external circuit.

2. **The correct answer is C.** The first sentence states that a good or service has value only because people want it.

3. **The correct answer is D.** The second sentence states that a toad's skin is both dry and rough.

4. **The correct answer is A.** The last sentence states that a nautical mile is equal to 6,080 feet, whereas an ordinary mile is 5,280 feet. Accordingly, a nautical mile is longer than an ordinary mile.

5. **The correct answer is B.** The third sentence states that for stereophonic sound, a different sound is recorded in each wall of the groove.

6. **The correct answer is A.** The business of publishing city directories is a private business operated for profit. As such, it is a commercial enterprise.

7. **The correct answer is B.** The passage says that enough data have been collected to draw the conclusion that the rural crime rates are lower than those in urban communities.

8. **The correct answer is B.** The passage lists many different uses for iron.

9. **The correct answer is C.** The spaces allow roads, sidewalks, and railroad tracks to expand in the summer and contract in winter without cracking or breaking.

10. **The correct answer is D.** The second sentence states that crime is the result of opportunity plus desire. Accordingly, to prevent crime, it is each individual's responsibility to prevent the opportunity.

11. **The correct answer is A.** The first sentence states that when there is a sharp rise in demand for new buildings, construction invariably lags behind; that is, there are fewer new buildings in proportion to buyers.

12. **The correct answer is D.** The last sentence states that when there is a sudden drop in the demand for new buildings, their prices fall because the available supply cannot be immediately curtailed.

13. **The correct answer is C.** The first sentence states that a large proportion of the people behind bars are not criminals but people who are being held until their trial in court.

14. **The correct answer is D.** The last sentence states that those who do wind up in detention tend to be the poor, the unemployed, the single, and the young.

15. **The correct answer is D.** The passage states that one who can show that he is a stable citizen with a job and a family will be released on "personal recognizance" and can often avoid the detention system. The detention system involves being detained or paying bail.

Items Answered Incorrectly: _____ ; _____ ; _____ ; _____ ; _____ ; _____ ; _____ ; _____ ; _____

Items Unsure Of: _____ ; _____ ; _____ ; _____ ; _____ ; _____ ; _____ ; _____ ; _____

Total Number Answered Correctly: _____

PART 5: MATHEMATICS KNOWLEDGE

1. C	6. B	11. D	16. B	21. C
2. C	7. D	12. C	17. C	22. B
3. B	8. A	13. D	18. C	23. A
4. A	9. A	14. B	19. D	24. A
5. A	10. D	15. D	20. B	25. C

1. **The correct answer is C.** There are 12 marbles in the box. 4 out of 12 are red = 1 out of 3 are red. The probability of picking a red marble is $\frac{1}{3}$.

2. **The correct answer is C.** If the sides are parallel, the angles are congruent.

3. **The correct answer is B.** A hexagon has 6 sides. $(n-2) \times 180° = (6-2) \times 180° = 720°$.

4. **The correct answer is A.** Subtract A^2 from both sides of the equation: $B^2 = X^2$, therefore $B = \pm X$.

5. **The correct answer is A.**

$6 + x + y = 20$

$x + y = 14 = k$; now substitute

$20 - 14 = 6$

6. **The correct answer is B.**

$\sqrt{75} = \sqrt{3 \times 25} = 5\sqrt{3}$

7. **The correct answer is D.** Since $20^2 = 400$ and $30^2 = 900$, then $\sqrt{400} = 20$ and $\sqrt{900} = 30$, then $\sqrt{745}$ is between those values.

8. **The correct answer is A.** $\angle 2$ and $\angle 1$ are supplementary angles. $m\angle 1 = 100°$. $\angle 1$ and $\angle 4$ are supplementary. $m\angle 4 = 80°$.

9. **The correct answer is A.**

$\frac{10^4}{10} = \frac{10000}{10} = 1000 = 10^3$

The base remains unchanged.

10. **The correct answer is D.**

$7x - 6 + 5x + 18 = 12x + 12 = 180°$

$12x = 180° - 12 = 168°$

$x = 14$

$5 \times 14 + 18 = 70 + 18 = 88°$

11. **The correct answer is D.**

$8 + 5(x - y) = 8 + 5x - 5y$

Since $x = y$, $5x = 5y$ and $5x - 5y = 0$

Substituting: $8 + 0 = 8$

12. **The correct answer is C.**

$S = 1$

$R = 3 \times 1$

$+ \ T = \dfrac{1}{3}$

$\overline{\qquad\qquad}$

$4\dfrac{1}{3}$

13. **The correct answer is D.** Each jacket can be worn with 5 pairs of pants. $3 \times 5 = 15$

14. **The correct answer is B.** If $m\angle 2 = 120°$, then $m\angle 1 = 60$ because they are a linear pair (add to 180°) $m\angle 1 = m\angle 3$ because they are corresponding angles. So, $m\angle 3 = 60°$.

15. **The correct answer is D.** The definition of a rectangle is a polygon with four sides, four right angles, and opposite sides equal in length. So, a quadrilateral is a rectangle only if it has four right angles and opposite sides equal in length.

16. **The correct answer is B.** Angles that are a linear and/or are supplementary add up to 180°. So,

$$6x + 19 + 5x - 4 = 180$$
$$11x + 15 = 180$$
$$11x = 165$$
$$x = 15$$

Plug x back in to find $m\angle 1$. $6(15) + 19 = 109°$.

17. **The correct answer is C.** 87 can be divided by 3 as well as by 1 and itself.

18. **The correct answer is C.** With the passage of time, the ratio of the ages of A and B decreases. Pick a pair of ages and try for yourself. A is 4; B is 2; the ratio of their ages is 4:2 or 2:1. In two years, A is 6 and B is 4. The ratio of their ages is 6:4 or 3:2.

19. **The correct answer is D.**

$$\begin{array}{r} x + 3 \\ \times\ 2x + 5 \\ \hline 2x^2 + 6x \\ 5x + 15 \\ \hline 2x^2 + 11x + 15 \end{array}$$

20. **The correct answer is B.**

$$\begin{array}{r} x + 3 \\ \times\ x + 2 \\ \hline x^2 + 3x \\ 2x + 6 \\ \hline x^2 + 5x + 6 \end{array}$$

21. **The correct answer is C.** Let x equal shorter side; $2x$ equals length of longer side. $6x = 90$; $x = 15$; longer side = $2x = 30$.

22. **The correct answer is B.** The formula for the area of a triangle is one half the base times the height.

23. **The correct answer is A.** If $2x = y$, then substitute either one into the equation for the other. So, for example:

$$(2x - 2x)4 + 6$$
$$= (0)4 + 6$$
$$= 6$$

24. **The correct answer is A.** Each square is 2 times the size of the previous square. If square B = 3, then square C = 6, and square A would be half square B, or $1\frac{1}{2}$. Adding up the values, $1\frac{1}{2} + 3 + 6 = 10\frac{1}{2}$.

25. **The correct answer is C.** By definition, a square must have four equal sides and four right angles.

Items Answered Incorrectly: _____ ; _____ ; _____ ; _____ ; _____ ; _____ ; _____ ; _____ ; _____

Items Unsure Of: _____ ; _____ ; _____ ; _____ ; _____ ; _____ ; _____ ; _____

Total Number Answered Correctly: _____

PART 6: ELECTRONICS INFORMATION

1. B	**5.** C	**9.** C	**13.** D	**17.** C
2. D	**6.** B	**10.** B	**14.** B	**18.** B
3. C	**7.** B	**11.** A	**15.** C	**19.** D
4. B	**8.** A	**12.** B	**16.** D	**20.** B

1. **The correct answer is B.** A three-way switch is a single-pole double-throw switch or two single-pole switches.

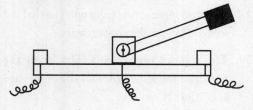

2. **The correct answer is D.** Leather gloves offer the best protection over the rubber gloves. The leather can withstand severe conditions before it will tear. The rubber acts as insulation.

3. **The correct answer is C.** A "mil" is short for milli or 1/1,000 of an inch.

4. **The correct answer is B.** The formula for determining the current in a parallel circuit is: It = I1 + I2 + I3 + … In. The current going through the lamps is 1 amp + 1 amp = 2 amps.

5. **The correct answer is C.** Never use a fuse having a higher rating than that specifically called for in the circuit. A fuse is a safety device used to protect a circuit from serious damage caused by too high a current.

6. **The correct answer is B.** Silver is a much better conductor of electricity than copper. However, gold is also used for tuner contacts because it will not tarnish. Silver can tarnish.

7. **The correct answer is B.** A "2-line return-call" electric bell circuit would have 2 bells, 2 metallic lines, 2 return-call push buttons, and 2 sets of batteries. It might look like this:

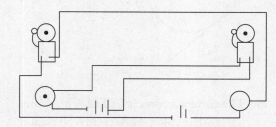

8. **The correct answer is A.** A LED (Light Emitting Diode) that is red is powered by 1.7 volts.

9. **The correct answer is C.** Grounding a fixture is a safety precaution used to lessen the chance of shock.

10. **The correct answer is B.** Higher, the current is the same through each resistor. The total resistance is found by simply adding up the resistance values of the individual resistors.

11. **The correct answer is A.** 4k4 is a non-standard value for a resistor.

12. **The correct answer is B.** A polarized plug is used so that the plug can only go into the receptacle in one way. The prongs are at an angle to one another.

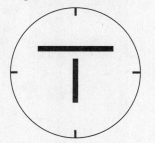

13. **The correct answer is D.** When reading an electric meter, you read the lower number just before the pointer. This meter would show 6872 kilowatt hours.

14. **The correct answer is B.** In a DC motor, the commutators are the metal contact points that the brushes come into contact with.

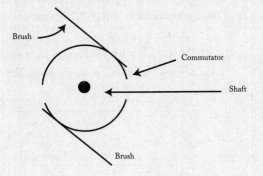

Brush · Commutator · Shaft · Brush

15. **The correct answer is C.** The neutral wire is whitish in color; the hot lead is black; and the ground wire is green.

16. **The correct answer is D.** Carbon, crystal, and dynamic are all types of microphones. Feedback is a condition caused when sound coming from a speaker is fed back into a microphone, causing noise.

17. **The correct answer is C.** This type of connector will join a flexible metallic conduit to a junction box. The wire is secured by tightening the compression screw. The locknut is tightened to secure the connector to the junction box.

18. **The correct answer is B.** Iron is a good magnetic material as are steel, nickel, and cobalt. Copper, tin, and brass are not.

19. **The correct answer is D.** Rosin is used to remove copper-oxide from wires so that the solder can join the copper wires.

20. **The correct answer is B.** The larger the capacitor the less ripple and the more constant the DC will be.

Items Answered Incorrectly: _____ ; _____ ; _____ ; _____ ; _____ ; _____ ; _____ ; _____ ; _____

Items Unsure Of: _____ ; _____ ; _____ ; _____ ; _____ ; _____ ; _____ ; _____ ; _____

Total Number Answered Correctly: _____

PART 7: AUTO & SHOP INFORMATION

1. C	6. A	11. C	16. A	21. D
2. D	7. C	12. D	17. C	22. C
3. B	8. C	13. A	18. D	23. D
4. A	9. B	14. C	19. D	24. B
5. B	10. B	15. A	20. C	25. A

1. **The correct answer is C.** The voltage regulator prevents the battery from overcharging by reducing the current from the alternator as the engine speeds up.

2. **The correct answer is D.** The four strokes of an internal combustion engine are the intake stroke, the compression stroke, the power stroke, and the exhaust stroke.

3. **The correct answer is B.** Vapor-lock usually occurs when the gasoline in the gas line has turned to vapor and the carburetor does not get enough gasoline.

4. **The correct answer is A.** The conditions described indicate that the battery is not fully charged. This may be corrected by recharging, or if necessary, replacing, the battery.

5. **The correct answer is B.** Overheating the brake shoe will cause the brake material to glaze and become slippery. Slippery brakes are dangerous because they take longer to stop a car.

6. **The correct answer is A.** Graphite, which is powdered carbon, is slippery and will not bind the small springs and metal parts of a lock.

7. **The correct answer is C.** After checking that the battery is not defective, the next logical reason for a car engine not to turn over is loose connections between the battery cables and the battery posts.

8. **The correct answer is C.** The intake manifold conducts the gas-air mixture to the cylinders and the exhaust manifold gets rid of the waste products from the engine.

9. **The correct answer is B.** When air flows past the venturi in the carburetor at high speed, a low pressure area is created that sucks the gas out of the fuel line. However, normal air pressure (about 15 pounds per square inch) pushes the fuel-air mixture from the carburetor to the cylinders.

10. **The correct answer is B.** If a car engine overheats and the radiator remains cold, it is more than likely a faulty thermostat. The purpose of the thermostat is to cut off the flow of coolant to the radiator when the engine is cold and allows it to flow once the coolant temperature rises. A stuck thermostat prevents the flow of coolant to the radiator, resulting in an overheated engine and a cool radiator.

11. **The correct answer is C.** If soap or talc were sucked into the engine, problems might arise. Heavy grease might not be taken in by a small leak. Oil can be burned in the engine if it were used to indicate a leak around the intake manifold.

12. **The correct answer is D.** If the intake manifold is warped, air would seep in. The carburetor would get a lean mixture of too much air and not enough gas. The engine would then run at a fast idle.

13. **The correct answer is A.** By placing a screw-driver at the end of a brace, you will have a much wider turning arc than by just using an ordinary screwdriver. The wider the turning arc, the more force that the screwdriver will exert. Screwdrivers with wide handles exert more force than those with narrow handles.

14. **The correct answer is C.** This is a Phillips-head screwdriver. It will turn Phillips-head screws with this shape:

15. **The correct answer is A.** A jointer plane is used for planing wood when close tolerances are required.

16. **The correct answer is A.** The number on the box of wood screws tells the thickness. The higher the number, the thicker the screw. A number 10 wood screw will be thicker than a number 6 wood screw.

17. **The correct answer is C.** Paint is made thinner or easier to apply by diluting it with turpentine. Linseed oil and varnish are not used as paint thinners.

18. **The correct answer is D.** The opened face on this tool shows that it is an open-end wrench.

19. **The correct answer is D.** Mastic, a glue, is applied to a wall with a serrated applicator. Then, the tiles are pressed into the mastic.

20. **The correct answer is C.** An Allen wrench is hexagonal and will fit into screw C.

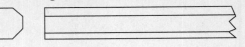

21. **The correct answer is D.** The smoothest finish can be obtained by sanding the wood with the grain.

22. **The correct answer is C.** The number of points on a saw tells the number of teeth per inch. For example, a 6-point saw has 6 teeth per inch and a 22-point saw has 22 teeth per inch.

23. **The correct answer is D.** A miter box is a tool for guiding a saw at the proper angle when making a miter joint in wood.

24. **The correct answer is B.** The carpenter's "hand screw" is shown in Figure B.

25. **The correct answer is A.** A brace and bit are used to drill holes while the other tools are used to smooth down wood.

Items Answered Incorrectly: _____ ; _____ ; _____ ; _____ ; _____ ; _____ ; _____ ; _____ ; _____

Items Unsure Of: _____ ; _____ ; _____ ; _____ ; _____ ; _____ ; _____ ; _____

Total Number Answered Correctly: _____

PART 8: MECHANICAL COMPREHENSION

1. D	6. B	11. C	16. A	21. A
2. A	7. C	12. D	17. A	22. A
3. D	8. A	13. B	18. A	23. D
4. B	9. D	14. C	19. A	24. D
5. C	10. B	15. C	20. C	25. B

1. **The correct answer is D.** Because the upper block is connected to an immovable hook, it must remain stationary.

2. **The correct answer is A.** The distortion of the cam causes the valve to rise when contact is made. The amount of this distortion is the length Y.

3. **The correct answer is D.** To move the pistons to the right, valves 1, 3, and 4 must be open. Valve 4 permits the air to enter the system; valve 3 allows the air to hit the left side of the piston; and valve 1 is an exhaust channel for the air.

4. **The correct answer is B.** When the water level rises past the safe area, the float turns on the sump pump. When the level of water in the sump goes down, the float also goes down and will shut off the sump pump.

5. **The correct answer is C.** The centrifugal force acts to pull the balls outward. Since the two balls are connected to a yolk around the center bar, this outward motion pulls the balls upward.

6. **The correct answer is B.** The piston is now in part of the compression stroke; $\frac{1}{4}$ turn will move it to full compression; $\frac{1}{2}$ more turn will move it to the end of the power stroke. Adding $\frac{1}{4} + \frac{1}{2} = \frac{3}{4}$ turn.

7. **The correct answer is C.** To tighten the bolt, turn it counterclockwise. To tighten the nut on the bolt the reverse is true—turn it clockwise.

8. **The correct answer is A.** Pressure is defined as $\frac{Force}{Area}$. For a given force, 20 lbs, the smaller the area, the greater the pressure produced. The smallest area is at position A, requiring the least force to lift the weight.

9. **The correct answer is D.** The try-cocks show the level of the water inside the boiler. They use the principle that water seeks its own level in a system.

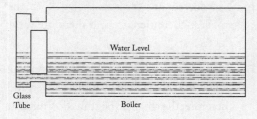

10. **The correct answer is B.** There are 8 holes in the circular cross-section of the flanged pipe. All circles have 360°. Thus, each hole is separated by 360°/8 or 45°.

11. **The correct answer is C.** The sum of the moments must be zero.

   Summing around the fulcrum we have:

   (6 ft. × 5 lbs) + (3 ft. × 10 lbs) = 6 ft. × F

   Combining terms, we get:
   60 (ft. – lbs) = 6 ft. × F

   Dividing both sides by 6: 10 lbs = F

12. **The correct answer is D.** The ball will move up if the arm holding it is pulled up. This will happen when the nut is tightened.

13. **The correct answer is B.** There are only 4 different types of symbols shown in the pictures:

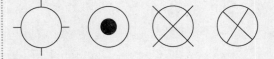

14. **The correct answer is C.** For every full rotation of the worm shaft, the gear will turn only 22°.

15. **The correct answer is C.** The problem here is that only part of a ruler is shown. Count 4 units on the 8th scale. This corresponds to $6\frac{1}{2}$ threads on the length to be threaded. Doubling the $6\frac{1}{2}$ threads (in $\frac{1}{2}$ inch) we get 13 threads in 1 inch.

16. **The correct answer is A.** Pulley A has the smallest circumference and therefore turns the fastest.

17. **The correct answer is A.** The larger the pulley, the more distance it must cover, and therefore, the smaller the rpm. If A turns at 2,000 rpm, B (twice as large) turns at 1,000 rpm; C is attached to B and turns at the same rate. Finally, D (8 times larger than C) turns at 1,000/8 or 125 rpm.

18. **The correct answer is A.** The weight is not centered but is closer to A. The distance from the center of the load to A is less than the distance from the center of the load to B. Therefore, A would support the greater part of the load.

19. **The correct answer is A.** Let x = force that must be applied.

$50 \times 1 = x \times 5$; $50 = 5x$; $x = \dfrac{50}{5} = 10$ lbs.

20. **The correct answer is C.** As brace C has the greatest area of support, it is the most secure.

21. **The correct answer is A.** A single fixed pulley is actually a first-class lever with equal arms. The mechanical advantage, neglecting friction, is 1.

22. **The correct answer is A.** Of the colors listed, white will reflect the most solar heat, thereby keeping down the inside temperature of the oil tank.

23. **The correct answer is D.** The metal key has the highest conductivity. Metals are the best conductors of heat. The other choices can be used as insulators.

24. **The correct answer is D.** Boiling Point = 100°, Freezing Point = 0°, 100° − 0° = 100°.

25. **The correct answer is B.** The formula for circumference of a wheel is $C = 2I\,r$. The wheel radius of the bike in front is larger. One revolution of the larger wheel will cover a greater linear distance along the road in a given period of time.

Items Answered Incorrectly: _____ ; _____ ; _____ ; _____ ; _____ ; _____ ; _____ ; _____ ; _____

Items Unsure Of: _____ ; _____ ; _____ ; _____ ; _____ ; _____ ; _____ ; _____ ; _____

Total Number Answered Correctly: _____

PART 9: ASSEMBLING OBJECTS

1. A	5. C	8. C	11. C	14. A
2. D	6. D	9. A	12. C	15. D
3. D	7. C	10. C	13. C	16. C
4. B				

1. The correct answer is A.

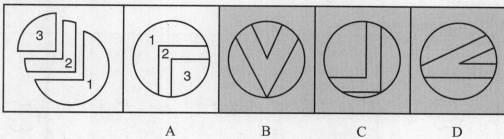

2. The correct answer is D.

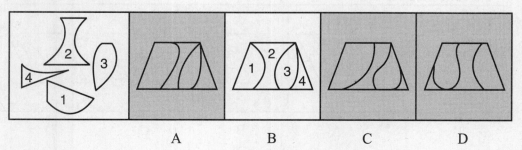

3. The correct answer is D.

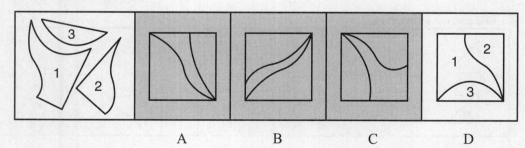

4. The correct answer is B.

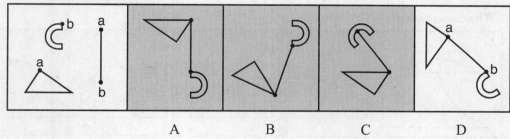

5. The correct answer is C.

6. The correct answer is D.

7. The correct answer is C.

8. The correct answer is C.

9. The correct answer is A.

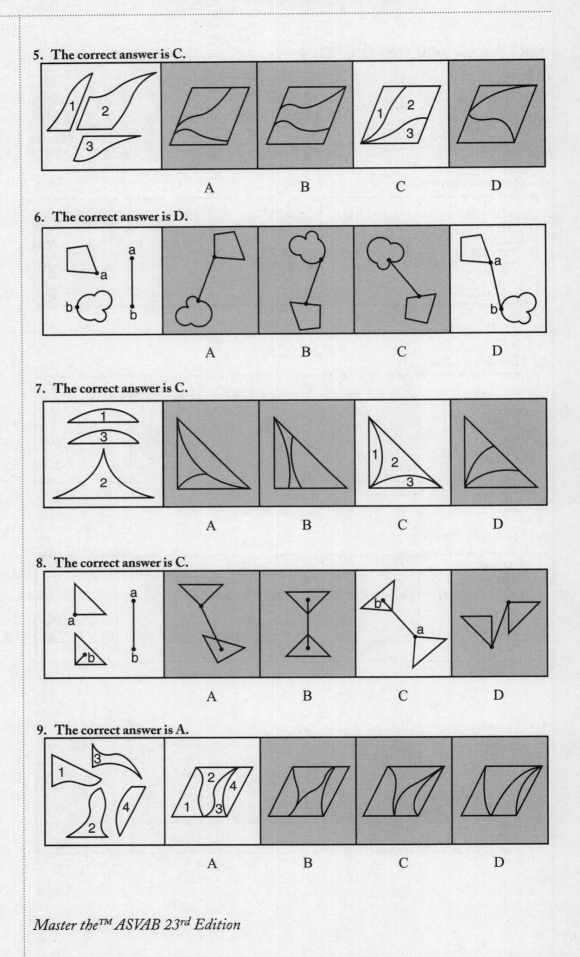

10. **The correct answer is C.**

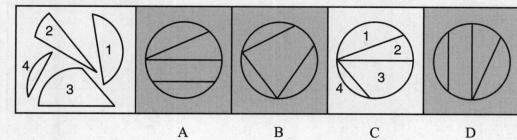

A   B   C   D

11. **The correct answer is C.**

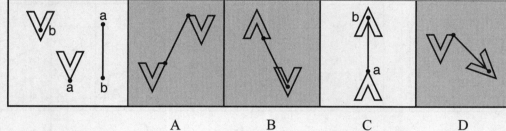

A   B   C   D

12. **The correct answer is C.**

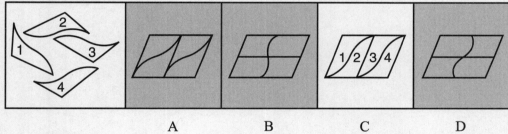

A   B   C   D

13. **The correct answer is C.**

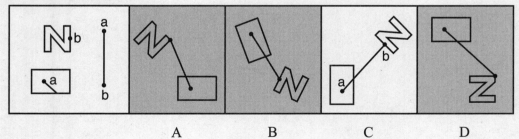

A   B   C   D

14. **The correct answer is A.**

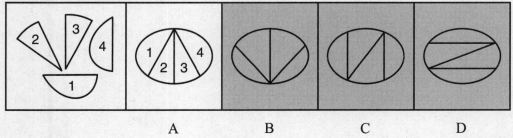

A   B   C   D

answers practice test 2

15. The correct answer is D.

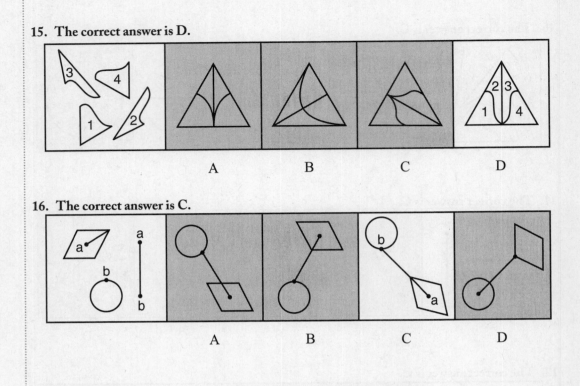

16. The correct answer is C.

Practice Test 3

Now that you have completed two practice tests, you should be feeling more confident about taking the ASVAB. You have keyed in on your strengths and weaknesses and have reviewed the subject material you need. This third test is another practice run through of the ASVAB.

Here are the guidelines again to help you make the most of this practice test:

- Take this test under "real" test conditions (time yourself, take it in a quiet room without distractions, and use the sample answer sheets).

- Time each test carefully and do not go over the time allotted for each section.

- Use the answer keys to get your test scores and to evaluate your performance on each test.

- Record the number of questions you answered correctly and incorrectly for each section in the answer chart provided at the end of the test. Also, record the number of questions you want to review further or were unsure about.

- Carefully review and understand the answer explanations to all questions you answered incorrectly.

- Don't forget to review each of the questions that you answered correctly but of which you may not be sure. This is a necessary step to gain the knowledge and expertise you need to get the highest scores possible on the real ASVAB tests.

- Transfer your scores for each section of Practice Test 3 to the Self-Evaluation Chart on page 22. This will enable you to track your progress as you continue to prepare for the actual test.

- Use the sample answer sheets provided to record your answers. If you want, you can cut them out to make them easier to use and to simulate actual test conditions.

ANSWER SHEET PRACTICE TEST 3

Part 1: General Science

1. Ⓐ Ⓑ Ⓒ Ⓓ   2. Ⓐ Ⓑ Ⓒ Ⓓ   3. Ⓐ Ⓑ Ⓒ Ⓓ   4. Ⓐ Ⓑ Ⓒ Ⓓ   5. Ⓐ Ⓑ Ⓒ Ⓓ
6. Ⓐ Ⓑ Ⓒ Ⓓ   7. Ⓐ Ⓑ Ⓒ Ⓓ   8. Ⓐ Ⓑ Ⓒ Ⓓ   9. Ⓐ Ⓑ Ⓒ Ⓓ   10. Ⓐ Ⓑ Ⓒ Ⓓ
11. Ⓐ Ⓑ Ⓒ Ⓓ   12. Ⓐ Ⓑ Ⓒ Ⓓ   13. Ⓐ Ⓑ Ⓒ Ⓓ   14. Ⓐ Ⓑ Ⓒ Ⓓ   15. Ⓐ Ⓑ Ⓒ Ⓓ
16. Ⓐ Ⓑ Ⓒ Ⓓ   17. Ⓐ Ⓑ Ⓒ Ⓓ   18. Ⓐ Ⓑ Ⓒ Ⓓ   19. Ⓐ Ⓑ Ⓒ Ⓓ   20. Ⓐ Ⓑ Ⓒ Ⓓ
21. Ⓐ Ⓑ Ⓒ Ⓓ   22. Ⓐ Ⓑ Ⓒ Ⓓ   23. Ⓐ Ⓑ Ⓒ Ⓓ   24. Ⓐ Ⓑ Ⓒ Ⓓ   25. Ⓐ Ⓑ Ⓒ Ⓓ

Part 2: Arithmetic Reasoning

1. Ⓐ Ⓑ Ⓒ Ⓓ   2. Ⓐ Ⓑ Ⓒ Ⓓ   3. Ⓐ Ⓑ Ⓒ Ⓓ   4. Ⓐ Ⓑ Ⓒ Ⓓ   5. Ⓐ Ⓑ Ⓒ Ⓓ
6. Ⓐ Ⓑ Ⓒ Ⓓ   7. Ⓐ Ⓑ Ⓒ Ⓓ   8. Ⓐ Ⓑ Ⓒ Ⓓ   9. Ⓐ Ⓑ Ⓒ Ⓓ   10. Ⓐ Ⓑ Ⓒ Ⓓ
11. Ⓐ Ⓑ Ⓒ Ⓓ   12. Ⓐ Ⓑ Ⓒ Ⓓ   13. Ⓐ Ⓑ Ⓒ Ⓓ   14. Ⓐ Ⓑ Ⓒ Ⓓ   15. Ⓐ Ⓑ Ⓒ Ⓓ
16. Ⓐ Ⓑ Ⓒ Ⓓ   17. Ⓐ Ⓑ Ⓒ Ⓓ   18. Ⓐ Ⓑ Ⓒ Ⓓ   19. Ⓐ Ⓑ Ⓒ Ⓓ   20. Ⓐ Ⓑ Ⓒ Ⓓ
21. Ⓐ Ⓑ Ⓒ Ⓓ   22. Ⓐ Ⓑ Ⓒ Ⓓ   23. Ⓐ Ⓑ Ⓒ Ⓓ   24. Ⓐ Ⓑ Ⓒ Ⓓ   25. Ⓐ Ⓑ Ⓒ Ⓓ
26. Ⓐ Ⓑ Ⓒ Ⓓ   27. Ⓐ Ⓑ Ⓒ Ⓓ   28. Ⓐ Ⓑ Ⓒ Ⓓ   29. Ⓐ Ⓑ Ⓒ Ⓓ   30. Ⓐ Ⓑ Ⓒ Ⓓ

Part 3: Word Knowledge

1. Ⓐ Ⓑ Ⓒ Ⓓ   2. Ⓐ Ⓑ Ⓒ Ⓓ   3. Ⓐ Ⓑ Ⓒ Ⓓ   4. Ⓐ Ⓑ Ⓒ Ⓓ   5. Ⓐ Ⓑ Ⓒ Ⓓ
6. Ⓐ Ⓑ Ⓒ Ⓓ   7. Ⓐ Ⓑ Ⓒ Ⓓ   8. Ⓐ Ⓑ Ⓒ Ⓓ   9. Ⓐ Ⓑ Ⓒ Ⓓ   10. Ⓐ Ⓑ Ⓒ Ⓓ
11. Ⓐ Ⓑ Ⓒ Ⓓ   12. Ⓐ Ⓑ Ⓒ Ⓓ   13. Ⓐ Ⓑ Ⓒ Ⓓ   14. Ⓐ Ⓑ Ⓒ Ⓓ   15. Ⓐ Ⓑ Ⓒ Ⓓ
16. Ⓐ Ⓑ Ⓒ Ⓓ   17. Ⓐ Ⓑ Ⓒ Ⓓ   18. Ⓐ Ⓑ Ⓒ Ⓓ   19. Ⓐ Ⓑ Ⓒ Ⓓ   20. Ⓐ Ⓑ Ⓒ Ⓓ
21. Ⓐ Ⓑ Ⓒ Ⓓ   22. Ⓐ Ⓑ Ⓒ Ⓓ   23. Ⓐ Ⓑ Ⓒ Ⓓ   24. Ⓐ Ⓑ Ⓒ Ⓓ   25. Ⓐ Ⓑ Ⓒ Ⓓ
26. Ⓐ Ⓑ Ⓒ Ⓓ   27. Ⓐ Ⓑ Ⓒ Ⓓ   28. Ⓐ Ⓑ Ⓒ Ⓓ   29. Ⓐ Ⓑ Ⓒ Ⓓ   30. Ⓐ Ⓑ Ⓒ Ⓓ
31. Ⓐ Ⓑ Ⓒ Ⓓ   32. Ⓐ Ⓑ Ⓒ Ⓓ   33. Ⓐ Ⓑ Ⓒ Ⓓ   34. Ⓐ Ⓑ Ⓒ Ⓓ   35. Ⓐ Ⓑ Ⓒ Ⓓ

Part 4: Paragraph Comprehension

1. Ⓐ Ⓑ Ⓒ Ⓓ   2. Ⓐ Ⓑ Ⓒ Ⓓ   3. Ⓐ Ⓑ Ⓒ Ⓓ   4. Ⓐ Ⓑ Ⓒ Ⓓ   5. Ⓐ Ⓑ Ⓒ Ⓓ
6. Ⓐ Ⓑ Ⓒ Ⓓ   7. Ⓐ Ⓑ Ⓒ Ⓓ   8. Ⓐ Ⓑ Ⓒ Ⓓ   9. Ⓐ Ⓑ Ⓒ Ⓓ   10. Ⓐ Ⓑ Ⓒ Ⓓ
11. Ⓐ Ⓑ Ⓒ Ⓓ   12. Ⓐ Ⓑ Ⓒ Ⓓ   13. Ⓐ Ⓑ Ⓒ Ⓓ   14. Ⓐ Ⓑ Ⓒ Ⓓ   15. Ⓐ Ⓑ Ⓒ Ⓓ

Part 5: Mathematics Knowledge

1. Ⓐ Ⓑ Ⓒ Ⓓ   2. Ⓐ Ⓑ Ⓒ Ⓓ   3. Ⓐ Ⓑ Ⓒ Ⓓ   4. Ⓐ Ⓑ Ⓒ Ⓓ   5. Ⓐ Ⓑ Ⓒ Ⓓ

6. Ⓐ Ⓑ Ⓒ Ⓓ   7. Ⓐ Ⓑ Ⓒ Ⓓ   8. Ⓐ Ⓑ Ⓒ Ⓓ   9. Ⓐ Ⓑ Ⓒ Ⓓ   10. Ⓐ Ⓑ Ⓒ Ⓓ

11. Ⓐ Ⓑ Ⓒ Ⓓ   12. Ⓐ Ⓑ Ⓒ Ⓓ   13. Ⓐ Ⓑ Ⓒ Ⓓ   14. Ⓐ Ⓑ Ⓒ Ⓓ   15. Ⓐ Ⓑ Ⓒ Ⓓ

16. Ⓐ Ⓑ Ⓒ Ⓓ   17. Ⓐ Ⓑ Ⓒ Ⓓ   18. Ⓐ Ⓑ Ⓒ Ⓓ   19. Ⓐ Ⓑ Ⓒ Ⓓ   20. Ⓐ Ⓑ Ⓒ Ⓓ

21. Ⓐ Ⓑ Ⓒ Ⓓ   22. Ⓐ Ⓑ Ⓒ Ⓓ   23. Ⓐ Ⓑ Ⓒ Ⓓ   24. Ⓐ Ⓑ Ⓒ Ⓓ   25. Ⓐ Ⓑ Ⓒ Ⓓ

Part 6: Electronics Information

1. Ⓐ Ⓑ Ⓒ Ⓓ   2. Ⓐ Ⓑ Ⓒ Ⓓ   3. Ⓐ Ⓑ Ⓒ Ⓓ   4. Ⓐ Ⓑ Ⓒ Ⓓ   5. Ⓐ Ⓑ Ⓒ Ⓓ

6. Ⓐ Ⓑ Ⓒ Ⓓ   7. Ⓐ Ⓑ Ⓒ Ⓓ   8. Ⓐ Ⓑ Ⓒ Ⓓ   9. Ⓐ Ⓑ Ⓒ Ⓓ   10. Ⓐ Ⓑ Ⓒ Ⓓ

11. Ⓐ Ⓑ Ⓒ Ⓓ   12. Ⓐ Ⓑ Ⓒ Ⓓ   13. Ⓐ Ⓑ Ⓒ Ⓓ   14. Ⓐ Ⓑ Ⓒ Ⓓ   15. Ⓐ Ⓑ Ⓒ Ⓓ

16. Ⓐ Ⓑ Ⓒ Ⓓ   17. Ⓐ Ⓑ Ⓒ Ⓓ   18. Ⓐ Ⓑ Ⓒ Ⓓ   19. Ⓐ Ⓑ Ⓒ Ⓓ   20. Ⓐ Ⓑ Ⓒ Ⓓ

Part 7: Auto & Shop Information

1. Ⓐ Ⓑ Ⓒ Ⓓ   2. Ⓐ Ⓑ Ⓒ Ⓓ   3. Ⓐ Ⓑ Ⓒ Ⓓ   4. Ⓐ Ⓑ Ⓒ Ⓓ   5. Ⓐ Ⓑ Ⓒ Ⓓ

6. Ⓐ Ⓑ Ⓒ Ⓓ   7. Ⓐ Ⓑ Ⓒ Ⓓ   8. Ⓐ Ⓑ Ⓒ Ⓓ   9. Ⓐ Ⓑ Ⓒ Ⓓ   10. Ⓐ Ⓑ Ⓒ Ⓓ

11. Ⓐ Ⓑ Ⓒ Ⓓ   12. Ⓐ Ⓑ Ⓒ Ⓓ   13. Ⓐ Ⓑ Ⓒ Ⓓ   14. Ⓐ Ⓑ Ⓒ Ⓓ   15. Ⓐ Ⓑ Ⓒ Ⓓ

16. Ⓐ Ⓑ Ⓒ Ⓓ   17. Ⓐ Ⓑ Ⓒ Ⓓ   18. Ⓐ Ⓑ Ⓒ Ⓓ   19. Ⓐ Ⓑ Ⓒ Ⓓ   20. Ⓐ Ⓑ Ⓒ Ⓓ

21. Ⓐ Ⓑ Ⓒ Ⓓ   22. Ⓐ Ⓑ Ⓒ Ⓓ   23. Ⓐ Ⓑ Ⓒ Ⓓ   24. Ⓐ Ⓑ Ⓒ Ⓓ   25. Ⓐ Ⓑ Ⓒ Ⓓ

Part 8: Mechanical Comprehension

1. Ⓐ Ⓑ Ⓒ Ⓓ   2. Ⓐ Ⓑ Ⓒ Ⓓ   3. Ⓐ Ⓑ Ⓒ Ⓓ   4. Ⓐ Ⓑ Ⓒ Ⓓ   5. Ⓐ Ⓑ Ⓒ Ⓓ

6. Ⓐ Ⓑ Ⓒ Ⓓ   7. Ⓐ Ⓑ Ⓒ Ⓓ   8. Ⓐ Ⓑ Ⓒ Ⓓ   9. Ⓐ Ⓑ Ⓒ Ⓓ   10. Ⓐ Ⓑ Ⓒ Ⓓ

11. Ⓐ Ⓑ Ⓒ Ⓓ   12. Ⓐ Ⓑ Ⓒ Ⓓ   13. Ⓐ Ⓑ Ⓒ Ⓓ   14. Ⓐ Ⓑ Ⓒ Ⓓ   15. Ⓐ Ⓑ Ⓒ Ⓓ

16. Ⓐ Ⓑ Ⓒ Ⓓ   17. Ⓐ Ⓑ Ⓒ Ⓓ   18. Ⓐ Ⓑ Ⓒ Ⓓ   19. Ⓐ Ⓑ Ⓒ Ⓓ   20. Ⓐ Ⓑ Ⓒ Ⓓ

21. Ⓐ Ⓑ Ⓒ Ⓓ   22. Ⓐ Ⓑ Ⓒ Ⓓ   23. Ⓐ Ⓑ Ⓒ Ⓓ   24. Ⓐ Ⓑ Ⓒ Ⓓ   25. Ⓐ Ⓑ Ⓒ Ⓓ

Part 9: Assembling Objects

1. Ⓐ Ⓑ Ⓒ Ⓓ   2. Ⓐ Ⓑ Ⓒ Ⓓ   3. Ⓐ Ⓑ Ⓒ Ⓓ   4. Ⓐ Ⓑ Ⓒ Ⓓ   5. Ⓐ Ⓑ Ⓒ Ⓓ

6. Ⓐ Ⓑ Ⓒ Ⓓ   7. Ⓐ Ⓑ Ⓒ Ⓓ   8. Ⓐ Ⓑ Ⓒ Ⓓ   9. Ⓐ Ⓑ Ⓒ Ⓓ   10. Ⓐ Ⓑ Ⓒ Ⓓ

11. Ⓐ Ⓑ Ⓒ Ⓓ   12. Ⓐ Ⓑ Ⓒ Ⓓ   13. Ⓐ Ⓑ Ⓒ Ⓓ   14. Ⓐ Ⓑ Ⓒ Ⓓ   15. Ⓐ Ⓑ Ⓒ Ⓓ

16. Ⓐ Ⓑ Ⓒ Ⓓ

answer sheet

PART 1: GENERAL SCIENCE

Time: 11 Minutes—25 Questions

> **Directions:** This is a test of 25 questions to find out how much you know about general science as usually covered in high school courses. Pick the best answer for each question, then blacken the space on your answer sheet that has the same number and letter as your choice.

Here are three sample questions.

1. Water is an example of a   Ⓐ Ⓑ ● Ⓓ
   A. solid.
   B. gas.
   C. liquid.
   D. crystal.

   Notice that answer space C has been marked for question 1. Now do practice questions 2 and 3 by yourself. Find the correct answer to the question, then mark the space that has the same letter as the answer you picked. Do this now.

2. Lack of iodine is often related to which of the following diseases?   Ⓐ Ⓑ Ⓒ Ⓓ
   A. Beriberi
   B. Scurvy
   C. Rickets
   D. Goiter

3. An eclipse of the sun throws the shadow of the   Ⓐ Ⓑ Ⓒ Ⓓ
   A. earth on the moon.
   B. moon on the earth.
   C. moon on the sun.
   D. earth on the sun.

   You should have marked choice D for question 2 and choice B for question 3. If you made any mistakes, erase your mark carefully and blacken the correct answer space. Do this now.

Your score on this test will be based on the number of questions you answer correctly. You should try to answer every question. Do not spend too much time on any one question.

When you begin, be sure to start with question number 1 in Part 1 in your test booklet and number 1 in Part 1 on your answer sheet.

1. Which one of the following is NOT a fruit?
   A. Potato
   B. Tomato
   C. Cucumber
   D. Green pepper

2. Which of the following are responsible for nitrogen fixation?
   A. Tomatoes
   B. Potatoes
   C. Peanuts
   D. Corn

3. Of the following, a condition NOT associated with heavy cigarette smoking is
   A. shorter life span.
   B. slowing of the heartbeat.
   C. lung cancer.
   D. heart disease.

4. You are most likely to develop hypothermia when
   A. it is very hot and you have nothing to drink.
   B. you are bitten by a rabid dog.
   C. you fall asleep in the sun.
   D. it is very cold and your clothes are wet.

5. If you are caught away from home during a thunderstorm, the safest place to be is
   A. in a car.
   B. under a tree.
   C. in an open field.
   D. at the top of a small hill.

6. During a thunderstorm, we see a lightning bolt before we hear the sound of the accompanying thunder chiefly because the
   A. eye is more sensitive than the ear.
   B. wind interferes with the sound of the thunder.
   C. storm may be very far away.
   D. speed of light is much faster than the speed of sound.

7. The scientific name *Homo sapiens* consists of the
   A. family and class.
   B. order and family.
   C. genus and species.
   D. species and domain.

8. The number of degrees on the Fahrenheit thermometer between the freezing point and the boiling point of water is
   A. 100 degrees.
   B. 212 degrees.
   C. 180 degrees.
   D. 273 degrees.

9. The energy transformation of chemical to electrical energy describes
   A. a power plant.
   B. a car battery.
   C. a rock at the top of a hill.
   D. plugging in a toaster.

10. During a tug-of-war contest, Team A beats Team B. The force exerted by Team A can be described as
    A. net force.
    B. ratio of force.
    C. product of force.
    D. equal force.

11. A vector is used to represent force. The length of the vector indicates its
   A. direction.
   B. magnitude.
   C. magnitude and direction.
   D. velocity.

12. Of the following, the statement that best describes a "high" on a weather map is that air
   A. extends farther up than normal.
   B. pressure is greater than normal.
   C. temperature is higher than normal.
   D. moves faster than normal.

13. The smallest particle of gold that still retains the characteristics of gold is a(n)
   A. molecule.
   B. proton.
   C. electron.
   D. atom.

14. Narcotics may be dangerous if used without supervision, but they are useful in medicine because they
   A. increase production of red blood cells.
   B. kill bacteria.
   C. relieve pain.
   D. stimulate the heart.

15. The primary reason why fungi are often found growing in abundance deep in the forest is that
   A. it is cooler.
   B. it is warmer.
   C. they have little exposure to sunlight for photosynthesis.
   D. they have a plentiful supply of organic matter.

16. The presence of coal deposits in Alaska shows that at one time Alaska
   A. had a tropical climate.
   B. was covered with ice.
   C. was connected to Asia.
   D. was formed by volcanic action.

17. If a person has been injured in an accident and damage to the back and neck is suspected, it is best to
   A. roll the person over so that he does not lie on his back.
   B. rush the person to the nearest hospital.
   C. force the person to drink water to replace body fluids.
   D. wait for professional help.

18. A 1,000-ton ship must displace a weight of water equal to
   A. 500 tons.
   B. 1,500 tons.
   C. 1,000 tons.
   D. 2,000 tons.

19. 52 weeks is the equivalent of
   A. 2 years.
   B. 365 days.
   C. 132 days.
   D. 4 years.

20. The temperature of the air falls at night because the earth loses heat by
   A. radiation.
   B. conduction.
   C. convection.
   D. rotation.

practice test 3

21. The normal height of a mercury barometer at sea level is
    A. 15 inches.
    B. 32 feet.
    C. 30 inches.
    D. 34 feet.

22. Nitrogen-fixing bacteria are found in nodules on the roots of the
    A. beet.
    B. potato.
    C. carrot.
    D. clover.

23. The vascular system of the body is concerned with
    A. respiration.
    B. sense of touch.
    C. circulation of blood.
    D. hormones.

24. In which of the following types of rocks are most fossils found?
    A. Igneous
    B. Metamorphic
    C. Sedimentary
    D. Volcanic

25. If you wish to cut down on saturated fats and cholesterol in your diet, which of the following foods should you avoid?
    A. Fish
    B. Dry beans and peas
    C. Cheese
    D. Spaghetti

STOP!
IF YOU FINISH BEFORE THE TIME IS UP,
YOU MAY CHECK OVER YOUR WORK ON THIS PART ONLY.

PART 2: ARITHMETIC REASONING

Time: 36 Minutes—30 Questions

> **Directions:** This test has 30 questions about arithmetic. Each question is followed by four possible answers. Decide which answer is correct, then blacken the space on your answer sheet that has the same number and letter as your choice. Use scratch paper to do any figuring.

Here are two sample questions.

1. A person buys a sandwich for 90¢, soda for 55¢, and pie for 70¢.   Ⓐ Ⓑ Ⓒ Ⓓ
   What is the total cost?
   A. $2.00
   B. $2.05
   C. $2.15
   D. $2.25

   The total cost is $2.15; therefore, choice C is the correct answer.

2. If 8 workers are needed to run 4 machines, how many workers are   Ⓐ Ⓑ Ⓒ Ⓓ
   needed to run 20 machines?
   A. 16
   B. 32
   C. 36
   D. 40

   The number needed is 40; therefore, choice D is the correct answer.

Your score on this test will be based on the number of questions you answer correctly. You should try to answer every question. Do not spend too much time on any one question.

Notice that Part 2 begins with question number 1. When you begin, be sure to start with question number 1 in Part 2 in your test booklet and number 1 in Part 2 on your answer sheet.

1. If pencils are bought at 70 cents per dozen and sold at 3 for 20 cents, the total profit on 6 dozen is
   A. 50 cents.
   B. 60 cents.
   C. 65 cents.
   D. 75 cents.

2. A certain type of siding for a house costs $10.50 per square yard. What does it cost for the siding for a wall 4 yards wide and 60 feet long?
   A. $800
   B. $840
   C. $2,520
   D. $3,240

3. A parcel delivery service charges $9.26 for the first 4 pounds of package weight and an additional $1.06 for each half pound over 4 pounds. What is the charge for a package weighing $6\frac{1}{2}$ pounds?
   A. $2.65
   B. $6.89
   C. $11.91
   D. $14.56

4. A typist uses lengthwise a sheet of paper 9 inches by 12 inches. She leaves a 1-inch margin on each side and a $1\frac{1}{2}$ inch margin on top and bottom. What fractional part of the page is used for typing?
   A. $\frac{21}{22}$
   B. $\frac{7}{12}$
   C. $\frac{5}{9}$
   D. $\frac{3}{4}$

5. A woman currently has a balance of $2,300 in her checking account. She had to withdraw $331.50 to pay a bill. What is her balance after the withdrawal?
   A. $1868.50
   B. $1958.50
   C. $1968.50
   D. $1988.50

6. An employee has of his $\frac{2}{9}$ salary withheld for income tax. The percent of his salary that is withheld is most nearly
   A. 16%.
   B. 18%.
   C. 20%.
   D. 22%.

7. On a blueprint in which 2 inches represent 5 feet, the length of a room measures $7\frac{1}{2}$ inches. The actual length of the room is
   A. $12\frac{1}{2}$ feet.
   B. $7\frac{1}{2}$ feet.
   C. $15\frac{3}{4}$ feet.
   D. $18\frac{3}{4}$ feet.

8. During a 25% off sale, an article sells for $375. What was the original price of this article?
   A. $93.75
   B. $468.75
   C. $500
   D. $575

9. The total length of fencing needed to enclose a rectangular area 46 feet by 34 feet is
   A. 26 yards, 1 foot.
   B. $26\frac{2}{3}$ yards.
   C. 52 yards, 2 feet.
   D. $53\frac{1}{3}$ yards.

10. A piece of wood 35 feet 6 inches long was used to make 4 shelves of equal length. The length of each shelf was
    A. 9 feet, $1\frac{1}{2}$ inches.
    B. 8 feet, $10\frac{1}{2}$ inches.
    C. 7 feet, $10\frac{1}{2}$ inches.
    D. 7 feet, $1\frac{1}{2}$ inches.

11. At the convenience store a shopper purchased 4 boxes of cereal at $2.98 each, 2 gallons of milk at $1.99 each, and a loaf of bread for $2.50. What was the total bill?
    A. $18.40
    B. $14.80
    C. $19.40
    D. $14.90

12. What is the simple interest on $600 at 8% for 2 years?
    A. $48
    B. $64
    C. $96
    D. $108

13. A worker makes $9.80 per hour for a 40-hour work week. He also earns $1\frac{1}{2}$ times the regular pay for overtime work. If he worked 50 hours last week, how much was his total paycheck?
    A. $488
    B. $688
    C. $392
    D. $588

14. How much does a salesperson earn for selling $68 worth of writing paper if she is paid a commission of 40% on her sales?
    A. $20.40
    B. $25.60
    C. $22.80
    D. $27.20

15. If a certain job can be performed by 18 clerks in 26 days, the number of clerks needed to perform the job in 12 days is
    A. 24.
    B. 30.
    C. 39.
    D. 52.

16. A carton contains 9 dozen file folders. If a clerk removes 53 folders, how many folders are left in the carton?
    A. 37
    B. 44
    C. 55
    D. 62

17. A man had $25. He saw some ties that cost $4.95 apiece. How many of these ties could he buy?
    A. 6
    B. 7
    C. 5
    D. 3

18. A man earns $20.56 on Monday; $32.90 on Tuesday; and $20.78 on Wednesday. He spends half of all that he earns during the three days. How much does he have left?
    A. $29.19
    B. $31.23
    C. $34.27
    D. $37.12

19. A flagpole that is 16 feet high has a shadow that is 4 feet long. A nearby flagpole is 24 feet high. How long is the shadow of the taller flagpole?
A. 4 feet
B. 6 feet
C. 8 feet
D. 10 feet

20. A customer bought a new computer with a $70 down payment and 10 more payments of $35 each. What was the total cost of the computer?
A. $320
B. $420
C. $460
D. $520

21. A crate containing a tool weighs 12 pounds. If the tool weighs 9 pounds, 9 ounces, how much does the crate weigh?
A. 2 pounds, 1 ounce
B. 2 pounds, 7 ounces
C. 3 pounds, 1 ounce
D. 3 pounds, 7 ounces

22. The area of a room measuring 12 feet by 15 feet is
A. 9 square yards.
B. 12 square yards.
C. 15 square yards.
D. 20 square yards.

23. A woman purchased a blouse for $10.98. She returned the blouse the next day and selected a better one costing $12.50. She gave the clerk a five-dollar bill to pay for the difference in price. How much change should she receive?
A. $3.58
B. $3.48
C. $2.52
D. $1.52

24. A man paid $52.50 to fill up his gas tank in April, $46.80 to fill it up in May, and $42.60 to fill it up in June. What was the average cost of a fill-up of gasoline?
A. $47.30
B. $49.30
C. $51.30
D. $53.30

25. In a 45-minute gym class, 30 boys want to play basketball. Only 10 can play at once. If each player is to play the same length of time, how many minutes should each play?
A. 8
B. 12
C. 15
D. 20

26. The library charges 5¢ for the first day and 2¢ for each additional day that a book is overdue. If a borrower paid 65¢ in late charges, for how many days was the book overdue?
A. 15
B. 21
C. 25
D. 31

27. How many slices of bread, each weighing 2 ounces, are needed to balance 2 pounds of apples?
A. 8
B. 12
C. 16
D. 24

28. If $\frac{1}{2}$ cup of spinach contains 80 calories and the same amount of peas contains 300 calories, how many cups of spinach have the same caloric content as a $\frac{2}{3}$ cup of peas?

   A. $\frac{2}{5}$

   B. $1\frac{1}{3}$

   C. 2

   D. $2\frac{1}{2}$

29. If it takes 30 minutes to type 6 pages, how many hours will it take to type 126 pages at the same rate?

   A. 6.3

   B. 10.5

   C. 15

   D. 25

30. A night watchman must check a certain storage area every 45 minutes. If he first checks the area as he begins a 9-hour tour of duty, how many times will he have checked this storage area?

   A. 10

   B. 11

   C. 12

   D. 13

STOP!
IF YOU FINISH BEFORE THE TIME IS UP,
YOU MAY CHECK OVER YOUR WORK ON THIS PART ONLY.

practice test 3

PART 3: WORD KNOWLEDGE

Time: 11 Minutes—35 Questions

> **Directions:** This test has 35 questions about the meanings of words. Each question has an underlined word. You are to decide which one of the four words in the choices most nearly means the same as the underlined word, then mark the space on your answer sheet that has the same number and letter as your choice.

Now look at the two sample questions below.

1. <u>Mended</u> most nearly means   Ⓐ Ⓑ Ⓒ Ⓓ
   A. repaired.
   B. torn.
   C. clean.
   D. tied.

   Repaired, choice A, is the correct answer. *Mended* means *fixed* or *repaired. Torn,* choice B, might be the state of an object before it is mended. The repair might be made by *tying,* choice D, but not necessarily. *Clean,* choice C, is wrong.

2. It was a <u>small</u> table.   Ⓐ Ⓑ Ⓒ Ⓓ
   A. Sturdy
   B. Round
   C. Cheap
   D. Little

   Little means the same as *small,* so choice D is the best answer.

Your score on this test will be based on the number of questions you answer correctly. You should try to answer every question. Do not spend too much time on any one question.

When you begin, be sure to start with question number 1 in Part 3 in your test booklet and number 1 in Part 3 on your answer sheet.

1. <u>Superiority</u> most nearly means
   A. abundance.
   B. popularity.
   C. permanence.
   D. excellence.

2. <u>Absurd</u> most nearly means
   A. disgusting.
   B. foolish.
   C. reasonable.
   D. very old.

3. Be careful, that liquid is <u>inflammable</u>!
   A. Poisonous
   B. Valuable
   C. Explosive
   D. Likely to give off fumes

4. <u>Conscious</u> most nearly means
   A. surprised.
   B. afraid.
   C. disappointed.
   D. aware.

5. <u>Impasse</u> most nearly means
   A. Blocked path
   B. Thoroughfare
   C. Corner
   D. Pathway

6. We <u>assumed</u> that Jack had been elected.
   A. Knew
   B. Wished
   C. Decided
   D. Supposed

7. <u>Counterfeit</u> most nearly means
   A. mysterious.
   B. false.
   C. unreadable.
   D. priceless.

8. <u>Expertly</u> most nearly means
   A. awkwardly.
   B. quickly.
   C. skillfully.
   D. unexpectedly.

9. <u>Loquacious</u> most nearly means
   A. Talkative
   B. Introverted
   C. Mean-spirited
   D. Sporadic

10. The children pledged <u>allegiance</u> to the flag.
    A. Freedom
    B. Homeland
    C. Protection
    D. Loyalty

11. The cashier <u>yearned</u> for a vacation.
    A. Begged
    B. Longed
    C. Saved
    D. Applied

12. <u>Summit</u> most nearly means
    A. face.
    B. top.
    C. base.
    D. side.

13. The driver <u>heeded</u> the traffic signals.
    A. Worried about
    B. Ignored
    C. Disagreed with
    D. Took notice of

14. <u>Malodorous</u> most nearly means
    A. Pleasant
    B. Fruity
    C. Foul-smelling
    D. Dull

practice test 3

15. <u>Imitate</u> most nearly means
   A. copy.
   B. attract.
   C. study.
   D. appreciate.

16. The <u>severity</u> of their criticism upset us.
   A. Harshness
   B. Suddenness
   C. Method
   D. Unfairness

17. <u>Negligent</u> most nearly means
   A. careful.
   B. thoughtful.
   C. clumsy.
   D. careless.

18. We made a very <u>leisurely</u> trip to California.
   A. Roundabout
   B. Unhurried
   C. Unforgettable
   D. Tiresome

19. The queen is <u>omnipotent</u>.
   A. All-powerful
   B. Knowledgeable
   C. Forceful
   D. Fair

20. <u>Familiar</u> most nearly means
   A. welcome.
   B. dreaded.
   C. rare.
   D. well-known.

21. He had an <u>acute</u> pain in his back.
   A. Dull
   B. Slight
   C. Alarming
   D. Sharp

22. <u>Bewildered</u> most nearly means
   A. worried.
   B. offended.
   C. puzzled.
   D. delighted.

23. <u>Conclusion</u> most nearly means
   A. theme.
   B. suspense.
   C. end.
   D. beginning.

24. She likes the <u>aroma</u> of fresh-brewed coffee.
   A. Flavor
   B. Warmth
   C. Fragrance
   D. Steam

25. The vagrant lived in <u>penury</u>.
   A. Affluence
   B. Extreme poverty
   C. The north
   D. The desert

26. <u>Amplified</u> most nearly means
   A. expanded.
   B. summarized.
   C. analyzed.
   D. shouted.

27. The vase remained <u>intact</u> after it was dropped.
   A. Unattended
   B. Undamaged
   C. A total loss
   D. Unmoved

28. Penicillin is a <u>potent</u> drug.
   A. Harmless
   B. Possible
   C. Effective
   D. Drinkable

29. <u>Terminate</u> most nearly means
   A. continue.
   B. go by train.
   C. begin.
   D. end.

30. The prisoner is a <u>notorious</u> bank robber.
   A. Convicted
   B. Dangerous
   C. Well-known
   D. Escaped

31. <u>Serrated</u> most nearly means
   A. Straight
   B. Notched
   C. Sharp
   D. Extensive

32. <u>Indigent</u> people are entitled to food stamps.
   A. Poor
   B. Lazy
   C. Angry
   D. Homeless

33. <u>Technique</u> most nearly means
   A. computed.
   B. engineered.
   C. calculation.
   D. method.

34. <u>Vocation</u> most nearly means
   A. school.
   B. examination.
   C. occupation.
   D. carpentry.

35. One should eat only <u>mature</u> fruits.
   A. Edible
   B. Washed
   C. Ripe
   D. Sprayed

STOP!
IF YOU FINISH BEFORE THE TIME IS UP,
YOU MAY CHECK OVER YOUR WORK ON THIS PART ONLY.

practice test 3

PART 4: PARAGRAPH COMPREHENSION

Time: 13 Minutes—15 Questions

> **Directions:** This test contains 15 items measuring your ability to obtain information from written passages. You will find one or more paragraphs of reading material followed by incomplete statements or questions. You are to read the paragraph(s) and select the lettered choice that best completes the statement or answers the question.

Here are two sample questions.

1. From a building designer's standpoint, three things that make a home livable are the needs of the client, the building site, and the amount of money the client has to spend.   Ⓐ Ⓑ Ⓒ Ⓓ

   According to the passage, to make a home livable
   A. the prospective piece of land makes little difference.
   B. it can be built on any piece of land.
   C. the design must fit the owner's income and site.
   D. the design must fit the designer's income.

   The correct answer is that the design must fit the owner's income and site, so choice C is the correct answer.

2. In certain areas, water is so scarce that every attempt is made to conserve it. For instance, on one oasis in the Sahara Desert, the amount of water necessary for each date palm tree has been carefully determined.   Ⓐ Ⓑ Ⓒ Ⓓ

   How much water is each tree given?
   A. No water at all
   B. Exactly the amount required
   C. Water only if it is healthy
   D. Water on alternate days

   The correct answer is exactly the amount required, so choice B is the correct answer.

Your score on this test will be based on the number of questions you answer correctly. You should try to answer every question. Do not spend too much time on any one question.

When you begin, be sure to start with question number 1 in Part 4 in your test booklet and number 1 in Part 4 on your answer sheet.

1. The prevention of accidents makes it necessary not only that safety devices be used to guard exposed machinery but also that mechanics be instructed in safety rules that they must follow for their own protection.

   The passage best supports the statement that industrial accidents
   A. are always avoidable.
   B. may be due to ignorance.
   C. usually result from inadequate machinery.
   D. cannot be entirely overcome.

2. Just as the procedure of a collection department must be clear-cut and definite, so the various paragraphs of a collection letter must show clear organization, giving evidence of a mind that has a specific end in view.

   The passage best supports the statement that a collection letter should always
   A. be divided into several paragraphs.
   B. express confidence in the debtor.
   C. be brief but courteous.
   D. be carefully planned.

3. The rights of an individual should properly be considered of greatest importance in a democracy until the activities of an individual come in conflict with the community interest or with the interest of society.

   According to this passage, in a democracy
   A. there is nothing of greater importance than the rights of the individual.
   B. there must be no conflict between the interest of the community and the rights of the individual.
   C. the rights of the individual are secondary to the interest of the community.
   D. the rights of the individual are generally incompatible with the interest of society.

4. Thomas Edison was responsible for more than 1,000 inventions in his 84-year life span. Among the most famous of his inventions are the phonograph, the electric light bulb, motion picture film, the electric generator, and the battery.

   According to the passage, Thomas Edison
   A. was the most famous inventor.
   B. was responsible for 84 inventions.
   C. invented many things in his short life.
   D. was responsible for the phonograph and motion picture film.

5. Scientists are taking a closer look at the recent boom in the use of wood for heating. Wood burning, it seems, releases high levels of pollutants. It is believed that burning wood produces a thousand times more CO, carbon monoxide, than natural gas does when it burns.

   According to the passage, CO is
   A. natural gas.
   B. wood.
   C. carbon monoxide.
   D. heat.

6. The location of a railway line is necessarily a compromise between the desire to build the line with as little expense as possible and the desire to construct it so that its route will cover that over which trade and commerce are likely to flow.

   The route selected for a railway line
   A. should be the one over which the line can be built most cheaply.
   B. determines the location of commercial centers.
   C. should always cover the shortest possible distance between its terminals.
   D. cannot always be the one involving the lowest construction costs.

7. A survey to determine the subjects that have helped students most in their jobs shows that word processing leads all other subjects in the business group. It also leads among the subjects college students consider most valuable and would take again if they were to return to high school.

   The paragraph best supports the statement that

   A. the ability to word process is an asset in business and in school.

   B. students who return to night school take word processing.

   C. students with a knowledge of word processing do superior work in college.

   D. success in business is assured to those who can word process.

8. Direct lighting is the least satisfactory lighting arrangement. The desk or ceiling light with a reflector that diffuses all the rays downward is sure to cause glare on the working surface.

   Direct lighting is least satisfactory as a method of lighting chiefly because

   A. the light is diffused causing eye strain.

   B. the shade on the individual desk lamp is not constructed along scientific lines.

   C. the working surface is usually obscured by the glare.

   D. direct lighting is injurious to the eyes.

9. In almost every community, fortunately, there are certain men and women known to be public-spirited. Others, however, may be selfish and act only as their private interests seem to require.

   The paragraph suggests that those citizens who disregard others are

   A. needed.

   B. found only in small communities.

   C. not known.

   D. not public-spirited.

10. Unfortunately, specialization in industry creates workers who lack versatility. When a laborer is trained to perform only one task, he or she is almost entirely dependent for employment on the demand for that particular skill. If anything happens to interrupt that demand, he or she is unemployed.

    The paragraph best supports the statement that

    A. the demand for labor of a particular type is constantly changing.

    B. the average laborer is not capable of learning more than one task at a time.

    C. some cases of unemployment are due to laborers' lack of versatility.

    D. too much specialization is as dangerous as too little.

Questions 11 and 12 are based on the following passage.

Because electric drills run at high speed, the cutting edges of a twist drill are heated quickly. If the metal is thick, the drill point must be withdrawn from the hole frequently to cool it and clear out chips. Forcing the drill continuously into a deep hole will heat it, thereby spoiling its temper and cutting edges. A portable electric drill can be used to drill holes in material too large to handle in a drill press.

11. According to the previous passage, overheating a twist drill will
   A. slow down the work.
   B. cause excessive drill breakage.
   C. dull the drill.
   D. spoil the accuracy of the work.

12. One method of preventing overheating of a twist drill, according to the previous passage, is to
   A. use cooling oil.
   B. drill a smaller pilot hole first.
   C. use a drill press.
   D. remove the drill from the work frequently.

Questions 13–15 are based on the following passage.

Many accidents and injuries can be prevented if employees learn to be more careful. Wearing shoes with badly worn soles or open toes can easily lead to foot injuries from tacks, nails, and chair legs. Loose or torn clothing should not be worn near moving machinery. When supplies are stored, they should be placed or piled so that nothing sticks out of the pile. If an employee is injured, no matter how small the injury, he or she should report it to the supervisor and have the injury treated. A small cut not attended to can easily become infected and can cause more trouble than some injuries that at first seem more serious. It never pays to take chances.

13. According to the passage, an employee who gets a slight cut should
   A. have it treated to help prevent infection.
   B. know that a slight cut becomes more easily infected than a big cut.
   C. pay no attention to it as it can't become serious.
   D. realize that it is more serious than any other type of injury.

14. According to the passage, you should NOT wear loose clothing when you are
    A. in a corridor.
    B. storing supplies.
    C. moving chairs.
    D. near moving machinery.

15. According to the passage, it is NOT true that
    A. by being more careful, employees can reduce the number of accidents.
    B. women should wear shoes with open toes for comfort when working.
    C. supplies should be piled so that nothing is sticking out from the pile.
    D. if an employee sprains his or her wrist at work, he or she should tell the supervisor about it.

STOP!
IF YOU FINISH BEFORE THE TIME IS UP,
YOU MAY CHECK OVER YOUR WORK ON THIS PART ONLY.

PART 5: MATHEMATICS KNOWLEDGE

Time: 24 Minutes—25 Questions

Directions: This is a test of your ability to solve 25 general mathematical problems. You are to select the correct response from the choices given. Then mark the space on your answer sheet that has the same number and letter as your choice. Use scratch paper to do any figuring.

Now look at the two sample problems below.

1. If $x + 6 = 7$, then x is equal to   Ⓐ Ⓑ Ⓒ Ⓓ
   A. 0
   B. 1
   C. −1
   D. $\frac{7}{6}$

   The correct answer is 1, so choice B is the correct answer.

2. What is the area of the square above?   Ⓐ Ⓑ Ⓒ Ⓓ
   A. 1 square foot
   B. 5 square feet
   C. 10 square feet
   D. 25 square feet

   The correct answer is 25 square feet, so choice D is the correct answer.

Your score on this test will be based on the number of questions you answer correctly. You should try to answer every question. Do not spend too much time on any one question.

When you are told to begin, be sure to start with question number 1 in Part 5 in your test booklet and number 1 in Part 5 on your answer sheet.

practice test 3

1. The cube of 8 is
   A. 128
   B. 256
   C. 512
   D. None of the above

2. How many different combinations of outfits are possible from a wardrobe that contains 3 shirts, 4 pants, and 5 pairs of shoes?
   A. 12
   B. 24
   C. 30
   D. 60

3. If the circumference of a circle has the same numbered value as its area, then the radius of the circle must be
   A. 1
   B. 5
   C. 2
   D. 0

4. Divide 2.454 by 0.06.
   A. 0.49
   B. 4.9
   C. 4.09
   D. 40.9

5. A car owner finds he needs 12 gallons of gas for each 120 miles he drives. If he has his carburetor adjusted, he will need only 80% as much gas. How many miles will 12 gallons of gas then last him?
   A. 90
   B. 150
   C. 96
   D. 160

6. The perimeter of a square with side r =
   A. $r^2 + r^2$
   B. $4r$
   C. r^4
   D. None of the above

7. A quadrilateral is a parallelogram only if
   A. both pairs of its opposite sides are parallel.
   B. it has four right angles.
   C. it has four right angles and four equal sides.
   D. it has at least one pair of parallel sides.

8. If $V = l \cdot w \cdot h$, then h =
   A. $\dfrac{l \cdot w}{V}$
   B. $\dfrac{V \cdot l}{w}$
   C. $\dfrac{V \cdot w}{l}$
   D. $\dfrac{V}{l \cdot w}$

9. 5% of 5% of 100 is
   A. 25
   B. 0.25
   C. 2.5
   D. 10

10. If $\dfrac{3}{8}$ of a number is 96, the number is
    A. 132
    B. 36
    C. 256
    D. 156

11. A line of print in a magazine article contains an average of 6 words. There are 5 lines to the inch. If 8 inches are available for an article that contains 270 words, how must the article be changed?

   A. Add 30 words

   B. Delete 30 words

   C. Delete 40 words

   D. Add 60 words

12. An angle has a measure five times that of its supplement. What is the measure of the angle?

   A. 60°

   B. 75°

   C. 120°

   D. 150°

13. If a jar is filled with water in one minute, how many minutes longer will it take to fill the jar?

   A. $\frac{1}{4}$

   B. $\frac{1}{3}$

   C. $\frac{1}{2}$

   D. $\frac{2}{3}$

14. If $2 - x = x - 2$, then $x =$

   A. -2

   B. 2

   C. 0

   D. $\frac{1}{2}$

15. What is the correct time if the hour hand is exactly $\frac{2}{3}$ of the way between 5 and 6?

   A. 5:25

   B. 5:40

   C. 5:30

   D. 5:45

16. A square is changed into a rectangle by increasing its length 10% and decreasing its width 10%. Its area

   A. remains the same.

   B. decreases by 10%.

   C. increases by 1%.

   D. decreases by 1%.

17. If all P are S and no S are Q, it necessarily follows that

   A. all Q are S.

   B. all Q are P.

   C. no P are Q.

   D. no S are P.

18. $(x + a)(x + b) =$

   A. $x^2 + (ab)x + a + b$

   B. $x^2 + (a + b)x + ab$

   C. $x^2 + (ab)x + ab$

   D. $x^2 + (a + b)x + a + b$

19. If $\frac{5}{4}x = \frac{5}{4}$, then $1 - x =$

   A. $-\frac{5}{4}$

   B. 1

   C. 0

   D. -1

20. Factor $a^2 - 2ab + b^2$

   A. $(a + b)^2$

   B. $(a - b)^2$

   C. $(a^2 + b^2)$

   D. $(a^2 - b^2)$

21. When 5.1 is divided by 0.017, the quotient is

   A. 30

   B. 300

   C. 3,000

   D. 30,000

practice test 3

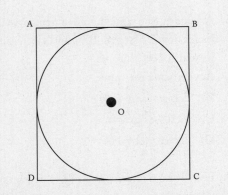

22. In the figure above, the area of circle O is 64π. The perimeter of square ABCD is
   A. 32
   B. 32π
   C. 64
   D. 16

23. Find the radius of a circle whose circumference is 90π.
   A. 45π
   B. 90π
   C. 90
   D. 45

24. Which of these is a prime number?
   A. 33
   B. 31
   C. 39
   D. 51

25. X is 5 years older than Y. With the passage of time, the
   A. ratio of the ages of X and Y will not change.
   B. ratio of the ages of X and Y decreases.
   C. ratio of the ages of X and Y increases.
   D. difference in their ages increases.

STOP!
IF YOU FINISH BEFORE THE TIME IS UP,
YOU MAY CHECK OVER YOUR WORK ON THIS PART ONLY.

PART 6: ELECTRONICS INFORMATION

Time: 9 Minutes—20 Questions

> **Directions:** This is a test of your knowledge of electrical, radio, and electronics information. There are 20 questions. You are to select the correct response from the choices given. Then mark the space on your answer sheet that has the same number and letter as your choice.

Now look at the two sample questions below.

1. What does the abbreviation AC stand for?   Ⓐ Ⓑ Ⓒ Ⓓ
   A. Additional charge
   B. Alternating coil
   C. Alternating current
   D. Ampere current

   The correct answer is alternating current, so choice C is the correct response.

2. Which of the following has the least resistance?   Ⓐ Ⓑ Ⓒ Ⓓ
   A. Wood
   B. Silver
   C. Rubber
   D. Iron

   The correct answer is silver, so choice B is the correct response.

Your score on this test will be based on the number of questions you answer correctly. You should try to answer every question. Do not spend too much time on any one question.

When you are told to begin, be sure to start with question number 1 in Part 6 in your test booklet and number 1 in Part 6 on your answer sheet.

1. Boxes and fittings intended for outdoor use should be of
   A. weatherproof type.
   B. stamped steel of not less than No. 16.
   C. standard gauge.
   D. stamped steel plated with cadmium.

2. A direct-current supply may be obtained from an alternating-current source by means of
   A. a frequency changer set.
   B. an inductance-capacitance filter.
   C. a silicon diode rectifier.
   D. None of the above

3. Fuses protecting motor circuits have to be selected to permit a momentary surge of
   A. voltage when the motor starts.
   B. voltage when the motor stops.
   C. current when the motor starts.
   D. current when the motor stops.

4. If you increase the voltage of the base of a transistor, it will
   A. turn on.
   B. turn off.
   C. remain the same.
   D. Cannot be determined

5. The voltage that will cause a current of 5 amperes to flow through a 20-ohm resistance is
   A. volt.
   B. 4 volts.
   C. 20 volts.
   D. 100 volts.

6. A 100n capacitor in parallel with a 10n produces
   A. 110n.
   B. 100n.
   C. 90n.
   D. Cannot be determined

7. The electronic symbol shown above usually represents a(n)
   A. resistor.
   B. inductor.
   C. capacitor.
   D. transformer.

8. If a live conductor is contacted accidentally, the severity of the electrical shock is determined primarily by
   A. the size of the conductor.
   B. the current in the conductor.
   C. whether the current is AC or DC.
   D. the contact resistance.

9. Locknuts are frequently used in making electrical connections on terminal boards. The purpose of the locknuts is to
   A. eliminate the use of flat washers.
   B. prevent unauthorized personnel from tampering with the connections.
   C. keep the connections from loosening through vibration.
   D. increase the contact area at the connection point.

10. As resistors are color-coded, a resistor with the color band red-red-red-gold will have the values of
    A. 22R 5%
    B. 22k 5%
    C. 220R 5%
    D. 2k2 5%

11. A material NOT used in the makeup of lighting wires or cables is
    A. rubber.
    B. paper.
    C. lead.
    D. cotton.

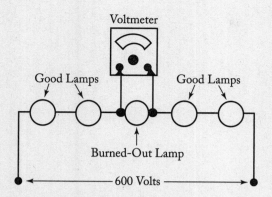

12. The reading of the voltmeter above should be
A. 600
B. 300
C. 120
D. 0

13. Silver is a better conductor of electricity than copper; however, copper is generally used for electrical conductors. The main reason for using copper instead of silver is its
A. cost.
B. weight.
C. strength.
D. melting point.

14. Direct current arcs are "hotter" and harder to extinguish than alternating current arcs, so electrical appliances that include a thermostat are frequently marked for use on "AC only." One appliance that might be so marked because it includes a thermostat is a
A. soldering iron.
B. floor waxer.
C. vacuum cleaner.
D. household iron.

15. An alternator is a(n)
A. AC generator.
B. frequency meter.
C. ground detector device.
D. choke coil.

16. Operating an incandescent electric light bulb at less than its rated voltage will result in
A. shorter life and brighter light.
B. brighter light and longer life.
C. longer life and dimmer light.
D. dimmer light and shorter life.

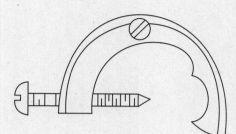

17. The device shown above is a
A. C-clamp.
B. test clip.
C. battery connector.
D. ground clamp.

18. When the electric refrigerator in a certain household kitchen starts up, the kitchen light at first dims considerably and then increases somewhat in brightness while the refrigerator motor is running; the light finally returns to full brightness when the refrigerator shuts off. This behavior of the light shows that most likely the
A. circuit wires are too small.
B. refrigerator motor is defective.
C. circuit fuse is too small.
D. kitchen lamp is too large.

19. A 10k resistor in parallel with 10k produces
A. 10k
B. 5k
C. 20k
D. Cannot be determined

20. The instrument by which electric power
may be measured is a(n)
  A. rectifier.
  B. scanner drum.
  C. ammeter.
  D. wattmeter.

STOP!
IF YOU FINISH BEFORE THE TIME IS UP,
YOU MAY CHECK OVER YOUR WORK ON THIS PART ONLY.

PART 7: AUTO & SHOP INFORMATION

Time: 11 Minutes—25 Questions

> **Directions:** This test has 25 questions about automobiles, shop practices, and the use of tools. Select the best answer for each question, then blacken the space on your answer sheet that has the same number and letter as your choice.

Here are three sample questions.

1. The most commonly used fuel for running automobile engines is   Ⓐ Ⓑ Ⓒ Ⓓ
   A. kerosene.
   B. benzene.
   C. crude oil.
   D. gasoline.

   Gasoline is the most commonly used fuel, so choice D is the correct answer.

2. A car uses too much oil when which parts are worn?   Ⓐ Ⓑ Ⓒ Ⓓ
   A. Pistons
   B. Piston rings
   C. Main bearings
   D. Connecting rods

   Worn piston rings cause the use of too much oil, so choice B is the correct answer.

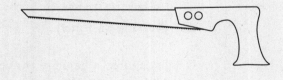

3. The saw shown above is used mainly to cut   Ⓐ Ⓑ Ⓒ Ⓓ
   A. plywood.
   B. odd-shaped holes in wood.
   C. along the grain of the wood.
   D. across the grain of the wood.

   The compass saw is used to cut odd-shaped holes in wood, so choice B is the correct answer.

Your score on this test will be based on the number of questions you answer correctly. You should try to answer every question. Do not spend too much time on any one question.

When you are told to begin, be sure to start with question number 1 in Part 7 in your test booklet and number 1 in Part 7 on your answer sheet.

1. Burned engine bearings result from
   A. lack of oil in the engine.
   B. lack of water in the engine.
   C. too much oil in the engine.
   D. too much water in the engine.

2. In an automobile distributor, the purpose of the rotor is to
   A. rotate the distributor cam.
   B. create a spark.
   C. distribute electricity to the spark plugs.
   D. rotate the distributor shaft.

3. Cam ground pistons are used primarily because
   A. they can be used in badly worn engines without reboring the cylinders.
   B. their use increases the compression ratio.
   C. their use aids in the lubrication of the cylinder walls.
   D. they eliminate piston slap in engine warm-up and permit expansion.

4. Having fuel injection in an automobile engine eliminates the need for
   A. spark plugs.
   B. a carburetor.
   C. a distributor.
   D. a manifold.

5. Water sludge in engine crankcase oil is most usually caused by
   A. using a low-viscosity oil.
   B. condensation in the crankcase.
   C. mixing different brands of motor oil.
   D. using a high-viscosity oil.

6. The purpose of an automobile's ignition coil is to
   A. smooth the current.
   B. increase the voltage.
   C. smooth the voltage.
   D. increase the current.

7. Setting the spark plug gap opening closer than normally required would probably result in
   A. smoother idling and increase in top engine speed.
   B. rougher idling and decrease in top engine speed.
   C. smoother idling and decrease in top engine speed.
   D. rougher idling and increase in top engine speed.

8. If a gasoline engine is continued in operation with a voltage regulator unable to check the output voltage of the alternator, the result would most likely be to
   A. "run down" the battery.
   B. reverse the current through the voltage coils.
   C. demagnetize the relay iron core.
   D. overcharge the battery.

9. On dismantling a gasoline engine, the piston rings were stuck in the grooves, not being free to rotate. This was most likely caused by
   A. operating the engine with spark setting in advanced position.
   B. the thermostat maintaining too low an engine temperature.
   C. dirty or contaminated lubricating oil.
   D. using the wrong type of spark plugs in the engine.

10. On the complete loss of oil pressure while a car is in operation, it is best that the car be
   A. pulled over to the side of the road and the engine stopped immediately for inspection.
   B. pulled over to the side of the road and a repair truck called to install a new oil pump.
   C. driven a few miles to your favorite garage.
   D. driven as usual for the entire day and be dropped off at the garage in the evening.

11. When painting, nail holes and cracks should be
   A. filled with putty before starting.
   B. filled with putty after the priming coat is applied.
   C. filled with paint by careful working.
   D. ignored.

12. The tool shown above is a
   A. punch.
   B. drill holder.
   C. Phillips-type screwdriver.
   D. socket wrench.

13. The length of a flat-head screw is defined as the length
   A. of the threaded portion.
   B. of the shank plus the threaded portion.
   C. of the complete screw.
   D. between the bottom of the head and the point.

14. If the head of a hammer has become loose on the handle, it should properly be tightened by
   A. driving the handle farther into the head.
   B. driving a nail alongside the present wedge.
   C. using a slightly larger wedge.
   D. soaking the handle in water.

15. End grain of wood should be sanded
   A. crosswise.
   B. with the grain.
   C. obliquely.
   D. with a circular motion.

16. The tool shown above is a(n)
   A. Allen-head wrench.
   B. double scraper.
   C. offset screwdriver.
   D. nail puller.

17. To install an expansion shield in a concrete wall, of the following, the proper tool to use is a
   A. bull nose chisel.
   B. star drill.
   C. chrome vanadium alloy cold chisel.
   D. rock wedge.

18. A method that can be used to prevent the forming of "skin" on a partially-used can of oil paint is to
   A. turn the can upside down every few months.
   B. pour a thin layer of solvent over the top of the paint.
   C. store the paint in a well-ventilated room.
   D. avoid shaking the can after it has been sealed.

19. Which of the saws is used to make curved cuts?

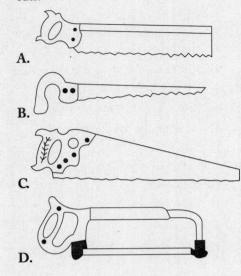

A.

B.

C.

D.

20. A wood screw that is tightened by using a wrench is called a

  A. lag screw.

  B. Phillips screw.

  C. monkey screw.

  D. carriage screw.

21. "Blistering" is generally caused by applying paint

  A. over a primer that has not completely dried.

  B. containing an improper binder for the pigment.

  C. that has been thinned too much.

  D. over a surface that has excessive moisture.

22. The plane to use in shaping a curved edge on wood is known as a

  A. jack.

  B. spoke shave.

  C. smooth.

  D. rabbet.

23. The wrench that is used principally for pipe work is

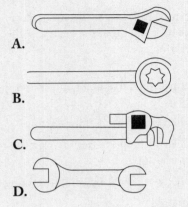

A.

B.

C.

D.

24. A lathe would be most useful in making which of the following items?

  A. Picture frame

  B. Kitchen cabinet

  C. Staircase

  D. Baseball batt

25. A squeegee is a tool that is used in

  A. drying windows after washing.

  B. cleaning inside boiler surfaces.

  C. the central vacuum cleaning system.

  D. clearing stoppages in waste lines.

STOP!
IF YOU FINISH BEFORE THE TIME IS UP,
YOU MAY CHECK OVER YOUR WORK ON THIS PART ONLY.

PART 8: MECHANICAL COMPREHENSION

Time: 19 Minutes—25 Questions

> **Directions:** This test has 25 questions about mechanical principles. Most of the questions use drawings to illustrate specific principles. Decide which answer is correct and mark the space on your answer sheet that has the same number and letter as your choice.

Here are two sample questions.

1. Which bridge is the strongest?

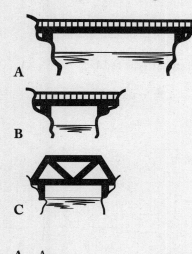

A. A
B. B
C. C
D. All are equally strong.

Ⓐ Ⓑ Ⓒ Ⓓ

Choice C is correct.

2. If all of the objects below are the same temperature, and your temperature is higher than the item's temperature, which will feel coldest?

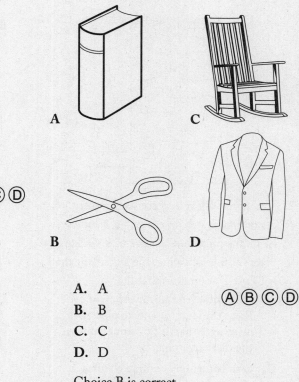

A. A
B. B
C. C
D. D

Ⓐ Ⓑ Ⓒ Ⓓ

Choice B is correct.

Your score on this test will be based on the number of questions you answer correctly. You should try to answer every question. Do not spend too much time on any one question.

When you are told to begin, be sure to start with question number 1 in Part 8 in your test booklet and number 1 in Part 8 on your answer sheet.

practice test 3

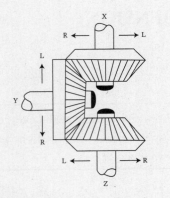

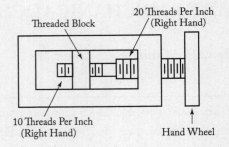

1. Which of the following is correct if gear Z in the figure above is turned to the right (R)?
   A. Gear Y turns L, and gear X turns R.
   B. Gear Y turns R, and gear X turns R.
   C. Gear Y turns L, and gear X turns L.
   D. Gear Y turns R, and gear X turns L.

3. In the figure above, the threaded block can slide in the slot but cannot revolve. If the hand wheel is turned 20 revolutions clockwise, the threaded block will move
   A. 1 inch to the left.
   B. $\frac{1}{2}$ inch to the left.
   C. 1 inch to the right.
   D. $\frac{1}{2}$ inch to the right.

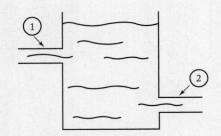

2. The figure above represents a water tank containing water. The number 1 indicates an intake pipe and 2 indicates a discharge pipe. Of the following, the statement that is LEAST accurate is that the
   A. tank will eventually overflow if water flows through the intake pipe at a faster rate than it flows out through the discharge pipe.
   B. tank will empty completely if the intake pipe is closed and the discharge pipe is allowed to remain open.
   C. water in the tank will remain at a constant level if the rate of intake is equal to the rate of discharge.
   D. water in the tank will rise if the intake pipe is operating when the discharge pipe is closed.

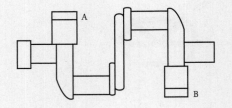

4. What is the function of A and B in the crankshaft shown in the drawing?
   A. They strengthen the crankshaft by increasing its weight.
   B. They make it easier to remove the crankshaft for repairs.
   C. They are necessary to maintain the proper balance of the crankshaft.
   D. They hold grease for continuous lubrication of the crankshaft.

5. Sweating usually occurs on pipes that
   A. contain cold water.
   B. contain hot water.
   C. are chrome plated.
   D. require insulation.

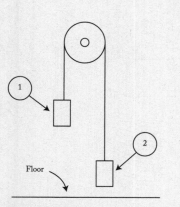

Floor

6. The above illustration represents a pulley, with practically no friction, from which two 10-pound weights are suspended as indicated. If a downward force is applied to weight 1, it is most likely that weight 1 will

A. come to rest at the present level of weight 2.

B. move downward until it is level with weight 2.

C. pass weight 2 in its downward motion and then return to its present position.

D. move downward until it reaches the floor.

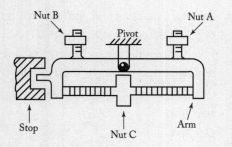

7. The arm in the above diagram is balanced exactly, as shown. If nut A is removed entirely, then, in order to rebalance the arm, it will be necessary to turn nut

A. C toward the left.

B. C toward the right.

C. B up.

D. B down.

8. The purpose of an air valve in a heating system is to

A. relieve the air from steam radiators.

B. prevent pressure from building up in a room due to the heated air.

C. control the temperature in the room.

D. allow excessive steam pressure in the boiler to escape to the atmosphere.

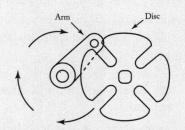

9. The above figure shows a slotted disc turned by a pin on a rotating arm. One revolution of the arm turns the disc

A. $\frac{1}{4}$ turn.

B. $\frac{1}{2}$ turn.

C. $\frac{3}{4}$ turn.

D. one complete turn.

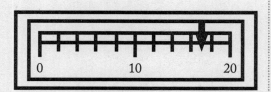

10. The reading shown on the above gauge is

A. 10.35

B. 13.5

C. 10.7

D. 17.0

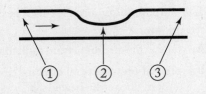

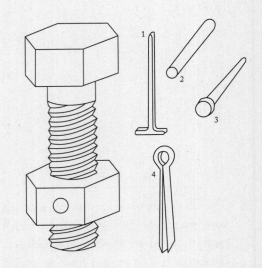

11. The figure above represents a pipe through which water is flowing in the direction of the arrow. There is a constriction in the pipe at the point indicated by the number 2. Water is being pumped into the pipe at a constant rate of 350 gallons per minute. Of the following, the most accurate statement is that

    A. the velocity of the water at point 2 is the same as the velocity of the water at point 3.

    B. a greater volume of water is flowing past point 1 in a minute than is flowing past point 2.

    C. the velocity of the water at point 1 is greater than the velocity at point 2.

    D. the volume of water flowing past point 2 in a minute is the same as the volume of water flowing past point 1 in a minute.

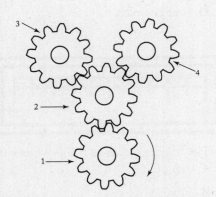

12. Four gears are shown in the figure above. If gear 1 turns as shown, then the gears turning in the same direction are

    A. 2 and 3.

    B. 2 and 4.

    C. 3 and 4.

    D. 2, 3, and 4.

13. The figure above shows a bolt and nut and four numbered pieces. If all of the pieces are long enough to go through the bolt, and if the circular hole extends through the bolt and through the other side of the nut, which piece must you use to fix the nut in a stationary position?

    A. 1

    B. 3

    C. 2

    D. 4

14. Assume that a gear and pinion have a ratio of 3:1. If the gear is rotating at 300 revolutions per minute, the speed of the pinion in revolutions per minute is most nearly

    A. 100

    B. 900

    C. 300

    D. 1,800

15. The wrecking bar is a first-class lever with curved lever arms. In the following figure, what is the theoretical mechanical advantage in using the wrecking bar to tear the crate open?

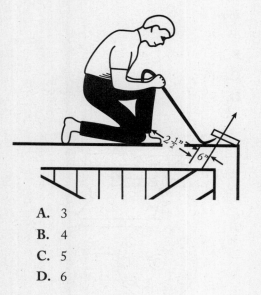

A. 3
B. 4
C. 5
D. 6

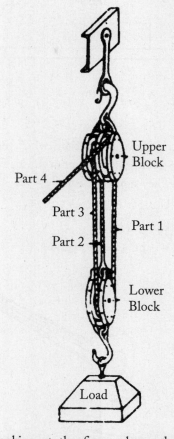

16. Looking at the figure above, determine which part of the rope is fastened directly to the block.
A. Part 1
B. Part 3
C. Part 2
D. Part 4

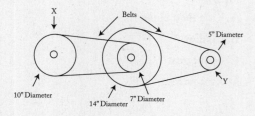

17. A double belt drive is shown in the figure above. If the pulley marked X is revolving at 100 rpm, the speed of pulley Y is
A. 800 rpm.
B. 200 rpm.
C. 400 rpm.
D. 25 rpm.

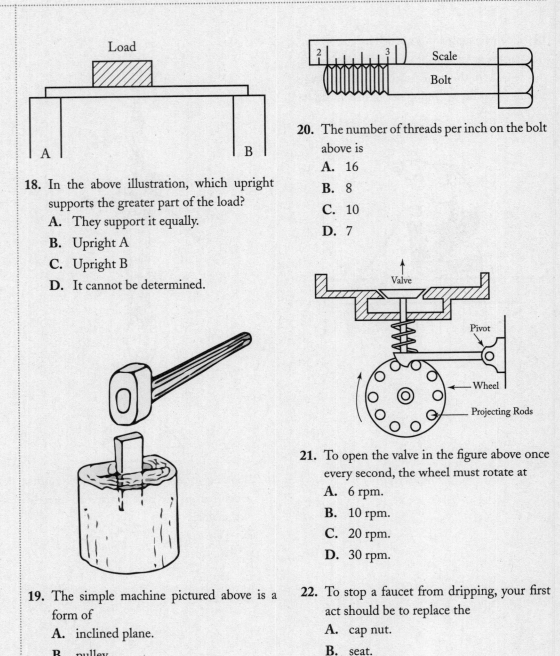

18. In the above illustration, which upright supports the greater part of the load?
   A. They support it equally.
   B. Upright A
   C. Upright B
   D. It cannot be determined.

19. The simple machine pictured above is a form of
   A. inclined plane.
   B. pulley.
   C. spur gear.
   D. torque.

20. The number of threads per inch on the bolt above is
   A. 16
   B. 8
   C. 10
   D. 7

21. To open the valve in the figure above once every second, the wheel must rotate at
   A. 6 rpm.
   B. 10 rpm.
   C. 20 rpm.
   D. 30 rpm.

22. To stop a faucet from dripping, your first act should be to replace the
   A. cap nut.
   B. seat.
   C. washer.
   D. spindle.

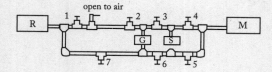

23. In the figure above, assume that all valves are closed. For air flow from R through G and then through S to M, open valves

A. 7, 6, and 5.

B. 7, 3, and 4.

C. 7, 6, and 4.

D. 7, 3, and 5.

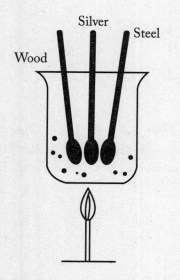

24. Which spoon above is hottest?

A. Wood

B. Silver

C. Steel

D. Silver and steel are equally hot.

25. There are twenty teeth on the front sprocket and ten teeth on the rear sprocket on the bicycle above. Each time the pedals go around, the rear wheel will go

A. halfway around.

B. around once.

C. around twice.

D. around four times.

STOP!
IF YOU FINISH BEFORE THE TIME IS UP,
YOU MAY CHECK OVER YOUR WORK ON THIS PART ONLY.

practice test 3

PART 9: ASSEMBLING OBJECTS*

Time: 9 Minutes—16 Questions

> **Directions:** This test contains 16 items measuring your ability to determine how an object will look when its parts are mentally assembled. Each item consists of five drawings. The problem is presented in the first drawing. Each problem is followed by four answers, only one of which is correct. Decide which answer is correct, then blacken the space on your answer sheet that has the same number and letter as your choice.

Now look at the two sample problems below.

1.

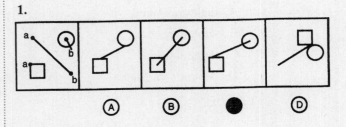

In the previous figure, the parts to be assembled are simple geometric figures (lines, squares, rectangles, etc.) that are labeled at one or more points with small letters. By matching corresponding letters on the different parts, you can see where the parts touch when the object is put together, or connected, properly.

Choice C is the correct answer.

2.

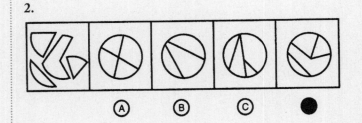

In this figure, the parts are not labeled. Instead, they fit together like pieces of a puzzle. Choice D is the correct answer.

Your score on this test will be based on the number of questions you answer correctly. You should try to answer every question. Do not spend too much time on any one question.

When you are told to begin, be sure to start with question number 1 in Part 9 in your test booklet and number 1 in Part 9 on your answer sheet.

---

*NOTE: This section is not included on paper-and-pencil versions of the ASVAB. It is included on the ASVAB computer-adaptive test (CAT) but may be eliminated in the future. Check with your recruiter for details.

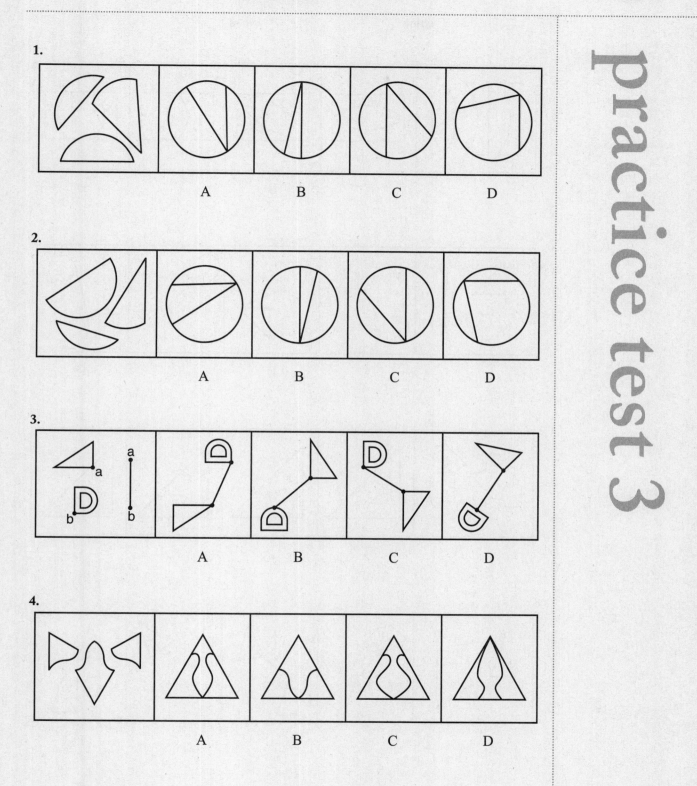

1.

A B C D

2.

A B C D

3.

A B C D

4.

A B C D

practice test 3

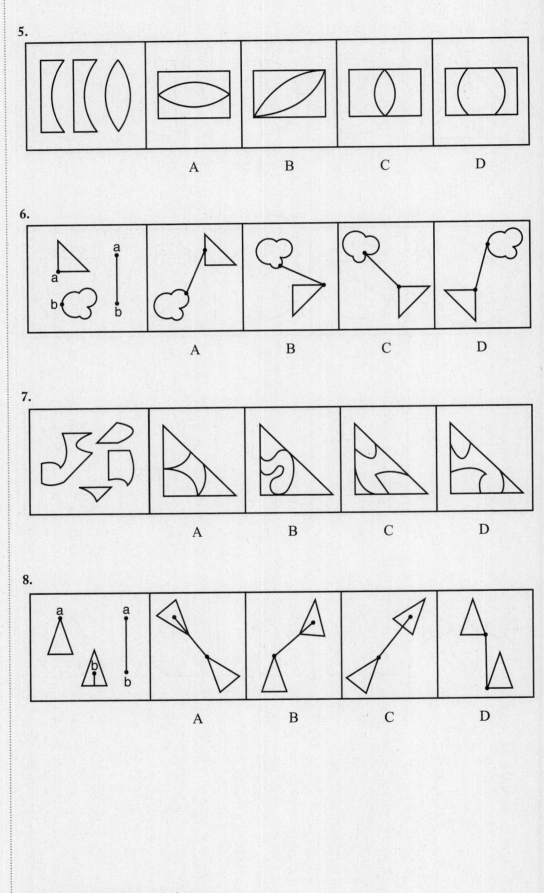

9.

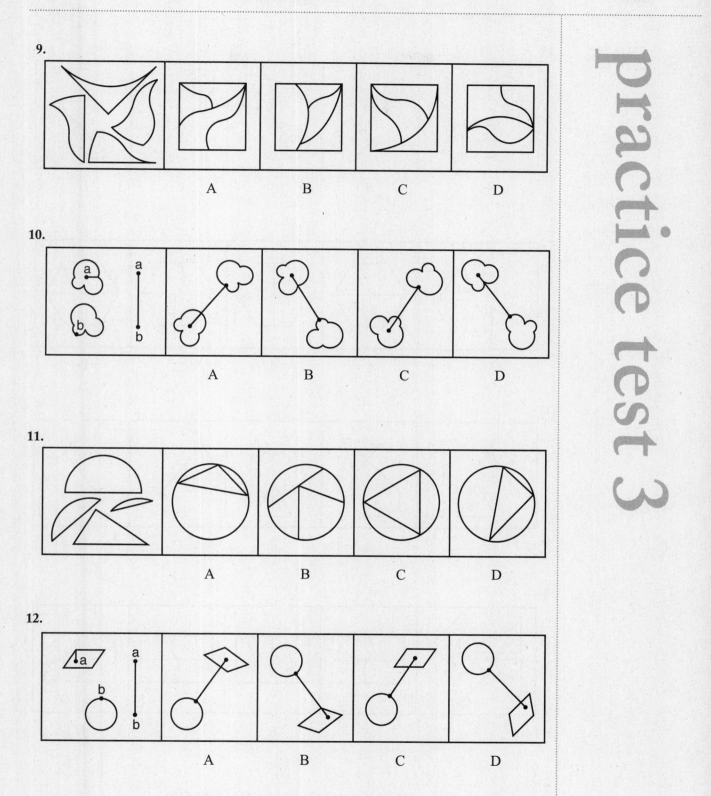

10.

11.

12.

practice test 3

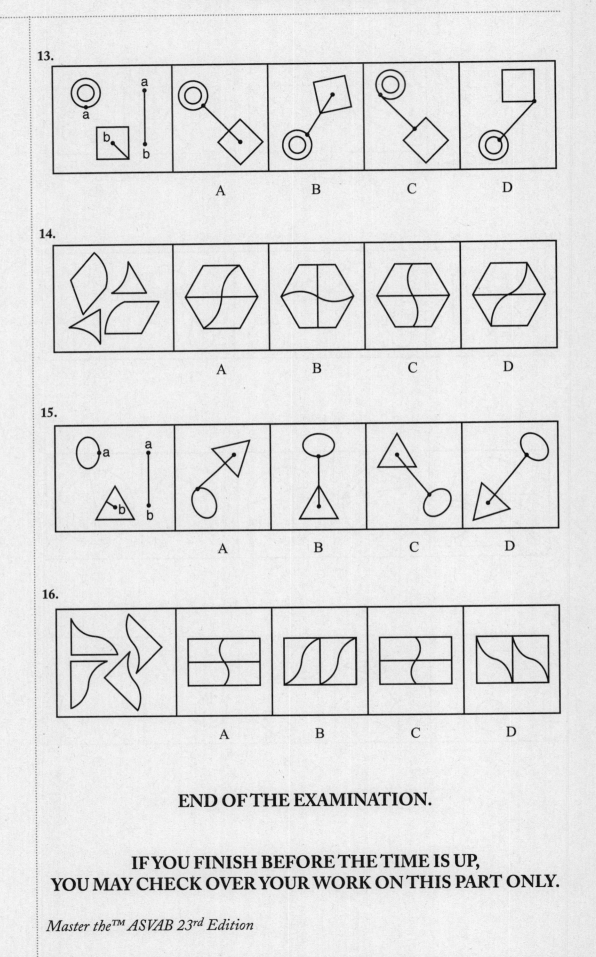

END OF THE EXAMINATION.

**IF YOU FINISH BEFORE THE TIME IS UP,
YOU MAY CHECK OVER YOUR WORK ON THIS PART ONLY.**

ANSWER KEYS AND EXPLANATIONS

PART 1: GENERAL SCIENCE

1. A	6. D	11. B	16. A	21. C
2. C	7. C	12. B	17. D	22. D
3. B	8. C	13. D	18. C	23. C
4. D	9. B	14. C	19. B	24. C
5. A	10. A	15. D	20. A	25. C

1. **The correct answer is A.** Fruits have seeds. Tomatoes, cucumbers, and green peppers have seeds. A potato is a tuber.

2. **The correct answer is C.** In a symbiotic relationship with the soil bacteria known as *rhizobia*, legumes (peanuts) form nodules on their roots (or stems,) to 'fix' nitrogen into a form usable by plants (and animals).

3. **The correct answer is B.** Cigarette smoking can speed up the heartbeat.

4. **The correct answer is D.** The prefix *hypo-* means *below* or *abnormally deficient*. Hypo-thermia is a condition in which the body's temperature falls well below the normal 98.6°F. If it is very hot and you have nothing to drink, you may become dehydrated and might develop *hyper*thermia, overheating.

5. **The correct answer is A.** Lightning is most likely to strike the highest object in an area. If you are standing in an open field or at the top of a small hill, you are likely to be the highest object and a good target. If you stand under a tree, lightning might hit the tree and cause it to fall on you. A car is grounded. If you are inside a car that is hit by lightning, you will only be frightened. The lightning will be transmitted into the ground by the car.

6. **The correct answer is D.** The speed of light is approximately a million times that of sound.

7. **The correct answer is C.** Scientific name are always the genus and the species. The scientific name for human beings is *Homo sapiens*.

8. **The correct answer is C.** Water boils at 212°F and freezes at 32°F.
$212° - 32° = 180°$.

9. **The correct answer is B.** A car's battery has stored energy in the form of sulfuric acid and in cells each with a cathode and anode, which can carry voltage necessary to power various systems of an automobile.

10. **The correct answer is A.** A net force is defined as the sum of all the forces acting on an object. The greater the force on one side of an object determines the direction of the force.

11. **The correct answer is B.** The length of the vector represents the magnitude of the force.

12. **The correct answer is B.** The "highs" on a weather map are based on barometric pressure. The greater the air pressure, the higher the mercury in the barometer.

13. **The correct answer is D.** An atom is the smallest part of an element that retains all the properties of the element.

14. **The correct answer is C.** The action of narcotics is to deaden pain.

15. **The correct answer is D.** Fungi do not contain chlorophyll, so they cannot produce their own food through photosynthesis. Because fungi must rely on decaying organic matter for their food, the forest is a hospitable home.

16. **The correct answer is A.** Coal is formed by the partial decomposition of vegetable matter under the influence of moisture, pressure, and temperature and in the absence of air. If there is coal in Alaska, there must once have been abundant vegetation in Alaska.

17. **The correct answer is D.** Damage to the neck and back is especially dangerous because the spinal cord is so vulnerable. Once the spinal cord is severed, paralysis is inevitable and irreversible, so if there is any question of back or neck injury, the person should be moved only by a skilled professional.

18. **The correct answer is C.** Like displaces like.

19. **The correct answer is B.** One year equals 52 weeks.
52 weeks × 1 month/4 weeks × 1 year/12 months = 1.0 year.

20. **The correct answer is A.** Radiation is the process by which energy is transferred in space.

21. **The correct answer is C.** Barometric pressure is expressed in inches. The range is generally from 28 to 31 inches.

22. **The correct answer is D.** Clover serves to return nitrates to the soil through the action of nitrogen-fixing bacteria in nodules on its roots.

23. **The correct answer is C.** The vascular system is the system of vessels for the circulation of blood. The respiratory system is concerned with respiration (breathing) and the endocrine system with hormones.

24. **The correct answer is C.** Fossils are found chiefly in sedimentary rock. When an organism falls in place and is covered and compressed by sand, mud, or soil, as the sediment hardens into rock, parts of the organism are preserved as fossil.

25. **The correct answer is C.** Milk and milk products, such as cheese and butter, are high in saturated fat and cholesterol.

Items Answered Incorrectly: _____ ; _____ ; _____ ; _____ ; _____ ; _____ ; _____ ; _____ ; _____

Items Unsure Of: _____ ; _____ ; _____ ; _____ ; _____ ; _____ ; _____ ; _____ ; _____

Total Number Answered Correctly: _____

PART 2: ARITHMETIC REASONING

1. B	**7.** D	**13.** D	**19.** B	**25.** C
2. B	**8.** C	**14.** D	**20.** B	**26.** D
3. D	**9.** D	**15.** C	**21.** B	**27.** C
4. B	**10.** B	**16.** C	**22.** D	**28.** D
5. C	**11.** A	**17.** C	**23.** B	**29.** B
6. D	**12.** C	**18.** D	**24.** A	**30.** D

1. **The correct answer is B.** 3 for 20¢ × 4 = 12 for 80¢

   80¢ − 70¢ = 10¢ profit per dozen

   10¢ × 6 doz. = 60¢ total profit

2. **The correct answer is B.** 60 ft. = 20 yd.

   The wall is 4 yd. × 20 yd. = 80 sq. yd.

   $10.50 × 80 = $840

3. **The correct answer is D.**

   $6\frac{1}{2}$ pounds − 4 pounds = $2\frac{1}{2}$ pounds

   There are 5 half-pounds in $2\frac{1}{2}$ pounds

   $9.26 + 5(1.06) = $9.26 + 5.30
   $$= $14.56$$

4. **The correct answer is B.** The whole paper is 9 in. × 12 in. = 108 sq. in. The paper she uses is

   9 in. − 1 in. − 1 in. = 7 in. × 12 in. −

   $1\frac{1}{2}$ in. − $1\frac{1}{2}$ in. = 9 in.

   The paper she uses is 7 in. × 9 in. = 63 sq. in. $\frac{63}{108} = \frac{7}{12}$ is used for typing.

5. **The correct answer is C.** $2,300 − $331.50 = $1968.50.

6. **The correct answer is D.** $0.2\bar{2}$ = approximately 22%

   $$\frac{2}{9} = 9\overline{)2.00}$$
   $$\begin{array}{r} .22\bar{2} \\ \underline{18} \\ 20 \\ \underline{18} \\ 2 \end{array}$$

7. **The correct answer is D.** 2 in. = 5 ft.; therefore,

   1 in. = $2\frac{1}{2}$ ft.;

   $7\frac{1}{2} \times 2\frac{1}{2} = 18\frac{3}{4}$ ft.

8. **The correct answer is C.** $375 is 75% of the original price.

   The original price = $375 ÷ 75%
   $$= $375 ÷ .75$$
   $$= $500$$

9. **The correct answer is D.**

   Perimeter = $2i + 2w$
   $$= 2(46 \text{ ft.}) + 2(34 \text{ ft.})$$
   $$= 92 \text{ ft.} + 68 \text{ ft.}$$
   $$= 160 \text{ ft.}$$

   $160 ÷ 3 = 53\frac{1}{3}$ yd.

10. **The correct answer is B.** First rename the feet as inches. 35 ft. 6 in. = 420 in. + 6 in. = 426 in.

    426 ÷ 4 = 106.5 in. per shelf = 8 ft. $10\frac{1}{2}$ in. per shelf

11. **The correct answer is A.** 4($2.98) + 2($1.99) + 1($2.50) = $18.40.

12. **The correct answer is C.** $600 × .08 = $48 × 2 = $96

13. **The correct answer is D.** $9.80 is regular pay.

    $1\frac{1}{2}($9.80) = 19.60 is overtime pay.

    40($9.80) + 10($19.60) = $588.

14. **The correct answer is D.** $68 × 40% = $27.20

15. **The correct answer is C.** Eighteen clerks can do the job in 26 days. Therefore, 1 clerk takes 18 × 26 = 468 days to do the job. To get the job done in 12 days will take 468 ÷ 12 = 39 clerks.

16. **The correct answer is C.** The carton contains 9 × 12 = 108 folders. 108 − 53 = 55 remain in carton.

17. **The correct answer is C.** $25 ÷ $4.95 = 5.05—he could buy 5 ties. $4.95 × 5 = $24.75. After buying 5 ties the man would still have 25¢ left.

18. **The correct answer is D.**

$ 20.56
 32.90
+ 20.78
$ 74.24 ÷ 2 = $37.12 left

19. **The correct answer is B.**

$\frac{16}{24} = \frac{4}{x}$ Cross multiply
$16x = 96$
$x = 6$ ft.

20. **The correct answer is B.** $70 + 10($35) = $420

21. **The correct answer is B.** 11 lb., 16 oz. − 9 lb., 9 oz. = 2 lb., 7 oz.

22. **The correct answer is D.** 12 ft. × 15 ft. = 4 yd. × 5 yd. = 20 yd.^{2}

23. **The correct answer is B.** $12.50 − $10.98 = $1.52 cost to upgrade the blouse; $5 − $1.52 = $3.48 change.

24. **The correct answer is A.**
$52.50 + $46.80 + $42.60 = $141.90
$141.90 ÷ 3 = $47.30

25. **The correct answer is C.** Only 10 boys can play at one time. Therefore, the 30 boys must be divided into 3 groups. Each group can then play 45 min. ÷ 3 = 15 min.

26. **The correct answer is D.** 65¢ − 5¢ for the first day = 60¢ for the other days. 60¢ ÷ 2¢ = 30 other days. The book was 31 days overdue.

27. **The correct answer is C.** 1 lb. = 16 oz.; 2 lb. = 32 oz.; 32 oz. ÷ 2 oz. = 16 slices.

28. **The correct answer is D.**

$\frac{1}{2}$ cup of spinach = 80 calories
$\frac{1}{2}$ cup of peas = 300 calories
1 cup of peas = 600 calories
$\frac{2}{3}$ cup of peas = 400 calories
400 ÷ 80 = 5 half cups of spinach
= $2\frac{1}{2}$ cups of spinach

29. **The correct answer is B.** 30 min. for 6 pages; 1 hr. for 12 pages; 126 ÷ 12 = 10.5 hrs.

30. **The correct answer is D.** 9 hrs. = 540 mins.; 540 ÷ 45 = 12. The night watchman stops at the storage area 12 times during his tour plus once at the beginning of his tour of duty for a total of 13 times.

Items Answered Incorrectly: _____ ; _____ ; _____ ; _____ ; _____ ; _____ ; _____ ; _____ ; _____

Items Unsure Of: _____ ; _____ ; _____ ; _____ ; _____ ; _____ ; _____ ; _____ ; _____

Total Number Answered Correctly: _____

PART 3: Word Knowledge

1. D	8. C	15. A	22. C	29. D
2. B	9. A	16. A	23. C	30. C
3. C	10. D	17. D	24. C	31. B
4. D	11. B	18. B	25. B	32. A
5. A	12. B	19. A	26. A	33. D
6. D	13. D	20. D	27. B	34. C
7. B	14. C	21. D	28. C	35. C

1. **The correct answer is D.** *Superiority* is *excellence.*

2. **The correct answer is B.** *Absurd* means *irrational, unreasonable,* or *foolish.*

3. **The correct answer is C.** *Inflammable* means *easily inflamed,* hence *explosive.*

4. **The correct answer is D.** *Conscious* means *mentally awake* or *aware.*

5. **The correct answer is A.** Literally, an *impasse* means *a blocked path,* but it can also mean *a point in negotiations where there is no solution.*

6. **The correct answer is D.** To *assume* is to *take for granted* or to *suppose.*

7. **The correct answer is B.** That which is *counterfeit* is an *imitation made with intent to defraud,* hence *false.*

8. **The correct answer is C.** That which is done *expertly* is done *skillfully.* It might also be done quickly but not necessarily so.

9. **The correct answer is A.** *Loquacious* most nearly means *talkative, chatty,* and *verbose.*

10. **The correct answer is D.** *Allegiance* means *devotion* or *loyalty.*

11. **The correct answer is B.** To *yearn* is to *have a great desire for* or to *be filled with longing.*

12. **The correct answer is B.** The *summit* is the *top.*

13. **The correct answer is D.** To *heed* is to *pay attention to* or to *take notice of.*

14. **The correct answer is C.** *Malodorous* means *foul-smelling, stinking, smelly,* or *foul.*

15. **The correct answer is A.** To *imitate* is to *copy.*

16. **The correct answer is A.** *Severity* means *seriousness, extreme strictness,* or *harshness.* It does not necessarily imply unfairness.

17. **The correct answer is D.** *Negligent* means *careless, inattentive,* or *remiss,* sometimes with disastrous results.

18. **The correct answer is B.** *Leisure* is *freedom from pressure.* The trip could be *leisurely* or *unhurried.*

19. **The correct answer is A.** *Omnipotent* means *all-powerful, invincible, unstoppable,* as well as, *supreme.*

20. **The correct answer is D.** *Familiar* means *well-known.* (Think of the word "family.")

21. **The correct answer is D.** An *acute* pain may well be alarming, but what makes it *acute* is its *sharpness.*

22. **The correct answer is C.** To be *bewildered* is to be *confused* or *puzzled.*

23. **The correct answer is C.** The *conclusion* is the *end*.

24. **The correct answer is C.** An *aroma* is a *pleasing smell* or *fragrance*.

25. **The correct answer is B.** *Penury* describes *extreme poverty* and *destitution*.

26. **The correct answer is A.** To *amplify* is to *enlarge* by adding illustrations or details, in short, to *expand*.

27. **The correct answer is B.** *Intact* means *unimpaired, whole*, or *undamaged*.

28. **The correct answer is C.** *Potent* means *powerful* or *effective*. The word that means *drinkable* is *potable*.

29. **The correct answer is D.** To *terminate* is to *end*. The *end* of a train line is the *terminus* or *terminal*.

30. **The correct answer is C.** *Notorious* means *well-known*, generally in an unfavorable sense.

31. **The correct answer is B.** Something that is *serrated* is *notched*. A knife's edge, for example, may be *serrated*.

32. **The correct answer is A.** *Indigent* means *needy* or *poor*. Indigent people might be lazy or homeless, but their indigence is their poverty. Indigent people might also become angry or *indignant*.

33. **The correct answer is D.** The *technique* is the *method* by which something is done.

34. **The correct answer is C.** One's *vocation* is one's *occupation* or *calling*.

35. **The correct answer is C.** That which is *mature* is *fully aged* or *ripe*.

Items Answered Incorrectly: _____ ; _____ ; _____ ; _____ ; _____ ; _____ ; _____ ; _____ ; _____

Items Unsure Of: _____ ; _____ ; _____ ; _____ ; _____ ; _____ ; _____ ; _____ ; _____

Total Number Answered Correctly: _____

PART 4: PARAGRAPH COMPREHENSION

1. B	4. D	7. A	10. C	13. A
2. D	5. C	8. C	11. C	14. D
3. C	6. D	9. D	12. D	15. B

1. **The correct answer is B.** The passage states that mechanics must be instructed in safety rules that they must follow for their own protection. This implies that industrial accidents may result from ignorance of safety rules.

2. **The correct answer is D.** If the collection letter must show clear organization and show evidence of a mind that has a specific end in view, it should be carefully planned.

3. **The correct answer is C.** When the activities of an individual come in conflict with the community interest, the individual's rights are no longer considered to be of greatest importance but actually become secondary.

4. **The correct answer is D.** The passage does not support any of the first three options but states Edison invented the phonograph and motion picture film.

5. **The correct answer is C.** The last sentence in the passage states that burning wood produces more CO, carbon monoxide, than natural gas does when it burns. CO is the chemical formula for carbon monoxide.

6. **The correct answer is D.** The key word is *compromise*. A railroad line must be built along logical trade and commerce routes even if construction is more expensive.

7. **The correct answer is A.** The survey showed that of all the subjects, word processing helped most in business. It was also considered valuable by college students in their schoolwork.

8. **The correct answer is C.** The second sentence states that direct lighting causes glare on the working surface.

9. **The correct answer is D.** The connective "Others, however," with which the second sentence begins, implies the converse of the first sentence. Some citizens are public-spirited; others, however, are not.

10. **The correct answer is C.** A laborer who has only one skill may find himself or herself unemployed if that skill is not in demand. A more versatile worker can find a job requiring another skill.

11. **The correct answer is C.** The third sentence states that heating the drill will spoil its temper and cutting edges.

12. **The correct answer is D.** The second sentence states that the drill point must be withdrawn frequently to cool it.

13. **The correct answer is A.** If an employee is injured, no matter how small the injury, he or she should have the injury treated. A small cut not attended to can easily become infected.

14. **The correct answer is D.** Loose or torn clothing should not be worn near moving machinery.

15. **The correct answer is B.** Wearing shoes with open toes can easily lead to foot injuries. Accordingly, they should not be worn.

Items Answered Incorrectly: _____ ; _____ ; _____ ; _____ ; _____ ; _____ ; _____ ; _____ ; _____

Items Unsure Of: _____ ; _____ ; _____ ; _____ ; _____ ; _____ ; _____ ; _____ ; _____

Total Number Answered Correctly: _____

PART 5: MATHEMATICS KNOWLEDGE

1. C	6. B	11. B	16. D	21. B
2. D	7. A	12. D	17. C	22. C
3. C	8. D	13. C	18. B	23. A
4. D	9. B	14. B	19. C	24. B
5. B	10. C	15. B	20. B	25. A

1. **The correct answer is C.** $8 \times 8 \times 8 = 512$

2. **The correct answer is D.** The fundamental counting principle states that if one event can occur in x way, and a second event can occur in y ways, and a third event can occur in z ways, and so forth, then the total number of ways an event can occur is $x \cdot y \cdot z$. So, $3 \cdot 4 \cdot 5 = 60$.

3. **The correct answer is C.** The formula to find the circumference of a circle is $2\pi r$. The formula to find the area of a circle is πr^2—the only number that has the same value when multiplied by 2 or squared is 2.

4. **The correct answer is D.** Dividing 2.454 by 0.06 on paper yields 40.9.

5. **The correct answer is B.** Right now he gets 120 mi. ÷ 12 gal. = 10 mpg. After carburetor adjustment, he will need 80% of 12, or 9.6 gal., to go 120 miles. He will then get 120 mi. ÷ 9.6 gal. = 12.5 mpg. 12 gal × 12.5 mpg = 150 miles on 12 gal.

6. **The correct answer is B.** Perimeter = $r + r + r + r = 4r$

7. **The correct answer is A.** By definition, a quadrilateral is a parallelogram only if both pairs of its opposite sides are parallel.

8. **The correct answer is D.** To solve for h, divide both sides of the equation by $l \cdot w$ which yields $\frac{v}{l \cdot w} = h$.

9. **The correct answer is B.** $100 \times 5\% = 5$; $5 \times 5\% = 0.25$

10. **The correct answer is C.**

$$\frac{3}{8}x = 96$$
$$3x = 96 \times 8 = 768$$
$$x = 256$$

11. **The correct answer is B.** 6 words per line × 5 lines per inch = 30 words per inch; 30 words per inch × 8 inches = 240 words. If the article has 270 words and there is space for only 240 words, then 30 words must be deleted.

12. **The correct answer is D.** Let x = measurement of supplement; $5x$ = measurement of angle.

$$x + 5x = 180°$$
$$6x = 180°$$
$$x = 30°$$
$$5x = 150°$$

13. **The correct answer is C.** If $\frac{2}{3}$ of the jar is filled in 1 minute, then $\frac{1}{3}$ of the jar is filled in $\frac{1}{2}$ minute. Since the jar is $\frac{2}{3}$ full, $\frac{1}{3}$ remains to be filled. The jar will be full in another $\frac{1}{2}$ minute.

14. **The correct answer is B.** The quickest way to answer this question is to try substituting the given values. If $x = 2$, then $2 - 2 = 2 - 2$ is a true statement.

To solve algebraically:
$$2 - x = x - 2 \text{ (add 2, add } x\text{)}$$
$$4 = 2x \text{ (divide by 2)}$$
$$2 = x$$

15. The correct answer is B.

$\frac{2}{3}$ of 60 min. = 40 min.

5 : 00 + 40 min. = 5 : 40

16. The correct answer is D. Assign arbitrary values to solve this problem:

A square 10 ft. × 10 ft. = 100 sq. ft.

A rectangle 9 ft. × 11 ft. = 99 sq. ft.

$100 - 99 = 1$; $\frac{1}{100} = 1\%$

17. The correct answer is C. Diagram this problem:

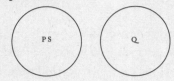

18. The correct answer is B.

$$\begin{array}{r} x + a \\ \underline{x + b} \\ x^2 + ax \\ \underline{+ \quad bx + ab} \\ x^2 + ax + bx + ab = x^2 + (a + b)x + ab \end{array}$$

19. The correct answer is C.

$\frac{5}{4}x = \frac{5}{4}$

$x = \frac{5}{4} \div \frac{5}{4} = \frac{\cancel{5}^1}{\cancel{4}_1} \times \frac{\cancel{4}^1}{\cancel{5}_1} = 1; 1 - 1 = 0$

20. The correct answer is B. $a^2 - 2ab + b^2 = (a - b)(a - b) = (a - b)^2$

21. The correct answer is B. $0.017\overline{)5.100}^{\,300.}$

To divide by a decimal, move the decimal point of the divisor to the right until the divisor becomes a whole number. Move the decimal point of the dividend to the right the same number of spaces. Place the decimal point of the quotient directly above the decimal point in the dividend.

22. The correct answer is C. The formula for the area of a circle is πr^2. In this problem, $r^2 = 64$ so $r = 8$. The circle is tangent with the square on all four sides; the radius is exactly $\frac{1}{2}$ the length of a side of the square. Each side, then, is 16 units long. The formula for the perimeter of a square is $P = 4s$, so $4 \times 16 = 64$.

23. The correct answer is A. The formula needed is $C = 2\pi r$, Circumference = 2 • π • radius. So, substitute 90π in the equation for C, $90\pi = 2\pi r$, then dividing both sides by 2π, the answer is 45.

24. The correct answer is B. A prime number is a number that has only two factors, 1 and itself. Since 31 has no other factors other than 1 and 31, it is a prime number.

25. The correct answer is A. If X is 5 years older than Y, then X will always be 5 years older than Y, therefore the ratio of their ages will not change.

Items Answered Incorrectly: _____ ; _____ ; _____ ; _____ ; _____ ; _____ ; _____ ; _____ ; _____

Items Unsure Of: _____ ; _____ ; _____ ; _____ ; _____ ; _____ ; _____ ; _____ ; _____

Total Number Answered Correctly: _____

PART 6: ELECTRONICS INFORMATION

1. A	**5.** D	**9.** C	**13.** A	**17.** D
2. C	**6.** A	**10.** B	**14.** D	**18.** A
3. C	**7.** C	**11.** B	**15.** A	**19.** B
4. D	**8.** D	**12.** A	**16.** C	**20.** D

1. **The correct answer is A.** Outdoor boxes and fittings must be weatherproof to withstand any problems caused by moisture.

2. **The correct answer is C.** A rectifier is a device that converts AC current into DC current by allowing the current to flow in only one direction while blocking the flow of electricity in the reverse direction.

3. **The correct answer is C.** The starting current of a motor is normally six times greater than its running current.

4. **The correct answer is D.** It is not enough information because it will depend on whether or not it was PNP or NPN. PNP and NPN sensors are 3-wire DC devices. The difference is in the type of transistor used in the sensor.

5. **The correct answer is D.** According to Ohm's law:

$V = IR$; $V = 5 \times 20$; $V = 100$ volts

6. **The correct answer is A.** The values are simply added.

7. **The correct answer is C.** The symbol is a standard one and shows the two conducting surfaces of a capacitor.

8. **The correct answer is D.** An electric shock is determined by the contact resistance. If a person is standing in water while being shocked, the shock will be severe because water reduces the amount of resistance and the electricity will flow freely through his body.

9. **The correct answer is C.** Locknuts are bent so that their metal edges will bite into the terminal board and will require the use of a wrench to loosen them.

10. **The correct answer is B.** The color combinations or RRRG will result in a value of 22k 5%.

11. **The correct answer is B.** Paper is not used in the makeup of a lighting wire because a small electrical charge could set it on fire.

12. **The correct answer is A.** No electricity flows through a burned-out bulb. However, the voltmeter acts as a bypass around the burned-out bulb and is therefore connected in series. It measures all of the voltage in the circuit. The voltage is 600 volts.

13. **The correct answer is A.** Silver is a much better conductor than copper. It is not used in wires because it is expensive.

14. **The correct answer is D.** A household iron is the only device that depends on a thermostat to control its use. An overheated iron will damage the clothing that it is supposed to press.

15. **The correct answer is A.** An alternator is a device that is found in automobiles. It is used to produce AC. In a car, the electronic circuitry changes AC to DC.

16. **The correct answer is C.** An incandescent electric light bulb is a typical light bulb found in the home. When the incandescent bulb, which is rated for 110 volts, is run at 90 volts, it will not burn as brightly. Because the 110-volt capacity is not being used, it will last longer.

17. **The correct answer is D.** This object is a ground clamp. It will be tightened around a cold water pipe. A grounding wire will be attached to the screw and thus stray electricity will be grounded.

18. **The correct answer is A.** When a refrigerator motor starts up, it draws considerable current. This takes current away from the bulb. Thicker wires would allow more electricity to pass through, but they would be too expensive and impractical.

19. **The correct answer is B.** Use the formula

$$R_{total} = \frac{(R1R2)}{(R1+R2)}$$
$$= \left(\frac{10 \times 10}{10+10} \right)$$
$$= \frac{100}{20}$$
$$= 5$$

20. **The correct answer is D.** Electric power is measured in units called *watts*. A watt is calculated by multiplying voltage by amperage. Watts are measured by a wattmeter.

Items Answered Incorrectly: _____ ; _____ ; _____ ; _____ ; _____ ; _____ ; _____ ; _____ ; _____

Items Unsure Of: _____ ; _____ ; _____ ; _____ ; _____ ; _____ ; _____ ; _____ ; _____

Total Number Answered Correctly: _____

PART 7: AUTO & SHOP INFORMATION

1. A	6. B	11. B	16. C	21. D
2. C	7. D	12. D	17. B	22. B
3. D	8. D	13. C	18. B	23. C
4. B	9. C	14. C	19. B	24. D
5. B	10. A	15. A	20. A	25. A

1. **The correct answer is A.** Engine bearings hold the crankshaft in place and are lubricated with engine oil. The oil lessens the friction caused by metal rubbing on metal and stops the metal from burning.

2. **The correct answer is C.** The rotor determines which spark plug ignites. It is located under the distributor cap. The rotor is connected by a shaft to the engine and is timed to ignite the spark plug at the top of the power stroke.

3. **The correct answer is D.** Piston slap occurs when a piston slams into the sides of the cylinder wall as it travels inside the cylinder. The piston rings keep the tight fit necessary between the wall and the piston. Properly ground pistons will move more smoothly.

4. **The correct answer is B.** The fuel-injection system eliminates the need for a carburetor by actually forcing the gas-air mixture into each of the cylinders instead of having the gasoline mix with the air in the carburetor and then go through the intake manifold.

5. **The correct answer is B.** Water in the crankcase is usually caused by condensation. A cracked engine block can also cause this condition, but this is not usual.

6. **The correct answer is B.** The ignition coil takes the low-voltage supplied by the car's battery and converts it to the high-voltage required to fire the spark plugs.

7. **The correct answer is D.** If the spark plug gap was set closer than required, the spark plugs would fire sooner than necessary. This would cause a rougher idle speed and a longer power stroke.

8. **The correct answer is D.** The device being described is a voltage regulator. When the battery becomes fully charged, a relay opens up so that the battery doesn't overcharge. A permanently closed voltage regulator will cause overcharging.

9. **The correct answer is C.** The piston rings form a seal around the piston and the wall of the cylinder. Dirty oil in the crankcase will stop the rings from working properly.

10. **The correct answer is A.** If an engine loses oil pressure, the car must be stopped immediately. Otherwise, it will overheat and become damaged.

11. **The correct answer is B.** Nail holes are filled with putty after applying the priming coat, before you apply the finishing coat of paint.

12. **The correct answer is D.** Although this tool looks like a screwdriver, the head fits into a hex nut and works like a socket wrench.

13. **The correct answer is C.** The length of a flat head screw is its entire length.

14. **The correct answer is C.** If you look at the top of a hammer where it is joined to the handle, you will see either the top of a wooden wedge or the top of a metal wedge. Driving another wedge into the handle will tighten the hammer.

15. **The correct answer is A.** The end grain of a block of wood is sanded crosswise.

16. **The correct answer is C.** The tool is an offset screwdriver. It is used for tightening screws in hard-to-reach places where a regular screwdriver cannot turn in a complete revolution.

17. **The correct answer is B.** A star drill is used to drill into masonry. Then an expansion shield is placed into the hole.

18. **The correct answer is B.** "Skin" forms when air combines with paint. To stop this from happening, pour a thin layer of solvent over the paint. The air will then be prevented from reaching the paint and forming a layer of skin.

19. **The correct answer is B.** Figure B is a keyhole saw used to make curved cuts; A is a backsaw; C is a rip or crosscut saw; and D is a hacksaw.

20. **The correct answer is A.** The diagram below illustrates how a lag screw can fit into the head of a wrench.

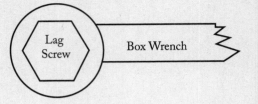

21. **The correct answer is D.** Paint adheres best to a dry surface. If the surface is wet when it is painted, the moisture becomes trapped. Blistering occurs when the trapped moisture expands and breaks through the paint.

22. **The correct answer is B.** A spoke shave is used to plane a dowel-shaped surface. The other planes are used to smooth flat surfaces.

23. **The correct answer is C.** Figure C is a pipe wrench; A is a crescent or expandable wrench; B is a ratchet wrench; and D is an open-end wrench.

24. **The correct answer is D.** A lathe is a machine that rotates a piece of wood to create a uniform circular design. The wood is rotated as it is cut with the blade(s) of the lathe. In this example, a baseball bat is the only rounded object.

25. **The correct answer is A.** A squeegee is a rubber wiper that removes water from a wet window.

Items Answered Incorrectly: _____ ; _____ ; _____ ; _____ ; _____ ; _____ ; _____ ; _____ ; _____

Items Unsure Of: _____ ; _____ ; _____ ; _____ ; _____ ; _____ ; _____ ; _____ ; _____

Total Number Answered Correctly: _____

PART 8: MECHANICAL COMPREHENSION

1. A	6. D	11. D	16. C	21. A
2. B	7. B	12. C	17. C	22. C
3. C	8. A	13. D	18. B	23. D
4. C	9. A	14. B	19. A	24. B
5. A	10. D	15. C	20. B	25. C

1. **The correct answer is A.** Here, right (R) can be thought of as how a point on the axle would appear to be moving. If gear Z moves to the right, gear Y will move in the opposite direction, to the left; and gear X will move in the opposite direction from gear Y, to the right.

2. **The correct answer is B.** If pipe 2 is open while pipe 1 is closed, then the level will drop to the lowest level of 2, leaving the volume below 2 still filled, having no way to discharge. All other statements are true.

3. **The correct answer is C.** The hand wheel tightens to the left when rotated clockwise since it is a right-handed thread. It goes 1 inch (20 revolutions = 1 inch). It then pulls the threaded block 1 inch in the opposite direction.

4. **The correct answer is C.** The function of A and B in the crankshaft is to counterbalance the weight for smooth piston motion.

5. **The correct answer is A.** Air surrounding a cold-water pipe contains water vapor at room temperature. The cold water cools the air in the immediate vicinity, reducing its ability to hold water vapor (warm air will hold more water than cool air). Water condenses on the cool pipe as sweat.

6. **The correct answer is D.** Newton's First Law of Motion states a body at rest will stay at rest unless acted on by an outside force. Conversely, a body in motion stays in motion unless acted on by an outside force. In this picture, both objects are at rest (equilibrium). When an outside force is added to weight 1, the equilibrium changes, moving the weight downward. Because the pulley has practically no friction, the weight strikes the floor.

7. **The correct answer is B.** if nut A were removed, it would be necessary to move nut C to the right to counter-balance the loss of the weight of nut A.

8. **The correct answer is A.** An air valve on a radiator removes air from the steam pipes. If air is trapped in the pipes, it prevents the steam from going to the radiator. This would prevent the radiator from producing heat.

9. **The correct answer is A.** Each time the rotating arm makes a complete revolution, it moves the slotted disc ¼ of a turn.

10. **The correct answer is D.** Each division marks 2 units: 20 units/10 divisions = 2 units/division. The pointer is $3\frac{1}{2}$ divisions above 10 or 2 units/division × $3\frac{1}{2}$ divisions = 7; 7 + 10 = 17.

11. **The correct answer is D.** The volume of water flowing at points 1, 2, and 3 must be the same because of the conservation of mass: mass in = mass out. Also, since no water is added or removed after point 1, there cannot be any change of volume.

12. **The correct answer is C.** Gear 1 turns clockwise; gear 2 turns counterclockwise; gears 3 and 4 turn clockwise.

13. **The correct answer is D.** By the process of elimination, numbers 1 and 3 are not shaped cylindrically and will wobble in the circular hole; number 2 may fall out if the assembly is tilted; but number 4, a cotter pin, will exert the proper tension to remain inside the hole without slipping.

14. **The correct answer is B.** Because of the ratio, the pinion will rotate 3 times for each rotation of the gear; 300 rotations of the gear will cause $300 \times 3 = 900$ rotations of the pinion.

15. **The correct answer is C.**
$2\frac{1}{2}$ ft. = 30 in.; $\frac{30}{6} = 5$; TMA = 5.

16. **The correct answer is C.** Begin with part 4, the line on which the force is directed; part 1 is the next strand; then part 3; and finally, attached to the lower block, is part 2.

17. **The correct answer is C.** *Step 1:* Pulley X revolves at 100 rpm (given). *Step 2:* Middle pulley (inner) rotates at $100 \times \frac{10}{7}$. (Remember that a larger pulley causes a smaller one to travel faster by the ratio of their diameters.)

    Step 3: Pulley Y travels at
    $\left(100 \times \frac{10}{7}\right) \times \frac{14}{5} = 400$ rpm.

18. **The correct answer is B.** Because the load is closer to upright A, it supports more of the load. If they were directly over A, all of the weight would be supported by A; then upright B could be removed completely.

19. **The correct answer is A.** An inclined plane is a sloping, triangular shape, used here as a wedge to force open an axe cut made in the wood.

20. **The correct answer is B.** The bolt thread makes one revolution per eighth of an inch, or has 8 threads in one inch.

21. **The correct answer is A.** Once every second = 60 times a minute. With 10 projecting rods on the wheel, the wheel must rotate at 6 rpm to make 60 rod contacts per minute.

22. **The correct answer is C.** The simplest and least expensive thing to do is to change the washer, which may have deteriorated because of excessive wear.

23. **The correct answer is D.** Choice A does not permit air flow through G and S; choice B does not permit air flow through S; choice C does not permit air flow through G; choice D is correct.

24. **The correct answer is B.** Wood is an insulator. Silver is a better conductor than steel.

25. **The correct answer is C.** One revolution of the rear wheel causes 10 teeth to rotate completely. But one revolution of the front sprocket causes 20 teeth to rotate completely, making the 10-teeth rear sprocket revolve twice.

Items Answered Incorrectly: _____ ; _____ ; _____ ; _____ ; _____ ; _____ ; _____ ; _____ ;_____

Items Unsure Of: _____ ; _____ ; _____ ; _____ ; _____ ; _____ ; _____ ; _____ ;_____

Total Number Answered Correctly: _____

PART 9: ASSEMBLING OBJECTS

1. D	5. A	8. D	11. B	14. D
2. A	6. C	9. C	12. B	15. D
3. C	7. D	10. B	13. B	16. B
4. D				

1. The correct answer is D.

2. The correct answer is A.

3. The correct answer is C.

4. The correct answer is D.

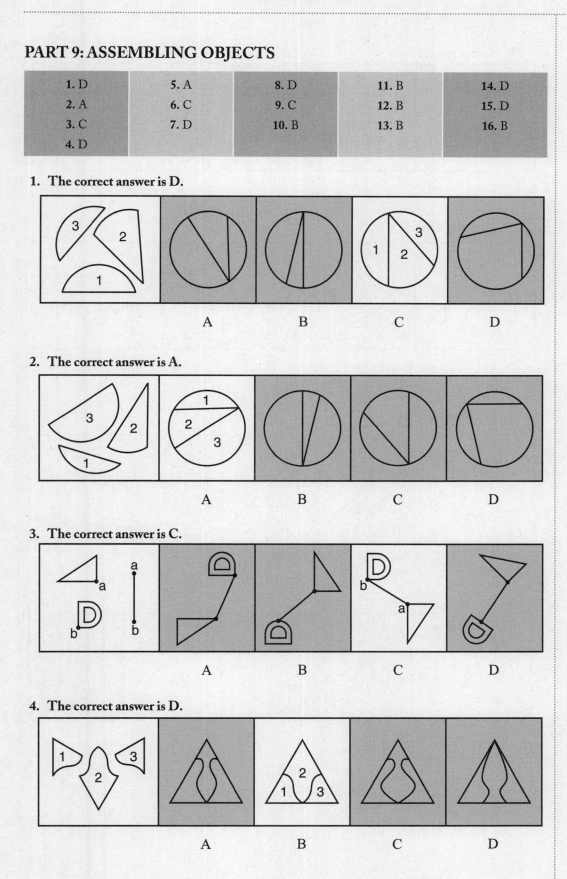

5. The correct answer is A.

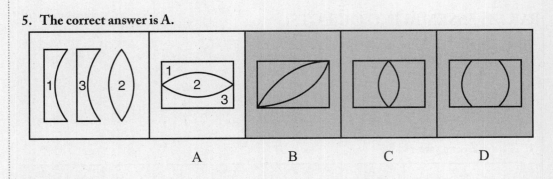

A   B   C   D

6. The correct answer is C.

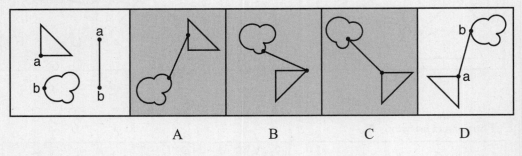

A   B   C   D

7. The correct answer is D.

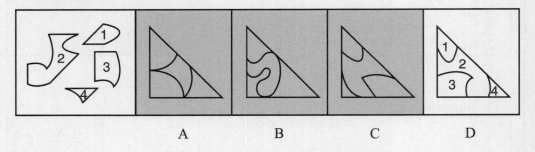

A   B   C   D

8. The correct answer is D.

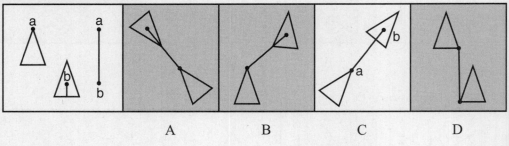

A   B   C   D

9. The correct answer is C.

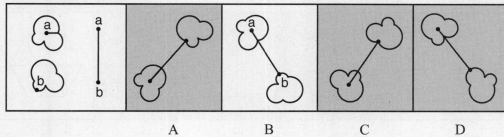

A   B   C   D

10. The correct answer is B.

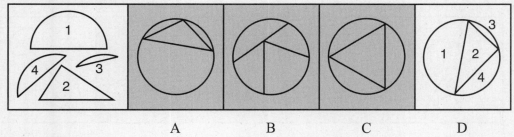

A   B   C   D

11. The correct answer is B.

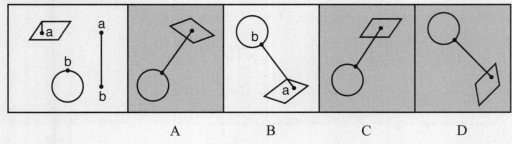

A   B   C   D

12. The correct answer is B.

A   B   C   D

answers practice test 3

13. The correct answer is B.

14. The correct answer is D.

15. The correct answer is D.

16. The correct answer is B.

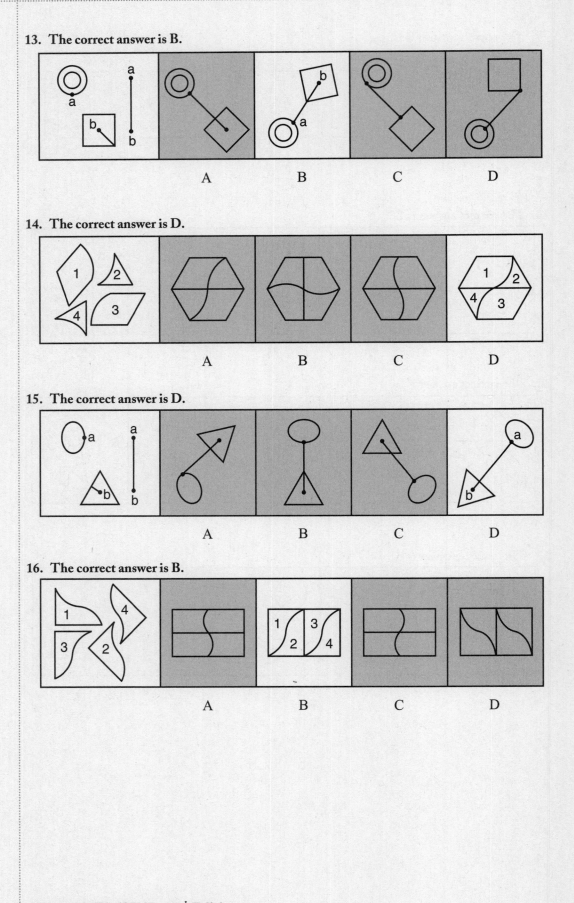

Practice Test 4

Here is your fourth opportunity to take a practice ASVAB test. All of your practice and preparation will be evident in your results of this final test. Once you have completed the test, review the scores you recorded for each Practice Test in the Self-Evaluation Chart. You can then determine if you feel prepared and confident enough for your test day or if you need further practice.

Here are the guidelines again to help you make the most of this practice test:

- Take this test under "real" test conditions (time yourself, take it in a quiet room without distractions, and use the sample answer sheets).

- Time each test carefully and do not go over the time allotted for each section.

- Use the answer keys to get your test scores and to evaluate your performance on each test.

- Record the number of items you answered correctly and incorrectly for each section in the answer chart provided at the end of the test. Also, record the number of questions you want to review further or were unsure about.

- Carefully review and understand the answer explanations to all questions you answered incorrectly.

- Don't forget to review each of the questions that you answered correctly but may not be sure of. This is a necessary step to gain the knowledge and expertise you need to get the highest scores possible on the real ASVAB tests.

- Transfer your scores for each section of Practice Test 4 to the Self-Evaluation Chart on page 22. This will enable you to track your progress as you continue to prepare for the actual test.

- Use the sample answer sheets provided to record your answers. If you want, you can cut them out to make them easier to use and to simulate actual test conditions.

485

ANSWER SHEET PRACTICE TEST 4

Part 1: General Science

1. Ⓐ Ⓑ Ⓒ Ⓓ   2. Ⓐ Ⓑ Ⓒ Ⓓ   3. Ⓐ Ⓑ Ⓒ Ⓓ   4. Ⓐ Ⓑ Ⓒ Ⓓ   5. Ⓐ Ⓑ Ⓒ Ⓓ
6. Ⓐ Ⓑ Ⓒ Ⓓ   7. Ⓐ Ⓑ Ⓒ Ⓓ   8. Ⓐ Ⓑ Ⓒ Ⓓ   9. Ⓐ Ⓑ Ⓒ Ⓓ   10. Ⓐ Ⓑ Ⓒ Ⓓ
11. Ⓐ Ⓑ Ⓒ Ⓓ   12. Ⓐ Ⓑ Ⓒ Ⓓ   13. Ⓐ Ⓑ Ⓒ Ⓓ   14. Ⓐ Ⓑ Ⓒ Ⓓ   15. Ⓐ Ⓑ Ⓒ Ⓓ
16. Ⓐ Ⓑ Ⓒ Ⓓ   17. Ⓐ Ⓑ Ⓒ Ⓓ   18. Ⓐ Ⓑ Ⓒ Ⓓ   19. Ⓐ Ⓑ Ⓒ Ⓓ   20. Ⓐ Ⓑ Ⓒ Ⓓ
21. Ⓐ Ⓑ Ⓒ Ⓓ   22. Ⓐ Ⓑ Ⓒ Ⓓ   23. Ⓐ Ⓑ Ⓒ Ⓓ   24. Ⓐ Ⓑ Ⓒ Ⓓ   25. Ⓐ Ⓑ Ⓒ Ⓓ

Part 2: Arithmetic Reasoning

1. Ⓐ Ⓑ Ⓒ Ⓓ   2. Ⓐ Ⓑ Ⓒ Ⓓ   3. Ⓐ Ⓑ Ⓒ Ⓓ   4. Ⓐ Ⓑ Ⓒ Ⓓ   5. Ⓐ Ⓑ Ⓒ Ⓓ
6. Ⓐ Ⓑ Ⓒ Ⓓ   7. Ⓐ Ⓑ Ⓒ Ⓓ   8. Ⓐ Ⓑ Ⓒ Ⓓ   9. Ⓐ Ⓑ Ⓒ Ⓓ   10. Ⓐ Ⓑ Ⓒ Ⓓ
11. Ⓐ Ⓑ Ⓒ Ⓓ   12. Ⓐ Ⓑ Ⓒ Ⓓ   13. Ⓐ Ⓑ Ⓒ Ⓓ   14. Ⓐ Ⓑ Ⓒ Ⓓ   15. Ⓐ Ⓑ Ⓒ Ⓓ
16. Ⓐ Ⓑ Ⓒ Ⓓ   17. Ⓐ Ⓑ Ⓒ Ⓓ   18. Ⓐ Ⓑ Ⓒ Ⓓ   19. Ⓐ Ⓑ Ⓒ Ⓓ   20. Ⓐ Ⓑ Ⓒ Ⓓ
21. Ⓐ Ⓑ Ⓒ Ⓓ   22. Ⓐ Ⓑ Ⓒ Ⓓ   23. Ⓐ Ⓑ Ⓒ Ⓓ   24. Ⓐ Ⓑ Ⓒ Ⓓ   25. Ⓐ Ⓑ Ⓒ Ⓓ
26. Ⓐ Ⓑ Ⓒ Ⓓ   27. Ⓐ Ⓑ Ⓒ Ⓓ   28. Ⓐ Ⓑ Ⓒ Ⓓ   29. Ⓐ Ⓑ Ⓒ Ⓓ   30. Ⓐ Ⓑ Ⓒ Ⓓ

Part 3: Word Knowledge

1. Ⓐ Ⓑ Ⓒ Ⓓ   2. Ⓐ Ⓑ Ⓒ Ⓓ   3. Ⓐ Ⓑ Ⓒ Ⓓ   4. Ⓐ Ⓑ Ⓒ Ⓓ   5. Ⓐ Ⓑ Ⓒ Ⓓ
6. Ⓐ Ⓑ Ⓒ Ⓓ   7. Ⓐ Ⓑ Ⓒ Ⓓ   8. Ⓐ Ⓑ Ⓒ Ⓓ   9. Ⓐ Ⓑ Ⓒ Ⓓ   10. Ⓐ Ⓑ Ⓒ Ⓓ
11. Ⓐ Ⓑ Ⓒ Ⓓ   12. Ⓐ Ⓑ Ⓒ Ⓓ   13. Ⓐ Ⓑ Ⓒ Ⓓ   14. Ⓐ Ⓑ Ⓒ Ⓓ   15. Ⓐ Ⓑ Ⓒ Ⓓ
16. Ⓐ Ⓑ Ⓒ Ⓓ   17. Ⓐ Ⓑ Ⓒ Ⓓ   18. Ⓐ Ⓑ Ⓒ Ⓓ   19. Ⓐ Ⓑ Ⓒ Ⓓ   20. Ⓐ Ⓑ Ⓒ Ⓓ
21. Ⓐ Ⓑ Ⓒ Ⓓ   22. Ⓐ Ⓑ Ⓒ Ⓓ   23. Ⓐ Ⓑ Ⓒ Ⓓ   24. Ⓐ Ⓑ Ⓒ Ⓓ   25. Ⓐ Ⓑ Ⓒ Ⓓ
26. Ⓐ Ⓑ Ⓒ Ⓓ   27. Ⓐ Ⓑ Ⓒ Ⓓ   28. Ⓐ Ⓑ Ⓒ Ⓓ   29. Ⓐ Ⓑ Ⓒ Ⓓ   30. Ⓐ Ⓑ Ⓒ Ⓓ
31. Ⓐ Ⓑ Ⓒ Ⓓ   32. Ⓐ Ⓑ Ⓒ Ⓓ   33. Ⓐ Ⓑ Ⓒ Ⓓ   34. Ⓐ Ⓑ Ⓒ Ⓓ   35. Ⓐ Ⓑ Ⓒ Ⓓ

Part 4: Paragraph Comprehension

1. Ⓐ Ⓑ Ⓒ Ⓓ   2. Ⓐ Ⓑ Ⓒ Ⓓ   3. Ⓐ Ⓑ Ⓒ Ⓓ   4. Ⓐ Ⓑ Ⓒ Ⓓ   5. Ⓐ Ⓑ Ⓒ Ⓓ
6. Ⓐ Ⓑ Ⓒ Ⓓ   7. Ⓐ Ⓑ Ⓒ Ⓓ   8. Ⓐ Ⓑ Ⓒ Ⓓ   9. Ⓐ Ⓑ Ⓒ Ⓓ   10. Ⓐ Ⓑ Ⓒ Ⓓ
11. Ⓐ Ⓑ Ⓒ Ⓓ   12. Ⓐ Ⓑ Ⓒ Ⓓ   13. Ⓐ Ⓑ Ⓒ Ⓓ   14. Ⓐ Ⓑ Ⓒ Ⓓ   15. Ⓐ Ⓑ Ⓒ Ⓓ

answer sheet

Part 5: Mathematics Knowledge

1. Ⓐ Ⓑ Ⓒ Ⓓ   2. Ⓐ Ⓑ Ⓒ Ⓓ   3. Ⓐ Ⓑ Ⓒ Ⓓ   4. Ⓐ Ⓑ Ⓒ Ⓓ   5. Ⓐ Ⓑ Ⓒ Ⓓ
6. Ⓐ Ⓑ Ⓒ Ⓓ   7. Ⓐ Ⓑ Ⓒ Ⓓ   8. Ⓐ Ⓑ Ⓒ Ⓓ   9. Ⓐ Ⓑ Ⓒ Ⓓ   10. Ⓐ Ⓑ Ⓒ Ⓓ
11. Ⓐ Ⓑ Ⓒ Ⓓ   12. Ⓐ Ⓑ Ⓒ Ⓓ   13. Ⓐ Ⓑ Ⓒ Ⓓ   14. Ⓐ Ⓑ Ⓒ Ⓓ   15. Ⓐ Ⓑ Ⓒ Ⓓ
16. Ⓐ Ⓑ Ⓒ Ⓓ   17. Ⓐ Ⓑ Ⓒ Ⓓ   18. Ⓐ Ⓑ Ⓒ Ⓓ   19. Ⓐ Ⓑ Ⓒ Ⓓ   20. Ⓐ Ⓑ Ⓒ Ⓓ
21. Ⓐ Ⓑ Ⓒ Ⓓ   22. Ⓐ Ⓑ Ⓒ Ⓓ   23. Ⓐ Ⓑ Ⓒ Ⓓ   24. Ⓐ Ⓑ Ⓒ Ⓓ   25. Ⓐ Ⓑ Ⓒ Ⓓ

Part 6: Electronics Information

1. Ⓐ Ⓑ Ⓒ Ⓓ   2. Ⓐ Ⓑ Ⓒ Ⓓ   3. Ⓐ Ⓑ Ⓒ Ⓓ   4. Ⓐ Ⓑ Ⓒ Ⓓ   5. Ⓐ Ⓑ Ⓒ Ⓓ
6. Ⓐ Ⓑ Ⓒ Ⓓ   7. Ⓐ Ⓑ Ⓒ Ⓓ   8. Ⓐ Ⓑ Ⓒ Ⓓ   9. Ⓐ Ⓑ Ⓒ Ⓓ   10. Ⓐ Ⓑ Ⓒ Ⓓ
11. Ⓐ Ⓑ Ⓒ Ⓓ   12. Ⓐ Ⓑ Ⓒ Ⓓ   13. Ⓐ Ⓑ Ⓒ Ⓓ   14. Ⓐ Ⓑ Ⓒ Ⓓ   15. Ⓐ Ⓑ Ⓒ Ⓓ
16. Ⓐ Ⓑ Ⓒ Ⓓ   17. Ⓐ Ⓑ Ⓒ Ⓓ   18. Ⓐ Ⓑ Ⓒ Ⓓ   19. Ⓐ Ⓑ Ⓒ Ⓓ   20. Ⓐ Ⓑ Ⓒ Ⓓ

Part 7: Auto & Shop Information

1. Ⓐ Ⓑ Ⓒ Ⓓ   2. Ⓐ Ⓑ Ⓒ Ⓓ   3. Ⓐ Ⓑ Ⓒ Ⓓ   4. Ⓐ Ⓑ Ⓒ Ⓓ   5. Ⓐ Ⓑ Ⓒ Ⓓ
6. Ⓐ Ⓑ Ⓒ Ⓓ   7. Ⓐ Ⓑ Ⓒ Ⓓ   8. Ⓐ Ⓑ Ⓒ Ⓓ   9. Ⓐ Ⓑ Ⓒ Ⓓ   10. Ⓐ Ⓑ Ⓒ Ⓓ
11. Ⓐ Ⓑ Ⓒ Ⓓ   12. Ⓐ Ⓑ Ⓒ Ⓓ   13. Ⓐ Ⓑ Ⓒ Ⓓ   14. Ⓐ Ⓑ Ⓒ Ⓓ   15. Ⓐ Ⓑ Ⓒ Ⓓ
16. Ⓐ Ⓑ Ⓒ Ⓓ   17. Ⓐ Ⓑ Ⓒ Ⓓ   18. Ⓐ Ⓑ Ⓒ Ⓓ   19. Ⓐ Ⓑ Ⓒ Ⓓ   20. Ⓐ Ⓑ Ⓒ Ⓓ
21. Ⓐ Ⓑ Ⓒ Ⓓ   22. Ⓐ Ⓑ Ⓒ Ⓓ   23. Ⓐ Ⓑ Ⓒ Ⓓ   24. Ⓐ Ⓑ Ⓒ Ⓓ   25. Ⓐ Ⓑ Ⓒ Ⓓ

Part 8: Mechanical Comprehension

1. Ⓐ Ⓑ Ⓒ Ⓓ   2. Ⓐ Ⓑ Ⓒ Ⓓ   3. Ⓐ Ⓑ Ⓒ Ⓓ   4. Ⓐ Ⓑ Ⓒ Ⓓ   5. Ⓐ Ⓑ Ⓒ Ⓓ
6. Ⓐ Ⓑ Ⓒ Ⓓ   7. Ⓐ Ⓑ Ⓒ Ⓓ   8. Ⓐ Ⓑ Ⓒ Ⓓ   9. Ⓐ Ⓑ Ⓒ Ⓓ   10. Ⓐ Ⓑ Ⓒ Ⓓ
11. Ⓐ Ⓑ Ⓒ Ⓓ   12. Ⓐ Ⓑ Ⓒ Ⓓ   13. Ⓐ Ⓑ Ⓒ Ⓓ   14. Ⓐ Ⓑ Ⓒ Ⓓ   15. Ⓐ Ⓑ Ⓒ Ⓓ
16. Ⓐ Ⓑ Ⓒ Ⓓ   17. Ⓐ Ⓑ Ⓒ Ⓓ   18. Ⓐ Ⓑ Ⓒ Ⓓ   19. Ⓐ Ⓑ Ⓒ Ⓓ   20. Ⓐ Ⓑ Ⓒ Ⓓ
21. Ⓐ Ⓑ Ⓒ Ⓓ   22. Ⓐ Ⓑ Ⓒ Ⓓ   23. Ⓐ Ⓑ Ⓒ Ⓓ   24. Ⓐ Ⓑ Ⓒ Ⓓ   25. Ⓐ Ⓑ Ⓒ Ⓓ

Part 9: Assembling Objects

1. Ⓐ Ⓑ Ⓒ Ⓓ   2. Ⓐ Ⓑ Ⓒ Ⓓ   3. Ⓐ Ⓑ Ⓒ Ⓓ   4. Ⓐ Ⓑ Ⓒ Ⓓ   5. Ⓐ Ⓑ Ⓒ Ⓓ
6. Ⓐ Ⓑ Ⓒ Ⓓ   7. Ⓐ Ⓑ Ⓒ Ⓓ   8. Ⓐ Ⓑ Ⓒ Ⓓ   9. Ⓐ Ⓑ Ⓒ Ⓓ   10. Ⓐ Ⓑ Ⓒ Ⓓ
11. Ⓐ Ⓑ Ⓒ Ⓓ   12. Ⓐ Ⓑ Ⓒ Ⓓ   13. Ⓐ Ⓑ Ⓒ Ⓓ   14. Ⓐ Ⓑ Ⓒ Ⓓ   15. Ⓐ Ⓑ Ⓒ Ⓓ
16. Ⓐ Ⓑ Ⓒ Ⓓ

PART 1: GENERAL SCIENCE

Time: 11 Minutes—25 Questions

> **Directions:** This is a test of 25 questions to find out how much you know about general science as usually covered in high school courses. Pick the best answer for each question, then blacken the space on your answer sheet that has the same number and letter as your choice.

Here are three sample questions.

1. Water is an example of a   Ⓐ Ⓑ ● Ⓓ
   A. solid.
   B. gas.
   C. liquid.
   D. crystal.

   Notice that answer space C has been marked for question 1. Now do practice questions 2 and 3 by yourself. Find the correct answer to the question, then mark the space that has the same letter as the answer you picked. Do this now.

2. Lack of iodine is often related to which of the following diseases?   Ⓐ Ⓑ Ⓒ Ⓓ
   A. Beriberi
   B. Scurvy
   C. Rickets
   D. Goiter

3. An eclipse of the sun throws the shadow of the   Ⓐ Ⓑ Ⓒ Ⓓ
   A. earth on the moon.
   B. moon on the earth.
   C. moon on the sun.
   D. earth on the sun.

   You should have marked choice D for question 2 and choice B for question 3. If you made any mistakes, erase your mark carefully and blacken the correct answer space. Do this now.

Your score on this test will be based on the number of questions you answer correctly. You should try to answer every question. Do not spend too much time on any one question.

When you begin, be sure to start with question number 1 in Part 1 in your test booklet and number 1 in Part 1 on your answer sheet.

1. Citrus fruits and tomatoes are good sources of
   A. Vitamin A.
   B. Vitamin B.
   C. Vitamin C.
   D. Vitamin D.

2. A meter stick can usually be balanced by placing a finger beneath the point marked
   A. 100 cm.
   B. 50 cm.
   C. 25 cm.
   D. 12.5 cm.

3. The chief nutrient in lean meat is
   A. starch.
   B. protein.
   C. fat.
   D. carbohydrates.

4. On the Celsius temperature scale, each Celsius degree represents what fraction of the temperature range between the freezing and boiling points of water?
   A. $\dfrac{1}{80}$
   B. $\dfrac{1}{100}$
   C. $\dfrac{1}{18}$
   D. $\dfrac{1}{10}$

5. The principal metal used to manufacture steel is
   A. iron ore.
   B. lead.
   C. iron.
   D. titanium.

6. "Shooting stars" are
   A. exploding stars.
   B. cosmic rays.
   C. planetoids.
   D. meteors.

7. Two children are seated on a seesaw. The first child, seated 4 feet from the center, weighs 80 pounds. If the second child weighs 40 pounds, how far from the center must that child sit to balance the seesaw?
   A. 1 foot
   B. 2 feet
   C. 8 feet
   D. 16 feet

8. The part of the digestive system in which most of the digested materials are absorbed into the bloodstream is the
   A. large intestine.
   B. liver.
   C. small intestine.
   D. stomach.

9. Skeletal muscles are joined to bones by tough connective tissue called
   A. cartilage.
   B. ligaments.
   C. muscle fibers.
   D. tendons.

10. Hearing an echo is most like seeing
    A. around the corner through a periscope.
    B. fine print under strong illumination.
    C. stars at night that are invisible in the daytime.
    D. one's image in a mirror.

11. Vitamin K is needed for
    A. energy release.
    B. formation of bones.
    C. normal blood clotting.
    D. normal metabolism.

12. If we start with 400 atoms of a radioactive substance, how many would remain after one half-life?
    A. 400
    B. 200
    C. 100
    D. 50

13. The primary reason designers seek to lower the center of gravity in automobiles is to
    A. reduce wind resistance.
    B. provide smoother riding.
    C. increase stability.
    D. reduce manufacturing costs.

14. Substances that hasten a chemical reaction without themselves undergoing change are called
    A. buffers.
    B. catalysts.
    C. colloids.
    D. reducers.

15. A hip joint is best described as a
    A. ball-and-socket joint.
    B. gliding joint.
    C. hinge joint.
    D. pivot joint.

16. AIDS is a disease caused by a
    A. bacillus.
    B. saprophyte.
    C. spirillum.
    D. virus.

17. Lack of Vitamin D is often related to which of the following diseases?
    A. Beriberi
    B. Scurvy
    C. Goiter
    D. Rickets

18. How old is a skeleton sample if the current amount of carbon in the bones is 3.135%? (Assume you started with 100% and the half-life of Carbon-14 is 5,730 years.)
    A. 5,000 years
    B. 11,460 years
    C. 28,650 years
    D. 57,300 years

19. A lead sinker weighs 54 grams in air, 23.8 grams in liquid A, and 28.6 grams in liquid B. From this information, what conclusions can be drawn concerning the densities of the two liquids?
    A. Liquid A has a greater density than liquid B.
    B. Both liquids are more dense than water.
    C. Both liquids are less dense than water.
    D. No conclusions can be drawn concerning the densities of the two liquids.

20. After adding a solute to a liquid, the freezing point of the liquid is
    A. lowered.
    B. the same.
    C. raised.
    D. inverted.

practice test 4

21. Organisms that sustain their life cycles by feeding off other live organisms are known as
    A. parasites.
    B. saprophytes.
    C. bacteria.
    D. viruses.

22. Chemicals that have been pumped into the air by industries cause air pollution. This leads to
    A. acid rains that destroy crops and animals.
    B. respiratory ailments in animals and people.
    C. possible changes in the climate.
    D. All of the above.

23. Carry out the following computation, and express the results in scientific notation 7.20×10^3 cm $\times$ 8.08×10^3 cm.
    A. 5.82×10^7 cm^3
    B. 58.2×10^7 cm^2
    C. 5.82×10^7 cm^2
    D. 5.82×10^6 cm^2

24. Photosynthesis is the process by which green plants manufacture carbohydrates from
    A. oxygen and nitrogen.
    B. carbon dioxide and water.
    C. oxygen and water.
    D. glucose and water.

25. When two or more elements combine to form a substance that has properties different from those of the component elements, that new substance is known as a(n)
    A. mixture.
    B. solution.
    C. alloy.
    D. compound.

STOP!
IF YOU FINISH BEFORE THE TIME IS UP, YOU
MAY CHECK OVER YOUR WORK ON THIS PART ONLY.

PART 2: ARITHMETIC REASONING

Time: 36 Minutes—30 Questions

> **Directions:** This test has 30 questions about arithmetic. Each question is followed by four possible answers. Decide which answer is correct, then blacken the space on your answer sheet that has the same number and letter as your choice. Use scratch paper to do any figuring.

Here are two sample questions.

1. A person buys a sandwich for $4.00, soda for $1.25, and pie for $1.75. What is the total cost?
   A. $6.85
   B. $6.95
   C. $7.00
   D. $7.15

   Ⓐ Ⓑ Ⓒ Ⓓ

   The total cost is $7.00; therefore, choice C is the correct answer.

2. If 8 workers are needed to run 4 machines, how many workers are needed to run 20 machines?
   A. 16
   B. 32
   C. 36
   D. 40

   Ⓐ Ⓑ Ⓒ Ⓓ

   The number needed is 40; therefore, choice D is the correct answer.

Your score on this test will be based on the number of questions you answer correctly. You should try to answer every question. Do not spend too much time on any one question.

Notice that Part 2 begins with question number 1. When you begin, be sure to start with question number 1 in Part 2 in your test booklet and number 1 in Part 2 on your answer sheet.

1. It takes a race car 54 seconds to go around a racetrack. If the car makes 20 laps around the track, how many minutes did it take?
   A. 14 minutes
   B. 16 minutes
   C. 18 minutes
   D. 20 minutes

2. How many 36-passenger buses will it take to carry 144 people?
   A. 4
   B. 3
   C. 5
   D. 6

3. The low temperature last night was −14°F and the high temperature today was 12°F at noon. What was the difference in the high and low temperatures for today?
   A. 14°
   B. 16°
   C. 24°
   D. 26°

4. A mechanic greased 168 cars in 28 days. What was his daily average of cars greased?
   A. 5
   B. 6
   C. 7
   D. 8

5. A jet plane traveled 1,400 miles in 3.5 hours. What was the speed of the plane?
   A. 360 miles per hour
   B. 80 miles per hour
   C. 400 miles per hour
   D. 420 miles per hour

6. Three workers assemble 360 switches per hour, but 5% of the switches are defective. How many good (nondefective) switches will these 3 workers assemble in an 8-hour shift?
   A. 2,736
   B. 2,880
   C. 2,944
   D. 3,000

7. The butcher made $22\frac{1}{2}$ pounds of beef into hamburger and wrapped it in $1\frac{1}{4}$ pound packages. How many packages did he make?
   A. 15
   B. 16
   C. 17
   D. 18

8. A salesman sold 4 computers at $240 each. He receives a commission on the sale of 15%. What was his commission?
   A. $144
   B. $164
   C. $124
   D. $184

9. It cost a couple $27 to go out for the evening. Sixty percent of this was for theater tickets. What was the cost for each ticket?
   A. $7.90
   B. $8.10
   C. $10.80
   D. $16.20

10. Soap, ordinarily priced at 2 bars for $0.66, may be purchased in lots of one dozen for $3.48. What is the savings per bar when it is purchased in this way?
    A. 4 cents
    B. 8 cents
    C. 16 cents
    D. 19 cents

11. Twenty students contribute $25 each for a Christmas party. Forty percent of the money is spent for food and drinks. How much is left for other expenses?
    A. $125
    B. $200
    C. $300
    D. $375

12. Two trucks left an intersection traveling in opposite directions. One truck held a speed of 60 miles per hour and the other truck held a speed of 50 miles per hour. After two hours how far apart were the two trucks?
    A. 110 miles
    B. 220 miles
    C. 165 miles
    D. 265 miles

13. The price of a $250 item after successive discounts of 20% and 30% is
    A. $125
    B. $130
    C. $140
    D. $180

14. If a laborer works from 7:15 a.m. to 3:45 p.m. with 1 hour off for lunch, his working time equals
    A. 7 hours.
    B. $7\frac{1}{2}$ hours.
    C. 8 hours.
    D. $8\frac{1}{2}$ hours.

15. A home has a tax rate of 2%. If the tax is $550, what is the assessed value of the home?
    A. $1,100
    B. $2,750
    C. $11,000
    D. $27,500

16. A delivery company employs 6 truck drivers. If each driver travels 250 miles a day, how many miles do all 6 drivers travel in a 5-day workweek?
    A. 750
    B. 1,500
    C. 7,500
    D. 15,000

17. The minute hand fell off a watch but the watch continued to work accurately. What time was it when the hour hand was at the 17-minute mark?
    A. 3:02
    B. 3:17
    C. 3:24
    D. 4:17

practice test 4

Part IV: Three ASVAB Practice Tests

18. A manufacturer has 3,375 yards of material on hand. If the average dress takes $3\frac{3}{8}$ yards of material, how many dresses can he make?
  A. 844
  B. 1,000
  C. 1,125
  D. 1,250

19. It costs $1 per square yard to waterproof canvas. What will it cost to waterproof a canvas truck cover that is 15 feet × 24 feet?
  A. $20
  B. $36
  C. $40
  D. $360

20. A part-time employee worked a total of $16\frac{1}{2}$ hours during 5 days of the past week. What was this employee's average workday?
  A. 3 hours
  B. 3 hours, 15 minutes
  C. 3 hours, 18 minutes
  D. 3 hours, 25 minutes

21. A driver traveled 100 miles at the rate of 40 mph, then traveled 80 miles at 60 mph. What is the total number of hours for the entire trip?
  A. $1\frac{3}{20}$
  B. $1\frac{3}{4}$
  C. $2\frac{1}{4}$
  D. $3\frac{5}{6}$

22. After an article is discounted at 25%, it sells for $112.50. The original price of the article was
  A. $28.12
  B. $84.37
  C. $150.00
  D. $152.50

23. I purchased a 12-foot board at the local hardware store. If I cut 4 sections of 2 feet and 6 inches from the 12-foot board, how much of the board would be left over?
  A. 1 foot
  B. 2 feet
  C. 3 feet
  D. 4 feet

24. If erasers cost 8¢ each for the first 250, 7¢ each for the next 250, and 5¢ for every eraser thereafter, how many erasers may be purchased for $50?
  A. 600
  B. 750
  C. 850
  D. 1,000

25. A plane left New York at 3:30 p.m. EST and arrived in Los Angeles at 4:15 p.m. PST. How long did the flight take?
  A. 7 hours, 15 minutes
  B. 6 hours, 45 minutes
  C. 3 hours, 45 minutes
  D. 3 hours, 15 minutes

26. The toll on the Island Bridge is $1 for car and driver and 75¢ for each additional passenger. How many people were riding in a car for which the toll was $3.25?
  A. 1
  B. 2
  C. 3
  D. 4

27. What is the total cost of 3 sheets of 23¢ stamps, 2 sheets of 50¢ stamps, and 4 sheets of 29¢ stamps if each sheet has 100 stamps?
  A. $265
  B. $275
  C. $285
  D. $295

28. An employee's net pay is equal to her total earnings less all deductions. If an employee's total earnings in a pay period are $497.05, what is her net pay if she has the following deductions: federal income tax, $90.32; FICA, $28.74; state tax, $18.79; city tax, $7.25; and pension, $1.88?

    A. $351.17

    B. $351.07

    C. $350.17

    D. $350.07

29. The price of a radio is $31.29, which includes a 5% sales tax. What was the price of the radio before the tax was added?

    A. $29.80

    B. $29.85

    C. $29.90

    D. $29.95

30. At the rate of 40 words per minute, how long will it take a typist to type a 3,600-word article?

    A. $1\frac{1}{2}$ hours

    B. $1\frac{3}{4}$ hours

    C. 2 hours

    D. $2\frac{1}{4}$ hours

STOP!
IF YOU FINISH BEFORE THE TIME IS UP, YOU
MAY CHECK OVER YOUR WORK ON THIS PART ONLY.

PART 3: WORD KNOWLEDGE

Time: 11 Minutes—35 Questions

Directions: This test has 35 questions about the meanings of words. Each question has an underlined word. You are to decide which one of the four words in the choices most nearly means the same as the underlined word, then mark the space on your answer sheet that has the same number and letter as your choice.

Now look at the two sample questions below.

1. <u>Mended</u> most nearly means   Ⓐ Ⓑ Ⓒ Ⓓ
   A. repaired.
   B. torn.
   C. clean.
   D. tied.

   Repaired, choice A, is the correct answer. *Mended* means *fixed* or *repaired*. *Torn*, choice B, might be the state of an object before it is mended. The repair might be made by *tying*, choice D, but not necessarily. *Clean*, choice C, is wrong.

2. It was a <u>small</u> table.   Ⓐ Ⓑ Ⓒ Ⓓ
   A. Sturdy
   B. Round
   C. Cheap
   D. Little

   Little means the same as *small*, so choice D is the best answer.

Your score on this test will be based on the number of questions you answer correctly. You should try to answer every question. Do not spend too much time on any one question.

When you begin, be sure to start with question number 1 in Part 3 in your test booklet and number 1 in Part 3 on your answer sheet.

1. Impartial most nearly means
   A. skewed.
   B. without bias.
   C. half.
   D. offensive.

2. To supersede most nearly means
   A. to come first.
   B. to be strong.
   C. to replace.
   D. to destroy.

3. Caution most nearly means
   A. signals.
   B. care.
   C. traffic.
   D. haste.

4. The fog horn sounded intermittently.
   A. Constantly
   B. Annually
   C. Using intermediaries
   D. At irregular intervals

5. He told us about a strange occurrence.
   A. Event
   B. Place
   C. Occupation
   D. Opinion

6. Deception most nearly means
   A. secrets.
   B. fraud.
   C. mistrust.
   D. hatred.

7. Did the storm cease during the night?
   A. Start
   B. Change
   C. Continue
   D. Stop

8. The crowd received him with acclaim.
   A. Amazement
   B. Applause
   C. Booing
   D. Laughter

9. The town will erect the bridge.
   A. Paint
   B. Design
   C. Destroy
   D. Construct

10. Relish most nearly means
    A. care.
    B. speed.
    C. amusement.
    D. enjoy.

11. Sufficient most nearly means
    A. durable.
    B. substitution.
    C. expendable.
    D. appropriate.

12. She will return in a fortnight.
    A. Two weeks
    B. One week
    C. Two months
    D. One month

13. Flaw most nearly means
    A. defect.
    B. mixture.
    C. surface.
    D. movement.

14. To attest to a story most nearly means
    A. to study.
    B. to recall.
    C. to state something is true.
    D. to record.

15. <u>Jeer</u> most nearly means
    A. peek.
    B. scoff.
    C. turn.
    D. judge.

16. <u>Alias</u> most nearly means
    A. enemy.
    B. sidekick.
    C. hero.
    D. other name.

17. <u>Impair</u> most nearly means
    A. direct.
    B. improve.
    C. weaken.
    D. stimulate.

18. To <u>hasten</u> most nearly means
    A. to hurry.
    B. to motivate.
    C. to stifle.
    D. to sadden.

19. We were told to <u>abandon</u> the ship.
    A. Relinquish
    B. Encompass
    C. Infiltrate
    D. Quarantine

20. <u>Resolve</u> most nearly means
    A. understand.
    B. decide.
    C. recall.
    D. forget.

21. <u>Ample</u> most nearly means
    A. plentiful.
    B. enthusiastic.
    C. well shaped.
    D. overweight.

22. <u>Havoc</u> most nearly means
    A. peace.
    B. safe.
    C. chaos.
    D. interruption.

23. <u>Sullen</u> most nearly means
    A. grayish yellow.
    B. soaking wet.
    C. very dirty.
    D. angrily silent.

24. <u>Rudiments</u> most nearly means
    A. basic procedures.
    B. politics.
    C. promotion opportunities.
    D. minute details.

25. <u>Clash</u> most nearly means
    A. applaud.
    B. fasten.
    C. conflict.
    D. punish.

26. I had a <u>lapse</u> in judgment.
    A. Consistency
    B. Temporary moral failure
    C. Decision
    D. Realization

27. His answer was a <u>superficial</u> one.
    A. Excellent
    B. Official
    C. Profound
    D. Cursory

28. Criminals try to <u>elude</u> the police.
    A. Escape
    B. Involve
    C. Follow
    D. Communicate with

29. <u>Terse</u> most nearly means
   A. concise.
   B. trivial.
   C. oral.
   D. lengthy.

30. She prepared a delicious <u>concoction</u> for us.
   A. Combination of ingredients
   B. Appetizer
   C. Drink made of wine and spices
   D. Relish tray

31. <u>Incessant</u> most nearly means
   A. occasional.
   B. disagreeable.
   C. constant.
   D. noisy.

32. <u>Solidity</u> most nearly means
   A. unevenness.
   B. smoothness.
   C. firmness.
   D. color.

33. <u>Increment</u> most nearly means a(n)
   A. improvisation.
   B. account.
   C. increase.
   D. specification.

34. The judge ruled it to be <u>immaterial</u>.
   A. Unclear
   B. Unimportant
   C. Unpredictable
   D. Not debatable

35. We <u>misconstrued</u> what she had said.
   A. Followed directions
   B. Pretended not to hear
   C. Acted to supervise
   D. Interpreted erroneously

STOP!
IF YOU FINISH BEFORE THE TIME IS UP, YOU
MAY CHECK OVER YOUR WORK ON THIS PART ONLY.

PART 4: PARAGRAPH COMPREHENSION

Time: 13 Minutes—15 Questions

> **Directions:** This test contains 15 items measuring your ability to obtain information from written passages. You will find one or more paragraphs of reading material followed by incomplete statements or questions. You are to read the paragraph(s) and select the lettered choice that best completes the statement or answers the question.

Here are two sample questions.

1. From a building designer's standpoint, three things that make a home livable are the needs of the client, the building site, and the amount of money the client has to spend.   Ⓐ Ⓑ Ⓒ Ⓓ

   According to the passage, to make a home livable
   A. the prospective piece of land makes little difference.
   B. it can be built on any piece of land.
   C. the design must fit the owner's income and site.
   D. the design must fit the designer's income.

   The correct answer is that the design must fit the owner's income and site, so choice C is the correct answer.

2. In certain areas, water is so scarce that every attempt is made to conserve it. For instance, on one oasis in the Sahara Desert, the amount of water necessary for each date palm tree has been carefully determined.   Ⓐ Ⓑ Ⓒ Ⓓ

   How much water is each tree given?
   A. No water at all
   B. Exactly the amount required
   C. Water only if it is healthy
   D. Water on alternate days

   The correct answer is exactly the amount required, so choice B is the correct answer.

Your score on this test will be based on the number of questions you answer correctly. You should try to answer every question. Do not spend too much time on any one question.

When you begin, be sure to start with question number 1 in Part 4 in your test booklet and number 1 in Part 4 on your answer sheet.

1. Numerous benefits to the employer as well as to the worker have resulted from physical examinations of employees. Such examinations are intended primarily as a means of increasing efficiency and production, and they have been found to accomplish these ends. The passage best supports the statement that physical examinations

   A. may serve to increase output.

   B. are required in some plants.

   C. often reveal serious defects previously unknown.

   D. are always worth more than they cost.

2. Examination of traffic accident statistics reveals that traffic accidents are frequently the result of violations of traffic laws—and usually the violations are the result of illegal and dangerous driving behavior rather than the result of mechanical defects or poor road conditions.

   According to this passage, the majority of dangerous traffic violations are caused by

   A. poor driving.

   B. bad roads.

   C. unsafe cars.

   D. unwise traffic laws.

3. Complaints from the public are no longer regarded by government officials as mere nuisances. Instead, complaints are often welcomed because they frequently bring into the open conditions and faults in operation and service that should be corrected.

   This passage means most nearly that

   A. government officials now realize that complaints from the public are necessary.

   B. faulty operations and services are not brought into the open except by complaints from the public.

   C. government officials now realize that complaints from the public are in reality a sign of a well-run agency.

   D. complaints from the public can be useful in indicating needs for improvement in operation and service.

4. In a pole-vaulting competition, the judge decides on the minimum height to be jumped. The vaulter may attempt to jump any height above the minimum. Using flexible fiberglass poles, vaulters have jumped as high as 18 feet $8\frac{1}{4}$ inches.

   According to the passage, pole vaulters

   A. may attempt to jump any height in competition.

   B. must jump higher than $\frac{1}{2}$ to win.

   C. must jump higher than the height set by the judge.

   D. must use fiberglass poles.

5. When gas is leaking, any spark or sudden flame can ignite it. This can create a "flash-back," which burns off the gas in a quick puff of smoke and flame. But the real danger is in a large leak, which can cause an explosion.

According to the passage, the real danger from leaking gas is a(n)
A. flashback.
B. puff of smoke and flame.
C. explosion.
D. spark.

6. A year—the time it takes the earth to go exactly once around the sun—is not 365 days. It is actually 365 days 6 hours 9 minutes $9\frac{1}{2}$ seconds, or $365\frac{1}{4}$ days. Leap years make up for this discrepancy by adding an extra day once every four years.

The purpose of a leap year is to
A. adjust for the fact that it takes $365\frac{1}{4}$ days for the earth to circle the sun.
B. make up for time lost in the work year.
C. occur every four years.
D. allow for differences in the length of a year in each time zone.

7. Any business not provided with capable substitutes to fill all important positions is a weak business. Therefore, a foreman should train each man or woman not only to perform his or her own particular duties but also to do those of two or three positions.

The paragraph best supports the statement that
A. dependence on substitutes is a sign of a weak organization.
B. training will improve the strongest organization.
C. the foreman should be the most expert at any particular job under him.
D. vacancies in vital positions should be provided for in advance.

8. In the business districts of cities, collections from street letter boxes are made at stated hours, and collectors are required to observe these hours exactly. Anyone using these boxes can rely with certainty on the time of the next collection.

The paragraph best supports the statement that mail
A. collections in business districts are more frequent during the day than at night.
B. collectors are required to observe safety regulations exactly.
C. collections are made often in business districts.
D. is collected in business districts on a regular schedule.

9. The increasing size of business organizations has resulted in less personal contact between superior and subordinate. Consequently, business executives today depend more on records and reports to secure information and exercise control over the operations of various departments.

The increasing size of business organizations has
A. caused a complete cleavage between employer and employee.
B. resulted in less personal contact between superior and subordinate.
C. tended toward class distinctions in large organizations.
D. resulted in a better means of controlling the operations of various departments.

10. Kindling temperature is the lowest temperature at which a substance catches fire and continues to burn. Different fuels have different kindling temperatures. Paper catches fire easily because it has a low kindling temperature. Coal, because of its high kindling temperature, requires much heat before it will begin to burn. Matches are tipped with phosphorus, or some other low kindling material, to permit the small amount of heat produced by friction to ignite the match.

The property of phosphorus that makes it ideal for use on matches is
A. its light color.
B. its high kindling temperature.
C. its low kindling temperature.
D. the fact that it contains carbon.

Questions 11 and 12 are based on the following passage.

Racketeers are primarily concerned with business affairs, legitimate or otherwise, and preferably those that are close to the margin of legitimacy. They get their best opportunities from business organizations that meet the needs of large sections of the public for goods and services that are defined as illegitimate by the same public, such as gambling, illicit drugs, etc. In contrast to the thief, the racketeer and the establishments he or she controls deliver goods and services for money received.

11. According to the passage, racketeering, unlike theft, involves
A. payment for goods received.
B. unlawful activities.
C. organized gangs.
D. objects of value.

12. It can be deduced that suppression of racketeering is difficult because
A. many people want services that are not obtainable through legitimate sources.
B. racketeers are generally engaged in fully legitimate enterprises.
C. victims of racketeers are not guilty of violating the law.
D. laws prohibiting gambling are unenforceable.

practice test 4

Questions 13–15 are based on the following passage.

The two systems of weights and measures are the English system and the metric system. The English system uses units such as foot, pound, and quart; the metric system uses meter, gram, and liter. The metric system was first adopted in France in 1795 and is now used by most countries in the world. In the metric system, the unit of length is the meter, which is one ten-millionth of the distance from the Equator to the North Pole. The British recently changed their system of weights and measures to the metric system; however, in the United States, there has been much opposition to this change. It would cost billions of dollars to change all our weights and measures to the metric system.

13. According to the passage, the metric system is used
   A. in all of Europe except Great Britain.
   B. in almost all countries of the world.
   C. in only a few countries.
   D. mostly in Europe.

14. The United States has not changed to the metric system because
   A. the system is too complicated.
   B. the change would be costly.
   C. the system is not accurate.
   D. it is difficult to learn.

15. The meter is equal to
   A. the distance from the Equator to the North Pole.
   B. $\frac{1}{1,000,000}$ of the distance from the Equator to the North Pole.
   C. $\frac{1}{10,000,000}$ of the distance from the Equator to the North Pole.
   D. $\frac{1}{100,000,000}$ of the distance from the Equator to the North Pole.

STOP!
IF YOU FINISH BEFORE THE TIME IS UP,
YOU MAY CHECK OVER YOUR WORK ON THIS PART ONLY.

PART 5: MATHEMATICS KNOWLEDGE

Time: 24 Minutes—25 Questions

> **Directions:** This is a test of your ability to solve 25 general mathematical problems. You are to select the correct response from the choices given. Then mark the space on your answer sheet that has the same number and letter as your choice. Use scratch paper to do any figuring.

Now look at the two sample problems below.

1. If $x + 6 = 7$, then x is equal to   ⒶⒷⒸⒹ
   A. 0
   B. 1
   C. −1
   D. $\frac{7}{6}$

   The correct answer is 1, so choice B is the correct answer.

2. What is the area of the square above?   ⒶⒷⒸⒹ
   A. 1 square foot
   B. 5 square feet
   C. 10 square feet
   D. 25 square feet

   The correct answer is 25 square feet, so choice D is the correct answer.

Your score on this test will be based on the number of questions you answer correctly. You should try to answer every question. Do not spend too much time on any one question.

When you are told to begin, be sure to start with question number 1 in Part 5 in your test booklet and number 1 in Part 5 on your answer sheet.

1. If you multiply $(2x + 1)$ and $(3x + 4)$, what will be the coefficient of x^2 ?
   A. 5
   B. 6
   C. 11
   D. 12

2. $(x + 1)(x + 2) =$
   A. $x^2 + 2x + 2$
   B. $x^2 + 3x + 2$
   C. $x^2 + 2x + 3$
   D. $x^2 + 3x + 3$

3. If $3x = -5$, then x equals
   A. $\frac{3}{5}$
   B. $-\frac{5}{3}$
   C. $-\frac{3}{5}$
   D. -2

4. The first digit of the square root of 59,043 is
   A. 2
   B. 3
   C. 4
   D. 5

5. A square is equal in area to a rectangle whose length is 9 and whose width is 4. Find the perimeter of the square.
   A. 24
   B. 26
   C. 34
   D. 36

6. A square has sides of length 4. What is the length of the diagonal?
   A. 4
   B. $4\sqrt{2}$
   C. 8
   D. $8\sqrt{2}$

7. $(4x + 1)(x + 3) =$
   A. $4x^2 + 3$
   B. $4x^2 + 11x + 3$
   C. $4x^2 + 12x + 3$
   D. $4x^2 + 13x + 3$

8. An angle has a measure twice that of its complement. What is the measure of the angle?
   A. 30°
   B. 45°
   C. 60°
   D. 75°

9. The perimeter of a rectangle is 44 inches. The length is 8 inches more than the width. What is the length?
   A. 7
   B. 8
   C. 15
   D. 22

10. Using the formula $A = \frac{1}{2}bh$, find the area of the triangle above.
    A. 17 ft^2
    B. 35 ft^2
    C. 70 ft^2
    D. 140 ft^2

11. Given the formulas $d = rt$ and $A = r + \dfrac{d}{t}$, which formula below correctly expresses the value of A without using t?

   A. $A = dr$

   B. $A = r + 2\dfrac{d}{t}$

   C. $A = 2r + d$

   D. $A = 2r$

12. Which of the following is a prime number?

   A. 23

   B. 27

   C. 39

   D. 51

13. The distance in miles around a circular course that has a radius of 35 miles is (use $\dfrac{22}{7}$ for pi)

   A. 156

   B. 220

   C. 440

   D. 880

14. The expression "3 factorial" equals

   A. $\dfrac{1}{9}$

   B. $\dfrac{1}{6}$

   C. 6

   D. 9

15. $\dfrac{(4 \text{ yards} + 14 \text{ feet} + 48 \text{ inches})}{4} =$

   A. 7.5 feet

   B. 15 feet

   C. 30 feet

   D. 120 feet

16. Solve for x: $\dfrac{2x}{7} = 2x^2$

   A. $\dfrac{1}{7}$

   B. $\dfrac{2}{7}$

   C. 2

   D. 7

17. Solve the following equation for C:

$$A^2 = \dfrac{B^2}{C + D}$$

   A. $C = \dfrac{B^2 - A^2 D}{A^2 B}$

   B. $C = \dfrac{A^2}{B^2} - D$

   C. $C = \dfrac{A^2 + D}{B^2 - D}$

   D. $C = \dfrac{B^2}{A^2} - D$

18. The perimeter of a rectangle is 90. One side of the rectangle is twice the length of the other side. What is the length of the shorter side?

   A. 15

   B. 20

   C. 25

   D. 30

19. Which one of the following is correct?

   A. Every rhombus is a square.

   B. Every rectangle is a square.

   C. Every square is a rhombus.

   D. Every trapezoid is a rectangle.

20. What is the area, in square inches, of a circle whose radius measures 7 inches? (use $\dfrac{22}{7}$ for pi)

   A. 22

   B. 44

   C. 154

   D. 616

practice test 4

21. Evaluate the expression $5a - 4x - 3y$ if $a = -2$, $x = -10$, and $y = 5$.

    A. +15

    B. +25

    C. −65

    D. −35

22. A small cog wheel having 6 cogs plays into another larger cog wheel having 14 cogs. When the small wheel has made 28 revolutions, how many has the larger cog wheel made?

    A. 10

    B. 12

    C. 14

    D. 16

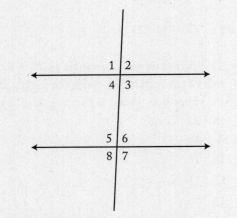

23. If $\angle 8 = 80°$ in the figure above, then $m\angle 2 =$

    A. 80°

    B. 100°

    C. 120°

    D. None of the above.

24. Solve for x: $\dfrac{x}{2} - \dfrac{x}{5} = 3$

    A. 2

    B. 3

    C. 52

    D. 10

25. If the radius of a circle is increased by 3, the circumference is increased by

    A. −3

    B. 3π

    C. 6π

    D. 6

STOP!
IF YOU FINISH BEFORE THE TIME IS UP,
YOU MAY CHECK OVER YOUR WORK ON THIS PART ONLY.

PART 6: ELECTRONICS INFORMATION

Time: 9 Minutes—20 Questions

Directions: This is a test of your knowledge of electrical, radio, and electronics information. There are 20 questions. You are to select the correct response from the choices given. Then mark the space on your answer sheet that has the same number and letter as your choice.

Now look at the two sample questions below.

1. What does the abbreviation AC stand for?　　　　ⒶⒷ©Ⓓ
   A. Additional charge
   B. Alternating coil
   C. Alternating current
   D. Ampere current

The correct answer is alternating current, so choice C is the correct response.

2. Which of the following has the LEAST resistance?　　　ⒶⒷ©Ⓓ
   A. Wood
   B. Silver
   C. Rubber
   D. Iron

The correct answer is silver, so choice B is the correct response.

Your score on this test will be based on the number of questions you answer correctly. You should try to answer every question. Do not spend too much time on any one question.

When you are told to begin, be sure to start with question number 1 in Part 6 in your test booklet and number 1 in Part 6 on your answer sheet.

1. The most likely cause of a burned-out fuse in the primary circuit of a transformer in a rectifier is
   A. grounding of the electrostatic shield.
   B. an open circuit in a bleeder resistor.
   C. an open circuit in the secondary winding.
   D. a short-circuited filter capacitor.

2. Four resistors in descending order are
   A. 22R, 270k, 2k2, 1M.
   B. 4k7, 10k, 47R, 330R.
   C. 5k6, 22R, 4R7, 3R3.
   D. 100R, 10k, 1M, 3k3.

3. To obtain a higher value of resistance, resistors are connected in
   A. reverse.
   B. forward.
   C. parallel.
   D. series.

4. Excessive resistance in the primary circuit will lessen the output of the ignition coil and cause the
   A. battery to short out and the generator to run down.
   B. battery to short out and the plugs to wear out prematurely.
   C. generator to run down and the timing mechanism to slow down.
   D. engine to perform poorly and be hard to start.

5. During a "short circuit," the
   A. current flow becomes very large.
   B. resistance becomes very large.
   C. voltage applied becomes very small.
   D. power input becomes very small.

6. The main reason for making wire stranded is
   A. to make it easier to insulate.
   B. so that the insulation will not come off.
   C. to decrease its weight.
   D. to make it more flexible.

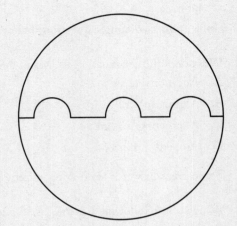

7. The oscilloscope image shown above represents
   A. steady DC.
   B. resistance in a resistor.
   C. AC.
   D. pulsating DC.

8. Voltage drop in a circuit usually results from
   A. inductance.
   B. capacitance.
   C. resistance.
   D. conductance.

9. Which of the following sizes of electric heaters is the largest one that can be used in a 120-volt circuit protected by a 15-ampere circuit breaker?
   A. 1,000 watts
   B. 1,300 watts
   C. 2,000 watts
   D. 2,600 watts

10. Of the following devices, which one will store an electric charge?
    A. Capacitor
    B. Inductor
    C. Thyristor
    D. Resistor

11. Of the nonmetallic elements listed, which one is the best conductor of electricity?
    A. Mica
    B. Carbon
    C. Formica
    D. Hard rubber

12. If an electric motor designed for use on AC is plugged into a DC source, what will probably happen?
    A. Excessive heat will be produced.
    B. It will operate the same as usual.
    C. It will continue to operate but will not get so warm.
    D. It cannot be predicted what will happen.

13. Most electrical problems involving voltage, resistance, and current are solved by applying
    A. Ohm's law.
    B. Watt's law.
    C. Coulomb's law.
    D. Kirchoff's voltage and current laws.

14. If every time a washing machine is started the circuit breaker must be reset, the best solution would be to
    A. oil the motor in the washer.
    B. replace the circuit breaker.
    C. tape the breaker switch closed.
    D. repair the timing mechanism.

15. Electronic circuits designed to produce high frequency alternating currents are usually known as
    A. oscillators.
    B. amplifiers.
    C. rectifiers.
    D. detectors.

16. The current in a circuit is 45mA. This is
    A. 0.45A.
    B. 0.0045A.
    C. 0.00045A.
    D. 0.045A.

17. 1,200mV is equal to
    A. 12v.
    B. 1.2v.
    C. 0.12v.
    D. 0.0012v.

18. Which of the following has the LEAST resistance?
    A. Silver
    B. Aluminum
    C. Copper
    D. Steel

19. In electronic circuits, the symbol shown above usually represents a
    A. transformer.
    B. capacitor.
    C. transistor.
    D. diode.

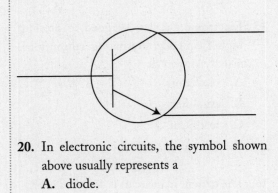

20. In electronic circuits, the symbol shown above usually represents a
   A. diode.
   B. magnetron.
   C. transistor.
   D. triode.

STOP!
IF YOU FINISH BEFORE THE TIME IS UP,
YOU MAY CHECK OVER YOUR WORK ON THIS PART ONLY.

PART 7: AUTO & SHOP INFORMATION

Time: 11 Minutes—25 Questions

Directions: This test has 25 questions about automobiles, shop practices, and the use of tools. Select the best answer for each question, then blacken the space on your answer sheet that has the same number and letter as your choice.

Here are three sample questions.

1. The most commonly used fuel for running automobile engines is   Ⓐ Ⓑ Ⓒ Ⓓ
    A. kerosene.
    B. benzene.
    C. crude oil.
    D. gasoline.

    Gasoline is the most commonly used fuel, so choice D is the correct answer.

2. A car uses too much oil when which parts are worn?   Ⓐ Ⓑ Ⓒ Ⓓ
    A. Pistons
    B. Piston rings
    C. Main bearings
    D. Connecting rods

    Worn piston rings cause the use of too much oil, so choice B is the correct answer.

3. The saw shown above is used mainly to cut   Ⓐ Ⓑ Ⓒ Ⓓ
    A. plywood.
    B. odd-shaped holes in wood.
    C. along the grain of the wood.
    D. across the grain of the wood.

    The compass saw is used to cut odd-shaped holes in wood, so choice B is the correct answer.

Your score on this test will be based on the number of questions you answer correctly. You should try to answer every question. Do not spend too much time on any one question.

When you are told to begin, be sure to start with question number 1 in Part 7 in your test booklet and number 1 in Part 7 on your answer sheet.

1. If an automobile engine is overheating,
   A. allow it to cool down.
   B. immediately remove the radiator cap.
   C. immediately pour cold water on the radiator.
   D. immediately pour cold water into the radiator.

2. A torsion bar might be found in the
   A. transmission.
   B. distributor.
   C. speedometer.
   D. suspension.

3. A black gummy deposit in the end of the tailpipe of an automobile indicates that
   A. the automobile "burns" oil.
   B. there is probably a leak in the exhaust manifold.
   C. the timing is late.
   D. there are leaks in the exhaust valves.

4. What occurs if cylinder heads are not torqued in the correct sequence?
   A. The intake manifold cracks.
   B. Valve clearance is reduced.
   C. It warps the head.
   D. It warps the piston rings.

5. If a car loses speed, lacks power, and a popping noise is heard, the problem is most likely
   A. a bad fuel supply.
   B. that ignition timing is off.
   C. a fouled spark plug.
   D. a bad ignition module.

6. The generator or alternator of an automobile engine is usually driven by the
   A. camshaft.
   B. flywheel.
   C. fan belt.
   D. cranking motor.

7. Of the following, which is the most likely cause if an engine is found to be missing on one cylinder?
   A. A clogged exhaust
   B. A defective spark plug
   C. An overheated engine
   D. Vapor lock

8. The head has broken off a bolt. The correct tools to use to remove the broken bolt are
   A. a screwdriver and locking pliers.
   B. an electric drill and easy-out extractor.
   C. a ball peen hammer and chisel.
   D. an acetylene torch and dead blow hammer.

9. It is best for an automobile's gas tank to be full or nearly full to prevent
   A. gasoline from vaporizing in the fuel lines.
   B. moisture from condensing in the gas tank.
   C. drying out of the fuel pump.
   D. loss of vacuum in the vacuum line.

10. The automotive power train includes all of the following EXCEPT the
    A. clutch.
    B. differential.
    C. steering gear.
    D. transmission.

11. An automobile handbrake is set tightly, and the engine is idling at 30 mph road speed. If you shift into high gear, release the clutch, and the engine continues to run about the same, what would most likely need repair?
    A. Clutch
    B. Throttle
    C. High gear
    D. Carburetor

12. The pistons of gasoline engines will some-times increase in size so that they "stick" in the cylinder. This is often caused by
    A. low engine operating temperature.
    B. overheating of the engine.
    C. worn oil rings.
    D. worn compression rings.

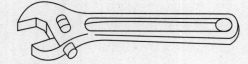

13. The tool shown above is a
    A. crescent wrench.
    B. monkey wrench.
    C. pipe wrench.
    D. torque wrench.

14. Concrete is usually made by mixing
    A. only sand and water.
    B. only cement and water.
    C. lye, cement, and water.
    D. rock, sand, cement, and water.

15. The set of a saw is the
    A. angle at which the handle is set.
    B. amount of springiness of the blade.
    C. amount of sharpness of the teeth.
    D. distance the points stick out beyond the sides of the blade.

16. The principal reason for "tempering" or "drawing" steel is to
    A. reduce strength.
    B. reduce hardness.
    C. increase strength.
    D. increase malleability.

17. Sheet metal is dipped in sulfuric acid to
    A. clean it.
    B. soften it.
    C. harden it.
    D. prevent it from rusting.

18. The cut of a file refers to the
    A. shape of its handle.
    B. shape of its edge.
    C. kind of metal of which it is made.
    D. kind of teeth it has.

19. When grinding a good point on a twist drill, it is necessary that
    A. the point be extremely sharp.
    B. both cutting edges have the same lip.
    C. a file be used for the entire cutting process.
    D. the final grinding be done by hand.

20. The tool used to locate a point directly below a ceiling hook is a
    A. plumb bob.
    B. line level.
    C. transit.
    D. drop gauge.

21. To remove a nail from a wall, the proper tool to use is a
    A. claw hammer.
    B. ball peen hammer.
    C. sledge hammer.
    D. dead blow hammer.

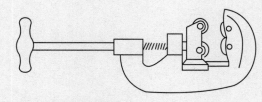

22. The tool above is a
    A. marking gauge.
    B. knurling tool.
    C. threat cutter.
    D. pipe cutter.

23. A high-speed grinder operator will check the abrasive wheel before starting the machine because
    - A. it must be wetted properly before use.
    - B. if cracked or chipped, it could injure someone.
    - C. a dry wheel will produce excessive sparks.
    - D. previous work may have clogged the wheel.

24. When marking wood, an allowance of $\frac{1}{16}$ inch to inch should be made to $\frac{1}{8}$ allow for
    - A. drying of the wood.
    - B. absorption of water by wood.
    - C. the width of the saw.
    - D. knots in the wood.

25. The tool shown above is used for
    - A. pressure lubricating.
    - B. welding steel plate.
    - C. drilling small holes in tight places.
    - D. holding small parts for heat treating.

STOP!
IF YOU FINISH BEFORE THE TIME IS UP,
YOU MAY CHECK OVER YOUR WORK ON THIS PART ONLY.

PART 8: MECHANICAL COMPREHENSION

Time: 19 Minutes—25 Questions

> **Directions:** This test has 25 questions about mechanical principles. Most of the questions use drawings to illustrate specific principles. Decide which answer is correct and mark the space on your answer sheet that has the same number and letter as your choice.

Here are two sample questions.

1. Which bridge is the strongest?

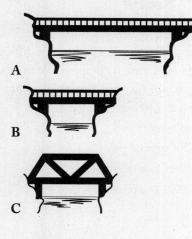

A. A

B. B

C. C

D. All are equally strong.

Ⓐ Ⓑ Ⓒ Ⓓ

Choice C is correct.

2. If all of the objects below are the same temperature, and your temperature is higher than the item's temperature, which will feel coldest?

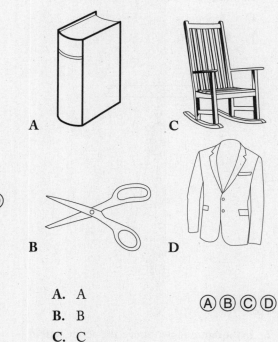

A. A

B. B

C. C

D. D

Ⓐ Ⓑ Ⓒ Ⓓ

Choice B is correct.

Your score on this test will be based on the number of questions you answer correctly. You should try to answer every question. Do not spend too much time on any one question.

When you are told to begin, be sure to start with question number 1 in Part 8 in your test booklet and number 1 in Part 8 on your answer sheet.

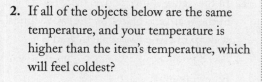

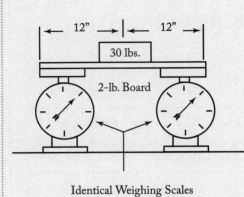

Identical Weighing Scales

1. In the figure shown above, the weight held by the board and placed on the two identical scales will cause *each* scale to read
   A. 8 pounds.
   B. 15 pounds.
   C. 16 pounds.
   D. 32 pounds.

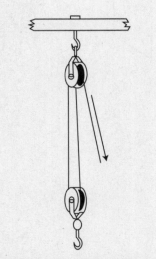

2. In the figure shown above, the pulley system consists of a fixed block and a movable block. The theoretical mechanical advantage is
   A. 1
   B. 2
   C. 3
   D. 4

3. A single movable block is being used in the figure shown above. The person is lifting a 200-pound cask with approximately how great a pull (disregard friction, weight of pulley, and weight of line)?
   A. 50-pound pull
   B. 100-pound pull
   C. 200-pound pull
   D. 250-pound pull

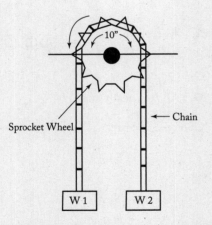

4. In the figure shown above, one complete revolution of the sprocket wheel will bring weight W2 higher than weight W1 by
   A. 20 inches.
   B. 30 inches.
   C. 40 inches.
   D. 50 inches.

5. The main purpose of baffle plates in a furnace is to
   A. retard the burning of gases.
   B. prevent escape of flue gases through furnace openings.
   C. change the direction of flow of heated gases.
   D. increase combustion rate of the fuel.

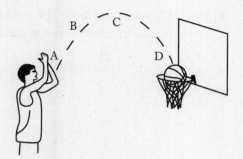

6. At which point was the basketball above moving slowest?
   A. A
   B. B
   C. C
   D. D

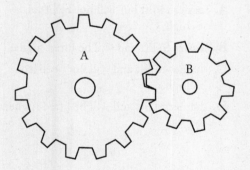

7. In the figure above, if gear A makes 14 revolutions, gear B will make
   A. 9 revolutions.
   B. 14 revolutions.
   C. 17 revolutions.
   D. 21 revolutions.

8. A characteristic of a rotary pump is
   A. valves that are required on the discharge side of the pump.
   B. it is usually operated at high speeds up to 3,600 rpm.
   C. a rapidly rotating impeller that moves the liquid through the discharge piping.
   D. two gears, meshed together and revolving in opposite directions that move liquid to the discharge pipe.

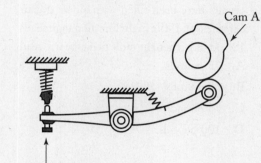

9. As cam A above makes one complete turn, the setscrew will hit the contact point
   A. once.
   B. twice.
   C. three times.
   D. not at all.

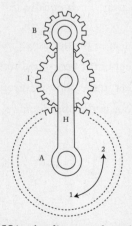

10. If arm H in the diagram above is held fixed as gear B turns in direction 2, gear
    A. A must turn in direction 1.
    B. A must turn in direction 2.
    C. I must turn in direction 2.
    D. A must be held fixed.

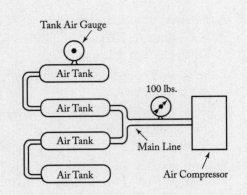

11. As shown in the figure above, four air reservoirs have been filled with air by the air compressor. If the main line air gauge reads 100 pounds, then the tank air gauge will read

A. 25 pounds.

B. 50 pounds.

C. 75 pounds.

D. 100 pounds.

12. In the figure above, a 150-pound man jumps off a 600-pound raft to a point in the water 12 feet away. Theoretically, the raft would move

A. 12 feet in the opposite direction.

B. 6 feet in the opposite direction.

C. 3 feet in the opposite direction.

D. 1 foot in the opposite direction.

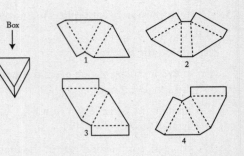

13. In the above illustration, the flat sheet metal pattern that can be bent along the dotted lines to form the completely closed triangular box is

A. 4

B. 2

C. 3

D. 1

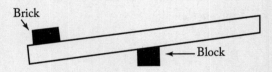

14. In the above diagram, if the block on which the lever is resting is moved closer to the brick, the brick will be

A. easier to lift but will not be lifted as high.

B. easier to lift and will be lifted higher.

C. harder to lift and will not be lifted as high.

D. harder to lift and will be lifted higher.

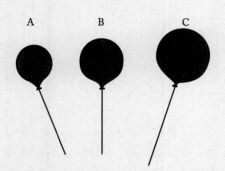

15. The amount of gas in the balloons is equal. The atmospheric pressure outside the balloons is highest on which balloon in the figure above?

A. A

B. B

C. C

D. The pressure is equal on all balloons.

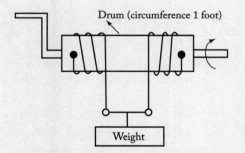

16. In the above figure, one complete revolution of the windlass drum will move the weight up

A. 6 inches.

B. 12 inches.

C. 18 inches.

D. 24 inches.

17. Liquid is being transferred from the above barrel to the bucket by

A. the vacuum at the lower end of the hose.

B. the difference between the fluid volumes in the barrel and the bucket.

C. air pressure on top of the liquid.

D. capillary action.

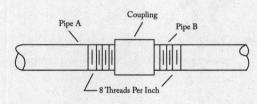

18. In the figure above, if pipe A is held in a vise and pipe B is turned 4 revolutions with a wrench, the overall length of the pipes and coupling will decrease

A. $\frac{1}{8}$ inch.

B. $\frac{1}{4}$ inch.

C. $\frac{3}{8}$ inch.

D. $\frac{1}{2}$ inch.

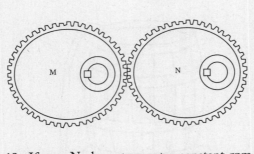

19. If gear N above turns at a constant rpm, gear M turns at

   A. the same constant rpm as N.

   B. a faster constant rpm than N.

   C. a slower constant rpm than N.

   D. a variable rpm.

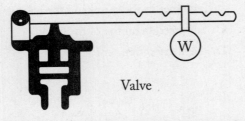

Valve

20. The figure above shows a lever-type safety valve. It will blow off at a lower pressure if weight W is

   A. increased.

   B. moved to the right.

   C. increased and moved to the right.

   D. moved to the left.

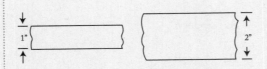

21. With the same water pressure, the amount of water that can be carried by the above 2-inch pipe as compared with the 1-inch pipe is

   A. the same.

   B. twice as much.

   C. 3 times as much.

   D. 4 times as much.

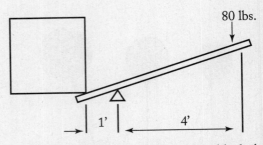

22. A pry bar is used to move a concrete block. A force of 80 pounds applied as shown above will produce a tipping force on the edge of the block of

   A. 80 pounds.

   B. 240 pounds.

   C. 320 pounds.

   D. 400 pounds.

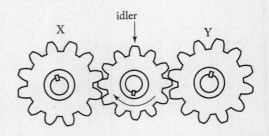

23. In the figure shown above, X is the driver gear and Y is the driven gear. If the idler gear is rotating counterclockwise, gear

   A. X and gear Y are rotating clockwise.

   B. X and gear Y are rotating counterclockwise.

   C. X is rotating clockwise, while gear Y is rotating counterclockwise.

   D. Y is rotating clockwise, while gear X is rotating counterclockwise.

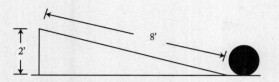

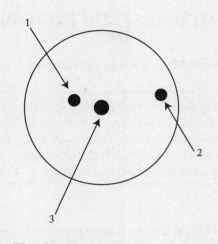

24. Neglecting friction, what effort is needed in the figure above to roll a barrel weighing 400 pounds up an incline 8 feet long and 2 feet high?

  A. 50 pounds

  B. 100 pounds

  C. 150 pounds

  D. 200 pounds

25. The figure above represents a revolving wheel. The numbers 1 and 2 indicate two fixed points on the wheel. The number 3 indicates the center of the wheel. Of the following, the most accurate statement is that point

  A. 1 makes fewer revolutions per minute than point 2.

  B. 1 will make a complete revolution in less time than point 2.

  C. 2 makes more revolutions per minute than point 1.

  D. 2 traverses a greater linear distance than point 1.

STOP!
IF YOU FINISH BEFORE THE TIME IS UP,
YOU MAY CHECK OVER YOUR WORK ON THIS PART ONLY.

practice test 4

PART 9: ASSEMBLING OBJECTS*

Time: 9 Minutes—16 Questions

> **Directions:** This test contains 16 items measuring your ability to determine how an object will look when its parts are mentally assembled. Each item consists of five drawings. The problem is presented in the first drawing. Each problem is followed by four answers, only one of which is correct. Decide which answer is correct, then blacken the space on your answer sheet that has the same number and letter as your choice.

Now look at the two sample problems below.

1.

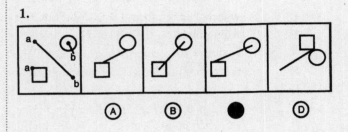

In the previous figure, the parts to be assembled are simple geometric figures (lines, squares, rectangles, etc.) that are labeled at one or more points with small letters. By matching corresponding letters on the different parts, you can see where the parts touch when the object is put together, or connected, properly.

Choice C is the correct answer.

2.

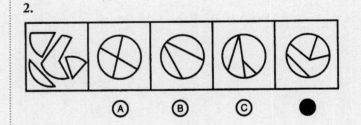

In this figure, the parts are not labeled. Instead, they fit together like pieces of a puzzle. Choice D is the correct answer.

Your score on this test will be based on the number of questions you answer correctly. You should try to answer every question. Do not spend too much time on any one question.

When you are told to begin, be sure to start with question number 1 in Part 9 in your test booklet and number 1 in Part 9 on your answer sheet.

---

*NOTE: This section is not included on paper-and-pencil versions of the ASVAB. It is included on the ASVAB computer-adaptive test (CAT) but may be eliminated in the future. Check with your recruiter for details.

1.

A   B   C   D

2.

A   B   C   D

3.

A   B   C   D

4.

A   B   C   D

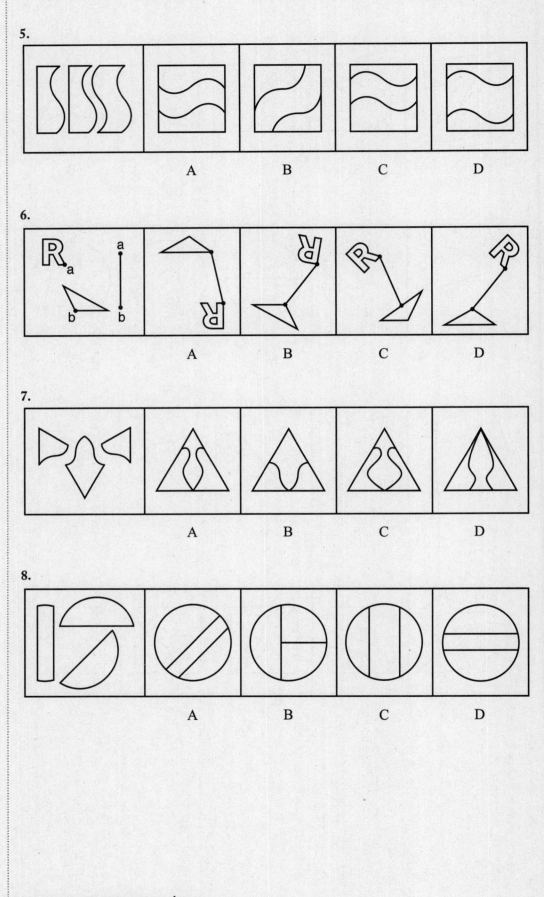

9.

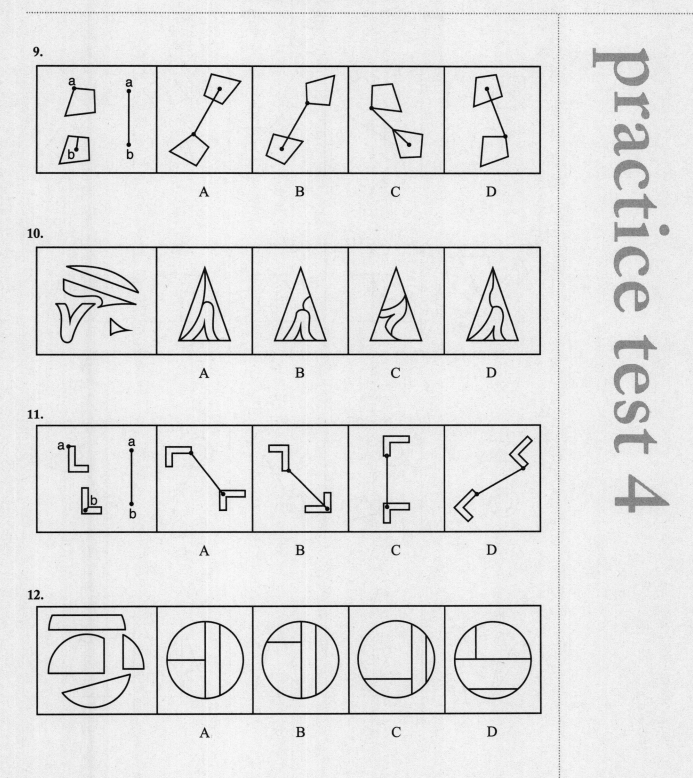

A   B   C   D

10.

A   B   C   D

11.

A   B   C   D

12.

A   B   C   D

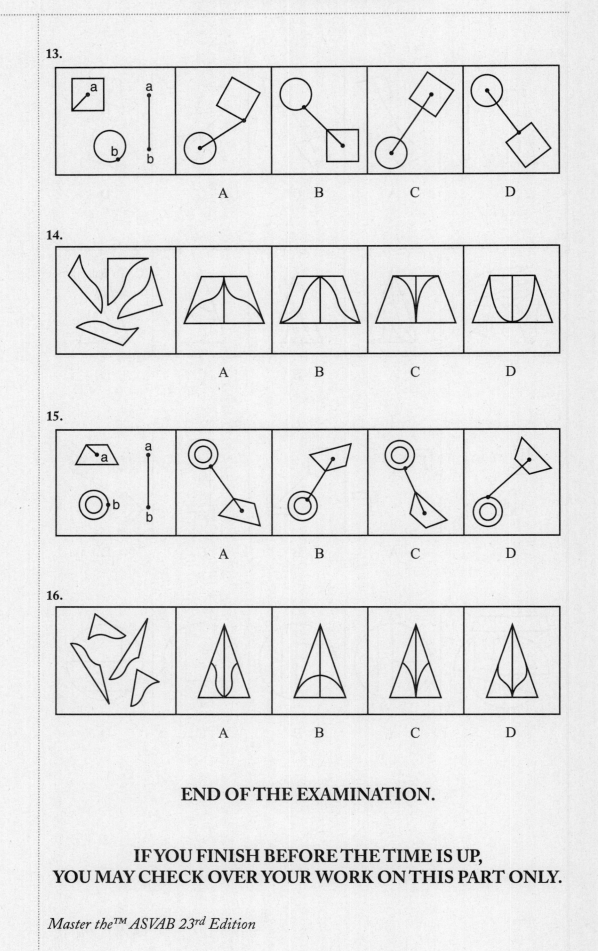

13.

A   B   C   D

14.

A   B   C   D

15.

A   B   C   D

16.

A   B   C   D

END OF THE EXAMINATION.

IF YOU FINISH BEFORE THE TIME IS UP,
YOU MAY CHECK OVER YOUR WORK ON THIS PART ONLY.

ANSWER KEYS AND EXPLANATIONS

PART 1: GENERAL SCIENCE

1. C	6. D	11. C	16. D	21. A
2. B	7. C	12. B	17. D	22. D
3. B	8. C	13. C	18. C	23. C
4. B	9. D	14. B	19. A	24. B
5. C	10. D	15. A	20. A	25. D

1. **The correct answer is C.** Citrus fruits and tomatoes prevent scurvy by providing the body with large quantities of Vitamin C.

2. **The correct answer is B.** A meter stick can be balanced on a finger placed on the 50 cm mark because it is half the distance of 1 meter. 100 centimeters equal 1 meter.

3. **The correct answer is B.** Meat provides much essential protein in the form the body needs. Protein is the principal nutrient in lean meat.

4. **The correct answer is B.** The freezing point of water is 0°C; the boiling point of water is 100°C. There is a 100° temperature range between the freezing and boiling points of water.

$$1° C = \frac{1}{100} \text{ of this range.}$$

5. **The correct answer is C.** Iron is the major component in the production of steel.

6. **The correct answer is D.** Meteors or "shooting stars" come into the earth's atmosphere from outer space with high velocity. The resistance offered by the earth's atmosphere makes these meteors incandescent in flight.

7. **The correct answer is C.** To balance the seesaw, the product of the weight and the distance from the weight to the fulcrum must be the same for both sides. Let x = distance from center of seesaw for the second child.

$$x \times 40 = 4 \times 80$$
$$40x = 320$$
$$x = \frac{320}{40} = 8 \text{ feet}$$

8. **The correct answer is C.** Most of the end products of digestion are absorbed into the bloodstream while traveling through the small intestine.

9. **The correct answer is D.** Skeletal muscles are joined to bones by tendons. Tendons are so attached that they pull on the bones and make them act like levers.

10. **The correct answer is D.** An echo is the repetition of a sound caused by the reflection of sound waves. An image is an optical appearance of an object produced by reflection from a mirror.

11. **The correct answer is C.** Vitamin K is a fat-soluble vitamin needed for normal blood clotting.

12. **The correct answer is B.** Half-life is defined as the amount of time it takes for half of a substance to undergo decay. A 400g sample undergoing one half-life decays by 50%. 200 is half of 400.

13. **The correct answer is C.** The primary reason for lowering the center of gravity in automobiles is to increase stability. Stability is increased largely by lowering the center of gravity and by increasing the width of the automobile.

14. **The correct answer is B.** A substance that changes the rate of a chemical reaction but is itself unchanged at the end of the reaction is called a catalyst.

15. **The correct answer is A.** The hip joint is a ball-and-socket joint that permits circular movement.

16. **The correct answer is D.** The virus that causes AIDS is called human immunodeficiency virus, or HIV.

17. **The correct answer is D.** Rickets is a disease in which bones and teeth are weak and poorly formed. It may be caused by insufficient Vitamin D in the diet.

18. **The correct answer is C.** 100% > 50 > 25 > 12.5 > 6.25 > 3.125 equals 5 half-lives. $5 \times 5,730 = 28,650$ years.

19. **The correct answer is A.** The denser the liquid, the less the weight of the lead sinker. Accordingly, liquid B has less density than liquid A.

20. **The correct answer is A.** The lowering of the freezing point of a solution is generally proportional to the solute particles in the solution. A practical application of this principle is the throwing of salt on a snow- or ice-covered sidewalk to help melt the snow or ice.

21. **The correct answer is A.** Organisms that live on or in the body of other live organisms from which food is obtained are called parasites.

22. **The correct answer is D.** As all the effects listed in choices A, B, and C result from air pollution, choice D (all of the above) is the most inclusive and therefore the best answer.

23. **The correct answer is C.** 7.20×10^3 cm $\times 8.08 \times 10^3$ cm $= 5.82 \times 10^7$ cm^2

24. **The correct answer is B.** Photosynthesis is the process by which green plants manufacture carbohydrates from carbon dioxide and water in the presence of sunlight and chlorophyll.

25. **The correct answer is D.** Substances are classified as elements or compounds. A compound is a substance composed of the atoms of two or more different elements.

Items Answered Incorrectly: _____ ; _____ ; _____ ; _____ ; _____ ; _____ ; _____ ; _____ ; _____

Items Unsure Of: _____ ; _____ ; _____ ; _____ ; _____ ; _____ ; _____ ; _____ ; _____

Total Number Answered Correctly: _____

PART 2: ARITHMETIC REASONING

1. C	7. D	13. C	19. C	25. C
2. A	8. A	14. D	20. C	26. C
3. D	9. B	15. D	21. D	27. C
4. B	10. A	16. C	22. C	28. D
5. C	11. C	17. C	23. B	29. A
6. A	12. B	18. B	24. B	30. A

1. **The correct answer is C.**

   54 seconds/lap = 20 laps = 1,080 seconds

   $1,080 \text{ seconds} = \dfrac{1 \text{ minutes}}{60 \text{ seconds}} = 18 \text{ minutes}$

2. **The correct answer is A.** $\dfrac{144}{36} = 4$ buses

3. **The correct answer is D.** The difference in temperature is high temperature – low temperature.

   $2°F - (-14°F) = 26°F$

4. **The correct answer is B.** $\dfrac{68}{28} = 6$ per day

5. **The correct answer is C.**

   Distance (d) = rate (r) × time (t)
   1,400 miles = r × 3.5 hours
   Divide by 3.5
   400 miles/hr = r

6. **The correct answer is A.**

   360 × 8 = 2,880 switches/8 hours

   2,880 × .05 = 144 defective switches

   2,880 – 144 = 2,736 good switches

7. **The correct answer is D.**

   $22\dfrac{1}{2} \div 1\dfrac{1}{4} = \dfrac{45}{2} \div \dfrac{5}{4} = \dfrac{\overset{9}{\cancel{45}}}{\underset{1}{\cancel{2}}} \times \dfrac{\overset{2}{\cancel{4}}}{\underset{1}{\cancel{5}}} = 18$ packages

8. **The correct answer is A.**
   $240 × 4 = $960 total sales
   $960 × 15% = $144

9. **The correct answer is B.** 60% of $27 = $16.20, the cost for 2 tickets; $\dfrac{\$16.20}{2} = \$8.10$, the cost for one ticket.

10. **The correct answer is A.** Cost per bar when purchased in small amounts = $0.33; $\dfrac{\$3.48}{12} = \$0.29$, cost per bar when purchased in lots of one dozen.

    $0.33 – $0.29 = $0.04, savings per bar

11. **The correct answer is C.** $25 × 20 = $500 in contributions

    $500 × .40 = $200 spent for food and drinks

    $500 – $200 = $300 remaining for other expenses

12. **The correct answer is B.**

    1st truck travels:
    60 miles/hr × 2 hours = 120 miles

    2nd truck travels:
    50 miles/hr × 2 hours = 100 miles

    120 miles × 100 miles = 220 miles

13. **The correct answer is C.**

    $250 × .20 = $50; $250 – $50 = $200

    $200 × .30 = $60; $200 – $60 = $140

14. **The correct answer is D.**

    7:15 to 12 noon = $4\dfrac{3}{4}$ hours

    12 noon to 3:45 = $3\dfrac{3}{4}$ hours

    $4\dfrac{3}{4} + 3\dfrac{3}{4} = 8\dfrac{1}{2}$ hours

15. **The correct answer is D.**

    Let x = assessed value of house

    $.02x = \$550.00$

    $x = \dfrac{550}{.02} = \$27.500$

16. **The correct answer is C.** 250 miles a day × 6 drivers = 1,500 miles a day

    1,500 miles a day × 5 days = 7,500 miles a week

17. **The correct answer is C.** The 17-minute mark is $\dfrac{2}{5}$ of the way between 3 and 4 o'clock. $\dfrac{2}{5}$ of 60 = 24; 24 minutes past 3 o'clock = 3:24

18. **The correct answer is B.**

    $3375 \div 3\dfrac{3}{8} = 3375 \div \dfrac{27}{8} = 3375 \times$

    $\dfrac{8}{27} = 125 \times 8 = 1,000$ dresses

19. **The correct answer is C.** 15′ × 24′ = 5 yards × 8 yards = 40 square yards

    40 square yards × \$1 = \$40

20. **The correct answer is C.**

    $16\dfrac{1}{2}$ hours = 15 hours + 90 minutes;

    $\dfrac{15}{5} = 3$ hours; $\dfrac{90}{5} = 18$ minutes;

    3 hours + 18 minutes = 3 hours, 18 minutes

21. **The correct answer is D.**

    100 miles @ 40 mph = $2\dfrac{1}{2}$ hours = $2\dfrac{3}{6}$ hours

    80 miles @ 60 mph = $1\dfrac{1}{3}$ hours = $1\dfrac{2}{6}$ hours

    $2\dfrac{3}{6}$ hours + $1\dfrac{2}{6}$ hours = $3\dfrac{5}{6}$ hours

22. **The correct answer is C.**

    Let x = original price

    $x \times .25 = 25x$

    $x - .25x = \$112.50$

    $.75x = \$112.50$

    $x = \dfrac{\$112.50}{.75} = \$150$

23. **The correct answer is B.**

    2 feet 6 inches × 4 sections = 10 feet.

    12 feet − 10 feet = 2 feet

24. **The correct answer is B.** 250 × .08 = \$20; 250 × .07 = \$17.50; 500 erasers cost \$37.50; \$50 − \$37.50 = \$12.50

    Let x = additional erasers purchased.

    $x \times .05 = 12.50$

    $x = \dfrac{2.50}{.05} = 250$; 500 + 250 $= 750$ erasers.

25. **The correct answer is C.** Time difference between New York and Los Angeles is 3 hours. 4:15 p.m. − 3:30 p.m. = 45 minutes; 3 hours + 45 minutes = 3 hours, 45 minutes for flight time.

26. **The correct answer is C.** Basic toll = \$1

    \$3.25 − \$1 = \$2.25 for extra passengers

    \$2.25 ÷ .75 = 3

27. **The correct answer is C.**

    Each sheet contains 100 stamps.

    3 sheets of 23¢ stamps cost \$ 69

    2 sheets of 50¢ stamps cost \$100

    4 sheets of 29¢ stamps cost <u>\$116</u>

                           \$285

28. **The correct answer is D.** Total earnings in pay period = \$497.05

    Deduct:

federal income tax	\$ 90.32
FICA	28.74
state tax	18.79
city tax	7.25
pension	<u>+ 1.88</u>
	\$ 146.98

                  497.05

              <u>−146.98</u>

              \$ 350.07

29. The correct answer is A.

Let x = price of radio before tax was added.

$x + .05x = \$31.29$

$1.05x = 31.29$

$x = \dfrac{32.29}{1.05} = \$29.80$

30. The correct answer is A.

$x = \dfrac{3600}{40} = 90$ minutes $= 1\dfrac{1}{2}$ hours

Items Answered Incorrectly: _____ ; _____ ; _____ ; _____ ; _____ ; _____ ; _____ ; _____ ; _____

Items Unsure Of: _____ ; _____ ; _____ ; _____ ; _____ ; _____ ; _____ ; _____ ; _____

Total Number Answered Correctly: _____

PART 3: WORD KNOWLEDGE

1. B	**8.** B	**15.** B	**22.** C	**29.** A
2. C	**9.** D	**16.** D	**23.** D	**30.** A
3. B	**10.** D	**17.** C	**24.** A	**31.** C
4. D	**11.** D	**18.** A	**25.** C	**32.** C
5. A	**12.** A	**19.** A	**26.** B	**33.** C
6. B	**13.** A	**20.** B	**27.** D	**34.** B
7. D	**14.** C	**21.** A	**28.** A	**35.** D

1. **The correct answer is B.** To be *impartial* means to be *without bias*, that is, *to remain neutral*.

2. **The correct answer is C.** *Supersede* means to *replace*. For example, the new law, written in 2018, supersedes the one written in 1968.

3. **The correct answer is B.** *Caution* means *care* or *watchfulness*.

4. **The correct answer is D.** The word *intermittently* means *recurring from time to time*.

5. **The correct answer is A.** The word *occurrence* is synonymous with *event* or *incident*.

6. **The correct answer is B.** *Deception* means *fraud* or *subterfuge*.

7. **The correct answer is D.** The word *cease* means *to stop* or *come to an end*.

8. **The correct answer is B.** The word *acclaim* is synonymous with *applause* or *approval*.

9. **The correct answer is D.** The word *erect* means to *build* or *construct*.

10. **The correct answer is D.** *Relish* means to *like* or *enjoy*.

11. **The correct answer is D.** *Sufficient* means *adequate, enough,* or *appropriate*.

12. **The correct answer is A.** The word *fortnight* means *fourteen days* or *two weeks*.

13. **The correct answer is A.** *Flaw* means *fault* or *defect*.

14. **The correct answer is C.** When someone *attests* to something, they are *stating that it is true*.

15. **The correct answer is B.** *Jeer* means to *deride, ridicule,* or *scoff*.

16. **The correct answer is D.** *Alias* means an *assumed* or *other name*.

17. **The correct answer is C.** *Impair* means to *make worse* or *weaken*.

18. **The correct answer is A.** *Hasten* means *to hurry, rush, accelerate,* or *speed*.

19. **The correct answer is A.** The word *abandon* means *to give up* or *relinquish*.

20. **The correct answer is B.** *Resolve* means *to determine* or *decide*.

21. **The correct answer is A.** *Ample* means *abundant* or *plentiful*.

22. **The correct answer is C.** *Havoc* most nearly means *chaos, destruction, mayhem,* or *disorder*.

23. **The correct answer is D.** *Sullen* means *morose* or *angrily silent*.

24. **The correct answer is A.** *Rudiments* means *basic principles* or *procedures*.

25. **The correct answer is C.** *Clash* means to *disagree* or *conflict*.

26. **The correct answer is B.** In this example, *lapse* refers to *a temporary moral failure*, but can also mean *a gap, space, delay,* or *break*.

27. **The correct answer is D.** The word *super-ficial* is synonymous with *shallow* or *cursory*.

28. **The correct answer is A.** *Elude* can mean to *escape*, *dodge*, *flee*, or *avoid*.

29. **The correct answer is A.** *Terse* means *concise* or *brief*.

30. **The correct answer is A.** The word *concoction* means *a combination of ingredients*.

31. **The correct answer is C.** *Incessant* means *unceasing* or *constant*.

32. **The correct answer is C.** *Solidity* means *firmness* or *the quality of being solid*.

33. **The correct answer is C.** *Increment* means an *addition* or *increase*.

34. **The correct answer is B.** The word *immaterial* means *unimportant*.

35. **The correct answer is D.** The word *misconstrued* means *misinterpreted* or *interpreted erroneously*.

Items Answered Incorrectly: _____ ; _____ ; _____ ; _____ ; _____ ; _____ ; _____ ; _____ ; _____

Items Unsure Of: _____ ; _____ ; _____ ; _____ ; _____ ; _____ ; _____ ; _____

Total Number Answered Correctly: _____

PART 4: PARAGRAPH COMPREHENSION

1. A	**4.** C	**7.** D	**10.** C	**13.** B
2. A	**5.** C	**8.** D	**11.** A	**14.** B
3. D	**6.** A	**9.** B	**12.** A	**15.** C

1. **The correct answer is A.** The passage states that physical examinations are intended to increase efficiency and production and that they do accomplish these ends.

2. **The correct answer is A.** The passage states that traffic violations are usually the result of illegal and dangerous driving behavior.

3. **The correct answer is D.** Complaints frequently bring into the open conditions and faults in operation and service that should be corrected.

4. **The correct answer is C.** The vaulter may attempt to jump any height above the minimum that is set by the judge.

5. **The correct answer is C.** The last sentence in the passage states that the real danger is in a large leak that can cause an explosion.

6. **The correct answer is A.** The time it takes the earth to go around the sun is $365\frac{1}{4}$ days rather than 365 days. Leap years correct for this discrepancy by adding an extra day once every four years.

7. **The correct answer is D.** The point of the passage is that a business should be prepared to fill unexpected vacancies with pre-trained staff members.

8. **The correct answer is D.** See the first sentence in the reading passage.

9. **The correct answer is B.** See the first sentence in the reading passage.

10. **The correct answer is C.** Phosphorus catches fire easily. Therefore, it has a low kindling temperature.

11. **The correct answer is A.** See the last sentence in the reading passage.

12. **The correct answer is A.** From the second sentence in the reading passage, it may be deduced that it is difficult to suppress racketeering because so many people want services that are not obtainable through legitimate sources.

13. **The correct answer is B.** See the second sentence in the reading passage.

14. **The correct answer is B.** See the last sentence in the reading passage.

15. **The correct answer is C.** A meter is one ten-millionth of the distance from the Equator to the North Pole.

One ten-millionth $= \dfrac{1}{10,000,000}$

Items Answered Incorrectly: _____ ; _____ ; _____ ; _____ ; _____ ; _____ ; _____ ; _____ ; _____

Items Unsure Of: _____ ; _____ ; _____ ; _____ ; _____ ; _____ ; _____ ; _____

Total Number Answered Correctly: _____

PART 5: MATHEMATICS KNOWLEDGE

1. B	**6.** B	**11.** D	**16.** A	**21.** A
2. B	**7.** D	**12.** A	**17.** D	**22.** C
3. B	**8.** C	**13.** B	**18.** A	**23.** A
4. A	**9.** C	**14.** C	**19.** C	**24.** D
5. A	**10.** B	**15.** A	**20.** C	**25.** C

1. **The correct answer is B.** Using the distributive property, $(2x + 1)(3x + 4)$ yields $6x^2 + 11x + 4$, so the coefficient of x^2 is 6.

2. **The correct answer is B.**

$$
\begin{array}{r}
x + 1 \\
\times\ x + 2 \\
\hline
x^2 + x \\
+ \quad\quad 2x + 2 \\
\hline
x^2 + 3x + 2
\end{array}
$$

3. **The correct answer is B.**

$$3x = -5$$
$$x = \frac{-5}{3} = -\frac{5}{3}$$

4. **The correct answer is A.** The first step to finding the square root of a number is to pair the digits to each side of the decimal point. If necessary, place 0 to the left of the first digit to form a pair and then solve with a modified form of long division.

$$\sqrt{059043}$$

As the square root of 05 is between 2 and 3, place 2 above the first pair. The first digit of the square root of 59,043 is 2.

5. **The correct answer is A.** Area of rectangle $= 9 \times 4 = 36$. Area of square $= 36$. Therefore, each side $= 6$ and the perimeter of the square $= 6 + 6 + 6 + 6 = 24$.

6. **The correct answer is B.** $4^2 + 4^2 = d^2$; $16 + 16 = d^2$; $16 \times 2 = d^2$; $\sqrt{16 \times 2} = d$; $d = 4\sqrt{2}$

7. **The correct answer is D.** Using the distributive property, $(4x + 1)(x + 3)$ yields $4x^2 + 13x + 3$.

8. **The correct answer is C.** Let angle of complement $= x$; let measure of angle $= 2x$; $2x + x = 90°$; $x = 30°$; $2x = 60°$.

9. **The correct answer is C.** The formula for the perimeter of a rectangle is $P = 2L + 2W$, then let width be x and the length be $x + 8$. Therefore:

$$
\begin{array}{ll}
44 = 2(x + 8) + 2(x) & \text{Substitute} \\
44 = 2x + 16 + 2x & \text{Distribute} \\
44 = 4x + 16 & \text{Subtract} \\
28 = 4x & \text{Divide} \\
7 = x &
\end{array}
$$

10. **The correct answer is B.** Substituting into the formula:

$$A = \frac{1}{2}(10)(7)$$
$$A = 35 \text{ ft}^2$$

11. **The correct answer is D.**

$$d = rt;\ A = r + \frac{d}{t};\ A = r + \frac{r\cancel{t}}{1\cancel{t}};$$

$$A = r + r;\ A = 2r$$

12. **The correct answer is A.** 23 is the only option that can be divided only by itself and 1.

13. **The correct answer is B.** If radius $r = 35$ miles, diameter $= 70$ miles.

$$\text{Circumference} = \frac{22}{\cancel{7}_1} \times \cancel{70}^{10} = 220 \text{ miles}$$

14. **The correct answer is C.** $3! = 3 \times 2 \times 1 = 6$

15. **The correct answer is A.** Since the multiple choice answers are in terms of feet, converting all measures in numerator gives:

$$\frac{(12 \text{ feet} + 14 \text{ feet} + 4 \text{ feet})}{4} = \frac{30 \text{ feet}}{4} = 7.5 \text{ feet}$$

16. **The correct answer is A.**

$$\frac{2x}{7} = 2x^2; \, 14x^2 = 2x; \, \frac{\overset{7}{\cancel{14}}x^2}{\underset{1}{\cancel{2}x}} = 1; \, 7x = 1; \, x = \frac{1}{7}$$

17. **The correct answer is D.**

$$A^2 = \frac{B^2}{C + D}; \, A^2(C + D) = B^2;$$

$$C + D = \frac{B^2}{A^2}; \, C = \frac{B^2}{A^2} - D$$

18. **The correct answer is A.** Let x = length of shorter side; let $2x$ = length of longer.

$$2x + x + 2x + x = 90; \, x = 15$$

19. **The correct answer is C.** A quadrilateral is a rhombus only if its four sides are congruent in length. A square has four congruent sides.

20. **The correct answer is C.**

Area $= \pi r^2 = \dfrac{2}{7} \times 7^2 = 22 \times 7 = 154$ sq. in.

21. **The correct answer is A.** $5a - 4x - 3y = 5(-2) - 4(-10) - 3(5) = -10 + 40 - 15 = +15$

22. **The correct answer is C.** More cogs means less revolutions (indirect proportion):

$$\frac{14}{7} = \frac{28}{x} \quad \text{Cross multiply,}$$

$$14x = 196 \quad \text{then divide}$$

$$x = 14$$

23. **The correct answer is A.** $\angle 8$ and $\angle 4$ are corresponding angles formed by parallel lines m$\angle 4 = 80°$. $\angle 4$ and $\angle 2$ are vertical angles and have equal measures. m$\angle 2 = 80°$.

24. **The correct answer is D.**

$$\frac{x}{2} - \frac{x}{5} = 3; \, \frac{5x}{10} - \frac{2x}{10} = 3; \, \frac{3x}{10} = 3; \, 3x = 30; \, x = 10$$

25. **The correct answer is C.** $C = \pi D = \pi \times 2r = 2\pi r$; if radius is increased by 3, $C = \pi \times 2(r + 3)$; $C = \pi \times (2r + 6) = 2\pi r + 6\pi$

Items Answered Incorrectly: _____ ; _____ ; _____ ; _____ ; _____ ; _____ ; _____ ;
_____ ; _____

Items Unsure Of: _____ ; _____ ; _____ ; _____ ; _____ ; _____ ; _____ ; _____ ; _____

Total Number Answered Correctly: _____

PART 6: ELECTRONICS INFORMATION

1. D	5. A	9. B	13. A	17. B
2. C	6. D	10. A	14. B	18. A
3. D	7. D	11. B	15. A	19. D
4. D	8. C	12. A	16. D	20. C

1. **The correct answer is D.** Consider the following filtered rectifier circuit with a short circuit across capacitor A:

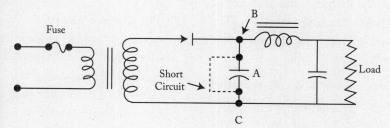

The current at point B, which would ordinarily flow through the load resistor, will now flow through the short circuit to C and back through the transformer. The short circuit has virtually no resistance, causing large currents to flow in both the primary and the secondary windings of the transformer. These large currents cause the fuse to burn out.

2. **The correct answer is C.** Descending order of resistors are 5k6, 22R, 4R7, 3R3.

3. **The correct answer is D.** To obtain a higher value of resistance, connect them in series.

4. **The correct answer is D.** Resistance in the primary circuit will reduce the current flow and reduce the voltage and current available at the spark plug. A "circuit" spark with as high a voltage and current as possible is necessary for easy starting and smooth performance.

5. **The correct answer is A.** The resistance of a short circuit usually consists of little more than the resistance of the circuit's copper wires since the load has been "shorted" or bypassed. This very low resistance results in very high current flow.

6. **The correct answer is D.** Wires larger than No. 10 AWG are usually stranded because a solid wire of that diameter is too stiff to make good connections or to "fish" readily through raceways.

7. **The correct answer is D.** The image shows the current rising and falling from some minimum value indicated by the straight-line portions of the image. The current, therefore, pulses without changing direction. AC involves a reversal of direction.

8. **The correct answer is C.** Ohm's law; $V = IR$ gives the voltage drop across a resistor. Inductance and capacitance do not produce a voltage drop. Conductance is the reciprocal of resistance. A high resistance has a low conductance.

9. **The correct answer is B.** Maximum wattage that will cause a 15-ampere breaker to trip is (15 amps) (120 volts) = 1,800 watts. Accordingly, 1,300 watts is the largest heater that will operate without causing the circuit breaker to trip.

10. **The correct answer is A.** A capacitor contains two conducting surfaces separated by an insulator and can, therefore, store static electrical charges. Caution should be exercised before touching capacitors. They should have their terminals "shorted" before being handled.

11. **The correct answer is B.** All the other materials are very good insulators. Carbon has some resistance but still conducts more readily than the others. Resistors may contain some carbon.

12. **The correct answer is A.** The windings in an AC motor are designed to offer a certain amount of impedance, which is a combination of inductive reactance and resistance, to the flow of AC. When DC is applied, only the pure resistance is available to limit the flow of current. Therefore, the direct current flow is larger than the alternating current would be at the same voltage. The increase in power consumption is dissipated as heat.

13. **The correct answer is A.** Ohm's law describes the relationship between the voltage, current, and resistance in a circuit: $V = IR$. The watts consumed by a circuit are the product of the voltage times the current. One ampere flowing for one second delivers one coulomb of electrical charge. Kirchoff's voltage and current laws concern the way voltages and currents around a circuit can be summed up.

14. **The correct answer is B.** Since the starting current drawn by the washing machine is usually six times greater than the running current, it is most likely that the circuit breaker is too small to permit the motor to start. Consult the various local laws governing the size of circuit breakers acceptable to permit motors of various ratings to start. These local laws are usually based on the National Electrical Code.

15. **The correct answer is A.** Oscillators capable of producing high-frequency AC may include crystals capable of producing particular frequencies or they may involve electronic components, such as capacitors and inductors, capable of being tuned to various frequencies.

16. **The correct answer is D.** 45mA is 45 milliamp, which is the equivalent to 0.045A. Divide by 1,000.

17. **The correct answer is B.** 1,200 millivolt is equivalent to 1.2v. Divide by 1,000.

18. **The correct answer is A.** All of the materials listed are conductors. Silver is the best, although it is not often used because of its high cost. The moving contacts in motor starters, however, are often made of silver, and it is widely used where low-resistance contacts are required.

19. **The correct answer is D.** The symbol shows a semiconductor diode. These usually contain silicon and sometimes germanium. They conduct only in the direction shown by the arrow. Currents flowing in the opposite direction meet with high resistance and are effectively blocked. For these reasons, silicon diodes are often used to rectify AC to DC.

20. The correct answer is C. The transistor contains semiconductor material. Two varieties, NPN and PNP, are manufactured. The one shown in the diagram is of the NPN type.

Items Answered Incorrectly: _____ ; _____ ; _____ ; _____ ; _____ ; _____ ; _____ ; _____ ; _____

Items Unsure Of: _____ ; _____ ; _____ ; _____ ; _____ ; _____ ; _____ ; _____ ; _____

Total Number Answered Correctly: _____

answers practice test 4

PART 7: AUTO & SHOP INFORMATION

1. A	6. C	11. A	16. C	21. A
2. D	7. B	12. B	17. A	22. D
3. A	8. B	13. A	18. D	23. B
4. C	9. B	14. D	19. B	24. C
5. A	10. C	15. D	20. A	25. B

1. **The correct answer is A.** If an engine overheats you must immediately stop the car. Not doing so will cause the metal to expand and damage the engine. If you pour anything on (or into) an overheated engine, the rapid cooling may cause the block to crack.

2. **The correct answer is D.** Torsion bars are used in the suspension to absorb shock by twisting.

3. **The correct answer is A.** When an automobile "burns" oil, it means that the engine oil consumption is excessive. This condition is manifested by the formation of a black gummy deposit in the end of the tailpipe.

4. **The correct answer is C.** Cylinder head torquing, or tightening, is accomplished in a specific order so that the head will fit closely to the engine block. Not doing so will lead to the cylinder head becoming warped.

5. **The correct answer is A.** The popping noise is most likely to be an intermittent supply of fuel reaching the cylinders. The lack of fuel causes the engine to lose power causing the car to slow down.

6. **The correct answer is C.** The generator or alternator is usually mounted at the front of the engine and is linked by a fan belt to the engine's crankshaft pulley.

7. **The correct answer is B.** Although all of the options may cause an engine to miss, a defective spark plug is the likely cause if the engine misses only on one cylinder.

8. **The correct answer is B.** The correct tools would be an electric drill with an easy-out extractor. An easy-out extractor is a reverse threaded drill bit used to remove broken bolts.

9. **The correct answer is B.** Moisture enters with the air, especially on damp days. Condensation forms inside the gas tank and collects in the bottom of the tank to form rust or create a thick sludge. Keeping the gas tank as nearly full as possible allows less room for formation of condensation.

10. **The correct answer is C.** The power train consists of the items used to conduct power from the pistons to the wheels.

11. **The correct answer is A.** If the clutch slips, the full power of the engine is not transmitted. The clutch needs to be repaired or replaced.

12. **The correct answer is B.** Pistons expand as the engine warms up. Pistons are designed to fit the cylinders, regardless of whether the pistons are cold or at working temperature. However, when the engine is overheated, the pistons may increase in size to such an extent that they "stick" in the cylinder.

13. **The correct answer is A.** The tool is an adjustable open-end wrench. One jaw is fixed; the other moves along a slide with a thumbscrew adjustment. The tool shown is also called a crescent wrench.

14. The correct answer is D. Concrete is made by mixing cement, sand, and broken rock with sufficient water to make the cement set and bind the entire mass.

15. The correct answer is D. The set of a saw refers to how much the teeth are pushed out in opposite directions from the sides of the blade.

16. The correct answer is C. Tempering brings steel to the desired hardness and strength.

17. The correct answer is A. Sheet metal is generally cleaned by using an industrial grade of sulfuric acid.

18. The correct answer is D. The cut of a file refers to the kind of teeth it has. It may have single-cut or double-cut teeth. The teeth also have different degrees of fineness.

19. The correct answer is B. In twist drill grinding, it is important to have equal and correctly sized drill-point angles, equal length cutting lips, correct clearance behind the cutting lips, and correct chisel-edge angle.

20. The correct answer is A. A plumb bob is a weight, often of lead, suspended from a cord and used to determine the vertical or plumb line.

21. The correct answer is A. A claw hammer has a "claw" on the opposite end of the striking surface that is designed to grab nail heads in order to extract nails.

22. The correct answer is D. The tool shown is a pipe cutter. Pipe cutters are used to cut pipe made of steel, brass, copper, wrought iron, and lead.

23. The correct answer is B. The operator should check the abrasive wheel before starting the machine for safety reasons. A cracked or chipped wheel may injure someone.

24. The correct answer is C. The allowance is made for the width of the saw.

25. The correct answer is B. The tool is a welding torch used in making metal-to-metal joints. Welding is generally done with material made of steel.

Items Answered Incorrectly: _____ ; _____ ; _____ ; _____ ; _____ ; _____ ; _____ ; _____ ; _____

Items Unsure Of: _____ ; _____ ; _____ ; _____ ; _____ ; _____ ; _____ ; _____ ; _____

Total Number Answered Correctly: _____

PART 8: MECHANICAL COMPREHENSION

1. C	**6.** C	**11.** D	**16.** B	**21.** D
2. B	**7.** D	**12.** C	**17.** C	**22.** C
3. B	**8.** D	**13.** C	**18.** D	**23.** A
4. C	**9.** A	**14.** A	**19.** A	**24.** B
5. C	**10.** B	**15.** A	**20.** D	**25.** D

1. **The correct answer is C.** 30 lb. + 2 lb. = 32 lb., the total weight equally supported by two scales. $\frac{32}{2} = 16$ lbs. the reading on each scale.

2. **The correct answer is B.** The number of parts of the rope going to and from the movable block indicates the mechanical advantage. In this case, it is 2.

3. **The correct answer is B.** The block is not fixed, and the fall is doubled as it supports the 200-lb. cask. Each half of the fall carries one half of the total load, or 100 lb. The person is lifting a 200-lb. cask with a 100-lb. pull.

4. **The correct answer is C.** The circumference of the wheel is 20 in. One complete revolution will raise W2 20 in. and lower W1 20 in., a difference of 40 in.

5. **The correct answer is C.** To increase the efficiency of heating gas, baffles cause gases to mix more thoroughly and thereby to come in closer contact with the heating elements in a furnace.

6. **The correct answer is C.** The vertical component of the momentum of the ball is zero only at position C.

7. **The correct answer is D.** Gear A has 15 teeth; gear B has 10 teeth.

    Let x = number of revolutions gear B will make.
    $$x \times 10 = 15 \times 14$$
    $$10x = 15 \times 14$$
    $$x = \frac{15 \times 14}{10} = 21$$

8. **The correct answer is D.** Two gears, moving together, turn in opposite directions. Liquid is thus forced through the pipe.

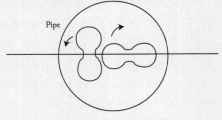

9. **The correct answer is A.** Study the diagram and note that with each complete turn of the cam, the setscrew will hit the contact point once.

10. **The correct answer is B.** Gear I would turn in direction 1 (opposite that of gear B), and gear A would turn in direction 2 (opposite that of gear I).

11. **The correct answer is D.** The pressure is uniform in the system given. If the main line air gauge reads 100 pounds, the tank air gauge will also read 100 pounds.

12. **The correct answer is C.** Let x = theoretical distance moved in the opposite direction.
    $$x \times 600 = 12 \times 150$$
    $$600x = 1800$$
    $$x = \frac{1800}{600} = 3 \text{ feet}$$

13. **The correct answer is C.** Figure 3, when folded on the dotted lines, forms the congruent triangles necessary to construct a closed triangular box.

14. **The correct answer is A.** If the block is moved toward the brick, the movement for a given force exerted will increase (being further from the force), making it easier to lift; the height will be made smaller, hardly raising the brick when moved to the limit (directly underneath it).

15. **The correct answer is A.** The greater the pressure outside the balloon, the less expansion within the balloon.

16. **The correct answer is B.** One complete revolution will raise the weight one foot, or 12 inches.

17. **The correct answer is C.** The siphon works, in part, because of air pressure on the top of the liquid.

18. **The correct answer is D.** If pipe B is turned 4 revolutions and there are 8 threads per inch, the overall length would decrease by 4 threads, or $\frac{1}{2}$ inch.

19. **The correct answer is A.** Gears M and N are eccentric oval gears that are identical in size, shape, and number of teeth. The point of contact of the gears shifts from the right to the left with each revolution. However, if gear N turns at a constant rpm, gear M will turn at the same constant rpm as N.

20. **The correct answer is D.** By reducing the length of the lever arm, you are reducing the effort and will permit the valve to blow off at a lower pressure.

21. **The correct answer is D.** The amount of water that can leave an outlet depends on the size or area of the opening. The area of a circular opening is proportional to the radius squared (area = πr^2). Therefore, the 2-inch pipe outlet will carry 4 times the amount of water as will the 1-inch opening. Mathematically,

$$\frac{\text{Area of 2-inch}}{\text{Area of 1-inch}} = \frac{\pi 2^2}{\pi 1^2} = \frac{\pi 4}{\pi 1} = 4.$$

22. **The correct answer is C.** Let x = tipping force. $80 \times 4 = x \times 1 = 320$ pounds

23. **The correct answer is A.** When two external gears mesh, they rotate in opposite directions. To avoid this, an idler gear is put between the driver gear and the driven gear.

24. **The correct answer is B.**

$$\text{IMA} = \frac{8}{2} = 4; \quad \frac{400}{4} = 100 \text{ lbs.}$$

25. **The correct answer is D.** Number 2 is a greater distance from the center than is number 1. Number 2 would therefore traverse a greater linear distance.

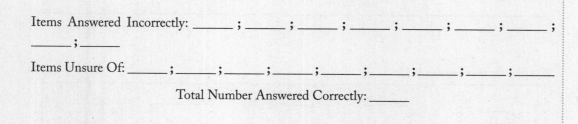

Items Answered Incorrectly: _____ ; _____ ; _____ ; _____ ; _____ ; _____ ; _____ ; _____ ; _____

Items Unsure Of: _____ ; _____ ; _____ ; _____ ; _____ ; _____ ; _____ ; _____

Total Number Answered Correctly: _____

PART 9: ASSEMBLING OBJECTS

1. A	5. A	8. D	11. B	14. B
2. B	6. D	9. A	12. B	15. A
3. B	7. B	10. A	13. B	16. A
4. C				

1. The correct answer is A.

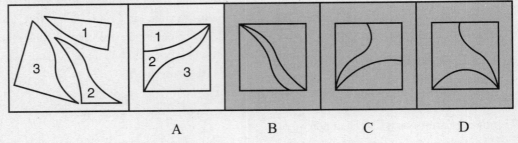

            A   B   C   D

2. The correct answer is B.

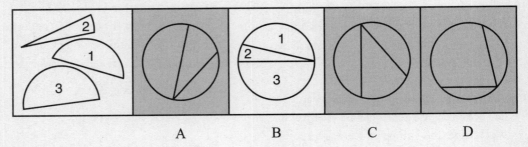

            A   B   C   D

3. The correct answer is B.

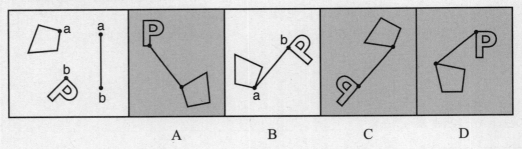

            A   B   C   D

4. The correct answer is C.

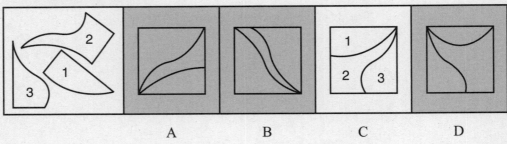

            A   B   C   D

5. The correct answer is A.

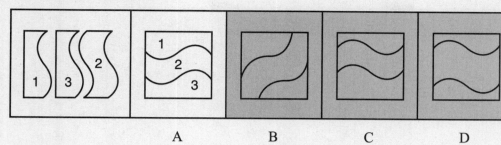

A   B   C   D

6. The correct answer is D.

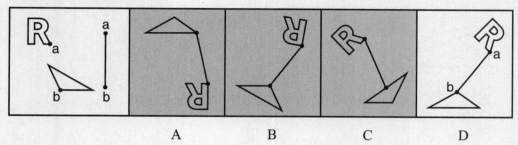

A   B   C   D

7. The correct answer is B.

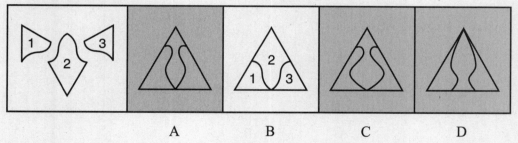

A   B   C   D

8. The correct answer is D.

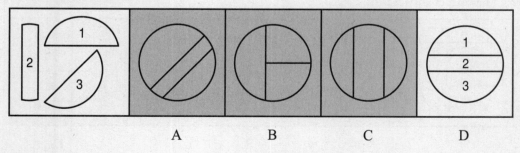

A   B   C   D

answers practice test 4

9. The correct answer is A.

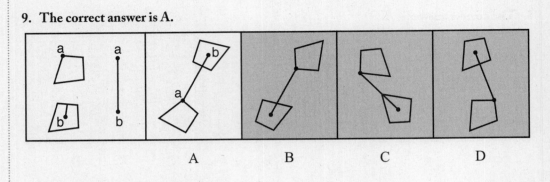

A   B   C   D

10. The correct answer is A.

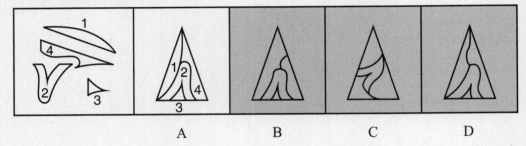

A   B   C   D

11. The correct answer is B.

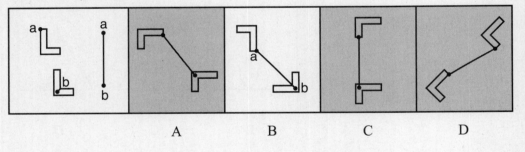

A   B   C   D

12. The correct answer is B.

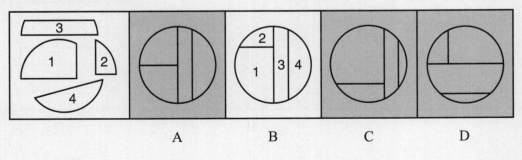

A   B   C   D

13. **The correct answer is B.**

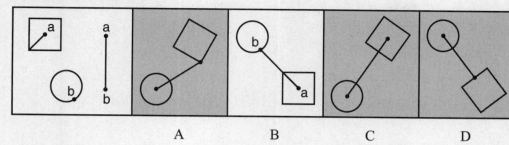

A   B   C   D

14. **The correct answer is B.**

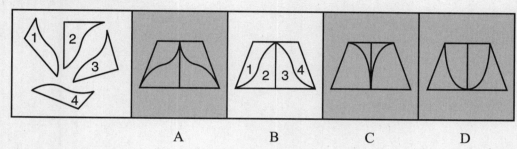

A   B   C   D

15. **The correct answer is A.**

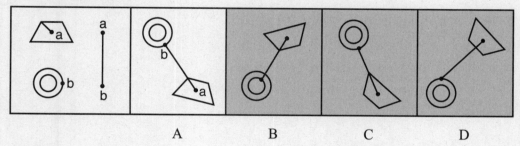

A   B   C   D

16. **The correct answer is A.**

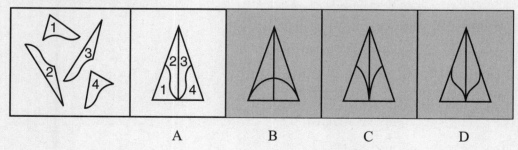

A   B   C   D

APPENDIXES

APPENDIX A: Military Enlisted Occupations and Civilian Counterparts

APPENDIX B: Enlisted Opportunities in the U.S. Military

APPENDIX C: Coding Speed

Military Enlisted Occupations and Civilian Counterparts*

Besides being the single largest employer in the nation, the military offers the widest choice of career opportunities. Together, the five services offer training and employment in more than 2,000 enlisted job specialties. To help you explore the enlisted world of work, these specialties are grouped into enlisted occupations. The occupations are organized into nineteen groups:

1. Accounting, Budget, and Finance
2. Arts, Communications, Media, and Design
3. Aviation
4. Business Administration and Operations
5. Combat Operations
6. Communications Equipment Technologists and Technicians
7. Construction, Building, and Extraction
8. Counseling, Social Work, and Human Services
9. Education and Training
10. Engineering and Scientific Research
11. Environmental Health and Safety
12. Healthcare Practitioners
13. Human Resources Management and Services
14. Information Technology, Computer Science, and Mathematics
15. Intelligence
16. International Relations, Linguistics, and Other Social Sciences
17. Law Enforcement, Security, and Protective Services
18. Legal Professions and Support Services
19. Mechanic and Repair Technologists and Technicians

This grouping is a convenient reference and index for locating the page numbers of all occupations that relate to a particular broad occupational group. For example, a person

---

* Information Provided by U.S. Department of Defense, Defense Manpower Data Center.

555

interested in the Law Enforcement, Security, and Protective Services group may quickly locate the page numbers of all enlisted occupations that fall within this group.

Each enlisted occupation contains a description that includes the following pertinent information:

- **Occupational Title**—The occupational title names the military occupation.

- **Military Service Representation**—The military services listed next to the title offer employment and training opportunities in the occupation. Not all services offer every military occupation.

- **Short Description**—As the name implies, provides a brief description of each occupation.

- **What They Do**—Typical tasks describe the main work activities in the occupation. Some of the activities listed may not apply to all services.

- **Helpful Attributes**—Helpful attributes include interests, school subjects taken, experience, and other personal characteristics that may be helpful for training and working in the military occupation. These are not actual requirements.

- **Training Provided**—Describes the type of training provided to prepare military members to perform their duties.

- **Work Environment**—Provides information about the environment in which you can expect to perform the various military occupations.

- **Civilian Counterparts**—Most military occupations are comparable to one or more civilian occupations because they have similar duties and require similar training. *Civilian Counterparts* identify these civilian occupations and the kinds of companies or organizations in which they are located. If you have a strong aptitude for a military occupation, you may have a strong aptitude for its civilian counterpart.

OCCUPATIONAL INDEX

Accounting, Budget, and Finance Occupations

    Finance and Accounting Specialists 559

Arts, Communications, Media, and Design Occupations

    Printing Specialists 560

    Audiovisual and Broadcast Technicians .562

    Broadcast Journalists and Newswriters 563

    Graphic Designers and Illustrators 564

    Musicians 565

    Photographic Specialists 567

    Arts and Media Directors 568

Aviation Occupations

    Flight Operations Specialists 569

    Air Crew Members 570

    Air Traffic Controllers 572

    Aircraft Launch and Recovery Specialists 573

    Flight Engineers. 574

Business Administration and Operations Occupations

    Administrative Support Specialists. 575

    Medical Record Technicians. 577

    Purchasing and Contracting Managers 578

Combat Operations Occupations

    Armored Assault Vehicle Crew Members 579

    Artillery and Missile Crew Members. 580

    Infantry. 581

    Special Forces 583

Communications Equipment Technologists and Technicians Occupations

    Avionics Technicians 584

    Electronic Instrument and Equipment Repairers. 586

    Communications Equipment Operators 587

    Radar and Sonar Operators 588

Construction, Building, and Extraction Occupations

    Building Electricians 590

    Heavy Equipment Operators 591

    Construction Specialists 592

    Plumbers and Pipe Fitters 593

    Surveying, Mapping, and Drafting Technicians. 595

Counseling, Social Work, and Human Services Occupations

    Caseworkers and Counselors 596

    Religious Program Specialists. 597

Education and Training Occupations

    Training Specialists and Instructors 599

    Teachers and Instructors. 600

Engineering and Scientific Research Occupations

    Meteorological Specialists 601

    Space Operations Specialists 602

    Unmanned Vehicle (UV) Operations Specialists 604

Environmental Health and Safety Occupations

    Environmental Health and Safety Specialists. 605

Ordnance Specialists 606

Water and Sewage Treatment Plant Operators 608

Emergency Management Specialists 609

Healthcare Practitioners Occupations

Dental Specialists 610

Medical Care Technicians 611

Medical Emergency Technicians 613

Optometric Technicians 614

Physical and Occupational Therapy Specialists 615

Human Resources Management and Services Occupations

Human Resources Specialists 616

Recruiting Specialists 618

**Information Technology, Computer Science, and
Mathematics Occupations**

Computer Systems Specialists 619

Intelligence Occupations

Intelligence Specialists 621

Interpreters and Translators 622

Geospatial Imaging Specialists 624

**International Relations, Linguistics, and Other
Social Sciences Occupations**

Interpreters and Translators 625

Foreign Affairs Specialists 626

Law Enforcement, Security, and Protective Services Occupations

Firefighters 628

Law Enforcement and Security Specialists 629

Legal Professions and Support Services Occupations

Legal Specialists and Court Reporters 630

Mechanic and Repair Technologists and Technicians Occupations

Electrical Products Repairers 632

Power Plant Electricians 633

Precision Instrument and Equipment Repairers 634

Ship Electricians 635

Weapons Maintenance Technicians 637

Divers 638

Non-Destructive Testers. 639

Machinists 641

Power Plant Operators 642

Survival Equipment Specialists 643

Welders and Metal Workers. 644

Aircraft Mechanics. 645

Automotive and Heavy Equipment Mechanics 647

Heating and Cooling Mechanics 648

Marine Engine Mechanics. 649

Powerhouse Mechanics. 650

ACCOUNTING, BUDGET, AND FINANCE OCCUPATIONS

Finance and Accounting Specialists

Army
Navy
Air Force
Marine Corps
Coast Guard

Short Description

Millions of paychecks are issued and large amounts of materials are purchased by the services each year. To account for military spending, exact financial records must be kept of these transactions. Finance and accounting specialists organize and keep track of financial records. They also compute payrolls and other allowances, audit accounting records, and prepare payments for military personnel.

What They Do

Finance and accounting specialists in the military perform some or all of the following duties:

- Use computers to perform calculations, record details of financial transactions, and maintain accounting records

- Review or audit financial records to check the accuracy of figures and calculations

- Prepare paychecks, earnings statements, bills, and financial accounts and reports

- Disburse cash, checks, advance pay, and bonds

- Organize information on past expenses to help plan budgets for future expenses

Helpful Attributes

Helpful school subjects include mathematics, statistics, bookkeeping, and accounting. Helpful attributes include:

- Ability to work with numbers
- Interest in using office machines such as computers and calculators
- Interest in work requiring accuracy and attention to detail

Training Provided

Job training consists of classroom instruction, including practice in accounting techniques. Course content typically includes:

- Accounting principles and procedures
- Preparation and maintenance of financial reports and budgets
- Statistical analyses to interpret financial data
- Computation of pay and deductions

Work Environment

Finance and accounting specialists work in offices on land or aboard ships.

Civilian Counterparts

Civilian finance and accounting specialists work for all types of businesses and government agencies. They perform duties similar to military finance and accounting specialists. Civilian finance and accounting specialists are also called accounting clerks, audit clerks, bookkeepers, or payroll clerks.

ARTS, COMMUNICATIONS, MEDIA, AND DESIGN OCCUPATIONS

Printing Specialists

Army
Navy
Marine Corps

Short Description

The military produces many printed publications each year, including newspapers, booklets, training manuals, maps, and charts. Printing specialists operate printing presses and binding machines to make finished copies of printed material.

What They Do

Printing specialists in the military perform some or all of the following duties:

- Reproduce printed matter using offset lithographic printing processes
- Prepare photographic negatives and transfer them to printing plates using copy cameras and enlargers
- Prepare layouts of artwork, photographs, and text for lithographic plates
- Produce brochures, newspapers, maps, and charts
- Bind printed material into hardback or paperback books using binding machines
- Maintain printing presses

Helpful Attributes

Helpful school subjects include shop mechanics and photography. Helpful attributes include:

- Interest in learning about printing
- Preference for doing physical work

Training Provided

Job training consists of classroom instruction, including practice in operating printing presses. Training length varies by specialty. Further training occurs on the job and through advanced courses. Course content typically includes:

- Photolithography techniques
- Operation of offset presses
- Techniques for making printing plates
- Binding techniques

Work Environment

Printing specialists work indoors in print shops and offices located on land or aboard ships.

Civilian Counterparts

Civilian printing specialists work for commercial print shops, newspapers, insurance companies, government offices, or businesses that do their own printing. They perform duties similar to military printing specialists. They may be called offset printing press operators, lithograph press operators, offset duplicating machine operators, lithograph photographers, or bindery workers.

Audiovisual and Broadcast Technicians

Army
Navy
Air Force
Marine Corps

Short Description

Television and film productions are an important part of military communications. Films are used for training in many military occupations. They are also used to record military operations, ceremonies, and news events. These productions require the teamwork of many technicians. Audiovisual and broadcast technicians perform many specialized tasks, ranging from filming to script editing to operating audio recording devices.

What They Do

Audiovisual and broadcast technicians in the military perform some or all of the following duties:

- Work with writers, producers, and directors in preparing and interpreting scripts
- Plan and design production scenery, graphics, and special effects
- Operate media equipment and special effect devices including cameras, sound recorders, and lighting
- Follow script and instructions of film or TV directors to move cameras, zoom, pan, or adjust focus

Helpful Attributes

Helpful school subjects include photography, graphics, art, speech, and drama. Helpful attributes include:

- Experience in school plays or making home movies
- Interest in creative and artistic work
- Preference for working as part of a team

Training Provided

Job training consists of instruction. Training length varies depending on specialty. Further training occurs on the job and through advanced courses. Course content typically includes:

- Motion picture equipment operation
- Audio recording
- Scripting and special effects techniques
- Maintenance of public address sound equipment

Work Environment

Audiovisual and broadcast technicians work in studios or outdoors on location. They sometimes work from aircraft or ships. They travel and work in all climates.

Civilian Counterparts

Civilian audiovisual and broadcast technicians work for film production companies, government audiovisual studios, radio and television stations, and advertising agencies. Their duties are similar to those performed by military journalists and newswriters. They may be called motion picture camera operators, audiovisual production specialists, sound mixers, recording engineers, and broadcasting and recording technicians.

Broadcast Journalists and Newswriters

Army
Navy
Air Force
Marine Corps

Short Description

The military publishes newspapers and broadcasts television and radio programs for its personnel and the public. These services are an important source of general information about people and events in the military. Broadcast journalists and newswriters write and present news programs, web-based programming, music programs, and radio talk shows.

What They Do

Broadcast journalists and newswriters in the military perform some or all of the following duties:

- Gather information for military news programs and publications
- Write radio and TV scripts, news releases, feature articles, and editorials
- Develop ideas for news articles
- Arrange and conduct interviews
- Collect information for commercial media use
- Select photographs and write captions for news articles
- Present news
- Produce press kits for release to civilian media outlets

Helpful Attributes

Helpful school subjects include English, journalism, speech, and media communications. Helpful attributes include:

- Ability to keep detailed and accurate records
- Ability to write clearly and concisely

- Interest in researching facts and issues for news stories
- Strong, clear speaking voice

Training Provided

Job training consists of classroom instruction. Course content typically includes:

- Newswriting and research
- Newspaper format and layout
- Photojournalism (writing news stories featuring pictures)
- Radio and television programming and production

Work Environment

Broadcast journalists and newswriters work in broadcasting studios on land or aboard ships, or sometimes outdoors, depending upon the research needed for their articles.

Civilian Counterparts

Broadcast journalists and newswriters work for newspapers, magazines, wire services, and radio and television stations. Their duties are similar to those performed by military journalists and newswriters. They may be employed as newscasters, disc jockeys, writers, directors, producers, or correspondents.

Graphic Designers and Illustrators

Army
Navy

Short Description

The military produces many publications, such as training manuals, newspapers, reports, and promotional materials. Graphic artwork is used in these publications and for signs, charts, posters, and TV and motion picture productions. Graphic designers and illustrators produce graphic artwork, drawings, web pages, and other visual displays.

What They Do

Graphic designers and illustrators in the military perform some or all of the following duties:

- Produce computer-generated graphics through understanding of electronic imaging equipment, multimedia and telecommunication software, image scanners, and digitizing devices
- Draw graphs and charts to represent budgets, numbers of troops, supply levels, and office organization
- Develop ideas and design posters and signs
- Help instructors design artwork for training courses
- Draw illustrations and cartoons for filmstrips and animation for films

- Make silkscreen prints
- Work with TV and film producers to design backdrops and props for film sets

Helpful Attributes

Helpful school subjects include art, drafting, desktop publishing, and geometry. Helpful attributes include:

- Ability to convert ideas into visual presentations
- Interest in artwork or lettering
- Neatness and an eye for detail
- Understanding of visual communication

Training Provided

Job training consists of classroom instruction, including practice in preparing graphic designs and illustrations. Further training occurs on the job. Course content typically includes:

- Introduction to graphics, lettering, drawing, and layout techniques
- Illustration and television graphics techniques
- Theory and use of color

Work Environment

Graphic designers and illustrators usually work in offices on land or aboard ships.

Civilian Counterparts

Civilian graphic designers and illustrators work for government agencies, advertising agencies, print shops, engineering firms, and large organizations that have their own graphics departments. They may be known as graphic arts technicians or commercial artists.

Musicians

Army
Navy
Air Force
Marine Corps
Coast Guard

Short Description

Music is an important part of military life. Service bands and vocal groups have a strong tradition of performing at ceremonies, parades, concerts, festivals, and dances. Musicians and singers perform in service bands, orchestras, and small groups. They perform many types of music, including marches, classics, jazz, and popular music.

What They Do

Musicians in the military perform some or all of the following duties:

- Play in or lead bands, orchestras, combos, and jazz groups
- Sing in choral groups or as soloists
- Perform for ceremonies, parades, concerts, festivals, and dances
- Rehearse and learn new music when not performing
- Play brass, percussion, woodwind, or string instruments

Helpful Attributes

Helpful school subjects include band, music theory, harmony, and other music courses. Helpful attributes include:

- Ability to play more than one instrument
- Ability to sing
- Poise when performing in public

Training Provided

Although musicians must be musically proficient to enter the service, music training is given to new band members. Job training consists of classroom instruction, including practice playing instruments. Training length varies depending on musical specialty. Further training occurs on the job through regular rehearsals and individual practice. Course content typically includes:

- Music theory
- Group instrumental techniques
- Sight-reading musical scores
- Dance band techniques

Work Environment

Musicians play indoors in theaters, concert halls, and at dances; outdoors at parades and open-air concerts. They also travel regularly.

Civilian Counterparts

Civilian musicians work for many types of employers, including professional orchestras, bands, and choral groups. They work in nightclubs, concert halls, theaters, and recording studios.

Photographic Specialists

Army
Navy
Air Force
Marine Corps

Short Description

The military uses photographs for many purposes, such as intelligence gathering and news reporting. The services operate photographic laboratories to develop the numerous photos taken by the military. Photographic specialists shoot and edit digital still photographs and also shoot and develop color or black and white still photographs.

What They Do

Photographic specialists in the military perform some or all of the following duties:

- Select camera, film, and other equipment needed for assignments
- Determine camera angles, lighting, and any special effects needed
- Take still photos of people, events, military equipment, land areas, and other subjects
- Develop, edit, duplicate or retouch digital or film photographs
- Maintain photographic equipment
- Transmit images via satellite, computer networks, telephone, or secure transmission systems

Helpful Attributes

Helpful school subjects include photography, chemistry, art, and mathematics. Helpful attributes include:

- Ability to recognize and arrange interesting photo subjects
- Accuracy and attention to detail

Training Provided

Job training consists of classroom instruction, including practice in taking and developing photographs. Length of training varies depending on the specialty. Further training occurs on the job and through advanced courses. Course content typically includes:

- Photographic processing and reproduction
- Principles of photojournalism
- Operation and maintenance of photographic equipment

Work Environment

Photographic specialists work both indoors and outdoors while photographing their subjects. They may take photos from aircraft or ships. They process photographs in photographic laboratories or studios on bases or aboard ships.

Civilian Counterparts

Civilian photographic specialists work for photography studios, newspapers, magazines, advertising agencies, commercial photograph developers, and large businesses. They perform duties similar to military specialists. Depending on the specialty, they may be known as photojournalists, aerial or still photographers, film developers, automatic print developers, or print controllers.

Arts and Media Directors

Navy
Marine Corps

Short Description

The services produce many motion pictures, video clips, and TV and radio broadcasts. These productions are used for training, news, and entertainment. Arts and media directors manage audiovisual projects. They may direct day-to-day filming or broadcasting or manage other directors.

What They Do

Arts and media directors in the military perform some or all of the following duties:

- Examine, select, and distribute photographs that are secure, timely, appealing, and artistic for reproduction
- Create or supervise creation of works of art in one or more visual arts media
- Plan and organize audiovisual projects, including films, video clips, TV and radio broadcasts
- Determine the staff and equipment needed for productions
- Set production controls and performance standards for audiovisual projects
- Direct the preparation of scripts and determine camera-shooting schedules
- Direct actors and technical staff during performances

Helpful Attributes

Helpful fields of study include audiovisual production, cinematography, communications, and graphic arts. Helpful attributes include:

- Ability to transform ideas into visual images
- Interest in organizing and planning activities
- Interest in planning and directing the work of others

Training Provided

Job training consists of classroom instruction. Training length varies depending on specialty. Course content typically includes:

- Public information management principles
- Management of military broadcasting facilities
- Motion picture and television production management

Work Environment

Arts and media directors usually work in studios or offices. They may direct film crews on location in military camps or combat zones.

Civilian Counterparts

Civilian arts and media directors work for television networks and stations, motion picture companies, public relations and advertising firms, and government agencies. They perform duties similar to those performed by military arts and media directors.

AVIATION OCCUPATIONS

Flight Operations Specialists

Army
Navy
Air Force
Marine Corps
Coast Guard

Short Description

The services operate one of the largest fleets of aircraft in the world. Hundreds of transport, passenger, and combat airplanes and helicopters fly missions every day. Accurate flight information keeps operations safe and efficient. Flight operations specialists prepare and provide flight information for air and ground crews.

What They Do

Flight operations specialists in the military perform some or all of the following duties:

- Process cross-country and local flight clearances, including examination for conformance with flight rules and regulations
- Keep flight logs on incoming and outgoing flights
- Keep air crew flying records and flight operations records
- Receive and post weather information and flight plan data
- Coordinate air crew needs, such as ground transportation
- Plan aircraft equipment needs for air evacuation and dangerous cargo flights
- Check military flight plans with civilian agencies
- Encode, decode, and post messages to airmen
- Maintain flight operations equipment in a tactical environment

Helpful Attributes

Helpful school subjects include general math and typing. Helpful attributes include:

- Ability to keep accurate records
- Interest in work involving computers
- Interest in work that helps others
- Ability to work as team member
- Interest in aircraft

Training Provided

Job training consists of classroom instruction. Training length varies depending on specialty. Further training occurs on the job and through advanced courses. Course content typically includes:

- Introduction to aviation operations
- Procedures for scheduling aircraft and assigning air crews
- Flight planning and airfield operations
- Preparing flight operations reports and records

Work Environment

Flight operations specialists work indoors in flight control centers or air terminals.

Civilian Counterparts

Civilian flight operations specialists work for commercial and private airlines and air transport companies. They perform duties similar to military flight operations specialists.

Air Crew Members

Army
Navy
Air Force
Marine Corps
Coast Guard

Short Description

The military uses aircraft of all types and sizes to conduct combat and intelligence missions, rescue personnel, transport troops and equipment, and perform long-range bombing missions. Air crew members operate equipment on board aircraft during operations. They normally specialize by type of aircraft, such as bomber, intelligence, transport, or search and rescue.

What They Do

Air crew members in the military perform some or all of the following duties:

- Operate aircraft communication and radar equipment
- Operate and maintain aircraft defensive gunnery systems
- Operate helicopter hoists to lift equipment and personnel from land and sea
- Operate and maintain aircraft in-flight refueling systems
- Maintain flight operations equipment
- Perform aircraft maintenance, weight and balance calculations
- Analyze and classify data
- Safeguard classified materials

Helpful Attributes

Helpful school subjects include mathematics and mechanics. Helpful attributes include:

- Ability to work as a team member
- Ability to work under stress
- Interest in flying
- Ability to work with mechanical and electrical systems

Training Provided

Job training consists of classroom instruction, including practical experience in aircraft systems operation and maintenance. Further training occurs on the job through actual flying time. There are additional courses covering air crew survival, scuba diving, parachuting, aircraft maneuvering, and combat crew training. Course content varies by specialty and may include:

- Operation of aircraft gunnery systems
- Operation of aircraft in-flight refueling systems
- Cargo, munitions, and fuel load planning
- Rescue and recovery operations

Work Environment

Air crew members work inside all sizes and types of aircraft based on land or aboard ships. They fly in all types of weather and in both hot and cold climates.

Civilian Counterparts

There are no direct civilian equivalents to military air crew members. However, some of the skills gained in the military could be useful in civilian government and private agencies that provide emergency medical services. Also, weight and load computation skills are useful for civilian air transport operations.

Air Traffic Controllers

Army
Navy
Air Force
Marine Corps

Short Description

Every day, hundreds of military airplanes and helicopters take off and land all over the world. Their movements are closely controlled in order to prevent accidents. Air traffic controllers direct the movement of aircraft into and out of military airfields. They track aircraft by radar and give voice instructions by radio.

What They Do

Air traffic controllers in the military perform some or all of the following duties:

- Operate radio equipment to issue takeoff, flight, and landing instructions
- Relay weather reports, airfield conditions, and safety information to pilots
- Use radar equipment to track aircraft in flight
- Plot airplane locations on charts and maps
- Compute speed, direction, and altitude of aircraft
- Maintain air traffic control records and communication logs

Helpful Attributes

Helpful school subjects include general mathematics, English, and typing. Helpful attributes include:

- Ability to make quick, decisive judgments
- Ability to work under stress
- Skill in math computation

Training Provided

Job training consists of classroom instruction. Training length varies depending on specialty. Additional training occurs on the job. Aircraft carrier air traffic controllers receive specialized training. Course content typically includes:

- Air traffic control fundamentals
- Visual and instrument flight procedures
- Radar and other landing approach procedures
- Communication procedures

Work Environment

Air traffic controllers work in land-based and shipboard control centers.

Civilian Counterparts

Civilian air traffic controllers work for the FAA in airports and control centers around the country. They perform duties similar to military air traffic controllers. They may specialize in specific areas, such as aircraft arrivals, departures, ground control, or en route flights.

Aircraft Launch and Recovery Specialists

Navy
Marine Corps
Coast Guard

Short Description

The military operates thousands of aircraft that take off and land on aircraft carriers all over the world. The successful launch and recovery of aircraft is important to the completion of air missions and the safety of flight crews. Aircraft launch and recovery specialists operate and maintain catapults, arresting gear, and other equipment used in aircraft carrier takeoff and landing operations.

What They Do

Aircraft launch and recovery specialists in the military perform some or all of the following duties:

- Operate consoles to control launch and recovery equipment, including catapults and arresting gear
- Operate elevators to transfer aircraft between flight and storage decks
- Install and maintain visual landing aids
- Test and adjust launch and recovery equipment
- Install airfield crash barriers and barricades
- Direct aircraft launch and recovery operations
- Operate and service aircraft ground-handling equipment and machinery
- Operate and service aircraft crash, firefighting, and rescue equipment

Helpful Attributes

Helpful school subjects include shop mechanics. Helpful attributes include:

- Ability to use hand tools and test equipment
- Interest in aircraft flight operations
- Interest in working on hydraulic and mechanical equipment

Training Provided

Job training consists of classroom instruction, including practice in maintaining launch and recovery equipment. Course content typically includes:

- Operating and maintaining launch and recovery equipment
- Installing crash barriers and barricades

Work Environment

Aircraft launch and recovery specialists work outdoors aboard ships while operating and maintaining launch and recovery equipment or holding visual landing aids for incoming aircraft. They are exposed to noise and fumes from jet and helicopter engines.

Civilian Counterparts

There are no direct civilian counterparts to military aircraft launch and recovery specialists. However, many of the skills learned are relevant to jobs performed by ground crews at civilian airports.

Flight Engineers

Army
Navy
Air Force
Marine Corps

Short Description

The military operates thousands of airplanes and helicopters. Pilots and air crew members rely upon trained personnel to keep aircraft ready to fly. Flight engineers inspect airplanes and helicopters before, during, and after flights to ensure safe and efficient operations. They also serve as crew members aboard military aircraft.

What They Do

Flight engineers in the military perform some or all of the following duties:

- Inspect aircraft before and after flights
- Plan and monitor the loading of passengers, cargo, and fuel
- Assist pilots in engine start-up, shut-down, and adjust power settings
- Compute aircraft load weights and fuel distribution and consumption
- Monitor engine instruments and adjust controls following pilot orders
- Check fuel, pressure, electrical, and other aircraft systems during flight
- Inform pilot of aircraft problems and recommend corrective action
- Compute take-off and landing limits
- Brief passengers on safety procedures
- Perform aircraft maintenance and aircraft system rigging

Helpful Attributes

Helpful school subjects include general mathematics and shop mechanics. Helpful attributes include:

- Ability to work as a member of a team
- Interest in working with mechanical systems and equipment
- Skill in using wiring diagrams and maintenance manuals
- Strong desire to fly

Training Provided

Job training consists of classroom instruction and practical experience in aircraft inspection. Further training occurs on the job during flight operations. Course content typically includes:

- Operation of aircraft systems
- Inspection of aircraft engines, structures, and systems
- Preparation of records and logs

Work Environment

Flight engineers live and work on air bases or aboard ships in all areas of the world. They fly in hot and cold climates and in all types of weather.

Civilian Counterparts

Civilian flight engineers work for passenger and cargo airline companies. They perform the same duties as in the military.

BUSINESS ADMINISTRATION AND OPERATIONS OCCUPATIONS

Administrative Support Specialists

Navy
Air Force
Marine Corps
Coast Guard

Short Description

The military must keep accurate information for planning and managing its operations. Paper and electronic records are kept on equipment, funds, personnel, supplies, and all other aspects of the military. Administrative support specialists record information, fill out reports, and maintain files to assist in the operation of military offices.

What They Do

Administrative support specialists in the military perform some or all of the following duties:

- Manage databases to capture, organize, and store information
- Proofread written material for spelling, punctuation, and grammatical errors
- Organize and maintain electronic and paper files and publications
- Order office supplies
- Greet and direct office visitors
- Sort and deliver mail to office workers
- Assist in planning, preparing, arranging, and conducting official social functions and activities
- Schedule training and leave for unit personnel
- Answer phones and provide general information
- Take meeting notes

Helpful Attributes

Helpful school subjects include English, math, and business administration. Helpful attributes include:

- Ability to organize and plan
- Interest in keeping organized and accurate records
- Interest in operating computers and other office machines
- Preference for office work

Training Provided

Job training consists of classroom instruction, including practice in various office functions. Further training occurs on the job. Course content typically includes:

- English grammar, spelling, and punctuation
- Keyboard and clerical skills
- Setting up and maintaining filing and publication systems
- Preparing forms and correspondence in military style
- Maintaining databases

Work Environment

Administrative support specialists work in office settings, both on land and aboard ships.

Civilian Counterparts

Civilian administrative support specialists work in most business, government, and legal offices. They perform duties similar to military administrative support specialists and are called receptionists, general office clerks, administrative assistants, executive assistants, or office managers.

Medical Record Technicians

Army
Air Force

Short Description

Medical records are important for health care delivery. To provide proper treatment, physicians need complete and accurate information about patient symptoms, test results, illnesses, and prior treatments. Medical record technicians prepare and maintain patient records, reports, and correspondence.

What They Do

Medical record technicians in the military perform some or all of the following duties:

- Fill out admission and discharge records for patients entering and leaving military hospitals
- Assign patients to hospital rooms
- Prepare daily reports about patients admitted and discharged
- Organize, file, and maintain medical records
- Prepare reports about physical examinations, illnesses, and treatments
- Prepare tables of medical statistics
- Maintain libraries of medical publications

Helpful Attributes

Helpful school subjects include general science and business administration. Helpful attributes include:

- Ability to communicate well
- Interest in using computers and other office machines
- Interest in work requiring accuracy and attention to detail

Training Provided

Job training consists of classroom instruction. Training length varies depending on specialty. Course content typically includes:

- Basic computer skills
- Medical terminology
- Medical records preparation and maintenance
- Maintenance of medical libraries

Work Environment

Medical record technicians work in admissions or medical records sections of hospitals and clinics. They work in land-based facilities and aboard ships.

Civilian Counterparts

Civilian medical record technicians usually work for hospitals, clinics, and government health agencies. They perform duties similar to military medical record technicians. However, civilian medical record technicians tend to specialize in areas such as admissions, ward, or outpatient records. Those working in admission or discharge units are called admitting or discharge clerks.

Purchasing and Contracting Managers

Army
Navy
Air Force
Marine Corps
Coast Guard

Short Description

The military buys billions of dollars worth of equipment, supplies, and services from private industry each year. The services must make sure their purchases meet military specifications and are made at a fair price. Purchasing and contracting managers negotiate, write, and monitor contracts for purchasing equipment, materials, and services.

What They Do

Purchasing and contracting managers in the military perform some or all of the following duties:

- Review requests for supplies and services to make sure they are complete and accurate
- Prepare bid invitations or requests for proposals for contracts with civilian firms
- Review bids or proposals and award contracts
- Prepare formal contracts, specifying all terms and conditions
- Review work to make sure that it meets the requirements of contracts

Helpful Attributes

Helpful fields of study include management and business or public administration. Helpful attributes include:

- Ability to develop detailed plans
- Interest in negotiating
- Interest in work requiring accuracy and attention to detail

Training Provided

Job training consists of classroom instruction. Training length varies depending on specialty. Further training occurs through advanced courses. Course content typically includes:

- Purchasing and accounting procedures
- Use of computers in contract administration
- Supply and financial management

Work Environment

Purchasing and contracting managers work in offices.

Civilian Counterparts

Civilian purchasing and contracting managers work for a wide variety of employers, including engineering, manufacturing, and construction firms. They perform duties similar to those performed by military purchasing and contract managers. They may also be called procurement services managers, purchasing directors, contracts administrators, or material control managers.

COMBAT OPERATIONS OCCUPATIONS

Armored Assault Vehicle Crew Members
Army
Marine Corps

Short Description

In peacetime, the role of armored units is to stay ready to defend our country anywhere in the world. In combat, their role is to operate tanks, amphibious assault vehicles, and other types of armored assault vehicles to engage and destroy the enemy. Armored units also conduct scouting missions and support infantry units during combat. Crew members work as a team to operate armored equipment and fire weapons to destroy enemy positions. They normally specialize by type of armor, such as tanks, light armor (cavalry), or amphibious assault vehicles.

What They Do

Armored assault vehicle crew members in the military perform some or all of the following duties:

- Drive armored land or amphibious assault vehicles in combat formations
- Locate, operate target sighting equipment and engage targets
- Operate communications and signaling equipment to receive and relay battle orders
- Gather and report information about enemy strength and target location
- Perform preventive and corrective maintenance on armored vehicles and mounted weapons systems
- Read maps and battle plans

Helpful Attributes

Helpful attributes include:

- Ability to follow directions and execute orders quickly and accurately
- Ability to work as a member of a team
- Ability to work well under stress
- Readiness to accept a challenge and face danger

Training Provided

Job training consists of classroom and field training under simulated combat conditions. Further training occurs on the job and through training exercises. Course content typically includes:

- Vehicle operations
- Armor offensive and defensive tactics
- Map reading
- Scouting and reconnaissance techniques
- Weapons training

Work Environment

Armored assault vehicle crew members, like other combat troops, work in all climates and weather conditions. During training exercises, as in real combat conditions, crew members work, eat, and sleep outdoors and in vehicles.

Civilian Counterparts

Although the job of armored assault vehicle crew member has no equivalent in civilian life, the close teamwork, discipline, and leadership experiences it provides are helpful in many civilian jobs.

Artillery and Missile Crew Members

Army
Navy
Marine Corps

Short Description

The military uses artillery and missiles to protect infantry and tank units, as well as to secure and protect land and sea positions from enemy attack. The personnel who operate these systems will usually specialize by type of weapon system such as cannons, howitzers, missiles, or rockets. Artillery and missile crew members position, direct, and fire these weapons to destroy enemy positions and aircraft.

What They Do

Artillery and missile crew members in the military perform some or all of the following duties:

- Operate computerized equipment to determine target locations
- Prepare ammunition for firing and load weapons
- Operate tactical vehicle
- Fire artillery and missile systems at enemy targets
- Clean and maintain weapons
- Test, remove, and replace fire control system components on launcher

- Mount communication components in vehicles and launchers
- Operate and perform operator maintenance on communications equipment

Helpful Attributes

Helpful attributes include:

- Ability to think and remain calm in stressful situations
- Ability to work as part of a team
- Interest in cannon and rocket operations
- Willingness to face danger

Training Provided

Job training consists of classroom instruction and field training under simulated combat situations. Training length varies depending upon specialty. Further training occurs on the job and through advanced courses. Course content typically includes:

- Methods of computing target locations
- Ammunition-handling techniques
- Weapon, missile, and rocket system operations
- Artillery tactics
- Maintenance programs

Work Environment

Artillery and missile crew members work under different conditions depending on the type of weapon system they use. Some crew members spend a lot of time in field training exercises, where they work, eat, and sleep outdoors and in tents. Others live and work aboard ships or submarines.

Civilian Counterparts

Although the job of artillery and missile crew member has no equivalent in civilian life, the close teamwork, discipline, and leadership experiences it provides are helpful in many civilian jobs.

Infantry

Army
Marine Corps

Short Description

The infantry is the main land combat force of the military. In peacetime, the infantry's role is to stay ready to defend our country. In combat, the role of the infantry is to capture or destroy enemy ground forces and repel enemy attacks. The infantry operates weapons and equipment to engage and destroy enemy ground forces.

What They Do

Infantry performs some or all of the following duties:

- Set up camouflage and other protective barriers
- Operate, clean, and store automatic weapons, such as rifles and machine guns
- Parachute from troop transport airplanes while carrying weapons and supplies
- Carry out scouting missions to spot enemy troop movements and gun locations
- Operate communications and signal equipment to receive and relay battle orders
- Drive vehicles mounted with machine guns or small missiles
- Perform hand-to-hand combat drills that involve martial arts tactics
- Dig foxholes, trenches, and bunkers for protection against attacks

Helpful Attributes

Helpful attributes include:

- Ability to stay in top physical condition
- Interest in working as a member of a team
- Readiness to accept a challenge and face danger

Training Provided

Infantry training starts with basic training of about 7 or 8 weeks. Advanced training in infantry skills lasts for another 8 weeks. While some of the training is in the classroom, most is in the field under simulated combat conditions. In reality, training for an infantry soldier never stops. Infantry soldiers keep their skills sharp through frequent squad maneuvers, target practice, and war games. War games conducted without live ammunition allow soldiers to practice scouting, troop movement, surprise attack, and capturing techniques.

Work Environment

Because the infantry must be prepared to go anywhere in the world they are needed, they work and train in all climates and weather conditions. During training exercises, as in real combat, troops work, eat, and sleep outdoors. Most of the time, however, they work on military bases.

Civilian Counterparts

Although the job of infantry has no equivalent in civilian life, the close teamwork, discipline, and leadership experiences it provides are helpful in many civilian jobs.

Special Forces

Army
Navy
Air Force
Marine Corps

Short Description

When the military has difficult and dangerous missions to perform, they call upon special forces teams. These elite combat forces stay in a constant state of readiness to strike anywhere in the world on a moment's notice. Special forces team members conduct offensive raids, demolitions, intelligence, search and rescue, and other missions from aboard aircraft, helicopters, ships, or submarines. Due to the wide variety of missions, special forces team members are trained swimmers, parachutists, and survival experts, in addition to being combat trained.

What They Do

Special forces team members in the military perform some or all of the following duties:

- Carry out demolition raids against enemy military targets, such as bridges, railroads, and fuel depots
- Clear mine fields, both underwater and on land
- Conduct missions to gather intelligence information on enemy military forces
- Conduct offensive raids or invasions of enemy territories
- Destroy enemy ships in coastal areas, using underwater explosives
- Perform land warfare, small unit tactics, mounted and dismounted operations
- Conduct mission planning, intelligence gathering, and interpretation
- Perform combat diving, paradrop and air operations, small boat operations, submarine and submersible operations
- Conduct all environment missions, including urban, desert, jungle, arctic, and mountain warfare

Helpful Attributes

Helpful attributes include:

- Ability to remain calm in stressful situations
- Ability to work as a team member
- Readiness to accept a challenge and face danger

Training Provided

Job training consists of formal classroom training and practice exercises. Additional training occurs on the job. Basic skills are kept sharp through frequent practice exercises under simulated mission conditions. Course content typically includes:

- Physical conditioning, parachuting, swimming, and scuba diving
- Using land warfare weapons and communications devices
- Explosives handling and disposal

Work Environment

Because special forces team members must be prepared to go anywhere in the world, they train and work in all climates, weather conditions, and settings. They may dive from submarines or small underwater craft. Special forces team members may also be exposed to harsh temperatures, often without protection, during missions in enemy-controlled areas. Most of the time, however, they work and train on military bases, ships, or submarines.

Civilian Counterparts

Although the job of special forces team member has no equivalent in civilian life, training in explosives, bomb disposal, scuba diving, and swimming may be helpful in such civilian jobs as blaster, police bomb disposal specialist, diver, or swimming instructor. The discipline and dependability of special forces are assets in many civilian occupations.

COMMUNICATIONS EQUIPMENT TECHNOLOGISTS AND TECHNICIANS OCCUPATIONS

Avionics Technicians

Army
Navy
Air Force
Marine Corps
Coast Guard

Short Description

Airplanes and helicopters have complex electrical and electronic systems for communication, navigation, and radar. Instruments, lights, weapons, landing gear, sensors, and many other aircraft parts are also controlled by electronics. Avionics technicians install, maintain, and repair electronic and electrical systems on all types of aircraft.

What They Do

Avionics technicians in the military perform some or all of the following duties:

- Troubleshoot aircraft electronics and electrical systems using test equipment
- Repair or replace defective components
- Inspect and maintain electronics and electrical systems
- Replace faulty wiring

- Install electronic components
- Repair or replace instruments, such as tachometers, temperature gauges, and altimeters
- Read electronic and electrical diagrams

Helpful Attributes

Helpful school courses include math and shop mechanics. Helpful attributes include:

- Ability to work with tools
- Interest in electronics and electrical equipment
- Interest in solving problems

Training Provided

Job training consists of classroom instruction, including practice in repairing avionics systems. Training length varies depending on specialty. Further training occurs on the job and through advanced courses. Course content typically includes:

- Electronics and electrical theory
- Troubleshooting procedures
- Installation techniques
- Avionics and electrical system maintenance

Work Environment

Avionics technicians usually work indoors, in aircraft hangars, airplanes, and repair shops. They may also work on aircraft parked outdoors.

Civilian Counterparts

Civilian avionics technicians work mainly for airlines and aircraft maintenance firms. They may also work for aircraft manufacturers and other organizations that have fleets of airplanes or helicopters. Their duties are similar to those of military aircraft electricians. They may also be called aircraft electricians.

Electronic Instrument and Equipment Repairers

Army
Navy
Air Force
Marine Corps
Coast Guard

Short Description

The military uses electronic instruments and equipment in many different areas, including health care, weather forecasting, and combat, to name a few. Electronics repairers maintain and repair instruments and equipment, such as computers, communications equipment, radar and sonar systems, precision measuring equipment, and biomedical instruments. Electronic instrument and equipment repairers normally specialize by type of equipment or instrument being repaired.

What They Do

Electronic instrument and equipment repairers in the military perform some or all of the following duties:

- Maintain, test, adjust, and repair electronic equipment using frequency meters, circuit analyzers, and other specialized test equipment.
- Install and repair circuits and wiring using soldering iron and hand tools
- Install computers and other data processing equipment
- Use technical guides and diagrams to locate defective parts and components of equipment
- String overhead communications and electric cables between utility poles
- Monitor the operation of air traffic control, missile tracking, air defense, and other radar and sonar systems to make sure there are no problems

Helpful Attributes

Helpful school subjects include math, electricity or electronic repair, shop mechanics, and physics. Helpful attributes include:

- Ability to apply electronic principles and concepts
- Interest in solving problems
- Interest working with electrical, electronic, and electrochemical equipment

Training Provided

Job training consists of classroom instruction, including practice in repairing electronic instruments and equipment. Training length varies depending on specialty. Course content typically includes:

- Mechanical, electronic, and electrical principles
- Maintenance and repair procedures

- Line installation and wiring techniques
- Use of test equipment

Work Environment

Electronic instrument and equipment repairers usually work in repair shops and laboratories on land or aboard ships.

Civilian Counterparts

Civilian electronic instrument and equipment repairers work for a variety of organizations, such as manufacturing firms, communications firms, commercial airlines, and government agencies. They perform the same kind of duties as military electronic instrument and equipment repairers. Depending on their specialty, they may be called electronics mechanics, telecommunications equipment installers and repairers, radio mechanics, or computer technicians.

Communications Equipment Operators

Army
Navy
Air Force
Marine Corps
Coast Guard

Short Description

The ability to relay information between air, sea, and ground forces is critical in the military. The military has sophisticated communications systems that use a variety of technologies and telecommunications equipment such as radios, telephones, antennas, satellites, and complex security and network devices. Communications equipment operators use these systems to transmit, receive, and decode messages at military locations throughout the world.

What They Do

Communications equipment operators in the military perform some or all of the following duties:

- Transmit, receive, and log messages according to military procedures
- Encode and decode classified messages
- Operate different types of telephone switchboards, satellite communications terminals, and network switches
- Set up and operate communications equipment and security equipment
- Monitor and respond to emergency calls
- Run state-of-the-art command, control, communications, and computer and signals intelligence/electronic warfare equipment
- Install, operate, and repair communications and security equipment

Helpful Attributes

Helpful school subjects include English and speech. Helpful attributes include:

- Ability to remain calm in an emergency
- Interest in working with codes
- Interest in working with communications equipment

Training Provided

Job training consists of instruction, including practice with equipment. Further training occurs on the job and through advanced courses. Course content typically includes:

- Installation and usage of various types of communications equipment
- Communications security
- Message encoding and decoding

Work Environment

Communications equipment operators may work either indoors or outdoors, depending on the specialty. They may be assigned to ships, aircraft, land bases, or mobile field units.

Civilian Counterparts

Civilian communications equipment operators work in airports, harbors, police stations, fire stations, telephone companies, telegraph companies, and many businesses. They may also work aboard ships. Their duties are similar to those of military communications equipment operators. They may be called radio operators, telephone operators, communication center operators, or switchboard operators, depending on their specialty.

Radar and Sonar Operators

Army
Navy
Air Force
Marine Corps
Coast Guard

Short Description

Radar and sonar devices work by bouncing radio or sound waves off objects to determine their location and measure distance. They have many uses, such as tracking aircraft and missiles, determining positions of ships and submarines, directing artillery fire, forecasting weather, and aiding navigation. Radar and sonar operators monitor sophisticated equipment. They normally specialize in either radar or sonar.

What They Do

Radar and sonar operators in the military perform some or all of the following duties:

- Detect and track position, direction, and speed of aircraft, ships, submarines, and missiles
- Analyze acoustic intelligence
- Set up and operate radar equipment to direct artillery fire
- Monitor early warning air defense systems
- Send and receive messages using electronic communication systems
- Analyze contact data to determine tactical intelligence
- Operate submarine sonar, oceanographic equipment, and submarine auxiliary sonar
- Detect, track, and classify surface and sub-surface contacts utilizing state of the art electronic equipment
- Participate in weapons handling functions

Helpful Attributes

Helpful school subjects include geometry, algebra, and science. Helpful attributes include:

- Ability to concentrate for long periods
- Ability to work under stress
- Interest in advanced communications and electronic equipment
- Detail oriented

Training Provided

Job training consists of classroom instruction and practice operating radar or sonar equipment. Training length varies by specialty. Further training occurs on the job and through advanced courses. Course content typically includes:

- Operation and maintenance of radar and sonar equipment
- Identification of ships, submarines, aircraft, and missiles
- Computation of aircraft or missile speed, direction, and altitude

Work Environment

Radar and sonar operators in the military primarily work indoors in security-controlled areas. They work in operations centers and command posts either on land or aboard aircraft, ships, or submarines. Some may work in a mobile field radar unit.

Civilian Counterparts

There are no direct civilian counterparts to military radar and sonar operators. However, workers in civilian occupations that use radar and sonar equipment in their jobs include weather service technicians, air traffic controllers, ship navigators, and ocean salvage specialists.

CONSTRUCTION, BUILDING, AND EXTRACTION OCCUPATIONS

Building Electricians

Army
Navy
Air Force
Marine Corps
Coast Guard

Short Description

The military uses electricity to do many jobs, including lighting hospitals, running power tools, and operating computers. Building electricians install and repair electrical wiring systems in offices, repair shops, airplane hangars, and other buildings on military bases.

What They Do

Building electricians in the military perform some or all of the following duties:

- Install and wire transformers, junction boxes, and circuit breakers, using wire cutters, insulation strippers, and other hand tools
- Read blueprints, wiring plans, and repair orders to determine wiring layouts or repair needs
- Cut, bend, and string wires and conduits (pipe or tubing)
- Inspect power distribution systems, shorts in wires, and faulty equipment using test meters
- Repair and replace faulty wiring and lighting fixtures
- Install lightning rods to protect electrical systems

Helpful Attributes

Helpful school subjects include science and math. Helpful attributes include:

- Ability to use hand tools
- Interest in electricity
- Preference for doing physical work

Training Provided

Job training consists of classroom instruction, including practice in the installation and repair of electrical wiring systems. Further training occurs on the job and through advanced courses. Course content typically includes:

- Fundamentals of electricity
- Electrical circuit troubleshooting
- Safety procedures
- Techniques for wiring switches, outlets, and junction boxes

Work Environment

Building electricians usually work indoors while installing wiring systems. They work outdoors while installing transformers and lightning rods.

Civilian Counterparts

Civilian building electricians usually work for building and electrical contracting firms. Some work as self-employed electrical contractors. They perform duties similar to military building electricians.

Heavy Equipment Operators

Army
Navy
Air Force
Marine Corps
Coast Guard

Short Description

Each year the military completes hundreds of construction projects. Tons of earth and building materials must be moved to build airfields, roads, dams, and buildings. Heavy equipment operators use bulldozers, cranes, graders, and other heavy equipment in military construction.

What They Do

Heavy equipment operators in the military perform some or all of the following duties:

- Drive bulldozers, road graders, and other heavy equipment to cut and level earth for runways and roadbeds
- Lift and move steel and other heavy building materials using winches, cranes, and hoists
- Dig holes and trenches using power shovels
- Operate mixing plants to make concrete and asphalt
- Spread asphalt and concrete with paving machines
- Drill wells using drilling rigs
- Place and detonate explosives
- Remove ice and snow from runways, roads, and other areas using scrapers and snow blowers
- Operate breaching/bridging systems

Helpful Attributes

Helpful school subjects include shop mechanics. Helpful attributes include:

- Interest in operating heavy construction equipment
- Preference for working outdoors

Training Provided

Job training consists of classroom instruction, including practice operating construction equipment. Further training occurs on the job and through advanced courses. Course content typically includes:

- Operation of different types of construction equipment
- Maintenance and repair of equipment

Work Environment

Heavy equipment operators work outdoors in all kinds of weather conditions. They often sit for long periods and are subject to loud noise and vibrations. They may work indoors while repairing equipment.

Civilian Counterparts

Civilian heavy equipment operators work for building contractors, state highway agencies, rock quarries, well drillers, and construction firms. Civilian heavy equipment operators may also be known as operating engineers, heavy equipment operators, well drillers, or riggers.

Construction Specialists

Army
Navy
Air Force
Marine Corps
Coast Guard

Short Description

The military builds many temporary and permanent structures each year. Lumber, plywood, plasterboard, and concrete and masonry (bricks, stone, and concrete blocks) are the basic building materials for many of these projects. Construction specialists build and repair buildings, bridges, foundations, dams, and bunkers. They work with engineers and other building specialists as part of military construction teams.

What They Do

Construction specialists in the military perform some or all of the following duties:

- Build and repair wood, concrete, and masonry structures; perform rough and finished carpentry and masonry
- Install sheet rock, paneling, ceramic tile, and millwork and trim, and perform paint and preservation
- Lay roofing materials, such as asphalt, tile, and wooden shingles
- Build forms: mix, place, and finish concrete for various types of projects
- Use hand and power tools, such as hammers, power saws, levels, and drills

- Operate and maintain carpentry and cabinet making shops
- Perform tasks required in combat and disaster preparedness or recovery operations

Helpful Attributes

Helpful school subjects include math, woodworking, and industrial arts. Helpful attributes include:

- Ability to work with blueprints
- Interest in using hand and power tools
- Preference for physical work
- Interest in construction projects

Training Provided

Job training consists of instruction, including practice with carpentry and masonry tools. Further training occurs on the job and through advanced courses. Course content typically includes:

- Building construction
- Masonry construction methods
- Types and uses of construction joints and braces
- Interpretation of blueprints and drawings
- How to mix and set concrete, mortar, and plaster
- Cabinetmaking

Work Environment

Construction specialists work indoors and outdoors on construction sites.

Civilian Counterparts

Civilian construction specialists usually work for construction or remodeling contractors, government agencies, utility companies, or manufacturing firms. They perform duties similar to military construction specialists. They may also be called bricklayers, stonemasons, cement masons, cement finishers, carpenters, or cabinetmakers.

Plumbers and Pipe Fitters

Army
Navy

Short Description

Military buildings and equipment require pipe systems for water, steam, gas, and waste. Pipe systems are also needed on aircraft, missiles, and ships for hydraulic (fluid pressure) and pneumatic (air pressure) systems. Plumbers and pipe fitters install and repair plumbing and pipe systems.

What They Do

Plumbers and pipe fitters in the military perform some or all of the following duties:

- Plan layouts of pipe systems using blueprints and drawings
- Bend, cut, and thread pipes made of lead, copper, and plastic
- Install connectors, fittings, and joints
- Solder or braze pipe and tubing to join them
- Install sinks, toilets, and other plumbing fixtures
- Troubleshoot, test, and calibrate hydraulic and pneumatic systems

Helpful Attributes

Helpful school subjects include math and shop mechanics. Helpful attributes include:

- Ability to work with detailed plans
- Preference for doing physical work

Training Provided

Job training consists of classroom instruction, including practice in repairing plumbing systems. Course content typically includes:

- Installation, operation, and repair of pipe systems
- Installation and repair of plumbing fixtures and boiler controls
- Maintenance and repair of hydraulic and pneumatic systems
- Methods of soldering, welding, silver brazing, and cutting

Work Environment

Plumbers and pipe fitters work both indoors and outdoors on land and aboard ships.

Civilian Counterparts

Civilian plumbers and pipe fitters usually work for mechanical or plumbing contractors or as self-employed contractors. Some plumbers and pipe fitters work for public utilities. Civilian plumbers and pipe fitters perform duties similar to those performed in the military.

Surveying, Mapping, and Drafting Technicians

Army
Navy
Air Force
Marine Corps
Coast Guard

Short Description

The military builds and repairs many airstrips, docks, barracks, roads, and other projects each year. Surveying, mapping, and drafting technicians conduct land surveys, make maps, and prepare detailed plans and drawings for construction projects. Surveys and maps are also used to locate military targets and plot troop movements.

What They Do

Surveying, mapping, and drafting technicians in the military perform some or all of the following duties:

- Draw maps and charts using drafting tools and computers
- Make scale drawings of roads, airfields, buildings, and other military projects
- Conduct land surveys and compute survey results
- Perform astronomic observation, measure azimuths, angles and determines deviations for target, connection and position area surveys with angular measuring equipment
- Build scale models of land areas that show hills, lakes, roads, and buildings
- Piece together aerial photographs to form large photomaps
- Use global positioning systems to collect location information from satellites
- Prepare, edit, and reproduce construction drawings
- Operate and perform maintenance on vehicles, radios, weapons, and all survey equipment

Helpful Attributes

Helpful school subjects include algebra, geometry, and trigonometry. Helpful attributes include:

- Ability to convert ideas into drawings
- Interest in maps and charts
- Interest in working with drafting equipment and computers
- Interest in working with surveying equipment

Training Provided

Job training consists of classroom instruction, depending on specialty. Further training occurs on the job and through advanced courses. Course content typically includes:

- Surveying and drafting techniques

- Geospatial interpretation
- Architectural and structural drawing

Work Environment

Surveying, mapping, and drafting technicians work both indoors and outdoors in all climates and weather conditions. Those assigned to engineering units sometimes work outdoors with survey teams. Those assigned to intelligence units may work on ships as well as on land.

Civilian Counterparts

Civilian surveying, mapping, and drafting technicians work for construction, engineering, and architectural firms and government agencies such as the highway department. Their work is used for planning construction projects such as highways, airport runways, dams, and drainage systems. They are also called cartographic technicians, and photogrammetrists.

COUNSELING, SOCIAL WORK, AND HUMAN SERVICES OCCUPATIONS

Caseworkers and Counselors

Navy
Air Force
Marine Corps

Short Description

Just like some civilians, some military personnel need assistance with various problems or concerns, including career decisions, family issues, substance abuse, or emotional problems. Caseworkers and counselors work with military personnel and their families to help them with their particular concerns. They may specialize by the type of counseling that they do, such as career guidance or alcohol and drug abuse prevention. They normally work as part of a team that may include social workers, psychologists, medical officers, chaplains, personnel specialists, and commanders.

What They Do

Caseworkers and counselors in the military perform some or all of the following duties:

- Interview personnel who request help or are referred by their commanders
- Identify problems and determine the need for professional help
- Counsel personnel and their families
- Administer and score psychological tests
- Help personnel evaluate and explore career opportunities
- Teach classes on human relations
- Keep records of counseling sessions

Helpful Attributes

Helpful school subjects include health, biology, psychology, sociology, social science, and speech. Helpful attributes include:

- Interest in working with people
- Patience in dealing with problems that take time and effort to overcome
- Sensitivity to the needs of others

Training Provided

Job training consists of classroom instruction, including practice in counseling. Further training occurs on the job and through advanced courses. Course content typically includes:

- Orientation to counseling and social service programs
- Interviewing and counseling methods
- Treatments for drug and alcohol abuse
- Psychological testing techniques

Work Environment

Caseworkers and counselors usually work in offices or clinics.

Civilian Counterparts

Civilian caseworkers and counselors work in rehabilitation centers, hospitals, schools, and public agencies. They are usually required to have a college degree in social work, psychology, or counseling. They may also be called employment counselors, social workers, human services workers, or substance abuse counselors.

Religious Program Specialists

Army
Navy
Air Force

Short Description

The military has personnel from many religions and faiths. The military provides chaplains and religious program specialists to help meet the spiritual needs of its personnel. Religious program specialists assist chaplains with religious services, religious education programs, and related administrative duties.

What They Do

Religious program specialists in the military perform some or all of the following duties:

- Assist chaplains in planning religious programs and activities
- Assist chaplains in conducting religious services
- Prepare religious, educational, and devotional materials
- Organize charitable and public service volunteer programs
- Maintain relations with religious communities and public service organizations
- Perform administrative duties for chaplains

Helpful Attributes

Helpful school subjects include English, public speaking, accounting, and typing. Helpful attributes include:

- Ability to express ideas clearly
- Interest in administrative work
- Interest in religious guidance
- Knowledge of various religious customs and beliefs
- Sensitivity to the needs of others

Training Provided

Job training consists of classroom instruction. Course content typically includes:

- Principles of religious support programs
- Guidance and counseling techniques
- Leadership skills
- Office procedures

Work Environment

Religious program specialists in the military usually work indoors. They also serve aboard ships or with land and air units in the field.

Civilian Counterparts

Civilian religious program specialists help manage churches and religious schools. Their duties are similar to those performed by military religious program specialists, including planning religious programs and preparing religious educational materials. They are also called directors of religious activities.

EDUCATION AND TRAINING OCCUPATIONS

Training Specialists and Instructors

Navy
Air Force
Marine Corps
Coast Guard

Short Description

The military trains new personnel in the job skills needed to begin their careers in the service. The military also offers advanced training and retraining to nearly all personnel. Instruction in electronics, health care, computer sciences, and aviation are just a few of the many vocational and technical areas for which the military has training programs. Training specialists and instructors teach classes and give demonstrations to provide military personnel with the knowledge needed to perform their jobs.

What They Do

Training specialists and instructors in the military perform some or all of the following duties:

- Prepare course outlines and materials to present during training
- Select training materials, such as textbooks and films
- Teach classes and give lectures in person, over closed-circuit TV, or on videotape
- Work with students individually when necessary
- Test and evaluate student progress
- Use weapons and equipment
- Manage training plans; develop, update, manage curriculum and field training exercises

Helpful Attributes

Helpful school subjects include public speaking and English. Helpful attributes include:

- Ability to communicate effectively, in writing and speaking
- Interest in counseling and promoting human relations
- Interest in teaching

Training Provided

Training consists of classroom instruction, including practice teaching. Length of training varies depending on specialty. Course content typically includes:

- Lesson planning
- Instructional methods
- Communications skills

Work Environment

Training specialists and instructors in the military work either indoors or outdoors, depending on the type of training they provide and their specialty area.

Civilian Counterparts

Civilian training specialists and instructors work for vocational and technical schools, high schools, colleges, businesses, and government agencies. Their duties are similar to those performed by military training specialists and instructors. Civilian training specialists and instructors may be called teachers, trainers, or training representatives.

Teachers and Instructors

Army
Navy
Air Force
Marine Corps
Coast Guard

Short Description

The military provides training and educational opportunities for all personnel. Teachers and instructors conduct classes in such academic subjects as engineering, physical science, social science, and nursing. Teachers and instructors teach military personnel subjects that are related to their military occupations.

What They Do

Teachers and instructors in the military perform some or all of the following duties:

- Develop course content, training outlines, and lesson plans
- Prepare training aids, assignments, and demonstrations
- Deliver lectures
- Conduct laboratory exercises and seminars
- Give tests and evaluate student progress
- Diagnose individual learning difficulties and offer help

Helpful Attributes

Helpful attributes include:

- Ability to express ideas clearly and concisely
- Interest in teaching
- Preference for working closely with people

Training Provided

No initial job training is provided to officers in this occupation.

Work Environment

Teachers and instructors usually work in classrooms and lecture halls.

Civilian Counterparts

Civilian teachers and instructors work in junior colleges, colleges, and universities. They perform duties similar to those performed in the military. They may teach several different courses within the same field of study.

ENGINEERING AND SCIENTIFIC RESEARCH OCCUPATIONS

Meteorological Specialists

Army
Navy
Air Force
Marine Corps
Coast Guard

Short Description

Weather information is important for planning military operations. Accurate weather forecasts are needed to plan troop movements, airplane flights, and ship traffic. Meteorological specialists collect information about weather and sea conditions for use by meteorologists. They make visual observations and take readings from weather equipment, radar scans, and satellite photographs.

What They Do

Meteorological specialists in the military perform some or all of the following duties:

- Launch weather balloons to record wind speed and direction
- Identify the types of clouds present and estimate cloud height and amount of cloud cover
- Take readings of barometric pressure, temperature, humidity, and sea conditions
- Operate radio equipment to receive information from satellites
- Plot weather information on maps and charts
- Forecast weather based on readings and observations
- Participate in the operation of a field artillery meteorological observation station

Helpful Attributes

Helpful school subjects include geography, mathematics, and physical science. Helpful attributes include:

- Ability to communicate effectively
- Interest in gathering and organizing information
- Interest in learning how weather changes
- Interest in working with formulas, tables, and graphs

Training Provided

Job training consists of classroom instruction. Training length varies depending on specialty. Advanced training in weather forecasting is available for some specialties. Course content typically includes:

- Basic meteorology (study of weather) and oceanography (study of the ocean)
- Methods for plotting weather data
- Analyzing radar and satellite weather information
- Preparation of weather reports

Work Environment

Meteorological specialists usually work in offices either on land or aboard ships. They work outdoors when making visual weather observations and launching weather balloons.

Civilian Counterparts

Civilian meteorological specialists work for government agencies (such as the U.S. Weather Service), commercial airlines, radio and television stations, and private weather forecasting firms. They perform duties similar to military meteorological specialists. Civilian meteorological specialists may also be called oceanographer assistants and weather clerks.

Space Operations Specialists

Navy
Air Force

Short Description

Orbiting satellites and other space vehicles are used for communications, weather forecasting, and collecting intelligence data. In the future, more and more military operations will involve space systems. Space operations specialists use and repair spacecraft ground control command equipment, including electronic systems that track spacecraft location and operation.

What They Do

Space operations specialists in the military perform some or all of the following duties:

- Transmit and verify spacecraft commands using aerospace ground equipment
- Monitor computers and telemetry display systems
- Analyze data to determine spacecraft operational status
- Repair ground and spacecraft communication equipment
- Assist in preparing spacecraft commands to meet mission objectives
- Operate data-handling equipment to track spacecraft

Helpful Attributes

Helpful school subjects include physics, geometry, algebra, and trigonometry. Helpful attributes include:

- Ability to work with formulas to solve math problems
- Interest in operating electronic equipment and systems
- Interest in space exploration
- Interest in working as part of a team

Training Provided

Job training consists of classroom instruction, including practice in spacecraft command and control operations. Course content typically includes:

- Operation of electronic transmitting, receiving, and computing equipment
- Analysis of data that indicate spacecraft operational status
- Application of electronic and satellite system principles
- Alignment of ground and spacecraft communication systems
- Space command and control system operational procedures

Work Environment

Space operations specialists work in space operations centers.

Civilian Counterparts

Civilian space operations specialists work for the National Aeronautics and Space Administration, the U.S. Weather Service, and private satellite communications firms. They perform duties similar to military space operations specialists.

Unmanned Vehicle (UV) Operations Specialists

Army
Navy
Air Force
Marine Corps

Short Description

The military uses remotely piloted unmanned vehicles for a variety of purposes, such as deep sea exploration, intelligence gathering, remote surveillance, and target applications. These vehicles are used in the air, on land, and at sea in operations or missions that could be dangerous for human operators onboard the vehicle. The military requires skilled operators and technicians to maintain and control these vehicles. Personnel normally specialize by the type of vehicle they operate, such as unmanned aerial vehicles, ground vehicles, surface vehicles, and undersea vehicles.

What They Do

Unmanned vehicle operations specialists in the military perform some or all of the following duties:

- Prepare and install equipment on or within the unmanned vehicle
- Operate, navigate, launch, track, and recover unmanned vehicles
- Operate equipment in remote receiving stations and ground control stations
- Coordinate with other personnel to complete the designated mission
- Perform pre-flight, in-flight, and post-flight checks and procedures
- Operate and perform operator-level maintenance on communications equipment, power sources, light and heavy wheel vehicle, and some crane operations

Helpful Attributes

Helpful attributes include:

- Enjoy working with tools
- Knowledge of electronic theory and schematic drawing
- Superior adaptability to three-dimensional spatial relationships

Training Provided

Job training varies depending on the position. Course content typically includes:

- Unmanned vehicle concepts and capabilities
- Operation of unmanned vehicles
- Basic preventative maintenance

Work Environment

Unmanned vehicle operations specialists work under a variety of conditions depending upon the type of vehicle and mission. Some specialists work in control stations or receiving stations on land, while others work aboard ships.

Civilian Counterparts

Unmanned vehicles are used in several civilian areas, such as mining, petroleum exploration, environmental research, and manufacturing. Civilian unmanned vehicle operations specialists perform duties similar to those of their military counterparts.

ENVIRONMENTAL HEALTH AND SAFETY OCCUPATIONS

Environmental Health and Safety Specialists

Army
Navy
Air Force
Marine Corps

Short Description

Each military base is a small community. The health and well-being of the residents and surrounding land is a major concern of the services. Keeping military work places and living areas sanitary helps to prevent illness. Environmental health and safety specialists inspect military facilities and food supplies for the presence of disease, germs, or other conditions hazardous to health and the environment.

What They Do

Environmental health and safety specialists in the military perform some or all of the following duties:

- Monitor storage, transportation, and disposal of hazardous waste
- Analyze food and water samples to ensure quality
- Conduct health and safety investigations of living quarters and base facilities for people and animals
- Provide training on industrial hygiene, environmental health, and occupational health issues
- Monitor noise and radiation levels at job sites
- Plan accident prevention and perform accident investigation

Helpful Attributes

Helpful school subjects include algebra, biology, chemistry, and general science. Helpful attributes include:

- Interest in gathering information
- Interest in protecting the environment
- Preference for work requiring attention to detail

Training Provided

Job training consists of classroom instruction, including practice in making health and sanitation inspections. Further training occurs on the job and through advanced courses. Training length varies depending on specialty. Course content typically includes:

- Identification of health hazards
- Inspection of food products and food service operations
- Inspection of wastewater and waste disposal facilities

Work Environment

Environmental health specialists work indoors while inspecting food facilities and buildings. They work outdoors while inspecting waste disposal facilities and field camps.

Civilian Counterparts

Most civilian environmental health and safety specialists work for local, state, and federal government agencies. Their duties are similar to the duties of military environmental health specialists. They may be called food and drug inspectors, public health inspectors, health and safety inspectors, or industrial hygienists.

Ordnance Specialists

Army
Navy
Air Force
Marine Corps

Short Description

Ordnance is a military term for ammunition and weapons. Ordnance includes all types of ammunition, missiles, toxic chemicals, and nuclear weapons. Ammunition and weapons must be handled carefully and stored properly. Ordnance specialists transport, store, inspect, prepare, and dispose of weapons and ammunition.

What They Do

Ordnance specialists in the military perform some or all of the following duties:

- Load nuclear and conventional explosives and ammunition on aircraft, ships, and submarines
- Inspect mounted guns, bomb release systems, and missile launchers
- Assemble and load explosives
- Defuse unexploded bombs
- Locate, identify, render safe, recover, or destroy hazardous U.S. and foreign munitions

Helpful Attributes

Helpful school subjects include general science and shop mechanics. Helpful attributes include:

- Ability to remain calm under stress
- Interest in working with guns and explosives

Training Provided

Job training consists of classroom instruction, including practice in ordnance maintenance. Training length varies depending on specialty. Further training occurs on the job and through advanced courses. Course content typically includes:

- Maintenance of nuclear weapons
- Handling, testing, and maintenance of missiles and rockets

Work Environment

Ordnance specialists work indoors and outdoors. They work in repair shops while assembling explosives and repairing weapons. They work outdoors while repairing equipment in the field and loading weapons on tanks, ships, or aircraft.

Civilian Counterparts

There are no direct civilian counterparts for many of the military ordnance specialties. However, there are many occupations that are related. For example, civilians work for government agencies and private industry doing research and development. Others work for police or fire departments as bomb-disposal experts. Some also work for munitions manufacturers and firearms makers. Ordnance specialists may also be called bomb disposal experts.

Water and Sewage Treatment Plant Operators

Army
Navy
Air Force
Marine Corps

Short Description

Military bases operate their own water treatment plants when public facilities cannot be used. These plants provide drinking water and safely dispose of sewage. Water and sewage treatment plant operators maintain the systems that purify water and treat sewage.

What They Do

Water and sewage treatment plant operators in the military perform some or all of the following duties:

- Operate pumps to transfer water from reservoirs and storage tanks to treatment plants
- Add chemicals and operate machinery that purifies water for drinking or cleans it for safe disposal
- Test water for chlorine content, acidity, oxygen demand, and impurities
- Regulate the flow of drinking water to meet demand
- Clean and maintain water treatment machinery
- Keep records of chemical treatments, water pressure, and maintenance

Helpful Attributes

Helpful school subjects include chemistry, math, and shop mechanics. Helpful attributes include:

- Interest in chemistry and pollution control
- Interest in working with mechanical equipment

Training Provided

Job training consists of classroom instruction, including practice operating water and sewage treatment equipment. Further training occurs on the job and through advanced courses. Course content typically includes:

- Operation of treatment systems
- Water testing and analysis
- Maintenance and repair of pumps, compressors, and other equipment

Work Environment

Water and sewage treatment plant operators work indoors and outdoors. They may be exposed to strong odors.

Civilian Counterparts

Civilian water and sewage treatment plant operators work for municipal public works and industrial plants. Their work is similar to military water and sewage treatment plant operators. Civilian plant operators usually specialize as water treatment plant operators, waterworks pump station operators, or wastewater treatment plant operators.

Emergency Management Specialists

Army
Navy
Air Force
Marine Corps
Coast Guard

Short Description

The military prepares for emergencies or natural disasters by developing detailed warning, control, and evacuation plans. Emergency management specialists prepare emergency plans and respond to all types of disasters, such as floods, earthquakes, hurricanes, or enemy attack.

What They Do

Emergency management specialists in the military perform some or all of the following duties:

- Assist in preparing and maintaining disaster operations plans
- Train military and civilian personnel on what to do in an emergency
- Operate and maintain nuclear, biological, and chemical detection and decontamination equipment
- Conduct surveys to determine needs in the event of an emergency
- Monitor disaster preparedness activities and training operations
- Serve as members of emergency response teams

Helpful Attributes

Helpful school subjects include algebra, chemistry, physics, geometry, and trigonometry. Helpful attributes include:

- Ability to communicate effectively
- Ability to plan and organize
- Ability to work calmly under stress

Training Provided

Job training consists of classroom instruction, including practice in the use of nuclear, biological, and chemical detection and decontamination equipment. Further training occurs on the job and through advanced courses. Course content typically includes:

- Defensive procedures for nuclear, biological, and chemical warfare
- Preparation of emergency plans

Work Environment

Emergency management specialists work indoors when conducting training sessions and preparing disaster plans. Sometimes they work outdoors while operating decontamination equipment and monitoring disaster training.

Civilian Counterparts

Civilian emergency management specialists work for federal, state, and local governments, including law enforcement and civil defense agencies. They perform duties similar to military emergency management specialists.

HEALTHCARE PRACTITIONERS OCCUPATIONS

Dental Specialists
Army
Navy
Air Force
Coast Guard

Short Description

Dental care is one of the health services provided to all military personnel. It is available in military dental clinics all over the world. Dental specialists assist military dentists in examining and treating patients. They also help manage dental offices.

What They Do

Dental specialists in the military perform some or all of the following duties:

- Help dentists perform oral surgery
- Prepare for patient examinations by selecting and arranging instruments and medications
- Help dentists during examinations by preparing dental compounds and operating dental equipment
- Clean patients' teeth using scaling and polishing instruments and equipment
- Operate dental X-ray equipment and process X-rays of patients' teeth, gums, and jaws
- Provide guidance to patients on daily care of their teeth
- Perform administrative duties, such as scheduling office visits, keeping patient records, and ordering dental supplies

Helpful Attributes

Helpful school subjects include biology and chemistry. Helpful attributes include:

- Ability to follow spoken instructions and detailed procedures
- Good eye-hand coordination
- Interest in working with people

Training Provided

Job training consists of classroom instruction, including practice in dental care tasks. Further training occurs on the job and through advanced courses. Course content typically includes:

- Preventive dentistry
- Radiology (X-ray) techniques
- Dental office procedures
- Dental hygiene procedures

Work Environment

Dental specialists in the military usually work indoors in dental offices or clinics. Some specialists may be assigned to duty aboard ships.

Civilian Counterparts

Civilian dental specialists work in dental offices or clinics. Their work is similar to work in the military. They typically specialize in assisting dentists to treat patients, provide clerical support (dental assistants), or cleaning teeth (dental hygienists).

Medical Care Technicians

Army
Navy
Air Force
Coast Guard

Short Description

The military provides medical care to all men and women in the services. Medical care technicians work with teams of physicians, nurses, and other health care professionals to provide treatment to patients. They help give patients the care and treatment required to help them recover from illness or injury. They also prepare rooms, equipment, and supplies in hospitals and medical clinics.

What They Do

Medical care technicians in the military perform some or all of the following duties:

- Provide bedside care in hospitals, including taking the body temperature, pulse, and respiration rate of patients
- Feed, bathe, and dress patients
- Prepare patients, operating rooms, equipment, and supplies for surgery
- Make casts, traction devices, and splints according to physicians' instructions
- Give medication to patients under the direction of physicians and nurses

Helpful Attributes

Helpful school subjects include general science, biology, and psychology. Helpful attributes include:

- Ability to follow directions precisely
- Ability to work under stressful or emergency conditions
- Interest in helping others

Training Provided

Job training consists of classroom instruction, including practice in patient care. Training length varies depending on specialty. Further training occurs on the job and through advanced courses. Course content may include:

- Patient care techniques
- Emergency medical techniques
- Methods of sterilizing surgical equipment
- Plaster casting techniques

Work Environment

Medical care technicians work in hospitals and clinics on land or aboard ships. In combat situations, they may work in mobile field hospitals.

Civilian Counterparts

Civilian medical care technicians work in hospitals, nursing homes, rehabilitation centers, psychiatric hospitals, or physicians' offices. They perform similar duties to those performed in the military. They may be called nurses' aides, orderlies, operating room technicians, orthopedic assistants, or practical nurses.

Medical Emergency Technicians
Army
Navy
Air Force

Short Description

In emergencies or in combat, physicians are not always immediately available to treat the injured or wounded. When a physician is not available, medical emergency technicians provide basic and emergency medical treatment. They also assist medical officers in caring for sick and injured patients.

What They Do

Medical emergency technicians in the military perform some or all of the following duties:

- Examine and treat emergency or battlefield patients
- Interview patients and record their medical histories
- Take patients' temperature, pulse, and blood pressure
- Prepare blood samples for laboratory analysis
- Keep health records and clinical files up to date
- Give shots and medicines to patients

Helpful Attributes

Helpful school subjects include chemistry, biology, psychology, general science, and algebra. Helpful attributes include:

- Ability to communicate effectively
- Ability to work under stressful conditions
- Interest in helping others

Training Provided

Job training consists of classroom instruction, depending on specialty. Further training occurs on the job and through advanced courses. Course content typically includes:

- Emergency medical treatment
- Basic nursing care
- Study of the human body
- Minor surgical procedures
- Clinical laboratory procedures
- Methods for diagnosing diseases

Work Environment

Medical emergency technicians usually work in hospitals and clinics on land or aboard ships. Medical emergency technicians may give emergency medical treatment in the field.

Civilian Counterparts

Civilian medical emergency technicians work in hospitals, clinics, nursing homes, and rehabilitation centers. They perform duties similar to those performed by medical emergency technicians in the military. Civilian medical emergency technicians are known for the type of work they do: emergency medical technicians treat victims of accidents, fire, or heart attacks; medical assistants work for physicians and perform routine medical and clerical tasks; medication aides give shots and medicine under the close supervision of physicians; and physician assistants perform routine examinations and treatment for physicians.

Optometric Technicians

Army
Navy
Air Force

Short Description

Optometry, or vision care, is one of the many health benefits available to military personnel. The military operates its own clinics to examine eyes and fit glasses or contact lenses. Optometric technicians assist optometrists in providing vision care. They work with patients and manage clinic offices.

What They Do

Optometric technicians in the military perform some or all of the following duties:

- Use and maintain ophthalmic instruments and equipment
- Perform screening tests
- Order eyeglasses and contact lenses from prescriptions
- Fit eyeglasses to patients
- Make minor repairs to glasses
- Place eye drops and ointment into patients' eyes
- Keep records in optometry offices

Helpful Attributes

Helpful school subjects include algebra, geometry, biology, and related courses. Helpful attributes include:

- Ability to communicate effectively
- Interest in work requiring accuracy and attention to detail

Training Provided

Job training consists of classroom instruction, including practice in optometric procedures. Further training occurs on the job. Course content typically includes:

- Preparing and fitting glasses and contact lenses
- Vision testing
- Maintenance of optometric instruments

Work Environment

Optometric technicians normally work in optometric clinics.

Civilian Counterparts

Civilian optometric technicians work in private optometry offices, clinics, and government health agencies. They perform duties similar to those performed by military optometric technicians. Optometric technicians are also called optometric assistants.

Physical and Occupational Therapy Specialists

Army
Navy
Air Force

Short Description

Physical and occupational therapy consists of treatment and exercise for patients disabled by illness or injury. Physical and occupational therapy specialists assist in administering treatment aimed at helping disabled patients regain strength and mobility and preparing them to return to work.

What They Do

Physical and occupational therapy specialists in the military perform some or all of the following duties:

- Test and interview patients to determine their physical and mental abilities
- Assist physical and occupational therapists in planning therapy programs and exercise schedules
- Fit artificial limbs (prostheses) and train patients in their use
- Provide massages and heat treatments to patients
- Teach patients new mobility skills
- Set up and maintain therapeutic equipment such as exercise machines and whirlpools

Helpful Attributes

Helpful school subjects include general science, biology, physiology, and psychology. Helpful attributes include:

- Ability to communicate effectively
- Interest in working with and helping people
- Patience to work with people whose injuries heal slowly

Training Provided

Job training consists of classroom instruction, including practice in applying therapy techniques. Further training occurs on the job and through advanced courses. Course content typically includes:

- Anatomy, physiology, and psychology (the study of the body, body functions, and the mind)
- Methods of therapy, including massage, electric therapy, and radiation therapy
- Handling and positioning of patients
- Principles of rehabilitation

Work Environment

Therapy specialists work in hospitals, clinics, and rehabilitation centers.

Civilian Counterparts

Civilian therapy specialists work in hospitals, rehabilitation centers, nursing homes, schools, and community health centers. They perform duties similar to military therapy specialists. Civilian therapy specialists often specialize in treating a particular type of patient, such as children, the severely disabled, the elderly, or those who have lost arms or legs (amputees).

HUMAN RESOURCES MANAGEMENT AND SERVICES OCCUPATIONS

Human Resources Specialists

Army
Navy
Air Force
Marine Corps
Coast Guard

Short Description

Personnel management helps individuals develop their military careers. It also serves the military's need to fill jobs with qualified workers. Human resources specialists collect and store information about the people in the military, such as training, job assignment, promotion, and health information. They work directly with service personnel and their families.

What They Do

Human resources specialists in the military perform some or all of the following duties:

- Organize, maintain, and review personnel records
- Enter and retrieve personnel information using computer terminals
- Assign personnel to jobs
- Prepare correspondence, organizational charts, and reports
- Provide career guidance
- Assist personnel and their families who have special needs
- Determine manpower requirements
- Evaluate organizational structure for effectiveness and efficiency
- Perform personal services

Helpful Attributes

Helpful school subjects include English, speech, and business administration. Helpful attributes include:

- Ability to compose clear instructions or correspondence
- Ability to follow detailed procedures and instructions
- Interest in working closely with others

Training Provided

Job training consists of classroom instruction. Further training occurs on the job and through advanced courses. Course content typically includes:

- Preparation of military correspondence and forms
- Personnel records management
- Computer update and retrieval procedures

Work Environment

Personnel specialists normally work in office settings on land or aboard ships.

Civilian Counterparts

Civilian personnel specialists work for all types of organizations, including industrial firms, retail establishments, and government agencies. They perform duties similar to military personnel clerks. However, specific jobs vary from company to company.

Recruiting Specialists

Army
Navy
Air Force
Marine Corps
Coast Guard

Short Description

Attracting young people with the kinds of talent needed to succeed in today's military is a large task. Recruiting specialists provide information about military careers to young people, parents, schools, and local communities. They explain service employment and training opportunities, pay and benefits, and service life.

What They Do

Recruiting specialists in the military perform some or all of the following duties:

- Interview civilians interested in military careers
- Describe military careers to groups of high school students
- Explain the purpose of the ASVAB (Armed Services Vocational Aptitude Battery) and test results to students and counselors
- Participate in local job fairs and career day programs
- Talk about the military to community groups
- Counsel military personnel about career opportunities and benefits

Helpful Attributes

Helpful school subjects include the social sciences, speech, psychology, and English. Helpful attributes include:

- Ability to speak before groups
- Ability to work independently
- Interest in working with youths

Training Provided

Job training consists of classroom instruction. Further training occurs on the job and through advanced courses. Course content typically includes:

- Recruiting procedures
- Interviewing techniques
- Public speaking techniques
- Community relations practices

Work Environment

Recruiting specialists work in local recruiting offices, on high school campuses and career centers, and in local communities. They may have to travel often.

Civilian Counterparts

Civilian recruiting specialists work for businesses of all kinds searching for talented people to hire. Recruiters also work for colleges seeking to attract and enroll talented high school students.

INFORMATION TECHNOLOGY, COMPUTER SCIENCE, AND MATHEMATICS OCCUPATIONS

Computer Systems Specialists

Army
Navy
Air Force
Marine Corps
Coast Guard

Short Description

The military uses computers to store and process data on personnel, weather, communications, finances, and many other areas, as well as to operate sophisticated equipment during combat and peacetime maneuvers.

What They Do

Computer systems specialists in the military perform some or all of the following duties:

- Install, configure, and monitor local and wide area networks, hardware, and software
- Collect, enter, and process information using computers
- Provide customer and network administration services, such as electronic mail accounts, user training, security, virus protection, and troubleshooting
- Use computer programs to solve problems
- Determine and analyze computer systems requirements
- Program information into languages that computers can read
- Develop, test, and debug computer programs
- Provide system analysis and maintenance
- Implement procedures to ensure computer and network security

Helpful Attributes

Helpful school subjects include computer science, math, and typing. Helpful attributes include:

- Ability to communicate effectively
- Ability to understand and apply math concepts
- Interest in solving problems
- Interest in work requiring accuracy and attention to detail

Training Provided

Job training consists of classroom instruction, depending upon the specialty area. Further training occurs on the job and through advanced courses in specific computer systems and languages. Course content typically includes:

- Use of computers and peripheral equipment
- Computer systems concepts
- Planning, designing, and testing computer systems
- Program structuring, coding, and debugging
- Use of current programming languages
- Computer security issues
- Network management

Work Environment

Computer systems specialists in the military work in offices or at computer sites on military bases or aboard ships.

Civilian Counterparts

Civilian computer systems specialists work anywhere that computer systems are used. They may be employed as network support technicians for large companies or as data processing technicians in local banks or school. Those who specialize in computer programming may work as programmers for software developers. The skills learned as a computer systems specialist are highly transferable to the civilian workforce.

INTELLIGENCE OCCUPATIONS

Intelligence Specialists

Army
Navy
Air Force
Marine Corps
Coast Guard

Short Description

Military intelligence is information needed to plan for our national defense. Knowledge of the number, location, and tactics of enemy forces and potential battle areas is needed to develop military plans. To gather information, the services rely on aerial photographs, electronic monitoring using radar, satellites, and sensitive radios, and human observation. Intelligence specialists gather and study the information required to design defense plans and tactics.

What They Do

Intelligence specialists in the military perform some or all of the following duties:

- Perform military action involving the use of electromagnetic energy to determine, exploit, reduce, or prevent hostile use of the electromagnetic spectrum

- Study foreign troop movements

- Operate sensitive radios to intercept foreign military communications

- Exploit imagery and geospatial data from satellite and airborne systems in support of military operations

- Participate in detecting, locating, tracking, and analyzing on-ground targets, rotary wing, and slow moving fixed wing aircraft

- Conduct information operations using foreign language skills and advanced computer systems

- Prepare intelligence reports, maps, and charts

- Install, operate, and conduct preventive maintenance of associated equipment and facilities

- Conduct investigations to detect, identify, assess, counter, exploit, and neutralize threats to national security

- Collect human intelligence (HUMINT) by interviewing, interrogating, or otherwise interacting directly with human sources of information

- Transcribe, translate, and interpret foreign language materials and provide cultural and regional guidance

Helpful Attributes

Helpful school subjects include algebra, geometry, trigonometry, and geography. Helpful attributes include:

- Ability to organize information
- Ability to think and write clearly
- Interest in gathering information and studying its meaning
- Interest in reading foreign cultures
- Interest in computers

Training Provided

Job training consists of classroom instruction, including practice in intelligence gathering. Training length varies depending on specialty. Further training occurs on the job and through advanced courses. Course content typically includes:

- Planning imagery and geospatial data from satellite and airborne systems
- Preparing intelligence reports, maps, and charts
- Analyzing aerial, satellite, and radar imagery
- Using computer systems
- Foreign language training

Work Environment

Intelligence specialists work in offices on land and aboard ships and in tents when in the field.

Civilian Counterparts

Civilian intelligence specialists generally work for federal government agencies such as the Central Intelligence Agency or the National Security Agency. Their duties are similar to those performed by military intelligence specialists. The analytical skills of intelligence specialists are also useful in other fields, such as research or business planning.

Interpreters and Translators

Army
Navy
Air Force
Marine Corps

Short Description

Some members of the military must be able to read and understand the many languages of the world. Information from foreign language media is important to the nation's defense. Interpreters and translators convert written or spoken foreign languages into English or other languages. They usually specialize in a particular foreign language.

What They Do

Interpreters and translators in the military perform some or all of the following duties:

- Translate written and spoken foreign language material to and from English, making sure to preserve the original meaning
- Interview prisoners of war, enemy deserters, and civilian informers in their native languages
- Record foreign radio transmissions using sensitive communications equipment
- Prepare written reports about the information obtained
- Translate foreign documents, such as battle plans and personnel records
- Translate foreign books and articles describing foreign equipment and construction techniques
- Install, operate, and maintain electronic equipment used to intercept foreign communications

Helpful Attributes

Helpful school subjects include speech, communications, and foreign languages. Helpful attributes include:

- Interest in reading and writing
- Interest in working with people
- Talent for foreign languages

Training Provided

Job training consists of classroom instruction, including practice in interpretation. Training length varies depending on specialty. Longer training is necessary for specialties that do not require foreign language fluency prior to entry. For these specialties, foreign language training for 6 to 12 months is provided. Further training occurs on the job and through advanced courses. Course content typically includes:

- Training in foreign language fluency
- Instruction in translation

Work Environment

Interpreters and translators normally work on military bases, aboard ships, or in airplanes.

Civilian Counterparts

Civilian interpreters and translators work for government agencies, embassies, universities, and companies that conduct business overseas. Their work is similar to the work of military interpreters and translators.

Geospatial Imaging Specialists
Army
Air Force

Short Description

Geospatial intelligence consists of imagery, imagery intelligence, and geospatial information (which includes mapping, charting, measuring, and representing the earth in 3D). The military relies on geospatial imagery specialists to gather imaging and geospatial information to describe, assess, and visually depict physical features and geographically reference activities on the Earth.

What They Do

Geospatial imaging specialists in the military perform some or all of the following duties:

- Uses multi-sensor imagery to conduct comparative analysis
- Analyzes terrain to determine trafficability and identify landing zones and defensive fortifications
- Determines type, function, status, location, significance of military facilities and activities, industrial installations, and surface transportation networks
- Determines present and future imagery collection requirements
- Prepares damage assessment reports detailing structural damage and weapons effects
- Maintains and uses geospatial databases, target materials, imagery, and other intelligence products
- Works with Unmanned Aerial System's (UAS) mission team to plan mission, maintain collection list, identify collection sequence, and provide specific targets' requirements

Helpful Attributes

Helpful fields of study include earth science and geography, mathematics, engineering and information technology. Helpful attributes include:

- Interest in computers
- Interest in earth science
- Strong critical thinking skills

Training Provided

Job training consists of classroom instruction. Course content typically includes:

- Imagery interpretation principles, techniques, and procedures for imagery exploitation, reports, and presentations
- Techniques of collating, analyzing, and evaluating imagery intelligence
- Use of national geospatial data, information and intelligence data systems and the maps, charts, grid systems, and interpreting equipment to solve geospatial intelligence problems

Work Environment

Geospatial imaging specialists usually work in office facilities. They may work in facilities in field camps or aboard ships.

Civilian Counterparts

Civilian geospatial imaging specialists generally work for federal government agencies such as the Central Intelligence Agency or the National Security Agency. They perform duties similar to those performed by military geospatial imaging specialists. They may specialize in areas such as agriculture, mining, healthcare, retail trade, urban planning, or military intelligence.

INTERNATIONAL RELATIONS, LINGUISTICS, AND OTHER SOCIAL SCIENCES OCCUPATIONS

Interpreters and Translators

Army
Navy
Air Force
Marine Corps

Short Description

Some members of the military must be able to read and understand the many languages of the world. Information from foreign language media is important to the nation's defense. Interpreters and translators convert written or spoken foreign languages into English or other languages. They usually specialize in a particular foreign language.

What They Do

Interpreters and translators in the military perform some or all of the following duties:

- Translate written and spoken foreign language material to and from English, making sure to preserve the original meaning
- Interview prisoners of war, enemy deserters, and civilian informers in their native languages
- Record foreign radio transmissions using sensitive communications equipment
- Prepare written reports about the information obtained
- Translate foreign documents, such as battle plans and personnel records
- Translate foreign books and articles describing foreign equipment and construction techniques
- Install, operate, and maintain electronic equipment used to intercept foreign communications

Helpful Attributes

Helpful school subjects include speech, communications, and foreign languages. Helpful attributes include:

- Interest in reading and writing
- Interest in working with people
- Talent for foreign languages

Training Provided

Job training consists of classroom instruction, including practice in interpretation. Training length varies depending on specialty. Longer training is necessary for specialties that do not require foreign language fluency prior to entry. For these specialties, foreign language training for 6 to 12 months is provided. Further training occurs on the job and through advanced courses. Course content typically includes:

- Interrogation (questioning) methods
- Use and care of communications equipment
- Procedures for preparing reports

Work Environment

Interpreters and translators normally work on military bases, aboard ships, or in airplanes.

Civilian Counterparts

Civilian interpreters and translators work for government agencies, embassies, universities, and companies that conduct business overseas. Their work is similar to the work of military interpreters and translators.

Foreign Affairs Specialists

Army
Navy
Marine Corps

Short Description

The military works with civil authorities and civilian populations in areas of operations in order to lessen their impact. Foreign affairs specialists support civil affairs and psychological operations while serving as liaison between the local population and the United States Government.

What They Do

Foreign affairs specialists in the military perform some or all of the following duties:

- Maintain and operate various voice and data communication devices

- Assess and determine the capabilities and effectiveness of foreign nations' government functions systems including governance, public health and welfare, infrastructure, rule of law, economic stability, and public education and information
- Research finished and current intelligence and open-source information
- Perform initial analysis of enemy foreign propaganda products and other media
- Assist in establishment of basic services in order to support in-country rehabilitation

Helpful Attributes

Helpful fields of study include political science, history, and international affairs. Helpful attributes include:

- Ability to express ideas clearly and concisely
- Interest in collecting and analyzing data
- Interest in living and working in a foreign country
- Interest in working closely with people

Training Provided

Job training is provided in some specialties. Training length varies by entry requirements and specialty area. Further training occurs on the job. Course content typically includes:

- Political and cultural awareness
- Development of foreign area expertise and language proficiency
- Organization and functions of diplomatic missions

Work Environment

Foreign affairs specialists work in offices of U.S. embassies and in the field on missions located overseas.

Civilian Counterparts

Civilians who perform work similar to the work of international foreign affairs specialists are employed mainly by government agencies, such as the Department of State. They work in U.S. embassies and missions overseas. Other civilian counterparts include political scientists, university instructors, and advisers to corporations doing business overseas.

LAW ENFORCEMENT, SECURITY, AND PROTECTIVE SERVICES OCCUPATIONS

Firefighters

Army
Navy
Air Force
Marine Corps

Short Description

Military bases have their own fire departments. Military firefighting units are responsible for protecting lives and property on base from fire. Firefighters put out, control, and help prevent fires in buildings, aircraft, and aboard ships.

What They Do

Firefighters in the military perform some or all of the following duties:

- Operate pumps, hoses, and extinguishers
- Force entry into aircraft, vehicles, and buildings in order to fight fires and rescue personnel
- Drive firefighting trucks and emergency rescue vehicles
- Give first aid to injured personnel
- Inspect aircraft, buildings, and equipment for fire hazards
- Teach fire protection procedures
- Repair firefighting equipment and fill fire extinguishers

Helpful Attributes

Helpful school subjects include health and general science. Helpful attributes include:

- Ability to remain calm under stress
- Ability to think and act decisively
- Willingness to risk injury to help others

Training Provided

Job training consists of classroom training, including practice in fighting fires. Further training occurs on the job. Course content typically includes:

- Types of fires
- Firefighting equipment operations
- Firefighting procedures
- First aid procedures
- Rescue procedures

Work Environment

Firefighters work indoors and outdoors while fighting fires. They are exposed to the smoke, heat, and flames of the fires they fight.

Civilian Counterparts

Civilian firefighters work for city and county fire departments, other government agencies, and industrial firms. They perform duties similar to those performed by military firefighters, including rescue and salvage work.

Law Enforcement and Security Specialists

Army
Navy
Air Force
Marine Corps
Coast Guard

Short Description

The military services have their own law enforcement and police forces. These specialists investigate crimes committed on military property or that involve military personnel. Military police do many of the same things as civilian officers, control traffic, prevent crime, and respond to emergencies. They also guard military bases and inmates in military correctional facilities.

What They Do

Law enforcement and security specialists in the military perform some or all of the following duties:

- Investigate criminal activities and activities related to espionage, treason, and terrorism
- Interview witnesses and arrest suspects
- Guard correctional facilities and other military installations
- Patrol areas on foot, by car, or by boat
- Perform fire and riot control duties
- Provide strategic weapons and cargo security
- Conduct customs and protective service operations

Helpful Attributes

Helpful school subjects include government and speech. Helpful attributes include:

- Ability to remain calm under pressure
- Interest in law enforcement and crime prevention
- Willingness to perform potentially dangerous work

Training Provided

Job training consists of classroom instruction. Training length varies depending on specialty. Course content typically includes:

- Civil and military laws
- Investigation and evidence collection procedures and techniques
- Prisoner control and discipline
- Use of firearms and hand-to-hand defense techniques
- Traffic and crowd control procedures

Work Environment

Law enforcement and security specialists in the military work both indoors and outdoors depending on their assignment. They may work outdoors while conducting investigations or patrolling facilities.

Civilian Counterparts

Civilian law enforcement and security specialists work for state, county, or city law enforcement agencies. They may also work in prisons, intelligence agencies, and private security companies. They perform similar duties to those performed in the military. They may be called police officers, detectives, private investigators, undercover agents, correction officers, or security guards.

LEGAL PROFESSIONS AND SUPPORT SERVICES OCCUPATIONS

Legal Specialists and Court Reporters

Army
Navy
Air Force
Marine Corps
Coast Guard

Short Description

The military has its own judicial system for prosecuting lawbreakers and handling disputes. Legal specialists and court reporters assist military lawyers and judges in the performance of legal and judicial work. They perform legal research, prepare legal documents, and record legal proceedings.

What They Do

Legal specialists and court reporters in the military perform some or all of the following duties:

- Research court decisions and military regulations

- Process legal claims and appeals
- Interview clients and take statements
- Prepare trial requests and make arrangements for courtrooms
- Maintain law libraries and trial case files
- Use a variety of methods and equipment to record and transcribe court proceedings
- Prepare records of hearings, investigations, court-martials, and courts of inquiry

Helpful Attributes

Helpful school subjects include business mathematics, typing, speech, and shorthand. Helpful attributes include:

- Ability to keep organized and accurate records
- Ability to listen carefully
- Interest in the law and legal proceedings

Training Provided

Job training consists of classroom instruction. Course content typically includes:

- Legal terminology and research techniques
- How to prepare legal documents
- High speed transcription
- Military judicial processes

Work Environment

Legal specialists and court reporters work in military law offices and courtrooms.

Civilian Counterparts

Civilian legal specialists and court reporters work for private law firms, banks, insurance companies, government agencies, and local, state, and federal courts. They perform duties similar to military legal specialists and court reporters. Civilian legal specialists and court reporters may also be called legal assistants, law clerks, paralegals, and court reporters.

MECHANIC AND REPAIR TECHNOLOGISTS AND TECHNICIANS OCCUPATIONS

Electrical Products Repairers

Army
Navy
Air Force
Marine Corps

Short Description

Much of the military's equipment is electrically powered. Electric motors, electric tools, and medical equipment require careful maintenance and repair. Electrical products repairers maintain and repair electrical equipment. They specialize by type of equipment.

What They Do

Electrical products repairers in the military perform some or all of the following duties:

- Maintain, test, and repair electric motors in many kinds of machines, such as lathes, pumps, office machines, and appliances
- Inspect and repair electrical, medical, and dental equipment
- Inspect and repair electric instruments, such as voltmeters
- Maintain and repair portable electric tools, such as saws and drills

Helpful Attributes

Helpful school subjects include math, electricity, and shop mechanics. Helpful attributes include:

- Ability to use tools
- Interest in electric motors and appliances
- Interest in solving problems

Training Provided

Job training consists of classroom instruction, including practice in repairing electrical products. Training length varies depending on specialty. Further training occurs on the job and through advanced courses. Course content typically includes:

- Maintenance and repair procedures
- Use of electrical test equipment

Work Environment

Electrical products repairers usually work in repair shops on land or aboard ships.

Civilian Counterparts

Civilian electrical products repairers work in many industries, including hospitals, manufacturing firms, and governmental agencies. They also work in independent repair shops. They perform duties similar to military electrical products repairers. They may be called electric tool repairers, electrical instrument repairers, electro-medical equipment repairers, or electric motor repairers.

Power Plant Electricians

Army

Navy

Short Description

Each military base—anywhere in the world—must have its own electricity. Power plant electricians maintain and repair electricity generating equipment in mobile and stationary power plants.

What They Do

Power plant electricians perform some or all of the following duties:

- Maintain and repair motors, generators, switchboards, and control equipment
- Maintain and repair power and lighting circuits, electrical fixtures, and other electrical equipment
- Detect and locate grounds, open circuits, and short circuits in power distribution cables
- Read technical guides and diagrams to locate damaged parts of generators and control equipment

Helpful Attributes

Helpful school subjects include electrical and electronic theory, math, and technical drawing. Helpful attributes include:

- Ability to use hand and power tools
- Interest in electricity
- Interest in working with machinery

Training Provided

Job training consists of classroom instruction, including practice in maintaining electrical power systems. Course length varies depending on specialty. Further training occurs on the job and through advanced courses. Course content typically includes:

- Generator and power plant operations
- Electrical generation and distribution
- Diesel generator operation, disassembly, inspection, and maintenance
- Principles of electrical and electronic circuitry

Work Environment

Power plant electricians work in repair shops on land, aboard ships, or wherever generating equipment needing repair is located.

Civilian Counterparts

Civilian power plant electricians often work for construction companies, manufacturers, and utility companies. They perform duties similar to military power plant electricians.

Precision Instrument and Equipment Repairers

Army
Navy
Air Force
Marine Corps

Short Description

The military uses precision instruments and equipment to perform a variety of functions. Some precision instruments are used to measure distance, pressure, altitude, temperature, underwater depth, and other physical properties. Other types of precision equipment include photographic and imaging equipment such as cameras, projectors, and film processing equipment. All of these items have many sensitive mechanisms which require regular attention to stay in good working order. Precision instrument and equipment repairers maintain and adjust these delicate items. They may specialize by the type of equipment that they work on.

What They Do

Precision instrument and equipment repairers in the military perform some or all of the following duties:

- Calibrate and repair instruments used in aircraft
- Perform field and sustainment-level maintenance and repair on microcomputers and electro-mechanical telecommunications equipment and Global Positioning Equipment
- Adjust and repair weapon aiming devices such as range finders, telescopes, periscopes, electronic azimuth determining devices, and nuclear, biological, and chemical (NBC) warning and measuring devices
- Diagnose and repair problems in all types of cameras and photo processing equipment
- Repair watches, clocks, and timers
- Calibrate electrical test instruments and other digital devices
- Perform maintenance on switchboards, telephones, associated wire instruments/equipment, night vision devices/equipment, laser and fiber optic systems

Helpful Attributes

Helpful school subjects include math, science, electronics, and shop mechanics. Helpful attributes include:

- Ability to solve mechanical problems
- Ability to use repair tools
- Interest in electronics, communications equipment, and digital services

Training Provided

Job training consists of classroom instruction, including practice in repairing precision instruments and equipment. Training length varies depending upon specialty. Further training occurs on the job and through advanced courses. Course content typically includes:

- Calibration and repair of precision measuring instruments
- Use of blueprints and schematics
- Test and repair of advanced communications and digital technologies
- Test and repair of aerial sensor equipment

Work Environment

Precision instrument and equipment repairers usually work in repair shops on land or aboard ships.

Civilian Counterparts

Civilian precision instrument and equipment repairers work in a variety of industries that use or repair precision instruments and equipment. They may work for manufacturing firms, airlines, machinery repair shops, photographic labs, or engineering firms. Civilian precision instrument and equipment repairers perform duties similar to military repairers. Depending on their specialty, they may also be called instrument mechanics, calibration specialists, digital camera repairers, or photographic equipment technicians.

Ship Electricians

Navy
Coast Guard

Short Description

Electrical systems supply power to operate ships and submarines. Lights, radar, weapons, and machinery all need electricity. Ship electricians operate and repair electrical systems on ships. They keep electrical power plants, wiring, and machinery in working order.

What They Do

Ship electricians in the military perform some or all of the following duties:

- Install wiring for lights and equipment
- Troubleshoot electrical wiring and equipment using test meters
- Operate and perform maintenance on generators, voltage and frequency regulators, controllers, distribution switchboards, and other electrical equipment
- Monitor and maintain electrical devices connected to the ship's main engines or nuclear reactors
- Rebuild electrical equipment
- Operate and maintain personal computers, electronics, and auxiliary equipment
- Maintain navigation data for use by the Strategic Weapons System

Helpful Attributes

Helpful school courses include math and shop mechanics. Helpful attributes include:

- Ability to use tools
- Interest in electricity and how electrical devices operate
- Interest in solving problems
- Interest in electronics and communication devices

Training Provided

Job training consists of classroom instruction, including practice repairing electrical systems. Further training occurs on the job and through advanced courses. Course content typically includes:

- Electrical theory
- Troubleshooting procedures
- Maintenance and repair procedures
- Reading diagrams and calculating amperage, voltage, and resistance levels

Work Environment

Ship electricians usually work indoors, aboard ships or submarines. They also work in ship repair shops on land.

Civilian Counterparts

Civilian ship electricians work for shipbuilding and drydock firms and shipping lines. They perform duties similar to military ship electricians. Other civilian electricians, such as building electricians and electrical products repairers, also perform similar work.

Weapons Maintenance Technicians

Army
Navy
Air Force
Marine Corps
Coast Guard

Short Description

Combat forces use many different types of weapons from small field artillery to large ballistic missiles. Weapons may be fired from ships, planes, and ground stations. Most modern weapons have electronic components and systems that assist in locating targets, aiming weapons, and firing them. Weapons maintenance technicians maintain and repair weapons used by combat forces.

What They Do

Weapons maintenance technicians in the military perform some or all of the following duties:

- Repair and maintain artillery, missile, multiple launch rocket systems, naval gun systems, and infantry weapons
- Clean and lubricate gyroscopes, sights, and other electro-optical fire control components
- Repair and maintain missile mounts, platforms, and launch mechanisms
- Perform field and sustainment level maintenance/repairs on the mechanisms/systems of tank turrets/weapons, fighting vehicles, towed/self-propelled artillery, and electronic, electrical, and cryogenic assemblies
- Maintain, operate, service, and repair weapons support systems such as power generation and distribution systems, environmental control, loading equipment, and associated interfaces
- Operate and maintain automated data processing equipment to perform munitions accounting, computations, and research
- Coordinate calibration and maintenance of associated missile systems test measurement diagnostic equipment
- Repair unserviceable optical and infrared components by aligning, adjusting, removing and replacing defective modules and assemblies
- Maintain and/or repair laser range finders, ballistic computers, laser observation devices, laser designators, and thermal imaging systems

Helpful Attributes

Helpful school subjects include science and math. Helpful attributes include:

- Ability to do work requiring accuracy and attention to detail
- Interest in working with electronic or electrical equipment
- Interest in working with weapon systems

Training Provided

Job training consists of classroom instruction and practical experience. Training length varies depending on specialty. Further training occurs on the job and through advanced courses. Course content typically includes:

- Electronic and mechanical principles and concepts
- Use of schematics, drawings, blueprints, and wiring diagrams
- Operation, testing, and maintenance of weapons systems and fire control systems

Work Environment

Weapons maintenance technicians work in workshops when testing and repairing electronic components. They may work outdoors while inspecting and repairing combat vehicles, ships, artillery, aircraft, and missile silos.

Civilian Counterparts

Civilian weapons maintenance technicians work for firms that design, build, and test weapons systems for the military. They perform duties similar to military weapons maintenance technicians. They may also be called avionics technicians, electronic mechanics, or missile facilities repairers.

Divers

Army
Navy
Marine Corps

Short Description

Sometimes, military tasks such as search and rescue, ship repair, construction, and patrolling must be done underwater. Divers in the military perform this work. They usually specialize either as scuba divers, who work just below the surface, or as deep sea divers, who may work for long periods of time in depths up to 300 feet.

What They Do

Divers in the military perform some or all of the following duties:

- Perform search and rescue activities
- Recover sunken equipment
- Patrol the waters below ships at anchor
- Inspect, clean, and repair ship propellers and hulls
- Assist with underwater construction of piers and harbor facilities
- Survey rivers, beaches, and harbors for underwater obstacles
- Use explosives to clear underwater obstacles
- Conduct underwater research

Helpful Attributes

Helpful school subjects include shop mechanics and building trades. Helpful attributes include:

- A high degree of self-reliance
- Ability to stay calm under stress
- Interest in underwater diving

Training Provided

Job training consists of classroom instruction, including practice in diving and repair work. Training length varies depending on specialty. Further training occurs on the job and through advanced courses. Course content typically includes:

- Principles of scuba diving
- Underwater welding and cutting
- Maintenance of diving equipment

Work Environment

Divers work underwater. However, they plan and prepare for work on land or aboard ships. Because diving is not usually a full-time job, divers often have another job specialty in which they work.

Civilian Counterparts

Civilian divers work for oil companies, salvage companies, underwater construction firms, and police or fire rescue units. They perform duties similar to divers in the military.

Non-Destructive Testers

Navy
Air Force
Marine Corps

Short Description

Military equipment is often placed under heavy stress. An airplane's landing gear absorbs heavy runway impact. Submarine hulls withstand tremendous pressure in the ocean depths. In time, stress may cause structural weakening or damage. Non-destructive testers examine metal parts for stress damage. They use X-rays, ultrasonics, and other testing methods that do not damage (are non-destructive to) the parts tested.

What They Do

Non-destructive testers in the military perform some or all of the following duties:

- Inspect metal parts and joints for wear and damage
- Take X-rays of aircraft and ship parts
- Examine X-ray film to detect cracks and flaws in metal parts and welds
- Operate ultrasonic, atomic absorption, and other kinds of test equipment
- Conduct oil analysis and heat damage tests to detect engine wear
- Prepare inspection reports

Helpful Attributes

Helpful school subjects include math and metal shop. Helpful attributes include:

- Interest in machines and how they work
- Thoroughness and dependability
- Interest in operating test equipment

Training Provided

Job training consists of classroom instruction, including practice in testing metal parts. Course content typically includes:

- Methods for inspecting parts and welds
- Operation of X-ray and film processing equipment
- Operation of ultrasonic test equipment
- Preparation of test reports

Work Environment

Non-destructive testers work indoors in laboratories and aircraft hangars. They also work outdoors in shipyards and in the field.

Civilian Counterparts

Civilian non-destructive testers work for commercial testing laboratories, airlines, aircraft maintenance companies, and industrial plants. They perform duties similar to military non-destructive testers and may be called radiographers.

Machinists

Army
Navy
Air Force
Marine Corps
Coast Guard

Short Description

Sometimes when engines or machines break down, the parts needed to repair them are not available. In these cases, the broken parts must be repaired or new ones made. Machinists make and repair metal parts for engines and all types of machines. They operate lathes, drill presses, grinders, and other machine shop equipment.

What They Do

Machinists in the military perform some or all of the following duties:

- Study blueprints or written plans of the parts to be made
- Use Computer Numerically Controlled (CNC) machines, and Computer Aided Drafting (CAD) to fabricate, repair, and modify metallic and nonmetallic parts
- Cut metal stock using power hacksaws and band saws
- Bore holes using drill presses
- Shape and smooth parts using grinders
- Measure work using micrometers, calipers, and depth gauges

Helpful Attributes

Helpful school subjects include math, general science, metal working, and mechanical drawing. Helpful attributes include:

- Ability to apply mathematical formulas
- Interest in making things and finding solutions to mechanical problems
- Preference for working with the hands

Training Provided

Job training consists of classroom instruction, including practice in machine operation. Further training occurs on the job and through advanced courses. Course content typically includes:

- Machine types and uses
- Machine setup and operation
- Uses of different metals
- Safety procedures
- Computer Numerically Controlled (CNC) machines, Computer Aided Drafting (CAD)

Work Environment

Machinists work in machine shops, which are often noisy.

Civilian Counterparts

Civilian machinists work for factories and repair shops in many industries, including the electrical product, automotive, and heavy machinery industries. They perform duties similar to military machinists.

Power Plant Operators

Navy
Air Force
Marine Corps
Coast Guard

Short Description

Power plants generate electricity for ships, submarines, and military bases. The military uses many different types of power plants. Many ships and submarines have nuclear power plants. Power plant operators control power generating plants on land and aboard ships and submarines. They operate boilers, turbines, nuclear reactors, and portable generators.

What They Do

Power plant operators in the military perform some or all of the following duties:

- Monitor and operate control boards to regulate power plants
- Operate and maintain diesel generating units
- Monitor and control nuclear reactors that produce electricity and power ships and submarines
- Operate and maintain stationary engines, such as steam engines, air compressors, and generators
- Operate and maintain auxiliary equipment
- Inspect equipment for malfunctions
- Operate the steam turbines that generate power for ships

Helpful Attributes

Helpful school subjects include math and shop mechanics. Helpful attributes include:

- Interest in nuclear power
- Interest in working with large machinery

Training Provided

Job training consists of classroom instruction, including practice in operating power plants. Nuclear specialties have training programs that last one year or more, covering all aspects of nuclear power plant operations. Course content typically includes:

- Operation of pressure boilers
- Operation and maintenance of reactor control systems
- Operation and maintenance of mechanical systems on nuclear powered ships and submarines

Work Environment

Power plant operators usually work indoors. They are subject to high temperatures and noise.

Civilian Counterparts

Civilian power plant operators work for power companies, factories, schools, and hospitals. They perform duties similar to military power plant operators. Depending on the specialty, they may also be called boiler operators, stationary engineers, nuclear reactor operators, or diesel plant operators.

Survival Equipment Specialists

Army
Navy
Air Force
Marine Corps
Coast Guard

Short Description

Military personnel often have hazardous assignments. They depend on survival equipment to protect their lives in case of emergencies. Survival equipment specialists inspect, maintain, and repair survival equipment such as parachutes, aircraft life support equipment, and air-sea rescue equipment.

What They Do

Survival equipment specialists in the military perform some or all of the following duties:

- Perform maintenance/repairs/riggings for aircraft and man-mounted systems, including emergency parachutes, seat survival kits, life rafts, life preservers, anti-exposure assemblies
- Pack parachutes for safe operation
- Repair life rafts and load them with emergency provisions
- Operate and maintain oxygen test stands, liquid oxygen convert test stands
- Stock aircraft with fire extinguishers, flares, and survival provisions
- Train crews in the use of survival equipment
- Assemble, maintain, and repair protective fabric components such as clothing and upholstery
- Operate and maintain sewing machines, including adjustment and lubrication

Helpful Attributes

Helpful school subjects include shop mechanics and science. Helpful attributes include:

- Ability to do work requiring accuracy and attention to detail
- Interest in working for the safety of others

Training Provided

Job training consists of classroom instruction, including practice in working with survival equipment. Further training occurs on the job and through additional courses. Course content typically includes:

- Parachute rigging techniques
- Repair of inflatable rafts and other survival equipment
- Maintenance of oxygen equipment
- Maintenance of air-sea rescue equipment

Work Environment

Survival equipment specialists in the military work in repair shops on land or aboard ships.

Civilian Counterparts

Civilian survival equipment specialists work for commercial airlines, parachute rigging and supply companies, survival equipment manufacturing firms, and some government agencies. They perform duties similar to military survival equipment specialists. Those that specialize in parachutes are called parachute riggers.

Welders and Metal Workers

Army
Navy
Air Force
Marine Corps

Short Description

Sheet metal is used as a building material in many military construction projects. Ships, tanks, and aircraft are made of heavy metal armor. Welders and metal workers make and install sheet metal products, such as roofs, air ducts, gutters, and vents. They also make custom parts to repair the structural parts of ships, submarines, landing craft, buildings, and equipment.

What They Do

Welders and metal workers in the military perform some or all of the following duties:

- Weld, braze, or solder metal parts together
- Repair automotive and ship parts using welding equipment

- Measure work with calipers, micrometers, and rulers

Helpful Attributes

Helpful school subjects include auto mechanics and industrial arts. Helpful attributes include:

- Interest in working with repair tools
- Preference for physical work

Training Provided

Job training consists of classroom instruction. Training length varies depending on specialty. Further training occurs on the job and through advanced courses. Course content typically includes:

- Sheet metal layout and duct work
- Procedures for cutting, brazing, and heat treating
- Operation and care of welding, soldering, and brazing equipment

Work Environment

Welders and metal workers work indoors in metalworking shops and aircraft hangars. They also work outdoors at construction sites, on ships, and in the field.

Civilian Counterparts

Civilian welders and metal workers may work for metal repair shops, auto repair shops, construction companies, pipeline companies, aircraft manufacturing plants, shipyards, and marine servicing companies. They perform duties similar to military welders and metal workers.

Aircraft Mechanics

Army
Navy
Air Force
Marine Corps
Coast Guard

Short Description

Military aircraft are used to fly hundreds of missions each day for transport, patrol, and flight training. They need frequent servicing to remain safe and ready to fly. Aircraft mechanics inspect, service, and repair helicopters and airplanes.

What They Do

Aircraft mechanics in the military perform some or all of the following duties:

- Service and repair helicopter, jet, and propeller aircraft engines

- Inspect and repair aircraft wings, fuselages, and tail assemblies
- Service and repair aircraft landing gear
- Repair or replace starters, lights, wiring, and other electrical parts
- Maintain fuel and lubrication systems as well as safety equipment and systems
- Perform maintenance on Metallic, Non-Metallic Flight Control System Components
- Keep detailed records

Helpful Attributes

Helpful school subjects include mathematics and shop mechanics. Helpful attributes include:

- Ability to use hand and power tools
- Interest in engine mechanics
- Interest in work involving aircraft

Training Provided

Job training consists of classroom instruction, including inspection and repair of aircraft engines and equipment. Training length varies depending upon the specialty. Further training occurs on the job and through advanced courses. Course content typically includes:

- Engine disassembly and repair
- Repair of hydraulic, fuel, and electrical systems
- Repair of aluminum, steel, and fiberglass airframes and coverings
- Precision measurement and equipment calibration

Work Environment

Aircraft mechanics work in aircraft hangars and machine shops located on air bases or aboard aircraft carriers.

Civilian Counterparts

Civilian aircraft mechanics work for aircraft manufacturers, commercial airlines, and government agencies. They perform duties similar to military aircraft mechanics. They may also be called airframe or power plant mechanics.

Automotive and Heavy Equipment Mechanics

Army
Navy
Air Force
Marine Corps
Coast Guard

Short Description

Keeping automotive and heavy equipment in good working condition is vital to the success of military missions. Automotive and heavy equipment mechanics maintain and repair vehicles such as jeeps, cars, trucks, tanks, and other combat vehicles. They also repair bulldozers, power shovels, and other construction equipment.

What They Do

Automotive and heavy equipment mechanics in the military perform some or all of the following duties:

- Troubleshoot problems in vehicle engines, electrical systems, steering, brakes, and suspensions
- Tune and repair engines
- Replace or repair damaged body parts, hydraulic arms or shovels, and grader blades
- Establish and follow schedules for maintaining vehicles

Helpful Attributes

Helpful school subjects include auto mechanics and industrial arts. Helpful attributes include:

- Interest in automotive engines and how they work
- Interest in troubleshooting and repairing mechanical problems
- Preference for physical work

Training Provided

Job training consists of classroom instruction. Training length varies depending on specialty. Further training occurs on the job and through advanced courses. Course content typically includes:

- Engine repair and tune-up
- Troubleshooting mechanical and electrical problems
- Repairing and replacing body panels, fenders, and radiators

Work Environment

Automotive and heavy equipment mechanics usually work inside large repair garages. They work outdoors when making emergency repairs in the field.

Civilian Counterparts

Civilian automotive and heavy equipment mechanics may work for service stations, auto and construction equipment dealers, farm equipment companies, and state highway agencies. They perform duties similar to military automotive and heavy equipment mechanics. They may also be called garage mechanics, transmission mechanics, radiator mechanics, or construction equipment mechanics.

Heating and Cooling Mechanics

Army
Navy
Air Force
Marine Corps
Coast Guard

Short Description

Air conditioning and heating equipment is used to maintain comfortable temperatures in military buildings, airplanes, and ships. Refrigeration equipment is used to keep food cold and to keep some missile fuels at sub-zero storage temperatures. Heating and cooling mechanics install and repair air conditioning, refrigeration, and heating equipment.

What They Do

Heating and cooling mechanics in the military perform some or all of the following duties:

- Install and repair furnaces, boilers, and air conditioners
- Recharge cooling systems with refrigerant gases
- Install copper tubing systems that circulate water or cooling gases
- Replace compressor parts such as valves, pistons, bearings, and electrical motors on refrigeration units
- Repair thermostats and electrical circuits

Helpful Attributes

Helpful school subjects include science, math, and shop mechanics. Helpful attributes include:

- Ability to use hand and power tools
- Interest in solving problems
- Interest in working on machines

Training Provided

Job training consists of classroom instruction, including practice in repair work. Training length varies depending on specialty. Additional training is available on the job and in advanced courses. Course content typically includes:

- Refrigeration theory
- Installation and repair of refrigeration and air conditioning units
- Installation and repair of furnaces and boilers
- Use of diagrams and blueprints

Work Environment

Heating and cooling mechanics may work inside repair shops. Frequently, they work wherever equipment is to be installed or repaired.

Civilian Counterparts

Civilian heating and cooling mechanics work for contractors that install home furnaces and air conditioners or for firms that repair refrigerators and freezers in homes, grocery stores, factories, and warehouses. Heating and cooling mechanics in civilian life often specialize more than those in the military. They may be called heating, air conditioning, refrigeration, or climate control mechanics.

Marine Engine Mechanics

Army
Navy
Marine Corps
Coast Guard

Short Description

The military operates many types of watercraft from small motor launches to large ships. Many of these vessels are powered by gasoline or diesel engines. Marine engine mechanics repair and maintain gasoline and diesel engines on ships, boats, and other watercraft. They also repair shipboard mechanical and electrical equipment.

What They Do

Marine engine mechanics in the military perform some or all of the following duties:

- Repair and maintain shipboard gasoline and diesel engines
- Locate and repair machinery parts, including valves and piping systems
- Repair ship propulsion machinery
- Repair and service hoisting machinery and ship elevators
- Repair refrigeration and air conditioning equipment on ships
- Repair engine-related electrical systems
- Operate, maintain, and repair auxiliary equipment and outside machinery, such as food preparation equipment, windlasses, and laundry equipment
- Operate and maintain marine boilers, pumps, forced draft blowers, and heat exchangers
- Perform test, transfers, and inventory of lubricating oils, fuels, and water

Helpful Attributes

Helpful school subjects include shop mechanics. Helpful attributes include:

- Ability to use hand and power tools
- Interest in fixing engines, machinery, and auxiliary equipment
- Preference for doing physical work

Training Provided

Job training consists of classroom instruction, including practice in marine engine maintenance and repair. Training length varies depending on specialty. Further training occurs on the job and through advanced courses. Course content typically includes:

- Internal combustion engine theory
- Repair of shipboard electronic and electrical machinery systems
- Service and repair of fuel injection systems
- Use and care of hand and power tools

Work Environment

Marine engine mechanics work aboard ships, normally in the engine or power rooms. Sometimes they work in repair centers on land bases. Working conditions in engine rooms tend to be noisy and hot.

Civilian Counterparts

Civilian marine engine mechanics work in many industries, including marine transportation, commercial fishing, and oil exploration and drilling. They perform duties similar to military marine engine mechanics.

Powerhouse Mechanics

Army
Navy
Air Force
Marine Corps
Coast Guard

Short Description

Power generating stations (powerhouses) provide electric power for military bases, ships, and field camps. There are many types of powerhouses, from small gas generators to large nuclear reactors. Powerhouse mechanics install, maintain, and repair electrical and mechanical equipment in power generating stations.

What They Do

Powerhouse mechanics in the military perform some or all of the following duties:

- Install generating equipment, such as gasoline and diesel engines, turbines, and air compressors
- Repair and maintain nuclear power plants
- Inspect and service pumps, generators, batteries, and cables
- Tune engines using hand tools, timing lights, and combustion pressure gauges
- Diagnose (troubleshoot) engine and electrical system problems
- Replace damaged parts such as fuel injectors, valves, and pistons

Helpful Attributes

Helpful school subjects include shop mechanics and math. Helpful attributes include:

- Interest in nuclear power
- Interest in repairing machines and equipment
- Preference for doing physical work

Training Provided

Job training for non-nuclear specialties consists of classroom instruction, including practice in repairing power generating equipment. Nuclear specialties have training programs that last one year or more, covering all aspects of nuclear power plant operations. Further training occurs on the job and through advanced courses. Training length varies depending on the specialty. Course content typically includes:

- Principles of electricity
- Gas and diesel engine theories
- Hydraulic (fluid pressure) and pneumatic (air pressure) system maintenance

Work Environment

Powerhouse mechanics work in equipment repair shops, power plant stations, or power generating rooms aboard ships. Sometimes they work outdoors while repairing substation generating equipment.

Civilian Counterparts

Civilian powerhouse mechanics work for a wide variety of employers, such as utility and power companies, manufacturing companies, and others that operate their own power plants. They perform duties similar to military powerhouse mechanics.

Enlisted Opportunities In The U.S. Military*

The military is the largest employer of high school graduates entering the work force full-time. Each year, approximately 200,000 young men and women, most of whom are recent high school graduates, join the enlisted forces of the Army, Navy, Air Force, Marine Corps, and Coast Guard.

Besides being the largest employer of young people in the nation, with total employment of more than 1.4 million enlisted men and women, the military offers the widest choice of career opportunities. Together, the five services offer training and employment in more than 2,000 enlisted job specialties, which have been grouped into military occupations in this book.

More than three-fourths of all military occupations have counterparts in the civilian world of work. For example, air traffic controller, aircraft mechanic, computer programmer, dental hygienist, and electronic technician occupations exist in both the military and civilian workforce.

GENERAL ENLISTMENT QUALIFICATIONS

The general qualifications for military enlistment are listed in the chart on page 654. The specific requirements may vary depending on the individual service.

Service Obligation

Joining the military involves entering into a legal contract called an *enlistment agreement*. The service agrees to provide a job, pay, benefits, and occupational training. In return, the enlisted member agrees to serve for a certain period of time, which is called the service obligation. The standard service obligation is eight years, which is divided between active military duty and reserve duty. Depending on the enlistment program selected, enlisted members spend between two and six years on active duty, with the balance of the eight-year obligation period spent in reserve status.

Enlistment Programs

Enlistment programs vary by service. The services adjust the programs they offer to meet changing recruiting needs. Major enlistment options include cash bonuses for enlisting in certain occupations and guaranteed choice of job training and assignments. Most individuals enter the military under the Delayed Entry Program (DEP), an option that is used by many

---

* Condensed from *Military Careers* and *Peterson's Guide to Joining the Military* 3rd Edition.

high school students who wish to enlist now but wait before entering into active duty. By enlisting under the DEP option, you can delay entry into active duty for up to one year. High school students often enlist under the DEP during their senior year and enter a service after graduation. Other qualified applicants choose the DEP because the job training they want is not currently available but will be within the next year.

General Enlistment Qualifications*	
Age	Must be between 17 and 35 years. Consent of parent or legal guardian required if 17.
Citizenship Status	Must be either (1) U.S. citizen, or (2) an immigrant alien legally admitted to the U.S. for permanent residence and possessing immigration and naturalization documents.
Physical Condition	Must meet minimum physical standards listed below to enlist. Some military occupations have additional physical standards.

	Height— For males: Maximum—6'8"
	                                Minimum—5'0"
	                For females: Maximum—6'8"
	                                Minimum—4'10"

	Weight—There are minimum and maximum weights, according to age and height, for males and females.
	Vision—There are minimum vision standards.
	Overall Health—Must be in good health and pass a medical exam. Certain diseases or conditions may exclude persons from enlistment—for example, diabetes, severe allergies, epilepsy, alcoholism, and drug addiction.
Education	High school graduation is desired by all services and is a requirement under most enlistment options.
Aptitude	Must make the minimum entry score on the ASVAB (Armed Services Vocational Aptitude Battery). Minimum entry scores vary by service and occupation.
Moral Character	Must meet standards designed to screen out persons likely to become disciplinary problems. Standards cover court convictions, juvenile delinquency, arrests, and drug use.
Marital Status and Dependents	May be either single or married.
Waivers	On a case-by-case basis, exceptions (waivers) are granted by individual services for some of the above qualification requirements.

* *Each service sets its own enlistment standards.*

Enlistment Contracts

The enlistment contract specifies the enlistment program you select. It contains the enlistment date, term of enlistment, and other options, such as a training program guarantee or a cash bonus. If the service cannot meet its part of the agreement (for example, to provide a specific type of job training), then you are no longer bound by the contract. If you accept another enlistment program, a new contract is written.

High School Graduates

The military encourages young people to stay in school and graduate. Research has shown that high school graduates are more likely to adjust to military life and complete an initial tour of duty. Therefore, the services accept few non–high school graduates.

ENLISTING IN THE MILITARY

There are four basic steps to the enlistment process. A summary follows. For detailed information about the enlistment process, including information about basic training, military pay, and benefits, refer to the most recent edition of *Peterson's Guide to Joining the Military*.

Step 1: Talking with a Recruiter

If you are interested in enlistment with a particular military service, you must talk with a recruiter from that service. Recruiters can provide detailed information about the employment and training opportunities in their service, as well as answer specific questions about service life, enlistment options, and other topics. They can also provide details about their service's enlistment qualification requirements.

If you decide to apply for entry into the service and the recruiter identifies no problems (such as a severe health problem), the recruiter will examine your educational credentials. You will then be scheduled for enlistment processing.

Step 2: Qualifying for Enlistment

Enlistment processing occurs at more than 60 Military Entrance Processing Stations (MEPS), located around the country. At the MEPS, you take the ASVAB if you have not already done so and receive medical examinations to determine if you are qualified to enter the service. The ASVAB is also administered at Mobile Examining Team (MET) sites.

ASVAB results are used to determine if you qualify for entry into a service and whether you have the specific Military Careers Score required to enter job specialty training programs. If you took the ASVAB at your school, you can use your scores to determine if you qualify for entry into the military services, provided the scores are not more than two years old. (There are provisions for re-taking the ASVAB if you need to, as long as a minimum of 30 days passes between tests.) Applicants with current ASVAB scores are not required to take the ASVAB a second time.

Step 3: Meeting with a Service Classifier

A service classifier is a military career information specialist who helps you select military occupations. For example, if you were applying for entry, the classifier informs you of service job training openings that match your aptitudes and interests. The classifier enters your ASVAB scores into a computerized reservation system. Based on your scores, the system shows the career fields and training you qualify for and when job training will be available.

After discussing job training options with the classifier, you select an occupation and schedule an enlistment date. Enlistment dates may be scheduled for up to one year in the future to coincide with job training openings. This option is called the Delayed Entry Program (DEP).

Following selection of a military training program, you sign an enlistment contract and take the oath of enlistment into the DEP, then return home until your enlistment date.

Step 4: Enlisting in the Service

After completing enlistment processing, most applicants are entered into the DEP and return to the MEPS on their scheduled enlistment date. At that time, applicants officially become "enlistees" (also known as "recruits") and proceed to a military base.

In the uncommon event that your guaranteed training program is not available on the reserved date, you have three options:

1. Make another reservation for the same training and return at a later date to enter the service.
2. Select another occupation and job training option.
3. Decide not to join the service and be free from any obligation.

MILITARY TRAINING

The military operates one of the largest training systems in the world. The five services sponsor nearly 300 technical training schools offering more than 10,000 separate courses of instruction.

The military generally provides four kinds of training to its personnel:

1. Recruit training
2. Job training
3. Advanced training
4. Leadership training

Recruit Training

Recruit training, popularly called basic training or "boot camp," is a rigorous orientation to the military. Depending on the service, recruit training lasts from eight to thirteen weeks and provides a transition from civilian to military life. The services train recruits at selected military bases across the country. Where an enlistee trains depends on the service and the job training to be received. Through basic training, recruits gain the pride, knowledge, discipline, and physical conditioning necessary to serve as members of the Army, Navy, Air Force, Marine Corps, and Coast Guard.

On reporting for basic training, recruits are divided into groups of 40 to 80 people. They then meet their drill instructor, receive uniforms and equipment, and move into assigned quarters.

During basic training, recruits receive instruction in health, first aid, and military skills. They also improve their fitness and stamina by participating in rigorous daily exercises and conditioning. To measure their conditioning progress, recruits are tested on sit-ups, push-ups, running, and body weight.

Recruits follow a demanding schedule throughout basic training; every day is carefully structured with time for classes, meals, physical conditioning, and field instruction. Some free time (including time to attend religious services) is available to recruits during basic training. After completing basic training, recruits normally proceed to job training.

For an in-depth look into basic training as well as how to get prepared for basic training, read *Peterson's Guide to Joining the Military*, 3rd Edition.

Job Training

Through job training, also called *technical* or *skill training*, recruits learn the skills they need to perform their job specialties. The military provides its personnel with high-quality training because lives and mission success depend on how well people perform their duties. Military training produces highly qualified workers, and, for this reason, many civilian employers consider military training excellent preparation for civilian occupations.

The type of job specialty determines the length of training. Most training lasts from ten to twenty weeks, although some nuclear specialties require more than one year of training.

Military training occurs both in the classroom and on the job. Classroom training emphasizes hands-on activities and practical experience, as well as textbook learning. For example, recruits who will be working with electronic equipment practice operating and repairing the equipment, in addition to studying the principles of electronics.

At their first assignments, enlisted members continue to learn on the job. Experienced enlisted members and supervisors help servicemen and servicewomen further develop their skills. In addition, the military offers refresher courses and advanced training to help military personnel maintain and increase their skills. As personnel advance in rank, they continue their training with leadership and management courses.

The Army, Navy, and Marine Corps offer apprenticeship programs for some job specialties. These programs consist of classroom and on-the-job training that meet U.S. Department of Labor apprenticeship standards. After completing an apprenticeship program, personnel receive a Department of Labor apprenticeship certificate. To military commanders and civilian employers, these certificates demonstrate that the worker has acquired specific skills and qualifications.

Advanced Training

Hundreds of advanced training courses have been developed by the services to improve the technical skills of the enlisted work force. These courses offer instruction in skills not covered in initial training. Advanced training also includes courses covering new or additional job-related equipment. Advanced training is especially important in high-technology areas where military technicians are constantly exposed to newer and more sophisticated equipment. Other advanced courses provide instruction in supervising and managing the daily operations of military units, such as repair shops or medical facilities.

Some advanced training involves classroom training, but the services also provide enlisted members with a wide choice of self-study correspondence courses. Some are general courses and address most duties of a job; others are designed to cover highly complex tasks or job-related skills. Self-study courses are particularly important to individual career advancement.

Leadership Training

Each service has schools and courses to help supervisors be more effective in managing the day-to-day operations of their units. These classes are designed primarily for noncommissioned officers. Courses include instruction in leadership skills, service regulations, and management techniques needed to train and lead other servicemembers.

The five services have similar systems for assigning personnel to jobs. Each system is designed to satisfy the staffing needs of the particular service. At the same time, the services attempt to meet the desires of the individual servicemember and provide opportunities for career development. The duty assignment process determines where enlisted personnel work, how often they move, and the opportunities open to them.

All services require their members to travel. Enlisted personnel are stationed in each of the fifty states and in countries all over the world. They are routinely reassigned after two-, three-, or four-year tours of duty. To many people, this is one of the attractive parts of service life, and many men and women join for the opportunity to travel, live in foreign countries, and see different parts of the United States.

PAY AND BENEFITS

Military personnel in all five services are paid according to the same pay scale and receive the same basic benefits. Military pay and benefits are set by Congress, which normally grants a cost-of-living pay increase once each year. In addition to pay, the military provides many of life's necessities, such as food, clothing, and housing or pays monthly allowances for them. The following sections describe military pay, allowances, and benefits in more detail.

Enlisted Pay Grades

Enlistees can progress through nine enlisted pay grades during their careers. Pay grade and length of service determine a servicemember's pay. The chart on pages 660–661 illustrates the insignia for the ranks in each service. The chart on page 662 lists pay grades (as of 2018) for each level of enlisted service.

New recruits begin at pay grade E-1, except in some cases individuals with college credits, who enlisted in certain technical occupations, or who participated in high school JROTC enter at a higher pay grade. Within six months, enlistees usually move up to E-2. Within the next six to twelve months, the military promotes enlistees to E-3 if job performance is satisfactory and other requirements are met. Promotions to E-4 and above are based on job performance, leadership ability, promotion test scores, years of service, and time in the present pay grade. Promotions become more competitive at the higher pay grades.

Incentives and Special Pay

The military offers incentives and special pay (in addition to basic pay) for certain types of duty. For example, incentives are paid for submarine and flight duty. Other types of hazardous duty with monthly incentives include parachute jumping, flight deck duty, and explosives demolition. In addition, the military gives special pay for sea duty, diving duty, special assignments, duty in some foreign places, and duty in areas subject to hostile fire. Depending on the service, bonuses are also paid for entering certain occupations.

Allowances

Most enlisted members, especially in the first year of service, live in military housing and eat in military dining facilities free of charge. Those living off base receive quarters (housing) and subsistence (food) allowances in addition to their basic pay. The monthly housing allowance for enlisted members depends on pay grade, number of dependents, and location. Housing allowances can be searched by ZIP code at www.dfas.mil. The food allowance is $369.39 per month. Because allowances are not taxed as income, they provide a significant tax savings in addition to their cash value.

Employment Benefits

Military personnel receive substantial benefits in addition to their pay and allowances. While they are in the service, enlisted members' benefits include health care, vacation, legal assistance, recreational programs, educational assistance, and commissary-exchange (military store) privileges. Families of servicemembers also receive some of these benefits. The chart on page 663 contains a summary of these employment benefits.

Insignia of the U.S. Armed Forces

Rank Level	Army		Navy / Coast Guard		Air Force		Marines	
E-1	Private	(no insignia)	Seaman Recruit (SR)		Airman Basic	(no insignia)	Private (Pvt)	(no insignia)
E-2	Private		Seaman Apprentice (SA)		Airman		Private First Class (PFC)	
E-3	Private First Class		Seaman (SN)		Airman First Class		Lance Corporal (LCpl)	
E-4	Specialist							
	Corporal		Petty Officer Third Class (PO3)		Senior Airman		Corporal (Cpl)	
E-5	Sergeant		Petty Officer Second Class (PO2)		Staff Sergeant		Sergeant (Sgt)	
E-6	Staff Sergeant		Petty Officer First Class (PO1)		Technical Sergeant		Staff Sergeant (SSgt)	
E-7	Sergeant First Class		Chief Petty Officer (CPO)		Master Sergeant		Gunnery Sergeant (GySgt)	
					Master Sergeant with first sergeant status			

Insignia of the U.S. Armed Forces (continued)

	Army		Navy		Air Force		Marine Corps	
E-8	Master Sergeant				Senior Master Sergeant		Master Sergeant (MSgt)	
	First Sergeant		Senior Chief Petty Officer (SCPO)		Senior Master Sergeant with first sergeant status		First Sergeant (1stSgt)	
E-9	Sergeant Major				Chief Master Sergeant		Master Gunnery Sergeant (MGySgt)	
	Command Sergeant Major		Master Chief Petty Officer (MCPO)		Chief Master Sergeant with first sergeant status		Sergeant Major (SgtMaj)	
E-9 (special)	Command Sergeant Major of the Army		Master Chief Petty Officer of the Navy (MCPON)		Command Chief Master Sergeant		Sergeant Major of the Marine Corps (SgtMajMC)	
					Chief Master Sergeant of the Air Force			

Basic Pay

The major part of an enlistee's paycheck is basic pay. Pay grade and total years of service determine an enlistee's pay. The following chart lists annual basic pay for each pay grade of enlisted service as of January 1, 2018. Cost-of-living increases generally occur once a year.

Years Of Service	Pay Grade								
	E-9	**E-8**	**E-7**	**E-6**	**E-5**	**E-4**	**E-3**	**E-2**	**E-1**
<2			2,944	2,546	2,333	2,139	1,931	1,836	1,599.90
2			3,213	2,802	2,490	2,248	2,052	1,836	
3			3,336	2,926	2,610	2,370	2,177	1,836	
4			3,499	3,046	2,733	2,490	2,177	1,836	
6			3,627	3,172	2,925	2,596	2,177	1,836	
8		4,235	3,845	3,454	3,126	2,596	2,177	1,836	
10	5,174	4,422	3,968	3,564	3,291	2,596	2,177	1,836	
12	5,291	4,539	4,187	3,777	3,310	2,596	2,177	1,836	
14	5,439	4,677	4,369	3,842	3,310	2,596	2,177	1,836	
16	5,613	4,828	4,493	3,889	3,310	2,596	2,177	1,836	
18	5,788	5,100	4,625	3,944	3,310	2,596	2,177	1,836	
20	6,069	5,237	4,676	3,944	3,310	2,596	2,177	1,836	
22	6,307	5,472	4,848	3,944	3,310	2,596	2,177	1,836	
24	6,556	5,602	4,940	3,944	3,310	2,596	2,177	1,836	
26	6,939	5,922	5,292	3,944	3,310	2,596	2,177	1,836	

Monthly Basic Pay Chart—Effective January 1, 2018

Note: E-1 with less than 4 months of service = 1,515.00

Summary of Employment Benefits for Enlisted Members

Vacation	Leave time of thirty days per year
Medical, Dental, and Eye Care	Full medical, hospitalization, dental, and eye-care services for enlistees and most healthcare costs for family members
Continuing Education	Voluntary educational programs for undergraduate and graduate degrees or for single courses, including tuition assistance for programs at colleges and universities
Recreational Programs	Programs include athletics, entertainment, and hobbies: • Softball, basketball, football, swimming, tennis, golf, weight training, and other sports • Parties, dances, and entertainment • Club facilities, snack bars, game rooms, movie theaters, and lounges • Active hobby and craft clubs and book and music libraries
Exchange and Commissary Privileges	Food, goods, and services are available at military stores, generally at lower costs than regular retail stores.
Legal Assistance	Many free legal services are available to assist with personal matters.

Retirement Benefits

For individuals who joined the U.S. military on or after August 1, 1986, there are two retirement options. After fifteen years of service, such a member must decide which of the two retirement plans he or she would prefer:

1. The first option is to receive a lump sum payment of $30,000 at this point, and then receive a pension after 20 years of service at the rate of 40 percent of the *average* of the highest three years' pay.

2. The second option is NOT to receive the cash bonus at fifteen years, but to wait and receive a pension after 20 years of service at the rate of 50 percent of the *average* of the highest three years' pay.

With either option, the percentage of pay increases if retirement is delayed beyond 20 years. The maximum percentage for retirement pay is 75 percent.

Today's military members may also contribute to a separate retirement plan in addition to the standard military retirement plan. Members contribute to the Thrift Savings Plan using "pre-tax" dollars. Unlike some plans, however, there are no matching funds from the government.

Veterans' Benefits

Veterans of military service are entitled to certain veterans' benefits set by Congress and provided by the Department of Veterans Affairs. In most cases, these include guarantees for home loans, hospitalization, survivor benefits, educational benefits (such as the Post-911 GI Bill), disability benefits, and assistance in finding civilian employment.

Coding Speed

The Coding Speed section of the ASVAB is used to evaluate Navy applicants only and is solely administered through the CAT-ASVAB. This section does not test prior knowledge but rather measures applicants' aptitude for several Navy careers including those requiring learning a foreign language. This speed-test requires applicants to choose the "code" that matches each word in a table. The act of matching these codes to the words is not difficult; the difficulty comes from the speed in which they must be matched.

Typically, there will be 84 questions in the Coding Speed section, however, as a timed speed-test, if questions are not answered quickly enough, the computer will move on to the next question. To improve your coding speed performance, practice the 84 questions in this section several times as you time yourself or have someone else time you. Your goal should be to reduce the time necessary to complete this section.

Start with the sample questions below and then complete the 84 questions which follow.

SAMPLE QUESTIONS

Mouse...4952	Blanket...8170	Song...9155
Crab...7891	Switch...2325	Lion...1978
Screwdriver...6799	River...5128	Tree...3282

S1. Mouse
- **A.** 8170
- **B.** 4952
- **C.** 2325
- **D.** 3282

Ⓐ Ⓑ Ⓒ Ⓓ

S2. Lion
- **A.** 7891
- **B.** 9155
- **C.** 3282
- **D.** 1978

Ⓐ Ⓑ Ⓒ Ⓓ

S1. **The correct answer is B,** as the code for mouse shown in the table is 4952.

S2. **The correct answer is D,** as the code for lion shown in the table is 1978.

House...4372	Automobile...8398	Bench...9575
Television...7209	Fireplace...2585	Floor...1976
School...6523	Modem...5190	Airplane...3092

1. House
   A. 6523
   B. 2585
   C. 3092
   D. 4372

2. Fireplace
   A. 9575
   B. 2585
   C. 5190
   D. 6523

3. School
   A. 6523
   B. 2585
   C. 3092
   D. 4372

4. Modem
   A. 9575
   B. 2585
   C. 5190
   D. 6523

5 . Automobile
   A. 6523
   B. 2585
   C. 4372
   D. 8398

6. Airplane
   A. 6523
   B. 2585
   C. 3092
   D. 4372

7. Floor
   A. 1976
   B. 5190
   C. 3092
   D. 4372

8. Bench
   A. 6523
   B. 2585
   C. 9575
   D. 1976

9. Television
   A. 9575
   B. 7209
   C. 3092
   D. 5190

Roof...9920	Window...7676	Baby...6014
Bottle...1120	Basket...9001	Picture...4727
Rabbit...2345	Clock...5611	Wall...1911

10. Clock
- **A.** 7676
- **B.** 5611
- **C.** 4727
- **D.** 9001

11. Bottle
- **A.** 1120
- **B.** 2345
- **C.** 5611
- **D.** 1911

12. Baby
- **A.** 2345
- **B.** 7676
- **C.** 6014
- **D.** 9920

13. Picture
- **A.** 7676
- **B.** 5611
- **C.** 4727
- **D.** 9001

14. Wall
- **A.** 1120
- **B.** 2345
- **C.** 5611
- **D.** 1911

15. Window
- **A.** 2345
- **B.** 7676
- **C.** 6014
- **D.** 9920

16. Basket
- **A.** 7676
- **B.** 5611
- **C.** 4727
- **D.** 9001

17. Rabbit
- **A.** 1120
- **B.** 2345
- **C.** 5611
- **D.** 1911

18. Roof
- **A.** 2345
- **B.** 7676
- **C.** 6014
- **D.** 9920

Door...4589	Wrench...9021	Dress...3267
Cradle...7832	Dirt...6262	Bread...8724
Refrigerator ...8256	Closet...1145	Glass...5791

19. Wrench
- **A.** 6262
- **B.** 8256
- **C.** 9021
- **D.** 5791

20. Refrigerator
- **A.** 8256
- **B.** 6262
- **C.** 4589
- **D.** 3267

21. Bread
- **A.** 3267
- **B.** 8724
- **C.** 7832
- **D.** 1145

22. Glass
- **A.** 6262
- **B.** 8256
- **C.** 9021
- **D.** 5791

23. Dress
- **A.** 8256
- **B.** 6262
- **C.** 4589
- **D.** 3267

24. Closet
- **A.** 3267
- **B.** 8724
- **C.** 7832
- **D.** 1145

25. Dirt
- **A.** 6262
- **B.** 8256
- **C.** 9021
- **D.** 5791

26. Door
- **A.** 8256
- **B.** 6262
- **C.** 4589
- **D.** 3267

27. Cradle
- **A.** 3267
- **B.** 8724
- **C.** 7832
- **D.** 1145

Hammer...9911	Book...6719	Picture...5116
Jar...7194	Computer...1492	Crate...7276
Truck...4329	Flower...3378	Fence...1960

28. Hammer
  A. 9911
  B. 3378
  C. 4329
  D. 7276

29. Computer
  A. 6719
  B. 1960
  C. 4329
  D. 1492

30. Jar
  A. 6719
  B. 5116
  C. 7194
  D. 9911

31. Flower
  A. 9911
  B. 3378
  C. 4329
  D. 7276

32. Fence
  A. 6719
  B. 1960
  C. 4329
  D. 1492

33. Book
  A. 6719
  B. 5116
  C. 7194
  D. 9911

34. Crate
  A. 9911
  B. 3378
  C. 4329
  D. 7276

35. Truck
  A. 6719
  B. 1960
  C. 4329
  D. 1492

36. Picture
  A. 6719
  B. 5116
  C. 7194
  D. 9911

Baby...9991	Saxophone...4509	Mayonnaise...5172
Frame...6823	Crater...1389	Road...4787
Trampoline...2013	Sofa...3258	Wing...1937

37. Saxophone
- **A.** 4509
- **B.** 4787
- **C.** 9991
- **D.** 2013

38. Sofa
- **A.** 9991
- **B.** 3258
- **C.** 6823
- **D.** 1389

39. Mayonnaise
- **A.** 4787
- **B.** 1937
- **C.** 1389
- **D.** 5172

40. Road
- **A.** 4509
- **B.** 4787
- **C.** 9991
- **D.** 2013

41. Frame
- **A.** 9991
- **B.** 3258
- **C.** 6823
- **D.** 1389

42. Wing
- **A.** 4787
- **B.** 1937
- **C.** 1389
- **D.** 5172

43. Trampoline
- **A.** 4509
- **B.** 4787
- **C.** 9991
- **D.** 2013

44. Baby
- **A.** 9991
- **B.** 3258
- **C.** 6823
- **D.** 1389

45. Crater
- **A.** 4787
- **B.** 1937
- **C.** 1389
- **D.** 5172

Dog...2525	Chicken...8198	Counter...4650
Stairwell...4012	Snowball...6595	Hair...3119
Movie...1941	Pie...3995	Thermostat...9104

46. Thermostat
   A. 9104
   B. 1941
   C. 3119
   D. 6595

47. Pie
   A. 2525
   B. 4012
   C. 3995
   D. 8198

48. Counter
   A. 4650
   B. 3119
   C. 2525
   D. 9104

49. Movie
   A. 9104
   B. 1941
   C. 3119
   D. 6595

50. Stairwell
   A. 2525
   B. 4012
   C. 3995
   D. 8198

51. Dog
   A. 4650
   B. 3119
   C. 2525
   D. 9104

52. Snowball
   A. 9104
   B. 1941
   C. 3119
   D. 6595

53. Chicken
   A. 2525
   B. 4012
   C. 3995
   D. 8198

54. Hair
   A. 4650
   B. 3119
   C. 2525
   D. 9104

Grill...2093	Blueberry...1698	Hamburger...7429
Bonfire...9213	Ticket...4729	Handrail...6392
Cracker...9867	Brick...8301	Jacket...3429

55. Blueberry
A. 8301
B. 1698
C. 6392
D. 9867

56. Cracker
A. 9213
B. 9867
C. 6392
D. 3429

57. Grill
A. 2093
B. 1698
C. 7429
D. 4729

58. Handrail
A. 8301
B. 1698
C. 6392
D. 9867

59. Jacket
A. 9213
B. 9867
C. 6392
D. 3429

60. Hamburger
A. 2093
B. 1698
C. 7429
D. 4729

61. Brick
A. 8301
B. 1698
C. 6392
D. 9867

62. Bonfire
A. 9213
B. 9867
C. 6392
D. 3429

63. Ticket
A. 2093
B. 1698
C. 7429
D. 4729

Candy...6329	Statue...3479	Fan...9312
Suitcase...4717	Rocket...1956	Earring...5901
Toothbrush...8119	Steeple...7727	Crown...6127

64. Steeple
- **A.** 7727
- **B.** 4717
- **C.** 5901
- **D.** 6127

65. Toothbrush
- **A.** 4717
- **B.** 8119
- **C.** 9312
- **D.** 1956

66. Candy
- **A.** 3479
- **B.** 4717
- **C.** 6329
- **D.** 8119

67. Earring
- **A.** 7727
- **B.** 4717
- **C.** 5901
- **D.** 6127

68. Rocket
- **A.** 4717
- **B.** 8119
- **C.** 9312
- **D.** 1956

69. Suitcase
- **A.** 3479
- **B.** 4717
- **C.** 6329
- **D.** 8119

70. Crown
- **A.** 7727
- **B.** 4717
- **C.** 5901
- **D.** 6127

71. Fan
- **A.** 4717
- **B.** 8119
- **C.** 9312
- **D.** 1956

72. Statue
- **A.** 3479
- **B.** 4717
- **C.** 6329
- **D.** 8119

Necktie...1009	Tablet...7923	Sweater...1672
Vase...4281	Straw...6929	Internet...9528
Party...8419	Helmet...2232	Map...5660

73. Party
  A. 8419
  B. 9528
  C. 5660
  D. 4281

74. Straw
  A. 1672
  B. 6929
  C. 1009
  D. 2232

75. Internet
  A. 9528
  B. 8419
  C. 1672
  D. 5660

76. Vase
  A. 8419
  B. 9528
  C. 5660
  D. 4281

77. Necktie
  A. 1672
  B. 6929
  C. 1009
  D. 2232

78. Map
  A. 9528
  B. 8419
  C. 1672
  D. 5660

79. Map
  A. 8419
  B. 9528
  C. 5660
  D. 4281

80. Helmet
  A. 1672
  B. 6929
  C. 1009
  D. 2232

81. Sweater
  A. 9528
  B. 8419
  C. 1672
  D. 5660

Laptop...7112	Carpet...7322	Cable...8719
Camera...5166	Alarm...9126	Container...4372
Desk...6316	Insect...2126	Sofa...1534

82. Laptop
- **A.** 5166
- **B.** 6316
- **C.** 7112
- **D.** 7322

83. Alarm
- **A.** 9126
- **B.** 2126
- **C.** 1534
- **D.** 6316

84. Container
- **A.** 1534
- **B.** 5166
- **C.** 7112
- **D.** 4372

ANSWER KEY

1. D	22. D	43. D	64. A
2. B	23. D	44. A	65. B
3. A	24. D	45. C	66. C
4. C	25. A	46. A	67. C
5. D	26. C	47. C	68. D
6. C	27. C	48. A	69. B
7. A	28. A	49. B	70. D
8. C	29. D	50. B	71. C
9. B	30. C	51. C	72. A
10. B	31. B	52. D	73. A
11. A	32. B	53. D	74. B
12. C	33. A	54. B	75. A
13. C	34. D	55. B	76. D
14. D	35. C	56. B	77. C
15. B	36. B	57. A	78. D
16. D	37. A	58. C	79. C
17. B	38. B	59. D	80. D
18. D	39. D	60. C	81. C
19. C	40. B	61. A	82. C
20. A	41. C	62. A	83. A
21. B	42. B	63. D	84. D

NOTES

NOTES

NOTES

NOTES

NOTES

NOTES